COOK'S

ILLUSTRATED

~ 2006 ~

$35.00

Published by
America's Test Kitchen
17 Station Street
Brookline, MA 02445

ISBN-13: 978-1-933615-11-0
ISSN: 1068-2821

To get home delivery of *Cook's Illustrated,* call 800-526-8442 inside the U.S., or 515-247-7571 if calling from outside the U.S., or subscribe online at www.cooksillustrated.com.

In addition to *Cook's Illustrated* Annual Hardbound Editions available from each year of publication (1993–2006), America's Test Kitchen offers the following cookbooks and DVD sets:

The America's Test Kitchen Family Cookbook

The Best Recipe Series
The Best 30-Minute Recipe
The Best Light Recipe
The Cook's Illustrated Guide to Grilling and
    Barbecue
Best American Side Dishes
Cover & Bake
The New Best Recipe
Steaks, Chops, Roasts, and Ribs
Baking Illustrated
Restaurant Favorites at Home
Perfect Vegetables
Italian Classics
The Best American Classics
The Best Soups & Stews

Additional books from America's Test Kitchen
The Best of America's Test Kitchen 2007
The Cook's Bible
*The Cook's Illustrated Complete Book of
    Pasta and Noodles*
834 Kitchen Quick Tips
The Kitchen Detective
1993–2006 Cook's Illustrated Master Index
2005 Cook's Country Annual Edition
2006 Cook's Country Annual Edition

**The America's Test Kitchen Series
(companion cookbooks and DVD sets
to our hit public television series)**
Test Kitchen Favorites
    (2007 season companion cookbook)
Cooking at Home with America's Test Kitchen
    (2006 season companion cookbook)
America's Test Kitchen Live!
    (2005 season companion cookbook)
Inside America's Test Kitchen
    (2004 season companion cookbook)
Here in America's Test Kitchen
    (2003 season companion cookbook)
The America's Test Kitchen Cookbook
    (2002 season companion cookbook)
The *America's Test Kitchen* 2006 Season
    4-DVD Boxed Set
The *America's Test Kitchen* 2005 Season
    4-DVD Boxed Set
The *America's Test Kitchen* 2004 Season
    4-DVD Boxed Set
The *America's Test Kitchen* 2003 Season
    4-DVD Boxed Set
The *America's Test Kitchen* 2002 Season
    4-DVD Boxed Set
The *America's Test Kitchen* 2001 Season
    2-DVD Boxed Set

To order any of our cookbooks listed above, give us a call at 800-611-0759 inside the U.S., or at 515-246-6911 if calling from outside the U.S.

You can order subscriptions, gift subscriptions, and any of our books by
visiting our online store at www.cooksillustrated.com

BC=Back Cover

COOK'S ILLUSTRATED INDEX 2006

Beef (cont.)

NUMBER SEVENTY-EIGHT

JANUARY & FEBRUARY 2006

COOK'S
ILLUSTRATED

Ultimate Chicken
Pot Pie
New One-Skillet Method

Flaky Biscuits 101

Perfecting All-Beef
Meat Loaf

Oven-Smoked Ribs

Best Chocolate
Mousse
Creamy, Silky, and Dark

Rating Grill Pans
Sizzle or Just Smoke?

Bistro-Style Potatoes

Breakfast Sausage Taste Test
Our Guide to Rice and Grains
Mushroom Side Dishes
Hot and Sour Soup
Better Huevos Rancheros
Lemon Bundt Cake

www.cooksillustrated.com

$5.95 U.S./$6.95 CANADA

02 >

0 7447 0 62805 7

CONTENTS

January & February 2006

www.cooksillustrated.com

HOME OF AMERICA'S TEST KITCHEN

Founder and Editor	Christopher Kimball
Executive Editor	Jack Bishop
Deputy Editor	Jolyon Helterman
Senior Editor	Adam Ried
Editorial Manager, Books	Elizabeth Carduff
Test Kitchen Director	Erin McMurrer
Senior Editors, Books	Julia Collin Davison
	Lori Galvin
Managing Editor	Rebecca Hays
Associate Editor, Books	Keith Dresser
Associate Editors	Erika Bruce
	Sean Lawler
	Sandra Wu
Web Editor	Lindsay McSweeney
Copy Chief	India Koopman
Test Cooks	Garth Clingingsmith
	David Pazmiño
	Rachel Toomey
	Diane Unger
	Nina West
	Sarah Wilson
Assistant Test Kitchen Director	Matthew Herron
Assistant Editor, Books	Charles Kelsey
Editorial Assistant, Books	Elizabeth Wray Emery
Editorial Assistant	Elizabeth Bomze
Assistant to the Publisher	Melissa Baldino
Kitchen Assistants	Maria Elena Delgado
	Nadia Domeq
	Ena Gudiel
Editorial Interns	Ellen London
	Lauren Oliver
Contributing Editors	Matthew Card
	Dawn Yanagihara
Consulting Editors	Shirley Corriher
	Guy Crosby
	Jasper White
	Robert L. Wolke
Proofreader	Jean Rogers
Design Director	Amy Klee
Marketing Designer	Julie Bozzo
Designer	Heather Barrett
Staff Photographer	Daniel van Ackere
Vice President Marketing	David Mack
Circulation Director	Bill Tine
Fulfillment Manager	Carrie Horan
Circulation Assistant	Elizabeth Dayton
Direct Mail Director	Adam Perry
Products Director	Steven Browall
E-Commerce Marketing Manager	Hugh Buchan
Marketing Copywriter	David Goldberg
Customer Service Manager	Jacqueline Valerio
Customer Service Representative	Julie Gardner
Vice President Sales	Demee Gambulos
Retail Sales Director	Jason Geller
Corporate Sponsorship Specialist	Laura Phillipps
Marketing Assistant	Connie Forbes
Vice President Operations	James McCormack
Senior Production Manager	Jessica L. Quirk
Project Manager	Anne Francis
Book Production Specialist	Ron Bilodeau
Production Assistants	Jeanette McCarthy
	Christian Steinmetz
	Matthew Warnick
Systems Administrator	Richard Cassidy
Internet Technology Director	Aaron Shuman
Web Producer	Lauren Record
Chief Financial Officer	Sharyn Chabot
Controller	Mandy Shito
Staff Accountant	Maya Santoso
Office Manager	Saudiyah Abdul-Rahim
Receptionist	Henrietta Murray
Publicity	Deborah Broide

2nd PRINTING IN CHINA

ITALIAN CHEESES The best known of Italy's hard cheeses are Parmigiano-Reggiano (the original Parmesan), a nutty, crumbly cow's-milk cheese, and Pecorino Romano, a salty, sharp sheep's-milk cheese—both ideal for grating. Grana Padano is a younger cow's-milk cheese, with a delicate flavor. Even less pungent is ricotta salata, which tastes nutty and milky. Asiago, a mild cow's-milk cheese, is marketed fresh, medium-ripe, or ripe, becoming crumblier as it ages. Provolone, from cow's milk, is eaten young or aged, after hanging to dry in gourd-shaped balls. Fresh mozzarella, once made with water-buffalo milk, is now generally made from cow's milk; soft and sweet, it should not be confused with supermarket "melting" mozzarella. A raw-cow's-milk cheese, Fontina Val d'Aosta is grassy, nutty, and excellent for melting. Taleggio, creamier and saltier, is distinguished by its runny interior. Gorgonzola, Italy's most famous blue cheese, is made from cow's milk; it's soft, creamy, and sweet when young and quite assertive when aged. Sweet, buttery mascarpone, from cow's milk, is closer to clotted cream than cheese.

COVER (*Cauliflower*): Elizabeth Brandon, BACK COVER (*Italian Cheeses*): John Burgoyne

For list rental information, contact: ClientLogic, 1200 Harbor Blvd., 9th Floor, Weehawken, NJ 07087; 201-865-5800; fax 201-867-2450.
Editorial Office: 17 Station St., Brookline, MA 02445; 617-232-1000; fax 617-232-1572. Subscription inquiries, call 800-526-8442.
Postmaster: Send all new orders, subscription inquiries, and change-of-address notices to Cook's Illustrated, P.O. Box 7446, Red Oak, IA 51591-0446.

LITTLE THINGS

During a recent church service in our small town in Vermont, the minister asked the congregation if there was anyone we ought to pray for. The mother of a teenage boy called out, "Let's all pray for teenagers!" On another occasion, Mike, a local farmer, was helping me hook up a brush hog to our tractor. When it slid right onto the power take-off without a hitch, he exclaimed, "That was as slick as a mitten!" Years ago, I jogged by Tom and Nancy's place in the early morning, followed by an amorous (or maybe just hungry) goat. Tom cried out, "That your new girlfriend?" Speaking of Tom, he once saw his beagle chasing a rabbit in circles—or so he thought; actually, the cottontail was sitting comfortably on a stump right in the middle of a briar patch, watching the dog run.

If you call Don Lewis's number in the fall, his answering machine is likely to say, "Well, the frost is on the pumpkin. . . ." On the wall of Axel's saphouse, there is a large mousetrap and a sign that says, "For Complaints, Push Here." The Wayside Country Store has a photograph on the wall of four donkeys that reads "Board of Directors." And nothing will ever beat John K's defroster, the one he jury-rigged in his rusty brown Rabbit. It was a votive candle stuck into the dashboard.

John's wife, Lucille, told me that one morning he got up early as usual to go the outhouse. (He used to phone in the local weather report while sitting in the two-holer.) He came back in a few minutes looking bewildered. "John," she asked, "What's wrong?" John looked like he'd seen a ghost and said, "I can't find it!" Lucille, still confused, asked, "Can't find what?" John shot back, "Can't find the outhouse!" A strong wind had picked it up and blown it into the next field.

Old-timers, of course, enjoy the little things, understanding the power of a simple word or phrase or gesture. When the last bale of hay was finally thrown up into the barn, I remember Charlie Bentley always calling out, "That's the one we've been looking for!" Back in the '60s,

when someone from the state agricultural department asked Bernie Squires if he knew where the Kimballs lived, Bernie got out from under his truck, walked over to the fence, and said, "Yup," then turned his back and walked away. Fraisher Mears used an apple branch for divining water, and he was known to start up a conversation with it, saying, "Tell me, Mr. Stick, how far is it?" Russell Bain had a saying about women and tractors, "Powder and paint make it what it ain't." There were two sisters, Big Helen and Little Helen: Little Helen was over six feet tall. The Woodcocks nailed a TV antenna to the top of their doghouse. Sonny Skidmore used to pick up a bathroom scale between his ham-sized hands and squeeze it until the needle jumped off the chart. Calvin Coolidge, stuck next to a dinner guest who had wagered she could get more than two words of conversation out of the tight-lipped Vermonter, said, "You lose."

In the country, life is made of the little things, stuff that nobody else has time to notice. One Saturday morning I was up early and walking by the lower pasture just before daybreak. Our six horses, normally slow moving and gentle, were galloping and skidding on the wet sod, rising up and pawing the air, kicking like broncos, and generally behaving like a bunch of kids. An hour later, when they came back to the barn for hay, they were as tame as usual.

That afternoon, I went out grouse hunting, and my 7-year-old, Emily, asked to come along. I said OK, but she would have to walk behind me since I would be carrying a loaded semi-automatic 20-gauge. I had to keep reminding her that it was dangerous to walk ahead until she finally said, "Mom would be really mad if you shot me." I allowed as how she would indeed be pretty mad. "After all," she stated firmly, "she went to a lot of trouble to have me."

Christopher Kimball

That weekend, all four kids were at home, including our two oldest girls, who are now off at boarding school. It was suppertime, and we were sitting around the table in front of a fire that felt particularly good, as the rain hadn't let up for 10 days. It was a simple supper: our own steak and potatoes, a salad from the garden, and a deep-dish apple pie made from the just-picked stock in the root cellar.

This reminded me of another table, the one at the Yellow Farmhouse. Back in the 1960s, I was sitting among farmers, Charlie and Floyd, the farmhands, Onie and Herbie, and the two dogs, Dixie and Bonnie, as the heat came from a green Kalamazoo wood cookstove. (Most Vermonters don't care for fireplaces—they suck up too much heat.) The one detail I remember most about those days was the cookies. Marie Briggs, the cook and baker, gave us only those cookies that weren't good enough to sell, so most of them had slightly burnt bottoms. Pretty soon, we all acquired a taste for dark-colored cookies, and to this day I like my pastry on the black side of brown.

We shouldn't be surprised that details define our personal history. The smell of yeast and wet dog. The heat from a wood cookstove. The way Floyd used to tell a story, elbows on his thighs, a cigarette dangling from his lip. Or, on this rainy evening, the taste of apple pie and with it the pleasures of a warm fire and the family table. Little things are economical, telling us who we were with a mere lick or glance. Even today, when I taste something dark and smoky, it's an invitation to noon dinner, to a place at the table where I learned to appreciate the commonplace—hard work, parsimony, self-reliance, and even the cookies that Marie couldn't sell down at the country store.

FOR INQUIRIES, ORDERS, OR MORE INFORMATION:

www.cooksillustrated.com

At www.cooksillustrated.com, you can order books and subscriptions, sign up for our free e-newsletter, or renew your magazine subscription. Join the Web site and you'll have access to 13 years of *Cook's* recipes, cookware tests, ingredient tastings, and more.

COOKBOOKS

We sell more than 40 cookbooks by the editors of *Cook's Illustrated*. To order, visit our bookstore at www.cooksillustrated.com or call 800-611-0759 (or 515-246-6911 from outside the U.S.).

COOK'S ILLUSTRATED Magazine

Cook's Illustrated magazine (ISSN 1068-2821), number 78, is published bimonthly by Boston Common Press Limited Partnership, 17 Station Street, Brookline, MA 02445. Copyright 2005 Boston Common Press Limited Partnership. Periodicals postage paid at Boston, Mass., and additional mailing offices, USPS #012487. POSTMASTER: Send address changes to Cook's Illustrated, P.O. Box 7446, Red Oak, IA 51591-0446. For subscription and gift subscription orders, subscription inquiries, or change-of-address notices, call 800-526-8442 in the U.S. or 515-247-7571 from outside the U.S., or write us at Cook's Illustrated, P.O. Box 7446, Red Oak, IA 51591-0446.

⇒ COMPILED BY SANDRA WU ⇐

Presizzled Bacon

I've noticed that fully cooked bacon is available at the supermarket. It seems to have a prolonged shelf life, but it's also quite expensive. Is it worth the price?

RITA WEINBERG
EAST BRUNSWICK, N.J.

➤ After a quick shopping trip, we managed to come up with three brands of shelf-stable bacon: Oscar Meyer, Hormel, and a generic house brand from a Boston-area supermarket. We conducted a blind tasting of these bacons in two applications: BLT (bacon, lettuce, and tomato) sandwiches and spinach salad with bacon dressing. As a point of comparison, we included in the mix one of our recommended brands of supermarket bacon—Boar's Head Naturally Smoked Sliced Bacon—to see if our panel of tasters would be fooled.

Straight out of the package, the precooked bacon ranged from thin and pale with a substantial amount of white fat to dark and crispy looking with spotty black sections and salt crystals. Although all three brands had been fully cooked, they still needed some manner of reheating and had to be refrigerated once opened.

Tasters overwhelmingly preferred the crisp-chewy texture and rich, meaty, salty-smoky flavor of the (fresh) Boar's Head bacon over any of the precooked varieties. Placing a distant second, the Oscar Mayer precooked bacon was mild in flavor, salty but not smoky, and "flaccid" in the BLT sandwich. When diced and added to the salad, it was alternately described as "meaty and smoky," "flavorless," and having "a strong bacon flavor, but tastes frozen." Not horrible—but not quite a glowing recommendation. The Hormel and the generic brand both came up short across the board, thanks to their chewy texture and "stale," "one-dimensional" flavor.

Our verdict? Aside from the advantages of being ready to eat in half the time of "raw" bacon and being convenient for

STRIP TEST
Is precooked bacon
a raw deal?

camping (or stockpiling in the pantry), we don't see much justification for buying these expensive strips.

Freezing Egg Whites

Can I freeze leftover egg whites and use them later? If so, what's the best way?

COLLEEN MONACO
SAN FRANCISCO, CALIF.

➤ Egg whites can be frozen and kept for later use (up to 12 months, according to the U.S. Department of Agriculture). While they can be frozen together in a solid mass in an airtight container, the test kitchen has found that it's much more convenient to freeze egg whites individually in an ice cube tray before transferring these "egg cubes" to a zipper-lock storage bag. Whatever amount you need can then be placed in an airtight container in the refrigerator overnight to thaw out. (Attempts to microwave the frozen whites at 50 percent power met with limited success; we had to be so careful not to accidentally cook sections of the whites that the time savings just wasn't worth it.)

Storage issues aside, we wondered how frozen egg whites would compare with their fresh counterparts in cooking applications. To find out, we made two versions of angel food cake and meringue, one using fresh and the other using frozen-and-thawed egg whites. We found that the frozen whites took longer to whip up to their soft-peak and stiff-peak stages and that they had a tendency to deflate a little when additional ingredients were incorporated.

In terms of baking, the fresh egg-white cake rose ¼ to ½ inch higher than the frozen egg-white cake, but the flavors of the cakes were virtually the same. Texturally, the frozen version came up short: less "bouncy," wetter, gummier, and too delicate on the tongue. As for the meringue disks, the one made with frozen whites had a wrinkly, deflated, and cracked appearance and a slightly gummier, chewier texture than its smooth-and-shiny fresh white counterpart. What's more, the frozen-white disk spread during cooking and therefore ended up too large and too flat.

Researching the topic further, we found out that very cold temperatures (anywhere below the optimal freezing temperature of 0 degrees

Fahrenheit) can hinder the functionality of the proteins needed to whip volume into egg whites, as can contamination by ice crystals—a danger even with supposedly "airtight" containers. The further the temperature falls, the worse the damage. Although we keep our test kitchen freezers as close to 0 degrees as possible, our egg whites apparently suffered at least minor damage.

So what do we recommend? By all means, freeze and use your leftover egg whites, but save them for applications that call for small amounts (egg wash) or that don't depend on volume (omelets).

Sharpening Granton Blades

Can granton-edge knives be honed like regular knives, or does maintaining their edge require a special tool or technique?

ADRIENNE ANCHETA
ANN ARBOR, MICH.

➤ Knives with granton blades (hollow-ground with oval recesses to create air pockets that reduce the friction between the blade and the food) can be sharpened and honed in the same way as any standard knife blade. According to four knife experts we contacted, no special product or technique is required. After sharpening a few of them ourselves, we agree. Even when you eventually sharpen your way down to the recessed areas, don't sweat it: The life of a granton-edge knife extends well beyond that of the crescent-shaped hollows of its blade. We used a granton-edge knife that had been worn down midway through the height of its grooves and a brand-new model to cut through a potato and an onion. Both knives sliced the vegetables easily, although lopping off the final bottom edge with the older knife sometimes required an extra draw or two of the blade thanks to the faintly scalloped edge.

INTO THE GROOVE?
No need to worry.

Spotting Trans Fat

I thought hydrogenated oil was the primary source of trans fat. But when I recently bought a bag of potato chips, the packaging advertised "0 grams trans fat" while the ingredient list included partially hydrogenated soybean oil. If I want to avoid trans fat, what should I look for?

KIM HUYNH
OAKLAND, CALIF.

➤ To find out whether a product contains trans fat—formed by adding hydrogen to vegetable oil to make it stay solid (rather than liquid) at room temperature—just look at the ingredient list on the label. According to the U.S. Food and Drug Administration, if "shortening," "partially hydrogenated vegetable oil," or "hydrogenated vegetable oil" is listed, the food contains trans fat. Although trans fat is great for keeping food items crispy and shelf-stable, it's also been linked to raised levels of LDL cholesterol (the bad kind), reduced levels of HDL cholesterol (the good kind), and increased risk of cardiovascular disease. In accordance with FDA guidelines, all conventional food products must declare trans fat content on their food labels by January 2006.

But a product's claim of "0 grams trans fat" is not a guarantee that it's free of these controversial fatty acids. Trans fat content is expressed as grams per serving to the nearest 0.5 gram below 5 grams and to the nearest gram above 5 grams. So if a serving contains less than 0.5 gram, it's expressed as 0 grams.

Cooking with Soy Milk

Can soy milk be substituted for regular milk in recipes?

JOANNE ARTMAN
MIDDLETOWN, PA.

➤ Soy milk is more watery than whole milk, which comes as no surprise given that most brands contain about half the fat.

To find out whether this creates problems in baking or cooking, we bought four widely available brands of "plain" soy milk and pitted them against whole milk in three applications: a cream pie filling, a yellow layer cake, and a béchamel sauce. Our lineup included Edensoy, Silk, 365 Organic, and WestSoy.

In the vanilla cream pie filling (cooked on the stovetop for 10 minutes), all brands but one, Edensoy, proved to be acceptable. Tasters found the Edensoy pie filling to be slightly "gelatinous" and "pasty," with a "cooked rice" flavor, and disliked its dark taupe color. By contrast, tasters praised Silk and 365 Organic for producing fillings that tasted the most like the real deal. Results were even more favorable in the yellow cake: Except for yielding a marginally drier texture overall than whole milk and a faint soy aftertaste, soy milk was a perfectly good substitute for whole milk here.

With the béchamel, it was a different story entirely. All the soy milk brands tanked for having

FAUX MILK
For more than just cereal and coffee?

a too-pronounced soy flavor and a cloying sweetness. Although these off flavors could be masked by the other ingredients in, say, a hearty lasagna, we wouldn't recommend using soy milk in this or any other savory application.

Our recommendation? If you'd like to substitute soy milk for whole milk in baked goods and desserts, it's fine to do so; the added inherent sweetness works in these recipes. Our overall favorite was Silk Organic Plain Soy Milk, found in the refrigerated section of major supermarkets. Just keep the stuff out of savory dishes.

Trickle-Down Theory

Is there any truth to the old myth that when you braise or roast a large piece of meat with a sheet of fat on the surface, the sheet of fat should face up? Does it help the meat self-baste?

KALIMAR MAIA
ARLINGTON, VA.

➤ In barbecue circles, the fat cap is almost always left face up, and many recipes repeat the same admonition when the meat is destined for the oven. But does it matter? We decided to test roasting a flat-cut brisket on a wire rack set over a baking sheet (so the bottom wouldn't sit in its own fat), uncovered, in a 275-degree oven. While we would never recommend cooking a brisket this way (it should always be braised or wrapped in foil to retain the most moisture), we hoped this extreme method could offer some insight. To minimize any variation from piece to piece in terms of fat distribution, toughness, and flavor, we cut one brisket in half lengthwise. One half roasted fat side up, the other fat side down.

After four hours, both briskets were fairly dry (no surprise), but the differences were telling. The brisket cooked fat side up was slightly more tender and yielded less resistance when poked with a fork. The melted fat basted the outer surfaces (the sides and bottom) of the brisket, making for a noticeably moister exterior, and the fat itself was more deeply browned, crispier, and more fully rendered. By contrast, the brisket cooked fat side down became dark, tough, and leathery, and its fat cap remained pale and firm.

More interesting, in the fat-side-up roast, tasters noticed little effect on moisture in the interior directly beneath the fat cap. After repeat tests yielded identical results, it was clear that the fat from the cap doesn't actually soak into the interior layers of meat (a myth perpetuated by some barbecue "experts"). As the rendered fat bathes the exterior, however, it does act as a natural protective barrier, reducing the amount of moisture that escapes from the surface. (By contrast,

only marbled fat and collagen that has been converted into gelatin can affect the texture of the interior.) So the next time you barbecue or braise a brisket or another piece of meat with a large layer of fat, remember to position it with the fat cap on top.

SEND US YOUR QUESTIONS We will provide a complimentary one-year subscription for each letter we print. Send your inquiry, name, address, and daytime telephone number to Notes from Readers, Cook's Illustrated, P.O. Box 470589, Brookline, MA 02447, or to notesfromreaders@bcpress.com.

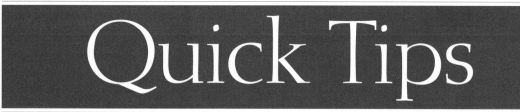

Quick Tips

⋑ COMPILED BY DAVID PAZMIÑO ⋐

Degreasing Pepperoni

Straight from the package, pepperoni often leave unsightly puddles of grease when baked atop a pizza. Kathryn Ryan of Annandale, Va., has figured out how to prevent this problem.

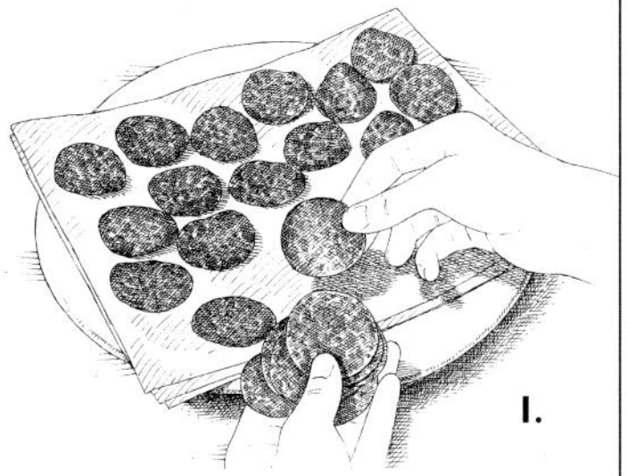

1.

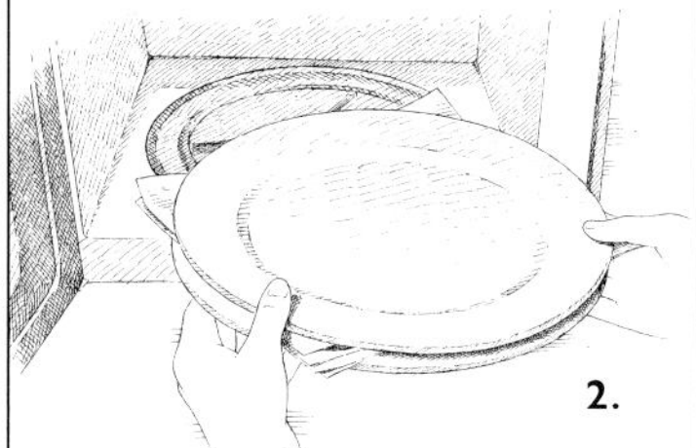

2.

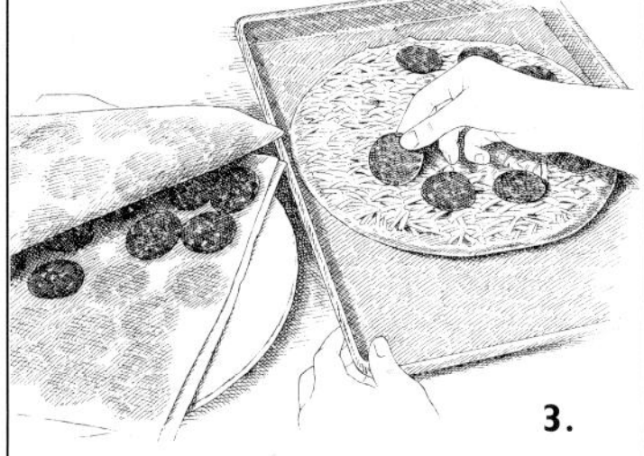

3.

1. Line a microwave-safe plate with a double layer of paper towels, place the pepperoni on top, then cover with two more paper towels and another plate to keep the meaty disks flat.
2. Cook for 30 seconds in a microwave on high, carefully remove the hot plate from the microwave, and uncover.
3. Place the degreased pepperoni on the pizza and bake according to the recipe.

Knife Savers

Instead of using a knife to break apart chocolate or frozen liquids, Stephen Hawk of Wheaton, Ill., keeps a cheap chisel from the local hardware store on hand. The chisel's sturdy edge does a better job—and keeps his knives' sharp, delicate edges out of harm's way.

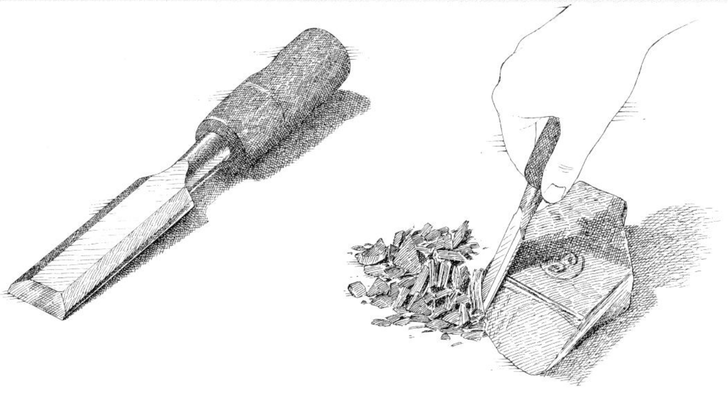

Place the chisel on chocolate or ice, angled away from you. Using short, quick strokes, chip into pieces of desired size.

A Crate Idea

Instead of discarding empty clementine orange containers, Marnie Coleman of Auburn, Maine, keeps the stackable crates in her pantry for storing onions, potatoes, and other items that benefit from exposure to air.

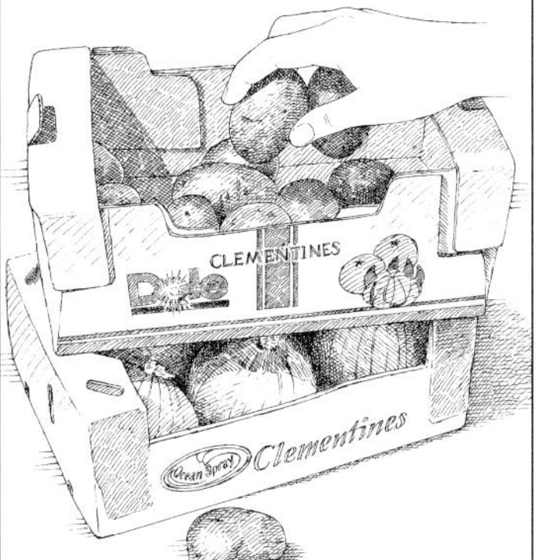

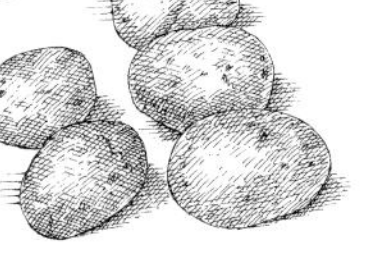

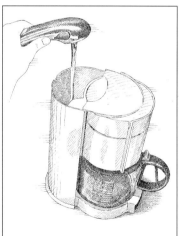

Puddle-Free Coffee Making

The poorly designed spouts of most modern coffee carafes make it difficult to pour water into the coffee-maker reservoir without splashing the countertop. Tired of the puddles, Karen Dailey of Hampton Bays, N.Y., fills the reservoir directly from the sink using the spray hose, avoiding the wet mess while also saving a step.

Uncracking Cracked Cheesecake

Even when every precaution is taken, the occasional cheesecake will develop unsightly cracks. Susan Secrest of Drexel, N.C., has discovered a simple method for repairing them.

1.

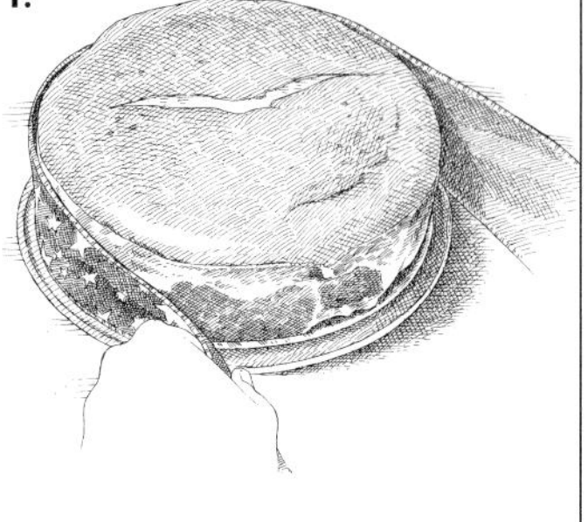

2.

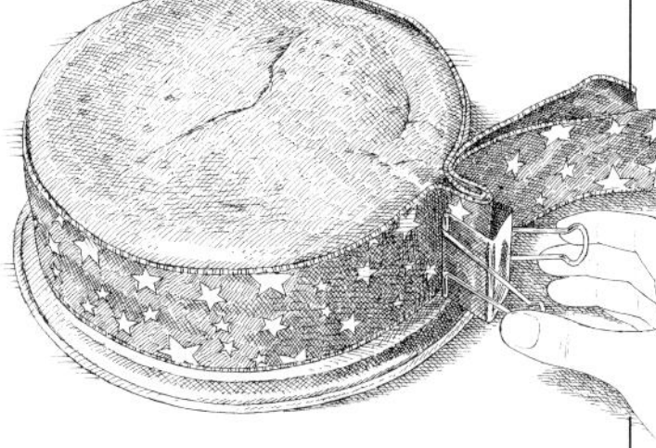

1. Remove the sidewall from the springform pan while the cheesecake is warm. Wrap a cloth ribbon snugly around the cake, preferably one that covers the sides completely (about 3 inches wide for most pans).
2. Secure the ribbon with a binder clip, and leave the ribbon in place until the cake has cooled completely.

Unsticking Sticky Pie Dough

Few things are more frustrating in the kitchen than having a rolled dough stick to the work surface. Rather than dirtying a bench scraper, Sterling Smith of San Ramon, Calif., makes do with the metal ruler he's used to measure the dough. Its thin edges pry the stubborn dough off just as well.

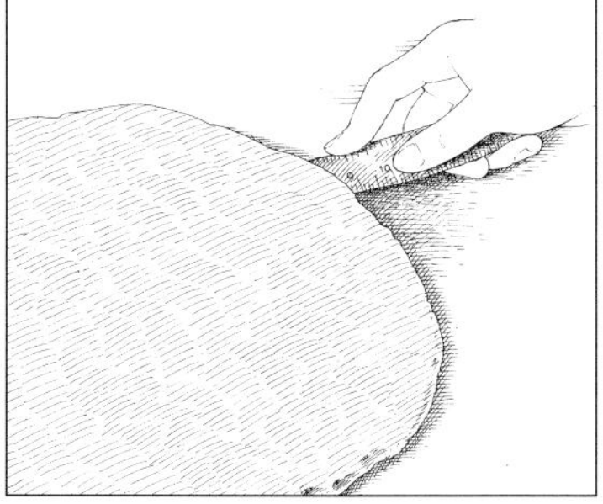

ILLUSTRATION: JOHN BURGOYNE

Send Us Your Tip We will provide a complimentary one-year subscription for each tip we print. Send your tip, name, and address to Quick Tips, Cook's Illustrated, P.O. Box 470589, Brookline, MA 02447, or to quicktips@bcpress.com.

No-Creep Pie Dough

After watching too many pie doughs inch their way across the counter while rolling them out between sheets of parchment paper, Cindy Ehlenfeldt of Charlestown, N.H., finally put a stop to it. She now places a nonstick silicone mat underneath the parchment paper, which makes for smooth, stable rolling.

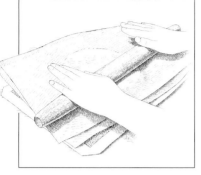

'Grounded' Nuts

Chopping nuts on a cutting board can send projectiles flying across the kitchen. Ginny Kluger of West Hartford, Conn., solves this problem by using a sharp-edged pastry blender to chop soft nuts like walnuts and pecans in a mixing bowl.

Wine-Glass Buffer Zone

Washing fragile glassware by hand is the best way to stave off breakage—unless it slips your grasp and crashes down into the sink. As a precautionary measure, Esther Cohen of Arlington, Mass., places rubber shelf liners in the sink for a breakage-free cleaning session.

Smarter Olive Retrieval

Dorothy Lorenc of Arlington, Texas, found an easy way to extract capers and olives from their narrow jars. She uses the small scoop of a melon baller to retrieve capers and the larger scoop for olives. As a bonus, the excess brine drains through the scoops' perforations.

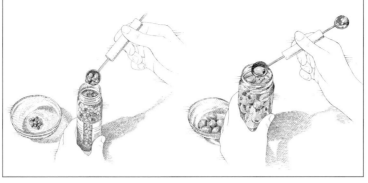

Drier Dinner Guests

Refilling guests' glasses with cold beverages usually means contending with dribbles from the pitcher. Heidi Berry of Port Townsend, Wash., has a unique solution.

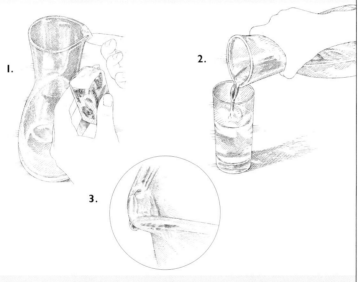

1. Smear a small dab of butter on the inside and outside edges of the pitcher's spout.
2. Pour the ice-cold beverage.
3. The butter stops drops of liquids just as they're about to take the plunge.

Seeding Hot Peppers

Using a knife to remove the seeds and ribs from a hot chile pepper takes a very steady hand. Evelyn Cantrell of Evansville, Wis., has come up with a safer and equally effective alternative.

1. Cut the pepper in half with a knife.
2. Starting opposite the stem end, run the edge of a small melon baller scoop down the inside of the pepper, scraping up seeds and ribs.
3. Cut off the core with the scoop.

No More Spouting Off

To prevent boiling water from sputtering from the spout of her metal teakettle, Therese Grundl of Sherman Oaks, Calif., runs the hot metal spout under cold water just before pouring out the contents.

Onions in the Mist

When browning small amounts of onion, there's a tendency for drying and scorching, even when using a high-quality pan. Brad Hutchinson of Bayville, N.Y., keeps small batches of onions moist with a plant mister, spritzing them lightly if they start to look dry. The water not only helps them caramelize evenly but also deglazes any flavorful brown bits (*fond*) stuck to the bottom of the pan.

Skillet Chicken Pot Pie

Many pot pie recipes treat the chicken and vegetables as mere hitchhikers in the rich, creamy sauce. We thought it was time to end the free ride.

≥ BY NINA WEST ≤

The dish that epitomizes my notion of comfort food is my Nana's chicken pot pie. Yet I was hard-pressed to find even one test kitchen colleague who shared my fondness for this combination of pie pastry, chicken, vegetables, and creamy velouté. The reason became abundantly clear after testing a dozen recipes. Even the few that avoided doughy toppings and pasty sauces fell short in the flavor department. The problem wasn't skimping on butter or cream; it was the absence of decent chicken or vegetable flavor. What's more, chicken pot pie is not a quick and easy dish: You have to make pie pastry, prepare the filling ingredients, and make a sauce. For all that work, it better be good—really good.

Getting More Chicken Flavor

The recipes I tried followed the same basic procedure: cook a *roux* (flour and butter), add broth and heavy cream, add poached breast meat and blanched vegetables, then bake the mixture beneath a topping. Problem one: For intense chicken flavor, poaching just wasn't going to cut it. I tried roasting, broiling, and pan-searing. I tried white meat, dark meat, and both. In the end, tasters liked the deep flavor imparted by oven-roasting a whole chicken; the dry, constant heat helped concentrate flavors. The downside? The nearly 1½-hour oven session. But by cutting the chicken into pieces, I could get the benefits of roasting while reducing the cooking time by half.

Using the usual *Cook's* roasting technique of pan-searing, then finishing in the oven, I realized I was creating the perfect conduit for deep chicken flavor: the pan juices and *fond* (the browned bits stuck to the pan), which I could save for building the sauce. I took a cue from gravy-making basics and placed a classic *mirepoix* (onion, celery, and carrot) in the bottom of the same skillet. Not only did the vegetables give the drippings more flavor, but they also served as a makeshift roasting rack that kept the chicken from stewing in its own juices in the oven.

Resting the chicken for 30 minutes ensured that enough juices were reabsorbed to keep the meat moist. One day, I accidentally let the chicken sit for an hour, and tasters perceived dramatically

Our one-skillet method produces a rich, flavorful chicken pot pie—and the skillet serves double duty as a pie plate.

increased tenderness. A fluke? After repeated tests yielded the same results, I investigated further. It turns out that while a moderate period of resting helps retain moisture, additional time tenderizes the meat. How? Mild residual heat continues to break down the connective tissue, and the meat becomes more tender (think slow-cooking pot roast at a very low temperature).

Vegetables, Sauce, and Crust

I wanted to avoid the blandness of blanched vegetables, and it occurred to me that traditional pot pie veggies (carrots, celery, onions, peas) were almost identical to the mirepoix I had been cooking. Why not use the same vegetables for the filling? Chilling the cooked vegetables (and chicken) before assembling the pie kept them from overcooking during the final stretch.

As for the sauce, I first deglazed the pan with canned broth to capture every bit of flavor. I then emptied the pan and made a traditional roux to thicken the sauce. After whisking my pan-juice-spiked broth back into the roux, I added ¾ cup heavy cream to give the sauce richness and body (milk was too thin, while a sauce made with half-and-half broke; see Kitchen Notes, page 30, for an explanation). The bright notes of parsley, thyme, and lemon rounded out the flavor profile.

So far I had done all my cooking in one pan. Why change now? I decided to top (and bake) the filling in the same skillet—a makeshift pie plate. Some recipes call for simply cutting out a few rounds of frozen puff pastry or rolling out biscuit dough. Not me: I was going for the ultimate chicken pot pie, so anything other than our homemade all-butter pie dough (September/October 2005) seemed to be missing the point. (That said, our winning store-bought crust makes an acceptable option if you can't bring yourself to roll out homemade pie dough; see Kitchen Notes, page 31.)

To make the dough work with the skillet's dimensions, I needed to chill the crust after rolling; freshly rolled dough was too unwieldy to wrangle onto the skillet. Unfortunately, chilling

One Skillet, Many Layers of Flavor

By cooking the chicken and vegetables, building the creamy sauce, and even baking the crust-topped pie all in the same 12-inch skillet, we ensure that every drop of flavor makes it into the final dish.

SEAR
Searing the chicken in the skillet develops the first layer of flavor: the deep brown fond.

ROAST
Roasting the chicken and vegetables in the same skillet releases flavorful juices that will be used in the sauce.

DEGLAZE
Deglazing the skillet infuses the broth with flavors from the fond, chicken, and vegetables.

the dough also extended the baking time from 15 minutes to almost 50—by which time the underside of the crust was soggy. Turning up the temperature for the first 15 minutes helped the crust set quickly, followed by lower heat to let the crust bake through more gently.

What did I end up with? A dish that transcends most people's memories of lackluster pot pie. Sure, it takes time and effort, but it is as superior to run-of-the-mill pot pie as *boeuf à la bourguignonne* is to Dinty Moore beef stew.

CHICKEN POT PIE
SERVES 6 TO 8

Our usual pie-crust procedures work fine with a cool 9-inch pie plate. But for a hot 12-inch skillet, we had to make some adjustments—for instance, eliminating the bottom crust and fluting the dough before sliding it over the filling.

 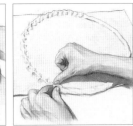 

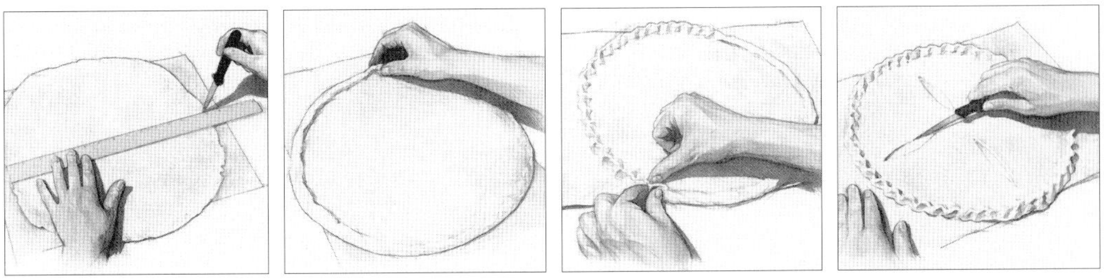

1. Roll out dough to rough 14-inch round on parchment. Mark center of top, bottom, and side arcs with knife.

2. Trim dough to precise 14-inch circle, connecting marks from step 1. Fold dough to form ½-inch perimeter rim.

3. Crimp folded dough between knuckle and fore-fingers to form 12-inch round with fluted edge.

4. Cut four oval-shaped vents, 3 inches long and about ½ inch wide. Decorate dough with cutouts.

Substitute 3 to 3½ pounds of bone-in, skin-on chicken parts for the whole chicken, if desired. We recommend chilling the rolled and shaped dough in the freezer. The dough can be prepared the day before and refrigerated. The chicken and vegetables can also be prepared the day before.

Dough
- 1⅔ cups (8¼ ounces) unbleached all-purpose flour, plus additional for work surface
- ¾ teaspoon table salt
- 10 tablespoons (1¼ sticks) cold, unsalted butter, cut into ½-inch pieces and frozen for 10 minutes
- 2 tablespoons sour cream
- 4–6 tablespoons ice water

Chicken and Vegetables
- 1 teaspoon vegetable oil
- 1 whole chicken (about 4½ pounds), cut into 4 pieces (2 breast pieces, 2 leg quarters, wings discarded) and trimmed of excess fat
- 24 frozen pearl onions, thawed, drained, and patted dry (about 1 cup, or 5 ounces)
- 1 medium onion, cut into ½-inch pieces (about 1 cup)
- 4 medium carrots, cut into ½-inch pieces (about 1½ cups)
- 3 medium ribs celery, cut into ½-inch pieces (about 1 cup)
  Table salt and ground black pepper

Sauce
- 4¼ cups low-sodium chicken broth
- 4 tablespoons unsalted butter
- ½ cup unbleached all-purpose flour
- ¾ cup heavy cream
- ¾ cup frozen peas (unthawed, about 3½ ounces)
- 2 teaspoons juice from 1 lemon
- 1 tablespoon minced fresh parsley leaves
- 1 teaspoon minced fresh thyme leaves
  Table salt and ground black pepper

1. **TO MAKE THE DOUGH:** Process flour and salt together in food processor until combined,

about 3 seconds. Add butter and pulse until size of large peas, about six to eight 1-second pulses.

2. Mix sour cream and 4 tablespoons ice water in small bowl until combined. Add half of sour cream mixture to flour mixture; pulse for three 1-second pulses. Repeat with remaining sour cream mixture. Pinch dough with fingers; if dough is floury, dry, and does not hold together, add 1 to 2 additional tablespoons water and process until dough forms large clumps and no dry flour remains, three to five 1-second pulses.

3. Turn dough onto work surface. Shape into ball and flatten to 5-inch disk; wrap in plastic and refrigerate until firm but not hard, 1 to 2 hours. (Dough can be refrigerated overnight.)

4. **TO ROAST CHICKEN AND VEGETABLES:** Adjust oven racks to lower-middle and upper-middle positions; heat oven to 450 degrees. Heat oil in heavy-bottomed 12-inch ovenproof skillet over medium-high heat until oil just begins to smoke; swirl skillet to coat evenly with oil. Brown chicken pieces skin side down until deep golden, 3 to 4 minutes; turn chicken pieces and brown until golden on second side, 3 to 4 minutes longer. Transfer chicken to large plate; drain all but 1 tablespoon fat.

5. Set skillet over medium heat. Add pearl onions and cook, stirring occasionally, until browned, about 3 minutes. Increase heat to medium-high and add onion, carrots, celery, and salt and pepper to taste; cook, stirring occasionally, until vegetables begin to brown, 2 to 3 minutes. Return chicken pieces to skillet skin side up and place in oven on lower-middle rack. Roast until thickest part of breast registers about 160 degrees on instant-read thermometer and thickest part of thigh and drumstick registers about 175 degrees, 18 to 25 minutes. Using potholder or oven mitt, remove skillet from oven. Transfer chicken to platter and let rest 1 hour. Set skillet with vegetables aside.

6. **TO ROLL OUT THE DOUGH:** (If dough has been chilled longer than 2 hours, let stand at room temperature for 15 minutes before roll-

ing.) Dust 16 by 12-inch sheet of parchment paper liberally with flour; roll, flute, and cut vent holes according to illustrations above. Transfer parchment and dough to baking sheet; chill in freezer until ready to use, at least 30 minutes (or refrigerate for 1 hour).

7. **TO MAKE SAUCE AND ASSEMBLE PIE:** While chicken rests, return skillet with vegetables to medium-high heat. Add chicken broth and any juices from chicken platter and bring to simmer, scraping sides and bottom of skillet with wooden spoon to loosen any browned bits. Pour contents of skillet through medium-mesh strainer set over large bowl; transfer vegetables from strainer to separate bowl and refrigerate. After fat rises to surface of broth, 15 to 20 minutes, skim with ladle or large spoon and discard. (You should have about 3½ cups broth.)

8. When chicken has rested, remove and discard skin. Using fingers or fork, pull chicken off bones into 2-inch shreds and 1-inch chunks; refrigerate until ready to use (you should have about 4½ cups chicken). Wipe skillet clean; melt butter over medium-high heat until foaming. Stir in flour and cook, stirring constantly, until mixture darkens slightly and becomes fragrant, about 1 minute. Slowly whisk in broth and cream and bring to boil; reduce heat to medium and simmer, stirring constantly, until sauce is thickened and coats back of spoon, 8 to 10 minutes. Off heat, add chicken, reserved vegetables, peas, lemon juice, parsley, thyme, and salt and pepper to taste; gently stir to combine. Remove dough from freezer, lift off parchment paper, and place dough on top of filling. Bake on upper-middle rack at 450 degrees until crust begins to brown around edges, about 15 minutes; reduce heat to 375 degrees and continue to bake until crust is golden brown and filling bubbles, 15 to 20 minutes more. Let cool 15 minutes before serving.

Go to www.cooksillustrated.com
- Key in code 1061 for our **Chicken Broth Tasting**.

COOK'S extra

Translating Huevos Rancheros

Getting this humble Mexican breakfast just right is easy when you have homemade tortillas and ripe tomatoes lying around. All we had were mediocre supermarket staples.

⇒ BY ERIKA BRUCE ⇐

Huevos rancheros, or "rancher-style eggs," is a dish born of ease and convenience: a quick, satisfying meal that makes use of leftover salsa and corn tortillas to serve as a simple Mexican breakfast alongside hearty refried beans. While there are many variations on this theme, most often the eggs are quickly fried, slipped onto a corn tortilla base, then napped with a fiery, roasted tomato-chile salsa.

North of the border, it's a different story: The huevos rancheros found on American brunch menus more closely resemble heaping plates of nachos. The eggs are lost under any number of untraditional ingredients—meat, gobs of melted cheese, shredded lettuce, and slices of avocado—the tortillas become soggy, the flavors are muddied.

But even with an authentic recipe, making this dish at home is no less problematic when the cook is faced with mediocre supermarket ingredients such as pale, mealy tomatoes and rubbery packaged tortillas. I wanted to do right by this dish and produce a version as close to authentic as I could with the materials at hand.

By crisping packaged tortillas, roasting tomatoes and chiles, and lightly poaching the eggs, we captured the spirit of the Mexican original.

The Salsa Dance

Salsa is the star in most authentic versions, so improving it was my first move. Traditionally, a cooked salsa is used (often fried in a little hot oil), and I thought canned tomatoes might give me better flavor than fresh. Armed only with the basics—tomatoes, jalapeños, and onions—I sautéed my way through a few simple salsas, substituting pureed, diced, and whole canned tomatoes for fresh. Pureed tomatoes were too thin and smooth, diced tomatoes were on the overly firm and chunky side, and whole tomatoes tasted too cooked. Tasters were looking for the bright, tart flavor that only fresh tomatoes can offer.

Back in the produce aisle, I reexamined my options. I tried diminutive cherry and oblong plum tomatoes as well as the usual round orbs. The cherry tomatoes held the most promise with their puckeringly tart flavor, but tasters couldn't get past the amount of skin and seeds in the salsa. The plum tomatoes had slightly more complexity than the round tomatoes and a more compact, less watery texture. In an effort to increase their flavor, I turned to the broiler; despite blackening and blistering their skins, the high heat did little to improve the flavor on the inside of the tomatoes. I decided to reduce the oven temperature and give the tomatoes more oven time. At 375 degrees, the tomatoes stayed intact, their flesh smooth and velvety.

Because I was now roasting the tomatoes and thus effectively enhancing their flavor (and then pulsing them in the food processor), I wondered if the chiles and onions would also benefit from roasting. I halved the jalapeños and cut the onions into thick wedges and tossed them with a little vegetable oil along with the tomatoes. Indeed, roasting improved their flavor, adding a deeper, sweeter intensity. Heady garlic was a welcome addition to this mix, as were cumin for its nutty flavor and cayenne pepper for extra zing. For more color and depth of flavor, I coated all the ingredients with a tablespoon of tomato paste before putting them in the oven. All I needed now was some brightness to round out the salsa. Once I had given the roasted vegetables a quick turn in the food processor, I added lime juice and fresh cilantro. As a final touch, I reserved one jalapeño and added it, finely chopped, at the end for a zesty, clean chile flavor.

Not So Over-Easy

After the rigmarole of roasting the salsa ingredients (though it was certainly worth the effort), I was chagrined to find that the simple fried-egg preparation I was expecting turned out to be a sloppy mess on the plate. Four gently fried eggs looked beautiful in the skillet but, once separated, appeared haphazard and irregular on top of a round tortilla—if I didn't break the yolks getting them there. While poaching the eggs is not traditional, I had seen this technique in a few recipes; indeed, these eggs were easily (and neatly) scooped out of their poaching liquid.

As I monitored my two adjacent cooking vessels full of bubbling liquid—poaching eggs and simmering salsa—I realized I might be able to make things even easier. Adding all the hot salsa to a skillet, I scooped out four small wells and cracked an egg into each, then fit a lid over the top for even cooking. Although the edges of the whites were disrupted from the bubbling salsa, the eggs were just as easily transferred to the plate as before. Lowering the heat while the eggs were poaching solved the frayed-edge matter, and I finally achieved the look I was after. Even better, the eggs benefited from the flavor boost, and I had only one pot to watch (and one less to wash).

When Bad Things Happen to Good Food

Beans, beef, cheese, guacamole, lettuce, olives, sour cream: To compensate for so-so ingredients, many recipes opt for overkill, turning this simple Mexican breakfast into an egg-adorned plate of "Extreme Nachos." Our version takes a simpler approach, fine-tuning flavor and texture for a few key ingredients. Huevos rancheros should be appetizing—not an appetizer.

Three Steps to Better Huevos Rancheros

ROAST
Slow-roasting improved the flavor of supermarket tomatoes while intensifying the other salsa ingredients.

TOAST
Crisping store-bought tortillas in the oven yielded the best texture—light and crispy, not tough or greasy.

POACH
Poaching the eggs in small wells made in the salsa improved their flavor and left us with just one pot to watch.

Tortilla Reform

Most authentic recipes call for fresh, handmade corn tortillas. I was stuck with all-but-stale supermarket versions. Some recipes attempt to "soften" the tortillas with a five-second shallow-fry, but this produced sodden, greasy results. Longer frying eliminated the sogginess but not the greasiness. Toasting the tortillas in a thin coating of oil in a skillet made them tough. Finally, I returned to the oven. Brushed lightly with oil, sprinkled with a little salt, and toasted until golden brown at 450 degrees, these tortillas were crisp and dry—a perfect foil for the soft, creamy poached eggs and the deep, roasted flavors of the fiery salsa. My translation was complete.

HUEVOS RANCHEROS
SERVES 2 TO 4

To save time in the morning, make the salsa the day before and store it overnight in the refrigerator. For extra-spicy salsa, add some of the reserved jalapeño ribs and seeds to taste. If you need to hold the tortillas for a short time, cover the baking sheet with foil. If you like, serve with refried beans (see Cook's Extra, at right, for our recipe).

- 3 jalapeño chiles, halved, seeds and ribs removed (see note above)
- 1½ pounds ripe plum tomatoes (about 8 medium), cored and halved
- ½ medium yellow onion, cut into ½-inch wedges
- 2 medium garlic cloves, peeled
- 1 tablespoon tomato paste
  Table salt
- 3 tablespoons vegetable oil
- ½ teaspoon ground cumin
- ⅛ teaspoon cayenne
- 3 tablespoons minced fresh cilantro leaves
  Ground black pepper
- 1–2 tablespoons juice from 1 or 2 limes, plus additional lime cut into wedges for serving
- 4 corn tortillas
- 4 large eggs

1. **FOR THE SALSA:** Adjust oven rack to middle position; heat oven to 375 degrees. Mince one jalapeño and set aside. In medium bowl, combine tomatoes, remaining jalapeños, onion, garlic, tomato paste, 1 teaspoon salt, 2 tablespoons oil, cumin, and cayenne; toss to mix thoroughly. Place vegetables cut side down on rimmed baking sheet. Roast until tomatoes are tender and skins begin to shrivel and brown, 35 to 45 minutes; cool on baking sheet for 10 minutes. Increase oven heat to 450 degrees. Using tongs, transfer roasted onions, garlic, and jalapeños to bowl of food processor. Process until almost completely broken down, about 10 seconds, pausing halfway through to scrape sides of bowl with rubber spatula. Add tomatoes and process until salsa is slightly chunky, about 10 seconds more. Add 2 tablespoons cilantro, reserved minced jalapeño, salt, pepper, and lime juice to taste.

2. **FOR THE TORTILLAS:** Brush both sides of each tortilla lightly with remaining tablespoon oil, sprinkle both sides with salt, and place on clean baking sheet. Bake until tops just begin to color, 5 to 7 minutes; flip tortillas and continue to bake until golden brown, 2 to 3 minutes more.

3. **FOR THE EGGS:** Meanwhile, bring salsa to gentle simmer in 12-inch nonstick skillet over medium heat. Remove from heat and make four shallow wells in salsa with back of large spoon. Break 1 egg into cup, then carefully pour egg into well in salsa; repeat with remaining eggs. Season each egg with salt and pepper to taste, then cover skillet and place over medium-low heat. Cook until desired doneness: 4 to 5 minutes for runny yolks, 6 to 7 minutes for set yolks.

4. **TO SERVE:** Place tortillas on serving plates; gently scoop one egg onto each tortilla. Spoon salsa around each egg, covering tortillas, but leaving portion of eggs exposed. Sprinkle with remaining cilantro and serve with lime wedges.

> COOK'S extra
> **Go to www.cooksillustrated.com**
> • Key in code 1062 for **Refried Beans**.

TASTING: Supermarket Refried Beans

Traditional *frijoles refritos* start with dried pinto beans that are cooked, "fried well" in lard, then mashed. It's not rocket science, but it's time-consuming, so many cooks opt for a store-bought version instead. We sampled six brands of refried beans to determine if any were worth a spot beside our *huevos rancheros*. Only two brands, Old El Paso Traditional and Ortega, use lard (the rest use vegetable oil), but to our tasters, lard offered no advantage in flavor or texture. Texture, however, turned out to be key—Spackle is still Spackle, even if it contains garlic and onions. But even the best brands mustered only enough points to earn our "Recommended with Reservations" rating. And whatever you do, steer clear of dehydrated, instant refried beans. These were consistently stale and unappealing.

–Garth Clingingsmith

RECOMMENDED WITH RESERVATIONS

TACO BELL Home Originals Refried Beans, $0.99 for 16 ounces
Described as "well seasoned" and "super-smooth" by some tasters; others found them salty and runny. Good or bad, they were "just like the ones at Taco Bell."

GOYA Traditional Refried Pinto Beans, $0.89 for 16 ounces
Earthy and "honest" flavor and a hearty "stick-to-your-ribs" texture earned these a close second. Naysayers called them pasty.

OLD EL PASO Traditional Refried Beans, $1.29 for 16 ounces
One of two samples prepared with lard, these beans were on the thick side without being pasty or "gluey."

NOT RECOMMENDED

ORTEGA Refried Beans $0.99 for 16 ounces
Thick and moist (perhaps because made with lard), these beans nonetheless lost lots of points for off-flavors ranging from bitter to "musty."

MEXICALI ROSE Homestyle Mexican Refried Beans, $3.50 for 7 ounces (cooked yield is 26 ounces)
The best instant beans we could find were universally disliked for their "tough skins," their stale flavor, and a texture reminiscent of "soggy saltines."

EDEN ORGANIC Refried Pinto Beans $1.79 for 16 ounces
Three ingredients (organic pinto beans, water, sea salt) needed more help than they got. These beans had a pale, mottled appearance, a gluey texture, and a flavor like "oatmeal gone bad."

Oven-Barbecued Ribs Worth Making

Most oven rib recipes slather on smoke-flavored sauce for an ersatz barbecue experience.
Could we get the smoky flavor and fork-tender texture of true barbecue indoors?

⇛ BY MATTHEW CARD ⇚

The barbecue season for much of the country is cruelly short. When the temperature plunges as fall drifts into winter, it's virtually impossible to maintain the modest grill temperatures required to turn tough cuts of meat tender. When the craving strikes for crisp-crusted, smoky spareribs in midwinter, many of us have just two options: Head to the local BBQ shack or attempt them in the oven. But is it really possible to replicate outdoor ribs inside?

Barbecue is as much cooking method as flavoring agent. The low temperature and steady blanket of hardwood smoke work almost like braising, rendering the collagen—a protein in meat's tough connective tissue—to rich-tasting, silky gelatin. The low temperatures and moist environment are easy to replicate in the oven; the smoke, by contrast, is not.

The indoor barbecued-rib recipes I found were a dubious lot. Most smothered racks in smoke-flavored sauce and baked them slowly. Sure, the ribs tasted OK—slather an old shoe in smoky sauce and it will taste good—but none possessed the deep, rich flavor of true barbecue. Others slicked the ribs with liquid smoke, smearing on a dry rub just before baking—not much better: There's a fundamental difference between ribs that *taste* of smoke and ribs that *are* smoked.

Smoke Gets in My Eyes

There was a third option: indoor smoking. Indoor smokers are essentially roasting pans fitted with a wire rack and a tight-fitting lid. Shredded wood chips are dusted across the pan bottom, the food is set on the rack, and the pan is sealed. The pan is heated on the stovetop to ignite the chips, after

Some recipes muster only the crisp-charred exterior and fall-apart tenderness of outdoor ribs. Ours replicates the smoke flavor, too.

which it enters the oven to finish cooking. Some indoor smokers we tested worked fairly well (see page 30), but the designs are so basic that I opted to rig one up from equipment I had on hand.

Before I got ahead of myself, I had to choose the ribs. For outdoor barbecue, I favor St. Louis–style spareribs—pork spareribs (located near the belly) trimmed of skirt meat and excess cartilage—and saw no reason to change.

Squeezing the ribs onto a wire rack in the kitchen's biggest roasting pan, I tossed in a handful of hickory chips and sealed it with foil. I slid the pan over a burner set on high and waited.

And waited. Smoke finally began seeping out from the foil long after I was afraid the pan would melt from such heat. Once the alarm sounded, I guessed the ribs were smoky enough and transferred the pan to a 250-degree oven to finish.

The ribs tasted smoky alright, but this method certainly had flaws: It was hard finding a pan large enough to fit the ribs, it took me three trips to find wood chips (during off-season, most hardware stores switch out grilling paraphernalia for snow shovels), and the billowing smoke made the test kitchen reek of hickory for days.

Could I move the entire process to the oven, thereby containing the smoke? With no direct high heat, I could also switch to a rimmed baking sheet, which had enough room for the ribs to lie flat. I cranked the oven to 400 degrees, slid the ribs inside, and, once again, waited for smoke. An hour passed without the faintest whiff. After 1½ hours, I pulled the pan out and found gray, greasy, gristly-looking ribs without a hint of smoke flavor.

Higher heat? After turning up the temperature in 25-degree increments, I finally smelled smoke at 500 degrees. Where there's smoke, there should be flavor, but no such luck. The oven still wasn't hot enough to ignite the wood.

Teatime

Desperate, I had a bottle of that wretched liquid smoke in hand when a colleague suggested another option: tea smoking. Chinese cooks smoke a variety of foodstuffs over smoldering black tea. So I replaced the wood chips with loose tea, closed the oven door, and—while the leaves didn't burn—the distinct aroma of tea that filled the kitchen surprised me. The ribs tasted faintly of it, too. Perhaps outright combustion wasn't necessary—"roasting" was enough to unlock the tea's flavor. Smoky-tasting Lapsang Souchong tea leaves, cured over smoldering pine or cypress boughs, seemed like the perfect candidate.

With the oven set to high heat (the leaves scattered across the bottom of the baking sheet), I could smell smoke in minutes. After 30 minutes, the ribs tasted decidedly smoky. Grinding the leaves to a fine powder (thereby maximizing the tea-to-baking-surface ratio) imbued the ribs with an even deeper flavor. Neither as sweet as hickory nor as sharp as mesquite, the tea perfumed the ribs with a rich smokiness far deeper than that lent by barbecue sauce or liquid smoke.

SHOPPING: Pork Ribs

SPARERIBS
Ribs from near the pig's fatty belly.
An acceptable choice, but needs a fair
amount of home trimming.

ST. LOUIS STYLE
Spareribs that have been trimmed
of skirt meat and excess cartilage.
Minimal fuss—our top choice.

BABY BACK
Smaller, leaner ribs from the (adult)
pig's back. Tender, but the meat dries
out too quickly for our recipe.

Homemade Indoor Smoker

You can crowd ribs into an indoor smoker, but we prefer our roomier makeshift version. Spread tea leaves on a rimmed baking sheet, place a wire cooling rack on top, followed by the ribs and heavy-duty foil. A pizza stone gets the tea smoking quickly.

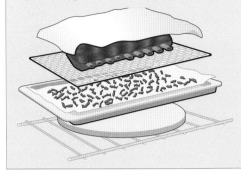

Full Steam Ahead

The ribs were smoky, but the high heat required to "roast" the tea had also made them inedibly tough. The solution lay in the freezer. Chilling the rib racks as the oven preheated cooled them enough that they could withstand a very high heat and quickly absorb "smoke" without toughening. After just half an hour at 500 degrees, my prechilled ribs had absorbed as much of the smoky flavor as possible, and I could decrease the oven temperature dramatically.

To cook the ribs, I experimented with temperatures ranging between 200 and 300 degrees; 250 degrees proved the best compromise between texture and time. Within two hours—including the "smoking" time—the ribs were fork-tender, though moist and gummy. A pass under the high heat of the broiler quickly turned the wet exterior into a chewy, crispy crust.

Following the lead of several recipes, I tried adding liquid to the pan (and resealing the foil to contain the steam) to see if an even moister environment could improve things. The ribs were ready in half the time. The moister the heat, the faster the heat transfer—right in line with the mechanics of braising. Water worked fine but added no flavor; beer and apple juice—both common "mops" used to keep the meat moist in outdoor barbecue—were better options. Beer brought a slightly boozy taste to the meat, but the juice added welcome sweet depth.

Where There's Smoke

Cured over smoldering pine or cypress, Lapsang Souchong tea brews up so smoky that, as a beverage, it's an acquired taste. But as a flavoring agent, it provides the smokiness missing in most indoor rib recipes. Loose tea leaves and tea bags work equally well. (Twining's Lapsang Souchong tea bags are widely available at supermarkets.)

JUST DON'T ADD WATER

Wet or Dry?

Smoky and tender but slightly bland, the ribs were ready for some spice. Barbecued ribs can be cooked "dry"—coated with spices and served as is—or "wet," brushed with sauce shortly before serving. I've always had a weakness for the latter, but tasters argued that the big-flavored sauce masked the tea's smokiness.

I knew I wanted to keep the rub simple to make way for the ribs' smoky, porky flavor so I started with the basics: salt, pepper, paprika, and brown sugar. I added a little cayenne for heat. Still too bland. Next I tried cumin, coriander, oregano, and chili powder and only really liked the depth lent by the chili powder. Finally, a thin slathering of mustard brought just the right tangy, sharp kick to the pork and, as an added bonus, helped the spices stick fast. For an extra level of flavor, I added a few cloves of minced garlic and a spoonful of ketchup.

All these ribs lacked now was the rosy, smoke-colored evidence of live-fire barbecue. Smoky-tasting to the bone, tender to a fault, and judiciously spicy, they were so good I might even make them in midsummer.

OVEN-BARBECUED SPARERIBS
SERVES 4

To make this recipe, you will need a baking stone, a sturdy baking sheet with a 1-inch rim, and a wire cooling rack that fits inside it. It's fine if the ribs overlap slightly on the rack. Remove surface fat to keep the ribs from being too greasy. Be careful when opening the crimped foil to add the juice, as hot steam and smoke will billow out.

Rub

- 6 tablespoons yellow mustard
- 2 tablespoons ketchup
- 3 medium garlic cloves, minced or pressed through garlic press (about 1 tablespoon)
- 2 teaspoons ground black pepper
- 1 tablespoon sweet paprika
- 1 tablespoon chili powder
- ½ teaspoon cayenne
- 1½ tablespoons kosher salt
- 3 tablespoons brown sugar

Ribs

- 2 racks St. Louis–style spareribs, 2½ to 3 pounds each, trimmed of surface fat, membrane removed (see illustrations above), each rack cut in half
- ½ cup Lapsang Souchong tea leaves (loose or from about 10 tea bags), ground to powder in spice grinder (about ¼ cup powder)
- ½ cup apple juice

1. Combine mustard, ketchup, and garlic in small bowl; combine pepper, paprika, chili powder, cayenne, salt, and sugar in separate small bowl. Spread mustard mixture in thin, even layer

THE MEMBRANE

For this recipe, we recommend removing the thin membrane that lines the concave side of the rib rack. The ribs are easier to manipulate (and eat), and the smoke penetrates both sides of the rack directly.

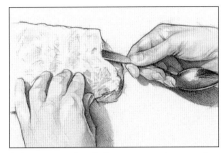

1. Insert spoon handle between membrane and ribs to loosen slightly.

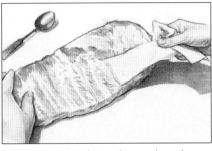

2. Using paper towel, grasp loosened membrane and pull away gently to remove.

over both sides of ribs; coat both sides with spice mixture, then wrap ribs in plastic and refrigerate for at least 8 hours and up to 24 hours.

2. Transfer ribs from refrigerator to freezer for 45 minutes. Adjust one oven rack to lowest position and second rack to upper-middle position (at least 5 inches below broiler). Place baking stone on lower rack; heat oven to 500 degrees. Sprinkle ground tea evenly over bottom of rimmed baking sheet; set wire rack on sheet. Place ribs meat side up on rack and cover with heavy-duty foil, crimping edges tightly to seal. Roast ribs directly on stone for 30 minutes, then reduce oven temperature to 250 degrees, leaving oven door open for 1 minute to cool. While oven is open, carefully open one corner of foil and pour apple juice into bottom of baking sheet; reseal foil. Continue to roast until meat is very tender and begins to pull away from bones, about 1½ hours. (Begin to check ribs after 1 hour; leave loosely covered with foil for remaining cooking time.)

3. Remove foil and carefully flip racks bone side up; place baking sheet on upper-middle oven rack. Turn on broiler; cook ribs until well browned and crispy in spots, 5 to 10 minutes. Flip ribs meat side up and cook until well browned and crispy, 5 to 7 minutes more. Cool for at least 10 minutes before cutting into individual ribs. Serve with barbecue sauce, if desired.

Hot and Sour Soup at Home

Spicy, bracing, rich, and complex, this classic Chinese soup has all the trappings of a full day in the kitchen. Not bad for a 20-minute dish.

≥ BY REBECCA HAYS ≤

The hot and sour soup we eat in Chinese-American restaurants today isn't much different from the Sichuanese original. Named for its potent peppery and vinegary flavors, the lightly thickened soup contains strips of pork, cubes of tofu, and wisps of egg. According to the cookbooks and Chinese-cooking experts I consulted, hot and sour soup encapsulates the Taoist principle central to Chinese culture: *yin* and *yang*, the notion of balancing the universe's opposing yet complementary forces. In the kitchen, that means creating balanced dishes by strategically combining flavors, textures, colors, and temperatures—some yin, some yang.

Balancing universal forces I'd have to leave to the philosophers. (All I was after was a good soup.) But balancing flavors, textures, and temperatures? That was familiar territory. At the very least, I figured, the yin/yang principle left me some leeway to explore stand-ins for hard-to-find ingredients that show up in some authentic versions—for instance, mustard pickle, pig's-foot tendon, and dried sea cucumber—without sacrificing the spirit of authenticity. So armed with thoughts of yin, yang, and the inventory of my local supermarket, I headed to the test kitchen to work on a balanced and (philosophically) authentic take on hot and sour soup.

Hot/Sour

The heat in hot and sour soup traditionally comes not from fresh chiles but from ground white (or sometimes black) peppercorns. Unlike chiles, pepper delivers direct spiciness but doesn't leave a lingering burn in its wake. An all-black-pepper soup was sharp but one-dimensional; a half-black, half-white combination was an improvement. Better still was a version made with a full teaspoon of distinctive, penetrating white pepper. Nice, but I suspected that a second heat source might deliver yet another layer of complexity. Sure enough, chili oil—a bit unconventional for this recipe—supported the white-hot heat of the pepper, laying the groundwork for the opposing flavor of vinegar. This yin/yang balancing act was turning out easier than I'd anticipated.

Hot and sour soup gets its complex flavors from strategically chosen ingredients—no long simmering required.

Until the very next experiment, that is. Made from toasted rice, Chinese black vinegar (the traditional sour component) has an elusive flavor that almost defies description. Because it can be difficult to find, I needed to identify a substitute. Emboldened by the success of my first improvisation, I raided the test kitchen pantry and assembled 14 bottles of vinegar. Drop by drop, I confidently sniffed and tasted my way through the lineup, ultimately deciding that balsamic, cider, malt, rice, and red wine vinegar most closely resembled black vinegar. Next, I supplemented the vinegars, alone and in combination, with everything from angostura bitters to molasses to vermouth to Worcestershire sauce. A smidgen of this, a drizzle of that, and so it went. Sadly, every concoction was exceedingly harsh. To adhere to the yin/yang principle, I needed a substitute that would support, not outshine, the pepper.

Resting my weary palate, I re-examined the black vinegar label and noticed an acidity level of 1.18 percent. Most American vinegars measure in the 5 to 7 percent range, so I would have to use a lot less of my substitute vinegars. After several more

rounds, I finally settled on a tablespoon each of dark, fruity balsamic and robust red wine vinegar as a workable substitute for 5 tablespoons of black vinegar. (That said, black vinegar is so unique that I recommend seeking it out.)

Textural Diversity

Now that I had carefully balanced the flavors of the soup, I turned my focus to texture. Cornstarch is the standard thickener, but a heavy hand resulted in a goopy gravy instead of a silky broth. I found that just 3 tablespoons yielded an agreeable, not-too-thick consistency that would gently support the other textures in the soup. To activate its thickening power, cornstarch is best added to the soup in the form of a cool slurry; the soup is then brought to a boil while being stirred constantly.

In addition to its role as thickener, cornstarch is believed by many Chinese cooks to play the part of meat (or protein) tenderizer. To test what seemed to me a dubious theory, I prepared two batches of soup, adding cornstarch to a simple soy sauce marinade for one julienned pork chop and omitting it in the marinade for another. The cornstarch-marinated pork was noticeably more tender. The cornstarch created a protective sheath that bought me the few extra minutes I needed to finish the soup without overcooking the pork.

After the pork is cooked and the soup thickened, beaten egg is drizzled in to create yet another complementary texture: fine, feath-

It's All about Balance

Warm and cool, crunchy and soft, sweet and pungent—in Chinese cuisine, striking a delicate balance between contrasting elements is often more crucial than ingredient specifics. The sources of this soup's namesake elements, hot and sour, vary from recipe to authentic recipe, but we achieved the most satisfying balance when we combined white peppercorns with black vinegar.

HOT   SOUR

ery shreds. The problem is that if the egg doesn't set immediately, it can blend into the soup and muddy the appearance of the broth. Wanting to make this step foolproof, I tried mixing the egg with vinegar and cornstarch. The vinegar instantly coagulated the egg, whereas the cornstarch, once again, was the miracle worker: The cornstarch molecules stabilized the liquid proteins, preventing them from contracting excessively when they hit the hot liquid. The result? Lighter, softer eggs. (See "Mysterious Powers of Cornstarch," below.)

Balancing Acts

Spicy, bracing, pungent, tender, fluffy—my soup was already replete with pleasing balances of flavor and texture. But I wasn't quite done yet. Almost all authentic hot and sour soup recipes start with reconstituted dried wood ear mushrooms and lily buds. Wood ear mushrooms, also known as tree ear or cloud ear, offer snappy texture but little else. I swapped in commonly available dried porcini and shiitake mushrooms, but their woodsy notes had a negative influence on the flavor equilibrium I'd worked so hard to achieve. Fresh, mild shiitake mushrooms were a better choice. Lily buds, or golden needles, are the dried buds of the tiger lily flower. Tangy, mildly crunchy canned bamboo shoots closely approximated the musky, sour flavor of lily buds and added textural variety (a crisp foil for the fluffy wisps of egg).

As for the tofu, I had one basic question: Must it be pressed? The answer was a simple yes. Spongelike tofu is full of water, and weighting it beneath a heavy plate yielded firmer, cleaner-tasting cubes. Marinating was a mistake; an occasional bite of plain, mild (yin) tofu was a necessary respite in the mostly yang soup.

Many recipes call for passing potent toasted sesame oil at the table, but a generous pour overwhelmed the other flavors. I took a low-risk approach and added a measured amount to the marinade for the pork. A sprinkle of raw, crisp, green scallions (raw versus cooked) symbolized a final embrace of the yin/yang philosophy. At last I could eat my soup—in peace.

HOT AND SOUR SOUP
SERVES 6 TO 8 AS AN APPETIZER

To make slicing the pork chop easier, freeze it for 15 minutes. We prefer the distinctive flavor of Chinese black vinegar; look for it in Asian supermarkets. If you can't find it, a combination of red wine vinegar and balsamic vinegar approximates its flavor. This soup is very spicy. For a less spicy soup, omit the chili oil altogether or add only 1 teaspoon.

- 7 ounces extra-firm tofu, drained
- 4 tablespoons soy sauce
- 1 teaspoon toasted sesame oil
- 3 tablespoons plus 1 ½ teaspoons cornstarch
- 1 boneless center-cut pork chop (½ inch thick, about 6 ounces), trimmed of fat and cut into 1 inch by ⅛-inch matchsticks
- 3 tablespoons plus 1 teaspoon cool water
- 1 large egg
- 6 cups low-sodium chicken broth
- 1 cup bamboo shoots (from one 5-ounce can), sliced lengthwise into ⅛-inch-thick strips
- 4 ounces fresh shiitake mushrooms, stems removed, caps sliced ¼ inch thick (about 1 cup)
- 5 tablespoons Chinese black vinegar or 1 tablespoon red wine vinegar plus 1 tablespoon balsamic vinegar (see note above)
- 2 teaspoons chili oil (see note above)
- 1 teaspoon ground white pepper
- 3 medium scallions, sliced thin

1. Place tofu in pie plate and set heavy plate on top. Weight with 2 heavy cans; let stand at least 15 minutes (tofu should release about ½ cup liquid). Whisk 1 tablespoon soy sauce, sesame oil, and 1 teaspoon cornstarch in medium bowl; toss pork with marinade and set aside for at least 10 minutes (but no more than 30 minutes).

2. Combine 3 tablespoons cornstarch with 3

tablespoons water in small bowl and mix thoroughly; set aside, leaving spoon in bowl. Mix remaining ½ teaspoon cornstarch with remaining 1 teaspoon water in small bowl; add egg and beat with fork until combined. Set aside.

3. Bring broth to boil in large saucepan set over medium-high heat. Reduce heat to medium-low; add bamboo shoots and mushrooms and simmer until mushrooms are just tender, about 5 minutes. While broth simmers, dice tofu into ½-inch cubes. Add tofu and pork, including marinade, to soup, stirring to separate any pieces of pork that stick together. Continue to simmer until pork is no longer pink, about 2 minutes.

4. Stir cornstarch mixture to recombine. Add to soup and increase heat to medium-high; cook, stirring occasionally, until soup thickens and turns translucent, about 1 minute. Stir in vinegar, chili oil, pepper, and remaining 3 tablespoons soy sauce; turn off heat.

5. Without stirring soup, use soupspoon to slowly drizzle very thin streams of egg mixture into pot in circular motion. Let soup sit 1 minute, then return saucepan to medium-high heat. Bring soup to gentle boil, then immediately remove from heat. Gently stir soup once to evenly distribute egg; ladle into bowls and top with scallions.

Go to www.cooksillustrated.com
• Key in code 1063 for our Soy Sauce Tasting.

SCIENCE: Mysterious Powers of Cornstarch

Most cooks keep a box of cornstarch on hand for a single purpose: thickening. So did we—until we noticed that cornstarch was working its magic in other ways as well. Predictably, adding cornstarch (3 tablespoons) to our soup thickened it. What was surprising, however, were the two other uses we found for cornstarch. Adding just 1 teaspoon of cornstarch to the pork marinade of soy sauce and sesame oil caused the marinade to cling to and coat the meat during cooking, creating a protective sheath that slowed the inevitable rise in temperature that separates moist, tender pork from dry, chalky pork jerky. And adding just ½ teaspoon of cornstarch to the egg that's drizzled into the soup at the end of cooking seemed to have a tenderizing effect. Cornstarch stabilizes liquid proteins when they're heated, staving off excessive shrinkage and contraction. So this last bit of cornstarch helped the eggs cook up lighter and softer. —R.H.

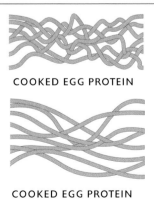

COOKED EGG PROTEIN

COOKED EGG PROTEIN WITH CORNSTARCH

Starch molecules keep proteins relaxed, yielding lighter and softer eggs.

Simplifying Potatoes Lyonnaise

Buttery, earthy, and sweet, this French bistro take on skillet potatoes and onions usually requires tons of time—and butter. Could we get away with using less of each?

> BY SANDRA WU <

One of the hallmark dishes of France's premier gastronomic city, *pommes de terre Lyonnaise* (aka potatoes Lyonnaise) is a study in simple elegance. Although originally conceived as a dish of economy (an easy way to use up leftover boiled potatoes), it came to represent the best of classic French bistro cuisine: buttery, browned potato slices interwoven with strands of sweet, caramelized onion and fresh, grassy parsley—a simple yet complex four-ingredient skillet potato dish.

The reality, however, is too often far removed from that buttery, earthy ideal. Most versions I tested were greasy and heavy rather than rich and complex. A few were so bad—with sodden spuds and waterlogged onions—that I was reminded how often the simplest dishes are the most difficult to execute properly. Each component would have to be handled with the utmost care.

Less Time, Less Butter

Having no leftover cooked potatoes on hand (the case with most home cooks), I wondered if I could proceed with raw spuds without precooking. Starting with a large skillet, I sautéed the raw slices on fairly high heat and got dismal results: The exteriors had cooked to a near-blackened crisp before the interiors got even remotely tender. On moderate heat, however, the potatoes took forever to develop a nice, browned crust. Cooking the potatoes covered got me closer to what I wanted. Still, they were too dry. Some sort of parcooking would have to be a first step.

Borrowing a technique used in the test kitchen for an American short-order classic (home fries), I began by microwaving the ¼-inch-thick slices of potato in a tablespoon of melted butter until

barely tender. This gave them the head start they needed. The time it took the potatoes to brown was now also sufficient to cook them through. Using just one more tablespoon of butter (most classic recipes call for 4 to 6 tablespoons), a simple brown-and-flip approach, and medium-high heat, I cooked the potatoes in less than 15 minutes.

Great color and cooking method, but the russet potatoes I'd been using often came out mealy. In a spud-to-spud taste test, creamy, golden-fleshed, medium-starch Yukon Gold potatoes beat out the high-starch russets and the "rubbery," low-starch Red Bliss by a comfortable margin.

Perfect Onions

Potatoes Lyonnaise would just be sautéed potatoes if not for the addition of onions, the definitive ingredient of dishes prepared *à la Lyonnaise*. For sweet, concentrated flavor, the onions would have to be cooked separately from the potatoes. Cooking them all the way through over medium-high heat dried them out. Covering the skillet and cooking on medium once they had released some moisture created an environment of gentle, moist heat. Deglazing the pan with a small amount of water gave them the chance to cook in their own flavorful juices.

To put the steps together in an efficient manner was easy. While the onions cooked, the potatoes began their warm-up in the microwave. Once the onions finished cooking and were removed to a nearby bowl, the potatoes had a turn in the pan. To meld the flavors, I added the onions back into the pan and briefly sautéed the two together. Now I had an updated version of a French classic that was good enough (and quick enough) to make even without leftover potatoes.

POTATOES LYONNAISE
SERVES 3 TO 4 AS A SIDE DISH

Toss the potatoes halfway through the microwave session to prevent uneven cooking. If using a lightweight skillet, you will need to stir the potatoes more frequently to prevent burning.

- 3 tablespoons unsalted butter
- 1 large onion (about 14 ounces), halved pole to pole and sliced ¼ inch thick (about 3 cups)
- ¾ teaspoon kosher salt (or ½ teaspoon table salt)
- 2 tablespoons water
- 1½ pounds medium Yukon Gold potatoes, peeled and sliced crosswise into ¼-inch rounds
- ¼ teaspoon ground black pepper
- 1 tablespoon minced fresh parsley leaves

1. Heat 1 tablespoon butter in 12-inch heavy nonstick skillet over medium-high heat. When foaming subsides, add onion and ¼ teaspoon salt and stir to coat; cook, stirring occasionally, until onions begin to soften, about 3 minutes. Reduce heat to medium and cook, covered, stirring occasionally, until onions are light brown and soft, about 12 minutes longer, deglazing with water when pan gets dry, about halfway through cooking time. Transfer to bowl and cover. Do not wash skillet.

2. While onions cook, microwave 1 tablespoon butter on high power in large microwave-safe bowl until melted, about 45 seconds. Add potatoes to bowl and toss to coat with melted butter. Microwave on high power until potatoes just start to turn tender (see photos, left), about 6 minutes, tossing halfway through cooking time. Toss potatoes again and set aside.

3. Melt remaining tablespoon butter in now-empty skillet over medium-high heat. When foaming subsides, add potatoes and shake skillet to distribute evenly. Cook, without stirring, until browned on bottom, about 3 minutes. Using spatula, stir potatoes carefully and continue to cook, stirring every 2 to 3 minutes, until potatoes are well browned and tender when pierced with tip of paring knife, 8 to 10 minutes more. Sprinkle with remaining salt and pepper.

4. Add onions back to skillet and stir to combine; cook until onions are heated through and flavors have melded, 1 to 2 minutes. Transfer to large plate, sprinkle with parsley, and serve.

The Path of Slight Resistance

A few crucial seconds in the microwave separate perfectly parcooked potatoes from overdone and underdone misfires. Because microwave ovens vary in terms of power, it's important to check the look and texture during cooking.

UNDERCOOKED
Potatoes look translucent and feel rubbery when bent.

JUST RIGHT
Mostly opaque potatoes resist slightly when bent.

OVERCOOKED
Potatoes yield easily when bent.

Improving Sautéed Mushrooms

Bland supermarket button mushrooms shrink and shrivel when sautéed.
We wanted more flavor and more mushrooms.

≥ BY SEAN LAWLER ≤

When I have the funds or good fortune to get my hands on a batch of freshly foraged chanterelles, I've learned it's best to keep their preparation very simple. It takes little beyond a hot pan and some butter and garlic to make the most of their intense flavor. In most markets, however, their availability is spotty, their quality questionable, and their price exorbitant. Besides the oversized portobello, which I generally reserve for grilling, the only affordable mushrooms I can always locate for a quick stovetop sauté are common white buttons. Given their mild flavor and rubbery texture, I've never considered them good for much beyond salads and takeout pizza. But was I being fair? With the right technique, perhaps abundant and affordable button mushrooms could also be delicious.

After a week of sautéing buttons by the bushel, it was clear to me that the problem was not the mushrooms but the recipes. Most are written for mushrooms of no particular type—wild, cultivated, or whatever is at hand—and so ignore certain characteristics of the common white button. These are, chiefly, an absorbent, spongy texture (which causes the mushrooms to soak up any and all fat in the pan) and a high water content (which then floods the skillet and hinders browning). While a handful of sliced shiitakes might be nicely browned after about 8 minutes in a hot skillet, white buttons are swimming in a lake of exuded mushroom liquid.

Sound sautéing theory told me to crank up the heat, extend the cooking time, and leave some breathing room in the skillet. These changes kept the mushrooms from stewing, but the yield was paltry. How could I cook just one batch of mushrooms in just one skillet and produce enough to feed at least four?

Unlike steaks or cutlets, which begin to sear immediately upon hitting a hot pan, button mushrooms don't begin to brown until their water has been driven off. This gave me an idea. What if I overloaded the skillet to start, the theory being that once the water evaporated and the mushrooms shrank, the pan would no longer be crowded. I was at first alarmed by the flood of liquid that resulted, but patience (and high heat) prevailed. After about 13 minutes (what most recipes give as a total cooking time for sautéed mushrooms), the skillet was dry, the mushrooms had shrunk to fit the skillet in a single layer, and browning had begun.

It seemed a short dash from here to the finish line: Keep the heat high, shake the pan occasionally, and cook the contents until well browned. But now the skillet was too dry. Even over a more moderate heat, the pan would begin to burn, which made the mushrooms taste bitter. The solution was simple enough. Once the mushrooms had given up their water, I lowered the heat and added a little fat to prevent burning. Just a few flavorful additions (garlic, herbs, wine, soy sauce, or bread crumbs) and the transformation of the basic white button mushroom was complete.

SAUTÉED MUSHROOMS WITH SHALLOTS AND THYME

SERVES 4

1	tablespoon vegetable oil
1½	pounds white button mushrooms, cleaned, stems trimmed, quartered if medium or halved if small
1	tablespoon unsalted butter
1	medium shallot, minced (about 3 tablespoons)
1	tablespoon minced fresh thyme leaves
¼	cup dry Marsala
	Table salt and ground black pepper

1. Heat oil in 12-inch skillet over medium-high heat until shimmering. Add mushrooms and cook, stirring occasionally, until mushrooms release liquid, about 5 minutes. Increase heat to high and cook, stirring occasionally, until liquid has completely evaporated, about 8 minutes longer. Add butter, reduce heat to medium, and continue to cook, stirring once every minute, until mushrooms are dark brown, about 8 minutes longer.

2. Add shallot and thyme and cook until softened, about 3 minutes. Add Marsala and cook until liquid has evaporated, about 2 minutes. Season with salt and pepper to taste; serve.

SAUTÉED MUSHROOMS WITH GARLIC, PARMESAN, AND BREAD CRUMBS

Pulse 2 slices white sandwich bread (torn into quarters) in food processor until coarsely ground. Heat 2 tablespoons butter in 12-inch skillet over medium-high heat until foaming. When foaming subsides, add bread crumbs and cook, stirring frequently, until dark brown, about 3 minutes. Transfer crumbs to small bowl and set aside. Using now-empty skillet, follow recipe for Sautéed Mushrooms with Shallots and Thyme through step 1. Add 2 teaspoons minced garlic (instead of shallot, thyme, and Marsala), and cook, stirring constantly, until fragrant, about 30 seconds. Season with salt and pepper to taste and transfer to medium bowl. Toss hot mushrooms with ½ cup shredded Parmesan until cheese melts. Toss with bread crumbs and 2 tablespoons minced fresh parsley; serve.

SAUTÉED MUSHROOMS WITH SESAME AND GINGER

2	tablespoons peanut oil
1½	pounds white button mushrooms, cleaned, stems trimmed, quartered if medium or halved if small
1	tablespoon sesame seeds, toasted
1	tablespoon minced or grated fresh ginger
2	tablespoons mirin (Japanese rice wine)
2	tablespoons soy sauce
1	teaspoon toasted sesame oil
2	scallions, sliced very thin on bias

1. Heat 1 tablespoon peanut oil in 12-inch skillet over medium-high heat until shimmering. Add mushrooms and cook, stirring occasionally, until mushrooms release liquid, about 5 minutes. Increase heat to high and cook, stirring occasionally, until liquid has completely evaporated, about 8 minutes longer. Add remaining tablespoon peanut oil, reduce heat to medium, and continue to cook, stirring once every minute, until mushrooms are dark brown, about 8 minutes longer.

2. Add sesame seeds and ginger and cook, stirring constantly, until ginger is fragrant, about 30 seconds. Add mirin and soy sauce and cook, stirring constantly, until liquid has evaporated, about 30 seconds. Remove from heat and stir in sesame oil. Transfer to serving dish, sprinkle with scallions, and serve.

Go to www.cooksillustrated.com
• Key in code 1064 for **Sautéed Mushrooms with Bacon and Pearl Onions**.

How to Cook Rice and Grains

Start by ignoring the directions on the box. Then consult our guide to match the right grain with the right cooking method.

BY SEAN LAWLER

About Rice

Color: All rice starts out as brown rice. For white rice, the fibrous bran layer and underlying germ are milled off—along with nutrients and natural oils. Less nutritious? Yes, but it's also more shelf-stable than the brown stuff.

Size: It matters. Long grain, medium grain, and short grain are three loosely defined categories based partly on length-to-width ratios, partly on texture and starch content, all of which determine how the rice cooks up.

Texture: Fluffy, sticky, or in between. The texture of cooked rice depends on the ratio of two starch molecules: *amylose* and *amylopectin*. High-amylose rices cook up firm, fluffy, and distinct; high-amylopectin rices come out tender and sticky. The former usually require more water (and cooking time) than the latter.

LONG GRAIN

MEDIUM GRAIN

SHORT GRAIN

BROWN RICE

LONG GRAIN

Includes most generic supermarket rice, as well as Basmati (an aged extra-long-grain rice from India), Texmati (a domestic alternative), and fragrant Thai Jasmine

How It Looks: Slender, elongated, four to five times longer than wide

How It Cooks: High amylose means a light, fluffy texture with firm, distinct grains, making it especially good for pilafs and salads. Some cooks use the "absorbtion method" (see page 17), but to our minds, just adding water is a missed flavor opportunity. We prefer the "pilaf method," a sauté-based method that brings out toasted, nutty flavors.

MEDIUM GRAIN

Includes generic medium-grain rice and specialty rices for dishes like risotto (Arborio) and paella (Valencia)

How It Looks: Fat, chalky grain, two to three times longer than wide

How It Cooks: Higher in amylopectin, medium-grain rice is tender and a bit sticky, and resists turning hard and crunchy as it cools (unlike long grain). It's versatile stuff. When simmered, the grains clump together, making it a good choice to accompany a stir-fry. But it also takes well to the pilaf method, especially in risottos and paellas.

SHORT GRAIN

Includes sushi rice

How It Looks: Opaque, almost round grains

How It Cooks: The softest, stickiest grain of the bunch (cooked), thanks to low amylose and high amylopectin. These qualities make it ideal for tossing with a light vinegar dressing and wrapping up in sushi rolls. Often steamed, but the basic "absorption method" works so long as the simmer is gentle.

BROWN RICE

How It Looks: Light brown bran layer intact (a few greenish grains are normal)

How It Cooks: The bran layer, valued for its fiber content, is also something of a nuisance: It slows absorption (brown rice takes nearly twice as long to cook as white) and cooks unevenly on the stovetop (we prefer the oven method). Whether short, medium, or long grain, brown rice has a pronounced chew, nutty flavor, and distinct grains.

TO RINSE OR NOT TO RINSE

For the fluffiest long-grain rice, rinse grains to remove some of the surface starches. Medium- and short-grain rices, by contrast, are supposed to be a bit sticky, so don't bother. Rinsing brown rice is pointless—with the bran layer intact, there's no exterior starch to wash away. Always rinse quinoa to remove *saponin*—a natural but bitter coating that protects each grain.

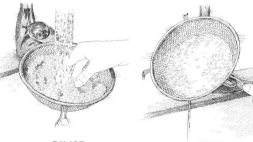

RINSE
Rinse rice under cold water in mesh strainer, stirring gently, until water runs clear.

TILT
Tilt the strainer to drain rice thoroughly.

About Other Grains

Dining on barley or bulgur was once strictly vegan territory. No longer. Thanks to wider availability, even confirmed carnivores are giving alternative grains their due as worthy side dishes. Here are some of the test kitchen's favorites.

PEARL BARLEY

Hulled whole grains of barley with the bran polished off. Chewy, with a mildly sweet, nutty flavor. A nice addition to hearty soups.

WHEAT BERRIES

Not berries at all, but whole, husked wheat kernels with bran layer and germ intact. Cooked wheat berries are firm, distinct, and quite chewy, making them great for cold salads.

BULGUR

Wheat berries that have been precooked, dried, stripped of their bran, and crushed into pieces. Commonly used to make salads like tabbouleh, this quick-cooking grain is not the same as cracked wheat, which has not been parcooked.

QUINOA

This spinach relative is sometimes called a "supergrain" because it contains eight essential amino acids. The tiny seeds expand to four times their size during cooking and turn out very light and fluffy.

WILD RICE

A difficult grain to categorize, wild rice is not quite the same as the domesticated rices described at left, although recent genetic research shows that they have much in common. "Real" wild rice is hand-harvested from lakes and rivers and costs as much as $9 per pound. We prefer not-so-wild wild rice—cultivated in man-made paddies—which has a more resilient texture and a much lower price. Cook wild rice at a bare simmer and check it often: It can go from chewy and underdone to mushy and "blown out" in a matter of minutes.

Four Methods for Cooking Rice and Other Grains

See the chart below for matching each grain with our preferred cooking method.

Absorption Method

Grains are simmered slowly in a measured quantity of liquid until tender. Combine grains, liquid, and salt (½ teaspoon per cup of raw grains) in heavy-bottomed saucepan. Bring to boil over medium-high heat. Reduce heat to low and simmer, covered, until grains are tender (see chart for times). Let stand off heat, covered, 10 to 15 minutes. Fluff with fork and serve.

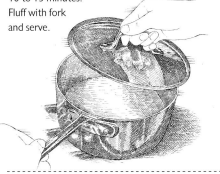

Pilaf Method

Cooking grains in hot butter or oil briefly before adding liquid to impart a toasted, nutty flavor. To make a true pilaf, sauté aromatics like onion and garlic and spices until fragrant before adding the grains.

1. Heat butter or oil (2 teaspoons per cup of raw grains) in saucepan over medium heat. Add grains and cook, stirring, until grains become chalky and opaque and stop sticking to pan, about 3 minutes.

2. Add liquid and salt (½ teaspoon per cup of raw grains), increase heat, and bring just to boil. Reduce heat to low, cover, and simmer until liquid is absorbed and grains are tender (see chart). Let stand off heat, covered, 10 to 15 minutes. Fluff with fork and serve.

Oven Method

Best for situations requiring prolonged, even heating, such as cooking brown rice or larger quantities of white rice.

1. Heat oven to 375 degrees with rack in middle position. Bring liquid to boil, covered, in saucepan over high heat.

2. Combine grains, boiling liquid, and salt (½ teaspoon per cup of raw grains) in baking dish and cover tightly with double layer of foil. Bake until grains are tender (see chart for times). Let stand 5 minutes, uncover, fluff with fork, and serve.

Pasta Method

Grains are cooked like pasta—in an abundant quantity of salted, boiling water. Best for very firm, chewy grains or for recipes in which a softer texture is desired, such as cold salads.

1. Bring 4 quarts water to a rapid boil over high heat. Add grains and 2½ teaspoons salt, reduce heat, and simmer until grains are tender (see chart for time).

2. Drain grains in strainer set in sink. Let stand in strainer 5 minutes before using or spread out on parchment-lined baking sheet to cool.

Cooking Rice and Other Grains (for 1 cup raw)

GRAIN	RINSE?	BEST METHOD	WATER	COOKING TIME	YIELD
long-grain rice	yes	pilaf	1½ cups	18–20 min	3 cups
medium-grain rice	no	pilaf, absorption	1⅓ cups	16–18 min	3 cups
short-grain rice	no	absorption	1¼ cups	16–18 min	2¾ cups
brown rice	no	oven	1½ cups	1 hr	2½–3 cups
pearl barley	no	pasta	4 quarts	25–30 min	3½–4 cups
wheat berries	no	pasta	4 quarts	1 hr	2–2½ cups
bulgur	no	absorption*	1½ cups	15 min	2–2½ cups
quinoa	yes	absorption	2 cups	15–20 min	3 cups
wild rice	no	absorbtion**	2 cups	35-45 min	3 cups

*Modified: Add bulgur to boiling water, then let steep, covered and off heat, for 15 minutes.

**Drain wild rice of excess liquid before using.

The Mystery of Meat Loaf

An all-beef meat loaf may be convenient, but it's also tough, dry, and dense.
We went through 260 pounds of beef to find the best way to lighten the loaf.

⇒ BY DAVID PAZMIÑO ⇐

All-beef meat loaf is an American classic that has as many variations as the Heinz ketchup that traditionally glazes it. But this humble approach has taken a back seat to loaves made from meat loaf mix: beef, pork, and veal. The reason for using a combination of meats was made abundantly clear as soon as we tasted an all-beef version. The texture was chewy, and the flavor was less interesting—more of a hamburger in the shape of a log. But when you can't find meat loaf mix or don't have it on hand for a quick, last-minute dinner, can an all-beef loaf make the grade?

From the Ground Up

I thought choosing the beef would be simple, but I was dizzy with the number of choices at the supermarket. Not only did ground beef come in several lean/fat percentage variations, but it was also often labeled according to the part of the animal it came from (see Kitchen Notes, page 30, for tips on buying ground beef).

Knowing that meat loaf turns dry and tough without fat, I focused first on the 80 percent lean/20 percent fat ground beef, our choice for hamburgers. Taking samples from three supermarkets, I proceeded to build a simple working recipe. Despite having the same lean/fat percentages, each sample produced a different meat loaf. Some were moist and tender, while others were gristly, with fibrous curds. When I turned

Two kinds of beef, frozen grated cheese, and a surprise ingredient transform dense, loaf-shaped hamburger into luxurious comfort food.

to ground beef from specific cuts—chuck, round, and sirloin—a clearer picture began to emerge. The chuck (20 percent fat) produced a moist but chewy loaf, with pieces of gristle. Ground round (15 percent fat) yielded more desirable results, but the flavor needed a boost. More pronounced

and natural beef flavor came through with the ground sirloin (90 percent lean), but to the detriment of the texture, which was dry, chalky, and chewy. The solution? A combo. After several tests, tasters agreed that equal parts ground chuck and sirloin (1 pound of each) provided just the right balance of juicy, tender meat and assertive beefy flavor.

I needed to choose a liquid component that would both add moisture and tone down beef's naturally livery flavor. While milk is the traditional choice, after sampling milk and other dairy products (buttermilk and yogurt), tasters agreed that none of them did much to mitigate off-notes. Beef broth was even worse, contributing an additional (metallic) off-taste. Chicken broth was the surprise winner, transforming the loaf from livery to savory.

Binding Decisions

Taking cues from other meat loaf recipes, I added cheese for its welcome flavor, moisture, and binding qualities. After testing eight kinds, I settled on Monterey Jack for its moderate moisture content and neutral cheese flavor (this was meat loaf, after all, not cheese loaf). Surprisingly, the method I used to break down the cheese proved critical. Dicing and shredding left visible "hot pockets" of cheese that oozed unappealing liquid once the loaf was cut. Grated cheese proved superior, and freezing the grated cheese kept it crumbly.

Many recipes forgo starchy binders, but a battery of tests made their advantages clear: lightening the texture, retaining moisture, and improving sliceability. I decided from the outset to pass on rice and potatoes (too much trouble) and focused instead on bread crumbs (dry and fresh), crackers, oats, croutons, cereal, and stuffing mix. The last three were quickly discarded for their too-pronounced flavors. Saltines emerged as the clear favorite, delivering a well-seasoned, tender loaf with good moisture.

I had now cooked 110 loaves, but the texture still seemed a bit tough. The solution came to me as I reviewed my testing notes. In early tests, I had experimented with reduced veal stock, a gelatinous ingredient chefs rely on to give savory recipes an unctuous texture. Of course, who has veal stock around except a restaurant? But what

RECIPE DIAGNOSIS: Troubleshooting Meat Loaf

Here are two problems we encountered when making meat loaf—and the steps we now take to avoid them.

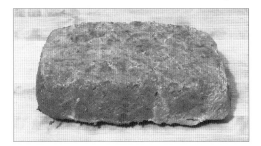

GRAY

PROBLEM: Sides of meat loaf remain crustless.
SOLUTION: Loaf pans expose only one side of the meat loaf to browning heat. By opting for a free-form loaf, we achieved an all-over browned crust.

GREASY

PROBLEM: Meat loaf sits in an unappealing pool of grease.
SOLUTION: Baking directly on a sheet pan provides no outlet for exuded grease. A foil base, poked with holes and set on a cooling rack, lets juices drain as the loaf cooks.

TECHNIQUE | CREATING A FREE-FORM 'LOAF PAN'

Allowing meat loaf to stew in its own juices makes for a greasy mess. Here's our solution: Fold heavy-duty aluminum foil to form a 10 by 6-inch rectangle. Center the foil on a metal cooling rack and place the rack over a rimmed baking sheet. Poke holes in the foil with a skewer (about half an inch apart). Spray the foil with nonstick cooking spray.

if I added *powdered* gelatin to the loaf to replicate the gelatinous qualities of the veal stock? I began adding unflavored powdered gelatin to the chicken broth before mixing it into the meat loaf. I tried a full packet, and, indeed, the texture was radically different—bouncy, like Jell-O. More tests revealed that a mere half-teaspoon was ideal, making the texture luxuriously smooth rather than gelatinously weird.

Finishing Touches

After sampling raw, sautéed, and caramelized onions, tasters agreed that sautéed onions produced the best flavor profile. Celery and garlic added a more complex savory flavor. Fresh thyme, paprika, soy sauce, and prepared mustard delivered an assertive flavor that married well with the beef. I cooked these seasonings along with the onions, celery, and garlic and deglazed the pan with tomato juice to create an intense, aromatic flavor.

The almost-finished meat loaf needed its crowning glory—a glaze. After experimenting with mustard, Worcestershire, steak sauce, and fruit, I settled on meat loaf's trusty and traditional sidekick: ketchup. Applied at the beginning of cooking, the glaze mixed unappealingly with the liquids seeping out of the loaf. Finishing with the glaze produced better results, especially when I placed the loaf briefly under the broiler.

As a final test, I tried the recipe using the ground beef variations I had previously discarded, but tasters weren't fooled: They overwhelmingly preferred the mixture of 80/20 chuck and 90/10 sirloin. (A loaf made entirely with 85/15 round was an acceptable but distant second.) But in any case, all-beef meat loaf had finally graduated from a compromise of convenience to truly luxuriant comfort food.

GLAZED MEAT LOAF
SERVES 6 TO 8

If you can't find chuck and/or sirloin, substitute any 85 percent lean ground beef. Handle the meat gently; it should be thoroughly combined but not pastelike. To avoid using the broiler, glaze the loaf in a 500-degree oven; increase cooking time for each interval by 2 to 3 minutes.

Meat Loaf

- 3 ounces Monterey Jack cheese, grated on small holes of box grater (about 1 cup)
- 1 tablespoon unsalted butter
- 1 medium onion, chopped fine (about 1 cup)
- 1 medium celery rib, chopped fine (about ½ cup)
- 1 medium garlic clove, minced or pressed through garlic press (about 1 teaspoon)
- 2 teaspoons minced fresh thyme leaves
- 1 teaspoon paprika
- ¼ cup tomato juice
- ½ cup low-sodium chicken broth
- 2 large eggs
- ½ teaspoon unflavored powdered gelatin
- 1 tablespoon soy sauce
- 1 teaspoon Dijon mustard
- ⅔ cup crushed saltine crackers
- 2 tablespoons minced fresh parsley leaves
- ¾ teaspoon table salt
- ½ teaspoon ground black pepper
- 1 pound ground sirloin
- 1 pound ground chuck

Glaze

- ½ cup ketchup
- 1 teaspoon hot pepper sauce
- ½ teaspoon ground coriander
- ¼ cup apple cider vinegar
- 3 tablespoons packed light brown sugar

1. Adjust oven rack to middle position; heat oven to 375 degrees. Spread cheese on plate and place in freezer until ready to use. Prepare baking sheet (see illustration above).

2. Heat butter in 10-inch skillet over medium-high heat until foaming; add onion and celery and cook, stirring occasionally, until beginning to brown, 6 to 8 minutes. Add garlic, thyme, and paprika and cook, stirring, until fragrant, about 1 minute. Reduce heat to low and add tomato juice. Cook, stirring to scrape up browned bits from pan, until thickened, about 1 minute. Transfer mixture to small bowl and set aside to cool.

3. Whisk broth and eggs in large bowl until combined. Sprinkle gelatin over liquid and let stand 5 minutes. Stir in soy sauce, mustard, saltines, parsley, salt, pepper, and onion mixture. Crumble frozen cheese into coarse powder and sprinkle over mixture. Add ground beef; mix gently with hands until thoroughly combined, about 1 minute. Transfer meat to foil rectangle and shape into 10 by 6-inch oval about 2 inches high. Smooth top and edges of meat loaf with moistened spatula. Bake until an instant-read thermometer inserted into center of loaf reads 135 to 140 degrees, 55 to 65 minutes. Remove meat loaf from oven and turn on broiler.

4. While meat loaf cooks, combine ingredients for glaze in small saucepan; bring to simmer over medium heat and cook, stirring, until thick and syrupy, about 5 minutes. Spread half of glaze evenly over cooked meat loaf with rubber spatula; place under broiler and cook until glaze bubbles and begins to brown at edges, about 5 minutes. Remove meat loaf from oven and spread evenly with remaining glaze; place back under broiler and cook until glaze is again bubbling and beginning to brown, about 5 minutes more. Let meat loaf cool about 20 minutes before slicing.

SCIENCE: How Gelatin Mimics Veal

Many meat loaf recipes call for three different meats (beef, pork, and veal), and each one has a core function. Beef contributes assertive beefiness, while pork adds dimension with flavor and extra fattiness. With veal, it's mostly about the gelatin—a viscous substance with natural water-retaining qualities that help keep a meat loaf moist and unctuous. Gelatin is formed when collagen, the protein in a cow's connective tissue, breaks down during cooking. Collagen is naturally present in cows of all ages, but the collagen in calves (the source of veal) is more loosely structured—and therefore converts to gelatin more easily—than the collagen in an adult cow. In our all-beef meat loaf, we successfully replicated the gelatinous qualities of veal by adding powdered gelatin.

So how does it work? Gelatin is a pure protein that suspends water in a meshlike, semisolid matrix. By slowing down the movement of liquids, gelatin has a stabilizing effect, making it harder for water and other liquids to be forced out, essentially fencing them in. In meat loaf, then, gelatin helps by (1) decreasing the amount of liquid leaking from the meat as the other proteins coagulate and (2) improving the textural feel by making the liquids more viscous even when very hot—sort of a transitional state between liquid and solid. That viscosity translates to a luxuriant texture in the mouth—much like reduced stock, or demi-glace—and the perception of greater richness, as if we had added more fat. –D.P.

WITHOUT GELATIN
Moisture leaks out of meat loaf, giving it a coarser, grainier texture.

WITH GELATIN
Moisture is suspended in a semisolid matrix, keeping the meat loaf juicy.

The Secrets of Flaky Biscuits

How do you get tender, flaky biscuits with truly distinctive layers? It's a pressing issue.

⇒ BY SEAN LAWLER ⇐

Most biscuit making is a study in simplicity and speed: A half-dozen staple ingredients mixed with a few brisk strokes take a quick trip through the oven to emerge hot and fluffy. But, truth be told, I've always found the appeal of such biscuits to be fleeting. Glory fades, alas, and hot biscuits cool. After savoring the first few bites, I start to wonder: Is that all there is?

Enter the ultra-flaky biscuit. Closer to pastry than dinner roll, this rich, elegant biscuit forgoes fluff in favor of a golden, crispy crust surrounding striated layers of tender, buttery dough. Perhaps because they require more work, truly flaky biscuits have become scarce, while their down-market imitators (supermarket "tube" biscuits) are alarmingly common.

Hard to Handle

What makes one biscuit "fluffy" and another "flaky"? My investigation was initially sidetracked by regional squabbling over the relative merits of butter versus lard, buttermilk versus milk, and brands of flour. Testing showed that while these choices do affect flavor and texture, they are not at the heart of the fluffy/flaky distinction. Instead, it is how those ingredients are handled.

Flaky Butter = Flaky Biscuits

Using a food processor to combine butter and flour may be easy, but the pebble-shaped pieces it creates result in uneven flakiness. Working the butter into the flour by hand yields large, flaky chunks of butter, which, when rolled into thin sheets, produce a biscuit with distinct layers.

PEBBLY PIECES ⟶ REGULAR BISCUITS

FLAKY SHEETS ⟶ FLAKY BISCUITS

To get this biscuit's distinct, tender layers to come out tall and even, we took a cue from puff pastry—and from business letters.

Rather than simple kneading, most recipes for flaky biscuits call for rolling and folding the dough, a technique used for puff pastry. Repeated multiple times, this action—like folding, then refolding a business letter—flattens the butter in the dough into thin sheets sandwiched between equally thin layers of flour. In the oven, the butter melts and steam fills the thin spaces left behind, creating a biscuit with flaky, buttery layers.

That was the theory, anyway. I cobbled together a simple working recipe using common ratios of cold butter, all-purpose flour, baking powder, and buttermilk, then set out to put it into practice. At first, I didn't even make it as far as the oven. My dough, like most biscuit doughs, was on the wet side, and any attempt to roll it thinner than 1 inch resulted in sticky, comic tragedy.

Counter Intelligence

It was a Catch-22. The dough had to be wet—a dry dough makes a dry biscuit—but it also had to be rollable. The only way I could successfully roll it was to scatter heaps of flour across the countertop, most of which ended up in the dough, which meant it was no longer wet. I needed to create a very thin, uniform layer of flour to keep the dough from sticking to the countertop during the crucial rolling process. The solution was a simple one. One morning, I gave the countertop a quick blast from a can of nonstick cooking spray. (My hope was that the spray coating would help the flour adhere more evenly to the counter.) I rolled out the next batch of dough, and, to my delight, it released easily—and without much flour sticking to it.

Now that I could manipulate the dough through a series of folds (or "turns," as they're called when making puff pastry), I wondered how many would be necessary. One set of turns didn't produce much layering, but by the time I completed a second set the cold butter in the dough had begun to soften and mix with the flour, resulting in biscuits that were short and crumbly instead of crisp and flaky. I didn't have the luxury of resting my dough in the refrigerator to firm up the butter, however, because the baking powder in the dough began reacting the moment the liquid and dry ingredients came together. Chilling the mixing bowl and all of the wet and dry ingredients (instead of just the butter) before mixing bought me the time I needed to complete a second set of turns with the cold butter still intact.

Two sets of turns yielded a biscuit that was moderately crisp and flaky, but I wanted more. I'd started with ½-inch cubes of butter that I put in the food processor along with the dry ingredients, turning the butter into small pebbles. The pebble shape is ideal for the small, irregular flakes in a pie crust but not for the pronounced layers I was after. Abandoning the food processor, I tried slicing the butter into very thin squares and—instead of cutting the squares into the flour with a pastry blender—I pressed each piece into the flour with my fingers, breaking them into flat, flaky pieces about the size of a nickel. As I rolled out this dough, I knew I was onto something—I could see the butter develop into long, thin sheets as I completed the turns. These biscuits really turned heads: As they rose they formed distinct, flaky layers with crispy browned edges.

Try a Little Tenderness

The biscuits now had a crisp and flaky crust but also a distracting chew. I suspected that swapping out some of the butter for shortening would have a tenderizing effect. After some testing, I settled on 2 tablespoons of shortening and 8 tablespoons of butter for a tender yet quite buttery biscuit.

The next problem was flavor. The cup-plus of buttermilk was too tangy. Switching to plain milk mellowed the flavor at the expense of the tenderness (from the buttermilk's acidity). Instead, I replaced some of the baking powder with baking soda, which reacted with the acidic buttermilk, taking the edge off of its tangy flavor.

By the end of testing, I had gained new appreciation for everyday drop-and-bake biscuits. But for a little extra effort, these ultra-flaky biscuits delivered rich flavor and textural interest worlds beyond their no-fuss brethren.

FLAKY BUTTERMILK BISCUITS
MAKES 12 BISCUITS

The dough is a bit sticky when it comes together and during the first set of turns. Set aside about 1 cup of extra flour for dusting the work surface, dough, and rolling pin to prevent sticking. Be careful not to incorporate large pockets of flour into the dough when folding it over. When cutting the biscuits, press down with firm, even pressure; do not twist the cutter. The recipe may be prepared through step 2, transferred to a zipper-lock freezer bag, and frozen for several weeks. Let the mixture sit at room temperature for 15 minutes before proceeding.

2¹/₂	cups (12¹/₂ ounces) unbleached all-purpose flour, plus additional flour for work surface
1	tablespoon baking powder
¹/₂	teaspoon baking soda
1	teaspoon table salt
2	tablespoons vegetable shortening, cut into ¹/₂-inch chunks
8	tablespoons (1 stick) cold unsalted butter, lightly floured and cut into ¹/₈-inch slices (see illustration at right), plus 2 tablespoons butter, melted
1¹/₄	cups cold buttermilk, preferably low fat

1. Adjust oven rack to lower-middle position; heat oven to 450 degrees. Whisk flour, baking powder, baking soda, and salt in large bowl.

2. Add shortening to flour mixture; break up chunks with fingertips until only small, pea-sized pieces remain. Working in batches, drop butter slices into flour mixture and toss to coat; pick up each slice of butter and press between floured fingertips into flat, nickel-sized pieces (see illustration at right). Repeat until all butter is incorporated; toss to combine. Freeze mixture (in bowl) until chilled, about 15 minutes.

3. Spray 24-inch-square area of work surface with nonstick cooking spray; spread spray evenly across surface with kitchen towel or paper towel. Sprinkle ¹/₃ cup of extra flour across sprayed area; gently spread flour across work surface with palm to form thin, even coating. Add all but 2 tablespoons of buttermilk to flour mixture; stir briskly with fork until ball forms and no dry bits of flour are visible, adding remaining buttermilk as needed (dough will be sticky and shaggy but should clear sides of bowl). With rubber spatula, transfer dough onto center of prepared work surface, dust surface lightly with flour, and, with floured hands, bring dough together into cohesive ball.

4. Pat dough into approximate 10-inch square; roll into 18 by 14-inch rectangle about ¹/₄ inch thick, dusting dough and rolling pin with flour as needed. Following illustrations below, using bench scraper or thin metal spatula, fold dough into thirds, brushing any excess flour from surface; lift short end of dough and fold in thirds again to form approximate 6 by 4-inch rectangle. Rotate dough 90 degrees, dusting work surface underneath with flour; roll and fold dough again, dusting with flour as needed.

5. Roll dough into 10-inch square about ¹/₂ inch thick; flip dough and cut nine 3-inch rounds with floured biscuit cutter, dipping cutter back into flour after each cut. Carefully invert and transfer rounds to ungreased baking sheet, spaced 1 inch apart. Gather dough scraps into ball; roll and fold once or twice until scraps form smooth dough. Roll dough into ¹/₂-inch-thick round; cut three more 3-inch rounds and transfer to baking sheet. Discard excess dough.

6. Brush biscuit tops with melted butter. Bake, without opening oven door, until tops are golden brown and crisp, 15 to 17 minutes. Let cool on baking sheet 5 to 10 minutes before serving.

TECHNIQUE | MAKING THE 'LAYERED LOOK' WORK FOR YOU

Getting biscuits with ultra-flaky layers is all in the handling of the dough—a strategic process of pinching, folding, and refolding creates stratified layers of air, fat, and flour.

  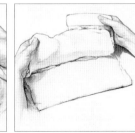 

SLICE
Cut butter (coated in flour to prevent sticking) into ¹/₈-inch-thick slices.

PRESS
Pinch butter slices between well-floured fingertips into flat, nickel-sized pieces.

FOLD
With scraper or metal spatula, fold dough into thirds (like a business letter).

REFOLD
Fold dough into thirds again, rotate 90 degrees, roll out, and repeat process.

Chocolate Mousse Perfected

Rich, frosting-like mousse is utterly delicious—for about two spoonfuls. Yet light and silky versions often lack decent chocolate flavor. Could we have the best of both worlds?

⇒ BY SANDRA WU ⇐

Chocolate mousse usually falls into one of two categories: rich, creamy, and dense, like a bittersweet chocolate truffle, or light and airy, but with all the flavor impact of chocolate milk. Neither is bad (I'd still eat them), but in my mind chocolate mousse is a dessert to be savored by the bowlful rather than reluctantly pushed away after a lick or two. Substantial chocolate flavor and a light, meltingly smooth texture should not be mutually exclusive.

Whisking my way through the gamut of chocolate mousse recipes, I was struck by the wide variations possible with the same basic ingredients: chocolate, eggs, sugar, and fat (butter, cream). Proportions and handling, apparently, were all that separated thick ganache from fluffy pudding.

Toward the Light

My perfect chocolate mousse was somewhere in between those two extremes, so my plan was to start with an average working recipe and adjust from there: Melt chocolate in a double boiler; whisk in egg yolks, butter, and heavy cream (for richness and smoothness); beat egg whites with sugar; then fold the soft peaks into the mixture (for silkiness). The resulting mousse was a fine start, but it was too dense, and the modest 4 ounces of chocolate proved little more than a tease.

Before embarking on the chocolate rampage I had planned, I decided to take a crack at lightening the texture. Where to begin? Of the recipe's six ingredients, butter, chocolate, cream, and

Heavy on chocolate flavor but light on texture, our chocolate mousse can be savored by the bowlful.

egg yolks were all likely culprits, although it was clear I needed more chocolate, not less. Given that some tasters had complained about a residual "waxy slickness" in the first few batches, my choice seemed obvious. Sure enough, when the butter was incrementally decreased—and, ultimately, eliminated—the texture lightened considerably and the waxiness was gone.

To correct the billowy marshmallow-like quality, I reduced the egg whites from four to two, which took the texture from airy to silky. But

four yolks now seemed like too many. By scaling down to two, I achieved a lighter, still-creamy mousse with good structure. Whipping the cream to soft peaks before adding it to the chocolate made up for some of the lost volume without reintroducing the "marshmallow effect."

Into the Dark

At last, the chocolate. For days, I subjected test kitchen staffers to a whirlwind of mousses made with various styles and brands. In the end, tasters found semisweet chocolate too sweet and one-dimensional (closer to milk chocolate than dark). Bittersweet chocolate, with its higher percentage of cocoa solids, provided the more complex flavor profile I was going for. As cocoa-solid percentage varies by brand, I standardized my recipe by using our winning supermarket dark chocolate, Ghirardelli, with 60 percent cocoa solids. (Some "premium" chocolates boast even higher percentages, and I wondered if substitution would be straightforward. It wasn't—see "Premium Chocolate Mousse," page 23.)

Armed with a shopping cart's worth of bittersweet chocolate, I set about slowly increasing the amount, in search of my mousse's breaking point. First, I tried bumping up the paltry 4 ounces I'd started with to 6 ounces. Mmm, nice—but nice wasn't enough. Seven ounces. Eight ounces. *Nine* ounces. At 9 ounces, I regrouped. The texture was suffering, and the mousse had become too sweet. I reduced the sugar (beaten with the egg whites) from 2 tablespoons down to 1. Better, but the dramatic increase in chocolate was still wreaking havoc on the texture.

I retreated to 8 ounces but immediately missed the more powerful flavor. What about a second form of chocolate? Adding an ounce of unsweetened chocolate made the mousse "starchy" and heavy. Two tablespoons of Dutch-processed cocoa powder, on the other hand, gave the mousse a fuller, more vibrant chocolate flavor—but it had a gritty texture.

Liquid Magic

Unwilling to sacrifice this intense, rounded flavor profile, I was determined to develop the infra-

Getting the Texture Right

There are as many different mousse textures as there are mousse recipes. Here's how some of them look.

DENSE
Butter, unwhipped cream, and too much chocolate are often the culprits in heavy, ganache-like mousse.

FLUFFY
Too many whipped egg whites produce an unappealing "marshmallow effect."

PERFECT
Going easy on the egg whites, omitting the butter, and adding a small amount of water yield just the right texture.

A Bittersweet Victory

The toughest challenge in making chocolate mousse is ramping up the chocolate without destroying the texture. Most recipes call it quits at just 4 or 5 ounces. We accommodated 8 ounces of bittersweet chocolate plus 2 tablespoons of cocoa—and the texture is silkier than ever.

SUBTLE HINT   **POWERFUL HIT**

structure necessary to support so much chocolate. The texture problem was creeping up early in the process: The melted chocolate turned thick and granular as soon as I whisked in the yolks, and seizing was not uncommon. No matter how slowly, quickly, or vigorously I whisked the mixture, it remained grainy. This compromised texture subsequently affected the incorporation of the egg whites as well, leaving the mousse riddled with white particles.

Something was giving my mousse the texture of a facial scrub—but what? I knew that liquid can cause melted chocolate to seize, but I was always careful not to let any steam from the double boiler contaminate the chocolate. Could it be the moisture-laden egg yolks? Well, that didn't make sense, given that I had reduced the number of yolks from four to two, and I'd had no problems with graininess back when I was using less chocolate. Besides, some recipes call for adding several tablespoons of coffee and other liquids at this stage, with no incidence of seizing.

After researching the subject further, I discovered that I had been only half-right: Liquids can cause melted chocolate to seize, but more important is the liquid-to-solid ratio. With small amounts of liquid, the solids absorb just enough moisture to form a gritty paste. But with more liquid (at least 1 tablespoon for every 2 ounces of chocolate), the dry cocoa solids become fluid. Suddenly, it all made sense. Early on, my recipe had just enough moisture from the 4 egg yolks and the butter to prevent 4 ounces of chocolate from becoming grainy. Once the butter was omitted, the yolks decreased, and the amount of chocolate increased, however, the story changed: The ratio of liquid to solid became too heavy on the solids.

To augment the liquid side of things, I was loath to add cream or any other source of fat. The solution was crystal clear (literally): water. I made several more batches, increasing the water (2, 4, 6, and 8 tablespoons) each time. The more water, the looser, glossier, and more manageable the mousse became. At 8 tablespoons, I was starting to undo the deep flavor I had achieved; at 6

tablespoons, the texture was perfect: light, ethereal, and chock full of chocolate.

Final Notes

All my mousse needed now was some final finessing of flavors. In other chocolate recipes, we have found that a small amount of instant espresso powder intensifies the chocolate experience. The trick worked here as well: One teaspoon added to the chocolate-cocoa-water mixture provided just the right boost. A mere 1/8 teaspoon of salt rounded out the mild sweetness.

Other common extras include vanilla and some sort of alcohol. Tasters flatly rejected vanilla for lending unwelcome floral notes to the mousse. Brandy was favored over rum and bourbon, and a meager tablespoon of the stuff (replacing an equal amount of water) added complexity without booziness. Finally, after making more than 100 batches, I had exactly the chocolate mousse I was looking for. Rich but not dense, chocolaty but not cloying, light and silky but not insubstantial, this perfectly balanced chocolate mousse could be devoured by the bowlful—or two.

DARK CHOCOLATE MOUSSE
MAKES 3 1/2 CUPS MOUSSE (6 TO 8 SERVINGS)

When developing this recipe, we used our winning supermarket brand of dark chocolate, Ghirardelli bittersweet, which contains about 60 percent cacao. If you choose to make the mousse a day in advance, leave it out at room temperature for 10 minutes before serving. Serve with very lightly sweetened whipped cream and chocolate shavings. A hand-held mixer can do the job of a standing mixer in this recipe, though mixing times may vary slightly.

- 8 ounces bittersweet chocolate, chopped fine
- 2 tablespoons cocoa powder, preferably Dutch-processed
- 1 teaspoon instant espresso powder
- 5 tablespoons water
- 1 tablespoon brandy
- 2 large eggs, separated
- 1 tablespoon sugar
- 1/8 teaspoon table salt
- 1 cup plus 2 tablespoons chilled heavy cream

1. Melt chocolate, cocoa powder, espresso powder, water, and brandy in medium heatproof bowl set over saucepan filled with 1 inch of barely simmering water, stirring frequently until smooth. Remove from heat.

2. Whisk egg yolks, 1 1/2 teaspoons sugar, and salt in medium bowl until mixture lightens in color and thickens

Like Water for Chocolate?

After trying every trick in the book to accommodate more chocolate, we found a surprisingly simple "solution."

slightly, about 30 seconds. Pour melted chocolate into egg mixture and whisk until combined. Let cool until just warmer than room temperature, 3 to 5 minutes.

3. In clean bowl of standing mixer fitted with whisk attachment, beat egg whites at medium-low speed until frothy, 1 to 2 minutes. Add remaining 1 1/2 teaspoons sugar, increase mixer speed to medium-high, and beat until soft peaks form when whisk is lifted, about 1 minute. Detach whisk and bowl from mixer and whisk last few strokes by hand, making sure to scrape any unbeaten whites from bottom of bowl. Using whisk, stir about one-quarter of beaten egg whites into chocolate mixture to lighten it; gently fold in remaining egg whites with rubber spatula until a few white streaks remain.

4. In now-empty bowl, whip heavy cream at medium speed until it begins to thicken, about 30 seconds. Increase speed to high and whip until soft peaks form when whisk is lifted, about 15 seconds more. Using rubber spatula, fold whipped cream into mousse until no white streaks remain. Spoon into 6 to 8 individual serving dishes or goblets. Cover with plastic wrap and refrigerate until set and firm, at least 2 hours. (The mousse may be covered and refrigerated for up to 24 hours.)

Premium Chocolate Mousse

While developing the recipe for Dark Chocolate Mousse, I stuck to our winning brand of supermarket chocolate, Ghirardelli, which contains about 60 percent cacao. I wondered what would happen if I switched to a high-end boutique brand, which contain 62 to 70 percent cacao. After one try, it looked like swapping in a premium chocolate wouldn't work. Directly substituting these inherently starchier, less sweet chocolates for the Ghirardelli left me with stiff, grainy mousse that was much more bitter than it was sweet. Chocolates with higher percentages of cacao contain more cocoa solids (hence the mousse's less-than-creamy texture) and, conversely, less sugar. To address these issues, I had to make these few minor adjustments: Increase the water to 7 tablespoons, add another egg, and up the sugar to 3 tablespoons (adding the extra 2 tablespoons of sugar to the chocolate mixture in step 1). The end result? Chocolate mousse for fans of truly dark chocolate. (See Cook's Extra below for the recipe.) –S.W.

Go to www.cooksillustrated.com
- Key in code 1066 for **Chocolate-Orange Mousse**.
- Key in code 1067 for **Chocolate-Raspberry Mousse**.
- Key in code 1068 for **Premium Chocolate Mousse**.

COOK'S extra

The Best Lemon Bundt Cake

Lemons are tart, brash, and aromatic. Why, then, is it so hard to capture these assertive flavors in a straightforward Bundt cake?

≥ BY ERIKA BRUCE ≤

Bundt cakes have a unique design that allows them to stand on their own, exclusive of fancy fillings or embellishments. This unfussy quality makes them perfect vehicles for showcasing simple flavors, whether rich chocolate or fragrant vanilla.

Lemon Bundt cakes are a different story: Whereas other flavoring agents can simply be increased to heighten their intensity, lemon flavor in cake is fleeting at best. Normally an assertive flavoring agent, lemon juice is drastically muted when exposed to the heat of the oven. And to complicate matters further, this highly acidic juice (few items in the kitchen compare) can wreak havoc on the delicate nature of baked goods.

A sampling of lemon Bundt cakes revealed the various ploys used to compensate for these problems. Some recipes simply drape a cloak of sweet, gloppy frosting over the cake. Others saturate it with a syrupy soak that makes for an overly sweet and sodden cake. Some manage to get a pungent flavor *inside* the cake by means of lemon extracts and oils, but these products can leave behind unpleasant, artificial aftertastes if used injudiciously. Flavor issues aside, I was also determined to come up with a cake that stayed true to proper Bundt cake texture: Unlike a light and fluffy layer cake (which is safely anchored by frosting), a Bundt cake must be firm enough to hold its own when sliced and served. At the same time, it should be less rich and compact than the typical pound cake. Could I strike this textural balance yet still achieve pure, vibrant lemon flavor?

Easy as 1-2-3-4

Many baking recipes are based on simple formulas, mnemonic tools used to pass down recipes through the generations. Bundt cakes commonly fall into the 1-2-3-4 cake category: 1 cup butter, 2 cups sugar, 3 cups flour, 4 eggs (plus 1 cup milk, a liquid component that sets both layer and Bundt cakes apart from pound cake). Almost two-thirds of the recipes I tried took advantage of this conveniently proportioned formula, which produced just the right volume but also made for a dry, uninspired texture—too crumbly and too coarse.

So began my battery of tests, starting with decreasing the flour and increasing the milk (to moisten) and eggs (for structure), all of which produced dense and gummy cakes. I had more

Our Lemon Bundt Cake is moist and rich enough to eat unglazed, but tasters liked the extra hit of lemon flavor.

luck increasing the butter, but 2½ sticks (tasters' favorite for richness and tenderness) left behind a greasy residue. I settled for an increase of just 2 tablespoons. Finally, replacing the milk with buttermilk yielded a lighter, more tender crumb and a nice, mild tang.

Most Bundt cakes follow the standard mixing technique of creaming butter and sugar, adding eggs, then alternating flour and liquid until combined. Could I streamline these steps? I tried several variations on the ultra-easy dump-and-stir method. But as soon as I bit into the rubbery, dense cakes, I knew that creaming was indeed necessary to achieve a light and even crumb. The whipping action aerates the batter, contributing lightness to the final cake.

Acid Reign

I was now ready to give this cake a hefty boost of flavor. My gut still told me that if I used enough lemon juice in the batter, at least some flavor would survive the 45 or 50 minutes in the oven. But after a generous ½ cup of potent lemon juice transformed the cake's texture into a fragile and crumbly mess, I was reminded that playing with acid is no casual affair. (Lemon juice has a pH of about 2.3, even stronger than vinegar.) Acids interfere with the formation of gluten, the protein that's so vital to a cake's structure. The more acidic the batter, the less structure in the cake, and the cakes I was now making were literally fall-apart tender. Fragile was not what I was going for. But I wondered if I could harness acid's gluten-weakening tendency to produce a *slightly* more delicate crumb. A modest 3 tablespoons of lemon juice did the trick.

Such a paltry amount had absolutely no effect on the cake's lemon flavor, however. So I turned to my next favorite part of the lemon, the zest (the yellow part of the peel; the white part, the pith, is very bitter and unpleasant). I noticed that most recipes called for a miniscule amount, using the zest from just one lemon to flavor a whole cake. Hoping the zest wouldn't affect texture in the way the juice had, I increased it steadily until tasters cried "Pledge!" I settled for three lemons' worth of zest for a floral,

The Great Yellow Cake Breakdown

Intricate contours aren't the only defining characteristic of a Bundt cake. While all yellow cakes are built from the same core ingredients—butter, eggs, flour, sugar—different proportions of fats and liquids yield strikingly different results. Here's how the basic cakes break down.

THE CAKE	THE FAT	THE LIQUID	THE RESULT
Pound	Lots	Not much	Rich and buttery, with a tight, compact crumb
Bundt	Moderate	Moderate	Moist and rich, but lighter than a pound cake
Layer	Moderate	Lots	Fluffy but rich, with a somewhat crumbly texture
Sponge	Not much	Lots	Light, with a springy, delicate texture

Lemon Anatomy 101

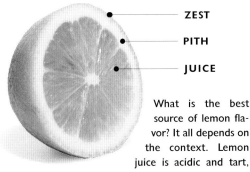

- ZEST
- PITH
- JUICE

What is the best source of lemon flavor? It all depends on the context. Lemon juice is acidic and tart, but that brightness is lost when exposed to heat; it's best used uncooked. (In baked items, juice provides tenderness only.) Better for baking is the thin, yellow zest layer, which contains floral, lemony oils. But avoid the bitter white pith, just beneath the zest.

perfumed lemon flavor that was not reminiscent of furniture polish.

I had one final adjustment to make. I had been removing the zest from the lemons using a Microplane rasp grater (which the test kitchen prefers to a box grater or traditional hand-held zester), but the fine strands of zest were showing up in the cake as yellow, fibrous specks. First, I tried mincing the strands with a chef's knife (reducing the zest to tiny flecks). Better, but not perfect; the flecks were still fibrous. The solution was a brief soak in the lemon juice after mincing, which softened the flecks nicely. After all, I wanted the taste of the zest, not the texture.

Trail Glazing

Now that I'd used as much lemon juice and zest in the cake itself as was palatable, I regrouped and concentrated on the exterior. Many recipes overdid it on the glazing or soaking front; I thought that a minimalist approach might do the trick. Using only basic ingredients—lemon juice and confectioners' sugar—I whisked together a simple glaze. Just the opposite of sweet and cloying, this glaze was too sour and overwhelmed the delicate flavor of the cake. I tried adding zest (too floral here), butter (too muting), and, finally, buttermilk, as it was already on hand. Supplementing some of the sour juice with the more mild yet tangy buttermilk smoothed out the flavor without dulling the brightness. But this now thick and gooey glaze felt heavy on top of such a tender cake. Thinning the glaze with more juice and buttermilk merely caused it to run off the top and sides, pooling underneath the cake rather than clinging to it. If the cake was still warm, however, the thick glaze melted into the cake and then dried into a thin, mottled shellac. To improve on the presentation, I reserved half of the glaze for use once the cake had cooled; now a more moderate amount of thick, white glaze stood out against the golden crust of the cake.

LEMON BUNDT CAKE
SERVES 12 TO 14

You will need between five and six tablespoons of lemon juice for this recipe. Because the amount of juice can vary from lemon to lemon, we suggest you first measure the juice from the three lemons you have zested, then juice a fourth lemon if necessary. Serve this cake as is or dress it up with lightly sweetened berries. The cake has a light, fluffy texture when eaten the day it is baked, but if well wrapped and held at room temperature overnight its texture becomes more dense—like that of pound cake—the following day.

Cake

	Grated zest plus 3 tablespoons juice from 3 lemons (see note above)
3	cups (15 ounces) unbleached all-purpose flour
1	teaspoon baking powder
1/2	teaspoon baking soda
1	teaspoon table salt
1	teaspoon vanilla extract
3/4	cup buttermilk, preferably low fat
3	large eggs plus 1 large yolk, at room temperature
18	tablespoons (2 1/4 sticks) unsalted butter, at room temperature
2	cups (14 ounces) sugar

Glaze

2–3	tablespoons lemon juice (see note above)
1	tablespoon buttermilk
2	cups (8 ounces) confectioners' sugar

1. **FOR THE CAKE:** Adjust oven rack to lower-middle position; heat oven to 350 degrees. Spray 12-cup Bundt pan with nonstick baking spray with flour (alternatively, brush pan with mixture of 1 tablespoon flour and 1 tablespoon melted butter). Mince lemon zest to fine paste (you should have about 2 tablespoons). Combine zest and lemon juice in small bowl; set aside to soften, 10 to 15 minutes.

2. Whisk flour, baking powder, baking soda, and salt in large bowl. Combine lemon juice mixture, vanilla, and buttermilk in medium bowl. In small bowl, gently whisk eggs and yolk to combine. In standing mixer fitted with flat beater, cream butter and sugar at medium-high speed until pale and fluffy, about 3 minutes; scrape down sides of bowl with rubber spatula. Reduce to medium speed and add half of eggs, mixing until incorporated, about 15 seconds. Repeat with remaining eggs; scrape down bowl again. Reduce to low speed; add about one-third of flour mixture, followed by half of buttermilk mixture, mixing until just incorporated after each addition (about 5 seconds). Repeat using half of remaining flour mixture and all of remaining buttermilk mixture. Scrape bowl and add remaining flour mixture; mix at medium-low speed until batter is thoroughly combined, about 15 seconds. Remove bowl from mixer and fold batter once or twice with rubber spatula to incorporate any remaining flour. Scrape into prepared pan.

3. Bake until top is golden brown and wooden skewer or toothpick inserted into center comes out with no crumbs attached, 45 to 50 minutes.

4. **FOR THE GLAZE:** While cake is baking, whisk 2 tablespoons lemon juice, buttermilk, and confectioners' sugar until smooth, adding more lemon juice gradually as needed until glaze is thick but still pourable (mixture should leave faint trail across bottom of mixing bowl when drizzled from whisk). Cool cake in pan on wire rack set over baking sheet for 10 minutes, then invert cake directly onto rack. Pour half of glaze over warm cake and let cool for 1 hour; pour remaining glaze evenly over top of cake and continue to cool to room temperature, at least 2 hours. Cut into slices and serve.

Go to www.cooksillustrated.com
- Key in code 1069 for our **Rating of Bundt Pans**.

TESTING: Are Nonstick Sprays Better Than Butter?

There's nothing worse than turning a Bundt pan over and seeing half a Bundt cake drop out. A coating of butter and flour does the trick, but we aren't wild about the crusty white "frost" it sometimes leaves behind on the cake. Could nonstick sprays do a better job?

We tested two nonstick cooking sprays (vegetable or canola oil under aerosol pressure) and two baking sprays (nonstick cooking sprays with a flour component) in our Lemon Bundt Cake and a classic génoise cake. The cooking sprays—Pam and Everbake—worked fairly well, but they weren't perfect. The baking sprays were a different story. With Pam for Baking No-Stick Cooking Spray ($2.99) and Baker's Joy ($2.99), every cake came out of the pan with nary a blemish. The uniformly blended flour-oil mixture made it easy to achieve an even coating, and the more solid texture of the baking sprays kept grease from pooling in crevices, which can dull the ridges of a Bundt cake. (This is especially important when using an intricately shaped pan; see Equipment Corner, page 32.) For less than $3, the winning baking sprays offer freedom from greasy palms, dirty flour sifters, and broken cakes. –Garth Clingingsmith

FLOUR POWER
Baking sprays with flour outperform butter and flour applied by hand.

Is Fresh Breakfast Sausage Best?

Precooked 'brown-and-serve' links couldn't taste better than fresh breakfast sausage, right? Several hundred sausages later, we made a few surprising discoveries.

⇒ BY ADAM RIED ⇐

Americans know breakfast sausage to be a mixture of ground meat (both lean and fat, and usually pork), salt, pepper, and spices that you fry up crisp and brown to accompany eggs or pancakes. A simple list of ingredients, maybe, but selecting a sausage can be a complicated affair. Shape (link, patty, roll, or bulk) and flavor (mild through "zesty") are just two of the obvious choices. But for our tasting we explored another option that many home cooks might not even consider: the choice between fully cooked sausage, which requires only a bit of heating (often referred to as "brown and serve"), and fresh sausage, which requires full cooking. Brown-and-serve sausage has two things going for it: It's less perishable than fresh, capable of withstanding months in the freezer, and it takes precious little time to prepare. But how much flavor do you have to sacrifice for such convenience?

In an informal poll, almost everyone in the test kitchen agreed that they would buy fresh over fully cooked, frozen breakfast sausage. That sounded like a challenge to me, so I conducted a tasting to find out if fresher really is better. These were the rules: pork only (nothing identified as beef, poultry, or meatless), in link form, and in the simplest possible flavor profile. Fresh and fully cooked sausages were prepared by panfrying according to package instructions. First, we evaluated the fresh sausages alone, then we sampled the fully cooked sausages along with the winning fresh sausage for reference.

Sausage Sleuthing

Fresh and brown-and-serve sausages are fabricated in much the same way, at least up to a point. Pork trimmings from several primal cuts are ground, blended with ice (to help maintain temperature) and water (for workability), and seasoned. Several experts stressed that the trimmings are not scraps but pieces of lean and fat removed from large primal cuts during the fabrication of retail cuts. Inquiries to manufacturers about specific types and grades of trimmings, lean-to-fat ratios, particle sizes, quantities of water, seasonings, and casings were unerringly met with the word "proprietary."

If sausages are to be sold as a brown-and-serve product, they are sent through gigantic cookers that often use steam and convection to cook them to 170 degrees. The sausages then may or may not be sent to a browning chamber, where gas-fired flame jets enhance both color and flavor. Some sources suggest that a less expensive way to color the steam-cooked sausages is to dip them in caramel coloring. The sausages are then quickly cooled and blast-frozen for packaging.

Sausage Surprise

With all this in mind, it came as a huge surprise that the fully cooked, brown-and-serve sausages did extremely well in the tasting, so well that the best sausage overall was the brown-and-serve product from Farmland, which scored a full two points higher (out of 10) than the highest-ranked fresh sausage—also from Farmland. After conversations with meat-processing experts, I concluded that the explanation for our findings is control.

Roger Mandigo of the University of Nebraska pointed out that fully cooked sausage introduces many variables, among them the evaporation of moisture, rendering of fat, and denaturing (reconfiguration) of proteins. But these variables are also opportunities for manufacturers to engineer the product. With specific appearance, flavor, and texture attributes in mind, manufacturers can manipulate the recipe, cooking temperature(s) and time, and humidity with great exactitude.

For instance, a Farmland representative mentioned one method that the company uses to help control the texture of its brown-and-serve sausage. Immediately after steam cooking, excess fat on the surface of the sausage is blown off at high pressure to reduce the perception of greasiness by the consumer. This kind of manipulation ensures a more consistent product when the sausages are reheated at home.

Robert Delmore Jr. at California Polytechnic State University mentioned another possible advantage of manufacturing brown-and-serve sausage. Oxidation of fat, he said, degrades flavor. Many companies combat this effect by adding preservatives such as propyl gallate, citric acid, butylated hydroxyanisole (BHA), and butylated hydroxytoluene (BHT), but the quick deep freeze that brown-and-serve sausages undergo during processing adds an extra level of protection against oxidation. Sure enough, our tasting bore out this theory, as tasters were more likely to use terms such as "off," "musty," "stale," and "not fresh" to describe the fresh sausage than the brown and serve.

Why Farmland?

Representatives from Farmland—makers of our favorite brown-and-serve and fresh sausages—were quick to offer a host of reasons for their product's superiority. One reason that stood out and tracked with my research was that their brown-and-serve sausages are browned with a flame rather than tinted with caramel coloring.

I next turned to the issue of fat, which provides both flavor and juiciness in sausage. We enlisted an independent food lab to measure fat content and uncovered large disparities. Some brands had as little as 22 percent fat, while others were nearly 50 percent fat (the maximum allowable amount, according to the U.S. Department of Agriculture). Comparing these figures with our tasting results, the success of Farmland makes a lot of sense.

With its relatively high fat content (44 percent), Farmland's fresh sausage was described by tasters as being juicy and tasting strongly of pork. (The two fresh sausages with higher fat contents, Hormel and Swift, failed for unrelated reasons.) In contrast, tasters considered Owens, near the bottom of the fat content scale at 23 percent, too bland. Likewise, many tasters found Jimmy Dean fresh sausage, with its relatively low fat content of 27 percent, to be dry. Among the brown-and-serve sausages, Farmland topped the fat ratings at nearly 41 percent, which helps explain why tasters found it to possess "big pork flavor" and juiciness.

Another point raised by the experts was seasoning. Tasters scrutinized every sample for saltiness, sweetness, and spiciness and marked down samples they perceived as too salty, sweet, or spicy. The lab could not analyze for specific spices, and none of the manufacturers we contacted would reveal their seasoning blend (there was that word "proprietary" again), but balance between salt, sweet, and spice was important to our tasters, who regarded Farmland favorably in this regard.

Selection 'Process'

What, then, to buy? If what you desire most in your pork breakfast sausage is convenience, you may now approach fully cooked, frozen products without fear of sacrificing flavor and reliable texture. This is one of those rare cases in which a "processed" food may in fact be superior to the "real thing."

TASTING BREAKFAST SAUSAGE

Twenty-three *Cook's Illustrated* staff members tasted 14 different supermarket pork sausages, including both fresh and frozen, fully cooked brown-and-serve samples. The sausages were pan-fried to the same degree of doneness (165 degrees on an instant-read thermometer), per the manufacturers' cooking instructions, and tasted warm. Fresh and fully cooked sausages were tasted separately, with one control in each lineup to confirm the validity of the tests. The top-rated fresh sausage was included in the tasting of fully cooked sausages as a point of reference. Tasters judged the sausages for meaty ("fresh pork") flavor, sweetness, and juiciness. **Sausages are listed below, separated by type, in order of preference.** The fat values were determined by independent lab tests.

BEST OVERALL SAUSAGE
FARMLAND Pork Sausage Links, Fully Cooked
➤ **$2.69 for 12 ounces** ➤ **Fat: 40.82%**
Tasters lauded this link for "big pork flavor," good balance of salt and sweet, and "nice, lingering spiciness." Accolades didn't end there; compliments were also garnered for tender, "super-juicy" meat.

FRESH SAUSAGES

RECOMMENDED

FARMLAND Original Pork Sausage Links
➤ **$1.89 for 12 ounces** ➤ **Fat: 43.99%**
Though saltiness was a common complaint, tasters found much to like in this link, which earned kudos for "straight-up pork flavor" and "spiciness that mellows with every bite." Pleasantly sweet and juicy.

RECOMMENDED WITH RESERVATIONS

BOB EVANS Original Links
➤ **$3.68 for 12 ounces** ➤ **Fat: 27.21%**
Some tasters likened the flavor of this "not-too-sweet" link to a hot dog, but most focused on obvious ("overwhelming") dried spice flavors, including coriander, white pepper, and sage.

OWENS Original Premium Pork Sausage Links
➤ **$3.75 for 12 ounces** ➤ **Fat: 22.46%**
Nicely balanced pork flavor, though some considered it too mild, even bland. Tasters collectively hated the texture: The words "gristly," "rubbery," and "spongy" were used repeatedly.

JIMMY DEAN Original Fresh Pork Sausage Links
➤ **$3.69 for 10 ounces** ➤ **Fat: 26.74%**
Several tasters picked up on a "cured," "hammy" flavor that even reminded one of "Chinese wontons," but many more declared this link to be bland and dry.

JONES All Natural Pork Little Sausages
➤ **$4.49 for 12 ounces** ➤ **Fat: 42.96%**
The smooth texture struck tasters alternately as greasy or juicy. Notes on the flavor were positive, with praise for "big" pork flavor. A vocal minority was stunned by salt: "Get me some OJ, stat!"

NOT RECOMMENDED

HORMEL Little Sizzlers Pork Sausage, Original
➤ **$2.69 for 12 ounces** ➤ **Fat: 47.17%**
Most tasters said "no thanks" to these "super-salty," overly spiced links, which were widely thought to resemble "Tater Tots" or "fish sticks."

SWIFT PREMIUM Fresh Pork Sausage
➤ **$3.59 for 12 ounces** ➤ **Fat: 47.66%**
Tasted "gamey" and "processed" to many panelists, one of whom even likened the sample to Slim Jim beef jerky. Saltiness was also a common complaint.

FULLY COOKED, FROZEN SAUSAGES

RECOMMENDED WITH RESERVATIONS

ARMOUR Brown 'N Serve Original Fully Cooked Sausage Links
➤ **$1.99 for 7 ounces** ➤ **Fat: 33.79%**
Armour's hallmark was tenderness, so much so that one taster thought the texture was "suspicious." A few complaints about saltiness, but most found the sweetness and saltiness well balanced and the pork flavor "decent."

OWENS Express Fully Cooked Regular Microwaveable Pork Sausage Links
➤ **$2.89 for 8 ounces** ➤ **Fat: 31.05%**
The middle-of-the-road fat content made for a middle-of-the-road link, with discernible flavors of pork and spice that some perceived as mild, even "boring." Texture viewed as fine and firm.

JONES Golden Brown Fully Cooked & Browned Sausage, Mild Links
➤ **$2.59 for 8 ounces** ➤ **Fat: 38.86%**
Pork flavor was lost on tasters, who cried "stale," "funky," and "bizarre." Comments on texture were split almost evenly between "greasy" and "juicy."

BOB EVANS Express Fully Cooked Original Microwaveable Pork Sausage Links
➤ **$2.59 for 8 ounces** ➤ **Fat: 28.70%**
Nearly every taster thought the casing was tough, giving the link "too much snap . . . like a hot dog." Most deemed the flavor fresh and subtle, though some complained of "massive sage overload."

NOT RECOMMENDED

SWIFT PREMIUM Sizzle 'N Serve Fully Cooked Sausage
➤ **$3.59 for 8 ounces** ➤ **Fat: 35.66%**
Tasters were overwhelmed by salt, so much so that several likened this link to a "salt lick." Tasters who could get beyond the salt were bothered by a "cafeteria flavor."

JIMMY DEAN Fresh Taste. Fast! Original Fully Cooked Pork Sausage Links
➤ **$4.19 for 9.6 ounces** ➤ **Fat: 36.15%**
Instead of pork flavor, more tasters noted hints of bacon, beef, and hot dogs, as well as a strong smokiness that "totally dominated."

Do Grill Pans Really Grill?

Grilling outside means bold flavors and attractive char marks—and waiting for decent weather. Can a grill pan transport the hot grate from the backyard to the stovetop?

≥ BY ADAM RIED ≤

Cooking over live fire imparts more than just flavor. Dishes made on the grill have that smoldering, come-hither look, too: The telltale charred, dark brown lines from the hot grate glorify foods just as neat pin-stripes accent the irresistible contours of a sexy Italian sports car.

When inclement weather (or lack of equipment) prohibits use of a grill, many recipe writers recommend the stovetop grill pan as the next best option. Basically a skillet (or sauté pan) with raised ridges splayed across the cooking surface, a grill pan is designed to deliver grill marks similar to those made on an outdoor grill. But while breathless recommendations from cookbook authors and other food writers are all well and good, I couldn't help but wonder: Was there more to cooking in grill pans than mere looks (those beguiling stripes)? Could they really replicate some of the flavor produced on a real grill?

Getting into the Groove(s)

First, I had to narrow the field: Grill pans come in a dizzying array of materials, shapes, and sizes—small and large, square and round, cast iron and aluminum, with stainless steel, enameled, and nonstick surfaces. I purchased representatives of each and embarked on a pretesting marathon that included pounds and pounds of beef, vegetables, and fish. Shape and size turned out to matter much less than material, and it soon became apparent that aluminum was the only way to go. Why? The aluminum pans were lighter and so easier to handle, and they produced more distinct grill marks than their cast-iron counterparts. (Which makes sense, given that aluminum conducts heat more efficiently than cast iron.) What's more, it took just one ultra-sticky round of glazed salmon to make me decide that nonstick aluminum is a better choice than a traditional surface. Scrubbing the sticky, burnt glaze and salmon fat

from between each and every ridge was, to put it politely, a major chore with both cast iron and stainless steel. (That said, for a great grill-pan cleaning aid, see "Grill Sponge: Good for Getting the Gunk Out?" below.)

The full testing, then, would focus on aluminum, nonstick-coated grill pans. An afternoon of shopping yielded eight models, with prices ranging from $40 to over three times as much. Some had wide ridges and others did not. Surely a few days at the stove would help determine the importance of design differences, not to mention settle my questions about the grill pans' ability to impart grilled flavor.

To gauge how well the pans produced attractive grill marks, I needed to cook something with a fairly uniform surface. Boneless chicken breasts? Eggplant planks? Not quite the uniformity I was looking for. But a trip to the home-improvement store produced exactly what I needed: standard two-by-four pine boards cut into 8-inch lengths. Back in the test kitchen, I opened all the windows, set the ventilation system on overdrive to dissipate the smoke, and spent two days burning grill marks into wood, as colleagues looked on in disbelief. It was an odd notion, but it worked. I ended up with an equitable and permanent memento of each pan's performance. In general, the pans with wider ridges produced wider, deeper grill marks than pans with narrow ridges.

Illustrative as the charred lumber was, I figured I'd better cook some real food, too. Full testing of the eight pans with hamburgers, flank steak, salmon fillets, swordfish steaks, chicken breast cutlets, panini (Italian-style grilled sandwiches), and sliced zucchini taught me a few things about cooking with grill pans.

First, to develop appetizing grill marks, the pan must be preheated. Second, it's best to use a modicum of fat. In my tests, a light coating of oil resulted in nicer stripes than dry food in a dry

Grate Expectations

After weeks of testing, we developed some clear preferences as to grill pan design.

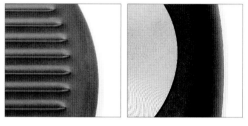

HOLLOW VICTORY
In general, ridges constructed by indenting the underside of the pan (left) produced superior grill marks to pans with solid disk bottoms (right).

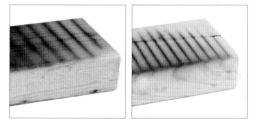

GO WIDE
Cooking wood planks let us compare pan performance on a level playing field and confirmed our observation that pans with wide ridges (left) produced more substantial char marks than those with slender ridges (right).

pan. (Besides, for safety's sake you should not overheat an empty nonstick pan.) Third, cooking foods with wide, flat surfaces will help any grill pan do its best. For instance, broad, flat swordfish steaks developed deeper, more consistent grill marks than salmon fillets, which have naturally uneven surfaces. Likewise, for hamburgers to develop dark, ruddy grill marks, the patties should be formed with perfectly flat surfaces.

All of our winners shared one trait. It wasn't price; the two least expensive models in the lineup—the $40 Calphalon and the $50 Anolon—were recommended. It wasn't material, since all the pans were aluminum. It was the design of the ridges. Our favorite pans had wide ridges (5/16 inch or more), which begat wide, substantial grill marks on the food—resulting in larger areas of caramelization and, thus, flavor. In contrast, pans with the narrowest ridges (3/16 inch or less), the Look and the Scanpan, produced thinner, less-developed marks. What's more, both

Grill Sponge: Good for Getting the Gunk Out?

The ridges of a grill pan—even a nonstick model—can be a cleaning nightmare, thanks to the charred, sticky gunk that collects in the crevices. So we were impressed when we came across the George Foreman Grill Sponge ($4.99 for three): Half polyester sponge, half scouring pad, its unique grooved shape is designed to fit easily between the ridges on George Foreman–brand indoor grills. Luckily, that also happens to be just the right size for cleaning all of our favorite grill pans, most of which have similarly wide spaces between the ridges. –Garth Clingingsmith

GROOVY PAD
This specialized sponge for grill pans is not just a gimmick.

RATING NONSTICK GRILL PANS

We tested eight nonstick aluminum grill pans (square shaped, whenever possible) and evaluated them according to the criteria listed below. When manufacturers offered more than one grill pan that satisfied our rubric, we chose their best-selling or recommended model. Tests were performed over gas burners on the professional-grade ranges in our test kitchen. The pans are listed in order of preference.

PRICE: Prices paid in Boston-area stores, national mail-order catalogs, or online stores.

MATERIAL: Materials from which the pan is made.

WEIGHT: As measured in the test kitchen, rounded to the nearest ounce.

RIDGE WIDTH: As measured in the test kitchen.

PERFORMANCE: We pan-grilled hamburgers; flank steaks; swordfish steaks; skinless, boneless chicken breast cutlets; glazed salmon; thick panini sandwiches; and sliced fresh zucchini. For each test, the color, evenness, and quality of the grill marks were most important. Scores of good, fair, or poor were assigned for each test, and the aggregate score determined the overall performance rating.

CLEANUP: After each test, we cleaned the pans by hand, with hot water and liquid dish detergent. Pans that washed up with little effort were rated good.

RECOMMENDED

Simply Calphalon Nonstick 13" Round Grill Pan
PRICE: $39.95
MATERIAL: Anodized aluminum with nonstick coating, steel handle

WEIGHT: 2 lb 11 oz
RIDGE WIDTH: 3/8"
PERFORMANCE: ★★★
CLEANUP: ★★★

TESTERS' COMMENTS: The wide-body of the lineup turned out an impressive flank steak, with wide, nicely developed grill marks. Best-in-class pricing and generous cooking area pushed it to the top slot.

Pampered Chef Professional Cookware 11" Square Grill Pan
PRICE: $95.00
MATERIAL: Anodized aluminum with nonstick coating, phenolic handle

WEIGHT: 3 lb
RIDGE WIDTH: 5/16"
PERFORMANCE: ★★★
CLEANUP: ★★★

TESTERS' COMMENTS: Gorgeous swordfish emerged from this pan, drawing a crowd of admirers, forks in hand and poised to pounce. Nary a misstep in any test. Available only from Pampered Chef sales reps.

Anolon Advanced 12" Covered Deep Round Grill Pan
PRICE: $49.95
MATERIAL: Anodized aluminum with nonstick coating, silicone rubber-coated stainless steel handle

WEIGHT: 3 lb 6 oz
RIDGE WIDTH: 5/16"
PERFORMANCE: ★★★
CLEANUP: ★★★

TESTERS' COMMENTS: An even-tempered performer that won't break the bank. Impressive showing on the burgers, swordfish, chicken cutlets, and zucchini.

Swiss Diamond 11" Square Grill Pan
PRICE: $129.99
MATERIAL: Cast aluminum with nonstick coating, phenolic handles

WEIGHT: 3 lb 14 oz
RIDGE WIDTH: 5/16"
PERFORMANCE: ★★★
CLEANUP: ★★★

TESTERS' COMMENTS: A heavy-searing star that produced beautiful grill marks. Its weight helped it overcome the cast design (we generally preferred hollow ridges).

All-Clad LTD. 11" Square Grille Pan
PRICE: $69.99
MATERIAL: Complete aluminum core with anodized aluminum exterior and nonstick interior, stainless steel handle

WEIGHT: 3 lb 6 oz
RIDGE WIDTH: 3/8"
PERFORMANCE: ★★
CLEANUP: ★★★

TESTERS' COMMENTS: Matched the other recommended pans in most ways, but stood out in none. Unevenly marked zucchini cost it a crucial performance point.

RECOMMENDED WITH RESERVATIONS

Berndes 12" Square Grill Pan
PRICE: $99.95
MATERIAL: Cast aluminum with nonstick coating on interior and exterior, phenolic handle

WEIGHT: 3 lb
RIDGE WIDTH: 3/8"
PERFORMANCE: ★★
CLEANUP: ★★★

TESTERS' COMMENTS: Closely spaced ridges are to thank for faint, uninspiring grill marks—and utter lack of charred flavor—in nearly every test.

Look Nonstick Square Grill Pan, 10½"
PRICE: $90.00
MATERIAL: Cast aluminum with nonstick coating, phenolic handle

WEIGHT: 3 lb 12 oz
RIDGE WIDTH: 3/16"
PERFORMANCE: ★★
CLEANUP: ★★★

TESTERS' COMMENTS: Grill marks? Pass the magnifying glass, please. Choked on both heavy and light searing tasks, with grill marks as disappointing on the fish as they were on the zucchini.

Scanpan Classic 10½" Nonstick Square Grill Pan
PRICE: $104.95
MATERIAL: Cast aluminum with nonstick coating, phenolic handle

WEIGHT: 3 lb
RIDGE WIDTH: 1/16"
PERFORMANCE: ★★
CLEANUP: ★★

TESTERS' COMMENTS: Tall, tight ridges made it harder to clean than some, and for what? Faint grill marks and a significantly lightened wallet.

the Look and the Scanpan performed worse in the sink as well. The valleys between the narrow ridges were tight and required an unwanted extra round of scrubbing and scraping to get clean, even though the surface was nonstick.

Finally, I noticed a fairly consistent correlation between performance and the method used to construct the ridges. There are two basic approaches: Either the ridges are punched into the metal from the bottom, leaving indentations open to the heat source, or the pan is cast from molten metal, meaning that the ridges are formed by the mold (see top photos, page 28). Cast pans have a solid bottom surface, without exposed indentations. In general, the pans with open indentations delivered better grill marks. Why? The interior of each ridge was directly exposed to the heat source, which facilitated heat transfer. (The exception to this rule is the Swiss Diamond, which has a solid bottom surface but was also the heaviest pan in the group.)

Flavor Face-Off

The recommended grill pans had proved their ability to dress a variety of foods for success in dark, even, nicely charred stripes. But did they deliver any advantage in terms of flavor? Happily, yes—though the grill pans could not caramelize food as efficiently as an outdoor grill and, hence, provided a subtler grill flavor. While our tasters liked the more robust flavor of the steaks and burgers we cooked outside, many tasters actually preferred the more delicate grilled flavor of zucchini cooked in the grill pans.

Are grill pans worth buying? Certainly, they can't replace a real grill. But for wintertime in the Snow Belt (or any time in the "Apartment Belt"), my tests proved that a grill pan can make a practical substitute, especially when you want to "grill" panini and fairly delicate foods such as fish or vegetables. And with its modest $40 price tag, wide ridges, and easily cleaned nonstick surface, our top-rated Calphalon grill pan makes the minor indulgence of a nonessential cookware item seem downright reasonable.

KITCHEN NOTES

⇒ BY ERIKA BRUCE ⇐

Shopping: Ground Beef

While developing our Glazed Meat Loaf recipe (page 19), we got the best texture by combining two types of ground beef: lean sirloin and fattier chuck. Easy enough, except that many supermarkets sell ground beef labeled not by primal cut (chuck, round, sirloin, and so on) but by lean/fat percentage. When we tried substituting the appropriate percentages (80/20 for chuck, 90/10 for sirloin), the resulting loaves had remarkably inconsistent textures; some turned out moist and tender, while others were gristly and fibrous.

Puzzled, we contacted Davey Griffin, a meat specialist at Texas A&M University, who explained that supermarkets have two choices when it comes to offering ground beef by lean/fat percentage. They can buy it ground and individually packaged at an off-site facility, or they can buy large amounts from a wholesaler in "chub packs," grinding them further in the store while adding some of their own "shop trim" to the mix. Unlike large off-site packing facilities, supermarket butchers don't usually have the expensive equipment required to measure fat content accurately, so their product is less consistent than beef that's ground off-site.

How much less? To find out, we bought 30 packages of ground beef from different grocery stores in the same chain: 10 labeled chuck, which naturally has about 20 percent fat; 10 labeled 80/20, packed and processed in-store; and 10 labeled 80/20, packed and processed off-site. Off they went to the lab for fat analysis.

A week later, we had surprising results. The packages of chuck were within 2 percent of the expected fat content. Not too shabby. The 80/20 beef packed off-site fell within the same range. But the 80/20 packed in-store? Way off the mark—by as much as 7 percent! No wonder our loaves were all over the map: For a recipe designed around 80/20 ground beef, "87/13" just didn't cut it. (That's like using regular milk in a recipe that calls for half-and-half.)

So for recipes that call for ground beef with specific fat percentages, we recommend buying packages labeled by primal cut or packaged by an off-site distributor. Look for the designation "Packed in [name of city]" on the label.

Breaking in Half (and Half)

In the test kitchen, we've found that half-and-half is not a suitable substitute for heavy cream when making sauces, soups, or casserole fillings, thanks to its tendency to break at high temperatures. We always assumed this was a matter of fat content—the principal proteins in dairy (called *casein*) coat the globules of fat, helping to stabilize the emulsion; the more fat, the more stable. But while testing dairy products in our Chicken Pot Pie (see page 7), we experienced no breaking problems when we tried a combination of milk and heavy cream that equaled the fat content of half-and-half. Why the difference?

Turns out, it's a matter of processing: Store-bought half-and-half is homogenized to prevent the separation of fat over a long shelf period. (The natural tendency of the fat in half-and-half is to separate into a top layer of cream if left standing.) This high-pressure treatment also disturbs the interaction between fat and casein, affecting the stability of half-and-half when exposed to high heat. Heavy cream is spared the homogenization process because it adversely affects foam formation (and so inhibits whipping).

TECHNIQUE | PREPARING FRESH PEARL ONIONS

We think frozen pearl onions taste just as good as fresh—and they're much less trouble. If you can find only fresh, here are some survival tactics.

1. Trim the root and stem end of each pearl onion and discard.

2. Boil for 1 minute, shock in ice water, then peel a thin strip from root to stem.

3. Remove any remaining outer skin—like peeling off a jacket.

TESTING EQUIPMENT: Just Smoke and Mirrors?

Although we came up with an indoor method to produce great smoky ribs (see Oven-Barbecued Spareribs, page 11), we wondered whether the indoor smokers on the market were worth an extra trip to the store and a hole burned in our pockets. We tested three models—two for the stovetop, one for the oven. Conceptually, the stovetop models make perfect sense: A closed chamber (similar to a large pot with a lid, fitted with an interior rack to hold the food) is placed over a burner; wood chips placed in the bottom of the chamber smoke the food. Despite turning out smoky, tender ribs to rival outdoor versions, the stovetop cookers had major flaws. One leaked enough smoke to overwhelm the test kitchen's industrial-grade ventilation hoods, while the other had a size and shape (small and round) that required us to cook the ribs in multiple batches.

The one option that wowed us was the SAVU Smoker Bag, which (like our recipe) kept the smoke in the oven. This simple system—a mixture of ground wood chips, hardwood syrup, and natural sugars contained within the walls of a large foil bag—allowed the smoke to pass through small perforations in the foil to get to the food contained within. The ribs emerged juicy, tender, and—after a quick run under the broiler—nicely crusted. –Garth Clingingsmith

SMOKE SIGNALS
The CAMERONS Stovetop Smoker ($37.95) is the right shape, but remove your smoke-alarm batteries.

TOO WELL ROUNDED
Smoke stays where it belongs in the VILLAWARE Stovetop Smoker ($69.99), but ribs aren't round.

BEST INDOOR SMOKER
SAVU Smoker Bags ($3.49 each) are virtually foolproof and produce well-balanced smokiness.

Reaching the Perfect Peak

We've always stressed the importance of whipping egg whites just to the soft-peak stage (no more, no less) before gently folding them into cake batters, mousses, or soufflés. Whisking causes the tightly wound egg proteins to relax and unwind, eventually overlapping, bonding, and trapping air in the form of loose bubbles—and thereby creating volume in the resulting dish. Overwhipping causes the protein strands to go from elastic to brittle, and much of the structure is lost.

That's all fine in theory, but how much damage does under- or overwhipping really inflict? To find out, we made several batches of our Grand Marnier Soufflé (September/October 2000) and Dark Chocolate Mousse (page 23), varying the egg-white consistency each time. The results were interesting. In the case of chocolate mousse, only the underwhipped whites (those that could not quite hold a soft peak when the whisk was lifted from the bowl) produced a mediocre texture—too loose and wet. Both soft-peak and overwhipped whites yielded acceptable mousses. But in the soufflé, the overwhipped whites showed their true nature—spongy and dry, with noticeably less volume after baking. The underwhipped whites didn't quite fill the soufflé dish, but this decrease in volume was barely perceptible after baking.

Our conclusion? For all recipes, baked or not, hitting the soft-peak stage spot-on is ideal. For baked applications, it's better to err on the side of slightly underwhipping, leaving the egg proteins elastic enough to respond well to the oven's heat. But when the whipped whites will not be baked—when pure volume is the goal—overwhipping is the lesser of two evils.

UNDERWHIPPED   OVERWHIPPED   JUST RIGHT

TASTING: Are All Store-Bought Pie Crusts Awful?

A flaky, buttery homemade pie crust is the ultimate crown for our Chicken Pot Pie (page 7), but it's also a fair amount of work. How much would we sacrifice by using a store-bought crust instead? To find out, we tried several types and brands—both dry mixes (just add water) and ready-made crusts, either frozen or refrigerated—in recipes for chicken pot pie and custard pie.

EASY AS . . .
PILLSBURY JUST UNROLL! PIE CRUSTS
$2.79 for two 9-inch crusts
The hard part is over, and the flavor and texture are fine.

WRONG PROBLEM
PILLSBURY PIE CRUST MIX
$1.39 for two 9-inch crusts
Saves mixing dry ingredients, but that's not the hard part.

The dry mixes, including Betty Crocker ($1.69), Jiffy ($0.99), Krusteaz ($3.28), and Pillsbury ($1.39), all had problems. Some were too salty, some were too sweet, and all required both mixing and rolling—not much work saved. Homemade pastry isn't much more difficult, and its flavor and texture are infinitely better. Frozen crusts, including Mrs. Smith's (also sold as Oronoque Orchards, $2.69) and Pillsbury Pet-Ritz ($2.69), were the ultimate timesavers (zero prep needed), but tasters found them pasty and bland, and it was nearly impossible to pry them from the flimsy foil "pie plate" in which they are sold. The one refrigerated contender, Pillsbury Just Unroll! Pie Crusts, wasn't bad. Though the flavor was somewhat bland, it wasn't offensive, and the crust baked up to an impressive flakiness. Better yet, this fully prepared product comes rolled up and is flexible enough to top a pie or line one of your own (nondisposable) pie plates. –G.C.

⇒ BY GARTH CLINGINGSMITH ⇐

EQUIPMENT TESTING
High-Design Bundt Pans
In our January/February 2004 testing of Bundt pans, NordicWare's Platinum Series Classic 12-Cup Bundt Pan ($32) carried the day, thanks to clean, distinctly defined contours. So it was with suspicion that we eyed the company's elaborate designs for Bundt cakes shaped like stars, cathedrals, and fleurs-de-lis. To find out how they measured up, we chose two designs, the chrysanthemum and the holiday tree, and made our Lemon Bundt Cake recipe (see page 25).

HARD TO HANDLE
Bakes great, but good luck inverting cake.

Our misgivings were for naught. Both pans browned well, and release was clean. There was just one problem: no handles, which made the fancy pans difficult to invert when removing the cake. (In a repeat test, we inadvertently "trimmed" one of the holiday trees by about an inch.) So we can recommend these high-design Bundt pans only tentatively—handles would seal the deal.

PRODUCT UPDATE
Cheap Nonstick Skillet
We weren't exactly thrilled when Farberware updated our favorite inexpensive nonstick skillet—the 12-inch Farberware Millennium 18/10 Stainless Nonstick—with a silicone handle. Oven safe only to 350 degrees, silicone handles limit a pan's use in the oven. So we tested our way to a worthy substitute: the Wolfgang Puck Bistro Omelet Pan. But, we've found the availability of the Wolfgang Puck pan to be

GET A GRIP
Were we too hard on soft handles?

spotty. Given that nonstick skillets do more egg scrambling and stir-frying than high-heat pan roasting, we took another look at the new Farberware Millennium. In a retest, the sturdy pan's stovetop performance matched that of the retired Millennium, and testers actually grew fond of the extra heat protection offered by the silicone handle. In light of the Farberware's wide distribution and reasonable $39.95 price, we've overcome our reservations. Just don't put it under the broiler.

EQUIPMENT TESTING
Panini Presses
A panini press (or grill press) is a heavy piece of metal used to make *panini*, Italian-style toasted sandwiches weighted down while they cook to yield a compact filling and crisp crust. Panini presses are heated along with the grill, grill pan, or skillet to reduce cooking time and make it unnecessary to flip the sandwich. For such a simple concept, there are plenty of design choices—heavy or light, round or square, cast iron or cast aluminum, smooth or ridged. We bought seven models and embarked on a panini marathon.

Weight turned out to be the most significant factor, with the heavy cast-iron presses beating out lighter aluminum models. Ridged surfaces made the handsome stripes that we prize, and rectangular presses were more practical than round for keeping sandwiches adequately covered. All-Clad's "Grille Pan" with Enameled Cast Iron Panini Press ($99.95) won top honors: The generously proportioned ridged press was the heaviest we tested and comes with a panini pan (a smaller version of the company's grill pan, see page 29). But if your panini habit doesn't warrant a $100 investment, the

square, ridged, cast-iron press from Le Creuset ($59.95) performed almost as well and can be used with most pans.

PRODUCT UPDATE
Baker's Secret Loaf Pan
Several readers asked what happened to the winning loaf pan from our 2000 testing, the Ecko Baker's Secret Non-Stick Loaf Pan. It's still around—just with a shorter name. After some corporate restructuring, Ecko and Baker's Secret (two World Kitchen brands) no longer share label space. The Baker's Secret Non-Stick Loaf Pan (8½ by 4½ inches, $3.69), our preferred model, is still available in most supermarkets.

Sources
The following are sources for items recommended in this issue. Prices were current at press time and do not include shipping. Contact companies directly to confirm prices and availability. Go to www.cooksillustrated.com for updates on sources.

Page 21: BISCUIT CUTTERS
• Ateco Plain Round Cutters 11 Piece Set: $14.99, item #23849, **Fante's Kitchen Wares Shop** (800-443-2683, www.fantes.com).

Page 28: GRILL SPONGE
• George Foreman Grill Sponge: $4.99 for 3, item #13307202, **Bed, Bath and Beyond** (800-462-3966, www.bedbathandbeyond.com).

Page 29: GRILL PANS
• Simply Calphalon Nonstick 13" Round Grill Pan: $39.95, item #200374, **Cooking.com** (800-663-8810, www.cooking.com).

Page 30: SMOKER BAGS
• SAVU Smoker Bag: $3.49, **Hot Diggity Cajun** (615-445-7823, www.smokerbags.com).

Page 32: BUNDT PANS
• NordicWare Bundt Pans:

Chrysanthemum, $32.00, and Holiday Tree, $32.00, NordicWare (877-466-7342; www.nordicware.com).

Page 32: NONSTICK SKILLET
• Farberware Millennium Soft Touch Stainless 12" Nonstick Skillet: $39.95, item #208669, Cooking.com.

Page 32: PANINI PRESSES
• All-Clad "Grille Pan" with Enameled Cast Iron Panini Press: $99.95, item #39902, **Cutlery and More** (www.cutleryandmore.com).

United States Postal Service
Statement of Ownership, Management, and Circulation
Publication Title: Cook's Illustrated
Publication Number: 1 0 6 8 - 2 8 2 1
Filing Date: 10/01/05
Issue Frequency: Bi-Monthly
Number of Issues Published Annually: 6 issues
Annual Subscription Price: $35.70
Complete Mailing Address of Known Office of Publication: 17 Station Street, Brookline, MA 02445
Telephone: 617-232-1000
Complete Mailing Address of Headquarters or General Business Office of Publisher: Same as publisher
Publisher: Christopher P. Kimball, Boston Common Press, 17 Station Street, Brookline, MA 02445
Editor: Same as publisher
Managing Editor: Jack Bishop, Boston Common Press, 17 Station Street, Brookline, MA 02445
Owner: Boston Common Press Limited Partnership, 17 Station Street, Brookline, MA 02445 (Christopher P. Kimball)
Known Bondholders, Mortgagees, and Other Security Holders: N/A
Publication Title: Cook's Illustrated
Issue Date for Circulation Data Below: September/October 2005

Extent and Nature of Circulation	Average No. Copies Each Issue During Preceding 12 Months	No. Copies of Single Issue Published Nearest to Filing Date
a. Total Number of Copies (Net press run)	900,721	950,621
b(1). Paid/Requested Outside-County Mail Subscriptions	661,681	87,517
b(2). Paid In-County Subscriptions	0	0
b(3). Sales Through Dealers and Carriers, Street Vendors, Counter Sales	90,152	87,517
b(4). Other Classes Mailed Through the USPS	0	0
c. Total Paid and/or Requested Circulation	751,833	805,698
d(1). Outside-County as Stated on Form 3541	4,316	3,955
d(2). In-County as Stated on Form 3541	0	0
d(3). Other Classes Mailed Through the USPS	0	0
e. Free Distribution Outside the Mail	4,138	4,388
f. Total Free Distribution	8,455	8,343
g. Total Distribution	760,288	814,041
h. Copies not Distributed	140,433	136,580
i. Total	900,721	950,621
j. Percent Paid and/or Requested Circulation	98.89%	98.98%

Publication of Statement of Ownership will be printed in Jan/Feb 2006 issue.
Signature: Date: 9/19/05

RECIPES
January & February 2006

COOK'S EXTRA: New Recipes Available on the Web
The following recipes are available free on our Web site. To access a recipe, go to www.cooksillustrated.com and enter the code listed after the recipe title.

Huevos Rancheros, 9

Oven-Barbecued Spareribs, 11

Glazed Meat Loaf, 19

Flaky Buttermilk Biscuits, 21

Dark Chocolate Mousse, 23

Chicken Pot Pie, 7

Hot and Sour Soup, 13

Potatoes Lyonnaise, 14

Sautéed Mushrooms with Sesame and Ginger, 15

Lemon Bundt Cake, 25

www.cooksillustrated.com

Join the *Cook's* Web Site and Get Instant Access to 13 Years of Recipes, Equipment Tests, and Tastings!

Web site members can also join the *Cook's* bulletin board, ask our editors cooking questions, find quick tips and step-by-step illustrations, maintain a private list of personal favorites (recipes, quick tips, tastings, and more), and print out shopping lists for all recipes.

Yours Free: As a paid Web site member, you will also receive our **2006 Buying Guide for Supermarket Ingredients.** Simply type in the promotion code **CB61A** when signing up.

Here's Why More Than 85,000 Home Cooks Subscribe to Our Web Site

Quick Search for 'Best' Recipes: Access to every recipe published since 1993.
Cook's Extra Recipes: Continued access to the recipes that don't fit in each issue of the magazine, including many flavor variations.
Updated Cookware Ratings: Charts of all buying recommendations published in the magazine (you can download them), plus frequent updates on new models and price changes.
Tasting Results: You'll have access to every tasting published in the magazine, in addition to tastings conducted for Web members only.
Questions for the Editors: Paid members can ask our editors questions by e-mail and are guaranteed a response.
Magazine/Book Customer Service: Pay invoices, give gifts, handle returns, check your subscription status, and more.
Visit Our Bookstore: Order any of our books online and also qualify for special offers.

AMERICA'S TEST KITCHEN TV SHOW

Join the millions of home cooks who watch our show, *America's Test Kitchen*, on public television every week. For more information, including recipes and a schedule of program times in your area, visit www.americastestkitchen.com.

Ricotta Salata

Fontina Val d'Aosta

Gorgonzola

Fresh Mozzarella

Asiago

Grana Padano

Mascarpone

Pecorino Romano

Provolone

Parmigiano-Reggiano

Taleggio

ITALIAN CHEESES

COOK'S
ILLUSTRATED

Pepper-Crusted
Filet Mignon

Quick Marinara
Long-Simmered Flavor in
Just 30 Minutes

Glazed Pork Chops

Better Chicken Kiev
No-Fry, No-Leak Method

Tasting Beef Broths

Best Old-Fashioned
Chocolate Cake

Rating Saucepans
$30 Pan Edges Pricier Models

Essential Bakeware 101
Garlic-Roasted Leg of Lamb
Easy Asian Potstickers
Pan-Roasted Broccoli
Multigrain Sandwich Bread

www.cooksillustrated.com

$5.95 U.S./$6.95 CANADA

04 >

0 7447 0 62805 7

CONTENTS

March & April 2006

COOK'S ILLUSTRATED
www.cooksillustrated.com
HOME OF AMERICA'S TEST KITCHEN

Founder and Editor Christopher Kimball
Executive Editor Jack Bishop
Deputy Editor Jolyon Helterman
Senior Editor Adam Ried
Editorial Manager, Books Elizabeth Carduff
Test Kitchen Director Erin McMurrer
Senior Editors, Books Julia Collin Davison
Lori Galvin
Managing Editor Rebecca Hays
Associate Editor, Books Keith Dresser
Associate Editors Erika Bruce
Sean Lawler
Sandra Wu
Web Editor Lindsay McSweeney
Copy Chief India Koopman
Test Cooks Garth Clingingsmith
David Pazmiño
Rachel Toomey
Diane Unger
Nina West
Sarah Wilson
Assistant Test Kitchen Director Matthew Herron
Assistant Editor, Books Charles Kelsey
Editorial Assistant, Books Elizabeth Wray Emery
Editorial Assistant Elizabeth Bomze
Assistant to the Publisher Melissa Baldino
Kitchen Assistants Maria Elena Delgado
Nadia Domeq
Ena Gudiel
Editorial Intern Ellen London
Contributing Editors Matthew Card
Dawn Yanagihara
Consulting Editors Shirley Corriher
Guy Crosby
John Dewar
Jasper White
Robert L. Wolke
Proofreader Holly Hartman

Design Director Amy Klee
Marketing Designer Julie Bozzo
Designer Heather Barrett
Staff Photographer Daniel J. van Ackere

Vice President Marketing David Mack
Circulation Director Bill Tine
Fulfillment Manager Carrie Horan
Circulation Assistant Elizabeth Dayton
Direct Mail Director Adam Perry
Products Director Steven Browall
E-Commerce Marketing Manager Hugh Buchan
Marketing Copywriter David Goldberg
Customer Service Manager Jacqueline Valerio
Customer Service Representative Julie Gardner

Vice President Sales Demee Gambulos
Retail Sales Director Jason Geller
Corporate Sponsorship Specialist Laura Phillipps
Marketing Assistant Connie Forbes

Production Director Guy Rochford
Senior Production Manager Jessica L. Quirk
Project Manager Anne Francis
Production Assistants Jeanette McCarthy
Christian Steinmetz
Matthew Warnick
Systems Administrator Richard Cassidy
Internet Technology Director Aaron Shuman
Web Producer Lauren Record

Chief Financial Officer Sharyn Chabot
Controller Mandy Shito
Staff Accountant Maya Santoso
Office Manager Saudiyah Abdul-Rahim
Receptionist Henrietta Murray
Publicity Deborah Broide

PICKLES

PICKLES For centuries, vegetables were pickled in seasoned brine as a means of preservation; nowadays, the flavor itself is the allure. Cucumbers, the most commonly pickled vegetable, run the gamut from mild-tasting, garlicky dill pickles to piquant, vinegary half- or full-sours. Sweet bread-and-butter pickles are brined in a sugary mix often containing onion, mustard and celery seeds, and turmeric (the source of their characteristic yellow color). Another sweet pickle is the gherkin, made from the same small cucumber as the French cornichon (which tends to be even smaller). Either brined or cured in salt, capers are the pickled flower bud of a thorny Mediterranean bush; caperberries, the fruit of the same plant, are about the size of a cocktail olive and can be used in the same fashion. A more familiar garnish—which turns a martini into a Gibson—is the delicately pickled pearl onion. Italian pepperoncini, also known as Tuscan peppers, often appear as part of an antipasto platter, offering mild heat along with tanginess.

COVER (*Leeks*): Elizabeth Brandon, BACK COVER (*Pickles*): John Burgoyne

For list rental information, contact: Specialists Marketing Services Inc., 1200 Harbor Blvd., 9th Floor, Weehawken, NJ 07087; 201-865-5800
Editorial Office: 17 Station St., Brookline, MA 02445; 617-232-1000; fax 617-232-1572. Subscription inquiries, call 800-526-8442.
Postmaster: Send all new orders, subscription inquiries, and change-of-address notices to Cook's Illustrated, P.O. Box 7446, Red Oak, IA 51591-0446.

2nd PRINTING IN CHINA

SAME TIME NEXT YEAR

Anyone who has spent time on a farm knows that a year has a rhythm to it, one that is determined by the weather. My mother, Mary Alice, who inherited a love of farming from her father, went so far as to create her own calendar with notes about planting garlic in the fall, when to add fuel stabilizer to chainsaws and mowers, and the best time to order baby chicks. Every day had a purpose and more than one task at hand, so when, for the first time in a year, the wood cookstove had to be fired up before sunrise and the air was so sharp it caught in your throat, it was time to turn the page on the calendar and get busy. There was work to do.

The advantage of this system is that you always know where you are in the grand scheme of things. It's time to tap the trees, site your gun, feed the bees, clean the pig house, call the ferrier, split the kindling, prune the trees, or plant the corn. Life runs on a schedule and you better not fall behind. If you do, the apples get coddling moth, the hay goes to seed, and you miss the good runs of sap. For old-timers, a good calendar was a matter of life and death. To us, it's more a matter of knowing your place.

Harley Smith just passed. His family used to own part of our farm, the part that was only good for summer pasture, up in the mountain hollows. But it has a strong spring, one that was piped down the mountain and under the dirt road to cool the large cans in the milk house. Harley and his wife, Dorothy, were good friends with Tom and Nancy, who lived just down the road. Every Friday night, they used to show up for dessert, and that's how the neighbors knew it was the end of the week: the sight of Harley's pickup in front of Tom's. It was the same routine every week. They would come over punctually at 7 P.M. (that's after dinner for local families), sit down, and then just stare for a bit. When

they had something to say, well, it got said, but long silences are a mark of respect. They expect you're smart enough to know when something just doesn't need to be talked about out loud—like when it's time to cut the cake or serve a second cup of coffee.

Our farm has just a few animals. We keep two Herefords, nine hens, two pigs in the summer, six horses, and two or more beehives, depending on how many survive the winter. When we're not around, Mike shows up to do daily chores: checking the run of spring water for the beefers, haying and graining the horses, mucking the stalls, and splitting wood for the sap house. Then there are the seasonal projects: spreading manure on the lower fields, tilling the corn, planting potatoes, pressing cider, making applesauce, fixing fences, haying, spraying the apple trees with dormant oil, weeding the strawberries, preparing the raised vegetable beds for spring planting, cleaning out the root cellar, boiling the sap, making and canning jams and jellies, checking the hives and extracting the honey, freezing bags of creamed corn . . . the list never ends.

If you pay attention, you find that nature has a schedule to keep as well, one that is easily tracked through the lesser observances. In late fall, it's the bare birches on the edge of the top meadows, highlighted in the late afternoon sun, waving back and forth, trying to keep the oaks and poplars from breaking free and running riot down the mountain. In winter, it's the site of our dimly lit farmhouse on a clear night, as Adrienne and I trudge up the hill after stalling the horses, anticipating the warm fire and a cup of tea. In spring, it's the color of the pond—a

Christopher Kimball

rippling milky-green—and the sound of partridges up in the pines across the brook, a circular calling that is easily mistaken for someone trying to start an old Farmall. And in summer, it's late shadows and children's games on the lawn at nightfall as stillness quenches notions of wanderlust.

Meanwhile, I still have my mother's calendar, the one that tells me when to clean out the garage and check the carrots in the root cellar. Sure, the seasons offer a good context for a living, a way of marking time and finding one's place in the grand cycle of things. It is no wonder, however, that our calendars are also marked by the lives of those closest to us. It's a familiar day when one of our children is old enough to baby-sit or strong enough to lug the heavy bucket of wet cornmeal to the pig trough before breakfast. And even leavings have a comforting pattern to them: the day a young child is first put on the school bus or a neighbor is returned to the rocky soil in an upper pasture.

On days when I consider breaking free of my appointed rounds, it occurs to me that our ghostly predecessors are probably vigilant, on the lookout to see if each of us is still productive. (I am dead certain that my mother will reappear and give me a good talking to if I ever forget to put the hens in at night, leaving them prey for fox and raccoon.) As for the next generation, we can secretly hope that our lives will be the making of a calendar, a map for living the good life. It is our daily to-do list, then, that truly binds one generation to the next. After all, the horses don't care who is carrying the grain bucket. Neither should we.

FOR INQUIRIES, ORDERS, OR MORE INFORMATION:

www.cooksillustrated.com

At www.cooksillustrated.com, you can order books and subscriptions, sign up for our free e-newsletter, or renew your magazine subscription. Join the Web site and you'll have access to 13 years of *Cook's* recipes, cookware tests, ingredient tastings, and more.

COOKBOOKS

We sell more than 40 cookbooks by the editors of *Cook's Illustrated*. To order, visit our bookstore at www.cooksillustrated.com or call 800-611-0759 (or 515-246-6911 from outside the U.S.).

COOK'S ILLUSTRATED Magazine

Cook's Illustrated magazine (ISSN 1068-2821), number 79, is published bimonthly by Boston Common Press Limited Partnership, 17 Station Street, Brookline, MA 02445. Copyright 2006 Boston Common Press Limited Partnership. Periodicals postage paid at Boston, Mass., and additional mailing offices, USPS #012487. POSTMASTER: Send address changes to Cook's Illustrated, P.O. Box 7446, Red Oak, IA 51591-0446. For subscription and gift subscription orders, subscription inquiries, or change-of-address notices, call 800-526-8442 in the U.S. or 515-247-7571 from outside the U.S., or write us at Cook's Illustrated, P.O. Box 7446, Red Oak, IA 51591-0446.

⇒ COMPILED BY SANDRA WU ⇐

Tip of the Iceberg

Can you advise me on the best way to store iceberg lettuce? I like to have it on hand for sandwiches, but it doesn't seem to last very long.

SUZANNE CANDREA
LITTLE SILVER, N.J.

➤ We tried four storage methods to see which was most effective at keeping iceberg lettuce fresh: wrapped in moist paper towels and stored in a plastic shopping bag, kept in its original perforated cellophane bag, stored in a zipper-lock plastic bag, and wrapped tightly in plastic wrap. For each method, we stored two samples, one unwashed with the core in, the other rinsed with the core removed.

After a week, all the samples were still mostly fresh and crisp except for minimal drying on the edges of the outermost leaves; the heads stored in the original packaging had wilted the most but were still usable. At the two-week mark, the differences were more apparent. The two samples wrapped in moist paper towels retained the crispest leaves. By contrast, the inner layers of the other samples had begun to dry out, becoming bendable and rubbery. Because moisture loss is often to blame when lettuce goes bad, it made sense that providing extra moisture (in the form of wet paper towels) was the winning method. More interesting was the fact that the plain old plastic shopping bag beat out the zipper-lock storage bag. Because the flimsy (and therefore slightly porous) shopping bag allowed a modicum of airflow, it prevented the buildup of too much moisture and delayed spoilage.

As far as washing and coring, the washed-and-cored lettuce evidenced a bit more browning, but minor trimming solved the problem. In the end, we recommend the effective—and more convenient—method of coring and washing iceberg lettuce and storing it, wrapped in moist paper towels, in a plastic shopping bag.

THROWING IN THE TOWEL
Maintaining moisture is key when storing lettuce.

Bottled Garlic

Have you tried garlic "juice," a product marketed as an alternative to fresh garlic?

HEATHER IRWIN
SAN FRANCISCO, CALIF.

➤ After doing a brief search on the Internet, we found the product you described, Garlic Valley Farms Cold Pressed Garlic Juice. According to the packaging, this mixture of garlic juice, sea salt, acetic acid, citric acid, and garlic flavor is equivalent to 150 cloves of garlic. The label says that eight sprays (or 1 teaspoon, if you remove the spray top and just pour it) offer the flavor equivalent of 1 garlic clove. Could this easy-to-use preparation stand in for real garlic?

To find out, we pitted one against the other in three applications—garlic toast, hummus, and aïoli—substituting the appropriate amount of garlic juice spray for each clove of garlic called for. In each recipe, nearly every taster found the garlic juice much too mild, especially in comparison to the fresh clove. When we increased the amount of juice by a few extra pumps in the hummus and the aïoli, tasters still preferred the fresh garlic for its pronounced but subtle heat, but they did find the garlic juice more acceptable as a substitute. As for the garlic toast, when more juice was used, the juice and the fresh clove got equally high marks.

In the end, because it's not possible to modify the sharpness, mellowness, or sweetness of the spray (as you can with fresh garlic by changing the size or shape of the cut or by cooking it), we don't recommend it as a regular substitute for fresh garlic. But given that it keeps for years, we might consider keeping a bottle on hand for use in emergency situations where just a small amount of garlic flavor is needed.

Alternative Oils

I'm curious about a product called Enova oil that claims to be better for you than traditional cooking oils. How does it measure up?

KRISTI KIYONAGA
SEATTLE, WASH.

➤ In the test kitchen, we never select a product based on its maker's claims that it's good for you. After all, for decades we were told that margarine was more healthful than butter based on the types of fat the two contain. Of course, we know now

GARLIC ON TAP
Juiced up enough to match the clove?

that butter is better, because some traditional margarines contain unhealthy trans fat. The maker of Enova also bases its claims of healthfulness on the types of fat it contains, in particular, that it has a higher ratio of *diacylglycerols* (a supposedly healthier fat molecule) to *triacylglycerols*, the latter being more likely to remain in your body as fat. Whether Enova really is a healthy alternative we cannot say, but it should be noted that Enova is not a reduced-fat oil. It contains 14 grams of fat per tablespoon, just like olive oil.

Being cooks, however, we can comment on its cooking properties. We compared the synthesized Enova oil with four other products in the following applications: fried chicken (versus shortening), french fries (versus peanut oil), pan-roasted broccoli (versus canola oil), and a simple vinaigrette (versus olive oil). In all four recipes, the Enova oil yielded results that were virtually identical in texture and appearance to the foods prepared with the other products. In terms of taste, panelists detected no difference between the two batches of fried chicken, but a few tasters felt that the Enova oil brought out a slightly sweeter, more potatoey flavor in the french fries, a sharper vinegar taste in the vinaigrette, and a faintly musty flavor in the broccoli.

This new oil doesn't come cheap: We paid $5.79 for a 20-ounce bottle. Should you go out and buy some? That depends on your faith, or lack thereof, in the American food industry. Our kitchen will continue to use oils such as peanut, olive, and canola, which, in addition to being widely available, are less expensive.

Stay-Fresh Chickens?

In the past, chicken purchased at the grocery store always had to be used within a few days. This still seems to be true of unwrapped poultry from the meat counter, but the shrink-wrapped chicken in the meat case often has a sell-by date as many as 10 days out. What's going on?

REX PARKER
PHILADELPHIA, PA.

➤ According to Brian Sheldon, professor in the department of poultry science at North Carolina State University, quality-control measures developed by the poultry industry over the last two decades to reduce the risk of food-borne pathogens have had the added benefit of extending refrigerator shelf life. Today, birds are processed with more water and antimicrobial agents, which wash away more contaminants and kill microorganisms. And rather than being packed on ice, many birds are now being chilled to the point that a thin crust of ice forms on their surface, a process that also extends shelf life. Another factor is that most large poultry companies package the birds at the processing plant prior to shipping rather than leaving it up to individual stores; this reduces the amount of handling (and thus exposure to bacteria and oxygen).

While some companies claim their birds have a shelf life of 12 or 14 days after processing (which includes shipping time, storage at the retail facility, and home refrigeration), the U.S. Department of Agriculture recommends cooking or freezing poultry within one or two days of purchase, no matter what its sell-by date. The sell-by date should not be considered a use-by date for the consumer but rather a general way for the store to determine how long to display an item for sale. There are no federal regulations governing calendar dating. While some states have regulations, the dates are often determined by the processor.

After scouring several local markets, we found three packages of store-brand chicken with different sell-by dates: one day out, four days out, and seven days out. We pan-roasted the chickens to see if we could taste any differences between them—we couldn't. So the next time you purchase poultry, don't be afraid to pick up a package with a soon-to-expire sell-by date (of course, you should not choose a package with an expired date). More important, once you get the chicken home, cook it as soon as possible, no matter what date is stamped on the label.

Clearing Up Clarified Butter
I buy ghee for making Indian dishes. Can I also use it in recipes that call for clarified butter?

LINDA TIEU
PASADENA, CALIF.

➤ While ghee is a form of highly clarified butter, clarified butter is not, in fact, ghee. Clarified butter (also known as drawn butter) is made by slowly melting unsalted butter over low heat so that the emulsion can be broken, most of the water evaporated, and the components separated according to density. Once the foam is skimmed off, the layer of clear golden butterfat underneath (clarified butter) is poured off from the layer of milk solids that have settled on the bottom of the pan. Ghee takes the process a step further by allowing butter to simmer until all the moisture is evaporated and the milk solids begin to brown, giving

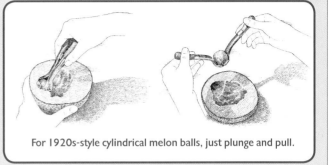

WHAT IS IT?

Two years ago, I inherited an old Victorian house from my uncle and found this gadget in a box among other kitchen tools. Could it be a corn kernel remover?
LISA LOGAN
ROCKVILLE, MD.

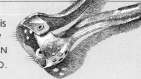

➤ Flipping through a book on antique kitchenware, we came across a description of your gadget. The item you've inherited is meant not for corn but for melons. This old-fashioned melon baller, from the 1920s, works in two steps: Hold the melon baller with the two handles together, inserting the cutting ring (a perforated oval about 1¼ by 1½ inches) into the flesh of the melon. Then pull the handles apart in opposite directions so that the two sides of the blade come together, cutting the melon into a cylindrical piece. Although less intuitive than modern melon ballers, this vintage tool can be used to create larger, tighter-shaped (though not perfectly round) pieces of fruit.

For 1920s-style cylindrical melon balls, just plunge and pull.

the butterfat a slightly nutty flavor and aroma. The product can be found in unrefrigerated jars at Indian and Middle Eastern markets, as well as at natural foods stores.

To see if ghee makes an adequate ready-to-use substitute for clarified butter, we made three batches of baklava using homemade clarified butter, homemade ghee, and store-bought ghee (Purity Farms brand). Tasters agreed that the only difference in the baklava made with ghee (both homemade and store-bought) was that it had a slightly richer, more buttery flavor. We found no problem with using ghee and clarified butter interchangeably.

Freezing Cream
Can I freeze heavy cream for later use?

BRIAN LATOUR
NEW YORK, N.Y.

➤ According to USDA guidelines, heavy cream can be frozen for up to four months. To see if freezing would change the flavor or texture of the cream, we froze several samples in 1-cup increments (in airtight containers) for three days and allowed them to thaw in the refrigerator before using them in three applications: fettuccine Alfredo, caramel sauce, and a whipped cream topping. These recipes were also made with fresh heavy cream for comparison.

After removing the frozen and thawed heavy cream from the refrigerator, we noticed a change in its appearance. Even though the cream was completely thawed, it had some grainy, hard flecks suspended within it. After further

research, we found that freezing can cause some of the cream's homogenized microscopic fat globules (invisible to the naked eye) to merge into larger, very visible fat globules. But once the cream was heated and reduced down in the Alfredo sauce, most tasters couldn't detect much of a difference between the two samples in terms of flavor or texture. A few tasters felt the Alfredo sauce made with fresh cream had a slightly richer, creamier texture with "more body," but both batches were given a thumbs up. The same went for the caramel sauce (made by adding hot, simmered cream and flavorings to a sugar syrup). Both versions were fine, with several people actually preferring the frozen version. The only application in which the frozen cream faltered was the whipped cream topping. Although the previously frozen cream took 15 seconds less to whip up to soft peaks, it didn't have the smooth, fluffy texture of the fresh. The small bits of fat that had separated out from the cream gave the final product a lumpy quality.

So where does that leave us? It's fine to use previously frozen cream in cooked recipes, but not when a fluffy whipped texture is paramount.

Vise-Grip Advice
Several eagle-eyed readers pointed out an error in one of the quick tips published in the November/December 2005 issue. The tool being used as a makeshift nutcracker is a pair of pump pliers, or Channellocks (a brand name), not a Vise-Grip, as stated in the text.

SEND US YOUR QUESTIONS We will provide a complimentary one-year subscription for each letter we print. Send your inquiry, name, address, and daytime telephone number to Notes from Readers, Cook's Illustrated, P.O. Box 470589, Brookline, MA 02447, or to notesfromreaders@bcpress.com.

Quick Tips

≽ COMPILED BY DAVID PAZMIÑO ≼

Smarter Knife Cleaning

Scrub pads do a fine job of removing gunk from knife blades but eventually damage the finish. To keep his knives shiny, Howard Fain of Providence, R.I., uses a wine cork instead. Angling the blade toward the cutting board, he simply rubs the cork over the knife to remove food residue, then washes the knife in hot, soapy water with a soft sponge.

Portion Control

Sharon Brown of Castle Rock, Wash., puts coffee filters to unusual but effective use by placing them between pancakes, pork chops, meat patties, and other items while stacking them for storage in the freezer. She can then easily remove individual portions without having to defrost the entire supply.

Foolproof Proof Box

When a chilly house makes it hard to proof dough for bread or pizza, Carolyn Dadaby of Boise, Idaho, looks to her microwave for help.

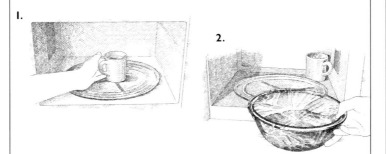

1. Place a coffee mug filled with ½ cup water in the microwave. Run the microwave on high power for about 1 minute.
2. Open the microwave, push the cup to a back corner, and set the dough inside. Close the door and let the dough rise. (The warmed mug will keep the interior between 80 and 90 degrees for up to 90 minutes.) Remove the dough once it has doubled in size or reached the desired volume in your recipe.

Standing (Up) Rib Roasts

Some standing rib roasts aren't so great at the "standing" part, especially smaller roasts, which have a tendency to tip over during cooking. Peter DeGroot of Ashland, Ore., avoids this problem by turning a skewer into a support bar.

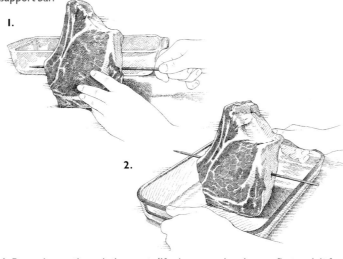

1. Run a skewer through the roast. (If using a wooden skewer, first soak it for about 20 minutes.)
2. Rest the ends of the skewer on the sides of the roasting pan and cook the roast. When ready to carve, simply remove the skewer.

Makeshift Fat Separator

Jim McLaughlin of Nokomis, Fla., has figured out a novel way to remove fat from pan drippings before making a sauce or gravy.

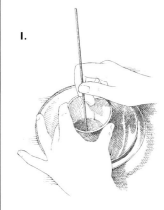

1. Pour the pan drippings into a paper coffee cup and place the cup in the freezer. Once the fat has separated and begun to solidify on top, after about 10 minutes, poke a hole in the bottom of the cup with the tip of a skewer.
2. Let the defatted drippings run out through the hole until the fat reaches the bottom of the cup.

Homemade Cooling Rack

When he needs extra cooling racks, Andrew Eberle of Lexington, Mass., places canning-jar rings on his countertop. The elevation of the rings allows for just enough air circulation.

Send Us Your Tip We will provide a complimentary one-year subscription for each tip we print. Send your tip, name, and address to Quick Tips, Cook's Illustrated, P.O. Box 470589, Brookline, MA 02447, or to quicktips@bcpress.com.

Impromptu Colander

With her salad spinner already on the countertop, Jeanette Camelio of Rochester, N.Y., realized she could use it to drain pasta rather than digging out her colander.

After cooking the pasta, pour it into the salad spinner insert and drain.

Soft Butter in a Jiffy

Need soft butter for baking but don't have time to wait? Deborah Jurgens of Medford, N.Y., has a solution. Place the cold butter in a plastic bag, then use a rolling pin to pound it to the desired consistency in a matter of seconds.

Don't Lose Your Tamper

Just because your espresso machine is seldom in use doesn't mean the tamper has to sit idle.

A. Emmy Russell of San Diego, Calif., measures brown sugar into measuring cups and packs it with her espresso tamper.

B. Kathy Wein of Collinsville, Ill., uses an espresso tamper to smash peppercorns, garlic, and olives.

A.

B.

Keeping Scrub Pads Dry

Andrew Garrett of Lexington, Mass., hates it when a wet steel-wool scrub pad leaves rust all over the countertop. His solution is to store the pad on an unpainted terra cotta planter base. The clay material absorbs any water that drips off the used pad, and the pad stays rust-free.

Muffin-Tin Shields

Tired of scrubbing off the burnt batter from her muffin tins, Andrea Mikeal of Bryan, Texas, opts for an ounce of prevention.

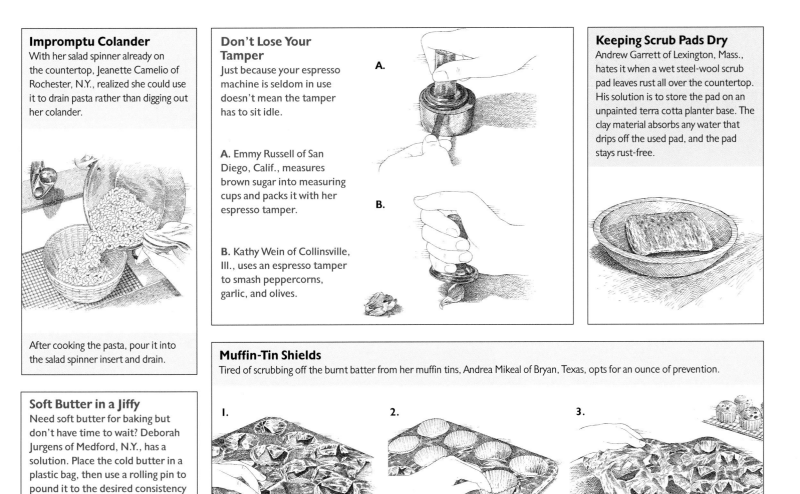

1. **2.** **3.**

1. Cover the muffin tin tightly with aluminum foil. Cut slits in each hole and press the foil into each indentation.
2. Drop paper or foil liners into each hole and fill with your favorite muffin batter.
3. After removing the muffins, simply peel off the dirty foil.

Not Full of Hot Air

Kevin Spears of Decatur, Ga., found a reason to dust off his old hot-air popcorn popper: to toast nuts. He places ¼ cup nuts in the popper and turns on the contraption for about one minute, until the nuts turn golden brown.

A Separate Piece

Robert Smythe of Swarthmore, Pa., has found an easy way to separate strips of bacon stuck together in the shrink-wrapped package.

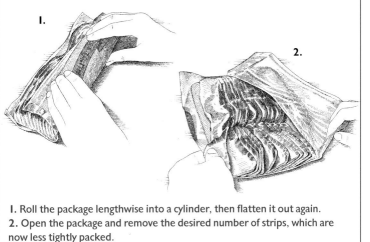

1.

2.

1. Roll the package lengthwise into a cylinder, then flatten it out again.
2. Open the package and remove the desired number of strips, which are now less tightly packed.

Shocking Discovery

When she runs out of ice to shock vegetables after blanching them, Julie Slayton Frank of Dover, N.H., reaches for a chilled ice cream maker insert, which she fills with cold tap water. After the vegetables are finished cooking, she shocks them in the cold water in the insert. The water remains cold for at least one batch of vegetables.

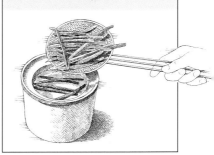

Pepper-Crusted Filet Mignon

Black peppercorns bring a welcome flavor boost—but also a punishing blast of heat—
to this mild-tasting cut. Could we lose the pain without giving up the flavor?

≥ BY SEAN LAWLER ≤

Filet mignon may be revered as the elite superstar of steaks, but it needs serious help in the kitchen to live up to that reputation on the palate. Chefs compensate for the relatively mild flavor of beef tenderloin—the lean, ultra-tender muscle from which filet mignon steaks are cut—by wrapping it in bacon or puff pastry, searing it to develop a dark, flavorful crust, and serving it with rich wine sauces or flavored butters.

Another popular way to dress up a filet is with a crust of cracked black peppercorns. Surveying a stack of published recipes, I envisioned the pleasing contrast of a thick center of pink, soft-as-butter beef and a crunchy, spicy coating—a peppery hit with every bite. The daydreaming ended as I recalled the test kitchen's prior frustrations with peppercorn crusts. Peppercorns fall off in the pan, interfere with the meat's browning, and—used in sufficient quantity to create a real crust—deliver punishing pungency.

Letting the cooked steaks rest on a wire cooling rack—instead of a plate—keeps the bottom crusts from turning soggy.

Remembrance of Steaks Past

Our earlier recipe (Steak au Poivre, September/October 2001) solved these problems by coating only one side of each steak with the cracked peppercorns. The overall heat level was reduced by half, and the uncoated side got nicely browned, contributing flavor to the steaks and providing the necessary *fond* (browned bits in the pan) to create the brandy-cream sauce that accompanies the classic French dish. A neat solution, but not one that could help me this time, I feared. That recipe used strip steaks cut from the loin that were, at most, an inch thick. Because the eye of the tenderloin muscle is small, filet steaks are usually cut almost twice as thick. I suspected a one-sided crust would not be sufficient, and a quick test proved it: Too many bites came with little or no crust. Flavor was also an issue. When I did get a bite with peppercorns, peppercorns were all I tasted.

Thick, lean, tender, mild—how best to use peppercorns to complement these traits without overwhelming them? I started with the test kitchen's standard technique for cooking a filet mignon: searing it first in a hot pan with a small amount of oil, then finishing in the oven.

Immediately, I encountered a problem. The cracked pepper kept the meat from making direct contact with the hot pan, so beneath the crust the steaks were unappealingly pale. I tried adding extra oil to the skillet, hoping it would bridge the gap between the pan and the meat, and this was a partial success. On the downside, peppercorns were still falling off. Next, I made a thick paste of cracked peppercorns and oil, which I rubbed over the raw steaks. Before cooking, I pressed down on each peppercorn-adorned steak through a sheet of plastic wrap. Problem solved.

Doctoring Pepper

Now I had steaks that were well browned and coated in an attractive pepper crust, but some tasters preferred to admire them from afar, as the overall heat level was still intense. Inspired by an article on blooming spices in infused oils, I wondered how heating my peppercorn-oil paste might affect its flavor, especially the spiciness. I brought the mixture to a gentle simmer in a saucepan, as aromas of flowers, chocolate, and toasted nuts wafted up. When I cooked up steaks coated with this mixture, I was amazed at the change. In place of the stinging heat was a pleasant warmth that spread slowly across my palate. (For an explanation, see "Taming Peppercorn Heat," page 7.) Now I could have a substantial peppercorn crust without the usual punishing heat.

Flavor Enhancers

To augment the flavor of the steaks' thick interior, I took a cue from the magazine's Grill-Roasted Beef Tenderloin recipe (September/October 2004), in which the meat is rubbed with salt an hour before grilling; the salt penetrated into the interior, seasoning it and drawing out a beefier flavor. I hoped this same technique would

---

Key Steps for Pepper-Crusted Filet Mignon

Choking heat, gray exteriors, peppercorns that fall off with the slightest provocation—we encountered all these problems during recipe development. To avoid them, take these steps.

SIMMER
Gently simmer the peppercorns in olive oil to mellow the heat.

COAT
Coat the tops and bottoms of the steaks with the pepper mixture, pressing the excess into the sides.

REST
Cover with plastic, pressing to make sure the peppercorns adhere. Let rest one hour.

BROWN
Sear the steaks in a well-oiled skillet until browned beneath the peppercorn layer.

ROAST
Finish cooking in a hot oven to ensure browning on the sides of the steaks.

work here, but rather than include a separate salting step I simply added a tablespoon of salt to the peppercorn paste and let the steaks sit, covered, for an hour before cooking. Sure enough, the meat became noticeably beefier—and flavorful enough to stand up to the assertive pepper crust.

As for accompaniments, the salting step bought me plenty of time to simmer a rich reduction sauce. Because it is so lean, filet mignon is also excellent with flavored butters.

PEPPER-CRUSTED FILET MIGNON
SERVES 4

While heating the peppercorns in oil tempers their pungent heat, this recipe is still fairly spicy. If you prefer a very mild pepper flavor, drain the cooled peppercorns in a fine-mesh strainer in step 1, toss them with 5 tablespoons of fresh oil, add the salt, and proceed. Serve with Port-Cherry Reduction or Blue Cheese–Chive Butter.

- 5 tablespoons black peppercorns, cracked (see illustration, right)
- 5 tablespoons plus 2 teaspoons olive oil
- 1 tablespoon kosher salt
- 4 center-cut filets mignons, 1 1/2 to 2 inches thick, 7 to 8 ounces each, trimmed of fat and silver skin

1. Heat peppercorns and 5 tablespoons oil in small saucepan over low heat until faint bubbles appear. Continue to cook at bare simmer, swirling pan occasionally, until pepper is fragrant, 7 to 10 minutes. Remove from heat and set aside to cool. When mixture is room temperature, add salt and stir to combine. Rub steaks with pepper mixture, thoroughly coating top and bottom of each steak with peppercorns. Cover steaks with plastic wrap and press gently to make sure peppercorns adhere; let stand at room temperature for 1 hour.

2. Meanwhile, adjust oven rack to middle position, place rimmed baking sheet on oven rack, and heat oven to 450 degrees. Heat remaining 2 teaspoons oil in 12-inch heavy-bottomed skillet over medium-high heat until faint smoke appears. Place steaks in skillet and cook, without moving steaks, until dark brown crust has formed, 3 to 4 minutes. Using tongs, turn steaks and cook until well browned on second side, about 3 minutes. Remove pan from heat and transfer steaks to hot baking sheet. Roast 3 to 5 minutes for rare, 5 to 7 minutes for medium-rare to medium. Transfer steaks to wire cooling rack and let rest, loosely tented with foil, for 5 minutes before serving.

PORT-CHERRY REDUCTION
MAKES ABOUT 1 CUP

- 1 1/2 cups port
- 1/2 cup balsamic vinegar
- 1/2 cup dried tart cherries
- 1 large shallot, minced (about 3 tablespoons)
- 2 sprigs fresh thyme
- 1 tablespoon unsalted butter
  Table salt

1. Combine first five ingredients in medium saucepan; simmer over medium-low heat until reduced to 1/3 cup, about 30 minutes. Set aside, covered.

2. While steaks are resting, reheat sauce. Off heat, remove thyme, then whisk in butter until melted. Season with salt to taste.

Go to www.cooksillustrated.com
- Key in code 3061 for the complete results of our **Tasting of Premium Filet Mignon**.
- This information is available until September 1, 2006.

COOK'S extra

TECHNIQUE
CRACKING PEPPERCORNS

Spread half of the peppercorns on a cutting board. Place a skillet on top. Pressing down firmly with both hands, use a rocking motion to crush the peppercorns beneath the "heel" of the skillet. Move the skillet back and forth, redistributing the peppercorns as needed. Repeat with the remaining peppercorns.

BLUE CHEESE–CHIVE BUTTER
MAKES ABOUT 1/2 CUP

- 3 tablespoons unsalted butter, softened
- 1 1/2 ounces mild blue cheese, room temperature
- 1/8 teaspoon table salt
- 2 tablespoons minced chives

Combine butter, cheese, and salt in medium bowl and mix with stiff rubber spatula until smooth. Fold in chives. While steaks are resting, spoon 1 to 2 tablespoons butter on each one.

SCIENCE: Taming Peppercorn Heat

Test-kitchen staffers with more sensitive palates were relieved to learn that the pungent heat of black peppercorns can be mellowed by a brief simmer in oil. I was pleased with the effect but curious as to the cause. Research revealed that the natural irritant in peppercorns is called piperine. As peppercorns age, the *piperine* is converted into closely related molecules (called isomers) that have different flavor characteristics and that are less irritating to the nose and throat. Left sitting at room temperature in your cupboard, the peppercorns may take years to undergo this reaction, but the hot oil serves as a catalyst, driving the conversion at hundreds of times its natural speed, quickly tempering the pepper's pungency. As a bonus, piperine and its isomers are oil-soluble, so that during the simmer some of the remaining pepper heat and flavor leaches out of the peppercorns into the surrounding oil. This oil can then be discarded to further reduce the heat of the dish. –S.L.

Rescuing Chicken Kiev

Crisply breaded and packed with herb butter, this Russian transplant was a star of the 1960s American restaurant scene. Can a home kitchen do it justice?

⋺ BY SANDRA WU ⋵

Popularized during the heyday of Manhattan's now-shuttered Russian Tea Room, chicken Kiev became one of the restaurant's premier offerings in the 1960s. The well-heeled were quite familiar with this elegant dish of pounded, breaded, and fried chicken breast stuffed with an herb butter that melted into a sauce. Although chicken Kiev's Ukrainian roots remain unclear, its current fate is hardly in dispute: It has become a greasy bundle of poultry with a sandy, disconcertingly peelable exterior and a greasy, leaky center. Commonly found in banquet halls and at catered events, this once-highbrow dish has become a self-parody.

The latter-day version, unfortunately, is what I had come to expect of chicken Kiev. My co-workers in the test kitchen were skeptics as well. But after preparing several cookbook versions, we realized that pairing a crisp-fried coating with a delicately flavored butter sauce was a great idea that deserved a revival.

By coating our Kievs with oven-crisped bread crumbs instead of a deep-fried shell, we put the focus where it belongs, on the rich herb-butter filling.

Leak Probe

Chicken Kiev has three distinct parts: the chicken, the butter, and the coating. The chilled butter is stuffed inside the boneless chicken breast, and the whole thing is rolled in a coating, then fried up crisp. As was clear from the flawed recipes I tried, getting the butter to survive cooking without leaking was key. So I started there.

Some recipes call for cutting a slit in the thickest part of the breast and inserting a disk of butter. That was easy, but it became apparent that providing any path of egress was a bad idea. One false move and the butter came streaming out—a dangerous proposition when frying in hot oil.

I had to encase the butter completely. Some recipes pounded the chicken, put a chilled disk of butter on top, then rolled the cutlet around it. This method worked much better, but it was hard to pound the chicken thin and wide enough to encase the butter without tearing the flesh. I next tried butterflying the breasts lengthwise (giving me cutlets twice as wide but half as thick as the original) before pounding. Much better: Less pounding meant less damage. Experimenting with various thicknesses, I settled on ¼ inch.

Flattened, my cutlets resembled large teardrops. Using a rolling-and-folding technique, I placed the butter disk just above the tapered end of the "teardrop" and proceeded as if wrapping a burrito: rolling the tapered end completely over the butter, folding in the sides, then continuing to roll until

I had a tight bundle. I was on the right track, but occasionally the folded-in sides refused to stay put. I quickly diagnosed the problem. The ¼-inch-thick sides, once folded over, were double the thickness of the rest of the bundle. Easy enough: I simply pounded the outer edges of the cutlets a little thinner (⅛ inch) than the rest. Obsessive precision? I'll admit it. But the foolproof result—no leaks—was worth it. (That said, pounding the cutlets down to a uniform ¼-inch thickness is almost as reliable.)

Crumby Coating

With four compact chicken bundles at the ready, I could focus on the exterior. I began with a standard breading procedure: dusting each stuffed cutlet with seasoned flour, dipping in beaten egg, then rolling in bread crumbs. But breading the chicken just after stuffing was a hazardous affair: The seam sometimes opened up, and the entire bundle became less compact (thus undoing all my anti-leak-protection work). Once, after leaving the unbreaded stuffed chicken in the refrigerator (uncovered) for an hour while I tended to other tasks, I noticed that the edges had begun to stick together, nearly gluing shut—much sturdier. From then on, I purposely placed the Kievs in the refrigerator to set up before attempting to bread them.

RECIPE DIAGNOSIS: Troubleshooting Chicken Kiev

Here are three problems we encountered while developing our recipe—and the steps we now take to avoid them.

'CORNDOGGY'

PROBLEM: Homogenized crust is reminiscent of a corndog.
SOLUTION: We had better results with coarse (not ultra-fine) crumbs and baking, not deep-frying.

LEAKY

PROBLEM: Compound butter leaks.
SOLUTION: Pounding the chicken thin (and thinner at the edges) and refrigerating to let the seams set produced butter-tight Kievs.

SPOTTY

PROBLEM: Pan-fried coating browns unevenly, and sides remain pale.
SOLUTION: Browning the bread crumbs before coating and baking the chicken yielded a uniform crust.

No matter what type of crumbs I used—fresh or dried, coarse or fine—deep-frying gave the Kievs a homogeneous, corndog-like quality. By the time the chicken was fully cooked, the exterior was a hard, tan-colored shell that desperately needed to be drained of grease. Not very appetizing. If only I could do away with deep-frying altogether. I tried pan-frying the bundles in a small amount of oil just until the crumbs became crisp. Once they were browned, I finished cooking them up to temperature in the oven. So far, so good—well, mostly. While the tops and bottoms of the chicken were nicely browned, it was hard to get the sides evenly colored without manhandling the Kievs, which often caused unraveling.

That's when I made the decision that would effectively transform my chicken Kiev from greasy banquet food to elegant dinner showpiece: toasting the bread crumbs in the oven first. Starting with already-browned bread crumbs meant I could skip the pan-frying step and cook the Kievs completely in the oven. I simply dredged the Kievs in seasoned flour, dipped them in egg, coated them with the browned bread crumbs, and threw them in the oven. No more frying, no more skillet, no more spotty browning.

Better Butter

All I had left to do was to perk up the plain filling. Traditional recipes stuff the Kievs with butter spiked with nothing more than parsley and chives. Tasters preferred the more aromatic minced shallots over chives and a small amount of chopped tarragon for a hint of sweetness. A squeeze of lemon juice tamed the rich butter with a bit of acidity, and Dijon mustard, whisked into the egg wash (for coating the chicken), provided another layer of flavor.

Years after my first disastrous encounter with chicken Kiev, my outlook had come full circle. This time, when fragrant, herb-speckled butter flowed from my crisply coated chicken, I sopped up every last drop, no longer compelled to blot it away with a paper napkin.

CHICKEN KIEV
SERVES 4

Unbaked, breaded chicken Kievs can be refrigerated overnight and baked the next day or frozen for up to one month. To cook frozen chicken Kievs, increase the baking time to 50–55 minutes (do not thaw chicken).

Herb Butter
- 8 tablespoons (1 stick) unsalted butter, softened
- 1 tablespoon minced shallot
- 1 tablespoon minced fresh parsley leaves
- 1/2 teaspoon minced fresh tarragon leaves
- 1 tablespoon juice from 1 lemon
- 3/8 teaspoon table salt
- 1/8 teaspoon ground black pepper

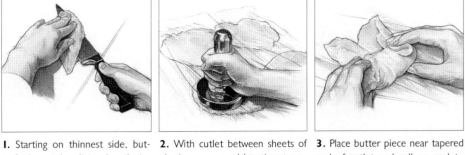

STEP-BY-STEP | BUILDING A BETTER CHICKEN KIEV

1. Starting on thinnest side, butterfly breast by slicing lengthwise almost in half. Open breast up to create a single, flat cutlet.

2. With cutlet between sheets of plastic wrap, pound (starting at center) to 1/4-inch thickness. Pound outer perimeter to 1/8 inch.

3. Place butter piece near tapered end of cutlet and roll up end to cover completely. Fold in sides and continue rolling to form cylinder.

4. After chilling one hour, dredge Kiev in flour, shaking off excess.

5. Roll flour-dredged Kiev in egg mixture, allowing excess to drip off.

6. Roll in toasted bread crumbs, pressing gently so crumbs adhere.

Chicken
- 4–5 slices white sandwich bread, cut into 3/4-inch cubes
  Table salt and ground black pepper
- 2 tablespoons vegetable oil
- 4 boneless, skinless chicken breasts (7 to 8 ounces each), tenderloins removed
- 1 cup all-purpose flour
- 3 large eggs, beaten
- 1 teaspoon Dijon mustard

1. **FOR THE HERB BUTTER:** Mix butter, shallot, herbs, lemon juice, salt, and pepper in medium bowl with rubber spatula until thoroughly combined. Form into 3-inch square on plastic wrap; wrap tightly and refrigerate until firm, about 1 hour.

2. **FOR THE CHICKEN:** Adjust oven rack to lower-middle position; heat oven to 300 degrees. Add half of bread cubes to food processor and pulse until cubes are coarsely ground, about sixteen 1-second pulses. Transfer crumbs to large bowl and repeat with remaining bread cubes (you should have about 3 1/2 cups crumbs). Add 1/8 teaspoon salt and 1/8 teaspoon pepper to bread crumbs. Add oil and toss until crumbs are evenly coated. Spread crumbs on rimmed baking sheet and bake until golden brown and dry, about 25 minutes, stirring twice during baking time. Let cool to room temperature (you should have about 2 1/2 cups bread crumbs).

3. Prepare cutlets, following illustrations 1 and 2 above. Unwrap butter and cut into 4 rectangular pieces. Place chicken breast cut side up on work surface; season both sides with salt and pepper. Following illustration 3, place 1 piece of butter in center of bottom half of breast. Roll bottom edge of chicken over butter, then fold in sides and continue rolling to form neat, tight package, pressing on seam to seal. Repeat with remaining butter and chicken. Refrigerate chicken, uncovered, to allow edges to seal, about 1 hour.

4. Adjust oven rack to middle position and heat oven to 350 degrees. Place flour, eggs, and bread crumbs in separate pie plates or shallow dishes. Season flour with 1/4 teaspoon salt and 1/8 teaspoon pepper; season bread crumbs with 1/2 teaspoon salt and 1/4 teaspoon pepper. Add mustard to eggs and whisk to combine. Dredge 1 chicken breast in flour, shaking off excess, then coat with egg mixture, allowing excess to drip off (illustrations 4 and 5). Coat all sides of chicken breast with bread crumbs, pressing gently so that crumbs adhere (illustration 6). Place on wire rack set over rimmed baking sheet. Repeat flouring and breading of remaining chicken breasts.

5. Bake until instant-read thermometer inserted into center of chicken (from top) registers 160 degrees, 40 to 45 minutes. Let rest 5 minutes on wire rack before serving.

Go to www.cooksillustrated.com
- Key in code 3063 for the results of our Meat Pounder Tests.
- This information is available until September 1, 2006.

Streamlining Marinara

Could we make a sauce with complex but fresh flavors—from scratch—in less than an hour?

⇒ BY DAVID PAZMIÑO ⇐

There's something great about a quick tomato sauce: fast, furious, and fresh. But what a quick sauce offers in convenience it lacks in the complexity of a slowly simmered tomato sauce, the best known of which may be marinara.

Unfortunately, complexity of flavor means lots of time in the kitchen, which is in short supply on a Tuesday night. My goal was to produce a multidimensional sauce in less than an hour, starting the clock the moment I entered the kitchen and stopping it when dinner was on the table. Weeding through hundreds of marinara recipes, I settled on testing not only a variety of "quick" versions but also some that were cooked for longer than an hour. The differences were readily apparent. The quick sauces were generally thin and lacked depth of flavor. The long-cooked sauces got the complexity right, but most relied on an ambitious laundry list of ingredients to achieve it—not to mention a lot of time. The sauce I was after had to capture some of these robust flavors within the confines of fairly quick cooking.

A Trick with Tomatoes

Because prime fresh tomatoes are available for such a limited time during the year, I opted for canned. But canned tomatoes take up nearly half an aisle at my supermarket. Which variety should I choose?

Crushed, pureed, and diced tomatoes offered the ultimate ease in sauce making: Open can, dump contents into pan. But all three options have downsides. Pureed tomatoes go into the can already cooked, which imparts a stale, flat flavor to the final sauce. Crushed tomatoes are generally packed in tomato puree: same problem. With these, my sauces came out tasting like unremarkable homemade versions of the jarred spaghetti sauces sold at the supermarket. With canned diced tomatoes, the problem was texture, not flavor. In the past, we've learned that manufacturers treat diced tomatoes with calcium chloride to keep them from turning to mush and losing their shape. That's fine for many dishes,

Slow, gentle simmering produces a great marinara, but we're much too impatient. Using unorthodox cooking methods, we cheated the clock.

but for recipes in which a smooth consistency is desired, calcium chloride does its job too well, making the tomatoes harder to break down—and the resulting sauces oddly granular.

The only choice left, then, was canned whole tomatoes. (While whole tomatoes are also treated with calcium chloride, the chemical has direct contact with a much smaller percentage of the tomato.) The big drawback of using whole tomatoes in a sauce is that they have to be cut up. Chopping them on a cutting board was a mess. The solution was to dump the tomatoes into a strainer over a bowl and then hand-crush them, removing the hard core and any stray bits of skin.

That's when I made the first of several decisions that would enable me to get long-simmered complexity in a short time. Most marinara recipes call for simply adding a can (or two) of tomatoes to the pot, juice and all—and some even call for throwing in a can of water. Now that I was separating the solids from the juice anyway, why not experiment with adding less of the reserved liquid? The trick worked: By adding only 2½ cups of the drained juice from two cans of whole tomatoes (rather than the full 3½ cups I had collected) and omitting the extra water, I managed to cut the simmering time by almost 20 minutes.

Up until now I had been following the standard marinara procedure of sautéing aromatics (onions and garlic) in olive oil in a saucepan before adding the tomatoes, liquid, and flavorings, then simmering. That's fine if you have all day, but I had only an hour. So I switched from a saucepan to a skillet, hoping the greater surface area would encourage faster evaporation and, thus, faster concentration of flavors.

It was faster, all right—down to just under an hour—but I felt that the sauce could use gutsier tomato flavor. Not only was the solution simple,

Getting Slow-Simmered Flavor Fast

The best marinaras have lots of complexity—and demand lots of cooking time. Here's how we sped up the process.

DRAIN JUICE

A can of tomatoes has more juice than solids. We jump-start flavor concentration by draining off almost a cup of juice beforehand.

CARAMELIZE SOLIDS

Caramelizing the tomato solids briskly in a large skillet before deglazing with liquid ingredients further deepens the flavor profile.

ADD RAW TOMATOES

Reserving a few uncooked tomatoes to add near the end of cooking contributes an extra note of freshness to the cooked sauce.

Do You Really Need a Hand Blender?

A hand, or immersion, blender can save time and effort: no need to blend in batches, no need to wash a food processor—just rinse it off and toss it back in the drawer. But which brand is best? To find out, we gathered nine models, priced between $13 and $90, and put them to the test. All nine blenders whirred the chunks out of our marinara sauce easily, so we upped the ante. Pureeing broccoli soup was a more telling task: A few models finished the job in just 30 seconds, while the weaker blenders were still batting around small chunks after a minute. (Several manufacturers advise against continuous running for more than a minute.) What separated the movers from the shakers was pesto. Only three blenders, two Brauns and a KitchenAid, dispatched the herbs and nuts in quick order.

So what makes a better hand blender? The differences aren't obvious. As we've found in past tests, wattage means nothing when it comes to most appliances: The 200- and 400-watt Braun models performed equally well. We did, however, end up with a few design preferences: Stainless steel shafts (rather than plastic) were not better performers, but they do resist staining and can be used in pots sitting over a flame. And come cleanup time, a removable blade end is best. In the end, KitchenAid's immersion blender ($49.99) was our favorite. Aside from a blending beaker, it offers no extras (some models come with fancy attachments), but it did as good as a job at blending as most traditional blenders. –Garth Clingingsmith

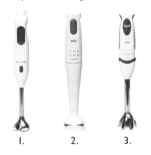

1.   2.   3.   4.   5.   6.   7.   8.   9.

FAVORITE HAND BLENDER

1. KITCHENAID, $49.99.
Minimal extras, but as good as many traditional blenders.

RECOMMENDED

2. BRAUN Multiquick, $34.95.
Great performance and value, but the plastic shaft can't be used over heat.

3. BRAUN Multiquick Professional, $79.95. That extra $45 doesn't mean better performance, just a few attachments.

RECOMMENDED WITH RESERVATIONS

4. CUISINART SmartStick, $69.99. Had trouble handling chunky pesto, a deal breaker for such an expensive model.

5. HAMILTON BEACH Turbo-Twister Mixing Stick, $19.99. A good value, but the plastic blade housing is less than ideal.

6. PROCTOR-SILEX, $12.99. The blade "cage" is somewhat cramped, leading to occasional clogging.

NOT RECOMMENDED

7. OSTER Hand Blender with Blending Cup, $23.99. Vibrations from the shakiest—and loudest—blender leave your hand quivering minutes after use.

8. FARBERWARE Special Select, $24.99. Refused to puree broccoli soup; bulky handle.

9. CUISINART Cordless, $49.95. Loose joints between three components and a lack of guts trumped the otherwise-attractive cordless feature.

---

but it was the key step in giving my quick sauce the complexity of a long-simmered one. Before adding the liquids and simmering, I sautéed the tomato meats until they glazed the bottom of the pan. Only then did I add the liquids, a normally routine step that, by essentially deglazing the pan, added crucial flavor to my sauce.

Balancing Acts

With the tomato flavor under control, it was time to develop more depth of flavor. Onions added a pleasant sweetness, but carrots, although sweet, also added an earthy flavor that diminished that of the tomatoes. Sugar, added at the end of cooking, proved to be the working solution to balance the flavors: too much and my sauce began to taste like it came out of a jar; too little and the acidity overwhelmed the other flavors. Tasters loved the robust, complex flavor of red wine, and a mere 1/3

cup was just the right amount. But not just any bottle: Wines with a heavy oak flavor rated lower than those with little to no oak presence. (Chianti and Merlot scored particularly high marks.)

I now had a good marinara ready to ladle and serve in less than an hour—about half the time of many recipes. Could I further bolster the complexity without adding minutes? On a hunch, I tried reserving a few of the uncooked canned tomatoes and adding them near the end of cooking. When I served this sauce alongside the earlier version, tasters were unanimous in their preference for the new sauce; just six tomatoes pureed into the sauce at the end added enough brightness to complement the deeper profile of the cooked sauce.

So far the sauce had little flavor from herbs beyond oregano. Fresh basil, also added at the end, contributed a floral aroma that comple-

mented the sauce's careful balance of sweet and acid. Adjusting the salt and pepper and adding extra-virgin olive oil rounded things out.

MARINARA SAUCE
MAKES 4 CUPS

This recipe makes enough to sauce more than a pound of pasta; leftovers can be refrigerated or frozen. Because canned tomatoes vary in acidity and saltiness, it's best to add salt, pepper, and sugar to taste just before serving. If you prefer a chunkier sauce, give it just three or four pulses in the food processor in step 4.

- 2 (28-ounce) cans whole tomatoes packed in juice
- 2 tablespoons olive oil
- 1 medium onion, chopped fine (about 1 cup)
- 2 medium garlic cloves, minced or pressed through garlic press (about 2 teaspoons)
- 1/2 teaspoon dried oregano
- 1/3 cup dry red wine, such as Chianti or Merlot
- 3 tablespoons chopped fresh basil leaves
- 1 tablespoon extra-virgin olive oil
  Table or kosher salt and ground black pepper
- 1–2 teaspoons sugar, as needed (see note above)

1. Pour tomatoes and juice into strainer set over large bowl. Open tomatoes with hands and remove and discard fibrous cores; let tomatoes drain excess liquid, about 5 minutes. Remove 3/4 cup tomatoes from strainer and set aside. Reserve 2 1/2 cups tomato juice and discard remainder.

2. Heat olive oil in large skillet over medium heat until shimmering. Add onion and cook, stirring occasionally, until softened and golden around edges, 6 to 8 minutes. Add garlic and oregano and cook, stirring constantly, until garlic is fragrant, about 30 seconds.

3. Add tomatoes from strainer and increase heat to medium-high. Cook, stirring every minute, until liquid has evaporated and tomatoes begin to stick to bottom of pan and brown fond forms around pan edges, 10 to 12 minutes. Add wine and cook until thick and syrupy, about 1 minute. Add reserved tomato juice and bring to simmer; reduce heat to medium and cook, stirring occasionally and loosening browned bits, until sauce is thick, 8 to 10 minutes.

4. Transfer sauce to food processor (or transfer to saucepan and insert immersion blender; see "Do You Really Need a Hand Blender?" left) and add reserved tomatoes; process until slightly chunky, about eight 2-second pulses. Return sauce to skillet and add basil and extra-virgin olive oil and salt, pepper, and sugar to taste.

Rethinking Roasted Leg of Lamb

Few roasts make as grand an entrance as roasted leg of lamb, but its charms quickly fade upon carving. We wanted the gristle (and gaminess) gone before we entered the dining room.

⇒ BY SARAH WILSON ⇐

For such a showstopping dish, roasted leg of lamb is remarkably easy to make: Salt, pepper, perhaps a few slivers of garlic—then into the oven it goes. A few hours later, out comes a juicy, deeply browned, primeval slab of meat with a rosy-pink interior. What's not to love?

Plenty, actually. What those fuss-free recipes fail to mention is that the simple-sounding last step—"carve and serve"—is anything but, thanks to the copious amounts of fat and sinew. Worse, unlike beef fat, which contributes rich, heady flavors as it renders, lamb fat is a key source of the musky flavor that even adventurous eaters can find off-putting.

I wanted a roasted leg of lamb without the gristle or the gaminess. I also wanted to avoid having to sequester myself in the kitchen to perform intricate surgery while my guests tapped their fingers.

On the Lamb

American supermarkets sell domestic, Australian, and New Zealand lamb, so I rounded up representatives of each for a taste test. Even before roasting, one difference was obvious: The domestic legs were three times as large. The size differential alone was reason enough to go domestic, but the tasting sealed the deal. ("Tastes like past-its-prime mutton," noted one test cook about the samples from Down Under.) The difference? Feeding habits. Australian and New Zealand lambs generally eat grass (rather than grain), a diet that yields noticeably gamier meat.

Next up, the cut. While tasters liked the dramatic presentation of a bone-in roast, carving was tricky, so I opted for boneless. I could buy either a whole leg or one of the two portions into which it's traditionally divided: the *shank end*, or middle part of the leg, which includes the top round, bottom round, and eye of round, and the *butt end*, or hip portion, which includes the sirloin. (The *shank* itself is a small section close to the hoof that is sold separately; see Kitchen Notes, page 30, for a shopping guide.) In terms of flavor and tenderness, tasters found little difference from section to section, so I settled on the meatier shank end.

The rewards of diligent trimming are reaped at serving time. Divided into three small roasts, our leg of lamb is gristle-free, and the gaminess is gone.

And All the Trimmings

Lamb's gamy flavor comes mostly from the fat. Theoretically, the more fat I removed, the milder the finished roast. So I sharpened my knives and set about putting this theory to the test. For the first round, I spent a modest amount of time trimming as much visible fat as I could—15 minutes, tops. I cooked a second one with no preparation beyond removing it from the package. Onto a roasting rack and into a hot oven they went. When the roasts emerged, both were crusty-brown and perfectly cooked, but the trimmed roast had a remarkably less gamy flavor.

I was on the right track, but the meat adjacent to the remaining fat still tasted musky, and some slices were riddled with gristle. I could do better. For the next test, I spent 10 more minutes on trimming, cutting into and around the lobes of meat. When I finished, the lamb looked clean, but all that butchering was taking a toll on the structure.

Instead of one cohesive slab of meat, the lamb had become a fragmented collection of meaty lobes. The finished roast had a meaty flavor almost as clean as that of beef, but the slices uncoiled unappealingly when carved.

I decided to revisit a recipe from my research that took the unorthodox approach of separating the lamb into three roasts, splitting the meat at the natural "seams" between the meaty lobes. I had initially rejected this method for being too fussy, but my diligently trimmed roast was most of the way there already. All I had to do was cut off the connective silver skin and roll and tie each lobe separately. I ended up with three tidy "mini-roasts" that had not a trace of gaminess once roasted! What's more, the presentation was flawless.

I repeated the recipe, this time separating the roasts at the natural seams before trimming, which made quicker work of the whole process. All in all, the butchering took close to half an hour, a fair amount of work. But given such a breathtaking payoff, and that all the work can be completed in advance, the consensus was that it was time well spent.

I made one other change. With the smaller roasts, which cooked quickly, it was difficult to get a deeply browned exterior by the time the interior reached a rosy medium-rare. I solved this problem by searing the three roasts on the stovetop in a skillet (impossible with the single large roast), then transferred the skillet to the oven to finish.

Sheep Trick

GARLIC + SALT + WATER

Brining doesn't do much for beef—its muscle fibers turn to mush—but the technique works wonders for lamb. The salt breaks down the fibers just enough to tenderize the meat, and the crushed garlic imbues it with deep flavor.

In with the Good

Now that I had removed unwanted flavors, I set about adding some good ones in the form of garlic and herbs. I tried inserting slivers of garlic into slits that I cut into the meat, but this technique yielded unevenly flavored meat, harsh and garlicky in one bite, faintly flavored in the next. I tried rubbing the lamb with garlic paste (both raw and roasted) and marinating for various intervals, but the flavor remained superficial. Tasters liked the flavor of the roasted garlic, but it didn't permeate the meat.

What about a flavorful brine? The test kitchen never brines beef because brining turns the protein fibers to mush, but I wondered how it would affect lamb. I added garlic to a basic brine (water, sugar, salt), then gave it a few hours to work its magic. Not only did brining season the meat throughout and infuse it with a delicate garlic flavor, but it improved the texture as well, bringing the lamb from oddly springy to pleasantly tender. Researching the topic further, I learned that the protein structures in beef are weaker than those in lamb, making beef more susceptible to a complete breakdown of fibers: Beef turns mushy, while lamb breaks down just enough to tenderize it.

To round out the garlic flavor, I revisited my roasted garlic paste. This time, however, I scored each brined roast on one side, slathered it with the paste, then rolled and tied it into a tidy log-shaped roast. The combination of the raw-garlic-infused brine and roasted garlic paste provided just the right level of complexity. A few sprigs of minced parsley, and the transformation from gamy, gristly mutton to elegant, subtly flavored showpiece was complete.

GARLIC-ROASTED LEG OF LAMB
SERVES 8 TO 10

Look for rolled, boneless leg of lamb wrapped in netting, not butterflied and wrapped on a tray. The desirable cut is the "shank end," which is the whole boneless leg without the sirloin muscle attached. If only bone-in or semi-boneless leg is available, ask your butcher to remove the bones for you. Plan on spending about 30 minutes trimming the lamb of fat and silver skin. This advance work is well worth the effort; your roasts will present elegantly and have a much cleaner flavor. (That said, even 10 minutes of trimming will improve the taste dramatically; see "Preparing the Lamb," below, for instructions.) If you opt for the more complete, 30-minute trim, you will have enough meat scraps left over to make a Roasted Garlic Jus, if desired. See Cook's Extra, below, for the recipe. The lamb can be trimmed, brined, rubbed with paste, and tied, then stored overnight in the refrigerator (do not season the meat). Allow the lamb to stand at room temperature for 30 minutes before proceeding with the recipe.

Lamb and Brine
- ¼ cup kosher salt (or 2 tablespoons table salt)
- ¼ cup sugar
- 12 medium garlic cloves, crushed
- 1 boneless leg of domestic lamb with sirloin muscle removed (5 to 7 pounds)

Garlic-Parsley Paste
- 2 medium garlic heads, outer papery skins removed and top third of head cut off and discarded
- 1 tablespoon olive oil
- 2 tablespoons minced fresh parsley leaves

  Kosher salt and ground black pepper
- 3 tablespoons vegetable oil

1. Combine salt, sugar, and crushed garlic with 2 quarts water in large bowl or container; stir until salt and sugar dissolve. Prepare lamb as shown through illustration 4 (at left). Submerge lamb in brine, cover, and refrigerate for 2 hours.

2. While lamb brines, adjust oven rack to middle position and heat oven to 400 degrees. Place garlic heads cut side up on sheet of aluminum foil and drizzle with olive oil. Wrap foil tightly around garlic; place on baking sheet and roast until cloves are very soft and golden brown, 40 to 45 minutes. When cool enough to handle, squeeze garlic head to remove cloves from skins. Mash cloves into paste with side of chef's knife. Combine 2 tablespoons garlic paste and parsley in small bowl. (Reserve remaining paste for Roasted Garlic Jus, if making; see Cook's Extra, below.)

3. Remove lamb from brine and pat dry with paper towels. Finish lamb preparation (illustrations 5 and 6). Season each roast with salt and pepper.

4. Heat vegetable oil in 12-inch ovensafe skillet over medium-high heat until shimmering. Place lamb roasts in skillet and cook until well browned on all sides, about 12 minutes total. Place skillet in oven and roast until instant-read thermometer inserted into center of each roast reads 125 degrees for medium-rare, or 130 to 135 degrees for medium to medium-well. (Roasting time will range from 8 to 25 minutes depending on size of roasts; begin checking after 7 minutes and transfer each roast to platter as it reaches desired temperature.) Let lamb rest, tented with foil, about 15 minutes. Snip twine off roasts, cut into ¼-inch slices, and serve.

STEP-BY-STEP | PREPARING THE LAMB

This process demands a sharp knife and a fair amount of patience. If you lack either one, you can simply separate the lamb into three roasts (as shown in illustration 1) and spend just 10 minutes trimming—concentrating on the exterior fat and gristle—then cut a deep, lengthwise pocket into each roast, rub the garlic-parsley paste on the interior surface, and tie the roasts with butcher's twine.

1. Unroll lamb. Following natural seams (delineated by lines of fat), separate into three smaller roasts, using sharp boning knife as needed.

2. Trim visible fat and gristle from exterior of each roast. With small, pointed cuts, penetrate deeper to remove interior pockets of gristle, fat, and silver skin. (Roasts open up and flatten slightly during trimming.)

3. As you trim meat, remove any large, meaty scraps that come loose from larger pieces (you will have about ¾ cup scraps). Reserve these for making Roasted Garlic Jus, if desired.

4. Lightly score inside of each roast, making ¼-inch-deep cuts spaced 1 inch apart in crosshatch pattern.

5. Rub scored surface of brined lamb with garlic-parsley paste, working paste into grooves.

6. Roll into compact roast, tucking in flaps, to form log shape. Tie with twine at 1-inch intervals.

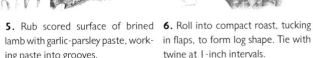

Go to www.cooksillustrated.com
- Key in code 3065 for **Roasted Garlic Jus.**
- Recipe available until September 1, 2006.

Perfect Potstickers

Can you really make great Chinese-restaurant dumplings at home? We wanted a light filling, the right wrapper, and the perfect mix of flavors.

⇒ BY SARAH WILSON ⇐

I can count on one hand the times I've had truly great potstickers. At their best, these staples of Chinese dim sum are soft, savory pillows filled with tender ground meat and crunchy cabbage spiked with a pleasing hit of garlic, ginger, and soy. But the usual fare is nowhere near so glorious: dense, flavorless meatballs wrapped in a doughy blanket.

Despite such grim prospects, most cooks (including me) prefer rolling the dice at a restaurant rather than taking on what would seem to be a grueling project at home. As I surveyed dozens of authentic potsticker recipes, however, I was surprised to find out how straightforward most were: Mix ground pork, cabbage, and seasonings; spoon it all into dumpling wrappers; then steam and fry in a wok. But time logged in the test kitchen revealed that tough fillings, bland flavors, and bad wraps are not just the bane of busy restaurants. Could I make this simple recipe more foolproof?

No Hard Fillings

First, I needed to lighten up the filling. Ground pork has a tendency to form a dense, solid mass when it's shaped and cooked, a phenomenon test kitchen staffers began calling "the meatball effect." One bite into the dumpling and the small, dense "meatball" hidden inside would fall out onto the plate. Not very appetizing. The scallions and cabbage, folded into the pork, are meant to mitigate this problem by providing moisture and textural variety, but they just weren't doing the trick.

I tried increasing the amount of cabbage. Tasters loved the looser consistency of the filling but complained that the cabbage flavor and texture were too dominant. Forgoing the raw cabbage I'd been using, I tried sautéing it briefly to mellow the sharp flavor, but tasters missed the crunch. I tried salting and draining the cabbage to get rid of excess moisture, a trick we often use in the test kitchen. This approach was a winner. After a 20-minute rest in the colander, the salted cabbage no longer dominated the filling, yet it still contributed a slightly bitter, crunchy edge.

Tasters continued to complain that the filling

A sequence of searing, steaming, then cranking up the heat produces potstickers with a pleasing balance of soft and crispy textures.

still seemed a bit hard and dense. This time I borrowed a trick from meat-loaf cookery and added lightly beaten egg whites to the pork/cabbage mixture. The theory is that the egg whites will puff up as they cook, almost like a soufflé, incorporating tiny air bubbles into the otherwise compact ground meat. Sure enough, the outcome was perfect: I now had a light and tender filling.

Wrapping Up

A thick, doughy wrapper, often encountered in restaurant versions, was out, but the wrapper had to survive the cooking process, so it couldn't be paper-thin. Two ready-made versions are widely available (I was unwilling to make wrappers from scratch). Wonton wrappers—made with flour, egg, and salt—are a bit thin for this application. I found the better choice to be gyoza wrappers. Made without egg, they are sturdier and hold up better when pan-fried. Also, the more substantial texture seemed a better match for the flavorful filling.

So far, I had been spooning the filling into the center of a round gyoza wrapper, folding it in half, then pressing the edges to seal. I placed the dumplings in a hot nonstick skillet seam side up to get a crisp, browned bottom, poured in some water, covered the pan, and let them steam until soft. Finally, I removed the cover to re-crisp the bottoms.

While mostly successful, this procedure did present a problem: The seam was drying out in the final stages of cooking. I increased the steaming time, but tasters still complained of toughness. The solution was easy. Instead of sautéing the dumplings standing straight up, I knocked them on their sides so that the seam would lie against the bottom of the pan. One side became crisp, while the rest of the dumpling remained pleasantly tender and chewy.

Placing 12 dumplings in a preheated skillet takes time and burns fingertips. By the time the

Choosing the Right Wrap

Tasters preferred the slightly chewy texture of gyoza-style wrappers to thinner wonton wrappers, but both styles produced terrific potstickers. Although we developed our recipe using round wrappers, square or rectangular wrappers can be used as well. Here's how to adjust filling amount and steaming time. Because the smaller wrappers yield more dumplings, you'll need to cook them in multiple batches. (For wrapping instructions, see page 15.)

WRAPPER	SIZE	FILLING AMOUNT	STEAMING TIME
Round gyoza	3¾ inches (diameter)	1 rounded tablespoon	10 minutes
Round wonton	3¾ inches (diameter)	1 rounded tablespoon	6 minutes
Square wonton	3⅜ inches square	2 rounded teaspoons	6 minutes
Rectangular wonton	3¼ by 2¾ inches	1 rounded teaspoon	5 minutes

last dumpling was in the pan, the first one was already browned, giving me an unevenly colored batch. The answer was to place the dumplings in a cold, lightly oiled skillet before turning on the burner. Success. To cook the second batch, I took the pan off the heat, wiped it out with bunched-up paper towels, and started the process again.

A few of the potstickers were not holding their filling well after steaming. While steaming one batch, I peeked under the lid and saw some of the dumplings ballooning out like blowfish. When I removed the lid, they seemed to deflate back to normal, but a few still had an air bubble trapped inside that kept the interior of the wrapper from making contact with (and clinging to) the filling. As a result, one bite would send the filling crashing down onto the plate. The solution? More diligence in removing all the air while filling the wrappers. Trying several approaches, I came up with the best sequence: Fold the meat-filled wrapper into a half-moon, pinch the middle closed, then carefully seal the remaining edges while lightly pressing the filling to ensure that no air remains.

All my potstickers needed now was the right dipping sauce—not the heavy-handed kind demanded by dumplings with ho-hum flavor but a simple, bracing blend of soy sauce, rice vinegar, mirin (a sweet Japanese cooking wine), and toasted sesame oil, with just a touch of chili oil to kick up the heat. Now my potstickers were not only light and flavorful but virtually foolproof as well.

The instructions below are for round wrappers, our preferred shape. If using square wrappers, fold diagonally into a triangle (step 2) and proceed with the recipe. For rectangular wrappers, fold in half lengthwise.

FILL
1. Place rounded tablespoon of filling in center of gyoza wrapper.

FOLD
2. After moistening edge of wrapper, fold it in half to make half-moon shape.

PINCH
3. With forefinger and thumb, pinch dumpling closed, pressing out any air pockets.

FLATTEN
4. Place dumpling on its side and press gently to flatten bottom.

POTSTICKERS
MAKES 24 DUMPLINGS, SERVING 6 AS FIRST COURSE

We prefer to use gyoza wrappers. You can substitute wonton wrappers, but the cooking time and recipe yield will vary (see the chart on page 14). Potstickers are best served hot from the skillet; we recommend that you serve the first batch immediately, then cook the second batch. To freeze potstickers, place filled, uncooked dumplings in the freezer in a single layer on a plate until frozen, then transfer to a storage bag. There's no need to thaw frozen potstickers; just proceed with the recipe.

Filling
- 3 cups minced napa cabbage leaves
- ¾ teaspoon table salt
- ¾ pound ground pork
- 6 tablespoons minced scallions (about 4 medium scallions, white and green parts)
- ⅛ teaspoon ground black pepper
- 4 teaspoons soy sauce
- 1½ teaspoons grated ginger
- 1 medium garlic clove, minced or pressed through garlic press (about 1 teaspoon)
- 2 egg whites, lightly beaten

- 24 round gyoza wrappers (see note above)
- 4 teaspoons vegetable oil

1. Toss cabbage and salt in colander or mesh strainer set over medium bowl. Let stand until cabbage begins to wilt, about 20 minutes; press cabbage gently with rubber spatula to squeeze out excess moisture. Combine cabbage and all other filling ingredients in medium bowl and mix thoroughly. Cover bowl with plastic wrap and refrigerate until mixture is cold, at least 30 minutes and up to 24 hours.

2. Place 4 wrappers flat on work surface (keep remaining wrappers covered with plastic wrap). Following illustration 1, above, place one slightly rounded tablespoon filling in center of each wrapper. Using pastry brush or fingertip, moisten edge of wrapper with water. Fold each wrapper in half; starting in center and working toward outside edges, pinch edges together firmly to seal, pressing out any air pockets (illustrations 2 and 3). Position each dumpling on its side and gently flatten, pressing down on seam to make sure it lies flat against work surface (illustration 4). Repeat to form 24 dumplings. (Filled dumplings can be refrigerated overnight in single layer on baking sheet wrapped tightly with plastic wrap.)

3. Add 2 teaspoons oil to 12-inch nonstick skillet and quickly spread oil with paper towel to distribute evenly. Arrange 12 dumplings in skillet, lying flat on one side, with all seams facing same direction, overlapping just slightly, if necessary. Place skillet over medium-high heat and cook, without moving, until dumplings are golden brown on bottoms, about 5 minutes. Reduce heat to low, add ½ cup water to skillet, and cover immediately. Cook, covered, until most of water is absorbed and wrappers are slightly translucent, about 10 minutes. Uncover skillet and increase heat to medium-high; cook, without stirring, until dumpling bottoms are well browned and crisp, 3 to 4 minutes more. Turn off burner and slide dumplings from skillet onto double layer paper towels, browned side down, to blot excess oil. Transfer to platter and serve immediately with Scallion Dipping Sauce. Let skillet cool until just warm, then wipe skillet clean and repeat with remaining dumplings and oil.

SCALLION DIPPING SAUCE
MAKES ¾ CUP

The sauce can be refrigerated overnight.

- ¼ cup soy sauce
- 2 tablespoons rice vinegar
- 2 tablespoons mirin
- 2 tablespoons water
- 1 teaspoon chili oil (optional)
- ½ teaspoon toasted sesame oil
- 1 medium scallion, white and green parts, minced

Combine all ingredients in bowl and serve.

Clearing the Air

During testing, we discovered that air left between wrapper and filling can cause "ballooning" during steaming, as the wrapper puffs up and away from the meat. The result? A messy first bite. Once we were mindful to press the air out before sealing the wrappers, our potstickers came out right every time.

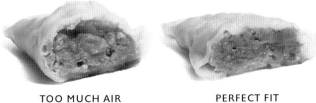

TOO MUCH AIR   **PERFECT FIT**

A Guide to Recommended Bakeware

Price doesn't always equal performance. The design details that prevent stuck muffins and burnt cookies may be the ones you least expected. BY SEAN LAWLER

MATERIAL WORLD: The Light, the Dark, and the See-Through

Though its manufacturers are loath to admit it, choosing quality bakeware is pretty simple. All the usual jargon about clad aluminum cores and anodized coatings remains in full force, but a dozen years of testing have left us even more skeptical than usual about bells and whistles when it comes to shopping for cake pans and cookie sheets. Here's what to look for—and what to avoid.

TEMPERED, OVENPROOF GLASS: Better known by the brand name Pyrex, thick tempered glass retains plenty of heat, so pans made from it ensure deep and even browning. They also make it easy to monitor the browning as it develops. Because Pyrex is scratch-resistant, you can cut and serve right from the pan with sharp knives and metal spatulas. What's not to like? Just the occasional explosion, a manageable risk as long as you take precautions (see "When Pyrex Explodes," page 17).

DARK-COLORED FINISHES: When it comes to metal pans, neither the type of metal nor its thickness matters much. What does matter is the color of the pan. Dark-colored nonstick pans allow metal to absorb more heat inside the oven than reflective, lighter-colored materials. The result: darker browning of baked goods, which is almost always a good thing. Combine that with the

TALL, DARK, AND HANDSOME
Dark-colored pans absorb heat well, yielding tall, nicely browned baked goods.

SQUAT AND PALE
Light-colored pans absorb less heat, inhibiting browning and rise.

clean release and easy cleanup of nonstick, and pans in this category are often the ones to beat.

LIGHT-COLORED FINISHES: A well-browned crust releases more easily from a pan than a pale crust. Because light-colored reflective pans brown more slowly than dark-colored pans, and because they also lack a nonstick coating, we're generally reluctant to recommend them. In a few situations, however, this controlled browning can be an advantage, such as when baking cookies. (Because it's only the bottom of a cookie that's in contact with the metal, it can easily burn before the rest of the cookie bakes through.)

INSULATED: To protect against overbrowning (not usually a problem for us), insulated pans incorporate a layer of air sandwiched between two sheets of metal. Unfortunately, this "insulation" works all too well: The pans produce pale, underdeveloped crusts. The interior chamber also becomes waterlogged if submerged in water during cleanup. What a pain.

SILICONE: These flexible, rubbery pans are the most useless things to appear in the kitchen since salad shooters. These "pans" don't brown well, and getting them into the oven when loaded down with batter is awkward.

BAKING PAN

Testing Notes: We stock plenty of these pans in the test kitchen, where they handle everything from lasagna to sticky buns. Sturdy Pyrex is our first choice here: dishwasher-safe, handy handles, and scratch-resistant. The 13 by 9-inch pan is the best all-around option, but the 17 by 11-inch model turns out super-sized casseroles, while the 8-inch- and 9-inch-square pans are good for smaller batches of cornbread or brownies.

What to Avoid:
- Aluminum pans, which can react with the acids in tomato-based recipes

★ TEST KITCHEN FAVORITE ★
PYREX Bakeware 13 by 9-Inch Baking Dish, $8.95

Go to www.cooksillustrated.com
- Key in code 3067 for **Mail-Order Sources for Recommended Bakeware.**
- This information is available until September 1, 2006.

CAKE PAN

Testing Notes: We're still searching for the ultimate cake pan: one with high, straight sides; a dark, nonstick finish; and handles, which most manufacturers consider unnecessary. Until then, both our test kitchen winner and "best buy" option (below) score two out of three. Nine-inch cake pans are the standard size, and you'll need two for most recipes. (If you want to bake in a square pan instead, drop down to the 8-inch size—the surface area is comparable to a 9-inch round pan.)

What to Avoid:
- Light-colored tinned or stainless steel pans, which brown and release poorly
- Sloped sides, which produce flared cakes that are impossible to split evenly

★ TEST KITCHEN FAVORITE ★
CHICAGO METALLIC Professional Nonstick, $14.95
➤ **BEST BUY:** The supermarket standard **BAKER'S SECRET** cake pan ($3.99) is a bit short and has sloped sides, but it browns and releases easily, has helpful handles, and boasts a winning price tag.

COOKIE SHEET

Testing Notes: When it comes to light- versus dark-colored metal bakeware, the cookie sheet is the exception. All of the dark-colored, nonstick cookie sheets we tested consistently overbrowned the bottoms of cookies. Light-colored sheets, on the other hand, were prone to sticking, but because we always bake cookies on parchment paper, we chose the (much) lesser of two evils.

What to Avoid:
- Dark finishes
- Lightweight sheets, which are prone to warping
- Sheets with only one handle (difficult to rotate during baking) or four sides (difficult to transfer cookie-loaded parchment paper from sheet to cooling rack)

★ TEST KITCHEN FAVORITE ★
VOLLRATH Cookie Sheet, $19.95

ILLUSTRATION: JOHN BURGOYNE

PIE PLATE

Testing Notes: Pie making is hard work—we understand why lots of cooks want to show off the finished product in a handsome, heavy piece of French ceramic pottery. (We're less certain why so many others trust their creations to flimsy EZ Foil disposable aluminum pans.) But neither option turns out evenly browned crusts as reliably as the trusty, inexpensive Pyrex. The Pyrex pie plate is scratch-resistant, its wide lip makes it easy to shape decorative fluted crusts, and its see-through glass is the best choice for monitoring a crust's browning progress.

What to Avoid:
- Ceramic pie plates
- Flimsy, disposable aluminum pie plates
- Opaque plates

★ **TEST KITCHEN FAVORITE** ★
PYREX (9-Inch) Pie Plate, $5.00

MUFFIN TIN

Testing Notes: Thanks to excellent heat absorption, dark-colored metal pans produce muffins and cupcakes that not only brown better but also rise higher and sport more nicely domed tops when compared with those baked in shiny, reflective tins. Choose a moderately priced muffin tin with reasonable heft (no more than 2 pounds).

What to Avoid:
- Flimsy pans that buckle when filled with heavy batter
- Heavy pans (some of our contenders weighed in at well over 2 pounds), which provide an unwelcome one-arm workout
- Silicone (see page 16)

★ **TEST KITCHEN FAVORITE** ★
WILTON Ultra-Bake, $9.99

LOAF PAN

Testing Notes: The refusal of much of the bakeware industry to embrace the good common sense of handles has always left us puzzled. Loaf pans are a good example. All of the dark, nonstick pans we tested browned nicely and released cleanly, so we gave the nod to those that are easy to carry as well. Though often referred to as "9 by 5-inch loaf pans," few meet those exact dimensions. We prefer pans with a width of just under 5 inches, which produce loaves with taller, rounder tops. Many recipes yield two loaves, so you might as well buy two pans.

What to Avoid:
- Pans without handles
- Light-colored pans, which deter browning

★ **TEST KITCHEN FAVORITE** ★
BAKER'S SECRET Non-Stick Loaf Pan
(8½ by 4½ inches), $3.99

FLUTED TART PAN

Testing Notes: We love these clever pans—the fluted edges and false bottom allow even a novice baker to turn out elegant-looking desserts with not much effort. But we can't condone splurging on pricey nonstick models when the generic tinned steel pans, sold in most stores for around $8, work just as well. (There's so much fat in buttery tart dough that it wouldn't stick to flypaper, much less a pan.) Our tart recipes are generally developed to fit a 9-inch pan, but 11-inch pans are also common.

What to Avoid:
- Nonremovable bottoms
- Expensive nonstick pans

★ **TEST KITCHEN FAVORITE** ★
Tinned Steel Fluted Tart Pan with
Removable Bottom, about $8

When Pyrex Explodes

Pyrex pie plates and baking dishes are standard issue in the test kitchen, but over the years we've learned that they are prone to shattering when exposed to sudden and extreme temperature changes. Naturally, this prohibits their use under a broiler or over direct stovetop heat, but the tempered glass bakeware is also vulnerable to sudden drops in temperature, known in the industry as downshock. Downshock would result from adding cold liquid to a hot Pyrex dish or from placing a hot dish directly on a cold or wet surface. It is considered safe, however, to transfer a Pyrex dish directly from the refrigerator or freezer to a hot oven, provided it has been properly preheated—some ovens use the broiler element to heat up to the desired temperature.

SHOCKING RESULTS
This pan went from hot to cold too quickly.

SPRINGFORM PAN

Testing Notes: The disappointing truth: All springform pans leak. This means that using them in a water bath can be problematic (we recommend double-wrapping the pan with aluminum foil to make it leakproof). We picked out the least leaky contenders, then chose the only model with helpful handles and a clear glass bottom to boot. Nine-inch pans are the standard size.

What to Avoid:
- Rimmed bottoms, which make it difficult to slide a spatula under the cake to remove it

★ **TEST KITCHEN FAVORITE** ★
FRIELING Handle-It (9-Inch) Glass Bottom
Springform, $31.95

KITCHEN WORKHORSE: Jellyroll Pan

In the test kitchen, we keep stacks of rimmed aluminum baking sheets (known as jellyroll pans—half-sheet pans, in restaurant lingo) and use them for a wide assortment of everyday tasks: roasting vegetables, catching drips in the oven, and, yes, baking the occasional jellyroll or sheet cake. Fitted with the right-sized wire cooling rack, this versatile pan can stand in for a roasting pan; it also makes an acceptable cookie sheet, though the rimmed design prevents a quick sliding of cookies to the cooling rack. Though similar pans are available in cookware shops in a variety of materials, sizes, and finishes, we purchase ours at a restaurant supply store in the industry standard size of 16 by 12 inches and recommend that you do the same. If you do buy retail, however, a good alternative is the WearEver Commercial Jellyroll Pan ($10.99).

Great Glazed Pork Chops

Thin boneless chops cook up dry and bland, but their convenience is enticing.
Could we turn them into a flavorful weeknight meal?

⇒ BY NINA WEST ⇐

We've grilled, seared, pan-roasted, and barbecued our way through plenty of pork in the test kitchen, and, through all this testing, we've developed some pretty solid opinions. Specifically, we like pork chops big, brined, and bone-in: The size makes them hard to overcook and good candidates for brining, which keeps them moist; cooking on the bone promotes meaty flavor.

That said, I wondered if we'd been too hasty in turning a blind eye to the thin boneless pork chop. After all, these chops are always available straight from the supermarket meat case (no attentive butcher required), they cook up quickly, and they're inexpensive. So what's the problem? A few hours of cooking reminded me. Most of the thin chops I cooked curled up unattractively in the pan as they surrendered their last ounce of moisture. The ones that remained juicy did so at the expense of good browning and, by extension, good flavor.

My goal was to find a way to take advantage of the convenience of thin boneless pork chops yet still have both a pronounced sear and a moist, juicy interior. Most important, I wanted the chops on the table in about 30 minutes. So out went brining, grilling, and pan-roasting; in went pan-searing, using only the stovetop. This would open up the opportunity to make a pan sauce, as I would likely end up with a nice *fond* (the brown bits left behind by the cooked meat on the surface of the skillet, which enhance the flavor of any sauce).

Searing Impaired?

Luckily, I had some experience to draw from. During our testing for Easy Pork Chops (March/April 2004), we found that to cook pork chops completely on the stovetop (without brining and without finishing in the oven), it's best to stick with chops ¾ inch thick or thinner. So far, so good. But the foolproof cooking method we developed—starting the chops in a cold pan and gently bringing them up to heat—wasn't so foolproof here. The difference? For that recipe,

To avoid overcooking such thin, lean chops, we quickly sear one side, then finish over lower heat, gently simmering them right in the glaze.

we used bone-in chops, which took on a lightly browned exterior just as the interior turned juicy and tender. The leaner boneless chops I was using cooked more quickly, and it was impossible to get adequate color within that time frame. What's more, back then we took pains to call for natural pork chops rather than enhanced chops (pork injected with a saline solution to keep it moist), which release excess juices during cooking and, thus, inhibit quick browning. I wanted my recipe to work well no matter what was available at the supermarket.

Consequently, I turned to our traditional searing method: high heat, smoking pan, even color on both sides of the meat. Unfortunately, the meat failed to stay flat and in direct contact with the pan. Instead, it curled up

and took on a spotty, light golden sear by the time it was cooked through. The first problem was easily solved when I slashed through the fat and the silver skin, which creates the bowing effect as it contracts. The second problem—lack of a dark, rich sear—was not so easy. I had thought I could get away with searing one side of the chop pretty heavily and putting a quick sear on the second side once the pan was nice and hot. The presentation side, after all, was what really counted. Although this method worked, the cooking time was critical: A few extra seconds were all the pan's high heat needed to take the chops from perfectly tender to dry and tough. Too close for comfort, but I was out of ideas. I decided to put the cooking method on hold for a bit while I experimented with the sauce.

Glazing Over

Exploring some options for pan sauces, I thought I would try a glaze. I whipped up a few simple ones, but they were too thick, sweet, and one-dimensional. While honey added a distinct depth of flavor, it tended to crystallize and become grainy. (See Kitchen Notes, page 30, for a detailed explanation of this phenomenon.) Instead, I settled on brown sugar. I tempered this sweet base with soy sauce, vinegar, Dijon mustard, and cayenne and then added

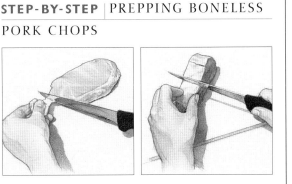

STEP-BY-STEP | PREPPING BONELESS PORK CHOPS

1. Trim excess fat off each chop with a sharp knife.

2. Cut two slits about 2 inches apart through fat and connective tissue.

Glazed and Confused

During testing, we learned as much from the flawed recipes as the ones that got things right. In the oven, the pork chops cooked through long before browning, and the glaze had no time to reduce properly (left). Another common problem was overpacking the glaze with sugar, yielding a sticky, gloppy mess (right).

PALE AND RUNNY

A STICKY MESS

apple cider for depth of flavor. Adding the juices from the resting pork was the final touch.

As good as this sweet and savory glaze tasted, the texture was inconsistent—at times too thick, at other times too thin. By adjusting the cooking time, I finally arrived at the point where the glaze both adhered well to the chops and was plentiful enough to spoon over them once they were plated.

Simmering Down

The recipe now called for searing the chops on the first side until well browned, turning them over, finishing on the other side, then removing them from the pan while I made the glaze. When I used thicker chops, however, I had to give them more time to sear on the "nonpresentation" side to get them up to the right temperature. A few times, I charred the pan and ruined the fond I needed for the glaze. Ah—the glaze! Perhaps if I added it to the pan earlier and turned down the heat, I could get a head start on its reduction, save time, *and* keep the fond from burning.

Not only did this trick work, but it gave me the insurance I'd been missing in my cooking method. Finishing the chops over moderate heat (rather than high heat) slowed things down just enough to give me a better chance of getting them out of the pan while they were still juicy. The precise cooking time became much less critical. What's more, unlike the high, relatively dry heat of sear-

ing, gently simmering the chops in the wet glaze over moderate heat seemed to help them retain their moisture, almost as though I were poaching them. Once the meat reached 140 degrees, a five-minute rest off the heat on a platter let the temperature rise a bit more and let the juices redistribute throughout the meat.

Finally, with a master recipe for glazed pork chops nailed down, I could develop a couple of interesting variations. Adding herbs, toasted seeds, beer, and various seasonings enhanced the baseline flavor in the glaze without disturbing its texture. Now I had three recipes for easy, foolproof pork that could make it from supermarket to weeknight dinner table in record time.

GLAZED PORK CHOPS
SERVES 4

If your chops are on the thinner side, check their internal temperature after the initial sear. If they are already at the 140-degree mark, remove them from the skillet and allow them to rest, tented with foil, for 5 minutes, then add the platter juices and glaze ingredients to the skillet and proceed with step 3. If your chops are closer to 1 inch thick, you may need to increase the simmering time in step 2.

Glaze
- ½ cup distilled white vinegar or cider vinegar
- ⅓ cup light brown sugar
- ⅓ cup apple cider or apple juice
- 2 tablespoons Dijon mustard
- 1 tablespoon soy sauce
- Pinch cayenne

Chops
- 4 boneless center-cut or loin pork chops, 5 to 7 ounces each, ½ to ¾ inch thick

- Table salt and ground black pepper
- 1 tablespoon vegetable oil

1. Combine all glaze ingredients in medium bowl; mix thoroughly and set aside. Following illustrations on page 18, trim chops and slash through fat and silver skin with sharp knife, making 2 cuts about 2 inches apart in each chop (do not cut into meat of chops). Pat chops dry with paper towels; season with salt and pepper.

2. Heat oil in heavy-bottomed 12-inch skillet over medium-high heat until smoking. Add pork to skillet and cook until well browned, 4 to 6 minutes. Turn chops and cook 1 minute longer; transfer chops to plate and pour off any oil in skillet. (Check internal temperature of thinner chops; see note above.) Return chops to skillet, browned side up, and add glaze mixture; cook until center of chops registers 140 degrees on instant-read thermometer, 5 to 8 minutes. Remove skillet from heat; transfer chops to clean platter, tent with foil, and let rest 5 minutes.

3. When chops have rested, add any accumulated juices to skillet and set over medium heat. Simmer, whisking constantly, until glaze is thick and color of dark caramel (heatproof spatula should leave wide trail when dragged through glaze), 2 to 6 minutes. Return chops to skillet; turn to coat both sides with glaze. Transfer chops back to platter, browned side up, and spread remaining glaze over chops. Serve immediately.

GLAZED PORK CHOPS WITH GERMAN FLAVORS

Toast ¾ teaspoon caraway seeds in small dry skillet over medium heat, stirring frequently, until fragrant, 3 to 5 minutes. Roughly chop seeds and set aside in small bowl. Follow recipe for Glazed Pork Chops, replacing cider or juice with ⅓ cup beer, reducing soy sauce to 2 teaspoons, and adding 3 tablespoons whole grain mustard (along with Dijon mustard), 1 tablespoon minced fresh thyme leaves, and reserved caraway seeds to glaze ingredients. Omit cayenne.

GLAZED PORK CHOPS WITH ASIAN FLAVORS

Toast 1 teaspoon sesame seeds in small dry skillet over medium heat, stirring frequently, until lightly browned and fragrant, 3 to 5 minutes; set aside in small bowl. Follow recipe for Glazed Pork Chops, replacing white or cider vinegar with ½ cup rice vinegar, omitting cider or juice, and adding 3 tablespoons each orange juice and mirin and 1 teaspoon finely grated fresh ginger to glaze ingredients. In step 3, stir another 2 teaspoons rice vinegar into glaze before returning chops to skillet. Before serving, garnish chops with reserved sesame seeds and 1 teaspoon toasted sesame oil.

Message in a Bubble

Getting the glaze right takes some finessing—a few extra seconds can mean the difference between luxurious texture and gooey mess. Our solution? Monitor the size of the bubbles, the color of the glaze, and the amount of exposed pan surface.

NOT YET
Pan surface has just a few small bubbles, and a spatula makes no trails.

JUST RIGHT
Increased bubbles, caramel color, and a spatula just starts to make trails.

TOO LONG
Many large bubbles, ultra-dark glaze, and plenty of exposed pan surface.

Better Pan-Roasted Broccoli

Pan-roasting works beautifully for many vegetables. So what's the problem with broccoli?

≥ BY SANDRA WU ≤

Pan-roasting broccoli is an intriguing idea, but that method (dry pan, high heat) often yields dried-out, shriveled florets and chewy stems—plenty of room for improvement.

The first step was to transform a head of broccoli into pieces that would cook evenly—trimming the florets into small pieces and the stalks into oblong coins. Next I assembled the pieces in an even layer in a hot, lightly oiled skillet. I had hoped the heat would promote caramelization and that the bit of oil would keep things from drying out, but it became clear that some moist heat (in other words, steam) was needed if the broccoli was to cook through without burning or drying out.

Once the pieces began to brown, I added water seasoned with salt and pepper, covered the skillet, and let the pieces steam. When the broccoli turned bright green, I removed the lid and let the excess moisture evaporate. Because the hardier stems take longer to cook than the delicate florets, I found that adding the pieces in a two-step process (browning the stems first, then tossing in the florets) prevented the florets from becoming limp.

After spending just 10 minutes at the stove, I had a flavorful broccoli dish with bright green florets and toasty-brown stems that were tasty enough to be eaten simply as is—but hearty enough to stand up to assertive flavorings.

PAN-ROASTED BROCCOLI

SERVES 4 AS A SIDE DISH

3 tablespoons water
1/4 teaspoon table salt
1/8 teaspoon ground black pepper
2 tablespoons vegetable oil
1 3/4 pounds broccoli, florets cut into 1 1/2-inch pieces, stems trimmed, peeled, and cut on bias into 1/4-inch-thick slices about 1 1/2 inches long (about 5 cups florets and 3/4 cup stems)

1. Stir water, salt, and pepper together in small bowl until salt dissolves; set aside. In 12-inch nonstick skillet with tight-fitting lid, heat oil over medium-high heat until just beginning to smoke. Add broccoli stems in even layer and cook, with-

out stirring, until browned on bottoms, about 2 minutes. Add florets to skillet and toss to combine; cook, without stirring, until bottoms of florets just begin to brown, 1 to 2 minutes longer.

2. Add water mixture and cover skillet; cook until broccoli is bright green but still crisp, about 2 minutes. Uncover and continue to cook until water has evaporated, broccoli stems are tender, and florets are tender-crisp, about 2 minutes more, and serve immediately.

PAN-ROASTED BROCCOLI WITH LEMON BROWNED BUTTER

1 recipe Pan-Roasted Broccoli
4 tablespoons unsalted butter
1 small shallot, minced (about 1 1/2 tablespoons)
2 medium garlic cloves, minced or pressed through garlic press (about 2 teaspoons)
1/4 teaspoon table salt
1/8 teaspoon ground black pepper
1 1/2 teaspoons juice from 1 lemon
1/2 teaspoon minced fresh thyme leaves

1. Follow recipe for Pan-Roasted Broccoli; transfer broccoli to medium bowl and set aside.

2. Melt butter in now-empty skillet over medium-high heat and continue to cook, swirling occasionally, until butter is browned and releases nutty aroma, about 1 1/2 minutes. Off heat, add shallot, garlic, salt, and pepper, and stir until garlic and shallot are fragrant, about 1 minute. Stir in lemon juice and thyme. Add broccoli to skillet, toss to coat with browned butter, and serve immediately.

PAN-ROASTED BROCCOLI WITH SPICY SOUTHEAST ASIAN FLAVORS

1 tablespoon creamy peanut butter
1 tablespoon hoisin sauce
2 teaspoons juice from 1 lime
2 medium garlic cloves, minced or pressed through garlic press (about 2 teaspoons)
1 teaspoon light or dark brown sugar
3/4 teaspoon Asian chili sauce
1 recipe Pan-Roasted Broccoli
1/4 cup coarsely chopped fresh basil leaves
2 tablespoons chopped roasted unsalted peanuts

One Vegetable, Two Different Worlds

TENDER FLORETS **HARDY STALKS**

The florets are cut into small pieces so that they cook quickly and evenly. The hardier stalks are sliced on the bias for maximum caramelization.

1. Stir together peanut butter, hoisin sauce, lime juice, garlic, brown sugar, and chili sauce in medium bowl until combined; set aside.

2. Follow recipe for Pan-Roasted Broccoli; during last minute of cooking, add basil and cook, stirring, until leaves wilt, about 30 seconds. Add peanut butter mixture and toss until broccoli is evenly coated and heated through, about 30 seconds. Transfer to serving dish, top with chopped peanuts, and serve immediately.

PAN-ROASTED BROCCOLI WITH CREAMY GRUYÈRE SAUCE

1 recipe Pan-Roasted Broccoli
1 tablespoon unsalted butter
1 medium shallot, peeled and sliced into thin rings (about 2 tablespoons)
1/2 cup heavy cream
1/2 teaspoon Dijon mustard
1/2 teaspoon dry sherry
Pinch cayenne
1/8 teaspoon table salt
3 tablespoons grated Gruyère cheese (about 3/4 ounce), plus additional 1 to 2 tablespoons
1 teaspoon juice from 1 lemon

1. Follow recipe for Pan-Roasted Broccoli; transfer broccoli to medium bowl and set aside.

2. Melt butter in now-empty skillet over medium heat. When foaming subsides, add shallot and cook, stirring frequently, until golden and softened, about 2 minutes. Stir in cream, mustard, sherry, cayenne, and salt. Increase heat to medium-high and cook until mixture bubbles and thickens, about 1 minute. Off heat, add cheese and lemon juice; stir until cheese is melted. Add broccoli and stir to reheat and coat. Transfer to serving dish, sprinkle with additional cheese, and serve immediately.

Old-Fashioned Chocolate Layer Cake

What ever happened to those towering slices of chocolate cake slathered with billowy frosting? We baked 130 cakes in search of the perfect wedge.

W hile almost everything has been super-sized in recent years, chocolate cakes have moved in the opposite direction, becoming denser, richer, and squatter. Many contemporary chocolate cakes are so intense that just a few forkfuls satisfy me. These cakes are delicious—a bad chocolate cake is hard to imagine—but sometimes I'd rather have a real piece of cake, not a confection.

When I think of the perfect chocolate cake, I remember childhood birthdays and the cakes my mother set before me once a year. They were tall, sweet, and chocolaty—the kind of cake you ate with a glass of milk, not a demitasse of espresso. Each towering slice had a tender, airy, open crumb and was frosted with silky-smooth wisps of chocolate heaven.

Like many mothers, mine started with a cake mix, but this style of old-fashioned chocolate cake has its roots in the American kitchen. While today's stylish cakes are dense and rich (and contain little or even no flour), the cake I had in mind would have a spongy but moist texture that offered a nice contrast with its thick coating of frosting.

Chocolate tends to weigh cakes down. To get the volume and texture we wanted, we borrowed a few tricks from old-time cookbooks.

Mixing It Up

I knew that the mixing method would be key to getting the right texture. Creaming—beating butter with sugar before whipping in the eggs and flour—is the most popular method for many home-baked cakes. The sugar crystals help whip air into the softened butter, which helps the cake rise in the oven. While this method is fine for yellow cake, the addition of so much melted unsweetened chocolate undoes the effects of creaming, and I found that the resulting cakes were fairly dense as well as a bit tough and dry. I tried various ways to lighten the load (more leavening, more eggs), but eventually I came to suspect that this method would never produce a fluffy, tender chocolate cake.

Next up on my list of mixing methods was "reverse creaming," which has come into vogue in recent years. Proponents tout reverse creaming as the best way to deliver maximum tenderness, and, in fact, this method has become the test kitchen's preferred way to prepare a yellow cake.

By mixing very soft butter with flour before adding any liquids, less gluten (the source of cake structure) can develop, yielding a tender and fluffy cake. When I tested reverse creaming with chocolate cake, the results were tender and fluffy, as promised, but the cake was too fragile to stand up to a billowy heap of frosting. I suspected that the additional moisture and fat provided by the chocolate were getting in the way.

How could I get volume, structure, and tenderness in the same cake? Stumped, I reconsidered a method I had previously dismissed—*ribboning*, a process of whipping eggs with sugar until they double in volume, then adding the butter, dry ingredients, and milk. The term refers to the ribbon-like strands that form (between the whisk and the batter) when the eggs and sugar are whipped. The technique is often the first step in making a French-style sponge cake, or génoise. Interestingly, many of the American cake recipes I had pulled from late-19th-century cookbooks relied on this technique. That's because chemical leaveners (baking soda and baking powder) were not yet widely used. The egg foam was responsible for aerating the cake. While I was planning on using a leavener for extra security, maybe this technique would deliver both the height and the structure I wanted.

I followed the basic génoise procedure of whipping eggs with sugar until light and fluffy, then adding the melted chocolate and butter, followed by the dry ingredients and milk. Finally, some success! The cake was a bit too dry and not quite chocolaty enough, but ribboning had yielded a better combination of structure and tenderness than any of the other methods I had tried. Clearly, achieving volume with eggs and sugar right at the beginning of mixing was key. And when I increased the liquid side of things by adding a full cup of buttermilk (which won out over regular milk), I had a fairly moist cake with good structure and spongy volume. Adding some cocoa powder to the flour mixture improved the chocolate flavor. Not perfect yet (the cake could still be more moist and chocolaty), but getting closer.

Proof in the Pudding

The solution to the moisture problem finally presented itself one evening as I combed yet

RECIPE TESTING: **Two Styles of Chocolate Cake**

THOROUGHLY MODERN
Modern chocolate cakes, like this one, are rich, dense, and squat and often covered with a truffle-like frosting.

UNABASHEDLY OLD-FASHIONED
Old-style chocolate layer cakes, like ours, stand much taller and are crowned by soft, billowy frosting.

MARCH & APRIL 2006

21

SECRETS TO OLD-FASHIONED CHOCOLATE LAYER CAKE

Some of the steps in our chocolate cake recipe may seem unconventional, but we think the moist, chocolaty results are worth bucking tradition.

Make Chocolate 'Pudding'
Mixing chocolate, cocoa, water, and sugar into a "pudding" in a double boiler boosts the chocolate flavor and adds moisture.

Ribbon Eggs and Sugar
Whipping eggs and sugar on high speed until they form "ribbons" (thin strands of batter) adds volume and fluffiness.

Tenderize with Butter
Adding soft butter to the batter makes for a tender cake.

Alternate Dry and Wet Ingredients
Adding the dry and wet ingredients in small batches helps to develop a more consistent crumb.

again through the stack of old chocolate cake recipes. Although some called for simply melting the unsweetened chocolate and mixing it into the batter, I came across a few references to chocolate "pudding" or "custard." This wasn't pudding or custard in the classic sense (chocolate, milk, eggs, sugar, cornstarch) but a simpler concoction of chocolate, water, and sugar. Probably taken up to keep the chocolate from burning, this technique was popular in the early 1900s. I found recipes using this technique in *The Settlement Cookbook* (1901)—one of the most important American cookbooks of its era—and in the first edition of the *Joy of Cooking* (1931). Although I could find few modern references to this method, I was reminded of the supermarket cake mixes used by my mother. They also had included powdered "pudding" for extra moisture. I'd always assumed this was just a gimmick, but maybe these cake-mix makers were on to something.

To test this theory, I made another cake using my working recipe, this time melting unsweetened chocolate and cocoa powder in hot water over a double boiler, then stirring in sugar until it dissolved. What came from the oven was the moistest chocolate cake yet, with a pronounced yet subtle chocolate flavor and a rich brown color. It was gloriously tall, and the crumb was open and spongy yet also tender and moist. Here was the cake I had been searching for!

Frosting Matters

I wanted a silky, voluminous frosting with good chocolate flavor to pair up with my tender, well-structured cake. I imagined the finished cake sitting on a cake stand on the counter of an old-time diner, barely fitting under its high glass dome. Frostings fall into three basic categories: meringue, buttercream, and ganache. Meringue and buttercream easily produce a frosting with great volume, but the emphasis is never really on the chocolate. I found that the beaten egg whites and sugar in a meringue frosting and the pound

of butter in most buttercreams overwhelmed the chocolate flavor. Ganache is all about chocolate—it can be as simple as heated cream poured over chopped sweetened chocolate—but its texture is usually quite dense. Could I make a ganache that was soft and billowy?

My first thought was to whip butter into the ganache once it had cooled. The frosting left a nice trail of peaks behind a spatula, but it wasn't as silky and glossy as I wanted—and it had a tendency to break into a clumpy mess. As the frosting set, it became too hard, forming a helmet-like

shell around my cake. Adding some corn syrup and sugar made the frosting more pliable and shiny, but the emulsion was still breaking. After a week of experimenting with various temperatures, times, and ingredients, the solution turned out to be a simple reversal of the conventional ganache procedure: I poured cold (rather than heated) cream into warm melted (rather than room-temperature) chocolate, waited until the mixture reached room temperature, then whipped it until fluffy. Success! My chocolate frosting was now creamy, billowy, and—most important—stable.

SCIENCE: The 'Pudding' Makes It Perfect

Unsweetened chocolate contains cocoa solids and cocoa butter, while cocoa powder contains mostly solids. We found that a combination of melted unsweetened chocolate and cocoa powder produced a cake with the best chocolate flavor. But the way we combined them proved key to our recipe's success.

Some recipes add the cocoa powder with the flour and other dry ingredients, but we found that this produced a cake with fairly weak chocolate flavor. After much trial and error, we discovered that cooking a mixture of melted unsweetened chocolate, cocoa powder, hot water, and sugar—what many older cookbooks call a chocolate "pudding"—improved the cake's flavor considerably.

At least one aspect of this phenomenon we had seen before. While developing other chocolate dessert recipes, we've found that adding hot water to cocoa solids before incorporating them into the recipe causes a "blooming" effect, enhancing the chocolate flavor in the final dish. Here, too, when the unsweetened chocolate and cocoa powder were combined with hot water, they formed an emulsion—tiny droplets of cocoa solids and cocoa butter dispersed in water. The result? A noticeably more chocolaty cake.

When we took the additional step of adding $1/2$ cup of sugar to the mix, however, the flavor enhancement was even more dramatic. What was going on? Research revealed that sugar's strong affinity for water was key. As soon as we dissolved the sugar in the pudding mixture, the sugar molecules bonded tightly with the water molecules, leaving the flavorful cocoa solids free to dissolve in the cocoa butter (the fat)—a better medium than water for conveying chocolate flavor. (Chocolate flavor molecules are more soluble in fat than in water.) Skip the pudding step and you'll have a cake that's diminished in chocolate flavor. –D.P.

ADD WATER
Blooming chocolate and cocoa powder in hot water gave us a cake with decent chocolate flavor.

STIR IN SUGAR
Adding sugar to the mix created a chocolate "pudding," resulting in even greater chocolate flavor.

My cake was all that I had imagined. The moist, tender, and airy cake layers were perfectly balanced by the light yet creamy frosting. While this cake can't really turn a grown man into an 8-year-old kid again, it might come close.

OLD-FASHIONED CHOCOLATE LAYER CAKE
SERVES 10 TO 12

For best results, don't make the frosting until the cakes are cooled, and use the frosting as soon as it is ready. If the frosting gets too cold and stiff to spread easily, wrap the mixer bowl with a towel soaked in hot water and mix on low speed until the frosting appears creamy and smooth. Refrigerated leftover cake should sit at room temperature before serving until the frosting softens.

Cake
12	tablespoons (1½ sticks) unsalted butter, very soft, plus extra for greasing pans
1¾	cups (8¾ ounces) unbleached all-purpose flour, plus extra for dusting pans
4	ounces unsweetened chocolate, coarsely chopped
¼	cup (¾ ounce) Dutch-processed cocoa powder
½	cup hot water
1¾	cups (12¼ ounces) sugar
1½	teaspoons baking soda
1	teaspoon table salt
1	cup buttermilk
2	teaspoons vanilla extract
4	large eggs, plus 2 large egg yolks

Frosting
16	ounces semisweet chocolate, finely chopped
8	tablespoons (1 stick) unsalted butter
⅓	cup sugar
2	tablespoons corn syrup
2	teaspoons vanilla extract
¼	teaspoon table salt
1¼	cups cold heavy cream

1. **FOR THE CAKE:** Adjust oven rack to middle position; heat oven to 350 degrees. Grease two 9-inch-round by 2-inch-high cake pans with softened butter; dust pans with flour and knock out excess.

Combine chocolate, cocoa powder, and hot water in medium heatproof bowl; set bowl over saucepan containing 1 inch of simmering water and stir with rubber spatula until chocolate is melted, about 2 minutes. Add ½ cup sugar to chocolate mixture and stir until thick and glossy, 1 to 2 minutes. Remove bowl from heat and set aside to cool.

2. Whisk flour, baking soda, and salt in medium bowl. Combine buttermilk and vanilla in small bowl. In bowl of standing mixer fitted with whisk attachment, whisk eggs and yolks on medium-low speed until combined, about 10 seconds. Add remaining 1¼ cups sugar, increase speed to high, and whisk until fluffy and lightened in color, 2 to 3 minutes. Replace whisk with paddle attachment. Add cooled chocolate mixture to egg/sugar mixture and mix on medium speed until thoroughly incorporated, 30 to 45 seconds, pausing to scrape down sides of bowl with rubber spatula as needed. Add softened butter one tablespoon at a time, mixing about 10 seconds after each addition. Add about one-third of flour mixture followed by half of buttermilk mixture, mixing until incorporated after each addition (about 15 seconds). Repeat using half of remaining flour mixture and all of remaining buttermilk mixture (batter may appear separated). Scrape down sides of bowl and add remaining flour mixture; mix at medium-low speed until batter is thoroughly combined, about 15 seconds. Remove bowl from mixer and fold batter once or twice with rubber spatula to incorporate any remaining flour. Divide batter evenly between prepared cake pans; smooth batter to edges of pan with spatula.

3. Bake cakes until toothpick inserted into center comes out with a few crumbs attached, 25 to 30 minutes. Cool cakes in pans 15 minutes, then invert onto wire rack. Cool cakes to room temperature before frosting, 45 to 60 minutes.

4. **TO MAKE FROSTING:** Melt chocolate in heatproof bowl set over saucepan containing 1 inch of barely simmering water, stirring occasionally until smooth. Remove from heat and set aside. Meanwhile, heat butter in small saucepan over medium-low heat until melted. Increase heat to medium; add sugar, corn syrup, vanilla, and salt and stir with heatproof rubber spatula until sugar

is dissolved, 4 to 5 minutes. Add melted chocolate, butter mixture, and cream to clean bowl of standing mixer and stir to thoroughly combine.

5. Place mixer bowl over ice bath and stir mixture constantly with rubber spatula until frosting is thick and just beginning to harden against sides of bowl, 1 to 2 minutes (frosting should be 70 degrees). Place bowl on standing mixer fitted with paddle attachment and beat on medium-high speed until frosting is light and fluffy, 1 to 2 minutes. Stir with rubber spatula until completely smooth.

6. **TO FROST CAKE:** Place one cake layer on serving platter or cardboard round. Spread 1½ cups frosting evenly across top of cake with spatula. Place second cake layer on top, then spread remaining frosting evenly over top and sides of cake. Cut into slices and serve.

EQUIPMENT TESTING:
Revolving Cake Stands

Frosting a layer cake is no easy task. Aside from a deft hand, the pros use a turntable-style cake stand. These stands elevate the cake, giving the baker a better view and making it possible to hold the spatula steady while rotating the stand—improving the likelihood of seamless frosting. We tested five models, listed below in order of preference. The ultimate stand (made by Ateco) consists of a metal table over an enameled cast-iron base. It costs $62.99—too much for the occasional birthday cake. A plastic version of the same stand is $43 cheaper and makes cake decorating just as easy. –Garth Clingingsmith

THE ULTIMATE
➤ ATECO Professional Icing Turntable ($62.99)
This metal stand is the best choice for pros.

BEST BUY
➤ ATECO Revolving Cake Stand ($19.95)
Plastic—but it does the job at a reasonable price.

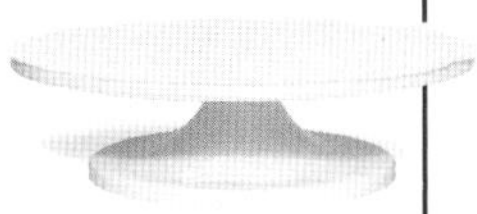

FLIMSY
➤ WILTON Revolving Cake Stand ($11.99)
Similar to our best buy but not as sturdy.

GIMMICKY
➤ WILTON Tilting Cake Turntable ($59.99)
Fine, but the tilting feature is silly—and it's pricey.

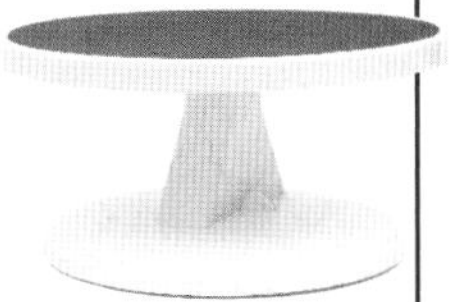

TOO SHORT
➤ WILTON Trim 'N Turn Cake Stand ($7.99)
This nearly flat stand is totally impractical.

Thermometer Watch: Getting the Frosting Just Right

The frostings below were made with exactly the same ingredients. The only difference was how soon the mixture was removed from the ice bath and whipped. Here are the resulting frostings when whipped at three different temperatures.

STILL TOO WARM
At 75 degrees, the frosting won't set up properly once whipped.

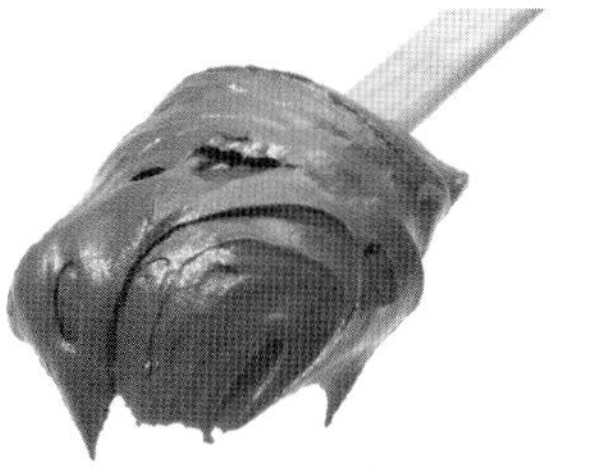

JUST RIGHT
At 70 degrees, the frosting whips up to a billowy, creamy consistency.

TOO COOL
At 65 degrees, the mixture has cooled too much and seizes once whipped.

Easy Multigrain Sandwich Bread

Some multigrain bread is better suited to propping open a door than making a sandwich.
We wanted a light but flavorful loaf—and we didn't want to spend all day making it.

⇒ BY ERIKA BRUCE ⇐

When it comes to multigrain bread, there are two distinct styles: the rustic free-form loaf found in artisan bakeries and your basic sandwich loaf. While the hearty, rustic loaves sport a thick, crunchy crust and a flavorful, chewy interior, re-creating this version at home requires lots of time (for an overnight sponge) and special equipment (a super-hot oven, a baking stone, and so on).

Sandwich-style multigrain bread, on the other hand, requires only a loaf pan and a modest amount of effort. The problem is that the hearty, multigrain flavor is usually sacrificed for the light, tender texture that is well suited to sandwiches, and you end up with all fluff and no substance. Even the small amount of effort necessary to make this loaf should yield something tastier than presliced supermarket bread.

After digging through cookbooks geared more toward the bread hobbyist than the casual cook, I found a few recipes that held promise. Lengthy ingredient lists, which included obscure grains, called for an excursion to the natural foods store, but the techniques were straightforward enough. Unfortunately, these doughs—full of heavy grains and whole grain flours—baked into poorly risen loaves, dense and heavy as bricks. I wanted a lighter loaf, tender enough for a sandwich yet with the sweet, nutty, complex flavor of bakery bread.

Loaves' Labors Lost

We wanted a multigrain bread with great flavor and a light, fluffy texture. Few of the recipes we found came through on both counts. Here are two of the offenders.

LIKE A BRICK
Great flavor, but a laundry list of ingredients weighs the loaf down into a dense, brick-like solid.

LIKE WHITE BREAD
Fluffy sandwich-style texture, but so little grain it's almost like plain old white bread.

Some multigrain loaves are fluffy but flavorless, while others are delicious but dense. We wanted the best of both worlds.

Gluten for Punishment

Using instant yeast for a quick rise, I started with our basic whole wheat sandwich bread recipe, calling for 6 cups of flour (roughly half whole wheat and half all-purpose), 2½ cups of water, ¼ cup of honey, and a tablespoon of salt. I replaced some of the flour with a generous cup of mixed grains (I'd work out the precise components later). The result was one dense and heavy loaf. It was obvious that the added grains were the problem. I knew that the sharp flakes of bran in whole wheat flour can actually slice through and weaken the matrix of gluten—a protein made when flour and water are mixed—that gives all breads their strength and structure. Apparently, the rough-edged grains were having the same effect. That plus their added weight were impeding the development of gluten. To get the light texture I was after, the bread needed more gluten.

Because the protein content of any flour is an indicator of how much gluten it will produce,

I thought first to switch out all-purpose flour (protein content of 10 to 12 percent) for bread flour (12 percent or more). But this only made the bread chewier, not less dense. Next I tried reducing the whole wheat flour to half of the amount of all-purpose; any less meant sacrificing flavor. (While whole wheat flour has a high protein content—about 14 percent—its density, like its bran flakes, can impede gluten development.) This step did alleviate some of the denseness, but the bread still felt heavy and dry. I added melted butter, which lubricated and tenderized the dough, but it didn't create more lift. I went so far as to add vital wheat gluten (made by stripping away most components of flour, leaving behind a whopping 75 to 80 percent pure protein). At last, I sliced into a well-risen loaf with a light, feathery crumb, but the wheat gluten left behind a bitter aftertaste. Frustrated, I moved on to kneading in hopes of finding a solution.

Working It Out

While the purist mode of some multigrain recipes requires kneading the dough by hand, I wanted to avoid a full workout. I pulled out my trusty standing mixer and mixed the dough on medium-high speed in an effort to kick-start the gluten development (gluten, once hydrated, is stretched and strengthened via mechanical action). But the texture was crumbly. I tried lowering the mixer speed and experimenting with timing: After three minutes of mixing, the bread hardly rose in the pans; after five minutes, the loaves had better height. I kept mixing until the dough became very elastic and bounced back when I poked it, a total of about 10 minutes. This dough rose well and sported a medium-holed, albeit still crumbly, texture.

Next, I ran through the gamut of traditional bread-mixing techniques to see if any proved helpful. Some recipes call for punching down the dough after the first rise, a step that redistributes the sugars (broken-down starches) that feed the yeast and get it working more rapidly. But speeding up the yeast action served only to give the bread a boozy flavor (alcohol is a byproduct of yeast metabolism). I then decided to try an autolyse, a

Scavenging for different grains (left) can be an invigorating challenge, but it also eats up precious time. We prefer the ease of one-stop shopping: One bag of hot cereal mix (right) has seven grains.

resting period just after the initial mixing of water and flour that gives the flour time to hydrate. This step proved vital, ramping up the development of gluten (which depends on water) and making the dough less tacky and so easier to work with and the baked loaf less crumbly. The bread now had a nice chew, without being tough.

Against the Grain

I was ready to tackle the grains. Driving all over town collecting one obscure grain here and another there was an onerous task. Could I pare down the list without losing the multidimensional flavor profile? I started with basic grains that were available at the supermarket: cornmeal, rolled oats, and rye flour. But this abridged grain mixture produced a loaf that was more of a muddy-tasting rye than a sweet, earthy multigrain bread. I returned to the supermarket in search of other options. As I scanned the shelves of steel-cut oats and Cream of Wheat in the hot cereal section, my eyes fell upon a package of 7-grain cereal, a handy mixture of ground whole grains, including the hard-to-find varieties. I quickly snatched up a package and headed back to the kitchen to see if it could deliver flavor as well as convenience.

Sure enough, the complexity was there—from the nutty flax seed to the tangy rye and sweet

wheat—but some of the grains remained distractingly hard and crunchy, even after baking. I tried soaking them for up to 24 hours before mixing them into the dough, but they seemed impervious to room-temperature water. Because these grains were meant to make a hot cereal, I tried cooking them per the package instructions, allowing the mixture to cool before adding my yeast, flours, and salt. But this dough was soupy and wet, requiring a startling 2 cups of additional flour before it became manageable.

Not discouraged, I tried using only the amount of water already called for in my bread recipe, bringing it to a boil, and pouring it over the grains. Once cooled, this thick porridge produced a dough with the right moisture content and a baked loaf with grains that added interesting textural contrast without cracking any teeth.

Now the only thing missing from my bread was the welcome (gentle) crunch of seeds. I tried poppy and sesame, but they were too small and got lost in the mix of grains. Sunflower and pumpkin seeds were better able to distinguish themselves from the crowd and added a nutty richness as well. Last, I rolled the shaped loaves in oats to give them a finished, professional look. While my tasters had undoubtedly suffered through plenty of barely edible loaves, in the end they could hardly believe that the ones they were eating hadn't been smuggled in from the bakery down the street. Not bad for just a few hours in the kitchen.

MULTIGRAIN BREAD
MAKES TWO 9 BY 5-INCH LOAVES

Don't confuse 7-grain hot cereal mix with boxed, cold breakfast cereals that may also be labeled "7-grain." Our favorite brands of 7-grain mix are

Bob's Red Mill and Arrowhead Mills. Leftover bread can be wrapped in a double layer of plastic wrap and stored at room temperature for 3 days; wrap with an additional layer of aluminum foil and the bread can be frozen for up to one month.

6¼	ounces (1¼ cups) 7-grain hot cereal mix (see note above)
20	ounces (2½ cups) boiling water
15	ounces (3 cups) unbleached all-purpose flour, plus extra for dusting work surface
7½	ounces (1½ cups) whole wheat flour
4	tablespoons honey
4	tablespoons unsalted butter, melted and cooled slightly
2½	teaspoons instant yeast
1	tablespoon table salt
¾	cup unsalted pumpkin or sunflower seeds
½	cup old-fashioned rolled oats or quick oats

1. Place cereal mix in bowl of standing mixer and pour boiling water over it; let stand, stirring occasionally, until mixture cools to 100 degrees and resembles thick porridge, about 1 hour. Whisk flours in medium bowl.

2. Once grain mixture has cooled, add honey, melted butter, and yeast and stir to combine. Attach bowl to standing mixer fitted with dough hook. With mixer running on low speed, add flours, ½ cup at a time, and knead until dough forms ball, 1½ to 2 minutes; cover bowl with plastic and let dough rest 20 minutes. Add salt and knead on medium-low speed until dough clears sides of bowl, 3 to 4 minutes (if it does not clear sides, add 2 to 3 tablespoons additional all-purpose flour and continue mixing); continue to knead dough for 5 more minutes. Add seeds and knead for another 15 seconds. Transfer dough to floured work surface and knead by hand until seeds are dispersed evenly and dough forms smooth, taut ball. Place dough into greased container with 4-quart capacity; cover with plastic wrap and allow to rise until doubled, 45 to 60 minutes.

3. Adjust oven rack to middle position; heat oven to 375 degrees. Spray two 9 by 5-inch loaf pans with nonstick cooking spray. Transfer dough to lightly floured work surface and pat into 12 by 9-inch rectangle; cut dough in half crosswise with knife or bench scraper. Follow illustrations 1 through 3 at left to shape loaves and coat with oats; cover lightly with plastic wrap and let rise until almost doubled in size, 30 to 40 minutes. (Dough should barely spring back when poked with knuckle.) Bake until internal temperature registers 200 degrees on instant-read thermometer, 35 to 40 minutes. Remove loaves from pans and cool on wire rack before slicing, about 3 hours.

STEP-BY-STEP | GETTING THE LOAF INTO SHAPE

1. With short side facing you, starting at farthest end, roll dough piece into log. Keep roll taut by tucking it under itself as you go.

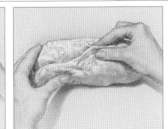

2. To seal loaf, pinch seam gently with thumb and forefinger. Spray loaves lightly with water or nonstick cooking spray.

3. Roll each dough log in oats to coat evenly. Place loaf seam-side down in greased loaf pan, pressing gently into corners.

Go to www.cooksillustrated.com
- Key in code 3068 for the results of our **Loaf Pan Tests**.
- This information is available until September 1, 2006.

COOK'S extra

ILLUSTRATION: YEVGENIY SOLOVYEV

Beefing Up Beef Broth

Several years ago, we all but banished beef broth from the test kitchen's pantry.
Is it time to lift the embargo?

⇒ BY THE COOK'S ILLUSTRATED TEST KITCHEN ⇐

Beef broth occupies a unique place in the history of *Cook's* tastings, and it's hardly a happy one. When we surveyed the field in 1998, tasters found every brand so dreadful that we all but banished supermarket beef broth from the test kitchen. Browse the magazine's archives, in fact, and you'll turn up only a handful of recipes that call for the stuff—and even then it's tempered with chicken broth in equal amounts (or more).

Was it really that bad? In a word, yes. The problem boiled down to an appalling lack of beef flavor. Lots of salt, plenty of vegetal flavors, a few metallic off-notes—but hardly anything that said beef beyond the brownish hue. When we learned that the U.S. Department of Agriculture requires only 1 part beef to every 135 parts water, we weren't surprised that most products came up short. (That translates to less than an ounce of beef for each gallon of water.) While commercial chicken broth, similarly, gets by on a paltry amount of poultry, chicken's less saturated fat goes much further when it comes to flavor than the same amount of beef. In fact, when we make homemade broth in the test kitchen, we use twice as much beef as chicken to flavor the same amount of liquid.

Since our original tasting of beef broths, an impressive collection of new products has hit the supermarket shelves, so we decided to take another taste. We were especially intrigued by the increased availability of beef "bases," stock concentrates (just add water) that were once used almost exclusively by restaurants. Could any of these make us reconsider our boycott of beef broth?

Where's the Beef?

Tasters sipped 13 beef broths—seven liquid broths and six made from concentrated bases—simply heated and served straight up. The top eight brands moved on to a full battery of tastings: plain (again), regular strength in a simple beef soup, and reduced in an all-purpose gravy.

The good news first: Some of these broths didn't taste half-bad! While they were still a far cry from the rich, heady flavors of a homemade broth, it was clear that commercial brews had come a far piece from the gustatory disaster of '98. In fact, Superior Touch, technically 1998's "winner," just barely squeaked past this year's elimination round, finishing in second-to-last place. (Most of the other repeats were eliminated early on.)

Even better, a few broths actually *tasted* like beef. Hints of mushroom, onion, other vegetables, and even chicken were still more common, but two brands—Redi-Base and Pacific—elicited consistent praise for assertive beefiness. In the end, those two broths came in first and second place (see the chart on page 27).

Interestingly, a distinctly beefy flavor profile was more important to tasters in the gravy tests than when the broths were tasted straight up. For instance, Knorr was the favorite in the soup tasting, just edging out Redi-Base and Pacific with its complex, "roasty" (though not necessarily beefy) flavor profile. But once reduced into a gravy, that "interesting complexity" became magnified in an unpleasant way, as tasters complained of strong, out-of-place notes that ranged from potato, mushroom, and soy to chocolate and corn nuts. This time around, Knorr plummeted in the ratings, while the beefier brands carried the day.

Taking Stock

So what makes a better beef broth? Our hopes of finding a clear pattern based on product type (that is, liquid broths versus concentrated bases) were quickly dashed after the final results were tallied. Although Redi-Base, our top finisher overall, was indeed a beef base, three bases ended up in the lower ranks, and two others failed even to make it past the elimination round. Likewise, the liquid broth contenders evidenced no discernible pattern.

What about the presence of beef itself? Foiled again. Virtually every product in the lineup included some form of beef near the top of the ingredients list, and every manufacturer we contacted was unwilling to provide additional details. To get around this roadblock, we sent samples to an independent lab to be analyzed for protein content—but to no avail. (The highest-protein brand came in last place overall, while the next-highest came in second.)

Frustrated, we canvassed industry experts to shed light on the beefy/not-so-beefy divide. The consensus was that it would be cost-prohibitive for broth makers to stray beyond the USDA's minimum beef-to-water ratio. Given that meager amount, manufacturers must rely on the magic of flavor chemistry to avoid a completely tasteless brew. Well, that explained the blandness of the one beef broth that opted for the all-natural route: It was eliminated by tasters in the preliminary round. The rest of the broths were chock-full of additives.

In our lineup, every broth contained a generous amount of the most common additive—salt. Most contained some form of sugar (including plain sugar, corn syrup solids, and maltodextrin). So far, so familiar. It was when we looked more closely at the less familiar ingredients that we stumbled upon our most important clues—namely, hydrolyzed vegetable protein and autolyzed yeast extract. Many sources we consulted lumped these additives together simply as "flavor enhancers," but more diligent digging revealed that they work quite differently.

Hydrolyzed vegetable protein (made by altering soybean, corn, or other vegetable molecules through a chemical reaction, hydrolysis) merely adds flavor complexity, sort of like adding spices or salt. By contrast, autolyzed yeast extract (made by allowing yeast enzymes to feed on carefully chosen sugars and proteins until they release flavor-enhancing compounds) works like MSG (monosodium glutamate). Rather than contribute additional flavors, yeast extract amplifies flavors already present, especially savory and meaty ones. "The molecules contained in yeast extract are true flavor potentiators," explained our food science consultant. "They literally boost the flavor of beef by as much as 20-fold. There is so little real beef protein and fat in commercial broth that [the product] wouldn't have much flavor without them." Put another way: By including yeast extract in the mix, that USDA recipe of just 1 part beef to 135 parts water could taste like 20 parts beef instead.

Where's the Yeast?

Suddenly, the pieces were falling into place. As we scanned the ingredients lists of our beef broths, we spotted a definite pattern. While many of the products contained yeast extract, they differed markedly in where it fell in the mix. (By law, ingredients must be listed in descending order by weight.) In our top four brands, yeast extract was placed second or third (just after beef or salt). Moving down the ranks, the placement of yeast extract began to fall dramatically—fifth,

TASTING SUPERMARKET BEEF BROTHS

Twenty-four test kitchen staffers tasted eight brands of beef broth and reconstituted beef broth made from concentrated bases plain, in a simple beef soup (in both cases with the sodium levels adjusted to parity), and cooked in a simple gravy reduction (with sodium levels left as is). Tasters rated each sample for beefy flavor, body, complexity, and overall likeability. Brands are listed below in order of preference. Sodium levels given are per 1-cup serving, based on package information.

In a preliminary round, tasters eliminated More Than Gourmet Glace de Viand Gold (base), Aromont Demi-Glace Beef Stock (base), Bear Creek Beef Base (base), Campbell's Beef Consommé (liquid), and Health Valley Organic Beef Flavored Broth (liquid) from our final lineup. In general, tasters downgraded these brands for unpleasant aromas and bland, sour, winey, and plasticky flavors.

RECOMMENDED

REDI-BASE Beef Base
- $5.95/8 ounces (makes 2$\frac{1}{2}$ gallons)
- Sodium: 690 mg

Tasters agreed on the presence of a "deep, dark, and hearty" character in the soup. Though many found the gravy salty, they also picked up a distinct beefiness, roasted flavor, and notes of onion and mushroom.

PACIFIC Beef Broth
- $2.69/32 fluid ounces
- Sodium: 570 mg

In both the soup and the gravy, tasters found "toasty" or roasted notes, though the gravy was considered mild and in need of extra salt. But this was one of the rare products that tasted truly beefy.

RECOMMENDED WITH RESERVATIONS

KNORR Beef Flavored Broth
- $4.99/30.4 fluid ounces
- Sodium: 860 mg

Scored higher marks as a soup—which tasters found sweet, "like caramelized onions," balanced with a slight acidity and a strong "vegetal" presence—than as a gravy, which one taster pronounced to be "wicked vegetal." In the gravy, tasters found, in addition to sweetness, notes of everything from "Chex Mix" to "BBQ potato chips."

SWANSON Lower Sodium Beef Broth
- $1.19/14 fluid ounces
- Sodium: 440 mg

"Cardboard comes to mind," declared one taster, who then joined the nearly unanimous cry to "please pass the salt." Even the salt-corrected soup struck numerous tasters as "nondescript" and "dull, dull, dull." At least there were no off-flavors.

NOT RECOMMENDED

SAVORY BASICS Beef Flavor Stock Concentrate
- $5.95/6 ounces (makes 1 gallon)
- Sodium: 570 mg

From "pallid" to "plain Jane," both the gravy and the soup were overwhelmingly decried as too light in color and too mild in flavor. While one detractor groaned "not worthy of the name gravy," many likened the flavor to that of chicken broth.

ORRINGTON Farms Gourmet Beef Soup Base and Food Seasoning
- $4.17/8 ounces (makes 2.8 gallons)
- Sodium: 570 mg

Detecting dried herbs and mushrooms, several tasters remarked that the bland gravy belonged on a TV dinner or grade-school hot lunch tray. "Archetypal cafeteria gravy," said one panelist. Others complained of metallic and "musty, stale" aftertastes.

SUPERIOR TOUCH Better Than Bouillon Beef Base
- $4.99/8 ounces (makes 2.4 gallons)
- Sodium: 730 mg

Our 1998 "winner" suffered in the rankings this time around, thanks to stiff competition from the beefier newbies. In the gravy, tasters picked up on mushrooms, soy, and salt. In the soup, most tasters couldn't get past vegetal, artificial, and other off-flavors.

COLLEGE INN Fat Free & Lower Sodium Beef Broth
- $0.99/14.5 fluid ounces
- Sodium: 450 mg

This gravy was characterized as bland and "thin" by most tasters, several of whom also picked up distinct artificial flavor notes. Referring to plasticky and metallic aftertastes, one panelist griped that it "tastes like the can it came in."

---

then 15th, then 10th, then 14th—and some of the brands eliminated in the first round lacked yeast extract altogether. What's more, our top five brands included no hydrolyzed vegetable protein (which the experts said can produce "metallic" off-tastes, a flaw we've often encountered in commercial beef broth). The rest of the brands included multiple forms of hydrolyzed vegetable protein—and a few of them were faulted for (you guessed it) metallic off-notes.

If yeast extract offers such a clear advantage in terms of flavor, why wouldn't all beef-broth manufacturers opt to include it in the mix? Quite simply: cost. Yeast extracts are far more expensive than hydrolyzed vegetable proteins, in large part because the technology is so much newer. According to industry literature, only in the last decade have food chemists begun to perfect yeast-extract science, and now yeast extract shows up on the ingredients lists of foods as varied as potato chips, salad dressing, processed sandwich meat, and chicken broth. Although

it's only speculation, this may be the reason that beef-broth products taste better than they did in 1998.

So which broth to stock? Based on our tests, just note the first few ingredients listed on the label. We found the winning combination to be beef plus a flavor amplifier—in the form of yeast extract—near the top of the list. In our lineup, Redi-Base Beef Base and Pacific Beef Broth conformed to these rules and, more important, tasted best to our panel.

The Little Nonstick Saucepan That Could

You can spend $100 on a 2-quart nonstick saucepan—but should you?

≥ BY ADAM RIED ≤

At home, my small saucepan sees plenty of action—making rice, heating milk, melting butter, or warming up a little soup. It may be the smallest pan in my kitchen arsenal—and the tasks may be basic—but it's by no means the least important. Because most of these tasks don't involve browning (and many involve sticky foods), in the test kitchen we use nonstick 2-quart saucepans almost exclusively. Do pans that cost close to $100 offer significant performance, stick-resistance, or design advantages over models costing a quarter as much? I decamped to the test kitchen with nine 2-quart nonstick saucepans to find out.

Test and Tell

I designed my initial tests around the smaller, less complicated jobs for which these small saucepans are suited best, including steaming rice, scalding cream, and making pastry cream (using a nonstick-friendly nylon or silicone whisk). The pastry cream test illustrated several design differences that separated those pans I'd reach for every day from those that would remain parked eternally in the cabinet. Pouring hot cream from a saucepan is much neater if the pan from which you're pouring has either a spout, like the pans from Look, Bialetti, and Revere, or a rolled lip, like the Cuisinart and Bialetti. An ample diameter and sloped sidewalls make it easier to carry out the constant whisking necessary to prevent pastry cream from scorching. Diameters (measured across the top) ranged from just shy of 7 inches for the Anolon to nearly 9½ inches for the Calphalon.

In the process of making pastry cream or rice, a pan can spend 30 minutes (or more) on the burner, so there's a clear advantage to handles that remain cool to the touch. All but three of the pans had hard thermal plastic or Santoprene (soft plastic) handles, which passed this test with no problem. Even the metal handles, which heated up alarmingly at the point of attachment, maintained a sufficiently comfortable temperature at the far end. While steaming rice, I also developed a preference for transparent lids, which make it easier to monitor cooking progress.

There are two common ways to attach a handle to a saucepan—with rivets or screws—but (to my mind) only one that works effectively. Simply put: Rivets are sturdier than screws.

The means by which the handle is attached to the pan constitutes a pet peeve for me. Rivets are a much more solid means of attachment than screws. The Calphalon, Cuisinart, Anolon, and Circulon handles were riveted securely in place, while the Revere handle appeared to be soldered. To my displeasure, the handles on all of the other pans in our group, including the pricey $95 Swiss Diamond, $85 Look, and $70 Berndes, were screwed into place, a fact that I find hard to tolerate on an expensive piece of cookware. Worse yet, the Look's handle was loose from the get-go.

Slow-and-Steady Wins the Race

To get at performance issues such as the evenness and speed of heat distribution, I sautéed chopped onions and cooked eggs in each pan. Weight, rather than materials (which were similar in all pans tested), was the deciding factor. The onions were lightly and evenly colored in the two heaviest pans, the Calphalon and the Look, each of which weighs close to 2½ pounds. In contrast, onions darkened faster in some of the lighter pans, including the Bialetti, Circulon, and Cuisinart, which all weigh 1¾ pounds or less. In the past, we have often downgraded heavy skillets for being too slow and unwieldy, but a heavy saucepan is actually a good thing. Even the heftiest pan in our lineup was easy to maneuver, and many saucepan tasks involve prolonged cooking over low heat, where gentleness, not speed, is paramount.

Fresh from the box, all of the pans exhibited excellent stick resistance. In fact, it wasn't until I subjected the pans to a purposeful abuse test, designed to bring about the sort of cooking mistake we all hope never to make, that I noticed any difference in the stick resistance of our pans. What evil did I visit upon our victims? Caramel. In each pan, I cooked sugar and water until it reached a deep amber hue. Caramel is no sin in and of itself, but what I did next was. I just walked away, leaving the sticky, sugary messes to harden overnight. I returned in the morning to face solid disks of caramel set hard into the pans, clinging with the force of epoxy. To remove the caramel, I tried bashing it with a wooden spoon and then whacked the pan upside down against the rim of a trash can with the hope that pieces of caramel would tumble out. If the caramel held fast after five tries, then I filled the pan with water, brought it to a boil, and melted it out.

Strictly speaking, I felt it would be unfair to count the results of this extreme trial in the chart on page 29, but it certainly separated the men from the boys; so I used this information to help break ties. In only two pans, the Revere and the Anolon, did I have to resort to boiling. On the other hand, the Calphalon and the Swiss Diamond pans discharged the caramel with ease.

In the end, the performance differences were subtle—most of the pans will do a fine job of heating up soup or making rice. Design differences were more significant, and the sturdy Calphalon pan—with its riveted handle, wide diameter, sloped sides, and superior nonstick coating—came out on top. The final factor, price, was the most decisive. The Calphalon pan costs just $30, a far cry from the second-place Swiss Diamond at $95.

Weighty Wisdom

Super-heavy pans heat up and respond to temperature changes very slowly. While that's a recipe for trouble when it comes to skillets (think quick sautés), it's a desirable trait in a small saucepan, a piece of cookware that specializes in slow-and-gentle tasks. In our tests, the heavier saucepans fared better than their lighter-weight brethren in terms of uniform, even cooking. The onions on top were cooked in one of the lightest pans in our lineup; those on the bottom were cooked in the winning Calphalon, our heaviest.

LIGHT PAN: SPOTTY AND SCORCHED

HEAVY PAN: EVENLY COOKED

RATING SMALL NONSTICK SAUCEPANS

We tested nine small nonstick saucepans (2-quart capacity, or as close as we could come in a given line) and evaluated them according to the criteria listed below. When manufacturers offered more than one saucepan that satisfied our rubric, we chose a competitively priced or best-selling model. Tests were performed over gas burners on the same range in our test kitchen. The pans are listed in order of preference.

PRICE: Prices paid in Boston-area stores, national mail-order catalogs, or online stores.
MATERIALS: Materials from which the pan is made.
WEIGHT: As measured in the test kitchen, without the lid.
DESIGN: We scalded half-and-half in each pan and then made pastry cream, which gave us a chance to evaluate handle comfort and heating qualities, the ease with which a whisk can be maneuvered in the pan, and whether the lip of the pan could aid in pouring liquid neatly, without spills or dribbles. Transparent lids that allowed us a view inside the pan were preferred, as were solidly attached handles.

PERFORMANCE: In addition to the pastry cream, we prepared long-grain white rice, which we expected to be evenly cooked with no hint of browning on the bottom, and eggs, which we expected to be moderately and evenly browned. In both cases, we expected the pan to release the food easily. Scores of good, fair, or poor were assigned for each test, and the aggregate score determined the overall performance rating. As a tiebreaker, we prepared caramel in each pan, left it to harden overnight, and then tried to remove the caramel without boiling water in the pan.

SAUTÉ SPEED: We started with a cold pan and sautéed $2/3$ cup chopped onions in 2 tablespoons olive oil over medium heat for 12 minutes. Pans that produced soft, pale gold onions with no burnt edges (indicating a medium to medium-slow sauté pace) were rated good, pans that produced onions that were barely colored and retained significant crunch (indicating a very slow sauté pace) were rated fair, and pans that produced onions that were dark brown, crisp, or burnt at the edges (indicating a fast sauté pace) were rated poor.

RECOMMENDED

OUR FAVORITE
Calphalon Contemporary Nonstick Short & Saucy 2½ Quart Shallow Saucepan with Cover
PRICE: $29.99
MATERIALS: Anodized aluminum with nonstick interior, tempered glass lid, stainless steel handle

WEIGHT:	2 lb 7 oz
DESIGN:	★★★
PERFORMANCE:	★★★
SAUTÉ SPEED:	★★★

TESTERS' COMMENTS: Heavy, solid, and priced right, this pan is a hybrid—part plain saucepan and part classic saucier—just as the name, shallow shape, and generous diameter suggest. Sauté pace was a little slow, though easy to control, and caramel nearly jumped out of the pan.

Swiss Diamond 2.2 Quart Covered Saucepan
PRICE: $94.99
MATERIALS: Cast aluminum with nonstick interior, vented tempered glass lid, thermal plastic handle

WEIGHT:	1 lb 12 oz
DESIGN:	★★★
PERFORMANCE:	★★★
SAUTÉ SPEED:	★★★

TESTERS' COMMENTS: Onions and eggs browned evenly and slipped out effortlessly, and this pan practically ejected the sticky caramel. But c'mon . . . for almost a hundred bucks, don't we deserve a riveted handle?

Berndes SignoCast Classic 2-Quart Saucepan
PRICE: $69.99
MATERIALS: Cast aluminum with nonstick interior and exterior, tempered glass lid, thermal plastic handle

WEIGHT:	1 lb 13 oz
DESIGN:	★★★
PERFORMANCE:	★★★
SAUTÉ SPEED:	★★★

TESTERS' COMMENTS: Flared sides and rounded corners meant easy whisking, and the nonstick finish performed well in the abuse test. Not cheap, though, and the handle is not riveted.

RECOMMENDED WITH RESERVATIONS

Bialetti Casa Italia Italian Collection 2 Quart Covered Saucepan
PRICE: $24.99
MATERIALS: Aluminum with nonstick interior, self-draining tempered glass lid, Santoprene handle

WEIGHT:	1 lb 5 oz
DESIGN:	★★★
PERFORMANCE:	★★
SAUTÉ SPEED:	★★

TESTERS' COMMENTS: This lightweight pan wasn't perfect (the onions overbrowned a bit), but given its low price, design features (rolled lip, pouring spout, glass lid, wide diameter, and stay-cool handle), and excellent performance in the caramel abuse test, we're willing to turn down the heat a little.

Circulon Total 2 Quart Covered Saucepan
PRICE: $40.00
MATERIALS: Anodized aluminum with nonstick interior, stainless steel lid, thermal plastic handle

WEIGHT:	1 lb 12 oz
DESIGN:	★★
PERFORMANCE:	★★★
SAUTÉ SPEED:	★★★

TESTERS' COMMENTS: The stainless steel lid lacked the see-through convenience of glass, a few pieces of onion over-browned, and the caramel required a soak to come clean. Deal breakers? Maybe not, but with stronger contenders in the lineup, we'd look elsewhere.

Anolon Advanced 2 Quart Covered Saucepan
PRICE: $60.00
MATERIALS: Anodized aluminum with nonstick interior, tempered glass lid, silicone-coated steel handle

WEIGHT:	2 lb
DESIGN:	★★
PERFORMANCE:	★★
SAUTÉ SPEED:	★★★

TESTERS' COMMENTS: Curiously, eggs cooked up a little dark, yet the onions, while impressively even, were on the light side. Run-of-the-mill nonstick performance was fine overall, but lacking in the caramel abuse test.

Cuisinart Chef's Classic Non-Stick Hard Anodized 2-Quart Saucepan
PRICE: $29.99
MATERIALS: Aluminum with anodized aluminum exterior and nonstick interior, tempered glass lid, stainless steel handle

WEIGHT:	1 lb 12 oz
DESIGN:	★★★
PERFORMANCE:	★★
SAUTÉ SPEED:	★

TESTERS' COMMENTS: Well designed, with riveted handle, rounded corners, rolled lip, and clear lid, but hotheaded in the sauté department—the onions came close to burning.

Revere Convenience 2-Quart Saucepan
PRICE: $23.99
MATERIALS: Stainless steel with multi-layer base and nonstick interior, stainless steel and tempered glass lid, thermal plastic handle

WEIGHT:	2 lb
DESIGN:	★★★
PERFORMANCE:	★★
SAUTÉ SPEED:	★★

TESTERS' COMMENTS: Nicely rendered with wide, almost 8-inch diameter, rounded corners, and pouring spouts, but performance didn't match design. Rice did not cook evenly, and onions and eggs were slightly darker than ideal. The caramel clung for dear life and had to be boiled away.

Look 7-Inch 2.5 Quart Covered Saucepan
PRICE: $85.00
MATERIALS: Aluminum with nonstick interior, tempered glass lid, thermal plastic handle

WEIGHT:	2 lb 5 oz
DESIGN:	★★
PERFORMANCE:	★★
SAUTÉ SPEED:	★★

TESTERS' COMMENTS: Handle was loose on delivery, and the lid was so ill-fitting that it flipped upside down on the pan with even the slightest provocation. Very slow sauté pace.

Glaze Anatomy

While developing the glaze for our Glazed Pork Chops (see page 19), we stumbled onto an interesting discovery. After testing different sweeteners, it came down to just two: brown sugar and honey. But while honey offered a distinct flavor profile that most tasters liked, its unpleasantly grainy texture in the glaze was no match for the smooth, glossy texture of the brown sugar glaze. What could explain honey's transformation from smooth and fluid to rough and grainy when reduced in a glaze (an effect not seen when baking with honey)?

Honey is composed of two separate simple sugar molecules, glucose and fructose, while brown sugar (and all granulated sugar made from cane or beets) consists of sucrose, a more complex sugar in which one molecule of glucose bonds to one molecule of fructose. Confused? We were, too, until a little research revealed that it all comes down to size: In a liquid solution, the smaller molecules of glucose (and, to a lesser extent, fructose) tend to pack together tightly and form crystals, whereas the larger, bulkier sucrose molecules are less likely to do so. Translation: Sucrose-laden brown sugar is the better choice for smooth, syrupy glazed chops.

LABEL WATCH
Two remarkably similar cans, two remarkably different tastes.

Read the Fine Print

The winning brand of canned whole tomatoes from our 2005 tasting was Progresso, which beat out the other brands with its firm texture, bright acidity, and fresh taste. Those qualities made it the natural choice for including in our Marinara Sauce (see page 11), and the development process went smoothly. Until one day, that is, when the once vibrant sauce suddenly became mysteriously lackluster and bland. At first, we thought Progresso was letting us down, but closer inspection of the cans revealed a subtle distinction. While the Progresso we originally tasted (which came out on top) was packed in tomato juice, these newer cans of tomatoes were in tomato puree. Puree (unlike juice) is cooked, and it usually gives the uncooked tomatoes packed in it a stale taste. Have we changed our recommendation? Not at all. It turns out that Progresso sells both styles, albeit in remarkably similar cans. Just read the fine print and select the tomatoes packed in juice.

TASTING: Dried Oregano

Dried oregano is one of a handful of dried herbs that we use frequently in the test kitchen. Does brand matter? To find out, we submitted seven brands to a series of taste tests that included a quick tomato sauce, our Marinara Sauce (see page 11), and plain cheese pizza (the oregano sprinkled right on top). But before we did any cooking at all, we tasted each of them the way herb experts do, making infusions out of the dried herb in hot water. When our seasoned tasters sampled these "herbal teas," they expressed eloquent surprise at the pronounced differences among Durkee ("an aggressive bite"), Spice Islands ("subtly piney"), Tone's ("biting" and "tannic"), McCormick ("floral, with citrus notes"), and the other brands. But the commentary turned much less precise ("not bad") once we moved on to real food. Even in the simpler applications—for instance, the quick tomato sauce—the nuances from brand to brand were mostly obliterated. Our recommendation? Unless you're serving oregano tea, any brand of dried oregano is fine. More important is making sure your herb container hasn't been sitting in the cupboard for longer than six months. –Garth Clingingsmith

HERBAL AGREEMENT
This oregano tastes just like the others.

On the Sheep

When we set out to develop our Garlic-Roasted Leg of Lamb recipe (see page 13), we figured shopping would be the least of our worries. A leg of lamb is a leg of lamb, right? Not so fast.

For starters, an entire leg of lamb consists of three main parts: Up near the hip is the *butt end* (which includes the sirloin, or hip meat); the bottom part is the *shank end*, with the shank (or ankle) at the very bottom. For our recipe, we wanted a boneless cut, and the shank end was

---

TECHNIQUE | THE ICING ON THE CAKE

Our Old-Fashioned Chocolate Layer Cake (see page 23) is perfectly suited to an informal presentation—just slather on the billowy frosting and serve. If you prefer a more tailored look, here are a few tips from the test kitchen.

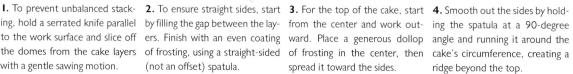

1. To prevent unbalanced stacking, hold a serrated knife parallel to the work surface and slice off the domes from the cake layers with a gentle sawing motion.

2. To ensure straight sides, start by filling the gap between the layers. Finish with an even coating of frosting, using a straight-sided (not an offset) spatula.

3. For the top of the cake, start from the center and work outward. Place a generous dollop of frosting in the center, then spread it toward the sides.

4. Smooth out the sides by holding the spatula at a 90-degree angle and running it around the cake's circumference, creating a ridge beyond the top.

5. To level off this ridge and clean up any other edges, scrape the spatula across the top of the cake one section at a time, cleaning the spatula as you go.

the easiest to work with and yielded almost three times as much meat.

But after receiving several blank stares—as well as an odd collection of diverse cuts of meat—from butchers, we realized that our nomenclature was getting lost in translation at the meat counter. Sometimes we wound up with just the shank itself, sometimes a strange, semiboneless hybrid of the shank end and butt end, replete with extra joints and muscles for us to navigate.

To avoid confusion and to eliminate the risk of running into regional differences in labeling, we recommend forgoing the shorthand terminology and just spelling it out for your butcher. After extensive research, we found that you can't go wrong asking for "a whole boneless leg of lamb, but without the sirloin attached." This approach is wordy, but worth it.

And remember to request an American leg of lamb, which is more widely available and almost always larger and less gamy than its Australian or New Zealand counterparts.

BUTT END
(includes sirloin)

SHANK END

SCRAMBLED LEGS

Even butchers get confused by lamb terminology. The meatier shank end is better. Ask for a whole boneless leg of lamb, but without the sirloin attached.

TASTING: Whole Wheat Flour

While baking loaf upon loaf of Multigrain Bread (see page 25), we wondered how much the brand of whole wheat flour mattered. To find out, we brought eight into the test kitchen to see how they baked up in bread and biscuits.

All eight of the flours delivered decent baked goods: Grind coarseness, not brand, turned out to be key—and the coarser the better. Our favorites were the graham flours, named for 19th-century health guru Dr. Sylvester Graham (of graham crackers fame). The coarsest flours sold in most supermarkets, graham flours packed the wheatiest punch. Stone-ground flours aren't quite as coarse, but they're less refined than flours ground with steel rollers (the standard grinding method) and scored nearly as well.

Third down on the grinding continuum are traditional whole wheat flours (which, like clockwork, we rated third-best). The more extensive grinding that traditional whole wheat flours undergo yields a smaller particle size, which means that more of the fat in the wheat kernel gets exposed to the air. That, in turn, results in more oxidation, which can contribute a slightly rancid flavor to finished baked goods. (Some tasters registered this oxidation as complexity; others detected "faint off-notes.")

Finally, there's white whole wheat flour. Ground from white wheat berries, this flour looks more yellow than bronze and has a milder flavor profile than regular whole wheat flours (made from red wheat). Some tasters found the resulting baked goods to be one-dimensionally sweet. While we wouldn't go so far as to recommend against this style of whole wheat flour, in the test kitchen, at least, we'll stick to the more flavorful, coarser varieties. —Garth Clingingsmith

WHEATY PUNCH
Whole Wheat
Graham Flour

TOO MILD?
White Whole
Wheat Flour

RECIPE UPDATE

Lemony Panna Cotta

Our recipe for **Panna Cotta** (July/August 2000) is a study in simplicity—milk and cream accented with sugar and vanilla, bound with gelatin, then chilled. Some readers wondered if they could add citrus for a change of pace. Immediately, we anticipated problems: High-acid ingredients like lemon or grapefruit juice can curdle dairy products. Intrigued by the challenge, we added various amounts of lemon juice, from 2 tablespoons to 1 cup. At 1 cup, the mixture was unbearably grainy as well as too sour. For the best texture, the magic number turned out to be ½ cup, but the lemon flavor was too weak. Previous research told us that lemon juice added too early in the cooking process essentially evaporates away. By adding the lemon juice after cooking, we maximized the impact. To round out the lemon flavor, we added some julienned lemon zest, then strained it before chilling.

GRAINY

CREAMY

Acids can destroy dairy texture. The top panna cotta has just ¼ cup more lemon juice than the bottom one.

The Diavola Inside

Chilly weather begets numerous reader requests about how to cook outdoor favorites indoors. Such is the case with **Chicken alla Diavola** (July/August 2003), a butterflied chicken dish that gets its "devilish" intensity from a fiery oil infused with garlic, black pepper, and red pepper flakes. The biggest challenge would be to re-create the effect of the grill's high heat to produce generous charring. For inspiration we looked to classic "chicken under a brick" recipes, in which the chicken is weighted to maximize the skin's contact with a hot skillet. With some adjustments, the method translated well. We placed about half of the garlic-pepper oil under the skin for flavor, seared the chicken per the original recipe, then slipped it in the oven skin side up. After resting and carving the bird, we drizzled each portion with extra infused oil and served the chicken with lemon wedges.

Flaky Biscuits with Flavorings

Our **Flaky Biscuits** (January/February 2006) have plenty of flavor on their own, but readers wondered how to introduce other flavors to these crispy, layered biscuits. Herbs or cheese were our first thoughts, but would these ingredients disturb the flaky layers we had so arduously developed? Eventually, we found that mixing 2 tablespoons of minced fresh herbs (we like rosemary and thyme) right into the flour and proceeding with the recipe was the optimal strategy. Adding Parmesan cheese the same way did not work as well. A mere 2 ounces of finely grated Parmesan yielded short, squat layered biscuits rather than the tall, striated beauties we were hoping for. After reducing the amount of cheese by half and adding only half of that to the dough (sprinkling the rest on the exterior), we arrived at a working variation, with distinct layers and cheesy flavor.

IF YOU HAVE A QUESTION about a recently published recipe, let us know. Send your inquiry, name, address, and daytime telephone number to Recipe Update, Cook's Illustrated, P. O. Box 470589, Brookline, MA 02447, or to recipeupdate@bcpress.com.

Go to www.cooksillustrated.com
- Key in code 30611 for **Lemon Panna Cotta**.
- Key in code 3069 for **Chicken alla Diavola Indoors**.
- Key in code 30610 for **Flaky Buttermilk Biscuits with Parmesan**.
- Recipes available until September 1, 2006.

EQUIPMENT CORNER

⇒ BY GARTH CLINGINGSMITH ⇐

NEW PRODUCT
Stovetop Cappuccino Maker

If you're not willing to dish out hundreds of dollars for a high-tech countertop espresso machine, the $89.99 Bialetti Mukka Express Stovetop Cappuccino Maker may be a viable lower-tech option: The top chamber, which holds the brewed espresso, also holds milk that steams simultaneously, thanks to a valve that releases pressurized steam. As the espresso enters the top chamber, it mixes with the milk while foam forms on top. Even the test kitchen's resident coffee snobs had to admit that the beverages tasted fine. The downsides? While the Mukka makes great steamed milk, the foam itself is a little flimsy—this gadget is better at lattes than its namesake cappuccinos. And don't try making a second latte too soon: Once it's hot, the bottom chamber is a pain (literally) to remove.

GOT MILK
This stovetop gadget makes decent lattes, but the cappuccinos need some work.

DO YOU REALLY NEED THIS?
Crème Brûlée Set

The prospect of moving custard-filled ramekins into and out of a water bath is enough to discourage some cooks from making crème brûlée at home. Chicago Metallic's Crème Brûlée Set ($19.95), an 8-inch-square baking dish with a rack designed to hold four ramekins, aims to make the task less precarious. As promised, the rack keeps the ramekins steady, and being able to transfer all four at once is a welcome benefit. What you gain in precision, however, you lose in flexibility. First, you can bake only four custards at

a time. Second, you're locked into using 3½-inch-wide ramekins (like the 6-ounce cups that come with this set); some crème brûlée fans prefer wider, shallower ramekins for a higher crust-to-custard ratio. Our verdict? Depends on your steadiness of hand. Either way, note that this "set" does not include a torch, which you'll have to buy separately.

DO YOU REALLY NEED THIS?
Le Creuset Doufeu Oven

Can a few cups of ice take the guesswork out of braising? That's the idea behind Le Creuset's oval-shaped Doufeu oven, which comes with a recessed lid meant to be filled with ice cubes during cooking. The ice creates condensation on the lid's dimpled underside that rains back down onto the food. By efficiently recycling the steam as a basting liquid, you can cook with less water or broth, yielding a stronger-flavored sauce. Well, that's the theory. Intrigued, we pitted the Doufeu against our favorite traditional Dutch oven (also Le Creuset) on several batches of braised meat. Even though it starts off with less water, the Doufeu ended up with more liquid every time. The meat was tender enough, but the extra retained liquid made for thinner and less flavorful sauces than those cooked in the regular (ice-free) Dutch oven. (Apparently, the Doufeu does its job *too* efficiently.) We'll stick with the regular Dutch oven, which allows moderate evaporation from the crack between the lid and the pot—our tried-and-true method for concentrating flavor.

COOL BRAISING
This Le Creuset pot has room for ice.

EQUIPMENT TESTING
Garlic Peelers

Kitchenware stores abound with new gadgets meant to make garlic peeling less tedious. The best known may be the simple rubber tube, which relies on hand friction to remove the skin of cloves placed inside. Oxo has updated the rubber tube, making it larger and swelling the middle to keep the cloves from falling out. The new tube works, but no better than the original. KitchenZone's bulb-shaped silicone pouch is another attempt to keep cloves where they belong, but digging them out of the tiny opening was a pain. The Chef'n Garlic Peeler (pictured) pushes a single clove through sharp plastic "blades" that are meant to strip the clove but end up slashing the peel and spewing out mutilated (but unpeeled) garlic. An electric version, the A1 Garlic Peeler, spins up to a full head of cloves around a central rubber bulb. All that speed and friction failed to peel more than half of the cloves—and it costs $35.

In the end, nothing worked better than the rubber tube—we like the one by E-Z-Rol ($7.99)—or the test kitchen's even cheaper method: whacking the cloves with the broad side of a knife ($0.00).

PRODUCT UPDATE
Same Grill, Different Name

Readers have complained about coming up empty-handed while trying to purchase the winning charcoal grill from our 2002 testing. We liked the New Braunfels Sante Fe Grill for its spacious size, easy fire-tending access, handy side tables, and movable charcoal grate (for varying levels of heat)—not to mention the reasonable price ($99). What happened? Just a name change. Char-Broil has taken over the line from New Braunfels, but the Char-Broil Sante Fe Charcoal Grill (still $99) is the same grill.

A SMASHING FAILURE
Chef'n Garlic Peeler left cloves unpeeled.

Sources

The following are mail-order sources for items recommended in this issue. Prices were current at press time and do not include shipping and handling. Contact companies directly to confirm prices and availability; visit www.cooksillustrated.com for updates.

Page 11: HAND BLENDERS
• KitchenAid Immersion Blender: $49.99, model #KHB100, Target Stores (www.target.com).
• Braun Multiquick Hand Blender: $34.95, item #197308, Cooking.com (800-663-8810, www.cooking.com).
• Braun Professional Multiquick Hand Blender: $79.95, item #197301, Cooking.com.

Page 23: CAKE STANDS
• Ateco Professional Icing Turntable: $62.99, item #8017, Fante's Kitchen Wares Shop (800-443-2683, www.fantes.com).
• Ateco Revolving Cake Stand: $19.95, item #189139, Cooking.com.

Page 25: 7-GRAIN HOT CEREAL
• 7-Grain Cereal: $2.19, item #1185C25, Bob's Red Mill (800-349-2173, www.bobsredmill.com).

Page 29: 2-QUART SAUCEPANS
• Calphalon Contemporary Nonstick Short & Saucy 2½ Quart Saucepan: $29.99, item #199926, Cooking.com.
• Swiss Diamond 2.2 Quart Saucepan: $94.99, item #SD02, A Cook's Wares (800-915-9788, www.cookswares.com).
• Berndes SignoCast Classic 2-Quart Saucepan: $69.99, item #B00008DGR5, Amazon.com (www.amazon.com).

Page 32: CAPPUCCINO MAKER
• Bialetti Mukka Express Cappuccino Maker: $89.99, item #9994, Fante's.

Page 32: CRÈME BRÛLÉE SET
• Chicago Metallic Commercial Crème Brûlée Set: $19.95, item #394883, Cooking.com.

Page 32: GARLIC PEELER
• E-Z-Rol Garlic Peeler: $7.99, item #11880, Fante's.

Page 32: CHARCOAL GRILL
• Char-Broil Sante Fe Charcoal Grill: $99.00, model #03308740, Home Depot (800-430-3376, www.homedepot.com).

RECIPES
March & April 2006

**New Recipes Available on
www.cooksillustrated.com**

COOK'S **extra**

The following recipes are available free until September 1, 2006. To access a recipe, go to www.cooksillustrated.com and enter the code listed after the recipe title.

AMERICA'S TEST KITCHEN TV SHOW

Join the millions of home cooks who watch our show, *America's Test Kitchen*, on public television every week. For more information, including recipes and a schedule of program times in your area, visit www.americastestkitchen.com.

Garlic-Roasted Leg of Lamb, 13

Pan-Roasted Broccoli, 20

Marinara Sauce, 11

Pepper-Crusted Filet Mignon, 7

Glazed Pork Chops, 19

Potstickers with Scallion Dipping Sauce, 15

Old-Fashioned Chocolate Layer Cake, 23

Multigrain Bread, 25

Chicken Kiev, 9

PHOTOGRAPHY: CARL TREMBLAY, STYLING: MARIE PIRAINO

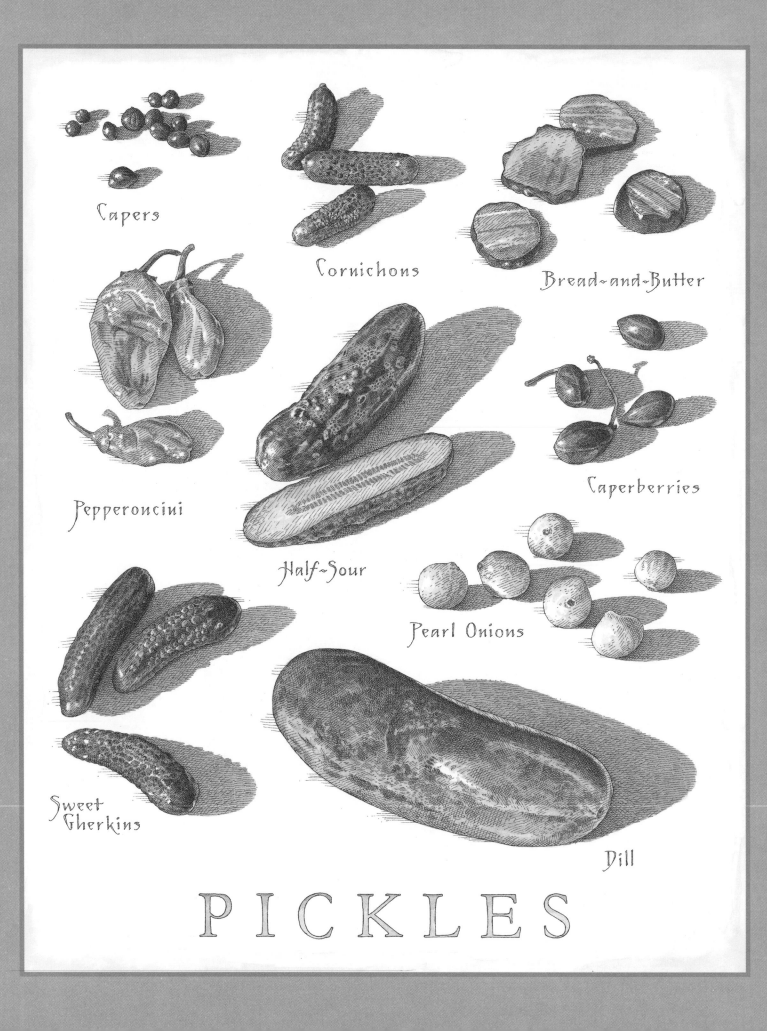

Capers

Cornichons

Bread~and~Butter

Pepperoncini

Caperberries

Half~Sour

Pearl Onions

Sweet
Gherkins

Dill

PICKLES

NUMBER EIGHTY

MAY & JUNE 2006

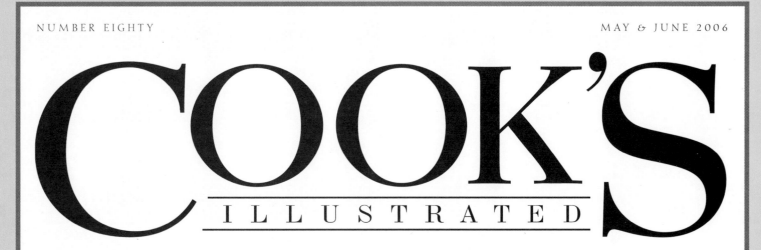

COOK'S
ILLUSTRATED

Grilled London Broil
Cheap Cut, Rich Flavor

Mashed Potatoes
with Olive Oil

Turtle Brownies
Dark, Chewy, and Rich

Moroccan Chicken

Illustrated Guide
to Cooking Pasta

Rating Vanilla
Ice Creams
Is Natural Really Better?

Grilled Tomato Salsa
Smoky Flavor in Minutes

Testing Kitchen Tongs
No-Mayo Chicken Salads
Fish and Chips at Home
Perfecting Veal Scaloppini
Best Strawberry Cream Cake

www.cooksillustrated.com

$5.95 U.S./$6.95 CANADA

0   74470 62805   7

0 6>

CONTENTS

May & June 2006

COOK'S
ILLUSTRATED
www.cooksillustrated.com
HOME OF AMERICA'S TEST KITCHEN

Founder and Editor Christopher Kimball
Executive Editor Jack Bishop
Deputy Editor Jolyon Helterman
Editorial Manager, Books Elizabeth Carduff
Test Kitchen Director Erin McMurrer
Senior Editors, Books Julia Collin Davison
Lori Galvin
Managing Editor Rebecca Hays
Associate Editor, Books Keith Dresser
Associate Editors Erika Bruce
Sean Lawler
Sandra Wu
Web Editor Lindsay McSweeney
Copy Chief India Koopman
Test Cooks Garth Clingingsmith
David Pazmiño
Rachel Toomey
Diane Unger
Sarah Wilson
Assistant Test Kitchen Director Matthew Herron
Assistant Editors, Books Charles Kelsey
Elizabeth Wray Emery
Editorial Assistant Elizabeth Bomze
Assistant to the Publisher Melissa Baldino
Editorial Intern Meredith Smith
Kitchen Assistants Maria Elena Delgado
Nadia Domeq
Ena Gudiel
Contributing Editors Matthew Card
Dawn Yanagihara
Consulting Editors Shirley Corriher
Guy Crosby
John Dewar
Jasper White
Robert L. Wolke
Proofreader Holly Hartman

Design Director Amy Klee
Art Director, Books Carolynn DeCillo
Senior Designer, Web/Marketing Julie Bozzo
Senior Designer, Magazines Heather Barrett
Designers Christian Steinmetz
Christine Vo
Staff Photographer Daniel J. van Ackere

Vice President Marketing David Mack
Circulation Director Bill Tine
Fulfillment Manager Carrie Horan
Circulation Assistant Elizabeth Dayton
Direct Mail Director Adam Perry
Products Director Steven Browall
E-Commerce Marketing Manager Hugh Buchan
Marketing Copywriter David Goldberg
Customer Service Manager Jacqueline Valerio
Customer Service Representative Julie Gardner

Vice President Sales Demee Gambulos
Retail Sales Director Jason Geller
Marketing Assistant Connie Forbes

Production Director Guy Rochford
Senior Production Manager Jessica L. Quirk
Project Manager Anne Francis
Production Assistants Jeanette McCarthy
Matthew Warnick
Systems Administrator Richard Cassidy
Internet Technology Director Aaron Shuman
Web Producer Lauren Record

Chief Financial Officer Sharyn Chabot
Controller Mandy Shito
Staff Accountant Maya Santoso
Office Manager Saudiyah Abdul-Rahim
Receptionist Henrietta Murray
Publicity Deborah Broide

ASIAN GREENS

ASIAN GREENS Once the province of specialty markets, Asian greens are becoming common staples in some supermarket produce aisles. Bok choy is mild and crunchy, with a high water content; the crisp white stalks require longer cooking than the tender greens. The diminutive baby bok choy can be used whole and is slightly sweeter than the mature version. Napa cabbage, with its crinkly, pale green leaves, is prepared in much the same way as bok choy, and both are well suited to stir-fries. Chinese broccoli is similar in appearance and texture to broccoli rabe, though its mild flavor has more in common with regular broccoli. The flat, pungent leaves of Chinese chives carry a garlicky flavor that mellows when cooked. Malabar spinach and Chinese water spinach have a mild flavor and can be stir-fried or eaten raw in salads. Tatsoi, with its mildly bitter, round leaves, and mizuna, often found in mesclun salad greens, both hail from Japan. Chinese parsley, better known in the West as cilantro, comprises the stems and leaves of the coriander plant and is a common ingredient in both Latin and Asian cuisines.

COVER (*Peppers*): Elizabeth Brandon, BACK COVER (*Asian Greens*): John Burgoyne

For list rental information, contact: Specialists Marketing Services, Inc., 1200 Harbor Blvd., 9th Floor, Weehawken, NJ 07087; 201-865-5800.
Editorial Office: 17 Station St., Brookline, MA 02445; 617-232-1000; fax 617-232-1572. Subscription inquiries, call 800-526-8442.
Postmaster: Send all new orders, subscription inquiries, and change-of-address notices to Cook's Illustrated, P.O. Box 7446, Red Oak, IA 51591-0446.

2nd PRINTING IN CHINA

ALL THE NEWS THAT FITS THE PRINT

In the event that some of you have become weary of my idyllic representation of Vermont country life, I offer a series of more unbiased and historically precise descriptions taken from a local newspaper that has records dating back to 1861. Kathy Wagner, one of our neighbors, assembled the relevant clippings and published them in a small booklet.

Before I leave you in the capable hands of the farmers, doctors, wives, clergymen, and others, I would simply quote Calvin Coolidge, who said, "[Vermonters] are a race of pioneers who have almost beggared themselves in the service of others. If the spirit of Liberty should vanish from other parts of our Union and the support of our institutions should languish, it could all be replenished from the generous store held by the people of the brave little state of Vermont." It may indeed be time, as Coolidge aptly predicted, that our nation should look to this hardy race of pioneers to replenish our sadly depleted stores.

September 4, 1867: "C. B. Hitchcock, the noted woodchuck hunter, is slaughtering a large number of the 'vermins' this season, having already killed upward of 150."

October 15, 1867: "Mr. Hitchcock outdone. A son of Mr. Harwood, aged 14 years . . . has caught . . . with the aid of a dog, 279 woodchucks."

November 19, 1867: "I noticed an article in the *Journal* entitled 'Mr. Hitchcock outdone.' Now . . . that is not the whole truth. The facts are these: Seymour Harwood, aged 14 years, has caught during the present season 320 woodchucks. Last year he caught 250; in 1865, 176; and in 1864, 191, making in the four seasons 937. Respectfully yours, subscriber."

December 22, 1868: "A correspondent writes concerning the character of a spiritualist who recently visited town. Her lectures were bold and open attacks upon the Bible and the religion of Christ. She left the town with a crowded wallet and a smiling face."

November 1, 1870: "A hailstorm about the first of August passed over the west and north part of town. Neighbor B was out in his field haying at the time, the storm coming suddenly, he burrowed under a cock of hay for protection. Forgetting the fate of Lotte's *[sic]* wife who looked back to see the storm of fire upon the cities of the plain, he peeked out to inspect into the mysteries of nature and ascertain the state of the weather, whereupon a frozen missile from the clouds took effect upon the exposed part, not a transformation into a pillar of salt, but a panoramic view of all the stars of the firmament and a sudden development of the bump of veneration. The consequences, however, were not very serious or lasting."

November 22, 1870: "A flock of turkeys belonging to a Mr. Barber recently flew from a big hill out over the valley in which his house stands and came with such velocity to the ground that 20 of them were killed."

July 13, 1871: "Manchester journeau printer I cend yew inklosed one dollar to pa for last yearz paper I don't reed the hournel but yew ma koncider me a subscriber for the nabers all say they luff to see it on the shelf thare ant much sed about your paper over the west cide but we east ciders tawk of getin up a klub to get the paper cheeper."

August 15, 1872: "The Congregational Church is unoccupied this season, the Methodists for some reason having failed to send a preacher."

January 2, 1873: "Recently a man named Towsley was seriously injured at R. S. Hurd's circular saw mill. His jaw was broken and his nose smashed. An intimate acquaintance with a circular saw when in motion is not very desirable."

July 15, 1875: "Mr. Editor: Not much worthy of note has transpired over here 'among the hills.' The boys generally find time to take their

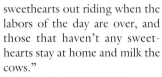

Christopher Kimball

sweethearts out riding when the labors of the day are over, and those that haven't any sweethearts stay at home and milk the cows."

November 16, 1876: "Bennett is having fortnightly hops at his home, where, for the small sum of $.50 a couple may dance until the 'wee small hours' and until they are 'all in a muck of sweat.'"

June 7, 1877: "Very many people have the impression that fowls will not eat the potato bug, but Mr. Thomas Hayes of this place saw his rooster poking around among his potatoes and supposing that the old fellow was digging them up, killed him, and finding the gullet very much distended opened it and found therein 107 veritable potato bugs. Mr. Hayes thinks now that he killed his best friend."

May 1, 1879: "'In times of old, when men were wise and women were bold, when bills were short and credit shorter, when from malt they brewed good porter,' lived Dr. Watkins. Like many others in his profession, he had a good practice but was a bad financier, a poor collector who seldom resorted to the law to collect a debt. But he did on one occasion sue a Mr. C, who had utterly refused to pay and who, the doctor supposed, was abundantly able. The doctor obtained judgment, Mr. C went to jail, stayed his six days, 'swore out' (agreed to pay his debts) as they called it, and was around as usual. It was winter and the snow was deep and the doctor's horse, old Whitey, got into the wrong track, the deep square-boxed cutter ran up on to a high snow drift, overturned, and actually imprisoned the old doctor. The identical Mr. C happened to be passing that way and righted matters at once, freeing the doctor. As he was leaving he asked, 'Doctor, how would you have got out without help?' The doctor coughed and said, 'I'd—I'd a swore out.'"

FOR INQUIRIES, ORDERS, OR MORE INFORMATION:

www.cooksillustrated.com

At www.cooksillustrated.com, you can order books and subscriptions, sign up for our free e-newsletter, or renew your magazine subscription. Join the Web site and you'll have access to 13 years of *Cook's* recipes, cookware tests, ingredient tastings, and more.

COOKBOOKS

We sell more than 40 cookbooks by the editors of *Cook's Illustrated*. To order, visit our bookstore at www.cooksillustrated.com or call 800-611-0759 (or 515-246-6911 from outside the U.S.).

COOK'S ILLUSTRATED Magazine

Cook's Illustrated magazine (ISSN 1068-2821), number 80, is published bimonthly by Boston Common Press Limited Partnership, 17 Station St., Brookline, MA 02445. Copyright 2006 Boston Common Press Limited Partnership. Periodicals postage paid at Boston, Mass., and additional mailing offices, USPS #012487. POSTMASTER: Send address changes to Cook's Illustrated, P.O. Box 7446, Red Oak, IA 51591-0446. For subscription and gift subscription orders, subscription inquiries, or change-of-address notices, call 800-526-8442 in the U.S. or 515-247-7571 from outside the U.S., or write us at Cook's Illustrated, P.O. Box 7446, Red Oak, IA 51591-0446.

NOTES FROM READERS

≥ COMPILED BY SANDRA WU ≤

Reading Meat Labels

I sometimes see meat at the supermarket labeled "lean" or "extra lean." What do these terms really mean?

KENIN COLOMA
GLENVIEW, ILL.

➤ According to the U.S. Department of Agriculture's Food Safety and Inspection Service, the terms *lean* and *extra lean* are used not only on meat but also poultry and seafood to convey information about fat content, including the amount of total fat, saturated fat, and cholesterol per 100-gram serving (about 3½ ounces). A "lean" designation means the product contains fewer than 10 grams of total fat, 4.5 grams of saturated fat, and 95 milligrams of cholesterol per serving. "Extra lean" indicates fewer than 5 grams of total fat, 2 grams of saturated fat, and 95 milligrams of cholesterol per serving. (Following these rules, 93 percent lean ground beef would technically be considered "lean," while "extra lean" beef would have to be more than 95 percent lean.) These designations can be used for any cut of meat as long as the packer includes nutritional information on the label. Whether they appear at all, however, is up to the individual packing company.

Freezing Cupcakes

What's the best way to freeze baked cupcakes?

ALLISON SACCONE
JERSEY CITY, N.J.

➤ When freezing baked cupcakes, we wanted to prevent the common problems of freezer burn, dryness, and gummy tops. Because the texture and consistency of frostings and icings can change drastically in the freezer, only plain (unfrosted) cupcakes should be frozen. Once thawed, they can be topped or decorated as desired.

We tried several methods of storing, freezing, and thawing our favorite yellow cupcakes. We froze them—individually and in groups of four—in four different ways: in a plastic zipper-lock bag with most of the air removed, in plastic wrap, in foil, and in plastic wrap and foil. After a week in the freezer, we took the cupcakes out to thaw on the countertop for 1½ hours until they reached room temperature; half of each sample was kept wrapped and the other half unwrapped.

Thawing the cupcakes wrapped—whether enclosed in foil, plastic wrap, or both or left in a zipper-lock bag—allowed condensation

to form between the wrapper and the tops, which turned gooey. Those that were unwrapped before thawing were as good as new. In terms of taste, there was little to differentiate one storage method from another. For longer periods of storage, where the likelihood of freezer burn increases, we recommend double-wrapping cupcakes in plastic wrap and foil (in groups or individually) before placing them in the freezer. And make sure to unwrap them before thawing.

Egg White Substitutes

What is your opinion about using liquid egg whites in desserts that call for many egg whites? I often feel guilty about throwing away a bunch of yolks.

BARBARA HART
YARMOUTH PORT, MASS.

➤ We purchased three widely available brands of pasteurized liquid egg whites—Papetti Foods All Whites, Eggology 100% Egg Whites, and Egg Beaters Egg Whites—and tested them against regular egg whites in four recipes: angel food cake, baked meringues, Italian meringue frosting, and scrambled egg whites. The Papetti Foods and Eggology products contain just egg whites; Egg Beaters contains small amounts of xanthan gum and triethyl citrate, which, according to the label, "enhance whipping."

Each sample varied in the amount of time it took to whip up to soft and stiff peaks (sometimes taking up to three times as long as fresh whites, even when beaten at a higher speed). Of all three brands, the cloudy-looking Papetti Foods product (which, to its credit, is labeled "not recommended for meringues or angel food cake") was the least consistent, needing the most time to whip up and only occasionally achieving stiff peaks. In contrast, Eggology was mostly on par with fresh egg whites. The Egg Beaters fell somewhere in between.

In all four applications, the Papetti Foods and Egg Beaters products failed to perform as well

as Eggology. The Papetti Foods almost always deflated into a soupy mess after other ingredients were whipped or folded in, rendering any application except the scrambled egg whites an abject failure. The Egg Beaters produced decent meringues but had a slightly chemical aftertaste when scrambled.

Overall, Eggology was the closest to fresh egg whites. The meringues and scrambled egg whites tasted identical to the real thing. The frosting was slightly less fluffy and more sticky and slick than the original but still acceptable. The angel food cake, however, failed miserably. Although only about ½ inch shy of the 3-inch-high cake made with fresh whites, the cake made with Eggology had a sunken center, sizeable slimy air pockets throughout, and a dense, gummy bottom half.

Moldy Cheese

Aside from cheese that contains cultivated mold, is it safe to eat cheese that has grown mold as long as I cut off the affected areas?

TERESA KAO
HOUSTON, TEXAS

➤ We spoke to Mary Keith, food and nutrition agent at the University of Florida Extension Service, to get some answers to your question. According to Keith, hard cheeses can generally be salvaged, but soft cheeses cannot. The toxins in the types of mold that grow on cheeses are mostly water-soluble, so they usually cannot travel far beyond the surface of harder cheeses with low moisture levels.

To remove surface mold from a hard cheese such as cheddar, the general rule is to cut off all visible mold as well as an inch of the surrounding area, being careful to keep the knife out of the mold itself to prevent cross-contamination of other areas of the cheese. Of course, this works only if you have a big piece of cheese. Small pieces on which the mold has grown on multiple sides should be discarded.

Soft cheeses such as goat cheese, Brie, or Camembert and wet, curd-like cheeses such as ricotta or cottage cheese should never be consumed once mold appears. Because most of the toxins produced by these uncultivated molds are water-soluble, they can easily travel beneath the surface of these high-moisture cheeses and contaminate the rest of the product. Cheeses that are injected with mold, such as blue cheese, should be discarded once they start becoming slimy or softer than usual or exhibiting strange odors or colors.

WHITES, BUT NO YOLKS
Are pasteurized egg whites as good as the real thing?

Our advice is never to buy more cheese than you can use in one or two weeks; the moister the cheese, the quicker it will spoil. As for storing most leftover cheese, we have found that wrapping it in parchment paper and then in foil is the most effective method, but a sealed zipper-lock bag is a very close (and much easier) second. Whichever method you choose, the cheese is best kept in the crisper drawer of the refrigerator. One more thing: Freezing doesn't kill mold. While freezing might slow down the mold's growth, it will not destroy any of the toxins the mold has already produced.

All about Farina

What's the difference between 2½-minute, 1-minute, and instant farina?

CHARLOTTE HURD
CUMBERLAND FORESIDE, MAINE

➤ Farina is a bland flour or meal made from the endosperm (the starchy part) of the wheat kernel and milled and sifted into a fine granular consistency resembling instant dried yeast or beige cornmeal. When cooked in boiling water and simmered until thickened (1 to 2½ minutes), farina becomes a protein-rich hot breakfast cereal. The quicker-cooking varieties are treated with an enzyme (papain, derived from papayas) or with disodium phosphate.

We tried the following four types of plain farina cereal, with cooking times ranging from 1 to 2½ minutes: Cream of Wheat instant hot cereal, Cream of Wheat 1-Minute Enriched Farina, Cream of Wheat 2½-Minute Enriched Farina, and Farina Mills Enriched Farina (2 minutes). While the Cream of Wheat instant hot cereal was noticeably salty and mushy, we thought the other three products were just fine.

Pastry Flour

How is pastry flour different from cake flour? What types of recipes does it work best in?

ANN DORFMAN
NEWTON, MASS.

➤ Pastry flour is a soft wheat flour with a protein content between those of all-purpose flour and cake flour. It is often used in pie crust and tender pastries. Whereas all-purpose flour is 10 to 12 percent protein, comes bleached or unbleached, and is a blend of hard and soft wheat flours, cake flour is 6 to 8 percent protein and is made from soft wheat flour that has been bleached to further weaken the protein (which is what gives baked goods their structure and chew). Pastry flour is 8 to 10 percent protein and, like cake flour, is made from soft wheat flour (but is usually not bleached).

We tried using pastry flour in a chiffon cake, scones, pie crust, and sugar cookies. Tasters lauded the pastry flour for giving the pie crust a flaky, delicate texture well suited for lining the bottom of a light lemon meringue or cream pie. In the equally butter-rich scones, the pastry flour contributed a tender, slightly crumbly, "light but cohesive" texture. It didn't fare so

NO SUBSTITUTE
But fine for crusts.

well in the other two recipes, however. The cookies spread too thin and became more crisp than chewy, while the chiffon cake didn't rise as high, was slightly gummy on the bottom inch, and had an eggy and creamy rather than light and fluffy texture. We also tried these recipes with whole grain pastry flour (milled with all of the bran included), but tasters generally disliked the "odd" brown color, "wheaty" flavor, and "granular" texture of all four baked goods made with this flour.

In the end, we recommend buying regular pastry flour for the tender, flaky texture it imparts to pie crust, tart pastry, scones, and other similarly buttery baked goods (such as biscuits and shortbread) but would stop short of substituting it for cake flour in cakes or all-purpose flour in cookies.

Reheating Pizza

I've noticed when reheating leftover pizza in the oven that the crust is crispier when reheated on parchment paper than on foil. Why is this?

CAROL ROSE
PITTSBURGH, PA.

➤ Before answering questions about the relative merits of foil and parchment, we wanted to test different techniques for reheating pizza. We started by testing three methods: heating pizza on a preheated baking stone, on a baking sheet, and directly on the oven rack with a baking sheet underneath to catch drips. Although we expected the last method to deliver a crisp crust, it didn't; the crust was soft and this method was quite messy. The baking sheet did a good job, but the crust was even more crisp when slices were warmed on a hot baking stone.

Could we adjust our baking sheet method to yield better results? Brushing the crust with oil before reheating just made it tough. Lining the pan with foil made the crust less crisp, but, as you found, parchment paper made the crust more crisp. In fact, when reheated on a parchment-lined baking sheet, the pizza was just as crisp as that heated on a preheated baking stone.

Why does parchment, and not foil, promote crispness? Absorbent parchment paper likely wicks away any moisture on the crust that might otherwise cause sogginess; with foil, the moisture has nowhere to go. Our recommendation is to reheat pizza in a 400-degree oven for six minutes on a baking sheet lined with parchment paper.

SEND US YOUR QUESTIONS We will provide a complimentary one-year subscription for each letter we print. Send your inquiry, name, address, and daytime telephone number to Notes from Readers, Cook's Illustrated, P.O. Box 470589, Brookline, MA 02447, or to notesfromreaders@bcpress.com.

WHAT IS IT?

I recently moved into an apartment with a kitchen drawer full of utensils left behind by the former tenants. I came across this bamboo tool, which looks like some sort of whisk. What is it used for?

JOHN HENRY RICE
PHILADELPHIA, PA.

➤ The item you've found is a *chasen*, a tea whisk carved from a single piece of bamboo that is used to prepare the *matcha* (a bitter, high-quality, stone-ground green tea powder) served in traditional Japanese tea ceremonies. The number and thickness of the splines vary depending on the consistency of the tea and where it will be served. (We found several places online to buy this tea whisk; see the source on page 32 for purchasing information.)

The basic procedure for preparing matcha is as follows: Place a small amount (about ½ teaspoon) of the green tea powder into a tea bowl (*chawan*) using a matcha tea spoon (*chashaku*). (For less formal home use, a measuring spoon and a large latte cup or deep soup bowl make decent substitutes.) Next, pour 4 to 6 ounces of hot (but not boiling) water over the tea. Gently whisk the tea and hot water together to dissolve the matcha. Once it is dissolved, hold the whisk vertically so that it barely touches the bottom of the bowl, and move it briskly back and forth until a frothy layer develops on top. Slowly lift and remove the whisk: Tea is served.

This tea whisk, or chasen, is used to make a frothy bowl of matcha (green tea).

Quick Tips

⪼ COMPILED BY DAVID PAZMIÑO ⪻

Handy Prep Cups

With small children who get lots of sniffles and sneezes, Kerry Roman of Pueblo, Colo., has lots of plastic cough-syrup cups. She saves these cups to measure out (and hold) small amounts of herbs, spices, and other ingredients in preparation for cooking—what the French call *mise en place.*

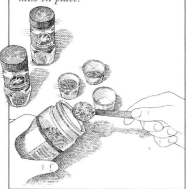

The Cut Stops Here

Eating Chinese food isn't the only use for wooden chopsticks. Luise Bolleber of Rochester, Minn., puts them to work as a guide when cutting decorative strawberry fans to use as a garnish.

Place a chopstick on a cutting board (straight-sided chopsticks work best). Position a strawberry in front of the chopstick. Holding the chopstick and the strawberry with one hand, slice through until the knife hits the chopstick. Continue making ⅛-inch-thick slices, fanning the slices on a plate.

Putting Down Roots

Tired of watching her ginger, carrots, and beets spoil in the vegetable drawer, Aria Arrizabalaga of Moscow, Idaho, figured out how to keep these root vegetables usable for several months.

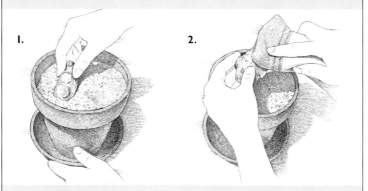

1. Fill a plastic container or clay pot with clean, dry sand. Bury ginger, carrots, or beets in the sand, and store the container in a dark, cool cupboard or in the refrigerator.
2. When you're ready to use a vegetable, just brush off the sand and peel.

Scratchless Steaming

Rather than scratching her saucepan's nonstick surface with the metal legs of a steamer insert, Amy Williams of Glenside, Pa., protects it with parchment paper.

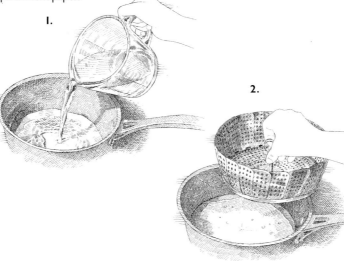

1. Cut a piece of parchment to fit the inside of your saucepan. Fill with 1 inch of water.
2. Place the steamer insert on top of the parchment. Bring to a simmer and steam your food, being careful not to let all the water evaporate.

Lump-Free Polenta

To avoid turning out lumpy polenta and hot cereal, John Barrett of Wakefield, Mass., relies on his funnel.

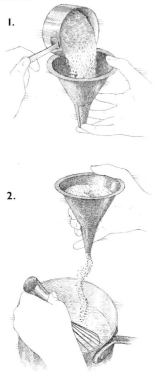

1. After bringing the liquid to a simmer, close off the bottom of a funnel with your finger, then fill it with the polenta meal or cereal called for in your recipe.
2. With the funnel in one hand and a whisk in the other, open the hole and let the grains slowly pour into the hot boiling liquid, whisking until the funnel is empty and the grains are smoothly mixed.

Measuring Spoon Roundup

Measuring spoons often come with flimsy rings that end up breaking. Joyce Wexler of Chicago, Ill., found that a simple "split" key ring keeps spoons together no matter how many times they go through the dishwasher.

Send Us Your Tip   We will provide a complimentary one-year subscription for each tip we print. Send your tip, name, and address to Quick Tips, Cook's Illustrated, P.O. Box 470589, Brookline, MA 02447, or to quicktips@bcpress.com.

ILLUSTRATION: JOHN BURGOYNE

Cleaner Squeeze Tops

Squeeze-bottle tops can get caked with ketchup, mayonnaise, or mustard. Susan Friesen of Abbotsford, B.C., Canada, washes the tops from empty bottles and stores them in a drawer. When the top of a new bottle gets dirty, she unscrews it, replaces it with a clean one, and throws the dirty top into the dishwasher.

Preserving Your Cookbooks

When the pages of her cookbook get soiled or moist from wayward recipe ingredients, Jeri Greenberg of Washington, D.C., uses this trick to keep them from sticking together.

1.

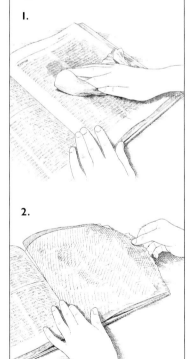

2.

1. Blot the pages dry with paper towels.
2. Slip a piece of waxed paper between the pages before closing.

Bread Box Cutting Boards

Jane Ashworth of Beavercreek, Ohio, hates pulling out and dirtying her large cutting board every time she wants freshly sliced bread. Instead, she keeps a custom-made plastic cutting board right in her bread box. Not only is it conveniently located, but it also needs little maintenance—just a quick wipe to clean off crumbs.

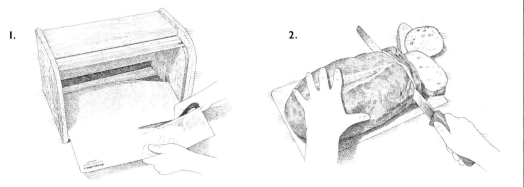

1. Cut a flexible plastic cutting board to fit inside your bread box.
2. Remove the cutting board when slicing bread, discarding any loose crumbs when finished.

Quick Tomato-Seed Removal

Roxanne Summer of Rockville, Md., uses the serrated edges of a grapefruit spoon to cut out the seeded portion of tomatoes after quartering them. She finds this more effective than using a regular spoon—and less messy than using her fingers.

No-Mess Tomato Chopping

Instead of chopping whole canned tomatoes on a cutting board and ending up with tomato juice all over the countertop, Kieran Joshi of Maynard, Mass., cuts them up right in the can with a pair of kitchen scissors.

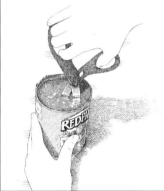

Exploiting the Loophole

Many kitchen towels come with a loop sewn into the hem. Linda Brown of Redmond, Ore., keeps a towel at the ready by hanging it from a button she has sewn into the waist of her apron for that purpose.

Makeshift Roasting Rack

Lacking a metal roasting rack that fits her roasting pan, Lydia Ma of Vancouver, B.C., Canada, makes do with aluminum foil.

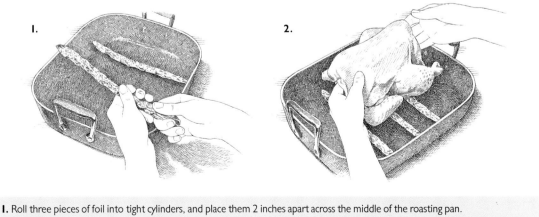

1. Roll three pieces of foil into tight cylinders, and place them 2 inches apart across the middle of the roasting pan.
2. Position the chicken so that it sits evenly atop the cylinders. Once the chicken is finished cooking, cool the foil rolls and discard.

Simplifying Moroccan Chicken

Time-consuming techniques and esoteric ingredients make cooking authentic
Moroccan chicken a daunting proposition. We had one hour and supermarket staples.

⇒ BY MATTHEW CARD ⇐

W hen most people think of Morocco, they envision dusty souks, spindly minarets, and men in flowing djellabas. Not me—I think with my stomach and see tagine. Tagines are exotically spiced, assertively flavored stews slow-cooked in earthenware vessels of the same name. They can include all manner of meats, vegetables, and fruit, though my hands-down favorite combines chicken with briny olives and tart lemon.

While I love tagine, it's not a dish I ever conceived of as American home cooking. Why? The few traditional recipes I had seen required time-consuming, labor-intensive cooking methods, a special pot (the tagine), and hard-to-find ingredients. I'm usually game for a day in the kitchen or a hunt for exotica, but isn't tagine, at its most elemental level, just stew?

A little research proved that I wasn't the first to take a stab at making tagine more accessible. While most of the recipes I tried lacked the depth of an authentic tagine, they did hold promise, proving that a Western cooking method (braising in a Dutch oven) was a serviceable substitution for stewing for hours in a tagine. I also discovered that the flavors I associated with Moroccan cooking weren't necessarily "exotic"—they were a strategic blending of ingredients I already had in my cupboard.

A Chicken in Every Pot

Almost all of the recipes I collected specified a whole chicken—broken down into pieces—and I soon found out why. Batches made entirely with white meat lacked the depth and character of those made with a blend of dark and white.

But when I cooked the white and dark meat in the same way—simmered partially submerged in broth—the white meat turned dry and stringy. Pulling out the white meat when it had just cooked through solved matters, but the close attention required was bothersome. There had to be an easier way.

That's when I thought of carrots. They were added to many of the recipes I had found and, if cut large enough, could raise the white meat pieces above the simmering broth. So I piled sev-

We used the spices and cookware already in our cupboards to create an authentic-tasting Moroccan tagine in less than an hour.

eral large carrot pieces into the bottom of the pot with the dark meat and set the white meat on top. With this method—and a five-minute head start for the dark meat—all the chicken was perfectly cooked and ready at the same time.

Some recipes called for rubbing the chicken with lemon and salt and letting the meat marinate before cooking; others employed salt alone or blended with spices. I found that adding spices at this point resulted in a muddy-flavored broth. Finally, while leaving the skin on the meat to brown it gave the braising liquid a deep flavor, pulling it off before simmering (the standard

Raising the Braise

When braising chicken parts, it can be hard to keep the white meat from turning dry and stringy. We solved this problem by layering the dark meat into the pot first, adding a layer of carrots, then setting the white meat on top of the carrots. The propped-up white meat sits above the braising liquid and cooks at a gentler pace than the dark meat below the surface.

Cook's method for braised chicken dishes) kept the dish free of rubbery skin.

Spices and Such

A large sliced onion and a few minced garlic cloves rounded out the basic flavors of the stew, and I finally felt ready to tackle the defining ingredients: spices, olives, and lemon. Many recipes called for a spice blend called *ras el hanout,* which translates loosely as "top of the shop" and may contain upward of 30 spices. I experimented with a broad range of spices until I landed on a blend that was short on ingredients but long on flavor. Cumin and ginger lent depth, cinnamon brought warmth that tempered a little cayenne heat, and citrusy coriander boosted the stew's lemon flavor. Paprika added sweetness but, perhaps more important, colored the broth a deep, attractive red. Thoroughly toasting the spices in hot oil brought out the full depth of flavors.

Finding the right olive proved harder than I anticipated. Big, meaty, green Moroccan olives were the obvious choice for the stew, but they were a rarity at any of my local markets. Other meaty green olives, like Manzanilla, Cerignola, and Lucques, were either too mild or too assertive to match the other flavors in the stew. Greek "cracked" olives, however, tasted great and were easy to find. (See Kitchen Notes, page 30, for the results of our green olive tasting.) When I added the olives to the stew too soon, their flavor leached out into the braising liquid, rendering them bland and bitter. Stirring in the olives just a few minutes before serving proved a better approach, as they retained their piquant flavor and firm texture.

The lemon flavor in authentic tagines comes from preserved lemon, a long-cured Moroccan

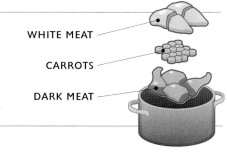

WHITE MEAT

CARROTS

DARK MEAT

condiment that's hard to find outside of specialty stores. "Quick" preserved lemons can be produced at home in a few days, but I wanted to keep my recipe as simple as possible. Part tart citrus, part pickled brine, traditional preserved lemon has a unique flavor that's tough to imitate. So I chose not to try; instead, I aimed for a rich citrus backnote in the dish. I added a few broad ribbons of lemon zest along with the onions, and the high heat coaxed out the zest's oils and mellowed them. Adding a lemon's worth of juice just before serving reinforced the bright flavor.

A spoonful of honey further balanced things, and chopped cilantro leaves freshened the flavors, but I felt the stew still lacked a certain spark. A last-minute addition of raw garlic and finely chopped lemon zest seemed to clinch it, as the sharpness brought out the best in each of the stew's components.

MOROCCAN CHICKEN WITH OLIVES AND LEMON
SERVES 4

Bone-in chicken parts can be substituted for the whole chicken. For best results, use four chicken thighs and two chicken breasts, each breast split in half; the dark meat contributes valuable flavor to the broth and should not be omitted. Use a vegetable peeler to remove wide strips of zest from the lemon before juicing it. Make sure to trim any white pith from the zest, as it can impart bitter flavor. If the olives are particularly salty, give them a rinse. Serve with couscous (see Cook's Extra, below, for a recipe).

1 1/4   teaspoons sweet paprika
1/2   teaspoon ground cumin
1/4   teaspoon cayenne
1/4   teaspoon ground ginger
1/4   teaspoon ground coriander
1/4   teaspoon ground cinnamon
3   strips lemon zest (each about 2 inches by 3/4 inch), plus 3 tablespoons juice from 1 to 2 lemons
5   medium garlic cloves, minced or pressed through garlic press (about 5 teaspoons)
1   whole chicken (3 1/2 to 4 pounds), cut into 8 pieces (4 breast pieces, 2 thighs, 2 drumsticks; wings reserved for another use) and trimmed of excess fat
    Table salt and ground black pepper
1   tablespoon olive oil
1   large onion, halved and cut into 1/4-inch slices (about 3 cups)
1 3/4   cups low-sodium chicken broth
1   tablespoon honey
2   medium carrots, peeled and cut crosswise into 1/2-inch-thick coins, very large pieces cut into half-moons (about 2 cups)
1   cup Greek cracked green olives (see page 30), pitted and halved
2   tablespoons chopped fresh cilantro leaves

EQUIPMENT TESTING: **Do You Really Need a Tagine?**
Tagines (the cooking vessel, not the stew) have lately enjoyed a fashionable comeback in cookware catalogs and food magazines. A shallower take on the Dutch oven, a tagine has a distinctive conical lid that makes for a dramatic presentation at the dinner table. According to tradition, the conical shape helps cooking performance as well: As steam rises during cooking, it condenses in the tip of the relatively cool lid (it's farther from the heat source than most lids) and drips back into the stew, conserving water in the process. Less steam loss means you can start off with less liquid to begin with and thus end up with more-concentrated flavors. Or so the story goes.

To put this theory to test, we brought equal amounts of water to a simmer in three tagines—a traditional terra cotta model ($34) and two modern versions from All-Clad ($199) and Le Creuset ($119.99)—put the lids on, and let the water "cook" over low heat. We included our favorite Dutch ovens (also All-Clad and Le Creuset) for comparison. After one hour, we measured the water left in each of the pots, and it was clear that the tagine's conical shape was not such an advantage after all. The big losers—literally—were the All-Clad Dutch oven and the traditional terra cotta tagine, which lost 16 percent and 30 percent of their water, respectively. (By contrast, the others lost only 8 to 9 percent.) More important than the shape of the pot were the lid's weight and fit: The leaky All-Clad Dutch oven had the lightest lid, while the base and lid of the handmade terra cotta tagine simply didn't fit together as precisely as their machine-made counterparts.

What does all this loss mean when it's more than water cooking? Not much, said our tasters, after sampling five batches of Moroccan chicken. Although the amount of liquid left behind in the stews varied, that variance translated to little discernible flavor difference. If you're a stickler for tradition, choose a tagine with a heavy, tight-fitting lid; our favorite was made by All-Clad. But a Dutch oven will do the job just as well. –Garth Clingingsmith

TOO TRADITIONAL?
The handmade lid of this traditional terra cotta tagine ($34) let steam leak out.

TOP TAGINE
All-Clad's tagine ($199) made a great Moroccan braise, but is it worth the price?

A FINE OPTION
Le Creuset's Dutch oven ($230) produces a tasty tagine—and its talents don't stop there.

1. Combine spices in small bowl and set aside. Mince 1 strip lemon zest; combine with 1 teaspoon minced garlic and mince together until reduced to fine paste; set aside.

2. Season both sides of chicken pieces liberally with salt and pepper. Heat oil in large heavy-bottomed Dutch oven over medium-high heat until beginning to smoke. Brown chicken pieces skin side down in single layer until deep golden, about 5 minutes; using tongs, turn chicken pieces and brown on second side, about 4 minutes more. Transfer chicken to large plate; when cool enough to handle, peel off skin and discard. Pour off and discard all but 1 tablespoon fat from pot.

3. Add onion and 2 remaining lemon zest strips to pot and cook, stirring occasionally, until onions have browned at edges but still retain shape, 5 to 7 minutes (add 1 tablespoon water if pan gets too dark). Add remaining 4 teaspoons garlic and cook, stirring, until fragrant, about 30 seconds. Add spices and cook, stirring con-stantly, until darkened and very fragrant, 45 seconds to 1 minute. Stir in broth and honey, scraping bottom of pot with wooden spoon to loosen browned bits. Add thighs and drumsticks, reduce heat to medium, and simmer for 5 minutes.

4. Add carrots and breast pieces (with any accu-mulated juices) to pot, arranging breast pieces in single layer on top of carrots. Cover, reduce heat to medium-low, and simmer until instant-read thermometer inserted into thickest part of breast registers 160 degrees, 10 to 15 minutes.

5. Transfer chicken to plate or bowl and tent with foil. Add olives to pot; increase heat to medium-high and simmer until liquid has thickened slightly and carrots are tender, 4 to 6 minutes. Return chicken to pot and add garlic-zest mixture, cilantro, and lemon juice; stir to combine and adjust seasoning with salt and pepper. Serve immediately.

MOROCCAN CHICKEN WITH CHICKPEAS AND APRICOTS

Follow recipe for Moroccan Chicken with Olives and Lemon, replacing 1 carrot with 1 cup dried apricots, halved, and replacing olives with 1 (15-ounce) can chickpeas, drained and rinsed.

Go to www.cooksillustrated.com
- Key in code 5061 for **Couscous Pilaf with Raisins and Almonds.**
- Key in code 5062 for the results of our **Paprika Tasting.**
- This information will be available until November 1, 2006.

Bringing Home Fish and Chips

Restaurant versions of England's favorite fast food rarely measure up. But trying it at home produced a greasy mess. Could we conquer our fear of frying?

≥ BY SEAN LAWLER ≤

On a recent visit to London, I was reluctant to join the throngs queuing up for England's most famous fast food: batter-fried fish, dumped onto a mound of fried potatoes and doused with malt vinegar. But when the food arrived, my attitude changed. Unlike any fried fish platter I'd ever ordered from a seaside shack, this one had large pieces of thick cod that were moist, delicate, and still steaming inside a crisp and tender coating. And, unlike fast-food fries, the "chips" were cut thick and served up crispy, with soft interiors.

With fish-and-chip shops like that one on every corner, most Britons wouldn't bother with the hassle and mess of deep-frying fish at home. But if I wanted to recreate my London experience stateside, I had no other choice, given the mediocre versions found in most American pubs. Along the way, I needed to figure out how to organize the process so that everything made it to the table at once.

Batter Up

Unsure how I would resolve this logistical challenge, I decided to focus first on developing a recipe for a batter that would perform two important functions. First, protection. A piece of plain fish dropped into hot oil overcooks almost instantly. While a coating of flour or bread crumbs provides a modicum of defense, a wet batter is the best defense because it completely coats the fish, allowing it to steam gently as it cooks. Second, the batter must form a coating that provides crisp contrast with the moist fish.

In the bulk of the recipes I surveyed, the batter (usually a 50/50 mix of flour and beer) excelled at the first task and flunked the second. The fish came out moist, but the coating was bready and thick. Worse, as the fish drained on paper towels, it continued to produce steam; minutes later, the crust was falling off the fish. I tried thinning the batter with more beer so that less steam would be trapped, but that brought new problems. The liquid in the batter began to boil almost immediately upon hitting the oil, and the coating failed to survive.

If I couldn't thin the batter, perhaps I could

We achieved the ideal contrast of light, crisp exterior and moist interior by carefully constructing our batter—and our cooking sequence.

adjust its structure. The obvious culprit behind the bready texture was gluten, the protein that gives bread its structure. What if I replaced some of the all-purpose flour with a starch that doesn't develop gluten? Various tests led me to a 3:1 ratio of flour to cornstarch. This thinner (but not wetter) mixture survived the hot oil and fried up crisp. Finally, a teaspoon of baking powder created tiny bubbles in the batter, giving the coating an airier texture.

One problem lingered: While the texture of the coating was great, it tended to puff away from the fish as it fried, ultimately flaking off in large pieces with the first bite. I had been drying the fish well and dredging it in flour before battering—techniques meant to stop this from happening—but it was still a problem. I tried spreading extra flour on a baking sheet, and, after dredging and battering each piece, I coated the fish with flour again. Success! The resulting coating had a slightly crumbly, irregular texture that clung tightly to the fish. A bit of cayenne for

spice and a sprinkle of paprika for color finished the deal.

Chipping Away

A recipe developed years ago at *Cook's* confirmed what any restaurant line cook knows well: The best fries are cooked twice. They're "blanched" in low-temperature oil to cook the centers, then finished in hotter oil to crisp the outsides to a golden brown. My plan was to blanch the fries, turn up the heat on the oil and fry the fish, then keep the fish warm while the fries finished.

There were two problems with this plan. First, the fish was not as crisp as it had been before. I suspected the "used" oil was the problem: The 3 pounds of potatoes I had already dumped into the oil released a lot of moisture, much of which bubbled away as steam but some of which remained in the oil, diluting it and thus diminishing its ability to make things crisp. The oil was in even worse condition after the fish had fried, which exacerbated the second problem: The blanched, oversized fries took about 10 minutes to turn golden brown and crisp, by which time the cooling fish was several minutes past its prime.

A colleague had developed a recipe for skillet potatoes that involved first parcooking sliced potatoes in a microwave. Could I parcook the fries to get rid of some of the excess water before the potatoes hit the oil? Yes, but if microwaved too long (until completely tender), the thick fries began to crumble and fall apart. They would still have to blanch in the oil, but the microwave head-start let me blanch at a higher temperature, partially browning the fries in advance to shave crucial minutes off of the final frying time. To further improve the quality of the oil, I tried adding some fresh oil to the pot just before frying the fish and found the crispness of the final products to be greatly improved.

This patchwork method—alternating the fish and the fries (see Recipe Shorthand, page 9)—was quick and easy, and it resulted in fish and chips that were done in sync. Finally, I had a recipe to keep me satisfied until my next trip across the Atlantic.

FISH AND CHIPS
SERVES 4

Ask your fishmonger to remove the thin tail portions of the fish. For safety, use a Dutch oven with at least a 7-quart capacity. Any beer will work in this recipe, even nonalcoholic beer, with the exception of dark stouts and ales. Serve with traditional malt vinegar or with tartar sauce.

- 3 pounds russet potatoes (about 4 large potatoes), peeled, ends and sides squared off, and cut lengthwise into ½ inch by ½-inch fries (see Kitchen Notes, page 30, for detailed instructions)
- 3 quarts plus ¼ cup peanut oil or canola oil
- 1½ cups all-purpose flour
- ½ cup cornstarch
- ½ teaspoon cayenne
- ½ teaspoon paprika
- ⅛ teaspoon ground black pepper
  Table salt
- 1 teaspoon baking powder
- 1½ pounds cod or other thick white fish fillet, such as hake or haddock, cut into eight 3-ounce pieces about 1 inch thick
- 1½ cups (12 ounces) cold beer

1. Place cut fries in large microwaveable bowl, toss with ¼ cup oil, and cover with plastic wrap. Microwave on high power until potatoes are partially translucent and pliable but still offer some resistance when pierced with tip of paring knife, 6 to 8 minutes, tossing them with rubber spatula halfway through cooking time. Carefully pull back plastic wrap from side farthest from you and drain potatoes into large mesh strainer set over sink. Rinse well under cold running water. Spread potatoes onto kitchen towels and pat dry. Let rest until room temperature, at least 10 minutes and up to 1 hour.

2. While fries cool, whisk flour, cornstarch, cayenne, paprika, pepper, and 2 teaspoons salt

in large mixing bowl; transfer ¾ cup of mixture to rimmed baking sheet. Add baking powder to bowl and whisk to combine.

3. In heavy-bottomed Dutch oven, heat 2 quarts oil over medium heat to 350 degrees. Add fries to hot oil and increase heat to high. Fry, stirring with mesh spider or slotted metal spoon, until potatoes turn light golden and just begin to brown at corners, 6 to 8 minutes. Transfer fries to thick paper bag or paper towels to drain.

EQUIPMENT TESTING: **High-End Deep Fryers**

From past tests, we know a decent deep fryer can be had for less than $80. Spend more and you'll get fancy features like oil filtration systems. But what about basic performance? To find out, we embarked on a french-fry marathon with six high-end models—Masterbuilt Turk'N'Surf ($199.95), Deni Multi-Fryer ($99.99), DeLonghi Dual Zone ($99.95), Waring Professional ($129.95), T-Fal Ultimate EZ Clean ($119.95), and DeLonghi Cool Touch ($129.95)—plus our favorite inexpensive model, the Oster Immersion ($79.95).

All the models turned out tasty fries—eventually. The difference between good performance and great hinged on oil capacity. The more capacity, the less severe the temperature drop once the food hit the oil, which allowed for fewer batches and quicker recovery between batches. For instance, the Masterbuilt, which holds 2 gallons of oil (enough to fry a 14-pound turkey!), dropped 34 degrees when we added a pound

of fries. In contrast, the DeLonghi Cool Touch, which uses a mere 1.3 quarts (it rotates food into and out of the oil), lost a whopping 114 degrees. What that means in practical terms is that the Masterbuilt can effectively cook an entire batch of fries; by the time the smallest model finished its fourth partial batch, the rest of the fries were soggy and limp.

Every model was equipped with a built-in thermostat—an essential feature, to our minds. But other "deluxe" features seemed extraneous. Transparent lids are nice in theory but quickly rendered useless by emanating steam. T-Fal's so-called EZ Clean—the oil is filtered and drained into a container—is anything but easy.

Ideally, we'd fry our fries in one batch, but pouring 2 gallons of oil into the Masterbuilt seems excessive. If you don't often fry fish and chips, the Oster—the cheap model—is all you really need.

—Garth Clingingsmith

BEST BUY	GAS GUZZLER	FILTERED OUT	SMALL FRY
The Oster Immersion ($79.95) offers all the fryer you need for most recipes.	The Masterbuilt ($199.95) was the best performer but required lots of oil.	The T-Fal ($119.95) had a fancy—but unnecessary—oil filtration system.	The DeLonghi Cool-Touch ($129.95) was innovative but lacked capacity.

4. Reduce heat to medium-high, add remaining quart of oil, and heat oil to 375 degrees. Meanwhile, thoroughly dry fish with paper towels and dredge each piece in flour mixture on baking sheet; transfer pieces to wire rack, shaking off excess flour. Add 1¼ cups beer to flour mixture in mixing bowl and stir until mixture is just combined (batter will be lumpy). Add remaining beer as needed, 1 tablespoon at a time, whisking after each addition, until batter falls from whisk in thin, steady stream and leaves faint trail across surface of batter. Using tongs, dip 1 piece fish in batter and let excess run off, shaking gently. Place battered fish back onto baking sheet with flour mixture and turn to coat both sides. Repeat with remaining fish, keeping pieces in single layer on baking sheet.

5. When oil reaches 375 degrees, increase heat to high and add battered fish to oil with tongs, gently shaking off excess flour. Fry, stirring occasionally, until golden brown, 7 to 8 minutes. Transfer fish to thick paper bag or paper towels to drain. Allow oil to return to 375 degrees.

6. Add all fries back to oil and fry until golden brown and crisp, 3 to 5 minutes. Transfer to fresh paper bag or paper towels to drain. Season fries with salt to taste and serve immediately with fish.

RECIPE SHORTHAND | GETTING THE FISH AND CHIPS IN SYNC

To ensure that the fish and chips are done at the same time, we crafted this sequence of steps that also minimizes mess.

| MICROWAVE POTATOES | RINSE POTATOES | FRY POTATOES | FRY FISH | FRY POTATOES AGAIN |

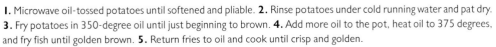

1. Microwave oil-tossed potatoes until softened and pliable. **2.** Rinse potatoes under cold running water and pat dry. **3.** Fry potatoes in 350-degree oil until just beginning to brown. **4.** Add more oil to the pot, heat oil to 375 degrees, and fry fish until golden brown. **5.** Return fries to oil and cook until crisp and golden.

Grilled Tomato Salsa

Could we transform out-of-season tomatoes into a sweet and smoky salsa?

⋟ BY ERIN MCMURRER ⋞

Grilled tomato salsa sounds terrific on paper. Who can argue with the idea of pairing traditional salsa's spicy heat and brightness with the smoky-sweet flavors that come from a quick stint on the grill? In practice, however, I found this recipe less alluring. Skins charred and curled off, tomatoes stuck to the cooking grate, and most versions had little smoke flavor. But even these disappointing tests held promise. If I could figure out a way to get the grilled flavor into the tomato without losing most of the tomato in the process, this recipe would be a great way to transform mediocre out-of-season tomatoes into something truly special.

First up, tomato choice: Beefsteak tomatoes were too watery. Cherry tomatoes were firm and sweet, but chasing them around on the grill was a losing proposition. Plum tomatoes were the meatiest of the bunch—and therefore the best suited to grilling. Because they could take the heat for a longer period of time, they could also take on more grilled flavor.

I first tried grilling the plum tomatoes whole, but it was hard to get a decent sear all the way around without losing most of the skin. Halving and seeding the tomatoes—and thereby exposing twice the surface area to the grill—produced a salsa with much more grilled flavor, but it was too dry. Next I tried halving the tomatoes but leaving the seeds in; this approach yielded a salsa with decent texture and grilled flavor, but I was losing a fair amount of flesh through the cooking grate. By grilling the halves cut side down first, then flipping them once well caramelized, the skin acted as a cradle that helped keep the flesh intact as the tomatoes continued to cook and soften.

I tried grilled and raw versions of red, white, yellow, and green onions. Tasters liked the red onions for their sweetness, and they liked them raw—their fresh bite adding a nice contrast to the softness of the grilled tomatoes. When it came to chiles, however, tasters preferred the deep flavor of grilled—not raw—jalapeños.

I now had a tomato salsa with good grilled flavor, but tasters wanted more. I turned to smoking, adding a foil packet of soaked wood chips to the hot coals. But because the tomatoes cooked so quickly, the foil-encased chips didn't have the time they needed to produce enough smoke. Next I tried doing away with the foil packet and tossed the soaked chips directly onto the coals—where they quickly ignited and proceeded to torch the tomatoes.

The solution was to build a modified two-level fire, with all the coals banked on one side of the grill. I added the chips to the hot coals once the tomatoes were safely situated over the cooler (coal-free) side of the grill and then covered the grill for just two minutes, which produced more than enough billowing smoke to boost the flavor of the tomatoes and chiles.

To balance and brighten the deep, smoky flavors of the tomatoes and chiles, I added a squeeze of lime juice, a handful of cilantro, and a bit of sugar, salt, and pepper. Given just 10 minutes to let the flavors meld, the salsa was so smoky and sweet that it was hard to believe that peak tomato season was months away.

SWEET AND SMOKY GRILLED TOMATO SALSA
MAKES ABOUT 3 CUPS

Sugar and lime juice should be added at the end to taste, depending on the ripeness of the tomatoes. For a spicier salsa, don't seed the grilled chiles. This salsa is a good match for tortilla chips but also goes well with grilled food and eggs. If serving the salsa with grilled meat or fish, grill the tomatoes and jalapeños, add more unlit coals, and then finish the salsa while you wait for the fire to intensify again before cooking the meat or fish. Mesquite wood chips are too potent for this recipe; we prefer hickory.

- 2 pounds plum tomatoes (10 to 12 medium), cored and halved pole to pole
- 2 large jalapeño chiles
- 2 teaspoons vegetable oil, plus additional for brushing cooking grate
- 1 cup wood chips, preferably hickory, soaked for 15 minutes
- 3 tablespoons minced red onion
- 2 tablespoons chopped fresh cilantro leaves
- 1 teaspoon table salt
- ¼ teaspoon ground black pepper
- 2 tablespoons extra-virgin olive oil
- ½ teaspoon sugar (see note above)
- 1–2 tablespoons juice from 1 lime (see note above)

1. Open top and bottom grill vents. Using large chimney, light 6 quarts charcoal (about 100 briquettes) and let burn until partially covered with layer of fine gray ash. Empty coals onto grill and build modified two-level fire by arranging all coals to cover one-half of grill. Position cooking grate over coals, cover grill, and heat until hot, about 5 minutes; scrape grate clean with grill brush.

2. Place tomatoes and chiles in bowl; drizzle with vegetable oil and toss to coat evenly. Using long-handled grill tongs, dip wad of paper towels lightly in vegetable oil and wipe hot side of grate. Place tomatoes cut side down over hot side of grill. Grill tomatoes until evenly charred and beginning to soften, 4 to 6 minutes, moving tomatoes from edges of grill to center as needed to make sure all tomatoes are evenly charred. Using tongs, flip tomatoes and grill until skin sides are charred and tomato juices bubble, 4 to 6 minutes more. As tomatoes finish charring, move to cooler side of grill, leaving firmer ones closer to coals and placing softer ones farther away (tomatoes should be very tender but not falling apart). While tomatoes are cooking, grill chiles over hot part of grill until skins are blackened on all sides, 8 to 10 minutes, turning as needed. Transfer to cooler side of grill.

3. When both tomatoes and chiles are on cooler side of grill, add soaked wood chips to hot coals and cover grill, positioning open lid vent over tomatoes. Cook for 2 minutes (smoke should billow through vents after about 30 seconds). Transfer vegetables to platter and let cool in single layer, at least 10 minutes.

4. Stem, peel, seed, and finely chop chiles. Pulse tomatoes in food processor until broken down but still chunky, about six 1-second pulses. Transfer tomatoes to bowl; stir in chiles, onion, cilantro, salt, pepper, and olive oil. Taste and add sugar and lime juice as needed to balance flavors. Let stand for 10 minutes and serve. (Salsa can be refrigerated in airtight container for up to 2 days; bring back to room temperature before serving.)

FOR GAS GRILL: Place wood chips in small disposable aluminum pan; set pan on edge of grill burner and position cooking grate. Ignite grill, turn all burners to high, cover, and heat until very hot and chips are beginning to smoke, about 15 minutes. (If chips ignite, use water-filled spray bottle to extinguish.) Scrape grate clean with grill brush. Continue with recipe from step 2, grilling tomatoes and chiles entirely over high heat on side of grill away from wood chips and with lid down, checking often to make sure they are not burning. Timing should be similar to that in charcoal recipe.

Grilled London Broil

Throwing a slab of cheap meat on the grill sounds easy, but the result can be more like chewing on a tire than on a nicely charred, tender steak.

≥ BY DAVID PAZMIÑO ≤

Anyone can grill up tender, rosy-pink, nicely charred steaks using pricey cuts from the rib or the loin; all they need is salt, pepper, oil, and a few licks from a hot flame. Try that simple approach with an inexpensive, large, and tough steak—like one labeled "London Broil"—and the meat usually turns into gray, livery chewing gum by the time it's developed a decent sear.

London broil is actually not a specific cut of meat; rather, it's a name given to various cheap cuts of beef that are cooked quickly, then sliced ultra-thin to mitigate some of the toughness. It's a marketing ploy of sorts—a way for supermarkets and butchers to unload unfamiliar steaks that home cooks aren't sure what to do with. Wanting to satisfy my caveman instincts for a grilled piece of meat without breaking the bank, I headed to the supermarket to search out this oversized cut.

Tough Choices
A utilitarian yellow or orange sticker proclaiming "London Broil" makes these steaks easy to spot among the many choices in the meat case. I commonly found it on three steaks: chuck shoulder, top round, and bottom round (see "Would the Real London Broil Please Stand Up?" below). Picking up all three, I checked out and made my way back to the test kitchen.

After firing up the grill and simply cooking the meat with salt, pepper, and oil, a few things

Carving grilled London broil into ultra-thin slices is just one of several tricks we used to transform a cheap steak into a terrific meal.

became apparent. Chuck shoulder steak, one of the test kitchen's perennial favorites, had great flavor, but when thinly sliced against the grain its three muscle groups left unappealing seams of fat in each slice. Move toward the rear of the animal and you get top round and bottom round steaks, which are more uniform in shape than

the chuck shoulder. Once the steaks were grilled, however, their toughness became apparent, and the meat itself was on the livery side. Still, these were the cheapest and thickest steaks I found, and they did develop a deep, dark, and evenly seared outer crust (especially the noticeably more uniform bottom round). Clearly, I had my work cut out for me.

'De-livering' Flavor
To solve the problem of livery flavor, I first turned to London broil recipes from the 1950s. The conventional wisdom was to immerse the meat in a vinaigrette-style marinade for two to 24 hours. I knew from previous testing that marinades do little for tenderness (the acids have the effect of "cooking" the proteins on the surface of the meat, making them drier after the real cooking) but thought that they might take care of the livery flavor of the meat. So I surrendered to tradition and dunked more than a dozen steaks in acidic baths flavored with a variety of ingredients, including red wine, Worcestershire sauce, balsamic vinegar, Italian dressing, and lemon juice. Although some of the marinades gave the steaks great flavor, they also squelched any beefiness. I wanted a steak that tasted like beef, not vinaigrette.

Up to this point, I had been testing all these marinades with steaks that had been simply salted and peppered. Had I overlooked the simplicity of salt as a possible solution? I coated steaks with various amounts of kosher salt (easier to

Would the Real London Broil Please Stand Up?

Coined in the early 1930s at Keen's Chophouse in New York City, the term "London broil" doesn't refer to a particular cut of meat at all. Rather, it's a generic label bandied about by butchers to sell large, cheap, unfamiliar steaks that might otherwise be ignored by customers. Over the years, a number of different steaks have been called London broil. For a while, flank steak was the most common, but flank's popularity on the grill and in stir-fries bumped its price into the $6.99-a-pound range—a bit too rich for London broil territory. Nowadays, you'll mostly see the still-cheap (roughly $3.99 a pound) chuck shoulder steak, top round steak, and bottom round steak labeled as London broil.

FLANK
Good and beefy, but its recent popularity has inflated prices.

CHUCK SHOULDER
Great flavor, but multiple muscle groups make for "gristly," unattractive slices.

TOP ROUND
Though "mineral-y" with a "tire-like toughness," top round is appealingly beefy.

BOTTOM ROUND
Similar to top round, but its uniform shape makes it even better for grilling; our favorite.

Coaxing the Best Out of London Broil

A tough, livery, unevenly browned slab of meat that buckles up when grilled? Not a very appealing combination. Instead of admitting defeat—and opting for pricey porterhouse—we stepped up to the challenge. Turns out a tough, cheap steak just needs a bit of old-fashioned pampering to smooth out its rough edges.

SALT RUBDOWN

Salt draws juices to the surface, where they eventually dissolve the salt; the juices are then reabsorbed in the form of a flavorful, concentrated "brine," bringing out beefy flavors and masking livery ones.

WARM BATH

Submerging the (wrapped) beef in warm water for the last hour of salting cuts the cooking time by almost 10 minutes—providing less opportunity for fatty acids to break down into off-tasting compounds.

MUSCLE RELAXATION

Flipping the meat once per minute keeps the long muscle fibers from contracting and buckling up, making it easier to achieve a good sear.

SLEEK CUT

Holding the knife perpendicular to the cutting board and slicing the meat diagonally (at a 45-degree angle) into ultra-thin slices shortens the long, tough muscle fibers, dramatically diminishing chewiness.

sprinkle evenly than table salt) and let them sit for short periods of time, eventually settling on 2 teaspoons of salt and four hours. Rather than salting the meat and putting it on a plate, I wrapped it tightly in plastic wrap. Once I took these steaks off the grill, tasters commented on their "beefiness" and "clean" flavors. Upon further research, I learned that the salt had drawn out the steak's juices, which mixed with the salt on the exterior and created a shallow "brine" that was reabsorbed by the meat over the four-hour period. The salt improved the flavor by accentuating the steaks' naturally beefy flavors and by masking some of the more unsavory (read: livery) off-notes.

Tenderizing Moments

I had done everything I could think of to combat the livery flavor, so I turned my attention to the other problem: the tough, chewy texture. I already knew that marinades with acid did little for the texture, but could there be other tenderizing ingredients? Scouring the cookbook literature for likely candidates, I decided to try yogurt, buttermilk, pineapple, papaya, kiwi, ginger, soda, commercial tenderizing powder, and a Jaccard (a sharp tool that breaks down meat).

After several tests with yogurt and buttermilk, it was apparent that the acids and enzymes in dairy were tenderizing the exterior of the meat but were doing nothing to the tough interior fibers. The enzymes in uncooked pineapple, papaya, kiwi, and ginger work similarly to acids in that they break down proteins. Unfortunately, they produced a similar outcome—softened exterior and tough interior, with overwhelming fruity and sour flavors left behind. Soda proved to be a dead end as well. Coca-Cola, Dr Pepper, and tonic water all dried out the meat, leaving it extremely tough and unpalatable.

The commercial tenderizer Adolph's, which

had worked so well on the thin cutlets called for in our Veal Scaloppini (see page 18), worked on only the outer quarter-inch of my steaks and left them tasting overly salty. If I couldn't break down the muscle fibers with chemicals, I figured I might as well try brute force. I turned to a Jaccard machine, a handheld device consisting of 48 small, pointy knives that cut up the tough fibers. After treating several pieces with the Jaccard (which resembles a medieval tool used for torture), the steak turned not merely tender but mushy.

Back to the drawing board, I decided to experiment with cooking techniques to solve the texture problem. At this point, I was employing the test kitchen's usual method for cooking a large piece of meat on the grill: searing it until well charred on the hot side of a modified two-level fire (that is, with the coals piled up on just one side of the grill), then moving it to the cooler (empty) side until it reached the right temperature. (Because bottom round is so lean, I took the additional step of brushing the exterior with oil to encourage charring—tough steaks get even tougher when overcooked.) Despite having a nice char and reaching an internal temperature of 120 degrees, the steaks all had discernible bands of gray meat surrounding a rosy, medium-rare interior. These predominant gray bands were simply overcooked meat, and they were the main reason tasters were experiencing the steaks as dry and tough. If I could turn out a more evenly cooked steak and eliminate these desiccated, chewy bands, I might be on my way to solving the problem of texture.

Harold McGee, in his book *On Food and Cooking* (1984), had the answer. He suggests increasing the temperature of the steak prior to cooking by soaking it in warm water—weird, yes, but worth a try. Increasing the temperature

of the raw meat from a refrigerator-chilly 40 degrees to 70 degrees would bring it closer to the finishing temperature of 120 degrees; this in turn would mean less time on the grill and a more evenly cooked and juicier steak. Before diving head first into the water, I thought it might be easier to simply leave the meat out at room temperature. After an hour, though, the internal temperature of the meat had increased by only 3 degrees. It took nearly six hours to reach 70 degrees—enough time for bacteria to multiply. I opted to try the quicker (and safer) method. Placing a steak wrapped in a plastic bag in a bucket of 100-degree water for just an hour brought the temperature up from 40 degrees to 70 degrees. It also decreased the grilling time from 22 minutes to just 13 (eight minutes on the hot side, five on the cooler). After resting, this pre-warmed steak revealed a gorgeous rosy interior as well as a decent char—and gone were the thick, overcooked gray bands near the edges.

But texture wasn't the only beneficiary of a shorter cooking time. The steaks cooked this way also tasted much less livery. After some careful research, I learned that the longer meat cooks, the more opportunity there is for the oxygen (stored in its proteins) to react with the fatty acids (stored in its fat) to produce the noxious, livery flavors and aromas that had plagued my steaks throughout recipe development. By reducing the cooking time, I was also able to rein in these reactions. Two birds with one stone!

Final Matters

The last nagging problem with the steak was the way that it curled and buckled on the grill. After spending four minutes over direct heat, the steak would start to curl. Making vertical slits along the edges didn't prevent the problem. I wondered what would happen if instead of flipping the steak only once I flipped it before the vertical muscle fibers had enough time to contract. After experimenting with different times, from 30 seconds to four minutes, I found that flipping the steak once every minute was perfect. The total searing time was 8 minutes (followed by 5 minutes on the cooler side), so the steak had to be flipped about eight times. This simple exercise was well worth it, as the meat now had an evenly cooked exterior with great color and flavor.

Now I had only to perform the last London broil ritual: tradition calls for slicing thinly against the grain. Unlike steaks that have a visible horizontal grain, the grain in top and bottom round steaks runs vertically; slicing them against the grain would require a dangerous parlor trick, standing the steak on one of its short sides and cutting thin slices across its face! Instead, the key was to shorten the grains by cutting thinly and diagonally, at a 45-degree angle (see photo on page 12), shortening the fibers and creating the impression of a more tender piece of beef.

In the end, getting a tender, flavorful, nicely charred steak out of a London broil meant using the same small arsenal of ingredients—salt, pepper, and oil—used on high-priced, well-marbled cuts of beef. The secret was in the finessing.

LONDON BROIL FOR A CHARCOAL GRILL
SERVES 4 TO 6

Tasters preferred bottom round for this recipe. While top round can be substituted, it is harder to get an even sear on its less uniform surface. We do not recommend cooking London broil beyond medium-rare. For the best texture, use a carving or slicing knife and cut the steak into very thin slices. (If you're stuck with a dull chef's knife, first cut the steak in half lengthwise, as shorter slices are easier to cut; see Kitchen Notes, page 31, for instructions.) If desired, serve with Sweet and Smoky Grilled Tomato Salsa (page 10) or Chimichurri Sauce (see Cook's Extra).

- 2 teaspoons kosher salt
- 1 bottom round steak, 2 to 2½ pounds and 1½ inches thick
- 1 tablespoon vegetable oil
- ½ teaspoon ground black pepper

1. Sprinkle both sides of steak evenly with salt; wrap tightly with plastic wrap and refrigerate for at least 3 hours (steak can be salted and refrigerated for up to 24 hours).

2. Fill large pot or bucket with 1 gallon warm water (about 100 degrees). Place wrapped steak into zipper-lock plastic bag, squeeze out excess air, and seal bag tightly. Place steak in water, covering with plate or bowl to keep bag submerged. Set aside for 1 hour.

3. About 20 minutes before grilling, light large chimney starter filled with charcoal (6 quarts, or about 100 briquettes) and allow to burn until coals are covered in thin, gray ash, about 20 minutes. Empty coals into grill and build modified two-level fire by arranging coals to cover one-half of grill with other half empty. Position cooking grate over coals, cover grill, and heat until hot, about 5 minutes; scrape grate clean with grill brush.

4. Remove steak from water and unwrap; brush both sides with oil (salt will have dissolved) and sprinkle evenly with pepper. Grill steak directly over coals, flipping steak with tongs once every minute, until dark brown crust forms on both sides, about 8 minutes. Move steak to cooler side of grill; cover grill and continue cooking until instant-read thermometer inserted into center of steak registers 120 degrees for rare to medium-rare, about 5 minutes, flipping steak halfway through cooking time.

5. Transfer steak to cutting board and let rest, tented with foil, about 10 minutes. Holding thin slicing knife at 45-degree angle to meat (see photo on page 12), slice very thinly and serve.

Go to www.cooksillustrated.com
- Key in code 5063 for our recipe for **Chimichurri Sauce**.
- This information will be available until November 1, 2006.

COOK'S **extra**

ILLUSTRATION: SEAN McNAUGHTON

SCIENCE:
Why Does Some Meat Taste Livery?

While developing the recipe for grilled London broil, one of my biggest hurdles was the presence of "iron-y" and livery flavors in the bottom round I was using. Through research, I learned that the more active a muscle is, the more oxygen it requires to function—and the more oxygen it stores in an iron-rich protein called myoglobin. So far, so good. The problem comes up when steaks cut from particularly active muscles (the bottom round, for instance, is from the leg) are heated. The heat releases the oxygen from the myoglobin, leaving it free to react with the fatty acids present in all meat to produce livery, iron-y flavors and aromas in the form of compounds called aldehydes. In short, what's causing the off flavors is oxidation. And the longer the cooking time and the higher the temperature, the more oxidation occurs.

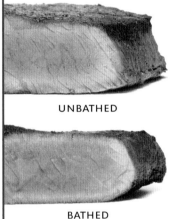

food science 101

heat + meat + time = livery flavors

UNBATHED

BATHED

Back in the test kitchen, we considered our options. While we don't usually give our steaks a bath before cooking, in the case of London broil, a warm soak really did the trick—by shortening the cooking time considerably. When we grilled a 1½-inch-thick bottom round steak straight from the refrigerator, it took about 22 minutes to achieve a medium-rare center; by that time, the steak had developed an overcooked, gray band around the perimeter (top photo). When we soaked the wrapped steak in 100-degree water for an hour first, we reached the same temperature in just 13 minutes—almost half the time! (That's because while the refrigerated steak started out at 40 degrees, the bathed steak started out at 70 degrees, giving it a big jump toward the endpoint of 120 degrees.) Instead of a tough gray band, our soaked steak had subtle gradations of rosy pink (bottom photo). And most important: The bottom round that cooked for about half the time tasted much less livery. –D.P.

LONDON BROIL FOR A GAS GRILL

Because gas grills generally produce less heat than charcoal grills, the steak requires a longer cooking time (and less frequent flipping) to develop a nice char. We have therefore omitted the step of warming the steak in water and employed metal skewers to keep it from buckling.

1. Sprinkle both sides of steak evenly with salt; wrap tightly with plastic wrap and refrigerate for at least 4 hours or up to 24 hours.

2. About 20 minutes before grilling, ignite grill, turn all burners to high, close cover, and heat until very hot, about 15 minutes. Scrape cooking grate clean with grill brush.

3. Unwrap steak; insert 3 metal skewers lengthwise through center of steak, spacing skewers about 1 inch apart. Brush both sides of steak with oil and sprinkle evenly with pepper. Place steak on hottest part of grill. Grill, flipping steak every 4 minutes, until instant-read thermometer inserted into center of meat registers 120 degrees for rare to medium-rare, 16 to 20 minutes.

4. Transfer steak to cutting board and let rest, tented with foil, about 10 minutes. Remove skewers. Holding thin slicing knife at 45-degree angle to meat, slice very thinly and serve.

Main-Dish Vegetable Stir-Fries

Stir-fried vegetables make a great side dish, but can they step up to the plate as an entree? Casting our carnivorous doubts aside, we raided the produce aisle.

≥ BY DAVID PAZMIÑO ≤

For a fast and easy weeknight dinner, it's hard to beat a stir-fry: Sliced meat and chopped vegetables are cooked quickly over high heat, then tossed with a bold-flavored sauce and served. Take out the meat, however, and this one-dish meal devolves into a side dish. The all-vegetable stir-fry has plenty of pleasing contrasts of flavor and texture but nothing substantial enough to anchor the dish firmly in entree territory.

Unlike many of my colleagues, I was convinced there was a way to make a satisfying meal out of nothing but stir-fried vegetables. It wasn't the meat they were missing from these all-veggie stir-fries, I reasoned, but the *meatiness*. And with a few strategically chosen vegetables, I thought I could change the mind of even the most unapologetic carnivore in the test kitchen.

Meaty Mushrooms

Scanning the produce aisle of my supermarket, it wasn't hard to figure out where to start. If it was meaty heft and texture I was after, mushrooms were the obvious choice—specifically, hearty portobellos. To capitalize on their bulk and meatiness, I cut them into wedges large enough to stand out from the other vegetables.

The only problem now was the gills, which often broke off and muddied the sauce. I tried cooking the mushrooms on the tops only (to keep the gills intact), but this technique left the mushrooms leathery and raw-tasting. Scraping the gills off with a spoon before cooking solved the problem (see illustration at right).

Now that I had settled on a cooking technique for my starring vegetable, it was time to move on to the supporting cast—and to more familiar territory. Taking the kitchen's tried-and-true procedure for stir-fries, I simply plugged in the meaty portobellos where the sliced beef or chicken usually went: Cook the portobellos in batches and set them aside; steam-sauté the longer-cooking vegetables (such as carrots and broccoli; see the

Cutting portobello mushrooms into large wedges gives them added heft and meatiness in a main-course stir-fry.

chart on page 15) and set them aside; stir-fry the softer vegetables (such as celery and bell pepper), greens (napa cabbage or bok choy), and aromatics (garlic and ginger); then add all of the vegetables back to the pan along with a flavorful sauce.

The technique worked without a hitch, but I thought the portobellos could still be more distinct from the other vegetables. Taking another cue from meat stir-fries, I experimented with marinades and coatings, but to no avail. Soaking the mushrooms in a soy-based marinade left them soggy, slimy, and difficult to sear. Dipping them in different combinations of egg and cornstarch created a distinct crust initially, but the mushrooms' high moisture content eventually made the crust unappetizingly chewy and wet. A simple sear proved best after all, but I wondered if a simple glaze (made from my existing sauce ingredients) might help. Adding soy sauce, chicken broth, and sugar as the mushrooms finished cooking yielded a shiny, flavorful glaze that provided just the boost they had been lacking.

Other Meat Stand-ins?

Surely portobellos were not the only vegetable that could anchor the dish. Summer squash was quickly ruled out: too watery and no substance. Sweet potatoes added bulk, but they remained starchy when stir-fried and fell apart when cooked through. Eggplant disintegrated into a mushy mess, but its meatiness was appealing enough for me to continue testing it. Dipping the eggplant first in beaten eggs and then in cornstarch provided just enough textural contrast to lift the eggplant out of vegetable obscurity. (For the recipe, see

---

STEP-BY-STEP | PREPARING VEGETABLES FOR STIR-FRYING

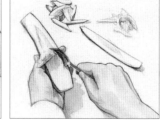

PORTOBELLO MUSHROOMS
After removing the stem, gently scrape the underside of the mushroom with a dinner spoon to remove the feathery gills, which can impart a muddy taste to the stir-fry.

ZUCCHINI
Halve zucchini lengthwise and gently scrape out the seeds from each half with a small spoon. Cut in half lengthwise again, then cut into 1/4-inch slices on a 45-degree bias.

NAPA CABBAGE
Separate leaves, removing the core of each leaf with a wedge-shaped cut. Slice the leafy greens crosswise into 3/4-inch strips. Cut the cores into 1/4-inch strips.

PHOTOGRAPHY: CARL TREMBLAY; ILLUSTRATION: RANDY GLASS

Choosing and Preparing Vegetables for a Stir-Fry

Portobello mushrooms are the mainstay in our stir-fries. As for the other vegetables, use those called for in the recipe or swap them with another vegetable from the same category below. We recommend using one longer-cooking vegetable paired with one quicker-cooking vegetable and a leafy green (either napa cabbage or bok choy).

LONGER-COOKING VEGETABLES (to yield 2 cups)	AMOUNT	PREPARATION
carrots	4 small	• peeled, sliced on bias 1/4 inch thick
broccoli	1/2 pound	• stalks discarded, florets cut into 1 1/4-inch pieces
cauliflower	1/2 pound	• core removed, florets cut into 1 1/4-inch pieces
asparagus	1 pound medium	• bottoms trimmed, cut on bias into 1 1/2-inch lengths
green beans	1/2 pound	• ends trimmed, cut on bias into 1 1/2-inch lengths
QUICKER-COOKING VEGETABLES (to yield 1 cup)		
bell pepper	1 medium	• stemmed, seeded, and cut into 1/2-inch dice
snow peas	3 ounces	• strings and tough ends trimmed
celery	3 medium ribs	• ends trimmed, cut on bias 1/2 inch thick
zucchini or summer squash	1 small	• seeded, quartered lengthwise, and cut on bias 1/4 inch thick
LEAFY GREENS (to yield 2 cups stems and 4 cups greens)		
bok choy or napa cabbage	1 small (about 1 pound)	• stems/cores and greens separated, stems/cores cut into 1/4-inch strips, greens into 3/4-inch strips

Cook's Extra on page 14.)

While not exactly a vegetable, firm tofu (soybean curd) seemed promising as an easy stand-in for the eggplant. In practice, however, the egg/cornstarch coating created a crust that was too thick and chewy; tasters wanted something thinner. Because it's packaged in water, tofu already has a significant amount of moisture, so what if I skipped the egg and simply dredged the tofu in the cornstarch? Not only was this method simple (no pressing or freezing, as so many other recipes required), but the results pleased even the skeptics who claimed they didn't like tofu.

Now when I head to the supermarket, I don't have to look beyond the produce aisle to assemble a quick meal that will satisfy my craving for a substantial main course.

STIR-FRIED PORTOBELLOS WITH GINGER-OYSTER SAUCE

SERVES 3 TO 4

This stir-fry cooks quickly, so have everything chopped and ready before you begin cooking. Serve with steamed white rice.

Glaze

- 2 tablespoons soy sauce
- 2 tablespoons sugar
- 1/4 cup low-sodium chicken or vegetable broth

Sauce

- 1 tablespoon soy sauce
- 1 cup low-sodium chicken or vegetable broth
- 3 tablespoons oyster-flavored sauce
- 2 teaspoons toasted sesame oil
- 1 tablespoon cornstarch

Vegetables

- 2 medium garlic cloves, minced or pressed through garlic press (about 2 teaspoons)
- 4 teaspoons minced fresh ginger
- 4 tablespoons vegetable oil
- 6–8 portobello mushrooms (each 4 to 6 inches), stems discarded, gills removed (see illustration on page 14), and cut into 2-inch wedges (about 7 cups)
- 2 cups sliced carrots or other longer-cooking vegetable from chart above
- 1/2 cup low-sodium chicken or vegetable broth
- 1 cup snow peas or other quicker-cooking vegetable from chart above
- 1 pound leafy greens from chart above
- 1 tablespoon sesame seeds, toasted (optional)

1. Whisk glaze ingredients in small bowl; whisk sauce ingredients in separate small bowl. In third small bowl, mix garlic and ginger with 1 teaspoon vegetable oil. Set bowls aside.

2. Heat 3 tablespoons vegetable oil in 12-inch nonstick skillet over medium-high heat until shimmering. Add mushrooms and cook, without stirring, until browned on one side, 2 to 3 minutes. Using tongs, turn mushrooms and reduce heat to medium; cook until second sides are browned and mushrooms are tender, about 5 minutes. Increase heat to medium-high; add glaze mixture and cook, stirring, until glaze is thick and mushrooms are coated, 1 to 2 minutes. Transfer mushrooms to plate; rinse skillet clean and dry with paper towels.

3. Heat 1 teaspoon vegetable oil in now-empty skillet over medium-high heat until beginning to smoke. Add carrots and cook, stirring occasionally, until beginning to brown, 1 to 2 minutes. Add 1/2 cup broth and cover skillet; cook until carrots are just tender, 2 to 3 minutes. Uncover and cook until liquid evaporates, about 30 seconds. Transfer carrots to plate with mushrooms.

4. Heat remaining teaspoon vegetable oil in now-empty skillet over medium-high heat until beginning to smoke. Add snow peas and bok choy stems or napa cabbage cores and cook, stirring occasionally, until beginning to brown and soften, 1 to 2 minutes. Add leafy greens and cook, stirring frequently, until wilted, about 1 minute. Push vegetables to sides of skillet to clear center; add garlic-ginger mixture to clearing and cook, mashing mixture with spoon or spatula, until fragrant, 15 to 20 seconds, then stir mixture into greens.

5. Return all vegetables to skillet along with sauce. Toss to combine and cook, stirring, until sauce is thickened and vegetables are coated, 2 to 3 minutes. Transfer to serving platter, top with sesame seeds, if using, and serve immediately.

STIR-FRIED PORTOBELLOS WITH SWEET CHILI-GARLIC SAUCE

SERVES 3 TO 4

Follow recipe for Stir-Fried Portobellos with Ginger-Oyster Sauce, replacing sugar in glaze with 2 tablespoons honey. For sauce, increase soy sauce to 3 tablespoons, reduce broth to 3/4 cup, and replace oyster-flavored sauce and sesame oil with 2 tablespoons honey, 1 tablespoon rice wine vinegar, and 1 teaspoon Asian chili sauce. Increase garlic to 4 teaspoons.

How to Stir-Fry Tofu

When coated with cornstarch and stir-fried, tofu develops a crisp exterior and a creamy interior. Most tofu is sold in 12- or 16-ounce blocks. To cut tofu for a stir-fry, hold a chef's knife parallel to the cutting board and cut the block in half horizontally to form two rectangular planks. Cut each plank into six squares, then cut each square diagonally into two triangles.

STIR-FRIED TOFU

Follow recipe for Stir-Fried Portobellos with Ginger-Oyster Sauce through step 1. Cut 1 container extra-firm tofu into 24 triangles (see note above). Heat 3 tablespoons vegetable oil in 12-inch nonstick skillet over medium-high until shimmering. While oil is heating, sprinkle 1/3 cup cornstarch evenly into baking dish. Place tofu on top of cornstarch and turn with fingers until evenly coated. When skillet is hot, add tofu in single layer and cook until golden brown, 4 to 6 minutes. Turn tofu with tongs and cook until second side is browned, 4 to 6 minutes more. Add glaze ingredients and cook, stirring, until glaze is thick and tofu is coated, 1 to 2 minutes. Transfer tofu to plate; rinse skillet clean and dry with paper towels. Proceed with recipe from step 3.

Essential Guide to Cooking Pasta

Cooking pasta seems simple—just boil water and wait—but cooking perfect pasta takes some finesse. Here's how we do it. BY SEAN LAWLER

PASTA BUYING GUIDE

ITALIAN PASTA

You have two basic choices—dried or fresh. Dried pasta is made from high-protein durum wheat flour, so it cooks up springy and firm and is suitable for thick tomato and meat sauces as well as concentrated oil-based sauces. Fresh pasta is made from softer all-purpose flour and is quite delicate. Its rough, porous surface pairs well with dairy-based sauces.

DRIED PASTA WINNER: RONZONI

Dried Semolina Pasta: No longer gummy and bland, American brands of semolina (which is coarsely ground durum wheat) pasta have improved so much that many bested their pricey Italian counterparts in our tasting.

➤ **COOKING TIPS:** When cooked to al dente, pasta retains some chew but is neither hard nor gummy at the center.

Fresh Egg Pasta: While your best bet for fresh pasta is still homemade, there are a few serviceable supermarket options. Our favorite brand is found in the refrigerator case, sealed in spoilage-retardant packaging and made from pasteurized eggs.

FRESH PASTA WINNER: BUITONI

➤ **COOKING TIPS:** Fresh pasta is easily overcooked, so taste early. Drain the pasta a few minutes before it reaches al dente, return it to the empty pot, and then cook with the sauce for another minute or two. The underdone pasta will absorb flavor from the sauce, and the starch from the pasta will help thicken the sauce.

Whole Wheat and Grain Pastas: Most of the whole wheat pastas we tried were gummy, grainy, or lacking in "wheaty" flavor, but there were a few that we really liked. Our favorite is made from a blend of whole wheat and regular flours. We were less thrilled about the alternative-grain pastas we tried. Made from

WHOLE WHEAT WINNER: RONZONI HEALTHY HARVEST

rice, corn, quinoa, and spelt, these products were plagued by shaggy, mushy textures and off flavors. If you're desperate to avoid wheat, try Tinkyáda Organic Brown Rice Pasta.

➤ **COOKING TIPS:** Cook and use as you would dried semolina pasta.

ASIAN NOODLES

Unlike Italian-style pasta, most Asian noodles are of a similar shape (long strands of varying thickness), but they can be made from a wide variety of flours. With some exceptions, they are usually best cooked like Italian pasta—in a large quantity of rapidly boiling, salted water, then drained (see specifics below). One note about judging doneness: In Asia, al dente is a foreign concept. Asian noodles are best cooked until completely tender (but not mushy).

Chinese Egg Noodles: These pale yellow, spaghetti-sized noodles are made from wheat flour and available dried, in the Asian ingredients aisle of your market, or fresh, usually with the produce. Sometimes labeled "lo mein" noodles or generic "Chinese-style" noodles. (Don't confuse them with the bags of curly dried American egg noodles.)

➤ **COOKING TIPS:** Chinese egg noodles are good for stir-fries, cold salads, or pan-fried noodle cakes. Except when used in fried noodle cakes, egg noodles should be drained, rinsed under cool, running water, drained again, then tossed with a few teaspoons of toasted sesame oil (to prevent clumping).

Udon Noodles: Available fresh or dried, udon are white, ropelike wheat noodles that are especially thick and starchy. They are best used for hearty soups, but unlike ramen (below), the noodles are cooked separately, not in the broth.

➤ **COOKING TIPS:** Udon noodles are made with quite a bit of salt, so there is no need to add salt to the cooking water. Because they are so starchy, they should definitely be rinsed after cooking.

Ramen Noodles: In Japan, the term *ramen* refers to a whole category of brothy noodle dishes, but in America we are limited to "instant ramen soup"—the

dried blocks of thin, wavy wheat noodles sold in cellophane with a seasoning packet.

➤ **COOKING TIPS:** Instant ramen noodles are first fried, then dried, so they cook in just a few minutes. We discard the seasoning packet, make our own broth (or doctor some canned chicken broth), and serve them topped with meat, seafood, or egg.

Somen Noodles: These very long, thin white noodles are made from wheat flour that has been lightly oiled and are usually sold dried. Traditionally, they are served iced, along with garnishes and a dipping sauce, but they can also be used in soups.

➤ **COOKING TIPS:** Like udon, somen should be rinsed after cooking and need no salt added to the cooking water.

Soba Noodles: Japanese soba noodles are thin, like Italian linguine, and made from a mixture of wheat flour and buckwheat flour, which imparts a brownish-gray color and earthy flavor. We prefer imported Japanese soba, which contain a higher percentage of buckwheat flour and therefore possess stronger flavor. Cooked soba noodles are added to broths to make soups, lightly dressed and served as salads (chilled, warm, or at room temperature), or eaten cold with dipping sauces.

➤ **COOKING TIPS:** No matter the application, soba noodles should be rinsed after cooking.

Rice Noodles: Chewy white rice noodles are especially popular throughout southeast Asia. American supermarkets generally carry only two sizes: thin, threadlike noodles (sometimes labeled "vermicelli" or "rice stick") and thicker, flat noodles about ¼ inch wide (confusingly, also called "rice stick"). Rice noodles are traditionally stir-fried (as in pad Thai) or served in soup.

➤ **COOKING TIPS:** If boiled, rice noodles overcook easily and tend to clump. We've had much better results soaking them in hot water until softened and pliable, draining them, then adding them directly to the soup or stir-fry. "Vermicelli" rice noodles need to soak for about five minutes, while thicker noodles need 15 to 20 minutes.

ITALIAN PASTA COOKING GUIDE

Pasta cooks quickly and should be served immediately, so have all the necessary ingredients and utensils assembled before you begin, including your dinner guests. As the Italians say, "People wait for pasta, not the other way around."

Oil: Unless you're serving a butter- or cream-based sauce, keep some extra-virgin olive oil on hand for drizzling over the sauced pasta for a final burst of flavor. Just don't waste it in the cooking water: It won't prevent the pasta from sticking (not a problem if you use enough water), but it will prevent the sauce from coating the pasta.

Water and Pot: You'll need 4 quarts of water to cook 1 pound of dried pasta. Any less and the noodles may stick. Pasta leaches starch as it cooks. Without plenty of water to dilute it, the starch coats the noodles, making them sticky.

The pot should be large, with at least a 6-quart capacity—to guard against boilovers. But forget expensive metal pots and fancy mesh inserts. A lightweight, inexpensive stockpot with sturdy handles and a lid does the job just fine.

Pasta: One pound of dried pasta generally serves four to six people as a main course, depending on whether the sauce is light (tomato sauce), rich (creamy Alfredo or hearty Bolognese), or bulked up with other ingredients such as vegetables or seafood.

Liquid Measuring Cup: In that last flurry of activity before saucing the pasta and getting dinner on the table, it's easy to forget to reserve some cooking water to thin the sauce, if needed. We often place a measuring cup in the colander as a reminder when we start to cook.

Colander: Once the pasta is drained, give the colander a shake or two, but don't shake the pasta bone-dry. The little bit of hot cooking water clinging to the pasta will help the sauce coat it. Another no-no: rinsing cooked pasta.

Salt: Properly seasoned cooking water is crucial for good flavor—use 1 tablespoon table salt (or 2 tablespoons kosher salt) per 4 quarts of water.

Sauce: Don't drop the pasta into the water until the sauce is nearly ready. Smooth sauces and sauces with very small bits, such as garlic and oil, are best with long strands of pasta. Chunkier sauces are best matched with short tubular or molded shapes.

Serving Bowls and Ladle: We like to serve pasta in wide soup bowls, as the edge provides an easy place to twirl noodles on a fork. To warm them before serving the pasta (especially important with cream sauces, which cool quickly and congeal), add a few extra cups of water to the pasta pot. When it boils, ladle about ½ cup of boiling water into each bowl and let stand while the pasta cooks.

Pasta Fork: Of the countless items of pasta paraphernalia we've tested over the years, the only one we recommend is a pasta fork, a long-handled, perforated spoon with ridged teeth. The wood variety is clunky and prone to splitting, but the plastic and stainless-steel versions are great. Not essential—basic tongs work fine—but we're glad we bought one.

Foolproof Veal Scaloppini

Supermarket veal cutlets are a far cry from the delicate fare served in restaurants. We set out to transform these convenient cutlets from tough to tender.

⇛ BY SARAH WILSON ⇚

Call them what you will—scaloppini, scallops, escalopes, or even schnitzel—these thinly sliced cutlets are remarkably easy to prepare. Gently pound the cutlets, sauté them quickly, and serve with a basic pan sauce. With its tender meat and delicate flavor, veal is a natural for this preparation. It's also a luxurious choice over the more popular and, frankly, more pedestrian substitute: chicken. Restaurants always seem to get this dish just right, pairing the lightly browned veal cutlets with a bracing lemon sauce or sweet Marsala reduction.

Usually, such a basic restaurant dish is a great candidate for an easy meal at home. Supermarkets always stock pristine pink veal cutlets ready to jump from package to pan. Sounds simple, but a quick sear told a different story. Bland flavor, tough meat, and slimy exterior were common complaints after my first round of testing.

A little digging revealed that the veal I was getting from the supermarket is from the shoulder or the leg, the two toughest parts of the calf, and quite unlike the veal scaloppini from the rib or loin served by top chefs. Executing this dish perfectly was going to be trickier than I thought. How could I re-create restaurant-quality veal scaloppini using supermarket-quality cutlets?

Veal Revealed

To understand the different cuts, I consulted my local butcher. He informed me that the prepared cutlets he receives from the meat supplier come in large vacuum-sealed packs, making it impossible to tell if the veal was cut from the shoulder or the leg. As the shoulder and leg are the muscles worked the most, they are naturally the toughest meat. I briefly reconsidered my decision to use supermarket cutlets, but the notion of slicing my own cutlets from a loin roast or rib chop seemed beyond the pale for weeknight cooking, especially for such a simple recipe. (I did decide to offer these hand-cut cutlets as an option; see "The Ultimate Scaloppini" on page 19.)

With this tougher cut of veal, I needed a surefire approach to tenderness. First, I tried soaking the veal in milk overnight. I hoped that the lactic acid in milk would help tenderize the meat. Unfortunately, tasters noticed little difference between soaked and unsoaked cutlets; in addition, the milk-soaked cutlets steamed, then burned in the pan. Next I tried a Jaccard, a handheld tenderizer that works by forcing multiple needles through the meat, breaking the tough fibers. This was slightly more effective, but tasters complained that these odd-looking cutlets reminded them of Salisbury steak.

Desperate, I reached for the shaker of meat tenderizer—Adolph's, the brand my mother used

By flouring only one side of the veal cutlets, we achieved a crisp crust without overcooking the delicate meat.

so many years ago. These cutlets were as tender as any I've ever tasted, and tasters were startled when I revealed my secret ingredient. (For details on how meat tenderizer works, see page 19.) This decidedly unglamorous product turned reasonably priced supermarket cutlets into cutlets every bit as tender as those found in restaurants. No home butchering, no high price tag: Not bad for a tenderizer that costs pennies per use.

Flour Makes a Difference

Cutlets seasoned with meat tenderizer and pepper and then sautéed failed to develop much of a crust. Dredging the seasoned cutlets in flour definitely helped. But by the time the cutlets were nicely browned, they were also overcooked. Less time in the pan yielded a pale, colorless exterior and bland flavor. To solve this problem, I tried cooking only the first side until golden brown, then flipping each cutlet and finishing. This method prevented overcooking, but the second, quickly cooked side was pasty. I finally found the answer: flouring just one side of the cutlet. The floured side obtained a rich, golden brown exterior, and the other side, now without flour, was no longer gummy.

After cooking three batches of veal there was plenty of *fond* (flavorful browned bits) in the pan, but these cutlets didn't afford me the luxury of spending 15 minutes on sautéing shallots and reducing liquids in the empty pan. To keep the veal tender and hot, I had to reverse the usual process and make the pan sauce in a separate saucepan *before* cooking the veal. Once the last batch was done, I poured the almost-finished sauce into the skillet and scraped the pan to incorporate the meaty flavors into my sauce. I finished the sauce with butter and herbs, and a minute later my sauced (and tender) cutlets were on the table.

COOK'S extra

Go to www.cooksillustrated.com
- Key in code 5065 for our recipe for **Tarragon-Sherry Cream Sauce.**
- Key in code 5066 for our article on the **safety of nonstick cookware.**
- This information will be available until November 1, 2006.

TASTING: Milk-Fed vs. Naturally Raised Veal

Veal calves traditionally have been fed a strict milk or formula diet, and their movement has been limited. As a result, milk-fed veal is white in color. (In general, the more muscle tissue is used, the darker it becomes.) In recent years, naturally raised veal calves, fed milk as well as grain and not given any antibiotics or hormones, have gotten people's attention. These animals are allowed more exercise, and their meat is pink.

Ethical and appearance concerns aside, we wondered if our tasters could tell the difference between milk-fed and naturally raised veal. In terms of flavor, our panel concluded that the two styles were indistinguishable. Texture was another matter. Tasters felt that the milk-fed veal was more tender, finding naturally raised veal a bit chewy. When we sprinkled the cutlets with meat tenderizer, however, the difference disappeared. –S.W.

PHOTOGRAPHY: CARL TREMBLAY

How Meat Tenderizers Work

The use of plants to tenderize meat dates back hundreds of years to the native peoples of what is now Mexico, who wrapped meat in papaya leaves. Both papaya and pineapple contain enzymes that break down collagen—the connective tissue that makes meat tough. These enzymes, papain (from papaya) and bromelain (from pineapple), are the active ingredients in bottles of meat tenderizer. We've dismissed these products in the past because they effectively tenderize only the outermost layer of a piece of meat—not much of an improvement for a thick, tough steak. But our ultra-thin veal cutlets were just the right thickness for the bottled tenderizer to penetrate completely.

To see if brand mattered, we gathered six tenderizers ("seasoned" and unseasoned varieties from Adolph's, Durkee, and McCormick) and headed to the kitchen with several pounds of tough veal cutlets. Adolph's and Durkee contain papain, while McCormick relies on bromelain to do the work. All of them worked equally well—neither the brand nor the type of enzyme made any difference. Should you opt for seasoned or unseasoned? While the extra spices aren't enough to ruin dinner, we'd just as soon do the seasoning ourselves.

–Garth Clingingsmith

TENDERNESS IN A BOTTLE

VEAL SCALOPPINI
SERVES 4

Cook the veal in batches to avoid overcrowding the skillet; because the size of packaged cutlets varies, each batch may contain as few as three cutlets or as many as six. A pan sauce (recipes follow) is a must; start preparing the sauce before cooking the cutlets, then finish in the skillet used to brown the cutlets. Because meat tenderizer contains sodium, it is unnecessary to salt the cutlets.

- 1 1/2 pounds veal cutlets, about 1/4 inch thick
- 3/4 teaspoon meat tenderizer
- 1/8 teaspoon ground black pepper
- 1/2 cup unbleached all-purpose flour
- 3 tablespoons vegetable oil

1. If cutlets are thicker than 1/4 inch, place between two sheets of plastic wrap or waxed paper and pound to even 1/4-inch thickness with skillet or meat pounder. If some cutlets are thinner than 1/4 inch, pound to even 1/8-inch thickness then fold in half. Blot cutlets dry with paper towels. Sprinkle tenderizer and pepper evenly over both sides of cutlets.

2. Place flour in rimmed baking sheet and spread to thin, even layer. Heat 1 tablespoon oil in 12-inch nonstick skillet over high heat until

---

The Ultimate Scaloppini: Very Tender, Very Expensive

To experience super-tender veal scaloppini without using meat tenderizer, you must buy a roast or chops from the loin or rib and butcher your own cutlets. Among these premium choices, the rib chop is probably the easiest to work with and the most widely available. But don't expect to save any money for your efforts. Supermarket cutlets from the leg or shoulder cost $10 to $20 per pound, depending on the market. Cutlets that you make yourself from rib chops will end up costing closer to $25 or $30 per pound. If the sticker shock doesn't stop you, here's how to make the most tender scaloppini imaginable.

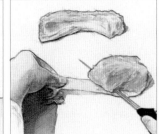

1. Start by trimming the bone from the meaty lobe of each rib chop.

2. Trim outside fat, but leave interior fat alone.

3. Slice meat in half horizontally, then pound to 1/4-inch thickness.

---

beginning to smoke. Dredge first batch of cutlets (see note above) in flour on one side only, shake off excess, and place in skillet, floured side down, making sure cutlets do not overlap. Cook, without moving cutlets, until well browned, 1 to 1 1/2 minutes. Flip with tongs and cook until second sides are no longer pink and cutlets feel firm when pressed, about 30 seconds. Transfer cutlets to platter and tent lightly with foil to keep warm. Repeat to cook remaining cutlets in 2 batches, using additional 1 tablespoon oil for each batch. (If skillet becomes too dark after cooking second batch, rinse before continuing.) Use paper towels to wipe away fat, liquid, or white matter in skillet without removing *fond*. Return pan to medium heat, finish pan sauce (recipes follow), pour over cutlets, and serve.

PORCINI-MARSALA PAN SAUCE
MAKES ABOUT 1 CUP

- 1/3 ounce dried porcini mushrooms, rinsed well (about 1/3 cup)
- 1/2 cup hot water
- 2 teaspoons vegetable oil
- 2 medium shallots, minced (about 1/3 cup)
- 1 cup dry Marsala
- 1 1/2 cups low-sodium chicken broth
- 2 tablespoons unsalted butter, cut into 4 pieces
- 1 tablespoon minced fresh chives
    Table salt and ground black pepper

1. Cover mushrooms with water in small microwave-safe bowl; cover with plastic wrap, cut several steam vents in plastic with paring knife, and microwave on high power for 30 seconds. Let stand until mushrooms soften, about 5 minutes. Lift mushrooms from liquid with fork and chop into 1/4-inch pieces (you should have about 3 tablespoons). Strain liquid through fine-mesh strainer lined with paper towel into medium

bowl. Set mushrooms and strained liquid aside.

2. Heat oil in medium saucepan over medium-high heat until shimmering. Add shallots and cook until beginning to soften, about 1 minute. Remove pan from heat and add Marsala. Return pan to high heat; simmer rapidly until liquid is reduced to 1/2 cup, about 4 minutes. Add mushrooms and strained soaking liquid and simmer until liquid in pan is again reduced to 1/2 cup, about 4 minutes. Add broth and simmer until liquid is reduced to 1 cup, about 8 minutes. Set aside.

3. After transferring last batch of cutlets to platter, pour sauce into empty pan and bring to simmer, scraping up browned bits on pan bottom. Off heat, whisk in butter, chives, and salt and pepper to taste. Pour sauce over cutlets and serve immediately.

LEMON-PARSLEY SAUCE
MAKES ABOUT 3/4 CUP

- 2 teaspoons vegetable oil
- 2 medium shallots, minced (about 1/3 cup)
- 1 1/2 cups low-sodium chicken broth
- 2 tablespoons minced fresh parsley leaves
- 2 tablespoons unsalted butter, cut into 4 pieces
    Table salt and ground black pepper
- 1–2 tablespoons juice from 1 lemon

1. Heat oil in medium saucepan over medium-high heat until shimmering. Add shallots and cook until beginning to soften, about 1 minute. Add broth and increase heat to high; simmer rapidly until liquid is reduced to 3/4 cup, about 8 minutes. Set aside.

2. After transferring last batch of cutlets to platter, pour sauce into empty pan and bring to simmer, scraping up browned bits on pan bottom. Off heat, whisk in parsley, butter, and salt, pepper, and lemon juice to taste. Pour sauce over cutlets and serve immediately.

A New Twist on Chicken Salads

A vinaigrette is a great remedy for the mayo rut. If only it would cling to the chicken.

≥ BY REBECCA HAYS ≤

For many cooks (myself included), mayonnaise is the go-to ingredient for turning last night's leftovers into chicken salad. Fine for a simple sandwich, but mayonnaise is more about luscious texture than interesting flavor, as the creamy fat tends to dull the impact of other ingredients, no matter how aggressively you empty your spice cabinet. Instead, I thought a vinaigrette-dressed chicken—something you might serve on a bed of greens as a light dinner—would have fresher, bolder flavors.

Yet it wasn't long before I ran into trouble: Because oil and vinegar separate so easily, they cling poorly to chicken, yielding greasy, watery salads. I hated to admit it, but my salads were crying out for the cohesiveness I had lost by ruling out mayonnaise. I needed to create an emulsion (a suspension of two liquids that don't naturally mix). Emulsification can be achieved through vigorous whisking—which disperses the oil in tiny droplets throughout the vinegar—but the most stable emulsions involve a third ingredient. This ingredient (called, logically enough, an emulsifier) gets in the way of the oil droplets, making it harder for them to collect in that all-too-familiar pool of oil that floats on top of many vinaigrettes. I successfully used sun-dried tomatoes, peanut butter, and roasted red peppers as emulsifiers.

Using a blender was key. A mechanical blade can reduce oil to small droplets more effectively than a whisk; the smaller the droplets, the more likely they are to maintain suspension in an emulsion. With bright, creamy dressings at the ready, I just stirred in handfuls of fresh vegetables, herbs, and toasted nuts to make these dinner salads come to life.

A Fuss-Free Roast Chicken

To make the right amount of chicken for our salad recipes, roast a 3- to 3½-pound chicken (seasoned with salt and pepper) in a 375-degree oven until an instant-read thermometer inserted in the thigh registers 165 to 170 degrees, about 1 hour, 10 minutes. When cool, pull the meat off the bones in 2-inch shreds, discarding fat and sinew. Don't dress the chicken while it's warm—it will absorb too much of the dressing. The chicken can be roasted, shredded, and refrigerated in an airtight container for up to 24 hours. For even less fuss, use a fully cooked supermarket rotisserie chicken.

CHICKEN SALAD WITH ASPARAGUS AND SUN-DRIED TOMATO DRESSING
SERVES 6

This recipe (and the two that follow) are best served over salad greens.

½ cup plus 1 tablespoon extra-virgin olive oil
¼ cup red wine vinegar
½ cup sun-dried tomatoes packed in oil, drained, rinsed, and minced
1 small garlic clove, minced or pressed through garlic press (about ½ teaspoon)
  Table salt and ground black pepper
½ pound asparagus, trimmed of tough ends and cut on diagonal into 1-inch pieces
1 cup chopped fresh basil leaves
5 cups shredded roast chicken, room temperature (see box below)
3 ounces goat cheese, crumbled (optional)
½ cup pine nuts, toasted

1. Puree ½ cup oil, vinegar, sun-dried tomatoes, garlic, ¼ teaspoon salt, and ½ teaspoon pepper in blender until smooth. Transfer to large bowl. (Dressing may be made ahead of time, covered, and refrigerated overnight. Whisk to recombine before using.)

2. Heat remaining tablespoon oil in 10-inch nonstick skillet over high heat until beginning to smoke; add asparagus, ¼ teaspoon salt, and ¼ teaspoon pepper; cook until asparagus is browned and almost tender, about 3 minutes, stirring occasionally. Transfer to plate to cool.

3. Add cooled asparagus and basil to vinaigrette; stir to combine. Add chicken and toss gently to combine; let stand at room temperature 15 minutes. Adjust seasoning with salt and pepper and sprinkle with goat cheese, if using, and pine nuts. Serve immediately.

THAI-STYLE CHICKEN SALAD WITH SPICY PEANUT DRESSING
SERVES 6

½ cup canola oil
3 tablespoons smooth peanut butter
½ cup juice from 3 to 4 limes
2 tablespoons water
  Table salt
3 small garlic cloves, minced or pressed through garlic press (about 1½ teaspoons)
2 teaspoons very finely grated fresh ginger
2 tablespoons light brown sugar
1½ teaspoons hot red pepper flakes
½ medium cucumber, peeled, seeded, and cut into 1 inch by ¼-inch matchsticks (about 1 cup)
1 medium carrot, peeled and grated on large holes of box grater (about ½ cup)
4 scallions, white and green parts sliced thin
3 tablespoons minced fresh cilantro leaves
5 cups shredded roast chicken, room temperature (see box below)
½ cup chopped roasted peanuts

1. Puree oil, peanut butter, lime juice, water, ¼ teaspoon salt, garlic, ginger, brown sugar, and red pepper flakes in blender until combined. Transfer to large bowl. (Dressing may be made ahead of time, covered, and refrigerated overnight. Whisk to recombine before using.)

2. Add cucumber, carrot, scallions, and cilantro to vinaigrette; toss to combine. Add chicken and toss gently to combine; let stand at room temperature 15 minutes. Adjust seasoning with salt and sprinkle with peanuts. Serve immediately.

SPANISH-STYLE CHICKEN SALAD WITH ROASTED RED PEPPER DRESSING
SERVES 6

½ cup extra-virgin olive oil
3 tablespoons sherry or balsamic vinegar
10 ounces jarred roasted red peppers, drained and diced medium (about 1⅓ cups)
1 small garlic clove, minced or pressed through garlic press (about ½ teaspoon)
  Table salt and ground black pepper
1 small shallot, minced (about 2 tablespoons)
3 tablespoons minced fresh parsley leaves
2 celery ribs, sliced very thin (about 1¼ cups)
½ cup roughly chopped pitted green olives
5 cups shredded roast chicken, room temperature (see box at left)
½ cup sliced almonds, toasted

1. Puree oil, vinegar, ⅔ cup roasted red peppers, garlic, ¼ teaspoon salt, and ½ teaspoon pepper in blender until smooth. Transfer to bowl.

2. Add shallot, parsley, celery, olives, and remaining ⅔ cup red peppers to vinaigrette; stir to combine. Add chicken and toss gently to combine; let stand at room temperature 15 minutes. Adjust seasoning with salt and pepper and sprinkle with almonds. Serve immediately.

Garlic and Olive Oil Mashed Potatoes

We loved the idea of adding extra-virgin olive oil and garlic to our mashed potatoes—but not the harsh flavors and pasty texture.

A heaping mound of rich yet fluffy traditional mashed potatoes is to many main dishes what a scoop of vanilla ice cream is to dessert: a great all-American side. But in the Mediterranean, another take on mashed potatoes exists that incorporates the distinct flavors of extra-virgin olive oil (used in lieu of dairy products like butter and cream) and garlic. For example, the Greeks have skordalia, a puree of cooked potatoes, extra-virgin olive oil, garlic, and lemon served meze-style as a spread or dip. I wanted to translate these same bold (but often overpowering) flavors into a light and creamy mashed potato side dish to partner with simple grilled meats or fish.

Back to Basics

First, I needed the ideal potato base, so I began with the test kitchen's established methods. Rather than simmering peeled, cut potatoes, I opted for whole potatoes in their jackets. This minimizes the opportunity for water to enter and bind with the potato's starch molecules, thus keeping the mashed potatoes from becoming thin, waterlogged, and bland.

While Yukon Golds provided a nice golden color and a creamy, dense texture, russet potatoes yielded lighter, fluffier mashed potatoes that my tasters preferred. To ensure that the potatoes would be silky smooth rather than gritty, I tested doneness in what we've found to be the most accurate way: When a knife blade slips in and out of the potatoes easily, they're done. Putting the drained, peeled, still-hot potatoes through a ricer or food mill rather than using a potato masher ensured a smooth, fine texture.

Bye-Bye, Bite

Extra-virgin olive oil and garlic can make for a bold and flavorful combo—or a full-frontal assault. By cooking most of the garlic in olive oil and leaving a modest portion uncooked, we achieved the right balance—complex, well-rounded flavor without the bite.

4 PARTS COOKED GARLIC + I PART RAW GARLIC = BALANCED FLAVOR

Oil Change?

I knew that replacing the full 1½ cups of fat (butter and half-and-half) in our traditional recipe with extra-virgin olive oil would be a disaster (more like potato-flavored olive oil). Reducing the oil to a little more than ½ cup made the mashed russets smooth and creamy without being watery, greasy, or pasty. Now the texture was right, but the flavor of the extra-virgin olive oil was still overwhelming, so I tried other options. Extra-light olive oil had all the flavor of vegetable oil, while regular olive oil was only slightly better. Stumped, I took a break from the olive oil problem to focus on the garlic.

Taking the Edge Off

I quickly learned that stirring raw minced garlic into the mashed potatoes made for a harsh flavor. Next, I tried smashing raw minced garlic with kosher salt into a smooth paste. This improved the texture by eliminating pockets of grainy garlic but did nothing for the harsh bite. Boiling whole peeled cloves reduced the flavor to almost nothing. Pan-toasting unpeeled cloves was a winner—the resulting flavor was sweet and roasted. Slowly cooking the garlic puree in oil over low heat, however, provided a similarly mild-sweet flavor with an added benefit: I had inadvertently made a mild garlic oil.

This was the solution I'd been looking for. The 10 tablespoons of raw extra-virgin olive oil I had been using was too potent, but using less than half that amount (4 tablespoons, or ¼ cup) to simmer the garlic tempered the oil's raw flavor (heat alters the oil's taste) and added a hint of garlic. Next, I added the cooked garlic oil to the potatoes along with the remaining 6 tablespoons of uncooked oil. The result? Very nice, but tame. The answer was to add just 1 teaspoon of freshly made garlic paste for a full—but not overwhelming—flavor.

To lighten and brighten these mashed potatoes without making them sour or overly citrusy, I added just a splash (2 teaspoons) of lemon juice. Smooth and creamy, with distinct but balanced flavors, my Mediterranean-style mashed potatoes were finally ready for side-dish duty.

GARLIC AND OLIVE OIL MASHED POTATOES
SERVES 6

As this dish is denser and more intensely flavored than traditional mashed potatoes, our suggested serving size is smaller than you might expect. These potatoes make a fine accompaniment to simply seasoned grilled meats, fish, and poultry.

- 2 pounds russet potatoes, unpeeled and scrubbed
- 5 medium garlic cloves, peeled
- 2 teaspoons plus ⅛ teaspoon kosher salt
- ½ cup plus 2 tablespoons extra-virgin olive oil
- ½ teaspoon ground black pepper
- 2 teaspoons juice from 1 lemon

1. Place potatoes in large saucepan with water to cover by 1 inch. Bring to boil over high heat; reduce heat to medium-low and cook at bare simmer until just tender (potatoes will offer very little resistance when poked with paring knife), 40 to 45 minutes.

2. While potatoes are simmering, mince 1 garlic clove (or press through garlic press). Place minced garlic on cutting board and sprinkle with ⅛ teaspoon kosher salt. Using flat side of chef's knife, drag garlic and salt back and forth across cutting board in small circular motions until garlic is ground into smooth paste. Transfer to medium bowl and set aside.

3. Mince remaining 4 cloves garlic (or press through garlic press). Place in small saucepan with ¼ cup olive oil and cook over low heat, stirring constantly, until garlic foams and is soft, fragrant, and golden, 5 minutes. Transfer oil and garlic to bowl with raw garlic paste.

4. Drain cooked potatoes; set food mill or ricer over now-empty saucepan. Using paring knife, peel skins from potatoes. Working in batches, cut peeled potatoes into large chunks and process through food mill or ricer into saucepan.

5. Add remaining salt, pepper, lemon juice, and remaining 6 tablespoons uncooked olive oil to bowl with garlic and cooked oil and whisk to combine. Fold mixture into potatoes and serve.

COOK'S extra

Go to www.cooksillustrated.com
- Key in code 5067 for our Illustrated Guide to Garlic.
- This information will be available until November 1, 2006.

MAY & JUNE 2006
21

Ultimate Turtle Brownies

Dark chocolate brownies, rich and chewy caramel, and sweet pecans—it's hard to go wrong with turtle brownies. But it's even harder to make them right.

⇒ BY DAWN YANAGIHARA ⇐

Undeniably, caramel and chocolate have an affinity. Add pecans to that union and the confectionery combination is so noteworthy that it has a name: a turtle. This appealing confection has also inspired professional brownie bakers, and turtle brownies now appear in bakeries and coffeehouses from coast to coast.

Venture to make them at home, however, and the results are uninspiring. The reason is simple enough: Most turtle-brownie recipes call for boxed brownie mixes and jarred caramel sauce, yielding lackluster results. I wanted something reminiscent of a candy turtle: rich, chewy, and chocolaty, with a bittersweet, toothsinking caramel and an abundance of pecans.

Brown(ie) Nosing

I began by choosing the type and amount of chocolate. Brownies made solely with cocoa had a one-dimensional flavor and a chalky texture. Unsweetened chocolate packed a punch, but the flavor quickly fell flat. Bittersweet chocolate gave the brownies complexity and a nuanced flavor that lingered, but lacked assertiveness. I landed on 4 ounces of bittersweet (for complexity) and 2 ounces of unsweetened chocolate (for assertiveness).

I now had to get the texture right by adjusting the quantities of eggs, flour, and leavener. The light, open texture of classic cakey brownies was easily overwhelmed by the caramel. On the other hand, a dense, fudgy brownie was more confectionery than baked good once paired with the caramel. I wanted something in between. Two whole eggs worked nicely to give the brownies structure without untoward lift. Three-quarters cup of all-purpose flour was ideal for producing a moist brownie with chew. The leavener of choice was baking powder; a half teaspoon gave the brownies the slightest amount of lift, for a distinct crumb without too much cakiness.

The final additions to the brownies were a generous amount of chopped pecans and—for yet another dimension of chocolate—a handful of chocolate chips. (Some tasters found the chocolate chips superfluous, so I made them an optional ingredient.)

With a thick blanket of homemade caramel and a toasted pecan half, the transformation from turtle candy to turtle brownie is complete.

Sticky Situation

With the brownie component complete, it was onward to the caramel. A common technique is to layer the caramel with the brownie batter (and sometimes swirl it in) before baking. With this method, though, the caramel is lost visually to the dark color of the chocolate, and the turtle brownie simply doesn't look the part.

I tried several tactics, including prebaking the bottom brownie layer and adding flour to the caramel to produce a distinct middle layer. It was all to no avail. I returned to layering and swirling, this time drizzling the baked brownies with additional caramel. Better, but they still didn't read as "turtle" brownies. Undaunted, I blanketed the entire surface of the chilled, baked brownies with caramel, then garnished each square with a toasted pecan half. Finally, tasters were appeased.

Still, this turtle had not crossed the finish line: The caramel sauce didn't have enough chew—or enough textural contrast with the brownie. I knew from trial and error that a typical caramel sauce was too fluid for a turtle brownie. Because the brownies would likely be eaten at room temperature—or slightly chilled—the caramel had to be viscous enough to hold its form. For the 1¼ cups of sugar needed to yield the right amount of caramel, I experimented with 1 cup—or 16 tablespoons—of cream and eventually worked my way down to a mere 6 tablespoons, which produced a caramel that was pleasantly chewy and gooey.

I had a couple of run-ins with gritty, crystallized caramels. Research suggested that adding some corn syrup would prevent this. Indeed, once I began adding 2 tablespoons of corn syrup to the sugar before cooking, I had no more problems. Butter is a common ingredient in caramel, so I tried versions with and without; 2 tablespoons made the caramel smoother and silkier in flavor and feel. A touch of vanilla and a small amount of salt finished things off. Turtle brownies had finally come out of their shell.

With Shortcuts Like These . . .

In the test kitchen, we're no snobs when it comes to recipe shortcuts. But for our Turtle Brownies, we quickly rejected the most common one: melting store-bought caramel candies into a sauce. Not only was the flavor insipid and the texture waxy, but individually unwrapping a sufficient number of candies—52 of them—made this "shortcut" not so short after all. Instead, we came up with a foolproof recipe for homemade caramel that takes less than 10 minutes.

'SHORTCUT' CARAMEL SAUCE
Waxy and insipid—and lots of
tedious unwrapping

Foolproof Caramel 101

Caramel has a reputation for being tricky, but it's actually quite straightforward if you know what to look for. Below is a handy visual guide.

CENTER SUGAR

1. Pour granulated sugar into center of saucepan, making sure granules don't touch sides.

DAMPEN WITH SPATULA

2. Gently stir with clean spatula until sugar is damp. Cover until mixture boils and sugar dissolves completely; remove lid.

PALE GOLDEN

3. Cook until bubbles show faint golden color, then lower heat. Full gold bubbles mean you've gone too far.

LIGHT AMBER

4. Cook for 1 to 3 minutes more, until mixture is light amber (the color of honey). Remove pan from heat.

MEDIUM AMBER

5. Add cream, butter, and vanilla, which will cause caramel to turn a darker shade of amber.

ULTIMATE TURTLE BROWNIES
MAKES TWENTY-FIVE 1½-INCH-SQUARE BROWNIES

To drizzle the caramel in step 4, use a ¼-cup dry measuring cup that has been sprayed with nonstick cooking spray. If the caramel is too cool to be fluid, reheat it in the microwave.

Caramel

- ¼ cup plus 2 tablespoons heavy cream
- ¼ teaspoon table salt
- ¼ cup water
- 2 tablespoons light corn syrup
- 1¼ cups (8¾ ounces) sugar
- 2 tablespoons unsalted butter
- 1 teaspoon vanilla extract

Brownies

- 8 tablespoons (1 stick) unsalted butter, cut into 8 pieces
- 4 ounces bittersweet chocolate, chopped
- 2 ounces unsweetened chocolate, chopped
- ¾ cup (3¾ ounces) unbleached all-purpose flour
- ½ teaspoon baking powder
- 2 large eggs, room temperature
- 1 cup (7 ounces) sugar
- ¼ teaspoon table salt
- 2 teaspoons vanilla extract
- ⅔ cup (about 2¾ ounces) chopped pecans
- ⅓ cup semisweet chocolate chips (optional)

Garnish

- 25 pecan halves (about 1½ ounces), toasted

1. **TO MAKE THE CARAMEL:** Combine cream and salt in small bowl; stir well to dissolve salt. Combine water and corn syrup in heavy-bottomed 2- to 3-quart saucepan; pour sugar into center of saucepan, taking care not to let sugar granules touch sides of pan. Gently stir with clean spatula to moisten sugar thoroughly. Cover and bring to boil over medium-high heat; cook, covered and without stirring, until sugar is completely dissolved and liquid is clear, 3 to 5 minutes. Uncover and continue to cook, without stirring, until bubbles show faint golden color, 3 to 5 minutes more. Reduce heat to medium-low. Continue to cook (swirling occasionally) until caramel is light amber and registers about 360 degrees on candy or instant-read thermometer, 1 to 3 minutes longer. Remove saucepan from heat and carefully add cream to center of pan; stir with whisk or spatula (mixture will bubble and steam vigorously) until cream is fully incorporated and bubbling subsides. Stir in butter and vanilla until combined; transfer caramel to microwaveable measuring cup or bowl and set aside.

2. **TO MAKE THE BROWNIES:** Adjust oven rack to lower-middle position; heat oven to 325 degrees. Lightly spray 9-inch-square baking pan with nonstick cooking spray. Cut 14-inch length extra-wide heavy-duty foil; fold cut edges back to form 8½-inch width. With folded sides face down, fit foil securely into bottom and up sides of baking pan, allowing excess to overhang pan sides. Spray foil with cooking spray.

3. Melt butter and bittersweet and unsweetened chocolates in medium heatproof bowl set over saucepan of barely simmering water, stirring occasionally, until smooth and combined; set aside to cool slightly. Meanwhile, whisk together flour and baking powder in small bowl; set aside. When chocolate has cooled slightly, whisk eggs in large bowl to combine; add sugar, salt, and vanilla and whisk until incorporated. Add melted chocolate mixture to egg mixture; whisk until homogenous. Add flour mixture; stir with rubber spatula until almost combined. Add chopped pecans and chocolate chips (if using); mix until incorporated and no flour streaks remain.

4. Following illustrations below, distribute half of brownie batter in prepared baking pan, spreading in even layer. Drizzle scant ¼ cup caramel over batter. Drop remaining batter in large mounds over caramel layer; spread evenly and into corners of pan with rubber spatula. Drizzle additional scant ¼ cup caramel over top. Using tip of butter knife, swirl caramel and batter. Bake brownies until toothpick inserted into center comes out with only a few moist crumbs attached, 35 to 40 minutes. Cool brownies in pan on wire rack to room temperature, about 1½ hours.

5. Heat remaining caramel (you should have about ¾ cup) in microwave until warm and pourable but still thick (do not boil), 45 to 60 seconds, stirring once or twice; pour caramel over brownies. Using spatula, spread caramel to cover surface. Refrigerate brownies, uncovered, at least 2 hours.

6. Using foil extensions, lift brownies from baking pan, loosening sides with paring knife, if needed. Peel away and discard foil. Using chef's knife, cut brownies into 25 evenly sized squares. Press a pecan half onto surface of each brownie. Serve chilled or at room temperature.

STEP-BY-STEP | TURTLE BROWNIE CONSTRUCTION

  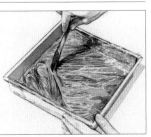

1. Add half of brownie batter to prepared baking pan and spread evenly.

2. Drizzle with scant ¼ cup warm caramel. Repeat steps 1 and 2.

3. Using tip of butter knife, swirl caramel and brownie batter.

Best Strawberry Cream Cake

What could possibly ruin the heavenly trio of cake, cream, and ripe strawberries? How about soggy cake, bland berries, and squishy cream?

BY ERIKA BRUCE

Nothing better showcases tangy, juicy strawberries than a strawberry cream cake. True, a simple strawberry shortcake puts the berries front and center, but its homespun, last-minute nature often doesn't suit a more dressed-up occasion. However, the concept is much the same: Fruit, cake, and cream are a winning combination, especially when artfully layered.

While I found no shortage of recipes for strawberry cream cakes that looked good, I was disenchanted by their lackluster taste and texture. The problem resided with either the cake itself, which collapsed under the weight of the filling, or the whipped cream, which squirted out the sides of the cake upon slicing. But most egregious, while my eyes told me there were strawberries in the cake, my taste buds remained unconvinced. I wanted a sturdy cake, a firm filling, and strawberry flavor fit for a starring role.

Supporting Character
With multiple layers, I needed a cake that was structurally sound. That meant butter cakes—rich but fragile—were out, so I moved on to sponge cakes. But tasters found the various sponge cakes I tried too lean and dry. I realized that what I wanted was the structure of a sponge cake coupled with the moistness and richness of a butter cake.

There was one sponge cake I had yet to try—the chiffon cake, an American invention introduced at Hollywood's Brown Derby restaurant in the 1920s and popularized by Betty Crocker in the 1940s. Similar to an angel food cake, a chiffon cake has more fat (in the form of egg yolks and vegetable oil) than most sponge cakes, making it high and light but also moist and tender.

When I baked the *Cook's* (May/June 1996) recipe for chiffon cake in a round cake pan (instead of the traditional tube pan), there was

COOK'S extra

Go to www.cooksillustrated.com
• Key in code 5068 for our **Cake Pan Equipment Test.**
• This information will be available until November 1, 2006.

Adding cream cheese and pureed strawberries between the cake's layers intensified its flavor and kept it stable enough to hold its form when sliced.

no way to hang it upside down while cooling to help the cake maintain its shape. The result was a sunken center and retracted sides. I tried increasing the flour and decreasing the liquid. The cake no longer sunk, but tasters felt it wasn't rich enough. The answer was to switch out the oil for butter, which produced a deeper, fuller flavor.

Berried Treasure
Most recipes call for folding the sliced strawberries into whipped cream. Tasters deemed this filling one-dimensional and felt that the flavors were muddied. I decided to treat the berries as a separate layer and began focusing on enhancing their flavor. Adding sugar to the naked berries was a must. Hoping strawberry jam might act as both sweetener and flavor enhancer, I found instead that it added a dull, cooked-berry quality.

Retracing my steps, I drew inspiration from the test kitchen's strawberry shortcake recipe, macerating the berries in sugar for an hour, mashing a portion, and folding this mash into the remaining berries. While this helped bind the berries, it also decreased their volume, allowing me to use four pints instead of the two I'd started with. The problem was that the macerated sliced berries became soft and were not visually appealing once added to the cake layers. The solution? Dividing the berries in half: One portion was sliced and used around the edges of the filling layers for visual appeal, while the other half was macerated, pulsed in a food processor, and spread over the center.

But I found that these processed berries exuded too much juice, which made the cake soggy. I tried straining off the excess liquid, but this was vital berry flavor going down the drain. My next step was to boil down the strained juices to evaporate the excess water, then add the syrupy remains back to the berries. This provided the perfect amount of soak for the cake, with no berry flavor lost. The final adjustment to flavor was some sweet liqueur (Kirsch was the favorite), cooked along with the strained juices to eliminate any boozy overtones.

Cream Sequence
With the strawberry and cake components securely in place, all I needed to fix was the insubstantial whipped cream layer. It needed more flavor and texture to stand up to the strawberries. Pastry cream was a popular suggestion, but I didn't want to add unnecessary cooking steps. Instead, I experimented with flavoring agents. Sour cream, yogurt, and cream cheese all offered a forward tang, but only cream cheese provided a boost in texture. When whipped with the heavy cream, cream cheese produced a stiff yet silky-smooth blend that helped anchor the cake layers. Even when sliced, the cake remained cohesive.

Not only did this cake meet all my expectations—sturdy yet moist chiffon cake, vibrant berries, and a robust, tangy cream—it even surpassed the classic yet humble strawberry shortcake.

PHOTOGRAPHY: CARL TREMBLAY

COOK'S ILLUSTRATED
24

STRAWBERRY CREAM CAKE
SERVES 8 TO 10

If using a cake pan, you will need one with straight sides that are at least 2 inches high; otherwise, use a springform pan. The cake portion can be made ahead of time, wrapped in a double layer of plastic wrap, and frozen; thaw the frozen cake, unwrapped, at room temperature for about two hours before proceeding with the recipe.

Cake

- 1¼ cups (5 ounces) cake flour
- 1½ teaspoons baking powder
- ¼ teaspoon table salt
- 1 cup (7 ounces) sugar
- 5 large eggs (2 whole and 3 separated), room temperature
- 6 tablespoons unsalted butter, melted and cooled slightly
- 2 tablespoons water
- 2 teaspoons vanilla extract

Strawberry Filling

- 2 pounds medium or large strawberries (about 2 quarts), washed, dried, and stemmed
- 4–6 tablespoons sugar
- 2 tablespoons Kirsch
- Pinch table salt

Whipped Cream

- 8 ounces cream cheese, room temperature
- ½ cup (3½ ounces) sugar
- 1 teaspoon vanilla extract
- ⅛ teaspoon table salt
- 2 cups heavy cream

1. **FOR THE CAKE:** Adjust oven rack to lower-middle position and heat oven to 325 degrees. Grease and flour round 9 by 2-inch cake pan or 9-inch springform pan and line with parchment paper. Whisk flour, baking powder, salt, and all but 3 tablespoons sugar in mixing bowl. Whisk in 2 whole eggs and 3 yolks (reserving whites), butter, water, and vanilla; whisk until smooth.

2. In clean bowl of standing mixer fitted with whisk attachment, beat remaining 3 egg whites at medium-low speed until frothy, 1 to 2 minutes. With machine running, gradually add remaining 3 tablespoons sugar, increase speed to medium-high, and beat until soft peaks form, 60 to 90 seconds. Stir one-third of whites into batter to lighten; add remaining whites and gently fold into batter until no white streaks remain. Pour batter into prepared pan and bake until toothpick or wooden skewer inserted into center of cake comes out clean, 30 to 40 minutes. Cool in pan 10 minutes, then invert cake onto greased wire rack; peel off and discard parchment. Invert cake again; cool completely, about 2 hours.

3. **FOR THE STRAWBERRY FILLING:** Halve 24 of best-looking berries and reserve. Quarter remaining berries; toss with 4 to 6 tablespoons sugar (depending on sweetness of berries) in medium bowl and let sit 1 hour, stirring occasionally. Strain juices from berries and reserve (you should have about ½ cup). In workbowl of food processor fitted with metal blade, give macerated berries five 1-second pulses (you should have about 1½ cups). In small saucepan over medium-high heat, simmer reserved juices and Kirsch until syrupy and reduced to about 3 tablespoons, 3 to 5 minutes. Pour reduced syrup over macerated berries, add pinch of salt, and toss to combine. Set aside until cake is cooled.

Here are some of the problems we encountered while developing our recipe—and the solutions we came up with.

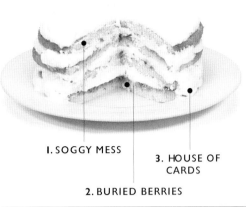

1. SOGGY MESS

3. HOUSE OF CARDS

2. BURIED BERRIES

1. **PROBLEM:** Tender butter cakes can't support filling.
   SOLUTION: A chiffon-style cake combined the rich flavor of a butter cake with the light-yet-sturdy texture of a sponge cake.

2. **PROBLEM:** Weak, one-dimensional strawberry flavor.
   SOLUTION: Making a flavorful berry "mash" and reducing the macerated juice in a saucepan helped concentrate and round out flavors.

3. **PROBLEM:** Filling squirts out when the cake is sliced, and layers fall apart.
   SOLUTION: Reducing the number of layers from four to three and fortifying the whipped-cream filling with cream cheese provided extra cohesiveness.

4. **FOR THE WHIPPED CREAM:** When cake has cooled, place cream cheese, sugar, vanilla, and salt in bowl of standing mixer fitted with whisk attachment. Whisk at medium-high speed until light and fluffy, 1 to 2 minutes, scraping down bowl with rubber spatula as needed. Reduce speed to low and add heavy cream in slow, steady stream; when almost fully combined, increase speed to medium-high and beat until mixture holds stiff peaks, 2 to 2½ minutes more, scraping bowl as needed (you should have about 4½ cups).

5. **TO ASSEMBLE THE CAKE:** Using large serrated knife, slice cake into three even layers. Place bottom layer on cardboard round or cake plate and arrange ring of 20 strawberry halves, cut sides down and stem ends facing out, around perimeter of cake layer. Pour one half of pureed berry mixture (about ¾ cup) in center, then spread to cover any exposed cake. Gently spread about one-third of whipped cream (about 1½ cups) over berry layer, leaving ½-inch border from edge. Place middle cake layer on top and press down gently (whipped cream layer should become flush with cake edge). Repeat with 20 additional strawberry halves, remaining berry mixture, and half of remaining whipped cream; gently press last cake layer on top. Spread remaining whipped cream over top; decorate with remaining cut strawberries. Serve, or chill for up to 4 hours.

STEP-BY-STEP | BUILDING A STRAWBERRY CREAM CAKE

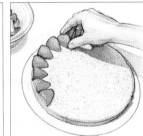

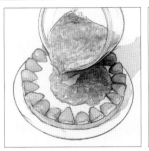

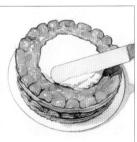

1. With serrated knife, use sawing motion to cut cake into 3 layers, rotating cake as you go.

2. Place sliced berries evenly around edges (they will be visible once layers are assembled).

3. Cover center of cake completely with half of pureed strawberries.

4. Spread one-third of whipped cream over berries, leaving ½-inch border. Repeat layering.

5. Press last layer into place, spread with remaining cream, and decorate with berries.

The Scoop on Vanilla Ice Cream

How about a heaping bowl of guar gum and pulverized spent vanilla pods? Can ice cream makers fool Mother Nature (and our tasters)? We scooped up 18 brands to find out.

⇒ BY JOLYON HELTERMAN ⇐

Broth makers do it with yeast extract. Tomato canners do it with calcium chloride. But when it comes to counting on the magic of food engineering to improve on Mother Nature, ice cream manufacturers really take the cake.

Sure, some supermarket vanilla ice creams attempt to get by on just the basics—"all natural" blends of cream, sugar, vanilla, and little else. But many cartons sport labels that read like highlights from a chemistry textbook. Some manufacturers substitute imitation vanilla extract for the real stuff, while others bet on visual appeal, using ground-up vanilla-bean specks to give the illusion of full flavor.

Does any of this hocus-pocus deliver a better product? To find out, we tasted 18 varieties, including 10 French-style (with egg yolks) and eight regular (yolkless) vanilla ice creams.

Creamy Secrets

As varied as the ice creams looked on paper, the side-by-side comparison was striking. Some were fluffy and light; others were dense and rich. A few had assertive vanilla notes that reminded tasters of "frozen, boozy eggnog." Several ice creams, on the other hand, seemed to be lacking in vanilla flavor altogether.

Contrary to expectations, the French vanilla ice creams—prized for the rich flavor and creamy texture that comes from egg yolks—did not sweep the competition. In fact, regular-style Turkey Hill Vanilla Bean just edged out French-style Edy's Dreamery (the winner of our 2001 French vanilla tasting) for first place. Yes, the French-style ice creams (with 12.5 percent to 17.0 percent butterfat) took five of the six top spots, while leaner

eggless vanilla ice creams (with 11.6 percent to 12.3 percent butterfat) took four of the five bottom places. But the top ranking of Turkey Hill Vanilla Bean (with just 12.1 percent butterfat) did not fit the neat pattern of more fat equals better quality.

Just as puzzling were tasters' comments about the texture of this yolkless winner. "What an amazingly gooey, creamy texture!" wrote one taster. "Nice eggy mouthfeel," said another. Double-checking the list of ingredients, I saw no evidence of any egg product. Even stranger, a quick skim through the rest of the comments revealed similar remarks about the "custardy" texture of a few of the other regular (yolkless) samples. Either my tasters were completely clueless, or there was something in these ice creams that was giving them (the ice creams) a faux-French demeanor.

Granting my colleagues the benefit of the doubt, I studied the labels and soon noticed a clear pattern. Every regular-style ice cream that had passed for French vanilla contained substances such as carob bean gum, carrageenan, guar gum, and mono- and diglycerides. Could these additives be mimicking the textural effect of egg yolks?

Turns out I was partly right. Carob bean gum, carrageenan, and guar gum are all stabilizers, added to ice cream to help keep ice crystals from forming and wreaking havoc on texture. Mono- and diglycerides, on the other hand, are emulsifiers, added to ice cream to keep the fat from separating—which, in turn, contributes a luscious, silky texture. Egg yolks, which naturally contain the emulsifier lecithin, serve this same function in French-style ice creams. So it was the mono- and diglycerides that

had fooled our panelists into praising the "custardy" texture of the eggless ice creams.

A much clearer picture was emerging: High fat content and egg yolks can give ice cream a rich, creamy texture, but the judicious use of stabilizers and emulsifiers goes a long way toward making up for the absence of either one. The ice creams in our lineup that got the lowest scores for texture have low fat content and no egg yolks, stabilizers, or emulsifiers (that is, the "natural" regular-style ice creams). Our winning ice cream, Turkey Hill Vanilla Bean, contains emulsifiers as well as two stabilizers. And runner-up Edy's Dreamery has egg yolks, stabilizers, and a high fat content. No wonder it received the highest score for texture in the entire lineup.

Looks Can Be Deceiving

Of course, ice cream is more than just creamy. Some of the best-textured contenders fumbled when it came to flavor. Although the occasional ice cream lost points for too-potent vanilla notes (especially "artificial" or "boozy" flavors), by the end of the tasting it was clear why "vanilla" is often synonymous with "plain." In fact, weak vanilla flavor was the reason cited most often by panelists for awarding an ice cream a low score.

There are three forms of vanilla found in supermarket vanilla ice creams. Natural vanilla extract is made by steeping ground vanilla beans in a solution of alcohol and water to extract more than 240 flavorful compounds, the most dominant of which is called vanillin. Imitation vanilla extract is made by synthesizing vanillin from either eugenol (found in clove oil) or lignin (a by-product of the paper industry). The third form is vanilla beans themselves.

Only two of the ice creams—Blue Bunny regular and Blue Bell French—contained imitation vanilla extract. One failed to make it out of the elimination round, and the other landed in next-to-last place in the main tasting. Clearly, natural vanilla is a key component in good ice cream. But how much is enough?

To answer this question, we had our lab examine all 18 samples for vanillin content and found that more vanillin generally translated to higher ratings from our tasters. The differences were fairly dramatic. On the low end, several ice creams contained only 2 milligrams of vanillin (per kilogram), and many of these were eliminated early on for weak

---

Air Apparent: Why Is Some Ice Cream So Fluffy?

All ice creams are aerated to make their texture lighter and softer. Federal regulations allow manufacturers to increase the volume of ice cream by up to 100 percent. The air added to the ice cream is called overrun. Premium brands with a dense texture (often sold in pint containers) have less overrun than fluffy brands (often sold in big containers).

Brands with low overrun (between 21 percent and 24 percent) took most of the top spots in our tasting (including second, third, and fourth), while brands with high overrun (between 78 percent and 97 percent) landed in the last four spots. But there was one brand that did not fit this neat pattern. Our taste-test winner, Turkey Hill Vanilla Bean, has 94 percent overrun (the second-highest in our tasting). It achieved better texture through better engineering (see story for details). So what does this mean in practical terms? A 10-ounce serving of Turkey Hill will tower over a regular sugar cone. A 10-ounce serving of second-place Dreamery (with 21 percent overrun) looks pretty skimpy by comparison. –J.H.

vanilla flavor (including Breyers Natural and Turkey Hill French). Other ice creams contained nearly 10 times as much. In the end, our winning Turkey Hill Vanilla Bean (4 milligrams) and second-place Edy's Dreamery (10 milligrams) represented the extremes of what our tasters considered the right amount of vanilla flavor. Ice creams with more than 10 milligrams tended to lose points for "extract overkill," while those with fewer than 4 milligrams had tasters asking "where's the flavor?"

Even more striking were the differences in vanilla-bean specks found in about half of our samples: In some, the specks looked like a uniform sprinkling of finely ground black pepper; in others, the pieces were large and less frequent. But seeing vanilla specks doesn't necessarily mean that you're going to taste vanilla.

My first clue that something was amiss came after running taste tests with and without blindfolds. When asked to pick the samples with the most vanilla flavor, tasters almost unanimously chose the samples with bean specks. But when I ran the same test with blindfolds, tasters chose samples without bean specks as having the most intense vanilla flavor. The lab confirmed these results. Not only were these visible vanilla specks not a reliable indicator of vanilla intensity, but the ice creams with bean specks generally contained *less* vanilla flavor! Additional research confirmed that these "vanilla bean specks" are the pulverized pods of spent vanilla beans—not the flavorful beans themselves—and carry little to no flavor.

The Cream of the Crop

So where did we come out? Turns out it is possible to pull one over on Mother Nature—and, when it comes to vanilla ice cream, some strategic engineering is actually a desirable thing. Our tasters liked both French-style ice creams with stabilizers and regular (yolkless) ice creams with stabilizers and emulsifiers. If you prefer your ice cream smooth, subtle, and balanced, Turkey Hill Vanilla Bean is our top choice, while those who like vanilla that packs more of a punch might opt for the second-place Edy's Dreamery.

TASTING VANILLA ICE CREAMS

Overrun was estimated by comparing the weight of 1 gallon of each ice cream to 9 pounds, the approximate weight of 1 gallon of commercial ice cream mix before processing. Vanillin content was determined by an independent laboratory; fat and sugar content (per ½-cup serving) are based on the labeling information. Ice creams are listed in order of preference from left to right within each category.

HIGHLY RECOMMENDED

TURKEY HILL All Natural Flavor Vanilla Bean (regular)
- Mono- and Diglycerides, Guar Gum, and Carrageenan
- **$4.99**/1.75 quarts **Fat:** 12.1%
  Sugar: 16 g **Vanillin:** 4 mg/kg
  Estimated Overrun: 94%

"Exactly what vanilla ice cream should taste like," said one panelist about the only yolkless contender in our top six. "Subdued vanilla," noted one taster, "but a very clean flavor, and an amazingly creamy, gooey texture."

EDY'S Dreamery Vanilla (French-style)
- Carob Bean Gum, Guar Gum, and Carrageenan
- **$3.69**/1 pint **Fat:** 14.2%
  Sugar: 24 g **Vanillin:** 10 mg/kg
  Estimated Overrun: 21%

Tasters gave Dreamery the top score for texture ("ultra-creamy and yummy"), clearly enhanced by three stabilizers and egg yolks, and praised its strong vanilla flavor. *This brand is called Dreyer's on the West Coast.*

RECOMMENDED

HÄAGEN-DAZS Vanilla (French-style)
- No Stabilizers or Emulsifiers
- **$3.79**/1 pint **Fat:** 17.0%
  Sugar: 21 g **Vanillin:** 15 mg/kg
  Estimated Overrun: 21%

Rich, creamy, and "buttery," this high-fat, "high-octane" brand was some tasters' favorite, but others found the vanilla flavor much too strong: fairly boozy, "like a good eggnog."

HÄAGEN-DAZS Vanilla Bean (French-style)
- No Stabilizers or Emulsifiers
- **$3.79**/1 pint **Fat:** 17.0%
  Sugar: 26 g **Vanillin:** 14 mg/kg
  Estimated Overrun: 21%

"So many vanilla specks it looks like Cookies 'n' Cream," said one taster. The strong, boozy flavor called to mind "rum steeped with vanilla," and this was the sweetest entry in the lineup. Some complaints about icy texture.

RECOMMENDED WITH RESERVATIONS

BEN & JERRY'S Vanilla (French-style)
- Guar Gum and Carrageenan
- **$3.49**/1 pint **Fat:** 14.6%
  Sugar: 19 g **Vanillin:** 4 mg/kg
  Estimated Overrun: 24%

Creamy, rich, and subtly flavored, but some found it too subtle in vanilla intensity. "Fatty but flavorless," complained one taster.

BLUE BUNNY Premium Natural Vanilla Bean (French-style)
- No Stabilizers or Emulsifiers
- **$3.24**/1.75 quarts **Fat:** 12.5%
  Sugar: 16 g **Vanillin:** 12 mg/kg
  Estimated Overrun: 78%

High vanillin and modest fat content were a recipe for major vanilla intensity. "Too much vanilla to eat a whole bowl," said one taster. Texture was on the icy side.

TURKEY HILL Philadelphia Style All Natural Vanilla Bean (regular)
- No Stabilizers or Emulsifiers
- **$4.99**/1.75 quarts **Fat:** 11.8%
  Sugar: 16 g **Vanillin:** 6 mg/kg
  Estimated Overrun: 88%

Lost points for a "lean and icy" consistency that its sibling (our winner) solved with stabilizers and emulsifiers.

BREYERS Extra Creamy Vanilla (regular)
- Carob Bean Gum and Guar Gum
- **$4.99**/1.75 quarts **Fat:** 11.6%
  Sugar: 14 g **Vanillin:** 2 mg/kg
  Estimated Overrun: 85%

The problem with this yolkless ice cream wasn't texture or richness; there just wasn't enough vanilla flavor.

BLUE BUNNY Premium Vanilla (regular)
- Carob Bean Gum, Guar Gum, Mono- and Diglycerides, and Carrageenan
- **$3.24**/1.75 quarts **Fat:** 11.8%
  Sugar: 15 g **Vanillin:** 26 mg/kg
  Estimated Overrun: 88%

One of two ice creams that used synthetic vanilla, this brand confounded tasters with its texture—"velvety" to some, "gummy" and "taffy-like" to others.

EDY'S Grand Vanilla Bean (regular)
- Cellulose Gum, Mono- and Diglycerides, Guar Gum, and Carrageenan
- **$4.79**/1.75 quarts **Fat:** 12.3%
  Sugar: 14 g **Vanillin:** 3 mg/kg
  Estimated Overrun: 97%

Tasters decried the "frozen Marshmallow Fluff" texture, and the abundance of vanilla specks belied the low vanillin content. *This brand is called Dreyer's on the West Coast.*

The Tong Show

Are the new design features on some tongs more than just gimmicks?
We tested 11 pairs to see if it was possible to improve on this kitchen workhorse.

⇒ BY ADAM RIED ⇐

Professional chefs often joke about having "asbestos hands" that can take the heat from searing-hot food and blazing-hot sauté pans. For those of us whose hands are made from skin, flesh, and bones, using a pair of kitchen tongs is a decidedly safer approach. In the test kitchen and our home kitchens alike, we use them to lift, flip, turn, rotate, and otherwise move every conceivable type of food while it cooks, from ramekins of custard in a water bath to small shrimp sautéing in a pan to gargantuan prime rib roasts emerging from the oven.

Believe it or not, tongs are no longer the straightforward affair they once were. Of course, you can still buy a basic model—two plain metal arms connected by a spring, with scalloped pincers for gripping—but you are just as likely to find tongs that fold in half, telescope, or pull double-duty as a spatula. Arms come cushioned or curved, and pincers can be nonstick-friendly and have various degrees of scalloping around the edges. With so many innovations, our question here was simple: Are these newfangled tongs any better than basic, old-school models?

Get a Grip

The business end of a pair of tongs, the pincers, can be smooth or scalloped, and we found that those with scalloped edges get a better grip on food. But that's not the end of the story. The shape of the scalloping can vary. Our tests showed that edges with deep, sharp scalloping were more likely to break through the delicate breading on a chicken cutlet or shred meat fibers on a pot roast than edges with wide, shallow scalloping. Pronounced scalloping did not necessarily spell disaster, but we preferred the gentler touch of wide, shallow scalloping.

Pincers that were slightly concave, or cupped, did a good job of grasping hard, irregularly shaped, and large objects. The nearly flat pincers of the KitchenAid tongs, for instance, had a tenuous hold on lobsters, ramekins, and pot roasts. Imagine shooting a basket while wearing a stiff oven mitt that limited the flex of your hand. Using your palm and fingers to cup the ball improves control; the same proved true with the pincers—the concavity helped tongs cradle the curved sides of the ramekins and lobsters.

Two of our contestants featured nonstick-friendly pincers, made of nylon on the Oxo (and heatsafe up to 400 degrees) and silicone on the Chef'n. The nylon Oxo really surprised testers, matching the aim and precision of the regular Oxo move for move until hard, slick lobsters slipped right out of the pincers. Because of their wide-body design and bulk, the silicone pincers on the Chef'n suffered the opposite problem—they were clumsy and imprecise for fine work such as moving a scallop or a spear of asparagus.

The Kuhn Rikon tongs had unique pincers, shaped like spatulas and made of wire. Unfortunately, unique does not equal effective. The flexible wire tines offered a poor grip on hard, large, and heavy items, and they were too wide to position small items accurately.

What's the moral of the pincer story? Whether you go nonstick-friendly or not, look for pincers with gentle concavity and wide, shallow scalloping.

Armed and Dangerous

The arms of several contenders featured unusual designs that, by and large, made little sense to our testers. We failed to see any advantage to the curved arms of the Chantal tongs, or the 10- to 14-inch telescoping arms of the Amco tongs (which could not be set to 12 inches, our preferred length). Worse yet, the G&S Design tongs, which fold up along the length of the tongs for easy storage, infuriated us by ratcheting downward under strain—bad news during the pot roast trials. The good news is that the soft cushioning on the arms of both the Oxo and the Chef'n models kept hands comfortable, firmly planted, and cool in case the tongs heated up during use. (Flipping frying chicken can make all-metal tongs unbearably hot.)

After all the testing was done, the Oxo tongs—both nonstick-friendly and regular—proved to be the best of show. If you wield your tongs with wild abandon (and worry about scratching your nonstick cookware), Oxo's nylon-tipped tongs ($9.95) may be the way to go. But if you really want just one pair that will do it all and are willing to use them gingerly when using nonstick cookware, you can't beat Oxo's regular, metal-tipped tongs ($9.95).

Tweezer Tongs: A Fine Job

Though appearance may suggest otherwise, those gigantic tweezers—nearly the same size as regular tongs—billed as "fine" or "precision" tongs were not invented so the Jolly Green Giant could pluck his eyebrows. Said to be the brainchild of Japanese cooks working with small morsels of raw fish or vegetables, fine tongs are billed similarly here—for precision work with delicate foods that require accuracy and the gentlest touch. We wouldn't think of replacing our all-purpose kitchen tongs with fine tongs, but we did wonder if they would make a useful supplement.

We tested four pairs—including the $36 Global Chef's Tweezers, $22 Rösle Fine Tongs, and $4 R.S.V.P.—on the most delicate foods in our tong trials: scallops, breaded cutlets, and asparagus spears. Long story short, none of the precision tongs outmaneuvered the best of the regular tongs, and four of the five testers said they'd never use them at home. –A.R.

PRECISION WORK ONLY
The Rösle Fine Tongs were the best we tested, but they aren't necessary unless you're a food stylist charged with adjusting strands of pasta a millimeter to the left or right.

A Pincer Is Worth a Thousand Words

After weeks of testing, we found that we could tell a lot about the performance of a pair of tongs just by noting the shape of its pincers. Tongs with flat pincers (left) had trouble keeping hold of awkward or bulky items, such as ramekins and pot roasts. In general, we preferred models with concave, scalloped pincers. Of those, we found that pincers with deep, sharp scalloping (middle) had a tendency to tear apart delicate foods. Our favorite style? Pincers with wide, shallow scalloping (right).

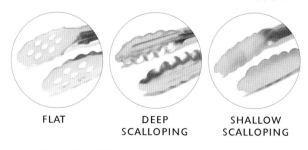

FLAT	DEEP SCALLOPING	SHALLOW SCALLOPING

RATING KITCHEN TONGS

We tested 11 pairs of 12-inch tongs (or as close to that size as possible from some manufacturers) and evaluated them according to the following criteria. A range of testers (large- and small-handed, more and less experienced) participated in the performance tests and evaluations of overall handle comfort, ease of use, and pincer design. Testers rated the tongs on a scale of 1 to 10, and those scores were averaged into ratings of good, fair, and poor. Scores were averaged to determine overall rank, and tongs are listed in order of preference.

PRICE: Prices paid in Boston-area retail, national mail-order, or online outlets.

CONSTRUCTION: Materials and style.

PINCER DESIGN: The pattern of the edge that comes into contact with the food.

PERFORMANCE, LARGE ITEMS: Testers lifted a cooked, 4½-pound beef roast from a deep pot of braising liquid and rated tongs for strength and grip security.

PERFORMANCE, SMALL ITEMS: Testers moved 1 pound of cooked asparagus in a skillet and rated tongs for precision and grasp.

PERFORMANCE, HARD ITEMS: Testers lifted 1¼-pound lobsters from tall pots and custard-filled ramekins (round and deep as well as oval and shallow) from a water bath and rated tongs for grip security.

PERFORMANCE, SOFT ITEMS: Testers turned both sea scallops and breaded chicken cutlets in a skillet and rated tongs for grip precision and gentleness.

HANDLE COMFORT: Testers evaluated handle comfort based on shape, materials, and fit in hand.

TESTERS' COMMENTS: These comments augment the information on the chart with observations about the tongs' design or performance in specific tests.

RECOMMENDED

	PERFORMANCE	TESTERS' COMMENTS
Oxo Good Grips 12-Inch Locking Tongs PRICE: $9.95 CONSTRUCTION: Stainless steel and Santoprene; spring-loaded, locking PINCER DESIGN: Shallow scallop	LARGE ITEMS: ★★★ SMALL ITEMS: ★★ HARD ITEMS: ★★★ SOFT ITEMS: ★★★ HANDLE COMFORT: ★★★	Missed a perfect score only because one picky tester thought the pincers bruised cooked asparagus—a minor complaint. Class valedictorian in every other respect.
Oxo Good Grips 12-Inch Tongs (Nylon Tips) PRICE: $9.95 CONSTRUCTION: Stainless steel, Santoprene, and nylon; spring-loaded, locking PINCER DESIGN: Shallow scallop	LARGE ITEMS: ★★★ SMALL ITEMS: ★★★ HARD ITEMS: ★★ SOFT ITEMS: ★★★ HANDLE COMFORT: ★★★	Nonstick-friendly and effective with everything but hard objects. We could get a (tenuous) grip on ramekins, but lobster was a no-go.
Edlund 12-Inch Locking Tongs PRICE: $9.25 CONSTRUCTION: Stainless steel; spring-loaded, locking PINCER DESIGN: Deep scallop	LARGE ITEMS: ★★★ SMALL ITEMS: ★★★ HARD ITEMS: ★★★ SOFT ITEMS: ★★ HANDLE COMFORT: ★★★	Described as light and natural; one tester remarked, "They just belong in your hand." Sharp, deeply defined scalloping can tear delicate foods.

RECOMMENDED WITH RESERVATIONS

	PERFORMANCE	TESTERS' COMMENTS
Vollrath 12-Inch One-Piece Utility Tongs PRICE: $7.65 CONSTRUCTION: Stainless steel with coated handle; nonlocking PINCER DESIGN: Shallow scallop	LARGE ITEMS: ★★ SMALL ITEMS: ★★ HARD ITEMS: ★★★ SOFT ITEMS: ★★ HANDLE COMFORT: ★★★	Performance equaled (surpassed, in fact) that of many of the locking tongs, but storage is less convenient. Some testers found the tension a bit too stiff.
Chantal Contoured Kitchen Tongs PRICE: $14.99 CONSTRUCTION: Stainless steel; spring-loaded, locking, curved handles PINCER DESIGN: Tapered	LARGE ITEMS: ★★ SMALL ITEMS: ★★★ HARD ITEMS: ★★★ SOFT ITEMS: ★★ HANDLE COMFORT: ★★	Several testers noted that the pincers shredded fibers on the surface of tender meat and the crust of chicken cutlets. The curved handles left testers more puzzled than impressed.
Amco Houseworks 10-Inch and 14-Inch Telescoping Tongs PRICE: $12.95 CONSTRUCTION: Stainless steel; spring-loaded, locking PINCER DESIGN: Small scallop	LARGE ITEMS: ★★★ SMALL ITEMS: ★★ HARD ITEMS: ★★ SOFT ITEMS: ★★ HANDLE COMFORT: ★★	Forget about picking up a roast with these tongs in the 10-inch position. Many testers disliked both lengths, finding that "the long is too long and the short is too short."
KitchenAid Utility Tongs PRICE: $9.99 CONSTRUCTION: Stainless steel; spring-loaded, locking PINCER DESIGN: Shallow scallop	LARGE ITEMS: ★★ SMALL ITEMS: ★★ HARD ITEMS: ★★ SOFT ITEMS: ★★ HANDLE COMFORT: ★★	The nearly flat pincers made for a compromised grip on large, hard, and soft objects alike (but created a nice spatula effect). Pincers and handles struck some testers as too broad.

NOT RECOMMENDED

	PERFORMANCE	TESTERS' COMMENTS
Chef'n Tongo 12-Inch Silicone Tongs PRICE: $14.99 CONSTRUCTION: Stainless steel and silicone; spring-loaded, locking PINCER DESIGN: Smooth	LARGE ITEMS: ★★ SMALL ITEMS: ★ HARD ITEMS: ★★ SOFT ITEMS: ★★ HANDLE COMFORT: ★★	Tongs with a double whammy: bulky pincers that were too flexible to be precise and arms that had a proclivity for pinching unsuspecting fingers.
Kuhn Rikon Easy-Lock Wire Tongs PRICE: $19.99 CONSTRUCTION: Stainless steel; locking PINCER DESIGN: Wire	LARGE ITEMS: ★ SMALL ITEMS: ★★★ HARD ITEMS: ★ SOFT ITEMS: ★★ HANDLE COMFORT: ★★	Hybrid spatula/pincers slid under asparagus and breaded cutlets easily but could neither fit around nor lift lobsters and pot roast.
G&S Design Compactables Locking Tongs PRICE: $16.99 CONSTRUCTION: Stainless steel and Santoprene; spring-loaded, locking PINCER DESIGN: Scalloped	LARGE ITEMS: ★ SMALL ITEMS: ★★ HARD ITEMS: ★★ SOFT ITEMS: ★★ HANDLE COMFORT: ★	The folding arms collapsed under the weight of the pot roast, causing a tidal wave of hot braising liquid when the meat dropped into the pot. Testers found the handles awkward.
Progressive Multi-Purpose (10-Inch) Kitchen Tongs PRICE: $1.99 CONSTRUCTION: Stainless steel/PVC-coated handles; scissor type, nonlocking PINCER DESIGN: Smooth	LARGE ITEMS: ★ SMALL ITEMS: ★ HARD ITEMS: ★ SOFT ITEMS: ★ HANDLE COMFORT: ★	When it comes to these hardware store standards, one word says it all: flimsy. More words? How about "misaligned, uncomfortable, and loose"?

KITCHEN NOTES

⇒ BY ERIKA BRUCE ⇐

Is It Done Yet?

Our preferred method for determining when boiled potatoes are fully cooked is to poke them with a paring knife (a fork merely wedges the potatoes open, making them fill up with water). But after cooking dozens of pounds of potatoes for Garlic and Olive Oil Mashed Potatoes (page 21), we realized that this technique wasn't quite foolproof—sometimes the potatoes were slightly underdone, marring our creamy mashed potatoes with granular bits. Because our paring knives are so sharp, we mistook the lack of resistance for fully cooked spuds. We found that an even better test was to poke the potato and then try to lift it out of the water. If it clung to the knife even for a second, back into the pot it went.

HOLD ON A SECOND
It's not ready yet.

Regular vs. Lower-Sodium Soy Sauce

Lower-sodium soy sauce contains as much as 37 percent less sodium than regular soy sauce. But is it also light on flavor? To find out, we compared Kikkoman regular soy sauce, our top supermarket brand, with its lower-sodium counterpart over plain white rice, in an uncooked dipping sauce with tuna steaks, and sautéed with bok choy.

Instead of tasting watered-down or bland, the lower-sodium soy sauce was surprisingly full-flavored. Over rice and in the dipping sauce for the tuna, tasters actually preferred it to regular soy sauce for its sweeter, "more complex" flavor. Given that the ingredient lists are virtually

STEP-BY-STEP | PREPARING POTATOES FOR FISH AND CHIPS

1. Trim each end. Carefully cut a thin slice from one side. Rotate the potato, and repeat with the remaining sides.

2. Cut each potato lengthwise into ½-inch slices.

3. Cut each potato slice into ½-inch batons.

identical, it was clear that with less salt, the nuances in the lower-sodium soy sauce became more pronounced. But when cooked (briefly, added toward the end of cooking), most of these delicate nuances were lost, and the end result was a milder-tasting side dish. In cooked recipes, such as our stir-fries on page 15, soy sauce functions as a seasoning (rather than a complex flavor component) and the regular soy sauce, with its additional sodium, is preferable.

Shopping for Strawberries

After purchasing several quarts of berries for Strawberry Cream Cake (page 25), we realized that few inhabitants of the produce aisle have as uncanny an ability to look perfect yet taste disappointingly bland. Unlike fruits such as bananas and peaches, which continue to ripen after picking (and are called climacteric), strawberries (nonclimacteric) don't get any sweeter once off the vine, so it's

vital to select the sweetest ones you can find. Strawberries continue to develop a deep red pigment (called anthocyanin), but a berry that looks redder is not necessarily a berry that tastes sweeter.

What, then, is the best way to pick out a ripe pint of strawberries? Being upstanding citizens, we would never officially recommend the most foolproof method—tearing open a berry or two to see if the red pigment extends all the way to the core, which

TASTING: Green Olives

Until we began developing our recipe for Moroccan Chicken (page 7), we were unaware of just how many green olive varietals were out there—from the $1.99-a-jar cocktail garnish to the $12.99-per-pound French import. Our curiosity (and taste buds) piqued, we scoured local supermarket shelves and returned with nearly two dozen jars and deli containers. We tried all of the olives plain, then cooked them in our Moroccan Chicken.

Straight from the container, the hands-down favorites were the imported (and somewhat expensive) French samples—Lucques and Picholines—for their buttery, bright flavor and al dente texture. The brawny Spanish Queens/Gordals were lackluster and mealy to some, "pleasantly mild" and soft to others. The Manzanillas (of martini fame) were faulted for an overwhelming pungency but praised for their meatiness.

There were two styles of Greek Conservolea—spice brined and salt brined—and both styles were "cracked," a method of curing that involves breaking the olive's flesh to extract a bitter compound called oleuropein. Tasters thought this curing method left the spice-brined Conservoleas lacking in olive flavor but found the salt-brined variety bright and full.

When incorporated into a cooked dish, most of the olives maintained their initial characteristics, with one exception. Rather than tainting our recipe with their initially unpleasant pungency and bitterness, the Manzanillas gained points for a newfound depth of flavor and meaty texture. Still superior in both categories, however, were the cracked, salt-brined Conservoleas (Divina was our favorite brand), which topped the charts for being "bright" and "snappy"—and which, at $3.79 a jar, left a little green in our wallets. –Elizabeth Bomze

CONSERVOLEAS
Bright and snappy

LUCQUES
Crisp and buttery

MANZANILLAS
Pungent and meaty

PICHOLINES
Tiny and bright

SPANISH QUEENS
Brawny and mild

is a reliable sign. (Or, better yet, stealing a quick taste.) The third-best method? Taking a whiff. A sweet, fruity aroma is a much better indicator of what lies beneath the rosy exterior than the rosy exterior itself.

A Dull Moment?

It might not seem like much, but the simple step of cutting Grilled London Broil (see the recipe on page 13) into ultra-thin slices is crucial for maximum tenderness. Best achieved with a very sharp carving, or slicing, knife, this task becomes all but impossible with a dull chef's knife. So what should you do if you're stuck with a not-so-sharp blade?

After the steak has rested, cut it in half lengthwise, then slice each half separately into very thin, even slices. The shorter slices are much easier to manage when you are working with an inferior knife.

1. Cut the steak in half lengthwise.   **2.** Cut each half crosswise into even slices.

EQUIPMENT TESTING : **Candy Thermometers**

Candy thermometers are designed for stovetop recipes where close monitoring of temperature is key—especially candy-making and deep-frying. The thermometer stays in the liquid during cooking. But which brand is best? To find out, we brought 13 models into the test kitchen and made multiple batches of caramel for our Turtle Brownies (page 23).

Thermometers with the simplest style—a plain glass tube—worked fine, but they are also fragile and the gradations were hard to read. What's more, a few models had a tendency to slide down and touch the bottom of the pan, giving a false reading. Similar thermometers with a metal "foot" to keep the thermometer off the pan bottom didn't work in a small (shallow) batch of caramel and were also hard to read. Dial-face thermometers required as much as 2½ inches of liquid—a rarity when making candies.

The best of the bunch were the digital models, which have easy-to-read consoles and alarm features that warn the cook when the caramel is done. But they tend to be top-heavy, with a precarious grip on the saucepan. Maverick's Redi-Chek Digital Oil & Candy Thermometer ($34.95) had the most reliable grip, and it's a decent choice. Essential? Probably not. An instant-read thermometer capable of registering temperatures up to 400 degrees—we like ThermoWorks' Thermapen ($79)—is just as reliable and can also be used to check the temperatures of roasts, breads, sauces, and more.

—Garth Clingingsmith

TIPPY TOP CHOICE
Digital thermometers: Easy to read but seem in danger of tipping over. Maverick's Redi-Chek ($34.95) was the best we found.

NOT-SO-EASY READING
Traditional candy thermometers: Hard to read, and some have a tenuous grip on the pan.

HIGH AND DRY
Dial-face thermometers: Require up to 2½ inches of liquid to register accurately—too much for our Turtle Brownies caramel.

RECIPE UPDATE

Sangría with White Wine

When readers asked how to make a white wine version of our **Best Sangría** (May/June 1998), we wondered if it would be as easy as swapping out red wine for white. After a few sips, it was clear that some fine-tuning was in order. The white sangría tasted too sweet and lacked the full body and distinctive "winey" profile of the red version. We quickly zeroed in on the difference in tannins—the source of the astringent flavors that are abundant in red wines but not in white wines. To temper the astringency of the red sangría, we had added a fair amount of sugar and Triple Sec orange liqueur, but that level of sweetness overwhelmed the less tannic white sangría. So we experimented with reducing the orange liqueur and sugar in increments. In the end, reducing just the orange liqueur proved key—both lessening the sweetness and diminishing competition from the liqueur's orange aromatics. The fuller body was easy to achieve. In a tasting of white sangrías made with several common varietals, tasters preferred Pinot Grigio and unoaked Chardonnay for their full body and fruity flavor profiles. (See Cook's Extra, below, for the recipe.)

Chicken Teriyaki . . . on the Grill

Several grill enthusiasts wondered if our **Chicken Teriyaki** (January/February 2005) could be adapted for the grill. Because our original recipe depends on charring boneless (but skin-on) thighs under the broiler, a high-heat grill option seemed like a no-brainer. We first tried a modified two-level fire, browning the skin first and finishing the chicken on the cooler side of the grill. However, thanks to flare-ups from the rendering fat, the chicken tended to scorch before it cooked through.

Unwilling to remove the skin to fix the problem (the ultra-crispy skin is what we like best), we came up with an alternate solution. Setting a disposable aluminum roasting pan in the center of the grill, with hot coals banked on two sides, we tried cooking the chicken directly over the pan, skin side up (with the cover on), until the internal temperature registered 160 degrees. At this point, the skin was not fully rendered, so we finished cooking the chicken directly over the charcoal with the skin side down. The area over the drip pan served as a "timeout zone" for the occasional flare-up—much rarer now that most of the fat had been rendered. The result was crispy skin that boasted deep, brown color—the perfect match for a spoonful of sweet, pungent teriyaki sauce. (See Cook's Extra, below, for the recipe.)

Raising the (Cookie) Bar

Inquiring readers wanted to know whether both of our chocolate chip cookie recipes could be made in bar form. The easy answer is yes—and no. The recipe for our **Thick and Chewy Chocolate Chip Cookies** (January/February 1996) transferred beautifully to a 13 by 9-inch baking pan: same proportions, just a slightly longer baking time. (See Cook's Extra, below, for the recipe.) But our more recently published **Thin, Crispy Chocolate Chip Cookies** (March/April 2001) were a different story. With substantially more sugar and butter and less flour (to help the cookies spread as dramatically as the words "thin" and "crispy" suggest), this dough lacked the structure to produce a decent bar.

—Compiled by Matthew Herron

IF YOU HAVE A QUESTION about a recently published recipe, let us know. Send your inquiry, name, address, and daytime telephone number to Recipe Update, Cook's Illustrated, P. O. Box 470589, Brookline, MA 02447, or write to us at recipeupdate@bcpress.com.

COOK'S extra

Go to www.cooksillustrated.com
- Key in code 5069 for **White Sangria**.
- Key in code 50610 for **Grilled Chicken Teriyaki**.
- Key in code 50611 for **Chocolate Chip Cookie Bars**.
- Recipes available until November 1, 2006.

EQUIPMENT CORNER

NEW PRODUCT: Simply Mash Potato Masher
Potato mashers generally come in one of two varieties: a flat perforated plate attached to a handle or wire loops (also flat) attached to a handle. You lift the masher, you mash the potatoes. Simple stuff, but Chef's Planet new Simply Mash Potato Masher ($9.95) represents an attempt to make the process even easier. The business end has 12 spokes that curve upward, giving the masher a natural rocking motion. By rocking the handle back and forth in a circular motion, the potatoes get mashed—no lifting required. Well, almost none: We had no luck achieving smooth potatoes without at least some pounding. Nothing beats a traditional masher—especially one with a flat, perforated plate, such as WMF's Profi Plus Masher ($15.99), winner of a previous kitchen test.

MASHLESS MASHER?
No match for traditional models

EQUIPMENT UPDATE: Food Mill
We emerged from our September/October 2002 rating of food mills with two winners: the ultimate, a $90 number from Cuisipro, and a much less expensive runner-up, the Moulinex Moulin à Légumes No. 2 ($15), which churned out nearly as smooth a puree. Moulinex, however, has become increasingly hard to find in the United States. For months, our search for a similarly inexpensive food mill came up fruitless. The cheap models we found were too small, flimsy, or too hard to turn, or they were too rough on foods. Finally, we came across R.S.V.P. Rotary Food Mill, which is suspiciously similar to Moulinex—same white plastic, same red handle, almost as modest a price ($19.95). In our tests, the R.S.V.P. mill proved every bit as good as our test kitchen's Moulinex at berry purees and applesauce. The Cuisipro is still our favorite, but the R.S.V.P. ranks as a "best buy."

EQUIPMENT TESTING: French Fry Cutters
While developing our recipe for Fish and Chips (page 8), we used a knife to cut the potatoes into proper "chip" shape. Could a french fry cutter make the job any easier? To find out, we rounded up four cutters and a few bushels of potatoes and went to work. Each design forces a potato through a crisscross of thin metal blades. The most basic of these relies on brute force—sort of like an apple corer. Once we trimmed the ends of the potato (to make it sit still), then pushed down hard, we got satisfactory results. But we did have to use a lot of muscle. We also tested lever-style cutters, which, despite the mechanics, require a good deal of oomph as well. The potatoes are placed in a horizontal hopper, and, with a pull of the lever, french fries shoot out from the blades. Pulling that lever is no easy task, and the hoppers couldn't accept potatoes longer than 4 inches.

If you've got the strength, the simple apple-corer-style cutters make quick work of turning russets into a pile of fries—and, in fact, are quicker than a knife. Of the two we tested, only the metal Cuisipro French Fry Cutter/Apple Corer ($19.95) seemed sturdy enough.

EQUIPMENT UPDATE: Baking Peels
In the March/April 2005 issue, we praised the Super Peel for its ability to get pizza and bread dough onto a baking stone without sticking or mishap. This clever peel relies on a pastry cloth liner that is threaded through the board like a conveyor belt. The dough is placed on the cloth, and, as the board is pulled back, the cloth rotates and gently deposits the dough onto the hot stone in the oven. While preparing materials for *Cooking at Home with America's Test Kitchen*, the companion book to this year's television series, we inadvertently put a "not recommended" label on this product. We stand by our original assessment of this product. While a well-floured regular peel will work after some practice, the Super Peel all but guarantees flawless transfer of sticky dough. We apologize for the confusion.

Sources

The following are mail-order sources for items recommended in this issue. Prices were current at press time and do not include shipping and handling. Contact companies directly to confirm prices and availability, and visit our Web site (cooksillustrated.com) for updates.

Page 3: CHASEN
- Chasen (Bamboo Whisk): $18, **In Pursuit of Tea** (866-878-3832, www.inpursuitoftea.com).

Page 3: PASTRY FLOUR
- King Arthur Flour Unbleached Pastry Flour (3 pounds): $2.95, item #3331, **King Arthur Flour** (800-827-6836, www.kingarthurflour.com).

Page 9: DEEP FRYERS
- Oster Immersion Deep Fryer: $79.95, item #212064, **Cooking.com** (800-663-8810, www.cooking.com).
- Masterbuilt Turk'N'Surf Turkey Fryer and Seafood Kettle: $199.95, item #SETFTV, **Masterbuilt Outdoor Products** (800-489-1581, www.masterbuilt.com).

Page 29: TONGS
- Oxo Good Grips 12-Inch Locking Tongs: $9.95, item #102087, **Cooking.com**.

Page 31: CANDY THERMOMETER
- Maverick Redi-Chek Digital Oil & Candy Thermometer: $34.95, item #201613, **Cooking.com**.

Page 32: POTATO MASHER
- WMF Profi Plus Potato Masher: $15.99, code #744004095906, (800-458-2616, www.thegadgetsource.com).

Page 32: FOOD MILL
- R.S.V.P. Rotary Food Mill: $19.95, item #435420, **Cooking.com**.

Page 32: FRENCH FRY CUTTER
- Cuisipro French Fry Cutter/Apple Corer: $19.95, item #137577, **Cooking.com**.

Page 32: BAKING PEEL
- Super Peel: $33.95, **Exoproducts** (518-371-3173, www.superpeel.com).

REVISED EDITION

**United States Postal Service
Statement of Ownership, Management, and Circulation**

1. Publication Title: Cook's Illustrated
2. Publication Number: 1 0 6 8 — 2 8 2 1
3. Filing Date: 10/01/05
4. Issue Frequency: Bi-Monthly
5. Number of Issues Published Annually: 6 issues
6. Annual Subscription Price: $35.70
7. Complete Mailing Address of Known Office of Publication: 17 Station Street, Brookline, MA 02445
   Contact Person: —
   Telephone: 617-232-1000
8. Complete Mailing Address of Headquarters or General Business Office of Publisher: Same as publisher
9. Full Names and Complete Mailing Addresses of Publisher, Editor, and Managing Editor
   Publisher: Christopher P. Kimball, Boston Common Press, 17 Station, Brookline, MA 02445
   Editor: Same as publisher
   Managing Editor: Jack Bishop, Boston Common Press, 17 Station Street, Brookline, MA 02445
10. Owner:
    Full Name: Boston Common Press Limited Partnership — Complete Mailing Address: 17 Station Street, Brookline, MA 02445
    (Christopher P. Kimball)
11. Known Bondholders, Mortgagees, and Other Security Holders: N/A
12. Tax Status: Has Not Changed During Preceding 12 Months
13. Publication Title: Cook's Illustrated
14. Issue Date for Circulation Data Below: September/October 2005

15. Extent and Nature of Circulation	Average No. Copies Each Issue During Preceding 12 Months	No. Copies of Single Issue Published Nearest to Filing Date
a. Total Number of Copies (Net press run)	900,721	950,621
b.(1) Paid/Requested Outside-County Mail Subscriptions Stated on Form 3541	661,681	718,181
b.(2) Paid In-County Subscriptions Stated on Form 3541	0	0
b.(3) Sales Through Dealers and Carriers, Street Vendors, Counter Sales, and Other Non-USPS Paid Distribution	90,152	87,517
b.(4) Other Classes Mailed Through the USPS	0	0
c. Total Paid and/or Requested Circulation	751,833	805,698
d.(1) Outside-County as Stated on Form 3541	4,316	3,955
d.(2) In-County as Stated on Form 3541	0	0
d.(3) Other Classes Mailed Through the USPS	0	0
e. Free Distribution Outside the Mail	4,138	4,388
f. Total Free Distribution	8,454	8,343
g. Total Distribution	760,288	814,041
h. Copies not Distributed	140,433	136,580
i. Total	900,721	950,621
j. Percent Paid and/or Requested Circulation	98.89%	98.98%

16. Publication of Statement of Ownership: Jan/Feb 2006 issue of this publication
17. Signature and Title of Editor, Publisher, Business Manager, or Owner — Date: 1/24/06

Instructions to Publishers

1. Complete and file one copy of this form with your postmaster annually on or before October 1. Keep a copy of the completed form for your records.
2. In cases where the stockholder or security holder is a trustee, include in items 10 and 11 the name of the person or corporation for whom the trustee is acting. Also include the names and addresses of individuals who are stockholders who own or hold 1 percent or more of the total amount of bonds, mortgages, or other unincorporated firm, give its name and address as well as those of each individual owner. If the publication is published by a nonprofit organization, give its name and address.
3. Be sure to furnish all circulation information called for in item 15. Free circulation must be shown in items 15d, e, and f.
4. Item 15h., Copies not Distributed, must include (1) newsstand copies originally stated on Form 3541, and returned to the publisher, (2) estimated returns from news agents, and (3), copies for office use, leftovers, spoiled, and all other copies not distributed.
5. If the publication had Periodicals authorization as a general or requester publication, this Statement of Ownership, Management, and Circulation must be published; it must be printed in any issue in October or, if the publication is not published during October, the first issue printed after October.
6. In item 16, indicate the date of the issue in which this Statement of Ownership will be published.
7. Item 17 must be signed.
Failure to file or publish a statement of ownership may lead to suspension of Periodicals authorization.

PS Form 3526, October 1999 (Reverse)

COOK'S ILLUSTRATED

32

RECIPES
May & June 2006

New Recipes Available on the Web

The following recipes are available free until November 1, 2006. Go to www.cooks illustrated.com and enter the code listed after the recipe title.

---

www.cooksillustrated.com

Start your 14-day FREE TRIAL MEMBERSHIP
Go to CooksIllustrated.com/SubTrial Today!

Your free trial membership to CooksIllustrated.com includes all these benefits and much more:

- Access to all 13 years of *Cook's Illustrated* recipes.
- Up-to-date equipment ratings and supermarket ingredient taste tests.
- NEW! GOOGLE-powered search engine that helps you find it fast! Search by recipe, course, or category.
- Options to SAVE your "favorites," CREATE menus, and PRINT shopping lists.
- NEW Menus! Wide range of menus covering all occasions. Only available to Web site members.

Join our 100,000 members and enhance your subscription to *Cook's Illustrated* magazine with a Web site membership.

Go to CooksIllustrated.com/SubTrial to begin your no-risk 14-day FREE TRIAL.

AMERICA'S TEST KITCHEN
Public television's most popular cooking show

Join the millions of home cooks who watch our show, *America's Test Kitchen*, on public television every week. For more information, including recipes and program times, visit www.americastestkitchen.com.

Spanish-Style Chicken Salad, 20

London Broil, 13

Fish and Chips, 9

Vegetable Stir-Fry, 15

Veal Scaloppini, 18

Sweet and Smoky Grilled Tomato Salsa, 10

Garlic and Olive Oil Mashed Potatoes, 21

Moroccan Chicken, 7

Ultimate Turtle Brownies, 23

Strawberry Cream Cake, 25

PHOTOGRAPHY: CARL TREMBLAY, STYLING: MARIE PIRAINO

Malabar
Spinach

Chinese
Water Spinach

Bok Choy

Tatsoi

Napa
Cabbage

Chinese Chives

Mizuna

Chinese
Broccoli

Chinese
Parsley

Baby
Bok Choy

ASIAN GREENS

NUMBER EIGHTY-ONE

JULY & AUGUST 2006

COOK'S
ILLUSTRATED

Foolproof Grilled
Hamburgers
You Can't Overcook Them!

Cuban BBQ Pork

Make-Ahead
Picnic Chicken
No More Rubbery Skin

Best Peach Crumble
Crisp Topping, Juicy Fruit

How to Grill Shrimp

Illustrated Guide
to Kitchen Knives

Rating Blenders
Bargain Model a Winner

Ketchup Taste Test
Grilling Onions 101
Best Pesto Pasta Salad
Creamy Key Lime Bars
Pizza Margherita

www.cooksillustrated.com

$5.95 U.S./$6.95 CANADA

0 8>

0 74470 62805 7

CONTENTS

July & August 2006

COOK'S ILLUSTRATED
www.cooksillustrated.com
HOME OF AMERICA'S TEST KITCHEN

Founder and Editor Christopher Kimball
Editorial Director Jack Bishop
Deputy Editor Jolyon Helterman
Editorial Manager, Books Elizabeth Carduff
Test Kitchen Director Erin McMurrer
Senior Editors, Books Julia Collin Davison
Lori Galvin
Managing Editor Rebecca Hays
Senior Editor Keith Dresser
Associate Editors Erika Bruce
Sean Lawler
Sandra Wu
Web Editor Lindsay McSweeney
Copy Chief India Koopman
Test Cooks Garth Clingingsmith
David Pazmiño
Rachel Toomey
Sarah Wilson
Assistant Test Kitchen Director Matthew Herron
Assistant Editors, Books Charles Kelsey
Elizabeth Wray Emery
Editorial Assistant Elizabeth Bomze
Assistant to the Publisher Melissa Baldino
Editorial Intern Meredith Smith
Kitchen Assistants Maria Elena Delgado
Nadia Domeq
Ena Gudiel
Contributing Editors Matthew Card
Elizabeth Germain
Dawn Yanagihara
Consulting Editors Shirley Corriher
Guy Crosby
John Dewar
Jasper White
Robert L. Wolke
Proofreader Debra Hudak

Design Director Amy Klee
Art Director, Books Carolynn DeCillo
Senior Designer, Web/Marketing Julie Bozzo
Senior Designer, Magazines Heather Barrett
Designers Christian Steinmetz
Christine Vo
Staff Photographer Daniel J. van Ackere

Vice President Marketing David Mack
Circulation Director Bill Tine
Fulfillment Manager Carrie Horan
Circulation Assistant Elizabeth Dayton
Direct Mail Director Adam Perry
Products Director Steven Browall
E-Commerce Marketing Manager Hugh Buchan
Marketing Copywriter David Goldberg
Customer Service Manager Jacqueline Valerio
Customer Service Representatives Julie Gardner
Jillian Nannicelli
Junior Developer Doug Sisko

Vice President Sales Demee Gambulos
Retail Sales Director Jason Geller
Corporate Marketing Manager Emily Logan
Marketing Assistant Connie Forbes

Production Director Guy Rochford
Senior Production Manager Jessica L. Quirk
Project Manager Anne Francis
Production Assistants Lauren Pettapiece
Matthew Warnick
Technology & Operations Director Aaron Shuman
Systems Administrator Paddi McHugh
Web Producer Lauren Record

Chief Financial Officer Sharyn Chabot
Controller Mandy Shito
Staff Accountant Maya Santoso
Office Manager Saudiyah Abdul-Rahim
Receptionist Henrietta Murray
Publicity Deborah Broide

2nd PRINTING IN CHINA

GRILLING SPICES Meat grilled over a hot fire takes on a flavorful exterior crust—even more so when first coated with a dry rub blended from carefully chosen ground spices. The intense, dry heat amplifies their flavor by coaxing out deep, toasted notes. Among the savory spices best suited for dry rubs are cumin, a small seed with a rich, mildly hot flavor; the more muted, floral coriander seed; star anise, with its distinct taste of spicy licorice; sweet anise-flavored fennel seed; and piquant mustard seed. While many of the delicate, sweeter spices diminish in flavor over the heat of the grill, cinnamon and allspice (which tastes of cinnamon, nutmeg, and clove) are exceptions, becoming even more complex. Freshly ground black pepper adds a pleasant heat and crunch to grilled meats, while dried and ground chiles such as ancho and chipotle (technically not spices) add a fiery depth. Also outside the spice realm are ground coffee and cocoa, both of which contribute welcome bitter notes.

COVER (*Watermelons*): Elizabeth Brandon, BACK COVER (*Grilling Spices*): John Burgoyne

For list rental information, contact: Specialists Marketing Services, Inc., 1200 Harbor Blvd., 9th Floor, Weehawken, NJ 07087; 201-865-5800.
Editorial Office: 17 Station St., Brookline, MA 02445; 617-232-1000; fax 617-232-1572. Subscription inquiries, call 800-526-8442.
Postmaster: Send all new orders, subscription inquiries, and change-of-address notices to Cook's Illustrated, P.O. Box 7446, Red Oak, IA 51591-0446.

AIN'T DEAD YET

I know that I am still alive because I get worked up about opening day at Fenway, double chocolate chip mint ice cream, bourbon and branch water, the first boil in sugaring season, and the opportunity to stand in a 35-degree trout stream in April. And I haven't forgotten the recipe for nutmeg doughnuts, the refrain from "In the Garden," why I get up in the morning, or who butters my bread. I still enjoy light pancakes, heavy lifting, cold weather, hot biscuits, hard rain, soft cheese, long days, short breads, the first snow, the last bale, the big storm, the small gesture, and a swift kick in the pants when I'm moving too slowly.

I can still remember my age, my middle name, my phone number, and my kids' birthdays but admit that for the life of me I can't remember why we need Lemon Pledge, automatic transmissions, Pop-Tarts, the Osmond family, think tanks, Hot Pockets, the Department of Homeland Security, or safety instructions for sunscreen, toothpaste, and shaving cream. I can also remember seeing the price of gas at 27 cents a gallon, paying a nickel for a cherry Coke at the soda fountain, riding in my father's Nash, watching Arthur Godfrey, and using the Winky Dink coloring kit to write on the screen of our small black-and-white TV set.

I'm still not old enough to understand string theory, anything about the Holy Ghost, toilet-bowl cleaner, restaurant critics, the Shriners, catalytic converters, AC versus DC, organic chemistry, smokeless tobacco, or the reason why women are in a panic to check their voice mail after only a weekend away.

Someday, when I am older, I hope I will be able to recognize the constellations, identify bird songs, tie a dozen sailor's knots, tell the difference between a ketch and a sloop, master the art of making puff pastry, and remember the names of people I have known for years. I also

still hold out faint hope of being invited to the White House, being included in a top 10 list, and having Reese Witherspoon call to say she wants me to costar in her next movie.

I am still looking forward to the future. That's when I'll finally finish my children's book, build my cabin, and complete the Dodge HEMI kit, with its 300 pieces, electric motor, and authentic HEMI sound chip. I will also finish organizing my garage, wax my car, have a serious talk with my son, clean my closets, and find time to scout for wild turkey and deer before the start of the season. The future will also be a good time to make amends, pay my dues, and think for myself.

In years to come, I also plan to ride horseback from our farm to Canada, run the Boston Marathon, and take my Indian motorcycle cross-country. I am still much too young, however, to consider motor homes, Florida, retirement communities, Arizona, Sansabelt pants, the idea of sitting down to dinner before sunset, San Diego, golf, cruises, letters from the AARP, and the pros and cons of burial versus cremation. I do hope, however, that if Martha Reeves is still around she will sing "Dancing in the Street" at my funeral. (If you get the chance, please mention this to my kids.) If she dies first, I promise to cook at her wake.

I know I am still young because my wife tells me daily to grow up, especially when I start planning the motorcycle trip. I am also confident that I have sufficient time left to recover from a steady diet of Slim Jims, bacon, fried buttermilk chicken, Old-Fashioned cocktails, and secondhand smoke. Someday, I know I will be able to

Christopher Kimball

jog three miles in less than 20 minutes, lose 10 pounds, stop purchasing relaxed-fit jeans, and start buying shorter belts. I will also lose my taste for cupcakes, Boston cream pie, raspberry bars, lemon meringue pie, Mallo Cups, and anything cooked in duck fat.

I also know that I ain't dead yet because "old people" are different from me. Their knees hurt, they plan their trips up and down stairs carefully (so as not to forget something on an upper floor), they worry about slipping on ice, they take every opportunity to visit a bathroom when traveling, and they find small children burdensome. (OK, well, maybe that list does seem a bit familiar.)

As further proof of my youth, I still don't understand my parents, save for retirement, or buy life insurance. I don't like Frank Sinatra, remember World War II, or argue about whether Franklin Roosevelt was a socialist. I do, however, note that when I discuss "where I was when Kennedy was shot" with my peers, younger people drift away. They do the same thing when the subject is Watergate, Sam Cooke, Fillmore East, Carnaby Street, *The Ed Sullivan Show*, Walter Cronkite, or *Meet the Beatles!* They just don't know their history.

I am just old enough, however, to know that of all the millions of kids my wife and I could have had, we had just the four we wanted. But I'm not yet wise enough to say the same thing about her (although it's true). And I am still too young to have learned humility, the art of being grateful, or an appreciation for the incredible miracle of life. Well, this all just takes time. And that's the great thing about being young. We think that we still have so much of it left.

FOR INQUIRIES, ORDERS, OR MORE INFORMATION:

www.cooksillustrated.com

At www.cooksillustrated.com, you can order books and subscriptions, sign up for our free e-newsletter, or renew your magazine subscription. Join the Web site and you'll have access to 13 years of *Cook's* recipes, cookware tests, ingredient tastings, and more.

COOKBOOKS

We sell more than 40 cookbooks by the editors of *Cook's Illustrated*. To order, visit our bookstore at www.cooksillustrated.com or call 800-611-0759 (or 515-246-6911 from outside the U.S.).

COOK'S ILLUSTRATED Magazine

Cook's Illustrated magazine (ISSN 1068-2821), number 81, is published bimonthly by Boston Common Press Limited Partnership, 17 Station St., Brookline, MA 02445. Copyright 2006 Boston Common Press Limited Partnership. Periodicals postage paid at Boston, Mass., and additional mailing offices, USPS #012487. POSTMASTER: Send address changes to Cook's Illustrated, P.O. Box 7446, Red Oak, IA 51591-0446. For subscription and gift subscription orders, subscription inquiries, or change-of-address notices, call 800-526-8442 in the U.S. or 515-247-7571 from outside the U.S., or write us at Cook's Illustrated, P.O. Box 7446, Red Oak, IA 51591-0446.

Strange Brews

In your supermarket coffee tasting story (November/December 2005) you blamed "quakers" for giving some coffees bad flavor. Couldn't you just remove the quakers before grinding a batch of beans?

MICHAEL CHANG
BALA CYNWYD, PA.

➤ Quakers are underdeveloped coffee beans that accidentally make it through the manufacturing process. Because they are less dense than healthy coffee beans, they roast up to a much lighter color, and they can impart a spoiled, rancid taste to a pot of coffee. Some manufacturers pay a premium to make sure quakers are sorted out before processing. What about removing them yourself? To see what effect this would have, we spent half an hour sifting through bags of whole-bean coffee (from a brand that evidenced a high number of quakers in our 2005 testing), separating the lighter-colored quakers from the rest. Then we brewed up two batches of coffee: one with the quakers left in; the other, quaker-free. After tasting one batch against the other, a few things were clear: The quaker-free sample was by no means perfect, but the "quakery" coffee was worse (described as more sour, astringent, and "rancid"). Our opinion is that while it won't hurt to remove any quakers you happen to see, spending half an hour hunched over a bag of coffee isn't worth the effort. Getting rid of a few bad beans isn't enough to transform a low-quality bag of coffee into a high-quality brew.

PICK OF THE BITTER
Should you bother sorting out blighted beans?

The Color of Corn Syrup

I don't use corn syrup very often and usually have only one type on hand at any given time. Can I substitute light corn syrup for dark (and vice versa)?

JON LEE
AUSTIN, TEXAS

➤ Derived from cornstarch, corn syrup is a thick liquid sweetener that was first bottled for home use by the maker of the Karo brand (in 1902). Karo remains the largest U.S. producer of corn syrup. Light corn syrup is a clear mixture of corn syrup and high-fructose corn syrup (added for greater sweetness) that has been clarified to remove all color and impurities, giving it a sweet, mild flavor. (Vanilla is also added.) Dark corn syrup is a mixture of corn syrup and refiners' syrup (a type of molasses), to which caramel color and flavor have been added to give it a deep brown color and stronger flavor.

We tried each type in three different recipes (oatmeal lace cookies, hot fudge sauce, and pecan pie) to determine whether the two varieties could be used interchangeably. Tasters detected few flavor differences in the samples. Those made with light corn syrup were lighter and chewier than the darker, crispier cookies made with dark corn syrup, but tasters found both acceptable. Colorwise, both samples of the hot fudge sauce and the pecan pie looked the same. In the hot fudge sauce, the dark corn syrup yielded a richer chocolate flavor and a slightly looser texture, but the differences were far from earth-shattering. In the pecan pie, several tasters found that the dark corn syrup made for a runnier texture and a richer, caramel flavor that masked some of the pecan flavor. Our conclusion? Yes, there are some subtle flavor and textural differences, but if you can't make it to the grocery store, go ahead and use whatever corn syrup you've got in the pantry.

Butcher–Block Care

Recently, I bought a used butcher-block worktable. What is the best method for cleaning and properly disinfecting a table like this?

ALAN SNYDER
OAKLAND, CALIF.

➤ Butcher-block tables, which function not only as a work space but as a cutting surface, must be cared for and treated in a manner similar to cutting boards. To reduce the growth of bacteria on your butcher block, be sure to scrub it with hot, soapy water after each use. The U.S. Department of Agriculture also recommends the periodic application of a solution of 1 teaspoon bleach per quart of water to sanitize the surface, which should then be rinsed off with cold water. To maintain the appearance of the wood surface, some manufacturers suggest applying a food-safe oil periodically (once every few weeks) using a clean cloth. The mineral oil soaks into the fibers of the wood, acting as a barrier to excess moisture. The experts we consulted recommend opting for mineral oil (make sure the container is labeled "food-grade") rather than more-volatile oils like vegetable oil and olive oil, which can turn rancid over time. For day-to-day use, we suggest reserving your butcher block for applications that don't involve fish, meat, or poultry. Instead, use a separate cutting board for these tasks, which will make cleaning much easier while reducing the risk of cross-contamination.

Coddled Eggs versus Poached

What's the difference between coddled eggs and poached eggs?

KHOI DINH
PHOENIX, ARIZ.

➤ Both coddling and poaching refer to cooking something gently in water heated to just below the boiling point. With eggs, the difference comes down to the shell: Poached eggs are cooked without the shell, directly in the simmering water (often with vinegar added to help the whites set). Coddling, on the other hand, involves cooking the eggs still protected by either their shell or individual covered containers called coddling cups. Lightly coddled eggs (cooked for about 45 seconds, just to thicken the yolks slightly) are commonly used in Caesar salad dressings to provide a more viscous texture, but they are sometimes cooked a few minutes more to a consistency resembling soft-boiled eggs (the whites are slightly more set) and eaten as is.

Fixing Frozen Cookies

Whenever I wrap and freeze baked soft chocolate cookies, the texture changes. After thawing, the sugar crystallizes and becomes crunchy. The cookies are smooth when they are hot out of the oven, so why would freezing leftovers affect the texture?

MERYL SHEPPARD
GREENSBORO, N.C.

➤ We baked two different recipes for chewy chocolate cookies, which we then froze and thawed at room temperature before comparing them with freshly baked cookies. We, too, noticed an unwanted crunchiness in the previously frozen versions. After doing some research, we learned that sugars become significantly more crystalline (less likely to dissolve) as the temperature drops. In the freezer, then, the extremely low temperature causes the sugars to begin to come out of solution and recrystallize.

But merely leaving the cookies out on the countertop to thaw did not provide enough heat to redissolve the sugar crystals. To get the cookies back into smooth, chewy shape, we tried "refreshing" them as we would most other frozen (prebaked) cookies: by placing them in a 350-degree oven for four to five minutes. Microwaving at full power for about 30 seconds also worked, but the distribution of heat was less even and only a few cookies could be refreshed at a time. Once the refreshed cookies cooled to room temperature, they were nearly as good as their fresh counterparts: chewy and crystal-free.

How 'Premium' Is Premium Butter?

Occasionally, I prefer to use butters with a higher percentage of fat, but many brands don't provide that information. Can you help?

SUE BISKNER
ROYAL OAK, MICH.

➤ There's been plenty of hype about the merits of "premium" butters (often called European-style butters), touted for their creamy texture and high fat content compared with regular butter. In the past, when the test kitchen conducted blind taste tests of both styles, tasters found only subtle differences when the butters were sampled plain (simply spread on toast), and those nuances disappeared entirely when they were used in cooking. Was our panel missing something?

It's when we hunkered down to calculate the percentages ourselves (dividing the amount of fat per serving by the 1-tablespoon serving size) that a clearer picture began to emerge. Initially, we were puzzled to find, as you did, that most manufacturers don't list fat percentage on the packaging—especially given that fat content is a key selling point. Even more surprising, the fat content of every butter we found—from the ubiquitous Land O' Lakes to the fanciest French beurre—fell between 11 grams and 12 grams per serving. Just a 1-gram difference. What's more, many of the so-called premium butters (including President, Kerrygold, Lurpak, and perhaps the best known, Plugrá) listed just 11 grams of fat per serving. How could it be that these self-proclaimed "premium" butters contained the same amount of fat as the generic (cheap) supermarket brands?

As it turns out, it all boils down to U.S. Food and Drug Administration labeling laws, which allow manufacturers to disclose fat content in grams rounded to the nearest whole number. That means a butter with "11 grams" of fat may contain between 80 percent and 82 percent fat (82 percent fat is generally considered the minimum fat content for a premium butter). No wonder our tasters noticed hardly any difference between cheap butter and premium butter in our

A SLIM DIFFERENCE?
"Premium" butters may not be that much more indulgent than regular butters.

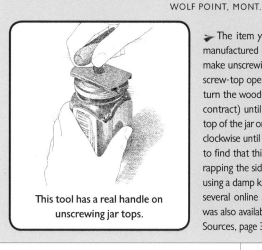

This tool has a real handle on unscrewing jar tops.

➤ The item you purchased is a Top-Off screw-top opener. First manufactured by Edlund Co. in 1932, this gadget is designed to make unscrewing stubborn jar and bottle tops easier. To adjust the screw-top opener to fit diameters of 1/2 inch to 4 1/2 inches, simply turn the wooden handle (clockwise to widen, counterclockwise to contract) until the two ends of the device wrap snugly around the top of the jar or bottle. To unscrew the top, turn the handle counterclockwise until the top is loosened. In our tests, we were surprised to find that this method works even better than the usual tricks of rapping the side of the jar on the countertop to loosen the seal or using a damp kitchen towel to get a better grip. Although we found several online auction sites selling this tool as an antique item, it was also available from the Vermont Country Store for $6.95. See Sources, page 32, for ordering information.

battery of blind taste tests—the difference comes down to less than two percentage points.

If you want a higher-fat butter, choose one with 12 grams of fat per serving rather than 11—which is guaranteed to be at least a few percentage points higher in fat content. In a 2004 tasting, our tasting panel liked the rich flavor and creamy texture of Land O' Lakes "Ultra Creamy" variety (which has 12 grams of fat).

Broiling Points

The broiler in my oven has two settings: low and high. I'm never sure which setting to use when a recipe calls for using the broiler.

NICK JONES
PHILADELPHIA, PA.

➤ In the test kitchen, we always use the highest setting when broiling. Most recipes, including ours, call for broiling only when quick, efficient browning is desired, so it only makes sense to go with the highest temperature. (Besides, it would be a mistake for us to offer a recipe requiring a setting that many in-oven broilers lack.)

Presumably, manufacturers came up with the low broiler setting as a way to account for the fact that some foods can take extreme heat better than others. We prefer the simpler (and more flexible) method of adjusting the distance of the oven rack from the broiler's heating element—the closer it is, the quicker it cooks. A few general guidelines: For roasting vegetables such as red peppers and asparagus, broiling about 4 inches from the heating element is optimal. For browning the tops of cheesy casseroles (like lasagna), make sure the top of the pan is at least 6 inches away. For breadcrumb toppings, which burn fairly easily, adjust the oven rack to the lower-middle position, 10 to

12 inches from the heating element. Poultry and fish will vary depending on the size of the pieces; the larger and thicker the pieces, the farther away they should cook. Because broiled foods can burn in mere seconds, start checking for doneness a little earlier than the recipe indicates.

Streaked Avocado

I've occasionally bought what I thought was a ripe avocado and then discovered it was streaked with brown lines inside. What causes this?

JACKIE MCDONOUGH
HOMER, ALASKA

➤ We contacted several avocado specialists, all of whom concurred that the brown, discolored streaks (which impart an unpleasant taste and texture) are caused by the increased concentration of an enzyme in certain parts of the fruit. This phenomenon tends to be most severe early and late in the season (which varies depending on the variety) as well as in fruit grown in cooler areas. Unfortunately, there is no reliable way to determine which avocados will be devoid of streaking except to try to purchase varieties that are at the peak of their harvesting season. (For the popular dark green Hass avocado, the season is April to October; for Fuerte, November to June; for Pinkerton, December to April.) Beware of fruit that feels soft or has air pockets, however: the former are either bruised or overripe, while the latter have probably sustained damage from improper handling.

SEND US YOUR QUESTIONS We will provide a complimentary one-year subscription for each letter we print. Send your inquiry, name, address, and daytime telephone number to Notes from Readers, Cook's Illustrated, P.O. Box 470589, Brookline, MA 02447, or to notesfromreaders@bcpress.com.

Quick Tips

⇒ COMPILED BY DAVID PAZMIÑO ⇐

Unlikely Deveining Tool

Even when grilling shrimp with the shell on, Katie Meadow of Oakland, Calif., likes to remove the gritty "vein" running down the back of the shrimp. Her solution is to straighten the shrimp as much as possible, grab the exposed end of the vein with flat-edged tweezers, and pull it out gently.

Perfect Tomato Slices

Cutting up a tomato into uniform slices can be tricky. Nicholas Ritrivi of New York, N.Y., has come up with a foolproof method to use when presentation counts.

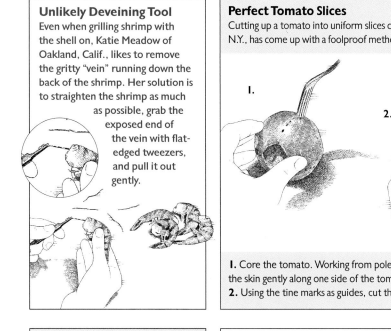

1. Core the tomato. Working from pole to pole, use the tines of a fork to pierce the skin gently along one side of the tomato.
2. Using the tine marks as guides, cut the tomato into even slices.

A Warmer Rest

Resting meat before carving is the key to getting the juiciest slices, but a chilly cutting board can make the temperature of the meat plummet. To keep heat loss under control, Nate Lusk of New York, N.Y., warms his cutting board under hot running tap water for a few minutes.

Saucepan Splash Guard

To keep simmering sauces from splattering onto the stovetop, Bruce Miller of Manchester, Conn., fashions a splash guard from a disposable aluminum pie plate.

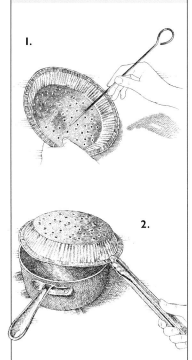

1. Using a metal skewer, poke at least a dozen holes in the pie plate.
2. Using tongs, invert the pie plate onto the pan. The holes allow the steam—not the splatters—to escape.

Tight Squeeze

Squeezing the entire contents out of a tube of tomato or anchovy paste can be difficult. To make it easier, Lynn Dickey of San Rafael, Calif., reaches for a wooden spoon with a round handle or a rolling pin.

Place the tube on a flat work surface. Starting at the far side of the tube and pressing down gently, roll the rolling pin (or wooden spoon handle) along the length of the tube.

De-Salting Nuts

Barbara Hantman of Philadelphia, Pa., has come up with a way to make salted nuts usable in recipes that call for the unsalted variety.

1. Rinse the shelled nuts in a strainer under cool water.
2. Spread the nuts evenly on a rimmed baking sheet and cook at 350 degrees for about 6 minutes, or until the nuts are dry and slightly toasted.

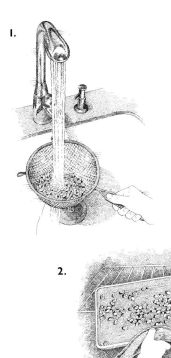

Send Us Your Tip We will provide a complimentary one-year subscription for each tip we print. Send your tip, name, and address to Quick Tips, Cook's Illustrated, P.O. Box 470589, Brookline, MA 02447, or to quicktips@bcpress.com.

ILLUSTRATION: JOHN BURGOYNE

Airy Onion Storage

Looking for a convenient way to store onions, shallots, and garlic in a dark, cool place with plenty of air circulation, Virginia Stautinger of Spring, Texas, brushed the dust off her little-used bamboo steamer. The baskets stack easily and allow just enough air circulation to prevent mold.

Using Salt to Prevent Flare-Ups

Fat sputtering up from a broiler pan can cause dangerous flare-ups. To prevent these flames, Christopher Steele of Woodland Hills, Calif., spreads a generous amount of kosher salt on the bottom of the pan.

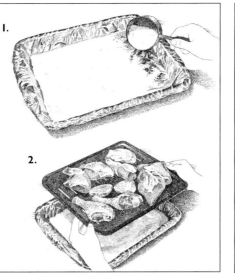

1. Cover the bottom of the broiler pan with aluminum foil and 2 cups of kosher salt.
2. Place the perforated rack on top. The salt layer catches any grease and prevents flare-ups.

Magnetic Lid Retrieval

When using a can opener, the lid sometimes drops into the can. David Leonard of Atlanta, Ga., doesn't dirty a butter knife to fish it out. Instead, he reaches for a handy tool hanging right on the refrigerator—a decorative magnet.

1. Use a can opener to remove the lid.
2. Place a magnet over the can—the lid comes right out, with no mess.

Cake Flip

John Carl Bowers of Brooklyn, N.Y., came up with this easy method for turning a cake out of an uncomfortably hot pan.

1. Place the cake pan on top of a large kitchen towel and top with an inverted plate.
2. Gather each corner of the towel and hold the ends together on the bottom of the plate. Gripping the towel tightly in one hand, lift the cake and the plate together.
3. Place your other hand on the bottom and gently invert the cake pan and plate onto the countertop. Lift off the pan to release the cake.

Easy-Bake Set

Tired of fumbling through his cabinets for baking ingredients, Arnold Baines of Kahului, Hawaii, keeps a plastic container stocked with the staples: vanilla extract, baking powder, baking soda, cinnamon, and so on. When it's time to bake, he simply retrieves all the necessary items from the container in one fell swoop.

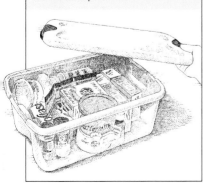

String behind the Scenes

When tying meat with butcher's twine, it can be hard to avoid contaminating the entire roll with dirty fingers. Instead of cutting the estimated amount needed ahead of time—and ending up with too much or too little—Jim Monaghan of Cape May, N.J., hides his solution behind closed doors.

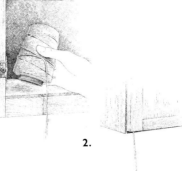

1. Place the roll of twine inside a cabinet in the corner behind the hinges.
2. Thread the twine out above the hinge and close the cabinet door. Pull the twine to tie your roast, cutting just the right amount.

Hung Out to Dry

Silicone baking mats clean up easily, but it can be hard to get them completely dry. Carolyn Cass of Burke, Va., attaches the mats to clothes-hanger clips and hangs them out to dry from a cabinet door or the edge of a pantry shelf.

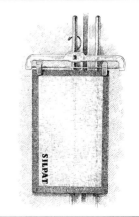

The Ultimate Picnic Chicken

How do you give cold picnic chicken great flavor without flabby, sticky skin?
As with James Bond's martinis, the secret is shaken, not stirred.

≥ BY SARAH WILSON ≤

Cold barbecued chicken is a picnic classic. Maybe because picnics offer so much more than food (fresh air, a nice view), most people don't care that this recipe often doesn't make culinary sense. Covered with sticky sauce, the chicken is hard to eat with a fork and impossibly messy eaten with hands. And because the chicken has been cooked and then chilled, the skin is flabby and the meat is so dry it squeaks. I wanted "picnic" chicken good enough to serve at my dining room table.

For starters, great picnic chicken ought to have moist, tender meat. I decided I also wanted the robust spicy and slightly sweet flavor of barbecue. On the other hand, I didn't want to have to light the grill for a dish that would be going straight to the fridge. The oven is a much easier option for a make-ahead recipe. After sampling several mediocre recipes from various cookbooks, I knew I had my work cut out for me: Turning this dish into something a lot better than worse-for-the-wear leftovers was going to be a tall order.

Cut and Dried

The first advance I made was as quick as it was dramatic. About 90 percent of the recipes I found called for slathering roasted, skin-on chicken with barbecue sauce and letting it sit overnight. Given that the main problem was soggy skin, this approach seemed counterintuitive. The few remaining recipes went the dry-rub route, relying on dried spices to provide traditional barbecue flavor. Although most got the flavor wrong—and were plagued by the same bland-meat problem as the wet-sauced versions—the skin was noticeably less soggy the next day. So dry rubs were in, sticky sauces were out.

Trying some simple combinations of chili powder, black pepper, paprika, cayenne, and a little brown sugar for that trademark barbecue sauce sweetness, I fiddled with the proportions until I was able to replicate the flavors of a good sauce.

Go to www.cooksillustrated.com
- Key in code 7061 for our **Creamy Buttermilk Coleslaw** recipe.
- Recipe available until January 1, 2007.

Coating the chicken overnight with a salty spice rub provides all the benefits of brining, with one important difference—no flabby skin.

By rubbing the spice mixture all over the chicken, even under the skin, I achieved the robust barbecue flavor I'd thought only barbecue sauce could deliver. When tasters sampled the chicken the next day, it drew raves for flavor, and there were no sticky fingers in sight. Unfortunately, the skin was flabby.

Clearly, I needed to spend more time trimming the fat before cooking the chicken. The breast and especially the thighs possess some excess fat that never quite renders properly, no matter how long the chicken cooks. Right out of the oven, that fat is mildly annoying; the coagulated mess you bite into the next day is disgusting.

The solution came in two parts. First, a simple but diligent trimming of the chicken pieces yielded improved results and took just a modicum of effort and time. Second, by slitting the skin with a sharp knife (and being careful not to cut into the flesh), I provided escape hatches for the melting fat during roasting; with a final blast of heat (I went all the way to 500 degrees) in the few last minutes, the skin was nicely rendered. The next day I found not tough, flabby skin but a thinner, flavorful coat on each piece of chicken. Although this skin was still less than crisp, I was making serious headway.

It Needs Salt

Up until now I had been following the test kitchen's standard procedure for roasting chicken, which includes brining (soaking in a solution of water and salt). Brining yields better flavor and moister meat, but the added moisture also makes for flabby skin. Omitting the brine in this recipe wasn't going to be easy, but perhaps I could get the salt into the meat without the water.

Back in our research library, I came across a technique used by Judi Rodgers, chef of San Francisco's Zuni Café. She salts all of her meat, vegetables, and even fish for up to three days depending on the size of the product. The salt is thought to draw moisture out of the product initially; then, after a few hours, the reverse happens, and the salt and moisture flow back into the flesh (see "Salting: Better than Brining?" page 7, for details). The test kitchen has used this technique successfully with some recipes for beef, a meat that we never brine, but I had never thought to try it with chicken.

Curious, I salted the chicken pieces, being careful not to under- or overseason, and then placed them in a covered dish in the refrigerator overnight. The next morning I added my spices and roasted the chicken. Tasters waited patiently as I allowed the chicken to cool to room temperature (after all, this dish wasn't going to be served hot). It was worth the wait. The chicken was well seasoned throughout and the meat very moist. Best of all, the skin was flavorful, delicate, and definitely not flabby. The salting had worked exactly as I'd hoped, both seasoning the meat and keeping it moist, even during high-heat roasting.

With the chicken where I wanted it to be, I worked on streamlining the recipe. I combined the spice rub with the salt and applied it at the same time, saving a step. I also placed the chicken pieces directly on the rack they'd be cooked on so they would be oven-ready the next morning. The final surprise, a completely unexpected bonus, was that after an overnight stay in the fridge some of the spice flavor had penetrated the meat along with the salt. Not only had I come up with a great recipe for picnic chicken, but I had stumbled across a fascinating alternative to brining, one that could produce moist meat that was also deeply flavored by means of a spice rub.

SPICE-RUBBED PICNIC CHICKEN
SERVES 8

If you plan to serve the chicken later on the same day that you cook it, refrigerate it immediately after it has cooled, then let it come back to room temperature before serving. On the breast pieces, we use toothpicks to secure the skin, which otherwise shrinks considerably in the oven, leaving the meat exposed and prone to drying out. We think the extra effort is justified, but you can omit this step. This recipe halves easily.

> 5 pounds bone-in, skin-on chicken parts (breasts, thighs, drumsticks, or a mix with breasts cut into 3 pieces or halved if small), trimmed of excess fat and skin
> 2 tablespoons kosher salt
> 3 tablespoons brown sugar
> 2 tablespoons chili powder
> 2 tablespoons sweet paprika
> 2 teaspoons ground black pepper
> 1/4-1/2 teaspoon cayenne

1. Following illustrations above, use sharp knife to make 2 or 3 short slashes in skin of each piece of chicken, taking care not to cut into meat. Combine salt, sugar, and spices in small bowl and mix thoroughly. Coat chicken pieces with spices, gently lifting skin to distribute spice rub underneath but leaving it attached

Salting Chicken 101

Salting is an effective method for seasoning chicken throughout and keeping it moist. Here are some tips for doing it right.

Plan ahead. Chicken salted for less than six hours cooked up dry. (Not enough time for the salt to travel into the chicken.) But beyond 24 hours, the added salt began to break down the interior muscle fibers and the meat cooked up mushy.

Get under the skin. Salting works best when the salt is applied directly to the meat; the skin acts as a barrier.

Don't oversalt. We had the best results when we coated the chicken with slightly more salt than we normally would use to season it. (After all, most of the salt ends up in the chicken.) **Our formula:** about 1 1/4 teaspoons kosher salt per 1 pound bone-in chicken.

GETTING CHICKEN INTO MAKE-AHEAD SHAPE

When chicken is eaten at room temperature or cooler, a fowl's usual flaws become magnified. For this recipe, we found that a modicum of extra prep work kept the flavor, texture, and appearance from suffering.

SCORE
Scoring the skin (but not the meat) provided outlets for melting fat, yielding more fully rendered, paper-thin skin.

RUB
Applying a salty spice rub both on the skin and beneath it ensured that neither exterior nor interior came out bland.

CHILL OUT
Air-drying the rubbed parts on a rack in the refrigerator overnight gave the flavors time to penetrate while also drying out the skin.

PIN DOWN
Securing the skin with toothpicks just before roasting kept the skin from shrinking up into an unattractive bundle.

to chicken. Transfer chicken skin side up to wire rack set over rimmed baking sheet, lightly tent with foil, and refrigerate 6 to 24 hours.

2. Secure skin of each breast piece with 2 or 3 toothpicks placed near edges of skin.

3. Adjust oven rack to middle position; heat oven to 425 degrees. Roast chicken until thickest part of smallest piece registers 140 degrees on instant-read thermometer, 15 to 20 minutes. Increase oven temperature to 500 degrees and continue roasting until chicken is browned and crisp and thickest parts of breast pieces register 160 degrees, 5 to 8 minutes longer, removing pieces from oven and transferring to clean wire rack as they finish cooking. Continue to roast thighs and/or drumsticks, if using, until thickest part of meat registers 170 to 175 degrees, about 5 minutes longer. Remove from oven; transfer chicken to rack and let cool completely before refrigerating or serving.

Salting: Better than Brining?

In the test kitchen, we're strong advocates of brining—soaking meat in a solution of salt and water before cooking. The meat absorbs water as well as salt, with the latter helping the meat retain the moisture as it cooks. With our Spice-Rubbed Picnic Chicken, however, brining made the skin soggy. To solve this problem, we turned to salting the chicken overnight, which helped the meat retain moisture as it cooked—and didn't harm the skin.

Chicken naturally contains some salt and lots of water, which coexist in a happy balance. In coating the chicken with salt, we threw off that balance. To restore order, or equilibrium, water in the meat moved to the surface, where it dissolved the salt.

But wouldn't drawing all that water out of the chicken make the situation worse, causing the meat to dry out? It certainly did—until we figured out the timing. When we tried cooking chicken that had been salted for three hours, the chicken cooked up drier than if we hadn't salted it. (The juices that had made it to the exterior simply evaporated in the oven.) But when we cooked the chicken after six hours, the story changed entirely. By that point, the exterior salt had pulled so much water to the surface that the balance of the salt concentration had changed. To restore equilibrium, the water simply changed directions, flowing back into the meat. But this time—and here's the key—the dissolved salt went along for the ride. Essentially, we had "brined" the chicken using its own juices instead of a bucket of water.

Once we successfully tapped into this means of delivering salt to the interior, we wondered if it was possible to deliver other flavors the same way. As it turns out, it all comes down to whether the flavoring agent is water-soluble (like salt) or fat-soluble. With the rub we used for our Spice-Rubbed Picnic Chicken, the salt and brown sugar, which dissolve easily in water, flowed right in, as did some of the distinguishing flavor compounds of the black pepper, cayenne, chili powder, and paprika. But the spiciness was waylaid at the surface. Capsaicin, the compound that gives chile peppers their spicy heat, is soluble only in fat, so it was unable to join the caravan. –S.W.

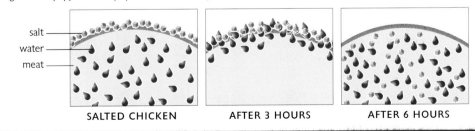

salt —
water —
meat —

SALTED CHICKEN   AFTER 3 HOURS   AFTER 6 HOURS

An Easier Way to Grill Shrimp

Grilling shrimp in their shells protects the delicate flesh, but seasonings are peeled away at the table. Could we deliver tender, flavorful grilled shrimp—without the shells?

⋟ BY REBECCA HAYS ⋞

It's no secret that shrimp can turn from moist and juicy to rubbery and dry in the blink of an eye, a consequence of their small size and lack of fat. Add the unpredictability of cooking over a live fire, and the challenge is magnified. Grilling shrimp in their shells to shield them from the coals' scorching heat works well, but I'm always disappointed when garlic, herbs, and other seasonings get stripped off at the table along with the shells, only to land in a discard pile. I wanted to experience tender, juicy, boldly seasoned grilled shrimp without having to lick my fingers.

Peel Out

I started by preparing the test kitchen's existing recipe for grilled shrimp, substituting peeled shrimp for shell-on. (I'd investigate flavorings later.) I followed every mandate, plumping the shrimp in a saltwater brine (which helps keep them moist), threading them onto skewers, brushing with oil, then quickly grilling over moderate heat. After a few minutes over the fire, the shrimp were tough and dehydrated—no surprise given their shell-free state. Also problematic was the absence of attractive (and flavorful) char marks.

Suspecting that brining was causing the shrimp to become waterlogged and, thus, hindering caramelization, I lit a new fire and grilled a batch of plain, unbrined samples. Sure enough, these shrimp began to pick up the flavor of the grill with a few faint, yet promising, marks.

Having discarded brining, I next built an especially hot fire by banking all the coals on one side of the grill. I seasoned a batch of shrimp with salt and pepper (plus a pinch of sugar to encourage caramelization), set them on the grate, and waited. And waited. Even with a screaming-hot fire, the only way to get sufficient charring was to leave the shrimp on the grill for four or five minutes, yet each passing minute brought me closer to shrimp jerky and farther from a decent dinner.

Shrimp cook so quickly because of their small size. Would jumbo shrimp afford me a few extra minutes? Thirty-seven dollars later, I had my answer. Producing a charred exterior and a tender interior on these hefty specimens was a snap, but with a cost of more than $25 per pound and spotty availability, there had to be a better way.

Grumblings to my colleagues about this dilemma were met first with empathy and then an idea. What if I crammed several normal-sized shrimp very tightly together on a skewer, creating a faux "jumbo" shrimp? Sure enough, this homemade giant shrimp cooked at a slightly slower pace, giving me the extra minutes of grilling time the shrimp needed for charring.

Trial by Fire

With a decent grilling method at hand, I could finally start investigating flavorings. Thus far, I'd been coating the shrimp in oil, but I wondered if yogurt, mayonnaise, coconut milk, or butter offered any advantages. Coconut milk was promising but too distinctive, so I stuck with relatively neutral olive oil. I tried to add personality to the oil with ground spices, but this was a mistake. During a moment of inattention, a flare-up torched the spice paste, turning it bitter. Minced garlic? Scorched. Fresh herbs? Scorched again.

As soon as each shrimp develops an attractive char, it goes into the pan of simmering sauce to finish cooking at a much gentler pace.

Scouring our library shelves, I reviewed every grilled seafood recipe I could find. I eventually happened upon a few recipes in which shellfish was given an initial sear over a hot fire, then transferred to a sauce waiting on the cooler side of the grill. Intrigued, I grilled a few shrimp and slid them into a sauce that simmered in a disposable aluminum pan. These shrimp were a tad overdone but, having soaked up the flavorful sauce, were good enough for two co-workers, who polished off an entire batch grill-side.

A few tries later, I started transferring the shrimp to the sauce *before* they were fully cooked. This way, I could concentrate on getting char marks, then switch to a more forgiving cooking method (gentle simmering in the sauce) until the shrimp were done. I finally had an infallible recipe that delivered everything I wanted in grilled shrimp: tender flesh, attractive charring, tons of flavor—and no shells.

CHARCOAL-GRILLED SHRIMP SKEWERS
SERVES 4 AS A MAIN COURSE, 6 AS AN APPETIZER

The shrimp and sauce (recipes follow) finish cooking together on the grill, so prepare the sauce ingredients while the coals are heating. To fit all of the shrimp on the cooking grate at once, you'll need three 14-inch metal skewers. Serve with grilled bread.

- 1½ pounds extra-large (21/25) shrimp, peeled and deveined, tails left on
- 2–3 tablespoons olive oil for brushing skewers
  Table salt and ground black pepper
- ¼ teaspoon sugar
- 1 recipe Spicy Lemon-Garlic Sauce or Charmoula Sauce (recipes follow)
  Lemon wedges for serving

1. Pat shrimp dry with paper towels. Thread shrimp onto 3 skewers, alternating direction of heads and tails (see illustration, page 9). Brush both sides of shrimp with oil and season lightly with salt and pepper. Sprinkle one side of each skewer evenly with sugar.

2. Light large chimney starter filled with charcoal (6 quarts, or about 100 briquettes) and allow to burn until coals are fully ignited and partially covered with thin layer of ash, about 20 minutes. Empty coals into grill; build modified two-level

TECHNIQUE | CROWDING
SHRIMP ONTO A SKEWER

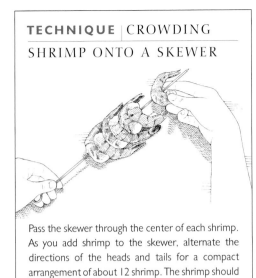

Pass the skewer through the center of each shrimp. As you add shrimp to the skewer, alternate the directions of the heads and tails for a compact arrangement of about 12 shrimp. The shrimp should be crowded and touching each other.

fire by arranging coals to cover one-half of grill, leaving other half empty. Position cooking grate over coals, cover grill, and heat until hot, about 5 minutes; scrape grate clean with grill brush.

3. Set disposable aluminum pan with sauce ingredients on hot side of grill and cook as directed; transfer pan to cooler side of grill. Place shrimp skewers, sugared sides down, on hot side of grate; use tongs to push shrimp together on skewer if they have separated. Grill shrimp, uncovered, until lightly charred, 4 to 5 minutes. Using tongs, flip and grill until second side is pink and slightly translucent, 1 to 2 minutes longer.

4. Using potholder or oven mitt, carefully lift each skewer from grill; use tongs to slide shrimp off skewers into pan with sauce. Toss shrimp and sauce to combine and transfer pan to hot side of grill; cook, stirring, until shrimp are opaque and

The Right Setup

With grilled shrimp, timing can be tricky. We solved the problem by setting up two cooking zones. On the hot side, we sear the shrimp over dry heat until almost done. On the cooler side, we keep a disposable pan of simmering sauce, where the shrimp finish cooking at a gentler pace. Crowding the shrimp on the skewers bought us a few extra minutes on the hot side, giving the shrimp better charring.

fully cooked, about 30 seconds. Remove from grill, add remaining sauce ingredients, and toss to combine. Transfer to serving platter and serve immediately with lemon wedges.

GAS-GRILLED SHRIMP SKEWERS

Follow step 1 of recipe for Charcoal-Grilled Shrimp Skewers. Turn all burners on gas grill to high, cover, and heat until very hot, about 15 minutes. Scrape grate clean with grill brush and proceed with step 3 of recipe, setting sauce aside off heat once hot and grilling shrimp with lid down, checking occasionally to make sure they're not burning (timing may be a few minutes longer than in charcoal grill recipe).

SPICY LEMON-GARLIC SAUCE
MAKES ENOUGH TO SAUCE 1 1/2 POUNDS SHRIMP

4	tablespoons unsalted butter, cut into 4 pieces
4	tablespoons juice from 2 lemons
1/2–3/4	teaspoon red pepper flakes
3	medium garlic cloves, minced or pressed through garlic press (about 1 tablespoon)
1/8	teaspoon table salt
	Disposable aluminum pan or pie plate
1/3	cup minced fresh parsley leaves

Combine butter, lemon juice, pepper flakes, garlic, and salt in pan. Cook over hot side of grill, stirring occasionally, until butter melts, about 1 1/2 minutes; transfer to cooler side of grill and proceed to grill shrimp, adding parsley just before serving.

CHARMOULA SAUCE
MAKES ENOUGH TO SAUCE 1 1/2 POUNDS SHRIMP

Charmoula is a traditional Moroccan spice blend.

4	tablespoons extra-virgin olive oil
1	small red bell pepper, stemmed, seeded, and diced very small (about 1/2 cup)
1/2	small red onion, minced (about 1/3 cup)
1	teaspoon paprika
1/2	teaspoon ground cumin
1/4	teaspoon cayenne
3	medium garlic cloves, minced or pressed through garlic press (about 1 tablespoon)
1/8	teaspoon table salt
	Disposable aluminum pan or pie plate
1/3	cup minced fresh cilantro leaves
2	tablespoons juice from 1 lemon

Combine oil, bell pepper, onion, paprika, cumin, cayenne, garlic, and salt in pan. Cook over hot side of grill, stirring occasionally, until vegetables soften, about 5 minutes (2 or 3 minutes longer if using gas grill); transfer to cooler side of grill and proceed to grill shrimp, adding cilantro and lemon juice just before serving.

Flat Skewers Skewer the Competition

When I first got the assignment to conduct an equipment test on skewers, I figured my editor had finally lost it. How much "performance" difference could there really be between one pointed stick and another? Once I'd surveyed the field—and tried out the designs with our recipes for Grilled Shrimp and Grilled Onions (page 18)—my attitude changed. It really is possible to buy bad skewers.

First of all, forget what most grilling books say: If you're cooking over very high heat, bamboo skewers will burn and break apart—no matter how long you soak them in water beforehand. We had better luck with metal skewers. They may cost more, but they're reusable and they can handle the heartiest kebabs without bending or breaking.

Not all metal skewers are created equal, however. We had a tough time flipping food on round skewers—the skewer itself turned just fine, but the food stayed in place. Flat skewers proved much more effective. Double-pronged skewers turned the food, but some were flimsy and most had a tendency to twist out of their parallel configuration. Other models took the sturdy concept too far, with bulky skewers that severed shrimp in half.

Our choice: Any flat, thin metal skewer will do. We particularly like Norpro's 12-inch Stainless Steel Skewers (six skewers for $10), which are just 3/16 inch thick. –Garth Clingingsmith

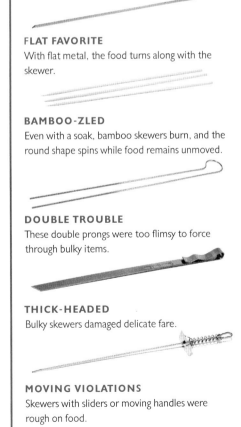

FLAT FAVORITE
With flat metal, the food turns along with the skewer.

BAMBOO-ZLED
Even with a soak, bamboo skewers burn, and the round shape spins while food remains unmoved.

DOUBLE TROUBLE
These double prongs were too flimsy to force through bulky items.

THICK-HEADED
Bulky skewers damaged delicate fare.

MOVING VIOLATIONS
Skewers with sliders or moving handles were rough on food.

Pizza Margherita at Home

Authentic recipes for this Neapolitan pizza call for an 800-degree oven, two days of proofing, and a dough expert's hands. We wanted real Margherita—hold the hassle.

≥ BY ERIKA BRUCE ≤

At American pizza parlors, it's the toppings that reign supreme. Slathered with tomato sauce, dripping with gobs of stretchy cheese, and loaded with mushrooms, olives, onions, pepperoni, pineapple, sausage, and more, the thick, chewy crust takes on a supporting role—in the most literal sense.

At Neapolitan pizzerias, by contrast, the crust is king. Thin, crisp, and shatteringly light, these rustic, wood-fired pizzas sport just a scattering of judiciously chosen toppings that serve as complements to the crust rather than as the main event. The most famous Neapolitan pizza is the Margherita, consisting of a crispy crust garnished with nothing more than a thin veil of tomato sauce, creamy mozzarella, and fresh basil.

But bringing this simple style of pizza home is anything but simple. Most authentic recipes depend on the stratospheric temperatures of a commercial oven, and the recipes aimed at home cooks tend to deliver the usual bready crust. The few that get the crust right require too much time and effort (multiple rising sessions, impossible-to-handle doughs). I wanted to re-create this Neapolitan classic without making it a project.

Beating the Clock

The crust is this pizza's foundation, so I began with the dough. I started with the most basic recipe: bread flour, water, yeast, and salt. From early tests, I discovered that a wet dough—with a high water content—created the best crust (and plenty of shaping headaches, but more on that later).

To achieve pizza Margherita's distinctively light, thin crust without a wood-fired oven, we spiked the dough with cake flour.

Secrets to Our Quick Recipe

CANNED TOMATOES
Doctor canned tomatoes to yield a speedy, no-cook topping.

FOOD PROCESSOR
Use a food processor to mix the dough to shorten kneading time.

The first place I shaved time was in the mixing of the dough. Authentic recipes call for up to 20 minutes of kneading in a standing mixer, but was this essential? To make a real dent in the kneading time, I tried replacing the standing mixer with a food processor. I was surprised that my tasters couldn't detect any differences between dough kneaded just 2 minutes in a food processor and dough kneaded 10 times longer in a mixer.

It turns out that pizza is more about tenderness and crispness than crumb structure. The slow kneading action of a standing mixer helps to develop gluten slowly and can produce rustic loaves with superior texture. However, when it comes to pizza, kneading is really mixing, and the food processor is just as capable as a standing mixer—and much faster.

Next up: Could I reduce the rising time? The simplest pizza dough takes at least two hours to double in volume, and many traditional recipes call for a pinch of yeast and an overnight rise. Once risen, the dough is divided into balls, rested again for about 45 minutes, then

shaped. Could I collapse these steps into one streamlined process? After several failed attempts, I found that I was able to shape the dough straight out of the food processor. This meant the balls of dough could rise and relax at the same time. A healthy amount of instant yeast cut the rising time to one hour.

Stick with Me

A rolling pin produces a uniformly flat pizza, while stretching achieves a thin center surrounded by thicker edges. The latter is characteristic of authentic Neapolitan pizza. While experts might find this method easy, I was having trouble with the wet, sticky dough. I backed off on the water until the dough became manageable. The result was a crust that was more bready than crisp. Because I couldn't handle a dough with more water, I would have to find another way to mimic its effect.

I thought that adding olive oil might produce the desired texture—crisp on the outside, tender on the inside—but instead the crust came out too soft and focaccia-like. My next thought was to abandon the bread flour I had been using in favor of all-purpose, which has a lower protein content and therefore produces a more tender dough. Sure enough, the dough was immediately easier on the hands and—once baked—on the teeth. I was on the right track, but I thought the dough could use even more tenderness. Because cake flour is the softest flour most home cooks keep on hand, I tried adding different amounts to the dough. In the end, a mixture of roughly 1 part cake flour to 2 parts all-purpose produced the light, thin texture I was after, and the dough was easy to handle.

Given the humble home oven I was using, these results made perfect sense. With its 800 degrees of wood-fired power, a Neapolitan pizzeria's commercial oven can cook a pizza Margherita in less than four minutes—not enough time for the high-protein dough to turn tough and overly chewy. In contrast, my regular oven—cranked up to its 500-degree max—took almost 10 full minutes, causing the high-protein bread-flour dough to toughen but leaving the softer cake-flour blend light and tender. (See "Great Pizza Without an 800-Degree Oven" below.)

Topping It Off

While I had imagined a sauce of tangy, sun-ripened fresh tomatoes, the requisite peeling, seeding, and pureeing were not my idea of quick and easy. Canned tomatoes were it, and the less cooking, the better. Diced tomatoes had the best texture when quickly pulsed in the food processor, forming a slightly chunky but uniform layer of sauce. Draining the pulsed tomatoes was essential to avoid a soggy crust. A little sugar, salt, fresh basil, and garlic rounded out the tomato flavor.

Because the crust took about 10 minutes to brown and crisp, the sauce had plenty of time to cook. Adding the fresh mozzarella halfway through the baking time was the only way to preserve its fresh creamy texture and milky flavor. All this pizza needed now was a sprinkling of basil, a drizzle of olive oil, and a dash of salt. Just an hour and a half from start to finish was quite reasonable, especially for pizza that tasted like it came all the way from Naples.

PIZZA MARGHERITA
MAKES TWO 12-INCH PIZZAS

This recipe requires a pizza stone and a peel. Convection ovens will produce a lighter, crispier pizza, and you will need to reduce the overall cooking time by a minute or two. You can shape the second dough round while the first pizza bakes, but don't add toppings until just before baking. You can let the dough rise overnight in the refrigerator if you like; place the dough balls on a floured baking sheet and cover with plastic wrap coated with nonstick cooking spray. If using mozzarella packed in brine, pat the cheese cubes dry before placing them on the pizza.

Dough
- 1¼ teaspoons instant yeast
- 1 cup (8 ounces) water, room temperature
- 1¾ cups (8¾ ounces) unbleached all-purpose flour, plus more for dusting work surface and peel
- 1 cup (4 ounces) cake flour
- 1½ teaspoons table salt
- 2 teaspoons sugar

Topping
- 1 (28-ounce) can diced tomatoes
- ½ teaspoon sugar
- 1 small garlic clove, minced or pressed through garlic press (optional)
- ¼ cup chopped fresh basil leaves
  Table salt
- 8 ounces fresh mozzarella (see note above), cut into 1-inch chunks
- 2 teaspoons extra-virgin olive oil

Getting the Dough Shape Just Right

1. Divide dough immediately after mixing and shape into smooth balls.

2. Flatten round into 8-inch disk to eliminate large air pockets.

3. Stretch outer edges with flattened fingers while giving quarter turns.

4. If dough develops weak spots, stretch edges using backs of hands.

1. **FOR THE CRUST:** Adjust oven rack to lowest position, set pizza stone on oven rack, and heat oven to 500 degrees. In liquid measuring cup, whisk yeast into water to dissolve. In food processor fitted with metal blade, process flours, salt, and sugar until combined, about 5 seconds. With machine running, slowly add liquid through feed tube; continue to process until dough forms satiny, sticky ball that clears sides of workbowl, 1½ to 2 minutes. (If after 1 minute dough is sticky and clings to blade, add 1 to 2 tablespoons all-purpose flour and continue processing. If dough appears dry and crumbly, add 1 to 2 tablespoons water and process until dough forms ball.) Divide dough in half and shape into smooth, tight balls (see photo 1, above). Place on floured counter or baking sheet, spacing them at least 3 inches apart; cover loosely with plastic wrap coated with nonstick cooking spray and let rise until doubled in volume, about 1 hour.

2. **FOR THE TOPPING:** In clean bowl of food processor, process tomatoes until crushed, two or three 1-second pulses. Transfer tomatoes to fine-mesh strainer set over bowl and let drain at least 30 minutes, stirring occasionally to release liquids. Just before shaping pizza rounds, combine drained tomatoes, sugar, garlic (if using), 1 tablespoon basil, and ¼ teaspoon salt in bowl.

3. **TO SHAPE AND COOK THE PIZZAS:** When dough balls have doubled in size, dust dough liberally with flour and transfer balls to well-floured work surface. Press one ball into 8-inch disk (photo 2). Using flattened palms, gently stretch disk into 12-inch circle, working along outer edge and giving disk quarter turns (photos 3 and 4). Lightly flour pizza peel; lift edges of dough round to brush off any excess flour, then transfer dough to peel. Spread thin layer of tomato topping (about ½ cup) over dough with rubber spatula, leaving ½-inch border around edge. Slide onto stone and bake until crust begins to brown, about 5 minutes. Remove pizza from oven with peel, close oven door, and top pizza with half of cheese chunks, spaced evenly apart. Return pizza to stone and continue cooking until cheese is just melted, 4 to 5 minutes more. Transfer to cutting board; sprinkle with half of remaining basil, 1 teaspoon olive oil, and pinch salt. Slice and serve immediately. Repeat step 3 to shape, top, and bake second pizza.

Great Pizza without an 800-Degree Oven

In Italy, pizza is serious business. Strict guidelines are placed on the designation of true Neapolitan pizza, and one of the requirements is a wood-fired oven reaching temperatures upward of 800 degrees.

To see what effect such extreme temperatures would have on my recipe, I borrowed a local pizzeria's commercial pizza oven. I baked my pizza and compared it with the pizzeria's (made with a dough that includes high-protein flour). Four minutes later, I expected two ultra-crisp pizzas to emerge, but mine was too soft, almost cakey. The crust made with high-protein flour was light, tender, and crisp. Back in the test kitchen, I made my recipe and the pizzeria's recipe (with the high-protein flour). This time the professional dough failed, yielding a tough, leathery crust.

Our recipe didn't work in an 800-degree oven, but it's ideal for a cooler conventional home oven.

Why did my recipe work well in a 500-degree test kitchen oven but not in an 800-degree commercial oven? And why didn't the professional recipe work in our oven? After some head scratching, I realized that time (not just temperature) has a big effect on the texture of the crust. In the super-hot professional oven, my dough cooked so quickly that it didn't have enough time to dry out and become crisp—high-protein flour was essential. Back in the test kitchen, the reverse was happening. The high-protein dough spent so much time in the oven that it became tough and crackery. The tenderizing, low-protein cake flour in my dough kept the interior of the crust soft while the prolonged baking time crisped the exterior. Apparently, you don't need an 800-degree oven to make great pizza Margherita—you just need the right dough for the job.–E.B.

Perfecting Cuban-Style Pork Roast

Garlicky, citrus-infused pork is a natural for the backyard grill. Unfortunately, so are dry meat, burnt skin, and faint flavors. We grill-roasted 200 pounds of pork to get it right.

≥ BY SANDRA WU ≤

Well known for its rum and cigars, Cuba is also home to another, lesser-known specialty of the Caribbean: citrusy, garlicky roasted meats. One of the best examples is *lechon asado*, or roast pork marinated in a flavorful mixture of citrus, garlic, olive oil, and spices. Tradition calls for a whole pig cooked on a spit over a wood fire, but many modern versions use a suckling pig, fresh ham, or pork shoulder instead. For convenience' sake, the project is sometimes brought indoors and roasted in the oven.

My goal was to re-create this bold-flavored dish, with its crackling-crisp skin, tender meat, and bracing garlic-citrus sauce. I wanted a recipe that could be made outdoors (great for large summer parties) as well as a variation that could be made indoors (for city dwellers and winter months). After testing half a dozen recipes in various cookbooks, I realized I had my work cut out for me. Burnt skin that peeled off, chewy meat so dry even the sauce couldn't save it, and marinades that failed to impart much flavor were common problems. This recipe is a project: If the texture and flavor aren't great, why bother?

Fire Away

Whether roasted on the grill or in the oven, Cuban-style roast pork has a texture somewhere between that of a juicy, sliceable American pork roast (which *Cook's* prefers cooked to about 145 degrees) and fall-apart-when-you-touch-it pulled pork (cooked to almost 200 degrees). The best authentic recipes I sampled called for an internal temperature of around 190 degrees, at which point the collagen and fat had mostly broken down and rendered but not quite to full-on disintegration. As for the cut, I went with the picnic shoulder (often simply labeled "pork shoulder"), an inexpensive, fatty, bone-in cut that comes with a generous amount of skin attached: The crispy skin, after all, is a hallmark of this dish. (See "Picking the Perfect Pork Roast," right.)

Go to www.cooksillustrated.com
COOK'S extra
• Key in code 7065 for our **Testing of Remote Meat Thermometers**.
• Available until January 1, 2007.

Unlike Carolina-style pulled pork, which falls apart in shreds, Cuban pork roast is sliced into juicy morsels.

The recipes I found for Cuban pork were a varied lot, but most followed the same sequence: Infuse the raw pork with flavor (with a marinade or wet paste), cook several hours on the grill using indirect heat, cut or slice into small pieces, then toss with a traditional mojo (pronounced "mo-ho") sauce, a garlicky vinaigrette that often serves double duty as a marinade. I would deal with flavor infusion later. First, I wanted to figure out the best way to cook the pork.

Letting the pork sit overnight in a working marinade of citrus juice, garlic, and olive oil, I proceeded to cook it over indirect heat, banking the coals on either side of the grill and placing the roast in between. Hours later, the interior had reached my target 190 degrees, but getting there was tedious. To keep the roast from turning too dark, I had to rotate it every 30 minutes or so—that's seven or eight times per session. Add that to the number of times I had to refuel to keep the charcoal from dying out, and the grill lid was lying on the ground almost as much as it was covering the pork.

There had to be a better way. I tried a modified two-level fire, banking all the coals on one side of the grill and cooking the pork over the side without the coals. This was an improvement, but I was still refueling too often. What if I started out with higher heat, then let the fire slowly die out? Unfortunately, ramping up the 4 quarts of coal I'd been using to a full chimney (6 quarts) brought the initial temperature of the grill to a scorching 450 degrees, giving me pork that was more Cajun-blackened than Cuban-roasted.

Discouraged, I wondered whether I should throw in the towel and focus on an oven method instead. After all, traditional Cuban-style roast pork was originally cooked outdoors more out of necessity than in the interest of flavor development (unlike, say, a smoky Carolina-style pulled

SHOPPING: Picking the Perfect Pork Roast

What's the best cut for Cuban-style pork? We tried them all. Widely available Boston butt (the upper portion of the front leg) was an attractive option thanks to its high fat content. But it comes with no skin attached, and the crisp, flavorful skin is one of the highlights of this dish. Fresh ham (from the rear leg) has skin but is usually too lean. We settled on the picnic shoulder (also called pork shoulder), a flavorful cut from the lower portion of the front leg that almost always comes bone-in—and with a fair share of fat and rind to boot.

BOSTON BUTT
Fatty but skinless

FRESH HAM
Great skin but too lean

PICNIC SHOULDER
Our choice: great skin, great fat

Bathed and Infused

Bland meat, dry interior, flavorless crust—three common problems with grill-roasted pork, each of which demands its own, customized solution. For the bland meat and dry interior, we combined a traditional brine (salt, sugar, and water) with a citrus marinade. To ratchet up the flavor of the crust, we coated the exterior with a potent garlic-citrus paste just before cooking.

BRINE

MARINADE **PASTE**

pork). Twelve test-kitchen staffers made the decision for me after I pitted a pork shoulder cooked on the grill (with all its requisite choreography) against one simply tossed into the oven. The oven version was tasty (so I included the recipe as an alternative), but the grill version was the clear favorite for its delicious charred flavor.

Keeping a Lid on It

The oven experiment had given me an idea. If tasters wanted grilled flavor, why not simply start out on the grill, then move the roast inside to finish? If I planned things right, maybe I could skip refueling altogether. Sure enough, starting with a two-thirds-full chimney allowed the pork to cook for almost three full hours before the coals died down. When I transferred the roast to a 325-degree oven, its internal temperature was around 130 degrees. Three hours later, out came a 190-degree pork roast with plenty of grilled flavor—and I'd used just one chimney of charcoal!

My recipe had gone from five charcoal replenishments to no charcoal replenishments, but I still had to fiddle with the roast every half-hour or so to keep the side closest to the coals from burning. Unwilling to leave well enough alone, I wondered if I could somehow protect the pork so that I could avoid the half-hourly rotations. Covering the roast completely with aluminum foil created a steam effect, which wreaked havoc on the crispiness of the skin. This roast needed dry heat. The solution was a foil "shield" (see photos on page 14), which allowed the heat to circulate around the meat yet kept it from turning black. More important, I had cut out the fuss: Now the grill stayed closed for the entire session.

Palates of the Caribbean

Half the recipes I had collected called for marinating the pork shoulder overnight (or even for two or three days); the other half went with a coating of wet paste. Each method had its advantages. The marinade penetrated deep into the meat, while the paste held fast to the exterior of the pork throughout cooking, yielding an assertively flavored crust (the marinade just slipped off). For

the best of both worlds, I opted for a combination.

Unfortunately, the wimpy marinade I was using—two or three fresh-squeezed limes and the same number of oranges, plus a few minced garlic cloves—just wasn't cutting it. I gradually increased the citrus and garlic until I was up to two heads of garlic and almost two dozen assorted oranges and limes. (With this more powerful formula, I found that I could get away with marinating the pork for just 12 hours rather than two or three days.) Tasters were appeased, but with carpal tunnel syndrome setting in, my hands were less enthusiastic. When I secretly eliminated the lime juice and replaced the fresh-squeezed orange juice with an equal amount from the carton, however, tasters couldn't tell the difference.

As for the exterior paste, the usual blend of mashed garlic, salt, pepper, oregano, cumin, olive oil, and orange juice, plus a shot of white vinegar for extra kick (basically, the components of a mojo sauce), worked just fine. Cutting fairly wide slits all over the pork proved to be the most effective method for trapping the paste's flavors.

All the Rest

I now had a solid (and fuss-free) cooking method and a great two-pronged technique for infusing flavor. The only problem remaining was an inconsistent texture. The sections of the meat closest to the crust (and, thus, near the exterior layer of fat) always came out moist and tender, but the leaner interior was less predictable. On a bad day, it could turn out so dry that even a generous slathering of mojo sauce barely saved it.

The test kitchen often relies on the magic of brining (soaking in a solution of salt and sometimes sugar) to remedy lean-meat texture problems, but I was already spending 12 hours soaking the pork in a marinade. The answer was simple: I took the test kitchen's basic formula for a brine, replaced some of the water with orange juice, and created a hybrid brine/marinade. I compensated for the diluted flavor (courtesy of the added water) by upping the soaking time from 12 hours to between 18 and 24 hours. The result was flavorful meat that came out tender even close to the bone.

Most large cuts of meat benefit from resting after cooking, which allows the juices to redistribute evenly throughout the meat. My Cuban pork roast was no exception. Compared side by side, a roast rested for 30 minutes was much juicier than one I sliced into immediately after cooking. Even more interesting is what happened when the roast rested for an entire hour: As expected, the exterior and the portions bordering knobs of fat

TECHNIQUE | BUILDING A FOIL 'SHIELD'

By protecting the pork roast with an aluminum foil shield, we kept it from getting too dark on the side closest to the heat—no rotation required.

I. Make two ½-inch folds on the long side of an 18-inch length of foil to form a reinforced edge. Place the foil on the center of the cooking grate, with the reinforced edge over the hot side of the grill. Position the roast, skin side up, over the cool side of the grill so that it covers about a third of the foil. **2.** Lift and bend the edges of the foil to shield the sides of the roast, tucking in the edges.

were delicious, but now the lean interior portions were every bit as moist. Patience really is a virtue.

All the pork needed now was a final splash of mojo sauce, which could be quickly mixed and cooled to room temperature while the pork rested. Made with many of the same ingredients used in the brine and paste, the mojo provided another bright, fresh hit of flavor. As I took a bite of the tangy, garlicky pork and a sip from an icy mojito, I knew my efforts had been worth it: This dish had finally gotten its mojo back.

CUBAN-STYLE GRILL-ROASTED PORK
SERVES 8 TO 10

Letting the cooked roast rest for a full hour will yield noticeably more tender meat. This roast has a crispy skin that should be served along with the meat. Top the meat with Mojo Sauce (recipe follows). Traditional accompaniments include black beans, rice, and fried plantains.

Pork and Brine
- 1 bone-in, skin-on pork picnic shoulder (7 to 8 pounds)
- 3 cups sugar
- 2 cups table salt
- 2 medium garlic heads, unpeeled cloves separated and crushed
- 4 cups orange juice

Garlic-Citrus Paste
- 12 medium garlic cloves, peeled and coarsely chopped (about ¼ cup)
- 2 tablespoons ground cumin
- 2 tablespoons dried oregano
- 1 tablespoon table salt
- 1½ teaspoons ground black pepper
- 6 tablespoons orange juice
- 2 tablespoons distilled white vinegar
- 2 tablespoons olive oil

1. TO BRINE THE PORK: With sharp paring knife, cut 1-inch-deep slits (about 1 inch long) all over roast, spaced about 2 inches apart. Dissolve sugar and salt in 6 quarts cold water in stockpot or large bucket. Stir in garlic and orange juice. Submerge pork in brine and refrigerate 18 to 24 hours.

2. TO APPLY THE GARLIC-CITRUS PASTE: Process garlic, cumin, oregano, salt, and pepper in food processor until they reach consistency of coarse paste, about ten 1-second pulses. With machine running, add orange juice, vinegar, and oil through feed tube and process until mixture forms smooth, wet paste, about 20 seconds. Remove pork from brine and rinse under cool running water; pat dry with paper towels. Rub paste all over pork and into slits. Refrigerate pork until ready to grill.

3. TO GRILL-ROAST THE PORK: Using chimney starter, light 4 quarts charcoal (about 60 briquettes) and burn until fully ignited and partially covered in gray ash, about 15 minutes. Empty coals into grill; build modified two-level fire by arranging coals to cover one-half of grill in even layer. Position cooking grate over coals, cover grill, and heat until hot, about 5 minutes; scrape grate clean with grill brush. Place roast with skin side up on cool side of grill and shield with foil according to photos above. Cover and cook until grill temperature falls to 225 degrees, 2 to 3 hours (coals will be gray and partially disintegrated). After 1¾ hours, heat oven to 325 degrees with rack in lower-middle position.

4. When grill temperature has fallen to 225 degrees, remove foil and transfer roast to wire rack set over rimmed baking sheet or to roasting pan with rack. Roast pork in oven until skin is browned and crisp and instant-read thermometer inserted into thickest part of meat registers 190 degrees, 2 to 3 hours. Transfer roast to cutting board and let rest 1 hour. To carve, first remove skin in one large piece. Scrape off and discard top layer of fat, then cut pork away from bone in 3 or 4 large pieces. Slice each piece against grain into ¼-inch slices. To serve skin, scrape excess fat from underside and cut into strips. Drizzle Mojo Sauce over pork just before serving.

CUBAN-STYLE GRILL-ROASTED PORK ON A GAS GRILL

1. Follow recipe for Cuban-Style Grill-Roasted Pork through step 2.

2. Turn all grill burners to high, close lid, and heat until hot, about 15 minutes. Scrape grate clean with grill brush. Turn off all except primary burner (burner that will remain on during cooking). Place roast with skin side up on cool side of grill, shielded with foil (see photos, left). Close cover and lower primary burner to medium or medium-high (grill temperature should be about 325 degrees). Cook until skin is browned and crisp and instant-read thermometer inserted into thickest part of meat registers 190 degrees, about 6 hours, rotating meat 180 degrees and removing foil shield halfway through cooking time. Follow resting and slicing instructions from step 4.

CUBAN-STYLE OVEN-ROASTED PORK

1. Follow recipe for Cuban-Style Grill-Roasted Pork through step 2. Heat oven to 325 degrees with rack in lower-middle position.

2. Place pork with skin side down on wire rack set over rimmed baking sheet or in roasting pan with rack. Cook, uncovered, 3 hours. Flip roast skin side up and continue to cook until instant-read thermometer inserted into thickest part of meat registers 190 degrees, about 3 hours more, lightly tenting roast with foil if skin begins to get too dark. Follow resting and slicing instructions from step 4.

MOJO SAUCE
MAKES 1 CUP

The sauce can be made while the cooked pork is resting or up to a day ahead of time and refrigerated in an airtight container. If chilled, let the sauce come to room temperature before serving.

- 4 medium garlic cloves, minced or pressed through garlic press (about 4 teaspoons)
- 2 teaspoons kosher salt
- ½ cup olive oil
- ½ teaspoon ground cumin
- ¼ cup distilled white vinegar
- ¼ cup juice from 1 to 2 oranges
- ¼ teaspoon dried oregano
- ⅛ teaspoon ground black pepper

1. Place minced garlic on cutting board and sprinkle with kosher salt. Using flat side of chef's knife, drag garlic and salt back and forth across cutting board in small circular motions until garlic is ground into smooth paste.

2. Heat olive oil in medium saucepan over medium heat until shimmering. Add garlic paste and cumin and cook, stirring, until fragrant, about 30 seconds.

3. Remove pan from heat and whisk in remaining ingredients. Transfer to bowl and cool to room temperature. Whisk sauce to recombine before serving.

Rescuing Sautéed Zucchini

This summertime staple cooks up soggy and bland in the skillet. Could we bail it out?

⇒ BY SEAN LAWLER ⇐

Grating zucchini is the best method for getting the water out, clearing the way for maximum flavor.

There's a reason zucchini usually gets tossed onto a hot grill, and it has nothing to do with the season. Confronted with the intense, dry heat of a live fire, the wettest vegetable in the garden (about 95 percent water) quickly expels excess moisture, leaving behind concentrated flavors. Try this trick on the stovetop and you'll get a panful of soggy summer-squash stew. While the high heat still works its magic, the lack of a slotted grate means there's no escape route for the liquid.

The secret to sautéed zucchini, then, is to extract as much water as possible *before* the squash hits the pan. The most common method is to salt thin-sliced zucchini, let it drain in a colander, then press the disks between paper towels. But even then, the disks may still be waterlogged enough to inhibit browning.

Several recipes I found called for shredding the zucchini on a box grater, squeezing the shreds in a kitchen towel, and cooking them in a hot skillet. The bad news first: These recipes all cooked up soggy, with an offputting steamed flavor. But given how much of the flavor-sapping liquid I was able to extract from the shreds, the method itself seemed promising.

Discarding the seedy, watery cores made the shreds noticeably drier, but the best solution was to incorporate techniques from the old salting/pressing method as well: tossing the shreds with salt, draining them in a colander, and wringing them out in a kitchen towel. I was pleasantly surprised to find that shredded zucchini needs only five minutes of draining, a far cry from the half-hour required by sliced disks.

By cranking up the heat and minimizing stirring, I had tender, lightly browned zucchini in less than five minutes. The only problem left to solve was a slightly clumpy, tangled texture, which made it tricky to distribute flavorful ingredients evenly. The key, I found, was to toss the raw shreds with olive oil before adding them to the pan.

ZUCCHINI WITH GARLIC AND LEMON
SERVES 4

Bread-Crumb Topping (optional)
- 2 slices white sandwich bread, torn into quarters
- 2 tablespoons unsalted butter

Zucchini
- 5 medium zucchini (about 8 ounces each), ends trimmed
  Table salt
- 1 small garlic clove, minced or pressed through garlic press (about ½ teaspoon)
- 1 tablespoon plus 1 teaspoon extra-virgin olive oil, plus extra for serving, if desired
- 1–2 teaspoons juice from 1 lemon
  Ground black pepper

1. **FOR THE BREAD CRUMBS** (optional): Pulse bread in food processor until coarsely ground. Heat butter in 12-inch nonstick skillet over medium-high heat until melted. Add bread crumbs and cook, stirring frequently with heat-proof rubber spatula, until golden brown, about 3 minutes. Transfer to small bowl and set aside.

2. **FOR THE ZUCCHINI:** Cut each zucchini crosswise into several pieces, each 2 to 3 inches long. Shred each piece on large holes of box grater, rotating as needed to avoid shredding seeds and core (which should be discarded); you should have about 10 cups shredded zucchini. Toss zucchini with 1½ teaspoons salt and place in colander set in medium bowl; let drain 5 to 10 minutes. Wrap zucchini in kitchen towel, in batches if necessary, and wring out excess moisture.

3. Place zucchini in medium bowl and break up any large clumps. Combine garlic with 2 teaspoons oil in small bowl; add mixture to zucchini and toss to combine thoroughly.

4. Heat remaining 2 teaspoons oil in 12-inch nonstick skillet over high heat until faint smoke appears. Add zucchini and spread evenly in pan with tongs; cook without stirring until bottom layer browns, about 2 minutes; stir well, breaking up any clumps with tongs, then cook until "new" bottom layer browns, about 2 minutes more. Off heat, stir in lemon juice and salt and pepper to taste. Serve immediately, drizzling with additional olive oil, if desired, and sprinkling with bread crumbs, if using.

ZUCCHINI WITH TOMATOES AND BASIL
SERVES 4

Combine 3 cored, seeded, and diced plum tomatoes, 1 small clove minced garlic, 1 teaspoon balsamic vinegar, 2 teaspoons extra-virgin olive oil, ¼ teaspoon salt and 2 tablespoons chopped fresh basil leaves in small bowl and set aside. Follow recipe for Zucchini with Garlic and Lemon from step 2, omitting garlic in step 3 and replacing lemon juice with tomato mixture in step 4. Transfer to serving platter, sprinkle with ¼ cup finely grated Parmesan, and serve immediately, drizzling with additional olive oil, if desired.

ZUCCHINI WITH SPICED CARROTS AND ALMONDS
SERVES 4

Follow steps 2 and 3 of recipe for Zucchini with Garlic and Lemon, omitting garlic in step 3. Heat 1 tablespoon extra-virgin olive oil in 12-inch nonstick skillet over medium heat until shimmering. Add 1 cup grated carrot and cook, stirring occasionally, until tender, about 5 minutes. Add ½ teaspoon coriander and ¼ teaspoon red pepper flakes and cook, stirring constantly, until fragrant, about 30 seconds. Increase heat to high; add zucchini and ½ cup golden raisins and spread evenly in pan with tongs. Cook until bottom layer browns, about 2 minutes; stir well, breaking up any clumps with tongs, then cook until "new" bottom layer browns, about 2 minutes more. Off heat, add ½ cup sliced, toasted almonds, and toss to combine. Stir in 1 to 2 teaspoons lemon juice and salt and pepper to taste. Serve immediately, drizzling with additional olive oil if desired.

Go to www.cooksillustrated.com
- Key in 7064 for our recipe for **Zucchini with Peas and Herbs.**
- Recipe available until January 1, 2007.

PHOTOGRAPHY: CARL TREMBLAY

Illustrated Guide to Kitchen Knives

Do you really need $400 worth of forged German steel? Here's our guide to choosing (and using) the essential knives—and which ones don't make the cut. BY SEAN LAWLER

THREE ESSENTIAL KNIVES

Manufacturers try to trap you into buying blocks with a dozen knives, but sharp shoppers invest only in the essentials.

8-INCH CHEF'S KNIFE

From chopping an onion to mincing herbs and butchering a chicken, this one knife will handle 90 percent of your kitchen cutting work.

Forged or Stamped?

Conventional wisdom dictates that forged blades—made by pouring molten steel into molds—are superior to cheaper stamped blades, which are punched out of a sheet of steel. Our tests showed that the forged/stamped distinction is less important than weight. Some testers liked the maneuverability of the lighter knives, while others preferred the sturdiness and balance of a heavier forged blade.

Bolster Basics

Most forged knives have a thick collar of metal near the handle called a bolster. Designed to balance the weight of the blade, it poses a problem for home sharpeners, as its thickness prevents the heel of the blade from passing through the sharpening channel. Over the course of many sharpenings (which gradually wear down the blade), the bolster may start to protrude, preventing the blade from making smooth contact with the cutting board.

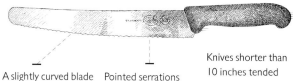

Material World

Most quality blades are made from high-carbon stainless steel, a hard metal that, once sharpened, tends to stay that way. (We recommend them.) Some purists prefer carbon steel knives, which may take a sharper edge initially but don't retain it for as long. Expensive ceramic blades are ultra-sharp but ultra-fragile.

Curve Appeal

Chef's knives with a long, gently sloping curvature better perform the rocking motion necessary for mincing and chopping than those with a relatively straight line that curves abruptly at the tip.

Getting a Handle on It

We prefer molded plastic handles over those made from wood (which collects grease and dirt) or metal (which can get slippery). Most of our test cooks prefer a simple shape (no "ergonomic" bumps and ridges) and a smooth texture rather than a "pebbled" finish. The handle should balance the weight of the blade, making a tight, comfortable seal with your hand. When shopping for a knife, try out both common grips (see "Two Basic Grips," page 17) before making your choice.

★ AND THE WINNERS ARE . . .★

The inexpensive, lightweight **FORSCHNER FIBROX** ($36) was the favorite among testers who fancy lighter knives. Those who like a sturdier forged blade preferred the **WÜSTHOF GRAND PRIX II** ($94)—still reasonably light.

3½-INCH PARING KNIFE

A paring knife is essential for tasks that require more dexterity and precision than a chef's knife can provide: peeling and coring apples, deveining shrimp, cutting citrus segments, and more.

The blade of a paring knife should be somewhat flexible for easy maneuvering into tight spots (such as tomato cores) and for handling curves when peeling and paring.

★ AND THE WINNER IS . . .★

With a paring knife, weight and balance are less important than a sharp, agile blade and a firm, comfortable grip. The **FORSCHNER FIBROX** ($5.95) has both for a low price.

10-INCH BREAD KNIFE

The pointed serrations of a good bread knife glide through crusty breads, bagels, and tomato skins to produce neat slices, while a poorly designed bread knife slips, stutters, and shreds its way through food.

A slightly curved blade keeps knuckles from scraping the cutting board, allowing a rocking motion to cut through tough crusts.

Pointed serrations give the blade a good grip on the food right away, while wavy serrations slide around before digging in.

Knives shorter than 10 inches tended to catch their tips on larger loaves; the blade should be rigid for stable cutting through tough crusts.

★ AND THE WINNER IS . . .★

The **FORSCHNER FIBROX** ($36) has it all, including the most comfortable handle.

OTHER RECOMMENDED KNIVES

Depending on what you cook, you may want to expand your arsenal to include some of these other useful blades.

BONING KNIFE

The slim, flexible blade of a boning knife is invaluable for sliding through joints, between bones, and under silver skin. Choose a blade between 5 and 7 inches, with a tapered tip and an easy-to-grip handle, such as the **Forschner Fibrox Boning Knife** ($18).

SLICING/CARVING KNIFE

A good carving knife does one thing only: cut thin, uniform slices from large cuts of meat. You either need one or you don't. Look for a straight, nonserrated edge with a uniform width (at least 1½ inches) from handle to rounded tip and a rigid 10-inch blade, like that of the **Chef Cutlery Legend 10-inch Granton Slicer** ($45, see page 32).

CLEAVER

About the only time we reach for a meat cleaver is when making homemade chicken stock—we've found the best way to release flavor from the bones is to hack them up. If you tackle this task regularly, consider the super-sharp, sturdy **Global** ($106) or the lighter-weight **LamsonSharp** ($40).

ELECTRIC KNIFE

Aside from carving large holiday roasts, electric knives do an excellent job cutting into foods that are made up of layers with distinctly firm and soft textures—such as pecan pie and quesadillas—which can get mashed by a regular chef's knife. (For perfectionists, admittedly.) The test kitchen winner is the **Black and Decker EK800 Slice Right** ($24.99).

KEEPING KNIVES SHARP

A knife loses its sharpness when the fine tip of the cutting edge gets knocked slightly out of alignment, which can happen any time the blade makes contact with food or a cutting board. The knife may "act dull" even though the edge is still quite sharp —it's just pointed in the wrong direction. This can happen very quickly if you are doing a lot of heavy cutting work, but the edge can be just as quickly restored by using a sharpening steel, which realigns the edge and removes slight irregularities.

Two ways to protect your knife's edge are to avoid hard cutting surfaces such as glass or acrylic (stick to wood and plastic cutting boards) and to keep them out of the dishwasher, where getting knocked around might damage their edge.

IS IT SHARP?

To determine if your knife needs to be sharpened, put it to the paper test.

1. Hold a folded, but not creased, sheet of newspaper by one end.
2. Lay the blade against the top edge at an angle and slice outward. If the knife fails to slice cleanly, try steeling it. If it still fails, it needs sharpening.

CHOOSING—AND USING—A STEEL

You should steel your knives regularly, before each use if possible, but sharpen them only when necessary. Traditional steels are lightly grooved, magnetized iron rods, but we prefer the newer diamond steels—hollow oval tubes coated with diamond dust. These grind trace amounts of metal from the knife with each swipe, partially sharpening the blade while straightening it and extending the period between sharpenings. However, keep in mind that steeling will only realign a fairly sharp blade; a dull knife has to be sharpened (see below).

1. Hold the steel perpendicular to the work surface, with the tip resting on a cutting board.
2. Place the heel of the blade against the steel, with the blade at a 20-degree angle away from it.
3. With a locked wrist and light pressure, slide the blade down the length of the steel in a sweeping motion, pulling the back of the blade toward you so that the entire length of the blade comes in contact with the steel.
4. Repeat the motion on the other side of the blade. Four or five strokes per side should realign the edge.

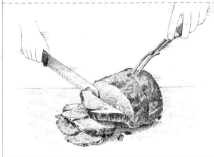

SHARPENING

There are two options for grinding a new edge on a knife at home:

1. **Sharpening stone.** This method is effective but takes some practice, and it's more work than many home cooks want to do. It involves a double-sided sharpening stone, some elbow grease, and about 15 minutes per blade. (For step-by-step instructions, see Cook's Extra, below at right.)
2. **Knife sharpener.** An electric home sharpener can restore the edge of even a seriously neglected blade, provided you buy one with a coarse regrinding wheel,

such as our favorite, the **Chef'sChoice 110** ($80). Some less expensive models feature only medium- and fine-grade slots, good for perking up a slightly dull blade but unable to grind a completely new edge. These machines do remove a certain amount of metal from the blade with each use, so use them no more than necessary.

BASIC KNIFE TECHNIQUES

TWO BASIC GRIPS

Handle Grip

With the handle grip, the thumb rests on the side of the handle opposite the index finger. This grip is the favored by test cooks with smaller hands. For those who work long hours with a knife, it also causes fewer calluses.

Blade Grip

Cooks with larger hands often prefer the blade grip, in which the thumb and index finger actually grip the heel of the blade. While this grip requires a bit more hand strength, it also provides more control over the tip of the blade.

SAFE SLICING WITH A 'GUIDING HAND'

By properly positioning the hand that is not holding the knife, you can prevent slippage, control the size of the cut, and protect your fingers.

In this "bear claw" position, the fingertips are curled back away from the knife to hold the food in place, while the knuckles rest against the side of the blade, providing guidance with no danger of being cut.

To cut multiple slices, use the curvature of the blade to guide the knife through a series of smooth cutting strokes. Some part of the blade should remain in contact with the cutting board at all times. During the upward motion, reposition the guiding hand to set up the next slice.

CAREFUL CARVING

The key to smooth, even cuts is a long stroke with very mild downward pressure. Let the knife do the work, and avoid short, sawing strokes, which yield ragged slices.

CHOPPING AND MINCING

This fast, continuous motion makes quick work of fresh herbs, onions, and the like. It begins with the handle held high and the knife tip on the cutting board, held gently in place with the guiding hand. The front half of the blade remains in contact with the cutting board at all times.

COOK'S extra

Go to www.cooksillustrated.com
- Key in code 70613 for our **Illustrated Guide to Sharpening Knives.**
- Available until January 1, 2007.

How to Grill Onions

Grilled onions usually cook up blackened outside and raw inside. Is there a better way?

> BY ELIZABETH GERMAIN <

Grilling onions is risky business. The rings have a tendency to slip through the grate, land on the hot coals, and go up in flames. Or they resist the pull of gravity and simply burn and blacken right where they are. They're almost always unevenly cooked: raw on the inside, leathery on the outside. And, inevitably, they're hard to manage on the grill—it's a process akin to herding cats.

My first thought was to start with a bit of precooking, but that seemed fussy. I tried grilling onions whole, halved, and quartered to keep them from falling through the grate, but with pieces this large, the outer layers tended to burn before the interiors finished cooking. And none offered an ideal level of caramelized exterior. Concluding that slices were the logical cut (they exposed the greatest surface area), I eventually chose a generous half-inch slice.

Hot fires incinerated the onions, and medium-hot fires often resulted in burned rings. Moderate heat was the best way to produce a gently caramelized exterior. I placed a foil pan over the onions to keep them surrounded by heat.

To stop the rings from plunging through the grate, I tried metal baskets, without much luck, but skewers proved key. (For the results of our skewer tests, see page 9.) To flip the skewers, I soon learned to ignore the rounded "handles," which let the slices spin. More effective was to grasp the centermost onion slice with tongs.

Does any onion variety work for grilling? Yes and no. Sweet, mild Vidalia onions have such a high water content that they came out gummy and insipid when grilled. Regular yellow and white onions have more bite, which mellowed after a stint over the hot coals, and red onions earned extra points for looks. But our surprise favorite was Spanish onions, which won over tasters with their meaty texture and "deep, complex" flavor profile.

CHARCOAL-GRILLED ONIONS
SERVES 4

A two-level fire in a charcoal grill allows you to cook an entree over the hotter side while grilling the onions over the cooler side. Serve unadorned or use in one of the recipes that follow.

2   large Spanish onions (about 2 pounds),
      cut crosswise into 1/2-inch rounds
3   tablespoons olive oil
      Kosher salt and ground black pepper
      Large disposable aluminum baking pan

1. Thread onions onto metal skewers; place on baking sheet and brush each side with oil. Season each side generously with salt and pepper.

2. Light large chimney starter filled with charcoal (6 quarts, or about 100 briquettes) and let burn until coals are fully ignited and partially covered with thin layer of ash, about 20 minutes. Empty coals into grill; build two-level fire by stacking two-thirds of coals in one half of grill and arranging remaining coals in single layer in other half. Place grill grate over coals, cover grill, and heat until grate is hot, about 5 minutes; scrape grate clean with grill brush. Place onions over cooler side of grill and cover with aluminum pan.

3. Grill onions, covered, until onion rounds are deep golden brown and just tender, 15 to 20 minutes, checking onions every 5 minutes and flipping and rotating skewers as needed to ensure even cooking. Transfer onions to platter and remove skewers; discard any outer charred rings. Serve hot, warm, or at room temperature.

GAS-GRILLED ONIONS

Heat grill with lid down and all burners set to high until very hot, about 15 minutes. Lower heat to medium and place onions on grill. Continue with step 3 of recipe for Charcoal-Grilled Onions, omitting disposable aluminum pan and keeping grill lid down except when checking onions.

SWEET AND SOUR GRILLED ONION RELISH WITH PARSLEY AND OLIVES
MAKES 4 CUPS

This relish makes a good accompaniment to grilled tuna.

Whisk together 2 tablespoons red wine vinegar, 2 tablespoons extra-virgin olive oil, 1 teaspoon sugar, and salt and pepper to taste in small bowl; set aside. Place 1 recipe Grilled Onions, cooled and chopped into 1/2-inch pieces, in medium bowl, along with 1 cup pitted and chopped kalamata olives, 1/2 cup raisins, 1/2 cup chopped fresh parsley, dressing, and additional salt and pepper to taste; stir to combine. Serve.

GRILLED ONION RELISH WITH ROQUEFORT AND WALNUTS
MAKES 4 CUPS

Serve this relish with grilled beef.

Whisk together 1 tablespoon balsamic vinegar, 1 tablespoon extra-virgin olive oil, and salt and pepper to taste in small bowl; set aside. Place 1 recipe Grilled Onions, cooled and chopped into 1/2-inch pieces, in medium bowl along with 6 ounces crumbled Roquefort cheese, 3/4 cup roughly chopped toasted walnuts, 1/4 cup chopped chives, dressing, and additional salt and pepper to taste; stir to combine. Serve immediately.

COOK'S extra
Go to www.cooksillustrated.com
• Key in code 7068 for our recipe for **Grilled Onion, Tomato, and Arugula Salad**.
• Recipe available until January 1, 2007.

Tips for Keeping Grilled Onions at Bay

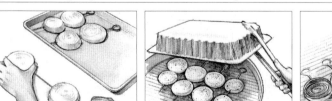

SAFETY LINE
You don't get credit for onions that plunge through the grates to an incendiary demise. Skewers keep the rings out of harm's way.

INSIDE JOB
Covering the onions with a foil pan creates an oven effect that cooks the interiors faster. (For gas grills, just use the lid.)

OFF THE HANDLE
It's awkward to flip a skewer by the rounded "handle." Instead, grasp a centrally located onion slice with tongs and gently turn it over.

Better Pasta Salad with Pesto

At its best, pesto is fresh, green, and full of herbal flavor. Could it stay that way even when added to an American pasta salad?

⇒ BY SANDRA WU ⇐

More light and refreshing than a cream-based sauce or a chunky ragù, pesto makes a top-notch accompaniment to pasta during the sultry summer months. There's nothing complicated about this uncooked Ligurian sauce, which consists of processed fresh basil, garlic, pine nuts, Parmigiano-Reggiano cheese, and olive oil. And tossing it with hot, just-cooked pasta couldn't be easier. But numerous issues arise once pesto is added to a pasta salad. The refrigerator dulls the color and flavor of the pesto, which turns greasy and clumpy as the pasta cools.

Perfecting the Pesto

I began by trying varying ratios of the five integral ingredients: basil, garlic (blanched briefly to tame its harsh bite), Parmesan cheese, olive oil (extra-virgin), and pine nuts (toasted to enhance their nutty flavor). I found that I had to use a lot of basil (between 3 and 4 packed cups) to achieve decent herbal flavor and the bulk needed for the pesto to cling to the pasta. But when made even a few hours ahead of time, the basil turned dark, muddy, and much less sprightly. Adding another green element seemed the obvious solution. Parsley is a common trick, but I needed to use so much that it began to compete with the basil flavor. I'd seen frozen chopped spinach used in one recipe. While it turned the pesto a nice, bright shade of green, it also made the texture stringy. The easy solution was to add a small amount of fresh baby spinach (1 cup added to 3 cups of basil), which provided a lovely bright green color

Two Secrets to Better Pesto Pasta Salad

It's not hard to make a pesto pasta salad taste good. To get the appearance and texture to live up to the vibrant flavors, we came up with two easy tricks.

BRIGHT COLOR
Supplementing the basil with baby spinach helped maintain the pesto's bright green color.

CREAMY TEXTURE
Adding a touch of mayonnaise turned the too-slick pesto creamy and cohesive.

and smooth texture without interfering with the basil flavor.

While the relatively thin consistency of traditional pesto might be fine for hot noodles, a thicker, creamier pesto was in order for room-temperature pasta. But no matter how much I fiddled with ingredient amounts, the pesto was always less than optimally creamy. Upping the quantity of cheese and pine nuts thickened the pesto, but these additions also made it salty, gritty, and pasty. Adding more oil to smooth out the mixture only made the pesto greasy.

Since this dish wasn't exactly an Italian classic, I decided to borrow a standard ingredient used in many American pasta salads: mayonnaise. The creamy, tangy condiment served as the perfect binder—so long as it was used in moderation. Six tablespoons was enough to provide a creamy, luscious texture.

Preparing the Pasta

The best pasta shapes for this dish have a textured surface with a concave nook or two that can trap the pesto and keep it from sliding off. With its stubby form, indented center, and jagged edges, farfalle made an excellent partner. Unlike hot pasta, which should generally be cooked until al dente, the pasta used in salads should cook slightly longer, until tender. (For tips on judging when shaped pasta is done, see Kitchen Notes, page 31.)

When the pesto was added straight to just-cooked pasta, it took an hour to reach room temperature. The hot pasta also "cooked" the basil, deadening its impact. Rinsing the pasta in cold water cooled it down quickly but made the surface of the pasta too slick to hold on to the pesto. The solution was to let the pasta cool in a single layer on a rimmed baking sheet, tossing in a splash of oil to prevent sticking.

All my pasta salad needed was some final flavor tweaking. Lemon juice cut through the richness, and an extra ½ cup of toasted pine nuts folded into the pesto-coated pasta added a sweet, nutty note as well as textural contrast. A pint of quartered cherry tomatoes or halved grape tomatoes contributed color and small bursts of freshness. Finally, I had translated a Ligurian mainstay into an American picnic classic.

PASTA SALAD WITH PESTO
SERVES 8 TO 10 AS A SIDE DISH

This salad is best served the day it is made; if it's been refrigerated, bring it to room temperature before serving. The pesto can be made a day ahead—just cook the garlic cloves in a small saucepan of boiling water for 1 minute. Garnish with additional shaved or grated Parmesan.

- ¾   cup pine nuts
- 2   medium garlic cloves, unpeeled
-     Table salt
- 1   pound farfalle (bow ties) pasta
- ¼   cup plus 1 tablespoon extra-virgin olive oil
- 3   cups packed fresh basil leaves (about 4 ounces)
- 1   cup packed baby spinach (about 1 ounce)
- ½   teaspoon ground black pepper
- 2   tablespoons juice from 1 lemon
- 1½   ounces Parmesan cheese, finely grated (about ¾ cup), plus extra for serving
- 6   tablespoons mayonnaise
- 1   pint cherry tomatoes, quartered, or grape tomatoes, halved (optional)

1. Bring 4 quarts water to rolling boil in large pot. Toast pine nuts in small dry skillet over medium heat, shaking pan occasionally, until just golden and fragrant, 4 to 5 minutes.

2. When water is boiling, add garlic and let cook 1 minute. Remove garlic with slotted spoon and rinse under cold water to stop cooking; set aside to cool. Add 1 tablespoon salt and pasta to water, stir to separate, and cook until tender (just past al dente). Reserve ¼ cup cooking water, drain pasta, toss with 1 tablespoon oil, spread in single layer on rimmed baking sheet, and cool to room temperature, about 30 minutes.

3. When garlic is cool, peel and mince or press through garlic press. Place ¼ cup nuts, garlic, basil, spinach, pepper, lemon juice, remaining ¼ cup oil, and 1 teaspoon salt in bowl of food processor and process until smooth, scraping sides of bowl as necessary. Add cheese and mayonnaise and process until thoroughly combined. Transfer mixture to large serving bowl. Cover and refrigerate until ready to assemble salad.

4. When pasta is cool, toss with pesto, adding reserved pasta water, 1 tablespoon at a time, until pesto evenly coats pasta. Fold in remaining ½ cup nuts and tomatoes (if using); serve.

Well-Done Burgers Done Well

These days, many backyard cooks prefer grilling burgers to medium-well and beyond.
But does well-done have to mean overdone?

⇒ BY MATTHEW CARD ⇐

As much as the test kitchen respects the U.S. Department of Agriculture, you won't catch us buying their cookbooks. While recipes like Parchingly Dry Pork Chops (cooked to the USDA's suggested 170 degrees) and No-Pink Porterhouse (also 170 degrees) may be appealing options for the squeamish, *Cook's* generally errs on the side of great taste, great texture, and common sense.

When it comes to hamburgers, however, we've become a little less cavalier. Given the real food-safety issues surrounding ground beef (bacteria on the exterior of a cut of beef get mixed in during grinding), we recognize that many backyard cooks (and test cooks) grill their burgers to medium-well and beyond—especially when kids are around. At the very least, it's a recipe one needs in the repertoire. What I wasn't willing to accept is the usual outcome of cooking ground beef beyond medium: tough, desiccated hockey pucks with diminished beefy flavor. Could I make them better?

By packing these burgers with an unexpected ingredient, we kept them moist and ultra-juicy even when cooked till well-done.

Here's the Beef

From the outset, I decided that this recipe should work with supermarket ground beef—nothing fancy. But which type was best? Supermarkets sell beef according to the ratio of lean meat to fat, the three most common categories being 80 percent lean (usually from the chuck, or front shoulder), 85 percent (usually from the round, or hind legs), and 90 percent (usually from the sirloin). I assumed that the fattier 80 percent lean chuck would be tasters' favorite, and a quick test confirmed it. The well-done chuck burgers were noticeably moister than the inedible versions made from the leaner sirloin.

Well, an "edible" well-done burger was a start. I wondered if adding more fat to the mix might help matters, so I prepared patties with chunks of butter, bacon fat, whole milk ricotta, and Boursin cheese added in. While each ingredient proved interesting, most of the burgers tasted too rich or

distinctly flavored—and the moisture factor was hardly affected. (However, the one made with bacon fat was such a hit that I kept it as a variation; see Cook's Extra, below.)

Down in Flames

I had always grilled my medium-rare burgers over the hottest fire I could muster, the goal being to sear the exterior quickly before the interior overcooked. Did a well-done burger call for a different strategy? Several tests later, I had mixed results. A moderate fire rendered a slightly juicier, more tender burger, but it lacked a flavorful sear. I might as well have baked it in the oven.

I tried all manner of multistep methods and multilevel fires, but no combination yielded a well-done burger that was both grill marked and juicy. I was unwilling to surrender either one.

Back at the drawing board, I decided to bone up on burger physics. Turns out the reason a medium-well or well-done hamburger becomes dry and tough is fairly simple. Collagen, a protein in muscle fiber, seizes when heated beyond 130 degrees

(about medium-rare) and squeezes the meat tissue, causing it to expel its juices. (Think of wringing the water out of a wet towel.) By the time the burger is well-done (about 160 degrees), it's as dry as the bun on which it's served.

Was there any way to stem this moisture loss? With poultry and pork, the solution is brining (soaking the meat in salted water), which adds both moisture and moisture-retaining salt to the interior. But that trick doesn't work well with beef: The muscle fibers turn to mush—an effect that's multiplied with already-ground beef.

If I couldn't force the meat to retain moisture, perhaps I could pack the patties with something better-suited to the task. That's when I (finally) began to think outside the box. After all, there were recipes in the test kitchen's archives that had already solved this very problem: meat loaf and meatballs, both of which include a panade, a paste made from bread and milk, to keep the ground beef from drying out. I tried mashing a slice of bread in a little milk to a stiff paste and folded it into the beef. Once grilled, these burgers were the best yet.

In my research, I'd seen all manner of flavorings added to burgers: mustard, Worcestershire sauce, garlic, onion soup mix, steak sauce, even applesauce. After sampling most of the possibilities (leaving the applesauce an unknown), tasters most liked the punch of minced garlic and the subtle tang of steak sauce, which contributed a deep, meaty flavor.

My last problem, more cosmetic than functional, was the burger's shape. As it cooked, it went through a transformation from flat puck to puffed-out semisphere. The fix was easy. Previous test kitchen efforts had found that if you make a

A Half-Ounce of Prevention . . .

Our quest for a juicy well-done burger ended when we hit upon a surprisingly effective addition—a bread-and-milk paste (or *panade*). A panade prevented the burger on the left from becoming dense and dried out, like the one on the right.

PHOTOGRAPHY: CARL TREMBLAY

depression in the center of the patty, it will puff slightly as it cooks and level out to form a flat top. Nicely grill marked and moist as could be, this well-done burger was finally well done.

WELL-DONE HAMBURGERS ON A CHARCOAL GRILL
SERVES 4

Adding bread and milk to the beef creates burgers that are juicy and tender even when well-done. (In fact, we recommend this method only for burgers that will be cooked to medium-well or well-done; see Cook's Extra, page 20, for our recipe for medium and medium-rare burgers.) For cheeseburgers, follow the optional instructions below. (See our tastings of presliced cheddar cheese below and presliced American cheese on page 30.)

1	large slice good-quality white sandwich bread, crust removed and discarded, bread chopped into ¼-inch pieces (about ½ cup)
2	tablespoons whole milk
¾	teaspoon table salt
¾	teaspoon ground black pepper
1	medium garlic clove, minced or pressed through garlic press (about 1 teaspoon)
2	teaspoons steak sauce, such as A-1
1½	pounds 80 percent lean ground chuck Vegetable oil for cooking grate
6	ounces sliced cheese, optional (see note above)
4	rolls or buns

1. Using large chimney starter, ignite 6 quarts charcoal (about 100 briquettes) and burn until covered with thin coating of light gray ash, about 20 minutes. Empty coals into grill; build modified two-level fire by arranging coals to cover half of grill. Position cooking grate over coals, cover grill, and heat grate for 5 minutes; scrape grate clean with grill brush. Grill is ready when coals are medium-hot (you can hold your hand 2 inches above grate for 3 to 4 seconds).

2. Meanwhile, mash bread and milk in large bowl with fork until homogeneous (you should have about ¼ cup). Stir in salt, pepper, garlic, and steak sauce.

3. Break up beef into small pieces over bread mixture. Using fork or hands, lightly mix together until mixture forms cohesive mass. Divide meat into 4 equal portions. Gently toss one portion of meat back and forth between hands to form loose ball. Gently flatten into ¾-inch-thick patty that measures about 4½ inches in diameter. Press center of patty down with fingertips until it is about ½ inch thick, creating slight depression in each patty. Repeat with remaining portions of meat.

4. Lightly dip wad of paper towels in oil; holding wad with tongs, wipe cooking grate. Grill burgers on hot side of grill, uncovered, until well seared on first side, 2 to 4 minutes. Using wide metal spatula, flip burgers and continue grilling, about 3 minutes for medium-well or 4 minutes for well-done. (Add cheese, if using, about 2 minutes before reaching desired doneness, covering burgers with disposable aluminum pan to melt cheese.)

Best Hamburger Buns

In a tasting of supermarket hamburger buns, we were surprised by the differences in flavor and texture. Sunbeam and Wonder were so airy that they all but deflated if grasped too indelicately, while heartier brands stood up well to wet condiments. But the dealbreaker was size: Of eight products, six measured less than 3½ inches across—a tight fit for most patties. Our favorite, Pepperidge Farm Premium Bakery Rolls (not the smaller "Classic" variety), had a generous 4½-inch diameter, hearty texture, "wheaty" taste, and the least amount of sugar in the lineup.—G.C.

While burgers grill, toast buns on cooler side of grill. Serve on buns with desired toppings.

WELL-DONE HAMBURGERS ON A GAS GRILL

Turn all burners to high, close lid, and heat until very hot, about 15 minutes. Use grill brush to scrape cooking grate clean. Lightly dip wad of paper towels in oil; holding wad with tongs, wipe cooking grate. Leave primary burner on high, turn other burner(s) to low. Follow recipe for Well-Done Hamburgers on a Charcoal Grill from step 2, grilling patties with lid down.

TASTING: **Presliced Cheddar Cheese**

Tangy, salty cheddar is the test kitchen's favorite cheese for topping a hamburger. Beckoned by the ease and convenience of presliced cheese, we rounded up nine packages from the supermarket dairy case. Whether tasted straight up, in grilled-cheese sandwiches, or on burgers, the "sharp" cheddars carried the day over their "mild" and "medium" counterparts. Aged for at least nine months, sharp cheddar cheese has a strong, tangy flavor that tasters preferred in every application. Mild and medium cheddars—aged for days rather than months—tasted more like mild Monterey Jack.

The biggest surprise came when tasters sampled two cheeses from Kraft that tasted nothing like the others. Prominently labeled "sharp cheddar," these two products were actually "pasteurized process cheese" loaded with added moisture and emulsifiers to make for smoother melting—a process identical to that used to make American cheese. The label simply refers to the intended flavor, but our tasters found nothing sharp about them, ranking them lowest in every round. Cheeses are listed in order of preference, from left to right. –Garth Clingingsmith

RECOMMENDED

TILLAMOOK Sharp Cheddar
Deemed the "cheddariest" by tasters, with a classic, slightly crumbly texture.

CABOT All Natural Sharp Cheddar
"Hearty," almost chewy texture was a nice foil for our burgers, as was the "great salty tang."

CRACKER BARREL Natural Sharp Cheddar
Lacked the tang of the Tillamook and Cabot but was much creamier.

RECOMMENDED WITH RESERVATIONS

SARGENTO Deli Style Medium Cheddar
Fullest flavor of the milder cheeses; "kid-friendly cheddar."

CABOT All Natural Mild Cheddar
A dead ringer for Monterey Jack cheese. Some found it "bland and rubbery."

TILLAMOOK Medium Cheddar
"Super-milky" but bland, with muted cheddar flavor.

HORIZON Organic Cheddar
"Bland-ola," said one taster. The mildest cheese in the lineup reminded tasters of many cheeses—but not cheddar.

KRAFT Deli Deluxe Sharp Cheddar
This processed cheese's waxy texture "sticks to your teeth," with an "oddly sweet" flavor.

KRAFT 2% Milk Singles Sharp Cheddar
As one taster summed up the taste of this processed cheese, "more Velveeta than cheddar."

The Best Key Lime Bars

Our first cracks at transforming Key lime pie into a cookie left us with a thick, dry crust— and too much lime on our hands. We wanted to raise the bar.

≥ BY DAWN YANAGIHARA ≤

Key lime pie is a brilliant pairing of rich and refreshing, sweet and tart, all in a buttery, crisp crumb crust. But what this classic dessert offers in elegance and simplicity it lacks in portability: I wanted a Key lime *bar*—all the appealing qualities of Key lime pie but without the need for a fork. I was an A-student in geometry, so making a round pie into square cookies shouldn't be too hard, right?

To get my footing, I started out with two recipes: one for Key lime bars made with cream cheese (typical of many recipes), the other for Key lime pie. The bars with cream cheese were heavy and dense, like a lime cheesecake. (Not quite what I had in mind.) As for the pie, I transformed it into bars by baking it in a square baking dish. Naturally, they set the flavor standard, but for a cookie, the filling was too soft and supple, the crust too thick, dry, and crumbly. Clearly, some fine-tuning would be required to get this transformation to come out right.

A sprinkling of lightly toasted coconut completes the balancing act of tart and creamy, soft and crispy, that defines great Key lime bars.

and, more often than not, eggs. I already knew that the *Cook's* Key lime pie filling didn't have a texture firm enough for bar cookies, but I was determined to make it work with some minor retooling. Leaving the condensed milk and lime juice in place, I tried everything that I thought might set the texture. The filling called for four egg yolks; I decreased the yolks, I added more, I omitted the yolks altogether. I tried whole eggs, no eggs, then a few egg whites, then several whites. That soft, pudding-like texture seemed inescapable. Next, I reached for the flour canister, thinking that some starch might help set things up. What the filling then had was a pasty, granular texture.

I took a moment to regroup. Then came the epiphany. I recalled the cheesecake lime bars that I'd made at the outset. The filling had neither eggs nor starch, yet it was sturdy—rigid, even. I made batches of lime bars with 8, 6, and 4 ounces of cream cheese incorporated into the filling. These were all thick and gluey, but I was onto something. I took the cream cheese down to 3, then 2 ounces. And there they were: lime bars with a firm, creamy, rich, finger-food-friendly filling.

One whole 14-ounce can of sweetened condensed milk provided all the sweetness the filling needed. I tried various amounts of lime juice, but ½ cup was best. It was enough to make the lime flavor sparkle without scaring away those with low tartness thresholds (like myself) and without thinning the filling. Concerning lime juice, fresh-squeezed Key lime juice, with its heady fragrance and pleasant acidity, was the favorite by a narrow margin; still, regular fresh lime juice held its own,

Animal Instinct

First things first: the crust. A graham cracker crust is traditional for a Key lime pie, so it was the obvious choice. But I was not enamored of the graham crust. Its flavor was too assertive (especially given the amount I needed to make a bar I could hold in my hand), and it didn't really complement the filling. I swapped in animal cracker crumbs, the test kitchen's crust of choice for coconut cream pie. Their more neutral flavor placed the lime flavor squarely in the limelight.

Whereas a pie crust can be tender and delicate, the crust for the bars needed sturdiness; this

meant increasing the butter, but not so much that the crust would become greasy. Brown sugar outdid granulated because it gave the crust a slightly richer, rounder flavor. As with all crumb crusts, this one required prebaking to firm it up, and 325 degrees proved the best temperature for producing an evenly browned crust.

Pie in the Sky?

With the crust firmly in place, I focused on the filling. Key lime pie filling is an easy mixture of sweetened condensed milk, lime juice, lime zest,

SCIENCE: **The 'Magic' of Sweetened Condensed Milk**

These days, convenience food products are everywhere, but the trend is hardly new. Back in 1856, American home cooks began taking advantage of sweetened condensed milk, a shelf-stable dairy product based on discoveries made centuries earlier by cooks in India and Latin America. Packed with calories and nutrients, this "magical" product has been credited with everything from reducing the infant mortality rate to nourishing Civil War soldiers. But today it's mostly about dessert-making convenience: Instead of reducing milk and sugar, you can just pop open a can—and there's no expiration date.

Sweetened condensed milk is made commercially by flash-heating fresh milk and evaporating it, using a specialized vacuum

drier (that's the "condensed" part). Once granulated sugar is added, the preservation process begins. The water-hungry granulated sugar and the natural sugar in the milk (lactose) pull in moisture from bacteria, killing them off in the process. The result is milk thickened to a gooey syrup—an ideal consistency for many desserts.

In our Key lime bar recipe, sweetened condensed milk offers an additional advantage: it keeps the filling from curdling. Curdling occurs when an acid (like lime juice) comes in contact with milk's protein strands and causes them to unwind and become entangled. In sweetened condensed milk, the sugar molecules coat these protein strands, which keeps them from entangling. If we'd used fresh milk instead, the creamy texture of the filling would have been compromised. –Elizabeth Bomze

PHOTOGRAPHY: CARL TREMBLAY

favored by some for standing up to the buttery crust and rich, creamy filling. A tablespoon of grated lime zest added lime essence; I minced it to keep its texture from being an annoyance. As for mixing the filling, it was easily accomplished by hand.

Some bar recipes include some sort of streusel or crunchy topping. A streusel didn't make sense, but I took a cue from the tropics and experimented with a toasted-coconut topping, which added a subtle textural contrast and more depth of flavor. The test kitchen was split over whether this topping was an improvement, so I left it optional. Finally, I had distilled the essence of a billowy slice of Key lime pie into a tidy, portable bar. Who said it's not cool to be square?

KEY LIME BARS
MAKES SIXTEEN 2-INCH BARS

If you cannot find fresh Key limes, use regular (Persian) limes. Do not use bottled lime juice. Grate the zest from the limes before juicing them, avoiding the bitter white pith that lies just beneath the outermost skin. The optional coconut garnish adds textural interest and tames the lime flavor for those who find it too intense. The recipe can be doubled and baked in a 13-by 9-inch baking pan; you will need a double layer of extra-wide foil for the pan (each sheet about 20 inches in length) and should increase the baking times by a minute or two.

Crust
- 5 ounces animal crackers
- 3 tablespoons packed light or dark brown sugar
  Pinch table salt
- 4 tablespoons unsalted butter, melted and cooled slightly

Filling
- 2 ounces cream cheese, room temperature
- I tablespoon grated lime zest, minced
  Pinch table salt
- I can (14 ounces) sweetened condensed milk
- I large egg yolk
- ½ cup Key lime or regular lime juice

Garnish (optional)
- ¾ cup shredded sweetened coconut, toasted until golden and crisp

1. Adjust oven rack to middle position and heat oven to 325 degrees. Cut about 12-inch length extra-wide heavy-duty foil; fold cut edges back to form 7½-inch width. With folded sides facing down, fit foil securely into bottom and up sides of 8-inch-square baking pan, allowing

Go to www.cooksillustrated.com
- Visit our Web site to see **video of a test cook preparing Key Lime Bars.**
- Available until January 1, 2007.

TASTING: **Are Key Limes Really Key?**

As their name suggests, Key limes bars are traditionally made from Key limes—a tiny, yellowish variety that grows only in tropical locales (like the Florida Keys, from which they got their name). Key lime aficionados herald the fruit's "distinctive" flavor and fragrance compared with conventional Persian limes, but we wondered if our tasters could tell the difference in a blind taste test.

Sampled plain, the Key lime juice tasted slightly less tart and bracing than its Persian counterpart, and a quick lab test confirmed that impression (the juice from the conventional limes had a lower pH than the Key lime juice, indicating higher acidity). When we made Key lime bars with both varieties, once again the Persian-lime version tasted a bit more tart, though tasters were split over which variety made the better bar. The deciding factor may be the amount of work involved: To get the half cup of lime juice called for in our bar recipe, we had to squeeze three Persian limes. With the Key limes, it took almost 20!

Both Key lime juice and regular lime juice are sold presqueezed in shelf-stable bottles, and we wondered whether these would do in a pinch. The short answer? No way. The four brands we tried were at best "bracingly bitter," and, in some cases, "just plain rancid." What's more, many baking recipes (including ours) call for the addition of zest—a tough proposition with a glass bottle. –Garth Clingingsmith

KEY LIMES
Subtle tartness, skimpy yield

REGULAR LIMES
Bracing tartness, generous yield

BOTTLED CONCENTRATE
Convenience at a bitter price

---

excess to overhang pan sides. Spray foil with non-stick cooking spray.

2. **TO MAKE THE CRUST:** In workbowl of food processor, pulse animal crackers until broken down, about ten 1-second pulses; process crumbs until evenly fine, about 10 seconds (you should have about 1¼ cups crumbs). Add brown sugar and salt; process to combine, ten to twelve 1-second pulses (if large sugar lumps remain, break them apart with fingers). Drizzle butter over crumbs and pulse until crumbs are evenly moistened with butter, about ten 1-second pulses. Press crumbs evenly and firmly into bottom of prepared pan. Bake until deep golden brown, 18 to 20 minutes. Cool on wire rack while making filling. Do not turn off oven.

3. **TO MAKE THE FILLING:** While crust cools, in medium bowl, stir cream cheese, zest, and salt with rubber spatula until softened, creamy, and thoroughly combined. Add sweetened condensed milk and whisk vigorously until incorporated and no lumps of cream cheese remain; whisk in egg yolk. Add lime juice and whisk gently until

incorporated (mixture will thicken slightly).

4. **TO ASSEMBLE AND BAKE:** Pour filling into crust; spread to corners and smooth surface with rubber spatula. Bake until set and edges begin to pull away slightly from sides, 15 to 20 minutes. Cool on wire rack to room temperature, 1 to 1½ hours. Cover with foil and refrigerate until thoroughly chilled, at least 2 hours.

5. Loosen edges with paring knife and lift bars from baking pan using foil extensions; cut bars into 16 squares. Sprinkle with toasted coconut, if using, and serve. (Leftovers can be refrigerated up to 2 days; crust will soften slightly. Let bars stand at room temperature about 15 minutes before serving.)

TRIPLE-CITRUS BARS

Follow recipe for Key Lime Bars, using 1½ teaspoons each grated lime zest, lemon zest, and orange zest (mince zest after measuring) and using 6 tablespoons lime juice, 1 tablespoon lemon juice, and 1 tablespoon orange juice.

STEP-BY-STEP | BUILDING KEY LIME BARS

I. Line pan with foil sling, then coat with cooking spray.

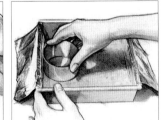

2. Press crumb mixture firmly and evenly into pan.

3. Pour filling into prebaked crust and spread into corners.

Improving Peach Crumble

Soggy topping and flavorless filling are the norm for this simple dessert. How do you make the crumble crisp and the peaches actually taste like, well, peaches?

≥ BY MATTHEW CARD ≤

They say first impressions are everything, and in the case of peach crumble and me, that might be true. It was elementary school and there it was: plopped onto my lunch tray, hard against the Salisbury steak, a sticky puddle of mushy fruit buried beneath a gloppy beige crust. Despite my young sweet tooth, I couldn't bring myself even to dip my fork in it, much less risk a bite.

It's not that I don't like peaches; just the contrary: I like them too much to see them so ill-served. In my opinion, peach crumble should consist of fresh-tasting, lightly sweetened peaches topped with a buttery, crisp, nutty-tasting crumble. So where do most recipes go so wrong?

Bottoms Up

There's a fundamental problem with peach crumble: the peaches. Few fruits are as finicky in flavor or texture, and some recipes try to address these problems by adjusting the amounts of sugar and thickener to suit the fruit's ripeness. More Hail Mary than sure thing, this approach worked when I was lucky—but I wasn't lucky very often.

Part of my solution came from a *Cook's* recipe for peach cobbler. The peeled peaches are sliced, tossed with sugar, and allowed to macerate for half an hour, then drained. The sugar draws off a fair amount of surprisingly mild-flavored juice, effectively minimizing the juices and maximizing the peaches' inherent sweetness.

The peaches required no additional sugar after the maceration (though I did add back a little of the sweet "juice," in which I dissolved the thickener), but they did need a little help flavorwise. Warm spices like cinnamon and nutmeg were common in the recipes I found, and tasters approved (of just a pinch of each). Salt helped define the flavors, as did a substantial splash of lemon juice. After a couple batches tasted too tart, I found it best to adjust the lemon juice to the flavor of the peaches.

As for thickener, flour was too starchy-tasting, so I moved on to instant tapioca and cornstarch. Both worked well, but the tapioca's "bouncy" texture proved a strange match for the silky peaches; cornstarch was a better fit. In the end, tasters liked a filling thickened with

Letting the rich, buttery topping spend some time cooking apart from the filling makes their eventual marriage that much stronger.

1¼ teaspoons, which barely bound the juices and gave the fruit a glossy sheen.

Flavor was one thing, texture something altogether different. Baking the filling for any more than 30 minutes at 350 degrees—an absolute minimum for a browned topping—and the peach slices deflated into mush. Thicker pieces (¾-inch wedges) retained a bit more bite and also saved on prep time.

Top Down

Some recipes blend the topping ingredients (butter, flour, sugar, spices) in a food processor, but why haul out equipment if it's not necessary? I added varying amounts of melted butter to different ratios of flour and sugar, but in each batch the texture was surprisingly hard—more gravelly streusel than crispy crumble. No matter how I altered

the ratio of ingredients, the topping was simply too hard. Defeated, I hauled out the food processor and gave up on melted butter.

Softened butter yielded a far softer though still crisp crumble. I found it best to let the processor run uninterrupted until the mixture formed a crumbly mass. (Pulsing failed to combine the dry ingredients with the butter beyond a sandy consistency.) The mixture broke apart easily into dense crumbs of varying size.

Pecans, walnuts, and almonds were all common in the recipes I found, and each had their merits, but tasters most appreciated the mild flavor of the almonds. Close but not quite there, I experimented with spices and flavorings, with little luck. The one standout was vanilla. A splash, processed with the dry ingredients, seemed to boost the topping's flavor magically—like a shot of MSG in a stir-fry.

A Simple Solution

Both filling and topping tasted good, but the topping was still too wet. A crisp top masked a pudgy, dumpling-like underbelly. Any oven temperature lower than 350 degrees took forever (and overcooked the fruit) and anything much above 400 degrees burned the crumble long before the fruit even bubbled (the juices must come to a boil to activate the thickening power of the cornstarch). A two-temperature approach—starting high to crisp the topping and dropping low to cook the fruit through—failed as well.

RECIPE DIAGNOSIS:
Overhauling Ho-Hum Peach Crumble

MACERATE

PROBLEM: Bland peaches
SOLUTION: Macerating the fruit in sugar and draining off excess juices helps to concentrate the peach flavor.

SEPARATE

PROBLEM: Soggy topping
SOLUTION: Baking the topping separately before sliding it onto the fruit filling keeps it crumbly and crisp.

Feeling deflated, I couldn't wrap my head around a way to cook these two incongruous elements together. I had tried everything I could think of, but the fact was that a crumble topping couldn't be cooked on top of steaming fruit and be expected to turn out crunchy and crisp.

But what if I cooked the topping separately and then married it to the filling? I spread the topping on a baking sheet (lined with parchment paper to make the transfer easier) and baked it crisp before showering it over the peaches. I slid the assembled crumble into the oven—on a lower rack, so that the crumble wouldn't over-brown—and cooked it just until the fruit bubbled about the edges. I cracked the crispy crust—now evenly browned top to bottom—and found the fruit firm and the juices perfectly thickened. The extra effort required to parbake the topping was nominal at worst and produced a far, far superior crumble than I had ever tasted.

PEACH CRUMBLE
SERVES 4 TO 6

Add the lemon juice to taste in step 2 according to the sweetness of your peaches. If ripe peaches are unavailable, you can substitute five 10-ounce bags of frozen peaches, thawed overnight in the refrigerator. The topping can be baked ahead of time, as directed in step 3, then cooled and stored in an airtight container. As directed in step 4, sprinkle the topping evenly over the fruit and continue to bake.

TECHNIQUE | TRANSFERRING THE BAKED CRUMBLE

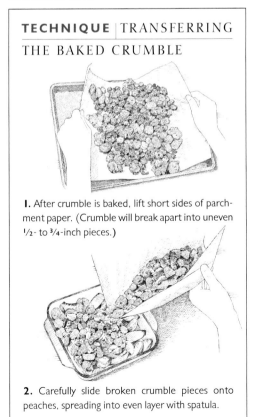

1. After crumble is baked, lift short sides of parchment paper. (Crumble will break apart into uneven ½- to ¾-inch pieces.)

2. Carefully slide broken crumble pieces onto peaches, spreading into even layer with spatula.

Filling

3½	pounds ripe but firm peaches (6 to 7 medium), peeled and pitted; each peach halved and cut into ¾-inch wedges (about 6½ cups prepared peaches)
⅓	cup (2⅓ ounces) granulated sugar
1¼	teaspoons cornstarch
3–5	teaspoons juice from 1 lemon (see note above)
	Pinch table salt
	Pinch ground cinnamon
	Pinch ground nutmeg

Topping

1	cup (5 ounces) unbleached all-purpose flour
¼	cup (1¾ ounces) plus 1 tablespoon granulated sugar
¼	cup (1¾ ounces) packed light or dark brown sugar
⅛	teaspoon table salt
2	teaspoons vanilla extract
6	tablespoons unsalted butter, cut into 6 pieces and very soft
½	cup sliced almonds

1. Adjust oven racks to lower and middle positions; heat oven to 350 degrees.

2. **FOR THE FILLING:** Gently toss peaches and sugar together in large bowl; let stand for 30 minutes, tossing several times. Drain peaches in colander set over large bowl. Whisk ¼ cup drained peach juice, cornstarch, lemon juice, salt, cinnamon, and nutmeg together in small bowl; discard excess peach juice. Toss juice mixture with peaches and transfer to 8-inch-square glass baking dish.

3. **FOR THE TOPPING:** While peaches are macerating, combine flour, sugars (reserving 1 tablespoon granulated sugar), and salt in workbowl of food processor; drizzle vanilla over top. Pulse to combine mixture, about five 1-second pulses. Add butter and half of nuts; process until mixture clumps together into large, crumbly balls, about 30 seconds, pausing halfway through to scrape down sides of workbowl. Sprinkle remaining nuts over mixture and combine with two quick pulses. Transfer mixture to parchment-lined baking sheet and spread into even layer (mixture should break up into roughly ½-inch chunks with some smaller, loose bits). Bake on middle rack until chunks are lightly browned and firm, 18 to 22 minutes.

4. **TO ASSEMBLE AND BAKE:** Grasping edges of parchment paper (following illustrations 1 and 2 at left), slide topping over peaches and spread into even layer with spatula, packing down lightly and breaking up any very large pieces. Sprinkle remaining tablespoon sugar over top and place on lower oven rack. Increase oven temperature to 375 degrees and bake until well browned and fruit is bubbling around edges, 25 to 35 minutes. Cool on wire rack until warm, at least 15 minutes; serve.

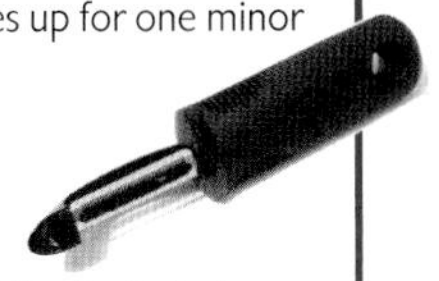

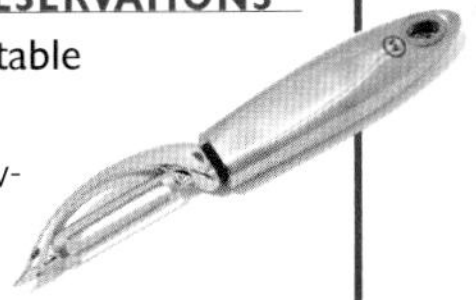

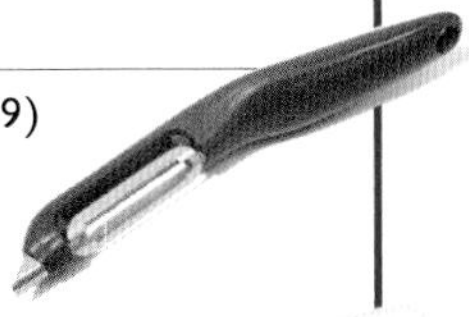

ILLUSTRATION: JOHN BURGOYNE

Is There a New King of Ketchup?

We measured pectin levels, calculated pH, and grabbed our Bostwick consistometer to explain the surprising results of our ketchup taste test.

> BY LEIGH BELANGER

You think you know ketchup. It's red, thick, sweet, salty, and tangy—and you can't imagine a burger and fries without it. And you think you know which brand tastes best. You probably have a bottle of Heinz in your fridge (this one brand accounts for nearly 60 percent of the domestic ketchup market), and it's often the only choice on restaurant tables, from truck-stop diners to four-star steakhouses.

What you probably don't know is that this classic American condiment began in Southeast Asia as a salty sauce made from anchovies. When British explorers first encountered Chinese *ke-tsiap*, Malaysian *kechap*, and Indonesian *ketjap*, the sauce was more like soy sauce or Worcestershire sauce than modern ketchup. Until the 19th century, British and American ketchup was often made from mushrooms, nuts, or fruit.

The first tomato-based ketchups were made from unripe tomatoes and were quite thin. In the late 19th century, H. J. Heinz offered an alternative made with ripe tomatoes, and transformed ketchup into the thick condiment we know today. With sweet, ripe tomatoes as the base for his ketchup, Heinz was able to add enough vinegar to preserve the product naturally. Balanced out with plenty of sweetener, ketchup as we know it was born.

Ketchup hasn't really changed for more than a century, so why run a tasting? Heinz is ketchup and ketchup is Heinz, right? True or not, no one in our test kitchen likes to accept things on face value. So I rounded up eight brands (all avail-

Slow Race Downhill

To measure consistency, we poured each sample into this troughlike device, called a Bostwick consistometer. With stopwatch in hand, we timed each sample as it crept along the trough. Most samples made it to the finish line in one to 2½ minutes, but two overly thick brands took more than eight minutes to travel the length of the trough.

A TOOL FOR GAUGING VISCOSITY

able nationwide and fairly traditional—no spicy mango ketchups allowed) and asked 29 tasters to taste them straight from the bottle (on spoons) and with hot french fries.

My panel had some shocking news for ketchup lovers. According to tasters, there's a better option than Heinz—and it's sitting right there on the shelves of your local supermarket. Hunt's, America's number two ketchup, was the clear winner of our tasting. Although Heinz's new organic ketchup was the runner-up, regular Heinz ketchup finished in the middle of the pack. The king of ketchups was being dethroned, and I wanted an explanation.

Tangy, Salty, and Sweet

As I read through the tasting sheets, I noticed a lot of comments (and complaints) about acidity. My tasters wanted a tangy ketchup, and several brands failed on this count. Since fat and protein (say, in a burger) temper ketchup's acidity, ketchup needs a pronounced tang to avoid tasting dull. Because tanginess was clearly a high priority for tasters, I got out the kitchen's trusty pH meter to test each sample. The three ketchups at the bottom of the ratings (see chart, page 27) were also the least acidic (higher pH translates to lower acidity). My first conclusion: A tangy ketchup is a good ketchup.

Next up on my list of items to examine was sodium. Product labels told the story here. Most brands contain 150 to 190 milligrams of sodium per tablespoon. However, two brands, World's Best and Westbrae, contain far less—just 40 milligrams and 10 milligrams, respectively. These brands landed at the bottom of the ratings. My second conclusion: A salty ketchup is a good ketchup.

Sweetness is another key ketchup trait, and the brands with less sugar fell to the bottom of the ratings. Top-rated Hunt's contains 4 grams of sugar per tablespoon. In contrast, World's Best (which is sweetened with maple syrup rather than the corn syrup and/or high-fructose corn syrup found in most brands) contains a measly gram of sugar per tablespoon. Bottom-dweller Westbrae (sweetened with fruit juice concentrate) contains just 2 grams of sugar per tablespoon. My third conclusion: A sweet ketchup is a good ketchup.

So my tasters wanted their ketchup tangy, salty, and sweet. Given ketchup's use as a condiment, it makes sense that tasters would want more of these key flavor components. But what about tomato flavor? Many of the experts I spoke with agreed that tomato growers are more concerned with the levels of tomato solids, the viscosity of their juice, and their color. After all, ketchup is made from tomato paste, which has been cooked long enough to evaporate most of the natural juices. As anyone who has tasted tomato paste knows, its cooked flavor is intense but not terribly nuanced, a quality more likely to be found in less processed tomato products, such as canned whole tomatoes.

Where did our tasters come out on tomato flavor? While they had much more to say about the above-mentioned acidity, saltiness, and sweetness, there were some complaints about "flat" tomato flavor. We sent the ketchups to a local food laboratory for an analysis of total solids (almost all of which would be tomato solids). Sure enough, the three lowest-rated brands had the lowest solids content, and our winning brand had the highest solids content. My fourth conclusion: A ketchup with more tomatoes is a good ketchup.

Besides providing color and thickness, tomatoes are a source of umami, the savory quality in "meaty" foods such as soy sauce and mushrooms that is related to the presence of the amino acid glutamate. Tomatoes are also a source of bitterness. Thus ketchup triggers all five major taste sensations: sweet, sour, salty, bitter, and umami. And so I reached my final conclusion about good-tasting ketchup: It has all five elements in perfect balance.

In the Thick of Things

Beyond flavor, my tasters were also very picky about consistency. Ketchup has to be thick enough to keep it from turning buns and fries soggy, but it shouldn't be pasty. Pectin is typically ketchup's only thickener.

To evaluate thickness, I sent samples to the lab to have the pectin levels measured. All but one fell within a fairly close range. The outlier, Westbrae, contained about 50 percent more pectin than the rest, and tasters' notes ("ugh, pasty, awful") confirmed that ketchup that's too thick is just plain "gross."

TASTING KETCHUPS

Twenty-nine members of the *Cook's Illustrated* staff tasted the ketchups on spoons and on french fries. The brands are listed below in order of preference. We measured pH in the test kitchen; higher numbers indicate less acidity. A local food laboratory analyzed samples for total solids and total pectin. We used a Bostwick consistometer (see photo on page 26) to rate thickness, measuring the time it took each sample to slide down this device. The longer the time, the thicker the ketchup.

RECOMMENDED

HUNT'S Ketchup
- $1.69 for 24 ounces
- pH: 3.82 solids: 33.76% pectin: 4939 mg/kg
- Bostwick: 2 minutes, 30 seconds

This "cherry red" ketchup scored the highest for both taste and texture and was the overall winner. Tasters praised the "inviting, smooth" texture and "tangy," "fresh" flavor. Some commented that this "well-balanced" sample tasted "exactly as it should."

HEINZ Organic Ketchup
- $1.99 for 15 ounces
- pH: 3.82 solids: 31.7% pectin: 4640 mg/kg
- Bostwick: 1 minute, 50 seconds

Tasters liked the "vinegary tang" of this organic sample. "Color and texture are perfect," wrote one taster. The consistency was praised as "not too heavy," while comments on the taste ranged from "tastes like ball-park ketchup" to "nice sweet/tart balance."

ANNIE'S Naturals Organic Ketchup
- $3.69 for 24 ounces
- pH: 3.81 solids: 32.43% pectin: 4696 mg/kg
- Bostwick: 56 seconds

This ketchup (sweetened with sugar rather than the usual corn syrup) received solid scores for taste, texture, and color. Tasters liked the "rich, hearty, and tangy flavor," but while some found it to have "just the perfect balance," others detected "odd smoky" notes. For texture, it was "not perfectly smooth but good."

RECOMMENDED WITH RESERVATIONS

DEL MONTE Ketchup
- $1.39 for 24 ounces
- pH: 3.65 solids: 32.12% pectin: 4966 mg/kg
- Bostwick: 1 minute, 10 seconds

Tasters were neither thrilled nor offended by this ketchup, giving it average marks in all categories. One taster called it "nothing out of the ordinary," while another said, "a little sweet but no big deal." Others described it as "a little watery," "a little sour," and "a little cooked."

RECOMMENDED WITH RESERVATIONS (cont.)

HEINZ Ketchup
- $1.69 for 24 ounces
- pH: 3.84 solids: 32.54% pectin: 4875 mg/kg
- Bostwick: 50 seconds

The standard bearer fell to the middle of the pack in our taste tests, losing points for being "bland" and "too sweet." Tasters were more positive about its "fry-dipping texture" and "smooth," "thick" consistency. Overall assessment: "unremarkable."

MUIR GLEN Organic Ketchup
- $3.49 for 24 ounces
- pH: 4.01 solids: 29.93% pectin: 3978 mg/kg
- Bostwick: 10 minutes, 4 seconds

Tasters who liked "untraditional" ketchup singled out Muir Glen for its "nice texture," but others found the texture "too pasty" and "way too thick." While some were put off by the abundance of "warm, cinnamon" spices, others enjoyed the "pleasant" flavor and said it "goes great with fries."

NOT RECOMMENDED

WORLD'S BEST Ketchup
- $2.99 for 10 ounces
- pH: 4.29 solids: 19.46% pectin: 4347 mg/kg
- Bostwick: 1 minute

The most "un-ketchup-like ketchup" in our tasting. Its "chunky" texture made one taster ask, "Did I just wander into the salsa tasting?" Many said it was "too sweet," and our pH test showed that it was the least acidic ketchup in the lineup.

WESTBRAE NATURAL
Fruit Sweetened Ketchup
- $2.39 for 14 ounces
- pH: 4.15 solids: 25.92% pectin: 7210 mg/kg
- Bostwick: 8 minutes, 9 seconds

This brand, sweetened with fruit juice concentrate, provoked strong negative comments. "No, no, no!" wrote one taster. Another described it as a "molasses and tomato train wreck." While many compared it to "bland" tomato paste, others found it "sour" and "too vinegary." One taster simply asked, "Why?"

But while pectin may be the only thickener in ketchup, it's not the only thing that can affect consistency. The amount of tomato solids and the presence of calcium (often added during the processing of tomato products) also play a role. Determined to quantify the thickness of each brand, I hit upon a promising lead when a source mentioned that the thickness of ketchup is actually regulated by the federal government. In fact, there's a tool used to measure consistency in ketchup (and other products), and I was able to borrow it from the food lab. Called a Bostwick consistometer (see photo on page 26), this stainless steel trough is marked with centimeters and measures the viscosity of foods. The federal regulation calls for ketchup to flow no more than 10 centimeters in 30 seconds at room temperature while the Bostwick is level on a flat surface.

Maybe government experts have all day, but I don't. Because none of the ketchups budged when the Bostwick was placed on a level surface, I decided to differentiate the "sort of" thick ketchups from the really thick ones by setting the consistometer at 28 degrees (so the ketchups would flow more quickly) and then timed each sample to see how long it took to travel 24 centimeters—the entire length of the trough. Most of the ketchups took between one and 2½ minutes to traverse the trough, but Muir Glen and Westbrae were noticeably slower, taking about 10 and eight minutes, respectively. Yes, ketchup should flow slowly, but there is such as thing as too thick and too slow.

A Better Balance

Ketchup is best when it's smooth, thick, and tangy, with balanced, bold flavors. The parameters are tight—not too thick or too thin, not too tangy or too sweet. Bright red but no chunks. Brands that deviated from this formula, such as World's Best and Westbrae, fell to the bottom of the rankings. They failed to meet tasters' expectations for this condiment we've all enjoyed since childhood.

The remaining brands might look alike, but our tasters noted some significant flavor differences. None were unacceptable, but Hunt's possessed a balance of sweet, sour, salty, bitter, and umami flavors that stood out among the pack. We now have a new brand of ketchup in the test kitchen.

Sizing Up Souped-Up Blenders

Have fancy features (and hefty price tags) finally made blenders an essential kitchen tool?

⇒ BY SCOTT KATHAN ⇐

In the test kitchen, our food processors are grinding, shredding, kneading, chopping, and mixing for several hours each day. In contrast, the test kitchen's blenders are apt to sit idle for days on end. We can't imagine pureeing soups, making smoothies, or whipping up an after-hours margarita without a blender, but the harsh reality is that the blender is slowly going the way of the hot-air popcorn popper.

Since blenders tend to collect their fair share of dust on the countertop, in the past we've recommended sturdy but reasonably priced models. A year ago, editors at our sister publication, *Cook's Country,* tested nine blenders priced at $50 or less and proclaimed the Braun PowerMax ($50) the champ—it is a great blender for the money.

But have we been too quick to dismiss blenders? We've recently noticed an increasing number of beautiful, high-end models in the marketplace, with newfangled blade and bowl designs, built-in timers, huge capacities, enhanced blades, and huge power ratings that promise to turn ice into snow in seconds, make peanut butter from whole nuts, pulverize spices, and grind entire bags of coffee. If one blender could do all this, maybe we'd be willing to take blenders more seriously and shell out some serious bucks for an upgrade. To give blenders their fair shake, we rounded up eight models, ranging in price from $100 to $399, and headed into the test kitchen.

A Chilling Discovery

Any testing of blenders has to begin with crushing ice and/or making frozen drinks, two tasks that food processors simply cannot perform. We filled each blender jar with 15 ice cubes and ran five 1-second pulses. We were shocked that only

two of these reportedly powerful and expensive blenders, the L'Equip and the Jenn-Air Attrezzi, produced a fine, chunk-free snow. To be fair, some models, like the Emerilware, instruct that crushing ice takes more than 60 seconds, but who wants to endure that much noise? After 15 seconds, the Emerilware and both Waring blenders still had several whole cubes of unprocessed ice, while the L'Equip and Jenn-Air models produced powder we'd be happy to ski on.

Making smoothies is another test that involves crushing frozen matter—this time, frozen mango chunks—along with fresh banana, orange juice, and yogurt. Fearing (after the ice-crushing test) that these pricey blenders were flashy but inadequate, we were relieved when four of them (L'Equip, Waring MegaMix, KitchenAid, and Vita-Mix) aced this test in less than the allotted 30 seconds. Oddly, the Jenn-Air Attrezzi—one of the two best ice crushers—was the only blender to fail this test, leaving behind large chunks of frozen mango and swirls of unblended yogurt.

Pureeing a simple soup of broccoli, onion, and broth was the last core test. Blenders outperform food processors when pureeing liquids for two reasons. First, a blender's four blades are arranged in multiple planes set at different angles, an arrangement that ensures more contact between food and blades, resulting in better-processed food (food processor blades are set on different planes at identical angles). Second, the mixture travels up and around the blender jar in a vortex, which helps to incorporate air, resulting in light, silky purees. The pureeing results were an exact match with the smoothie test, with only the Jenn-Air leaving behind chunks of broccoli and onion.

Until now, we'd been gearing our tests toward blenders' inherent strengths—frozen drinks and liquid purees. It was time to enter new territory. We decided to make hummus from canned chickpeas, toasted sesame seeds, garlic, olive oil, salt, and lemon juice. Could these fancy blenders step up to the task? For the most part, yes. Only the Emerilware was left with unprocessed chunks of chickpeas and sesame seeds.

A few instruction manuals claimed that these super-blenders can make peanut butter from raw peanuts, so we decided to push our blenders to the limit. Filling each jar with amounts ranging from ½ cup to 4 cups of roasted peanuts, we pulsed the nuts 5 times, then processed them on low speed for 45 seconds. With the exceptions of the Waring MegaMix and the Vita-Mix, no other blender even came close.

Revving Up

Why were some models excelling at some tests and failing at others? We had two main areas to investigate: power and design.

Manufacturers typically indicate motor power in horsepower or watts (both measure power; one horsepower equals 746 watts). In previous tests of countertop appliances, we discovered that the wattage listed on the package has little, if any, correlation to performance. That's because this number is a measurement of the power *consumed* by the blender motor, not the power *generated* by it. Our blender tests confirmed this: The 500-watt Jenn-Air Attrezzi, for example, was better at crushing ice than the 1,380-watt Vita-Mix.

Data for output wattage—a better indicator of performance—is not disclosed by manufacturers and is very difficult to measure. We wondered if the speed of the blades might explain our tests results, so we purchased a hand-held laser tachometer to take rpm (revolutions-per-minute) readings of the blender blades. The laser measured rpm by reading a piece of reflective tape we adhered to one of the blades in each blender. To get an accurate reading, the tachometer required that everything in the background be completely black, so we administered a healthy dose of black spray paint to the blades and bottoms of each blender jar. (Gray margaritas, anyone?) Our rpm findings ranged from 10,832 for the Jenn-Air Attrezzi to 27,364 for the Vita-Mix, with most of the blenders coming in at around 20,000 rpm.

A Truly Super Blender

The $945 Vorwerk Thermomix TM21 is a high-end European appliance that is a combination food processor, blender, mixer, self-stirring burner, scale, and steamer. But does it do any of this well? In a word, yes. Although its motor consumes only 600 watts, the Thermomix's blending and food-processing ability is fantastic (it would have placed first in our blender rating). It aced our ice-crushing, hummus, and soup-pureeing tests—and we could cook the soup in the machine before we pureed it. Being able to heat and stir simultaneously is a huge bonus that lends itself especially well to sauce making; our béarnaise and hollandaise sauces came out beautifully. The built-in digital scale is a handy touch. Steaming—you attach a basket above the main jar—is the one function that we would just as soon do without.

The Thermomix would be most useful in a tight-quartered kitchen with no other appliances, say, in a cabin or even on a boat. In a kitchen that already has a stove and a blender or food processor, however, we would opt to spend our $945 on something else. –S.K.

How We Rated the Blenders

We tested eight high-end blenders and the inexpensive Braun PowerMax (winner of a previous test) and evaluated them according to the following criteria. Blenders are listed in order of preference.

PRICE: Prices paid in Boston-area retail, national mail-order, or online outlets.

POWER/SPEED: Wattage is from the manufacturer; rpm (revolutions per minute) was measured in the test kitchen with a hand-held laser tachometer.

JAR: Material and maximum capacity.

ICE CRUSHING: Fifteen ice cubes were processed with five 1-second pulses.

SMOOTHIE: Banana, frozen mango, orange juice, and yogurt were blended for 30 seconds on high speed.

SOUP PUREE: Chunky broccoli soup was processed for 30 seconds on high speed (or on the "puree" setting when applicable).

HUMMUS: A chickpea mixture was processed for one minute on high speed (or on the "chop" setting when applicable).

PEANUT BUTTER: Peanuts were pulsed five times, then processed on low speed for 45 seconds.

Do higher rpm's equal better performance? The test was fun, but the blender with the lowest rpm (the Jenn-Air) was one of only two models to ace the ice-crushing test, presumably a test where speed and power are important. It seems what separates a so-so blender from a superior blender is design, not brawn.

Design Matters

Blenders normally have four blades. While one of our blenders, the Emerilware, boasted six blades, this feature proved to be more "sham" than "Bam!" (the Emerilware blender finished last in our kitchen tests). The other model that strayed from the standard blade design was the Jenn-Air; its inverted jar shape (large at the bottom, tapered at the top) has room for extra-large blades, which would seem to explain why this blender excelled at crushing ice.

But the Jenn-Air's wide base was also its downfall, as it explains why this blender left behind bits of mango and broccoli in the smoothie and soup tests. Our four top-rated blenders all have jars that taper at the bottom; blenders with straight-sided jars or jars that flared at the base landed at the bottom of our ranking. Why is jar design so important? Tapered jars funnel food down into the blades and yield nearly flawless purees—the reason you want a blender in the first place.

It turns out that a tapered jar is more important than any bell or whistle. In fact, jar design is so critical that the tapered Braun PowerMax ($50) held its own against more powerful blenders and finished second. For $134, you could buy our top-performing blender from L'Equip, which has a similar jar design (only bigger) and ever-so-slightly better performance. But until a markedly better blender comes along, we'll stick with the inexpensive Braun for the usual blender tasks—and rely on our food processor for everything else.

RATINGS	
GOOD:	★★★
FAIR:	★★
POOR:	★

RATING BLENDERS

RECOMMENDED

	PERFORMANCE	TESTERS' COMMENTS
L'Equip R.P.M. PRICE: $134 INPUT POWER/SPEED: 900 watts, 18,653 rpm JAR: Plastic, 56 ounces	ICE CRUSHING: ★★★ SMOOTHIE: ★★★ SOUP PUREE: ★★★ HUMMUS: ★★★ PEANUT BUTTER: ★	Excelled at every task except peanut butter, and did so in less time than most. Liked the manual power dial. Only complaint—and it's minor—is that it can take a few tries to nestle the jar into the base.
BEST BUY **Braun PowerMax** PRICE: $49.99 INPUT POWER/SPEED: 525 watts, 21,368 rpm JAR: Glass, 58 ounces	ICE CRUSHING: ★★★ SMOOTHIE: ★★★ SOUP PUREE: ★★★ HUMMUS: ★★ PEANUT BUTTER: ★	Made short work of all tests except peanut butter. The unique triangular-shaped jar makes it especially easy to rest the jar in the base (a problem with some other models).
Waring 2-Speed MegaMix Specialty PRICE: $249.95 INPUT POWER/SPEED: 746 watts, 24,591 rpm JAR: Plastic, 48 ounces	ICE CRUSHING: ★ SMOOTHIE: ★★★ SOUP PUREE: ★★★ HUMMUS: ★★★ PEANUT BUTTER: ★★★	Very loud, especially with hard items. Movement for ice crushing seemed "too violent"; the ice cubes were blown off the blades, never to return. The only blender to excel in making peanut butter, but poor ice crushing is a flaw.
Vita-Mix 5000 PRICE: $399 INPUT POWER/SPEED: 1380 watts, 27,364 rpm JAR: Plastic, 68 ounces	ICE CRUSHING: ★★ SMOOTHIE: ★★★ SOUP PUREE: ★★★ HUMMUS: ★★ PEANUT BUTTER: ★★	Best smoothie maker. Stands out because of its large size and huge jar. The stirrer, which can be inserted through the lid, is helpful for making peanut butter.
KitchenAid Pro Line Chef's Blender PRICE: $239.99 INPUT POWER/SPEED: 746 watts, 16,130 rpm JAR: Plastic, 48 ounces	ICE CRUSHING: ★★ SMOOTHIE: ★★★ SOUP PUREE: ★★★ HUMMUS: ★★ PEANUT BUTTER: ★	A solid all-around performer. Design is simple and controls very intuitive—although we can't imagine ever using the medium speed (pulse, high, and low are enough for most tasks).

RECOMMENDED WITH RESERVATIONS

	PERFORMANCE	TESTERS' COMMENTS
Cuisinart SmartPower Premiere PRICE: $199.90 INPUT POWER/SPEED: 600 watts, 21,496 rpm JAR: Glass, 50 ounces	ICE CRUSHING: ★★ SMOOTHIE: ★★ SOUP PUREE: ★★ HUMMUS: ★★ PEANUT BUTTER: ★	Keypad controls are easy to clean, but it's annoying to have to push "on" before selecting your speed level. Occasional leakage from the bottom of the jar.

NOT RECOMMENDED

	PERFORMANCE	TESTERS' COMMENTS
Jenn-Air Attrezzi PRICE: $209.99 INPUT POWER/SPEED: 500 watts, 10,832 rpm JAR: Glass, 72 ounces	ICE CRUSHING: ★★★ SMOOTHIE: ★ SOUP PUREE: ★ HUMMUS: ★★ PEANUT BUTTER: ★	Inverted design (wider at the base) made retrieving processed ingredients difficult; we had to unscrew the base of the jar and remove the blades to empty it. Too many buttons.
Waring Pro PBB PRICE: $129 INPUT POWER/SPEED: 390 watts, 19,973 rpm JAR: Glass, 40 ounces	ICE CRUSHING: ★ SMOOTHIE: ★★ SOUP PUREE: ★★ HUMMUS: ★★ PEANUT BUTTER: ★	Narrow cloverleaf shape made retrieving food awkward. Blender feels tipsy when resting on its base, but it never rocked off. While the retro look is cool, poor performance is not. Relatively small jar.
Emerilware PRICE: $99.95 INPUT POWER/SPEED: 500 watts, 22,326 rpm JAR: Glass, 50 ounces	ICE CRUSHING: ★ SMOOTHIE: ★★ SOUP PUREE: ★★ HUMMUS: ★ PEANUT BUTTER: ★	Too many button options—hard to tell which buttons to use for what task. And is there really a need for a milk-shake button? More damning, poor performance at several key tasks sunk this blender to the bottom of rankings.

KITCHEN NOTES

≥ BY ERIKA BRUCE ≤

Sizing Up Garlic

Because of garlic's intense flavor, the size of the cloves can really make an impact on your cooking. Along with the number and size of the cloves, our recipes offer teaspoon or tablespoon measurements for garlic, so there's no doubt that you're using the right amount in our Pasta Salad with Pesto (page 19) or Cuban-Style Grill-Roasted Pork (page 14). And regardless of size, don't forget to remove any green sprouts from the center of the clove; a blind tasting (both raw in aïoli and cooked with pasta and olive oil) revealed that the sprouts add an unpleasant bitterness. The photos below are to scale; the yields refer to the amount one clove produces when minced.

Small clove yields ½ teaspoon

Medium clove yields 1 teaspoon

Large clove yields 2 teaspoons

Extra-large clove yields 1 tablespoon

NOTE: Garlic shown at actual size.

Shake and Bake

A pizza peel is the handiest tool for getting pizzas in and out of the oven. In the past, we have eliminated any problems with dough sticking to the peel by placing a sheet of parchment in between. But for really crisp and well-browned Pizza Margherita (page 11), we found the parchment paper just got in the way (it stuck to the tacky dough and wrinkled up, and it prevented the direct contact with the hot stone necessary for the crispiest crust). Yet without parchment, we experienced our fair share of pizza mishaps; the dough either stuck to the peel on its own or became glued on by an errant drop of sauce, resulting in shapes that looked more like calzone than pizza. Without sacrificing a crisp bottom crust, we needed to find a foolproof solution for perfect pizzas every time.

Dusting the peel with flour was a must, but too much made for a floury pizza; cornmeal also worked well, like mini ball bearings, but it was distractingly crunchy between the teeth. We found the best solution was actually mechanical: a simple, quick shake over the countertop (rather than halfway into the hot oven) told us if there were any sticky spots. Then a quick swipe of the bench scraper under the dough both released the stuck areas and redistributed the flour underneath. And, of course, be sure the entire peel is dry; wipe up any dollops of sauce or liquid that could form potential speed bumps on the way into the oven.

It's Not Easy Staying Green

When making Pasta Salad with Pesto (page 19), storing leftover basil won't be an issue—the large bunches available at the supermarket will be easily used up. But what about those occasions when only two or three leaves are needed to season a dish? We wondered how long we could keep leftover store-bought basil and what would be the best way to store it.

Store basil wrapped in a damp towel, but don't seal the bag.

Since leaving basil out on the counter wasn't an option (it wilted within hours) we were stuck with refrigerator storage, which is about 15 degrees colder than the recommended temperature for basil. We tested storing basil in unsealed zipper-lock bags (to prevent build-up of moisture, which can cause basil to turn black), both plain and wrapped in damp paper towels (our preferred method for most leafy greens). After three days in the refrigerator, both samples were still green and perky.

But after one week, only the towel-wrapped basil was still fresh looking and tasting. Don't be tempted to rinse basil until just before you need to use it; when we performed the same tests after rinsing, the shelf life was decreased by half.

Jarred Tomatoes?

While recently shopping for canned diced tomatoes, we noticed a newcomer on the shelves: Del Monte Petit Diced jarred tomatoes. Claiming to be minimally processed and more like fresh, this new product was crying out for a taste test, so we pitted it against the real thing (in a fresh tomato salsa) and against Del Monte's canned counterpart (in a quick-cooked sauce for pasta).

For the salsa, tasters preferred the texture of fresh tomatoes because they were less watery, but the jarred tomatoes held their own in terms of flavor, especially when paired with potent onion and lime juice. In the

TASTING: Presliced American Cheese

We admit it. Many of us in the test kitchen top our burgers with—gasp—American cheese. Defined as a "process" cheese product with a minimum requirement of 51 percent actual cheese (the rest is mostly emulsifiers and stabilizers), American cheese can range dramatically in color, flavor, and texture. Coming to terms with our guilty pleasure, we decided to taste four widely available brands (in the guise of grilled cheese sandwiches) to find out which one we liked best.

We sampled Sara Lee, Land O' Lakes, Kraft, and Borden and included both the "yellow" and "white" varieties where available. The Sara Lee American Slices, both the Land O' Lakes American Yellow and White, and the Kraft Deli Deluxe White Slices rated highest for cheesy flavor. Not coincidentally, cheese culture (live bacteria added to milk to spur the formation of cheese curds) was higher on their ingredient lists than on those for Kraft Singles or the Borden Singles, which didn't taste anything like cheese. And while across the board the textures were slightly rubbery, we found that there was a distinct difference between gooey goodness (the first group) and just plain slimy (the second group). As for color, it came down to a matter of personal preference.

THE BIG CHEESE

When buying American cheese, look for "cultured pasteurized milk" or "cheese culture" as the first or second ingredient.

LOW CULTURE

If the "cultured" ingredients are far down on the ingredient list, American cheese won't have much "cheese" flavor.

ILLUSTRATION: JOHN BURGOYNE

Sweetened Condensed Milk

In our recipe for Key Lime Bars (page 23), sweetened condensed milk—a shelf-stable reduction of milk and sugar—plays a key role in keeping the filling creamy and sweet. (For a scientific explanation of this role, see page 22.) But does it matter which brand? We bought five different cans—Borden's Eagle Brand Regular, Lowfat, and Fat Free, as well as Parrot and Carnation (both full-fat brands)—and headed to the test kitchen to taste multiple batches of Key lime bars and Key lime pie filling.

Most of the ingredient labels were identical (just whole milk and sugar), with the exception of the Borden's reduced-fat and nonfat options (made with lowfat or nonfat milk), and the Parrot brand (which contains soybean oil). Surely our tasters would detect the difference, right? To our surprise, tasters were just as happy eating desserts fattened up with soybean oil and reduced-fat products, although they did notice a more assertive lime flavor in the latter. In the end, any of these sweetened condensed milk products will do. Stick with the whole-milk option for maximum creaminess, but the leaner options won't significantly lower the bar. –Elizabeth Bomze

---

pasta sauce, the jarred tomatoes fell flat—the tomato pieces were smaller than the canned, yet they remained separate and distinct, refusing to come together into a cohesive sauce. Apparently, the smaller dice meant more surface area was exposed to calcium chloride, a firming agent also added to canned diced tomatoes, yielding a firmer texture—good when trying to find a substitute for less-than-stellar fresh tomatoes in a raw dish but not so good for cooked applications.

For salsa, use Del Monte jarred tomatoes when fresh tomatoes are out of season.

Loosen That Bow Tie

We like our pasta with a little bite (or al dente) when it is served hot, but for cool pasta salad, we prefer pasta that is more tender than chewy. A quick nibble would normally suffice to see if the pasta was just past al dente, but with farfalle, our favorite shape for Pasta Salad with Pesto (page 19), the pinched centers required closer inspection. If a cut through the middle revealed a chalky white line (the color of uncooked pasta), the bow ties were not quite done, and needed more cooking.

Citrus Squeeze

Squeezing our way through literally hundreds of limes (for Cuban-Style Grill-Roasted Pork, page 14, and Key Lime Bars, page 23), we realized this was an opportune time to determine the most effective method for juicing this little fruit. We tested squeezing by hand against a citrus juicer, in which the lime half is twisted over a ridged, conical head set over a bowl; a simple wooden reamer, which is manually turned inside the fruit; and a citrus squeezer, a device that presses the lime half inside-out to extract the juice.

With the exception of hand squeezing (which was less than half as effective), each method yielded the same amount of juice. But when we factored in ease of use and speed, the squeezer pressed ahead of the competition. An added bonus: All the bits of pulp were contained in the well of the press rather than dropping down into the juice.

Are there any tricks for yielding more juice? We tried rolling the limes on the counter, heating them in the microwave, and poking them with a fork; while these tips may help when squeezing by hand, none made a bit of difference in yield (or ease) when using a hand-held squeezer. In fact, we found cold limes straight out of the refrigerator to yield the most juice—the firm flesh split open more readily than when warm and more pliable.

A hand-held citrus squeezer is the best tool for juicing limes.

RECIPE UPDATE

Peach Barbecue Sauce

Several readers asked us to combine the savory smokiness of our **Barbecued Pulled Chicken** (July/August 2005) with the sweetness of fruit. Adding some jam to the recipe's spicy barbecue sauce seemed like a promising idea. We replaced the apple cider and molasses (the sweet components in our original sauce) with water and various fruit-based jams, jellies, and preserves. Most of our tasters found all three to be interchangeable, although the jellies were a little sweeter. Our favorite was peach preserves or jam, followed by apricot preserves or jam. The only flavor that didn't work was orange marmalade, which was simply overpowering. To allow the fruit flavor to come through, we reduced the amount of chili powder from 1½ tablespoons to 2 teaspoons. See Cook's Extra, below, for the recipe.

German Chocolate Sheet Cake

Fans of our **German Chocolate Cake** (January/February 2005) wondered if this recipe could be translated to a sheet cake. Yes, those towering layers of chocolate cake separated by the sticky coconut-pecan filling look impressive, but they do require a fair amount of work, including the ability to split cake layers in half neatly, so we were happy to oblige with a simpler recipe. It turns out that the batter, which is designed for two 9-inch round cake pans, fits perfectly into a 13 by 9-inch pan and requires just five minutes more baking time. As for the filling, it's equally good as a thick layer of frosting for a sheet cake and requires no adjustments. See Cook's Extra, below, for the recipe.

TRADITIONAL   **STREAMLINED**

The traditional cake has four layers and requires some tricky construction. A sheet cake looks more humble but still tastes good.

Brown Rice Paella

Could we make a decent version of our **Paella** (May/June 2005) recipe with brown rice? To find out, we replaced the rice called for in our original recipe (Valencia or Arborio) with an equal amount of long-grain brown rice. Because brown rice has the bran and germ still intact, it usually takes much longer to cook than white rice and requires more liquid. For our paella recipe, we found it necessary to bake the rice in the oven for an additional 30 minutes (before adding the browned chicken and chorizo). However, the amount of liquid in the recipe (from the chicken broth, tomatoes, and wine) was just fine. It turns out that because our paella is baked in a lidded Dutch oven, very little liquid can escape from the pot, so the same amount will cook white or brown rice—as long as the brown rice gets some extra time. See Cook's Extra, below, for the recipe.

–Compiled by Matthew Herron

IF YOU HAVE A QUESTION about a recently published recipe, let us know. Send your inquiry, name, address, and daytime telephone number to Recipe Update, Cook's Illustrated, P.O. Box 470589, Brookline, MA 02447, or write to recipeupdate@bcpress.com.

COOK'S extra

Go to www.cooksillustrated.com
- Key in code 70610 for **Brown Rice Paella**.
- Key in code 70611 for **German Chocolate Sheet Cake**.
- Key in code 70612 for **Peach Barbecue Sauce**.
- Recipes available until January 1, 2007.

≥ BY GARTH CLINGINGSMITH ≤

DO YOU REALLY NEED THIS? Wood Soaker

We always recommend soaking wood chips or chunks before tossing them onto lit charcoal. The absorbed moisture keeps the wood from igniting and quickly burning up, allowing a slow smolder that produces plenty of smoke. Tossing the wood into a water-filled mixing bowl has always worked for us, but we wondered whether Weber's new Wood Chip Soaker ($9.99) was a better option. Shaped like a super-sized travel mug, the soaker has a perforated lid that twists down over the wood, keeping every chip below the water line. Does it work? To find out, we soaked a pound of wood chunks each in the soaker, in a bowl, and in a water-filled zipper-lock bag. After a two-hour soak, all the wood gained about 2 ounces of water, no matter the method, and the three batches had identical lifespans when tossed atop the coals. To our minds, then, there's no need for a dedicated wood soaker. But at $10, it's hardly a splurge for those who want to keep their mixing bowls (or storage bags) off the patio.

ALL WET
This mug is for soaking wood chips.

EQUIPMENT UPDATE Carving Knife

In last year's rating of carving, or slicing, knives (May/June 2005), we cut our way through pounds of poultry and beef. Serrated blades shred the meat rather than slice it, while pointed tips and narrow blades allow too much agility, making it hard to maintain an even stroke. In the end, we liked a wide, nonserrated blade, a rounded tip, an even breadth from tip to handle, and nothing longer than 10 inches. But almost as soon as we crowned the Forschner 10-inch Carving Knife our winner, it was discontinued, and we've made do with the 12-inch version—until now: Chef Cutlery has introduced a 10-inch slicer ($50) that performs just as well the Forschner.

EQUIPMENT TEST Grill Spatulas

Flipping burgers on the grill can be tricky—or so it would seem, given the number of spatulas designed to make the task easier. The basic difference between a regular spatula and a "grill spatula" is a few extra inches of handle to keep hands farther from the heat. While flipping cheeseburgers in our back alley, testers were most comfortable with handle lengths of 12 inches or longer (and least comfortable with one 7-inch model).

Most of the fancier designs weren't that helpful. Raised sidewalls, meant to keep food from slipping off, were an elegant solution to a seemingly made-up problem. Spatula/tong hybrids proved too much trouble: The tong half got in the way during spatula tasks—rudely "de-cheesing" two of our cheeseburgers. The most gimmicky spatula of the bunch, Charcoal Companion's Mr. BBQ 4-in-1 Spatula ($9.95) actually handled core tasks well. Testers weren't impressed with its "tenderizer" (metal spokes that riddle the meat with tiny holes) or its chintzy grill scraper, but the cutting edge made quick work of halving a hamburger. And we can think of plenty of uses for the bottle opener built into the base of a generous 14½-inch handle—especially at a weekend barbecue.

NEW PRODUCT Outdoor Pizza Maker

The VillaWare PizzAgrill BBQ Pizza Maker ($99.95) aims to turn a gas grill into an outdoor pizza oven. A metal stand that secures a baking stone onto the grill grate, the Pizza Maker produced an excellent crust—the bottoms of our pizzas were deeply browned and crisp—but a grill turns out to be a poor pizza oven. After preheating, both the stone and the temperature of the air inside the grill were well above 500 degrees. However, upon opening the grill to slide on a pizza, the air temperature plummeted to about 300 degrees and failed to recover by the time the crust's bottom was on the verge of burning. The cheese melted slightly, but there was nothing close to the crusty caramelization produced by an indoor oven. When we feel like pizza but don't feel like cranking up the oven, we'll stick to grilled pizza cooked directly over the coals.

DO YOU REALLY NEED THIS? Mango Splitter

Removing the flesh from a mango in tidy pieces can challenge even a seasoned pro's knife skills. When we came across Oxo's mango splitter, we gave it a whirl. Similar to an apple corer—it's pressed down onto the fruit like a two-handed (ultra-sharp) cookie cutter—this gadget has a central hole shaped to match the narrow contours of a mango pit. At first, we had a terrible time balancing the mango for the initial cut, but once we trimmed the bottom flat, the splitter plunged through the fruit easily and cleanly. Try as we might, we couldn't round up a

MUST-HALVE TOOL
This mango gadget really works.

mango too small or large, and the mango splitter never left extra fruit on the pit by overestimating the pit's size. The Oxo Mango Splitter ($11.95) is one of those rare kitchen gadgets that works.

Sources

The following are mail-order sources for items recommended in this issue. Prices were current at press time and don't include shipping and handling. Contact companies to confirm prices and availability, and visit our Web site (www.cooksillustrated.com) for updates.

Page 3: JAR OPENER
• Twister Jar Opener: $6.95, item #42238, **The Vermont Country Store (802-362-8460, www.vermontcountrystore.com).**

Page 9: SKEWERS
• Norpro Stainless Steel Skewer Set (12"): $10 for 6, item #NP1933, **Golda's Kitchen (866-465-3299, www.goldaskitchen.com).**

Page 13: CHIMNEY STARTERS
• Weber Rapid Fire Chimney Starter: $16.99, item #139750, **Barbecues Galore (800-752-3085, www.bbqgalore.com).**
• Steven Raichlen Best of Barbecue Ultimate Chimney Starter: $29.99, model #SR8041, **The Barbecue Store (888-789-0650, www.barbecue-store.com).**

Page 17: KNIFE SHARPENER
• Chef'sChoice Knife Sharpener 110: $79.95, Sku #101779, **Cooking.com (800-663-8810, www.cooking.com).**

Page 25: SERRATED PEELER
• Messermeister Serrated Swivel Peeler: $5.50, item #154005, **Sur La Table (800-243-0852, www .surla table.com).**

Pages 28, 29: BLENDERS
• Vorwerk Thermomix TM21: $945, **Authorized Thermomix Distributors (772-223-9639).**
• L' Equip R.P.M. Blender: $134, item #213303, **Cooking.com.**
• Braun PowerMax Jug Blender: $49.99, item #5034; **Essentials.com (800-924-4950, www.theessentials.com).**

Page 32: WOOD CHIP SOAKER
• Weber Wood Chip Soaker: $9.99, model #18800, **Weber (888-469-3237, www.webergrills.com).**

Page 32: CARVING KNIFE
• Chef Cutlery Legend 10" Granton Slicer, Wide, Stiff Blade: $45, part #M14310, **Professional Cutlery Direct (800-859-6994, www.pcd.com).**

Page 32: GRILL SPATULA
• Charcoal Companion 4-in-1 Spatula: $9.95, item #CC1017, **The Barbecue Store (888-789-0650, www.barbecue-store.com).**

Page 32: MANGO SPLITTER
• Oxo Good Grips Mango Splitter: $11.95, item #411725, **Cooking.com.**

RECIPES

July & August 2006

New Recipes Available on the Web

The following recipes are available free until January 1, 2007. To access a recipe, go to www.cooksillustrated.com and enter the code listed after the recipe title.

Well-Done Hamburgers, 21

Cuban-Style Grill-Roasted Pork, 12

Grilled Shrimp Skewers, 8

Pasta Salad with Pesto, 19

Grilled Onions, 18

Spice-Rubbed Picnic Chicken, 7

Zucchini with Tomatoes and Basil, 15

Pizza Margherita, 11

Key Lime Bars, 23

Peach Crumble, 25

PHOTOGRAPHY: CARL TREMBLAY, STYLING: MARIE PIRAINO

Coriander

Coffee

Mustard Seed

Cocoa

Chipotle Chile

Black Peppercorns

Fennel Seed

Allspice

Star Anise

Cinnamon

Ancho Chile

Cumin

GRILLING SPICES

⇒ COMPILED BY SANDRA WU ⇐

Powdered versus Fresh Lemon Juice

Have you ever tried a powdered lemon product called True Lemon? How does it compare with fresh lemon juice?

ELLEN BIDDLE
SOUTH BURLINGTON, VT.

➤ True Lemon is a powdered "crystallized lemon substitute" made of citric acid, maltodextrin, lemon juice, lemon oil, and ascorbic acid intended for use in cooking and baking and as a seasoning. It is available in a 2.85-ounce shaker-top jar (equivalent to the juice from 20 lemons) and in individual-serving-sized packets. Following the manufacturer's guidelines, we tested this product against real lemon juice in lemonade, glazed lemon cookies, and hot tea with honey and lemon.

Does powdered lemon juice offer "true" lemon flavor?

Our tasters unanimously found that the True Lemon did not measure up to the real deal in lemonade. While the "real lemon" lemonade was bright, tart, and lemony, the True Lemon lemonade tasted (and looked) like "sugar water," with a hint of "fake" lemon flavor. We got similar results with the lemon cookies: The intensely fresh tang of real lemon juice that came through especially well in the icing became muted and slightly "artificial" when True Lemon was used. In the tea, however, a small amount of the powder proved to be a decent replacement for a squeezed slice of lemon.

When it comes to getting true lemon flavor, we prefer reaming fresh lemons, especially when making recipes that require lots of juice. For beverages that need only a splash of lemon juice, however, a sprinkle of the powdered stuff will work in a pinch.

Eggs across the Pond

In Europe, eggs are kept on the counter, while here in America we are told to keep them refrigerated. Can you explain?

TOTO SMITH
LOVELAND, COLO.

➤ According to the U.S. Department of Agriculture, all eggs sold in U.S. supermarkets must be washed and sanitized before being transported and stored at temperatures no higher than 45 degrees Fahrenheit. They must remain refrigerated (the USDA recommends storing eggs at 40 degrees) for two main reasons: to keep existing bacteria from rapidly multiplying and to stop additional bacteria from entering through the shell, made porous because washing removes a protective outer layer called the cuticle. Because eggs sold in the European Union are never washed, they can be stored unrefrigerated in a cool, dry place. But here in the States, don't even think about keeping your eggs out on the counter.

Recipe-Speak: 'Off Heat'

Sometimes there isn't a convenient or safe place to put a hot pan. If a recipe says "off heat" or "remove from heat," do I really need to take the pan off the burner, or can I just turn it off?

MIKE PETRUCELLI
PLYMOUTH, IND.

➤ We went into the test kitchen and brought a saucepan of water to a boil several times, recording its temperature change over a three-minute period as it sat on top of the same burner (turned off) as opposed to sitting on a trivet on the countertop. Left on the hot grate of the gas burner, the water in the saucepan remained 10 degrees higher than when the pan was removed to the countertop. When the pan was left on an electric burner, the temperature difference was even greater: The water remained 30 degrees hotter.

While these temperature differences probably won't matter for large pots of stew or pasta sauce, we wondered if they could adversely affect more delicate, heat-sensitive recipes. To find out, we made three batches each of a simple pan sauce and a vanilla custard pie filling, one batch taken completely off the heat when directed by the recipe, one left on the hot grate of a gas burner, and one left on the hot coil of an electric burner. In the 30 seconds that the skillet and saucepan sat on the gas burner while additional ingredients

To take a pan "off heat," don't just turn off the burner. Move the pan to another surface.

were whisked in, no adverse reaction occurred in either the sauce or the custard. When left on the electric burner (which retains heat for a longer period of time), however, the sauce became darker and clumpier, with a slightly oily rather than rich and glossy texture, and the custard became thick and pasty.

So the next time a recipe calls for adding an ingredient "off heat," don't just turn off the burner (especially if it's an electric burner). Take the extra two seconds to move the pan completely off the heat, either onto a trivet or a cool, unused burner.

A Better Way to Weigh Pasta

I tend to buy pasta in bulk and keep it in big containers on the counter. When I need a pound of penne, I just weigh out what I need. But spaghetti is harder to fit on a scale. Do you have any tips?

GARY LEUNG
CHICAGO, ILL.

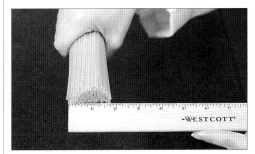

To measure out 1 pound of spaghetti without a scale, gather a bundle with a diameter of 1¾ inches.

➤ Tall, spacious containers—such as an empty coffee canister—work well for holding thin pasta upright on the scale, and this method is much less precarious than arranging it on a plate or in a large bowl. (Place the canister on the scale, tare it to zero, then place the pasta inside.) Another option is to gather a bundle of pasta into the shape of a cylinder and measure its diameter. We've found that a pound of either regular spaghetti or angel hair pasta measures 1¾ inches across, a pound of spaghettini (thin spaghetti) measures 1½ inches, and a pound of fettuccine measures 2 inches.

Improvised Cooling Racks

Once or twice a year, I bake a lot of pies. The problem is, I own just one cooling rack. Do I need to buy more racks, or is there an alternative?

BRIDGET MARSHALL
DENTON, TEXAS

FUTURE PLANS

Early spring was dry—not much snowmelt—and in April the Battenkill River was at August levels instead of overflowing onto the hay fields and Christmas tree farms along its banks. I was planning a float trip down to Rexleigh Bridge soon after fishing season opened but decided to hold off until the water level improved. (My lone outing in waders uncovered no hatch and nary a nibble even when I tied on my go-to fly, the White Zonker.) Of course, that all changed when the rain arrived in May. The seed corn rotted in the ground and had to be replanted. Hay got soaked and knocked down in the fields. Farmers who took a chance and mowed in hopes of baling before a storm got caught out. Our bees didn't have much of a chance to get to the apple blossoms or the lilacs. And our herb garden sprouted an unexpected crop of mushrooms.

Some years back, one of our neighbors, Jean, ordered her own headstone and had it set in a cemetery up in Wallingford, Vt. She then had a stone carved for her companion, Jack, and had it set next to hers. The carver, Michael Fannin from Tinmouth, transformed the marble slab for Jean's stone into a poster of sorts, a carved-in-stone impression of a country life. On the bottom, a lotus plant sprouts upward, a sign of the spiritual life. On the top are shooting stars (her first horse was named Shooting Star), and in the middle is a winged angel of death, its round face curiously childlike. Because Jean loves bird watching, she also had two birds cut into the marble. The inscription, of course, is not finished, but Jean thinks it ought to read something like this: "Died in 2040, in the 99th year of her life." Being a woman of determination, she even has a final date in mind.

My plans for the future are more immediate. The first cup of coffee in the morning. A few minutes with a good book. Some ripe fruit after dinner. Or the possibility that my 8-year-old, Emily, might be lying in wait for me by the front door when I come home from work, shouting "Boo!" as I walk in and then asking, hopefully, if she truly scared me. It is true that my more long-term plans seem to get up and walk out the door as soon the future starts to take shape, much like an ill-bred horse that turns up scarce on the day he is to be traded back to his old riding stable. The future knows that I am coming and it doesn't like it one bit.

Maybe it's simply a function of having the wrong sorts of plans. Charlie Bentley, the dairy farmer I used to work for back in the 1960s, decided soon after being born that he was going to work hard, he wasn't going to complain, and he wasn't going to covet anybody else's happiness. Those plans seem to have worked out pretty well for him, at least so far. Maybe the secret is to just pass on specificity when it comes to plans and concentrate on the big picture instead. Otherwise, like one neighbor of ours, you might end up surprised to find yourself divorced and remarried, with your ex-husband looking down at you from his new house on a hill right across the road.

Then again, Jean does seem to have a good plan, and it seems to be working out fine. When I went to see her headstone with her last Memorial Day, she showed me the beautiful view she and

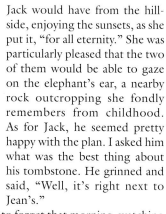

Christopher Kimball

Jack would have from the hillside, enjoying the sunsets, as she put it, "for all eternity." She was particularly pleased that the two of them would be able to gaze on the elephant's ear, a nearby rock outcropping she fondly remembers from childhood. As for Jack, he seemed pretty happy with the plan. I asked him what was the best thing about his tombstone. He grinned and said, "Well, it's right next to Jean's."

I can't seem to forget that morning, watching the two of them in the Green Hill Cemetery, chatting enthusiastically about their peaceful future, side by side, as if they were kids planning a fishing trip. Jack was a bit unsteady on the uneven side hill, but Jean just stood there and beamed, as if the certainty of these two headstones had removed the uncertainty from everyday life.

It also occurred to me that something as profound as true love is as fickle as a 22-inch brown trout in the Battenkill—catching it is more a matter of chance than good planning. And that's why I was so taken with Jean's notion of setting such a fleeting notion in stone. So when I got home, Adrienne was surprised when I suggested that we call Michael Fannin and get our headstones carved and planted as soon as possible. After some persuading, she took to the idea, and we decided on a small plot at the top of our mountain, one with a good view across New York State to the Adirondacks.

I guess it was about time to start planning our future together.

FOR INQUIRIES, ORDERS, OR MORE INFORMATION:

www.cooksillustrated.com

At www.cooksillustrated.com, you can order books and subscriptions, sign up for our free e-newsletter, or renew your magazine subscription. Join the Web site and you'll have access to 14 years of *Cook's* recipes, cookware tests, ingredient tastings, and more.

COOKBOOKS

We sell more than 40 cookbooks by the editors of *Cook's Illustrated*. To order, visit our bookstore at www.cooksillustrated.com or call 800-611-0759 (or 515-246-6911 from outside the U.S.).

COOK'S ILLUSTRATED Magazine

Cook's Illustrated magazine (ISSN 1068-2821), number 82, is published bimonthly by Boston Common Press Limited Partnership, 17 Station St., Brookline, MA 02445. Copyright 2006 Boston Common Press Limited Partnership. Periodicals postage paid at Boston, Mass., and additional mailing offices, USPS #012487. POSTMASTER: Send address changes to Cook's Illustrated, P.O. Box 7446, Red Oak, IA 51591-0446. For subscription and gift subscription orders, subscription inquiries, or change-of-address notices, call 800-526-8442 in the U.S. or 515-247-7571 from outside the U.S., or write us at Cook's Illustrated, P.O. Box 7446, Red Oak, IA 51591-0446.

CONTENTS

September & October 2006

www.cooksillustrated.com

HOME OF AMERICA'S TEST KITCHEN

2nd PRINTING IN CHINA

NEW ENGLAND HEIRLOOM APPLES

NEW ENGLAND HEIRLOOM APPLES Early Colonists brought apples to New England, and at one time hundreds of varieties flourished in the area. Today reduced to just a few, "heirloom" apples are found mostly at small orchards and farmers markets. The smallish Red, or Winter, Winesap gets its name from its spicy, wine-like flavor. This crisp, juicy variety is excellent for cooking and eating, as is its relative, the tart-sweet Stayman Winesap. Once the most widely planted apple in the United States, the small, tart Baldwin is great for baking. Another oldie-but-goodie, the all-purpose Rhode Island Greening was Benjamin Franklin's preferred apple. The Ben Davis has good keeping properties and is well suited for baking. Another good storing apple is the tender, crisp, and juicy Northern Spy. The deeply flavored Tolman Sweet can grow to be quite large and is a favorite for making cider. The McIntosh still graces supermarket shelves and is excellent for eating and for making applesauce (it breaks down readily when cooked). This apple has several familiar offspring, including the Cortland, Empire, Macoun, and Spartan varieties.

COVER (*Cabbages*): Elizabeth Brandon, BACK COVER (*New England Heirloom Apples*): John Burgoyne

For list rental information, contact: Specialists Marketing Services, Inc., 1200 Harbor Blvd., 9th Floor, Weehawken, NJ 07087; 201-865-5800.
Editorial Office: 17 Station St., Brookline, MA 02445; 617-232-1000; fax 617-232-1572. Subscription inquiries, call 800-526-8442.
Postmaster: Send all new orders, subscription inquiries, and change-of-address notices to Cook's Illustrated, P.O. Box 7446, Red Oak, IA 51591-0446.

COOK'S ILLUSTRATED

Founder and Editor Christopher Kimball
Editorial Director Jack Bishop
Deputy Editor Jolyon Helterman
Test Kitchen Director Erin McMurrer
Managing Editor Rebecca Hays
Senior Editors Keith Dresser
Lisa McManus
Associate Editors Erika Bruce
Sandra Wu
Copy Chief India Koopman
Test Cooks Garth Clingingsmith
David Pazmiño
Sarah Wilson
Market Research Manager Melissa Baldino
Assistant Test Kitchen Director Matthew Herron
Assistant Editor Elizabeth Bomze
Editorial Assistant Meredith Smith
Kitchen Assistants Maria Elena Delgado
Nadia Domeq
Ena Gudiel
Contributing Editors Matthew Card
Dawn Yanagihara
Consulting Editors Shirley Corriher
Guy Crosby
John Dewar
Jasper White
Robert L. Wolke
Proofreader Sheila Neylon

Web Managing Editor Katherine Bell
Web Editor Lindsay McSweeney

Editorial Manager, Books Elizabeth Carduff
Senior Editors, Books Julia Collin Davison
Lori Galvin
Test Cooks, Books Rachel Toomey
Megan Wycoff
Assistant Editors, Books Charles Kelsey
Elizabeth Wray Emery

Design Director Amy Klee
Art Director, Books Carolynn DeCillo
Senior Designer, Web/Marketing Julie Bozzo
Senior Designer, Magazines Heather Barrett
Designers Jay Layman
Christine Vo
Matthew Warnick
Staff Photographer Daniel J. van Ackere

Vice President Marketing David Mack
Circulation Director Bill Tine
Fulfillment Manager Carrie Horan
Circulation Assistant Elizabeth Dayton
Direct Mail Director Adam Perry
Products Director Steven Browall
E-Commerce Marketing Manager Hugh Buchan
Marketing Copywriter David Goldberg
Junior Developer Doug Sisko
Customer Service Manager Jacqueline Valerio
Customer Service Representatives Julie Gardner
Jillian Nannicelli

Vice President Sales Demee Gambulos
Retail Sales Director Jason Geller
Corporate Marketing Manager Emily Logan
Partnership Account Manager Allie Brawley
Marketing Assistant Connie Forbes

Production Director Guy Rochford
Senior Production Manager Jessica L. Quirk
Project Manager Anne Francis
Production Assistant Lauren Pettapiece
Technology & Operations Director Aaron Shuman
Systems Administrator S. Paddi McHugh

Chief Financial Officer Sharyn Chabot
Human Resources Manager Adele Shapiro
Controller Mandy Shito
Staff Accountant Maya Santoso
Office Manager Saudiyah Abdul-Rahim
Receptionist Henrietta Murray
Publicity Deborah Broide

NUMBER EIGHTY-TWO

SEPTEMBER & OCTOBER 2006

COOK'S
ILLUSTRATED

Roast Chicken and Vegetables
Perfect Chicken, Perfect Vegetables

Grilled Prime Rib

Best Dinner Rolls
Rich, Buttery, and Easy

Pork Tenderloin
Simple Skillet Method

Quick Tomato Sauces

Applesauce Cake
Big Apple Flavor

Rating Sauté Pans
Pricey Models Feel the Heat

Knowing When Food Is Done
Cider Vinegar Taste Test
Better Crêpes Suzette
Chicken and Rice, Latino-Style
Perfecting Mushroom Lasagna

www.cooksillustrated.com

$5.95 U.S./$6.95 CANADA

0 74470 62805 7

10>

➤ The reason most recipes for pie (and other baked goods) call for a cooling rack is to allow for proper airflow both above and beneath the item to make sure it cools quickly rather than retaining residual heat. We prefer the firmly welded chrome cooling and icing racks used by commercial bakeries. Still, we understand that buying five or six racks for the occasional baking spree is not necessarily practical.

Over the years, we've come across several clever ideas for makeshift cooling racks using common kitchenware. When in need of an extra cooling surface, the following work well in a pinch to provide adequate air circulation underneath the pie plate or cookie sheet: overturned muffin tins, inverted dozen-size empty egg trays set side by side, empty 28-ounce tin cans opened on both ends, and canning-jar rings.

Thawing Frozen Beef Patties

I like to buy bulk packages of ground beef and freeze individual burgers so they are ready for the grill, but sometimes I forget to defrost them. Should I thaw them in a microwave before grilling, or can I just toss them on the fire?

DAVID YANG
NEW YORK, N.Y.

➤ We used our trusty recipe for charcoal-grilled hamburgers to compare freshly made patties with patties that were frozen and then defrosted in the microwave and patties that went straight from the freezer to the grill.

When using the microwave, we found that setting the unit to 30 percent power helped the patties thaw evenly, preventing overcooked exteriors and partially frozen interiors. Individual patties took one to two minutes to defrost, while a large plate of four took five to eight minutes (checked every minute after hitting the five-minute mark). These microwave-defrosted burgers took about the same amount of time to cook as the freshly formed patties, acquired nice grill marks, and tasted just fine. The frozen patties, however, took nearly twice as long to cook on the grill, browned unevenly (the edges and part of the center browned while the area in between remained rather pale), and retained their slightly indented appearance rather than flattening out. They also exuded more liquid and cooked less evenly than either the fresh or the defrosted burgers.

So if you form and freeze ground beef into patties, we recommend thawing them in the refrigerator the night before or defrosting them in the microwave and grilling them immediately afterward.

What's Good about Garlic Presses

Your recipes call for mincing or pressing garlic through a press. Is one method better?

LAURA LOU GIFFORD
CHIPPEWA FALLS, WIS.

➤ Here in the test kitchen, we go through large quantities of minced garlic every day, so we like the convenience and speed a garlic press offers. In terms of flavor and quality, a good garlic press can break down cloves more finely and evenly than an average cook using a knife, which means better distribution of garlic flavor throughout any given dish. (If you're very proficient with your chef's knife, you can obtain a similarly fine and even mince.) All told, we think the garlic press is the best tool for the job. Our favorite press, the Zyliss Jumbo Garlic Press (for the results of our testing, see Equipment Corner, page 32), is comfortable to use while providing evenly processed garlic.

Beyond their main function, garlic presses can also be used to make a smooth paste of individually roasted garlic cloves, oil-packed sun-dried tomatoes, pitted olives, or capers; to mash anchovies; to mince canned chipotle peppers; and to prepare small amounts of onion or shallot juice.

Substitute for Greek Yogurt

I recently ran across a recipe that called for Greek yogurt. I looked everywhere and couldn't find it. Can regular yogurt be used as a substitute?

DIANE HENRY
CHESAPEAKE, VA.

➤ Greek yogurt is thicker and creamier and has more than twice the fat of typical full-fat American-style yogurts. Most brands of full-fat plain yogurt contain between 7 and 9 grams of fat per 1 cup serving, while FAGE Total Classic Greek yogurt (the most widely available brand in the United States) contains 23 grams of fat. Nearly all the whey (the watery liquid that separates from the solids) is strained out of Greek yogurt, giving it a rich, smooth texture that is slightly thicker than that of sour cream. In terms of flavor, Greek yogurt is fairly mild, with a slight tang. These qualities make it ideal for dips and spreads such as tzatziki sauce (a garlicky yogurt-cucumber sauce that becomes too watery when made with regular unstrained yogurt) or for serving drizzled with honey and sprinkled with nuts (a classic Greek dessert). Although Greek yogurt can be made

When strained for at least 24 hours, regular whole milk yogurt (top) makes a good substitute for thicker, creamier Greek yogurt (bottom).

with sheep's milk or goat's milk, the FAGE Total brand is made from cow's milk and is also available in skim, 2 percent, and light varieties.

To make our own version of Greek yogurt (essentially creating yogurt cheese), we strained full-fat plain yogurt in a fine-mesh strainer lined with several layers of cheesecloth (paper towels or coffee filters also work) and set over a bowl to catch the whey. After 24 hours (in the refrigerator, covered with plastic wrap), the yogurt had reduced in volume by about half and achieved a thick, rich consistency closely resembling that of Greek yogurt. Its taste was pretty close as well.

SEND US YOUR QUESTIONS We will provide a complimentary one-year subscription for each letter we print. Send your inquiry, name, address, and daytime telephone number to Notes from Readers, Cook's Illustrated, P.O. Box 470589, Brookline, MA 02447, or to notesfromreaders@bcpress.com.

WHAT IS IT?

I found this small aluminum tray at a flea market a few months ago. Is it used to poach quail eggs?

DONNA VORHEES
IPSWICH, MASS.

➤ The article you found is not an egg poacher, but it is used for heating another type of shelled food: snails. Six inches in diameter, the escargot plate, or *escargotière*, you found is made of stainless steel, though many today are ceramic. Here's how it is used: First, the prepared snails (soaked, blanched, and simmered in a court-bouillon if fresh, or just straight from the can) are stuffed back into their shells along with an herb-garlic compound butter. A few minutes before serving, each buttered escargot is placed in one of the recessed sections of the plate before being baked or broiled until the butter melts and the escargots are warmed through. The escargots can be eaten directly from the plate (set on top of another plate, a trivet, or a hot pad) with the help of escargot tongs, which maintain a grip on the shell while the snail is removed with an escargot fork. We found several styles of escargot plates as well as the tongs and fork online. See Sources on page 32 for ordering information.

This escargotière, or escargot plate, is used for heating and serving hot, buttered snails.

≈ COMPILED BY DAVID PAZMIÑO ≈

Dried Berries in a Flash

Instead of waiting for strawberries or other fruits to dry before dipping them in melted chocolate, Phyllis Kirigin of Croton-on-Hudson, N.Y., lays her just-washed berries on paper towels and blasts them with a blow-dryer turned to the "no heat" setting.

How to Skin an Eggplant

Removing the charred skin from a roasted eggplant can be frustrating and time-consuming. Christopher Cox of Tallahassee, Fla., uses plastic wrap to make quick work of this job.

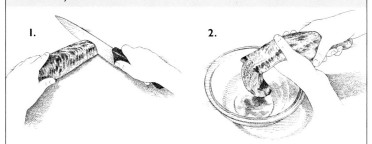

1. After roasting the eggplant over a direct flame or under a broiler until completely soft, cool to room temperature, then wrap it in two layers of plastic wrap. Cut off the top inch of the eggplant at the stem end.

2. Holding the plastic wrap as you would a tube of toothpaste, squeeze out the eggplant flesh, leaving the skin attached to the inside of the plastic wrap.

Steak Elevator

Most recipes call for resting steaks after cooking to allow the internal juices to redistribute. Inevitably, some of these juices leak out, ruining the nice crust. Matt Prager of New York, N.Y., uses a bowl to elevate the meat up and out of its juices.

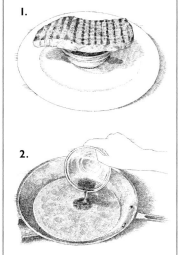

1. Place a small bowl in the center of a plate, and prop the steak on top.
2. Pour the collected juices into a pan to make a sauce.

Measuring by the Spoonful

Dipping a measuring spoon into a dry ingredient, then sweeping across the top with a knife to level it off, is the best way to get an accurate measurement. But it can also be a messy (and sometimes tricky) proposition. Two readers found ways to tidy things up.

Finding it impossible to get a measuring spoon into many jars, Hope Eisman of Brooklyn, N.Y., uses a paper coffee filter as an intermediary.

Rather than dirtying a counter when measuring baking powder or cocoa from a jar or box, Olivia Williams of Walla Walla, Wash., opts for this simple solution.

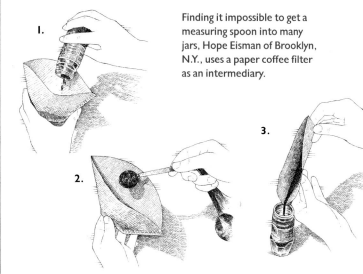

1. Holding a cone-shaped coffee filter in one hand, pour in a generous amount of the spice.
2. Dip the measuring spoon into the spice, using a straight edge to level it off.
3. Holding the coffee filter at an angle and pinching one corner, carefully pour the excess back into the spice container.

Run a double strip of masking tape across the opening of the container. Scoop up a heaping spoonful of the ingredient and level it off by scraping it against the tape.

Quicker Blanched Spinach

When a recipe calls for blanching spinach, it means boiling lots of water for a mere 30-second plunge. Deb Brownstein of Seattle, Wash., speeds things up by heating the water in a teakettle and pouring it over the spinach, placed in a colander.

Boil 4 to 6 cups of water in a teakettle. Place 1 pound of cleaned and stemmed spinach in a colander set in the sink. Pour the boiling water over the spinach in a steady stream to wilt. Shock the spinach with cold running water, squeeze out excess moisture, then use as directed in the recipe.

Send Us Your Tip We will provide a complimentary one-year subscription for each tip we print. Send your tip, name, and address to Quick Tips, Cook's Illustrated, P.O. Box 470589, Brookline, MA 02447, or to quicktips@bcpress.com.

ILLUSTRATION: JOHN BURGOYNE

Keeping Food Warm

Tired of burning butter for popcorn and scorching her mashed potatoes while trying to keep them warm over low heat, Jesse Kimball of Philadelphia, Pa., found an easy way to tame the flame. He places a cast-iron skillet over a low flame, then places the saucepan right in the skillet.

A Cut Above

Slicing a particularly hearty—or crusty—sandwich in half can force the fillings out the sides of the bread. Joan Hedman of Chandler, Ariz., offers this solution.

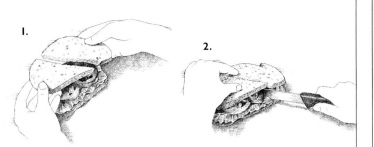

I. **2.**

1. Using a bread knife, cut the top slice of bread in half before placing it onto the assembled sandwich.
2. Gently hold the pieces together and use the existing cut to guide the knife through the filling and the bottom slice of bread.

Crisper Casserole Crusts

To keep a casserole topping crisp while traveling to a potluck dinner, Yvonne Sledge of Anchorage, Alaska, places a paper towel or clean dish towel over the top of the dish before wrapping it in foil. Steam from the hot casserole is absorbed by the towel instead of condensing on the foil and dripping back onto the casserole.

Crumb-Free Cake Layers

After cutting a cake round in half for a layer cake, it can be tricky to keep the top layer intact upon removal. Suzanne Marlow of Montreal, Quebec, came up with this foolproof method to keep the layers neat.

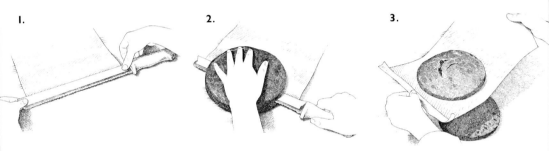

I. **2.** **3.**

1. Use masking tape to attach a 10-inch-wide piece of parchment paper to the nonserrated edge of a long serrated knife.
2. Cut the cake layer in half, dragging the paper through the cake as you cut.
3. Detach the tape from the knife, leaving the parchment between the cake layers. Lift up the cake to move it before frosting.

Spot-Free Glassware

For sparkling stemware free of water spots, Mindy Goldsborough of Gaithersburg, Md., washes the glasses by hand and rinses them with distilled water, which has none of the spot-producing impurities of regular tap water.

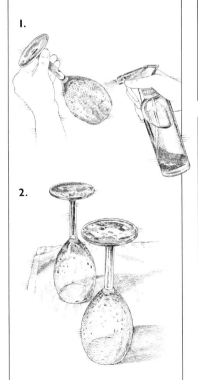

I.

2.

1. Fill a squirt bottle with distilled water. Rinse the glasses inside and out with the water.
2. Air-dry the glasses, first upside down, then right side up.

Spice Organizer

Anyone who lacks the storage space for a traditional spice cabinet or rack might want to follow the example of Margaret Gammon of Owen Sound, Ontario, who devised an efficient organizational system that keeps all of her spices at hand.

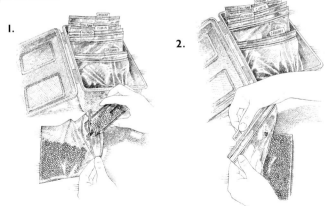

I. **2.**

1. Fill a small plastic zipper-lock storage bag with the desired dried herb or spice.
2. Attach a self-adhesive file-folder tab to the top of the bag, and organize the bags in a plastic container or shoe box in alphabetical order.

Easier Morning Coffee

Tired of tracking down a measuring cup every morning to make coffee, Kevin McCann of Sparks, Nev., figured out a better option: premeasuring the coffee into individual coffee filters. He stacks the coffee-filled filters back into an empty coffee can or another airtight container and stores it in the freezer. All he has to do is grab one of the filters from the freezer and pop it into the coffee maker.

How to Cook Prime Rib Outdoors

Getting a deep, flavorful crust on this costly cut of meat can be a messy, smoky ordeal in the kitchen. How about taking it outside?

≽ BY SARAH WILSON ≼

Prime rib of beef is what I call special-occasion food: It's pricey, it's impressive, and it feeds a crowd. But there's another reason home cooks rarely splurge on this deluxe roast. To make the most of prime rib's superior marbling—the thin lines of intramuscular fat that flavor and tenderize as they melt away—most recipes call for long cooking at a low temperature. (Otherwise, the outermost sections overcook by the time the center reaches medium-rare.) The downside is a gray-brown exterior that's neither appealing nor flavorful.

In the test kitchen, we solve this problem by searing the roast on all sides quickly in a hot skillet before tossing it into a 250-degree oven. It's an effective method for getting a delicious charred crust without ruining the interior, but it's one that can be messy (sputtering grease), cumbersome (flipping a 7-pound roast with tongs), and a challenge to anything less than a state-of-the-art ventilation system (billowing smoke).

To make this project less daunting, I decided to take a crack at moving the proceedings outside. Not only would the grill make the smoke a moot issue, but perhaps I could harness that smoke to intensify the contrast between the crust and the meltingly tender interior.

Taming the Flames

Given the test kitchen's success using the hybrid stovetop/oven method for prime rib, my plan was to translate the approach to the grill. With a hot fire on one side of the grill and the other side free of coals (a modified two-level fire), I mimicked the stovetop technique, searing the roast for 20 minutes on all surfaces, using tongs to stand it on each end to get the flat sides. Once the exterior was browned, I moved the roast to the cooler side of the grill and let it cook, covered, until the center reached medium-rare.

This first attempt was problematic, to say the least. I had a terrible time with flare-ups during

Beyond the well-charred, intensely smoky salt crust lies a generous slab of meltingly tender—and perfectly cooked—premium beef.

the searing process, as the roast's thick layer of fat rendered and dripped down onto the coals. And while the center of the roast reached a perfect medium-rare, the meat had a thick gray band around the perimeter (especially close to the cut sides), indicating that the roast had cooked at too high a temperature.

Had I been wrong about the high-heat sear? I tried placing the roast opposite the hot coals (without an initial sear), replacing the lid, and waiting. As the coals died down, the beef's temperature crept up to medium-rare (125 degrees) without developing an overcooked gray band. The downside was the crust. The two cut (flat) sides were adequately browned, but the fat-laden perimeter had an unappealing grayish look.

The answer was to combine the best ideas of each method. I clearly needed to spend some time searing the roast, but leaving the two cut sides unseared shaved 10 minutes from the process and avoided the awkward step of standing the roast up with tongs. What's more, reducing the time the roast spent directly over hot coals went a long way toward eliminating the over-

cooked gray bands. To minimize flare-ups while searing the fat-covered perimeter, I had the butcher trim the fat layer down to a thin ⅛ inch.

Many recipes call for cooking a rib roast on the bone, working from the idea that deeper flavor is developed this way. Here, though, tasters noticed little flavor advantage. (Given a rib roast's huge meat-to-bone ratio and the intense flavor imparted by a live fire, that's not so surprising.) However, the bones turned out to be more important as protection, keeping the underside from overbrowning. Unwilling to give up the convenience of a boneless roast (easier carving), I had my butcher remove the bones and then tie them back onto the meat with twine.

Crust to Glory

Now that the interior was right, it was time to improve the crust. To achieve a greater contrast in flavor and texture, I experimented with coating the exterior with a generous layer of salt. When done right, a salt coating promotes crust development by drawing out moisture from just below the surface, letting it evaporate faster once the searing process begins.

Salting for just one hour did nothing, but salting for too long was a bigger problem: After six hours, the moisture had dissolved the exterior salt and started to carry it deep into the roast. While that's a trick the test kitchen has used in some recipes as an alternative to brining, with prime rib it delivered an unwelcome "cured" effect (think really, really expensive corned beef). Salting the roast for three hours (one hour in the fridge, two hours at room temperature) was just right.

What about other flavors? I tried a spice rub, but the spices were too strong for this deluxe cut. Much better were garlic and herbs, especially piney rosemary. But the real coup came when I tried adding a modest amount of smoke flavor with wood chunks. Although skeptics objected in principle ("Why treat a premium roast like a pork shoulder?"), one bite ended the controversy. The smoke flavor penetrated only about half an inch into this huge roast—basically, the outer crust—leaving the majority of the pink interior untainted.

Finally, I had dramatic contrast in flavor and

PHOTOGRAPHY: CARL TREMBLAY

texture: In every slice, there was a crunchy, salty crust, a thin layer of smokiness, and a generous expanse of pink, juicy premium beef. Not only was the flavor experience more intense using this grill-roasting method, but I had kept the smoke and mess out of the kitchen. I may never make prime rib indoors again.

GRILL-ROASTED PRIME RIB FOR CHARCOAL GRILL
SERVES 6 TO 8

Your butcher can remove the bones and trim excess fat from the roast; just make sure that the bones are packed up along with the meat, as you need them to protect it from overbrowning. If the only roast you can find is boneless, fashion a protective "bone" from aluminum foil (see Kitchen Notes, page 30, for instructions). Letting the roast stand at room temperature for 2 hours prior to grilling helps it cook evenly. Serve the roast as is or with Horseradish Cream Sauce (see Cook's Extra, page 6). For instructions on cooking a whole prime rib, also see Cook's Extra, page 6.

- 1   first-cut (3- or 4-rib) beef standing rib roast (about 7 pounds), meat removed from bones, bones reserved, exterior fat trimmed to ⅛ inch
- 1   tablespoon vegetable oil
       Ground black pepper
- ¼   cup kosher salt
       Twine for tying roast, cut into four or six 2½-foot lengths (depending on number of bones)
- 2   (3-inch) wood chunks
       Disposable aluminum roasting pan

1. Rub roast with oil and season generously with pepper. Spread salt on rimmed baking sheet; press roast into salt to coat evenly on all sides. Tie meat back onto bones exactly from where it was cut, passing two lengths of twine between each set of bones and knotting securely. Refrigerate

roast, uncovered, for 1 hour, then let stand at room temperature 2 additional hours.

2. Meanwhile, soak wood chunks in water for 1 hour; drain. About 20 minutes before grilling, open top and bottom grill vents. Using chimney starter, ignite 4 quarts charcoal briquettes (about 60 coals) and burn until partially covered in thin, gray ash, about 15 minutes. Empty coals into grill; build modified two-level fire by arranging coals to cover one-half of grill. Place disposable roasting pan on empty side of grill. Position cooking grate over coals, cover grill, and heat until hot, about 5 minutes; scrape grate clean with grill brush.

3. Place roast on grate over hot side of grill and sear on fat-covered sides until well browned, turning as needed, 8 to 10 minutes total. (If flare-ups occur, move roast to cooler side of grill until flames die down.) When thoroughly browned, transfer roast to cooler side of grill, bone side down, with tips of bones pointed away from fire. Place soaked wood chunks on coals. Cover grill, positioning top vent over roast to draw smoke through grill. Grill-roast (do not remove lid for at least 1½ hours) until instant-read thermometer inserted into center of roast reads 125 degrees for medium-rare, 2 to 2½ hours.

4. Transfer roast to cutting board and let rest 20 minutes, lightly tented with foil. Remove strings and bones, cut into ½-inch-thick slices, and serve.

GRILL-ROASTED PRIME RIB FOR GAS GRILL

1. Follow recipe for Grill-Roasted Prime Rib for Charcoal Grill through step 1.

2. Soak 2 cups wood chips in water for 30 minutes; drain. Place wood chips in small disposable aluminum pan; set aside. About 20 minutes before grilling, ignite grill, turn all burners to high, cover, and heat until very hot, about 15 minutes. Scrape grate clean with grill brush.

3. Continue with recipe from step 3, turning off all but primary burner (burner that will remain on during cooking), placing pan with wood chips

TAMING THE GRILL'S HEAT

After searing the roast's fat-covered perimeter directly over the coals, transfer it to the cooler side, with the tips of the bones facing away from the fire.

on primary burner, and cooking with lid down once roast has been seared and positioned on cool side of grill as directed.

GRILL-ROASTED PRIME RIB WITH GARLIC-ROSEMARY CRUST

Combine ½ cup extra-virgin olive oil, ¼ cup minced garlic, and ¼ cup minced fresh rosemary leaves in bowl. Follow recipe for Grill-Roasted Prime Rib, brushing paste onto roast after searing in step 3.

SHOPPING: Locating the Prime Rib

There are 13 beef ribs, numbered in ascending order from the front of the animal to the back. The first five ribs are the chuck section (1 through 5), the next seven are the rib section (6 through 12), and the 13th is part of the loin. Ribs 6 through 12, the rib section, are sold as prime rib. A seven-rib prime rib roast can weigh as much as 20 pounds, enough for at least 16 guests. For smaller crowds, butchers often divide the whole prime rib into two smaller portions.

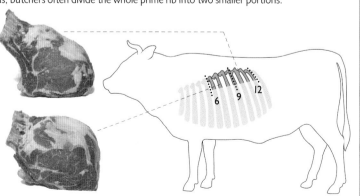

FIRST CUT: OUR FAVORITE
The first-cut roast consists of ribs 10 through 12 (sometimes rib 9 is included, too). Its large center eye of meat and beefy flavor make this our preferred cut.

SECOND CUT: TOO GRISTLY
The second-cut roast consists of ribs 6 through 8 (sometimes rib 9 is included, too). Lots of flavor, but the additional fat and gristle make it less appealing.

The Ultimate Dinner Rolls

Why bother making dinner rolls unless they are really rich, really soft, and really good?

≥ BY DAWN YANAGIHARA ≤

In my experience, homemade dinner rolls are often the difference between the preparation of an ambitious meal and an overambitious one. When there isn't any oven space, the sink is full of dirty pots and pans, and I'm feeling overextended, dinner rolls are the first item to be dropped from the menu. And I'd sooner opt for no rolls than serve mediocre ones made from quickie recipes that employ shortcuts like lightning-fast rises. Yes, these fast recipes turn out rolls that look the part, but they don't allow enough time for the dough to develop much flavor. In truth, they're not much better than the rolls you can buy at the supermarket. If I'm going to make my own dinner rolls, they have to be worth the effort.

Now, to be clear, when I say dinner rolls, I don't mean the coarse, crusty artisanal kind. I mean rich, soft, tender, airy, semisweet, pull-apart all-American dinner rolls, the kind that are as soft and plush as down pillows. I had one main goal in mind: I wanted to develop a formula that would produce the best such rolls without any shortcuts that would deny them full development of flavor. And, as a secondary objective, I would try to develop a recipe that could be prepared largely in advance so as to free up time and space for meatier kitchen pursuits. That way, perhaps dinner rolls would have a better shot at making it to the table.

There's a multitude of roll recipes out there. I carefully selected a few that showed promise. None failed, but none was ideal either. There were dry and lean rolls; rolls as fluffy as cotton candy; dull, boring rolls that were sandwich bread in disguise; and rolls that reeked of yeast. I rolled up my sleeves and got to work.

Flavor Building

I learned enough from my initial tests to devise a working recipe. It was very basic: milk, melted butter (much tastier than oil), eggs, yeast, sugar, salt, and flour kneaded together in a standing mixer for a few minutes. The dough rises, is shaped, rises again, and is finally baked.

I began by testing the main ingredient: flour. One recipe called for some cake flour, and I thought it was worth trying to see if it would

Rich, soft, and tender—with mild sweetness—these dinner rolls are best served warm with a pat of butter.

help the rolls develop a light, tender crumb. After experimenting, though, I found that even a small amount of cake flour made for overly soft rolls without adequate structure. The rolls with the best texture—tender and airy yet also resilient—were made with all-purpose flour.

Many roll recipes use milk as the liquid, and for good reason. With water, the rolls were lean, dry, and bland. Buttermilk made them taste funky. With milk, the rolls were soft, tender, and rich. I heeded the advice that many baking experts give about scalding—or heating—the milk and skimming off the "skin" that forms on the surface. This step did indeed result in rolls with a bit more height and a lighter crumb.

Most soft dinner roll recipes call for a single egg. I found that two eggs produced more flavor and better texture. Butter is primarily responsible for the richness in rolls. Most of the recipes in my research folder used 4 tablespoons, but my tasters thought these rolls were too dry and lean. Six tablespoons proved the ideal amount: The rolls

now tasted sweet and buttery but weren't so unctuous that they competed with the main course.

While I found most published recipes to be light on eggs and butter, the amounts of sugar and salt in these recipes were downright skimpy. I ended up using more sugar (6 tablespoons) than any other recipe I could find. Likewise, flavorful rolls demand a decent amount of salt; I settled on 1½ teaspoons.

Roll Playing

Just by getting the ingredients right, my rolls were certainly better than most. It makes sense that flavorful rolls demand liberal amounts of eggs, butter, sugar, and salt. But I had other ideas about how to improve their flavor further.

I realized my dough was similar to the queen mother of rich breads: brioche. Traditionally, brioche, rich with eggs and laden with butter, undergoes multiple rises, the second of which is a slow, cold rise in the fridge that allows the yeast to work its magic slowly so the flavors have time to develop. Could I learn something from brioche recipes?

My first thought was to take shaped and partially risen rolls and let them finish rising in the fridge; then the next day they could simply be brought to room temperature and baked. I soon discovered that it was impossible to predict how much the rolls would rise in the fridge. I needed a more reliable method.

I made more dough, allowed it to rise, and shaped more rolls. This time I put them in the fridge straight away, without any secondary rise. The following day I took out the rolls and let them rise. When placed in a sunny window in the test kitchen (roughly 80 degrees), the rolls rose unevenly and tasted "boozy." At cool room temperature, a languid pace of six or seven hours let the rolls rise evenly; once baked, their flavor was superb.

To make sure that all this time (but not much hands-on effort) was indeed worthwhile, I made a batch of same-day rolls for the sake of comparison. Both batches had the same open, airy texture, but the rolls left to rise overnight had a rounder, richer, more complex flavor—the result of allowing the flavors in the dough to develop slowly in the refrigerator overnight.

If You Can't Help the Heat, Get out of the Kitchen

These rolls rise for several hours on the counter, so getting the temperature right is crucial. At cool room temperature (68 degrees), the dough rounds should double in size after six or seven hours, yielding light, fluffy rolls upon baking. If they rise in a spot that's too warm, the exterior will race ahead of the interior, the rolls will rise unevenly, and a pan full of dense, misshapen rocks will emerge from the oven. If the heat in your kitchen is unpredictable, try a less conventional cool spot—like a basement or a spare bedroom.

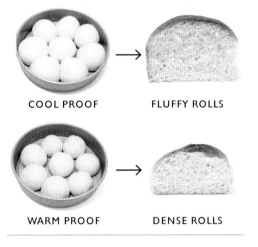

COOL PROOF   **FLUFFY ROLLS**

WARM PROOF   **DENSE ROLLS**

Yes, my rolls are two days in the making and they require a little planning (what kind of bread doesn't?). But their superior flavor is worth the modest investment. And the unforeseen bonus can't be overlooked: A night in the fridge means that the bulk of the work can be completed a day in advance (two days, even, I later found out). The day of serving, the rolls don't demand any attention, just a little counter space, then a quick brush with melted butter and 15 minutes in a 400-degree oven. Now a hectic kitchen is no excuse for the absence of dinner rolls.

BEST AMERICAN DINNER ROLLS
MAKES SIXTEEN 3-INCH ROLLS

For this recipe, the dough is made and the rolls are shaped and refrigerated a day or two before being baked and served. Be sure to plan accordingly, as the refrigerated rolls require about six hours to rise before they're ready for baking. For the best flavor, let the rolls rise at cool room temperature, about 68 degrees. Depending on the brand, instant yeast is marketed as "rapid rise," "quick rise," or "perfect rise" yeast, or sometimes as bread machine yeast; if it's necessary to use active dry yeast in its place, see page 30 for more information. If your cake pans have a dark nonstick finish, bake the rolls in a 375-degree oven to moderate the browning. This dough should be moister than most; resist the urge to add more flour than is needed to keep the dough from sticking to your hands. Made on a humid day, the dough may require more flour than if made on a dry day.

¾	cup whole milk
6	tablespoons unsalted butter, melted, plus 2 tablespoons, melted, for brushing on rolls before baking
6	tablespoons sugar
1½	teaspoons table salt
2	large eggs, room temperature
2¼	teaspoons (1 packet) instant (rapid rise) yeast
3	cups (15 ounces) unbleached all-purpose flour, plus additional flour as needed (see note above)

1. **TO MAKE THE DOUGH:** Bring milk to boil in small saucepan over medium heat; let stand off heat until skin forms on surface, 3 to 5 minutes. Using soup spoon, skim skin off surface and discard. Transfer milk to bowl of standing mixer and add 6 tablespoons melted butter, sugar, and salt; whisk to combine and let mixture cool. When mixture is just warm to the touch (90 to 100 degrees), whisk in eggs and yeast until combined.

2. Add flour to bowl; using dough hook, mix on low speed on standing mixer until combined, 1 to 2 minutes. Increase speed to medium-low and knead about 3 minutes more; when pressed with finger, dough should feel tacky and moist but should not stick to finger. (If dough is sticky, add another 1 to 3 tablespoons flour.) Continue to knead on medium-low until cohesive, elastic dough has formed (it should clear sides of bowl but stick to bottom), 4 to 5 minutes longer.

3. Transfer dough to lightly floured work surface. Knead dough by hand 1 to 2 minutes to ensure that it is well kneaded. Dough should be very soft and moist but not overly sticky. (If dough sticks excessively to hands and work surface, knead in flour a tablespoon at a time until dough is workable.) Lightly spray medium bowl with nonstick cooking spray. Transfer dough to bowl; lightly coat surface of dough with cooking spray and cover with plastic wrap. Let dough rise in warm, draft-free location until doubled in volume, 2 to 3 hours.

4. **TO SHAPE THE ROLLS:** Coat two 9-inch round cake pans with cooking spray; set aside. Turn dough out onto lightly floured work surface. Pat dough into rough 12 by 10-inch rectangle (see illustration 1, below), gently pressing out air; starting from edge farthest from you, roll dough into cylinder (illustration 2). Using palms, roll dough back and forth until cylinder is about 18 inches long and of even thickness. Using bench scraper or chef's knife, cut cylinder in half crosswise, then cut each half into 8 evenly sized pieces (illustration 3).

5. Working with one piece at a time and keeping remaining pieces covered with plastic wrap or kitchen towel, form dough pieces into smooth, taut rounds (illustration 4). Set piece of dough on unfloured area of work surface. Loosely cup hand around dough (not directly over it); without applying pressure to dough, move hand in small circular motions. (Tackiness of dough against work surface and circular motion should work dough into smooth, even ball.) Arrange shaped rolls in prepared cake pans (one in center and seven spaced evenly around edges) (illustration 5); cover cake pans with plastic wrap lightly coated with cooking spray, then cover pans securely with foil. Refrigerate at least 24 or up to 48 hours.

6. **TO BAKE THE ROLLS:** Remove foil (but not plastic wrap) from cake pans; let rolls rise in draft-free cool room-temperature location until doubled in volume (rolls should press against each other), 6 to 7 hours. When rolls are nearly doubled in volume, adjust oven rack to lower-middle position and heat oven to 400 degrees. Remove plastic wrap. Brush rolls with 2 tablespoons melted butter; bake until deep golden brown, 14 to 18 minutes. Cool rolls in pans on wire rack about 3 minutes, then invert onto rack; re-invert rolls and cool 10 to 15 minutes longer. Break rolls apart and serve warm.

STEP-BY-STEP | GETTING DINNER ROLLS SHAPED JUST RIGHT

1. Pat dough into 12 by 10-inch rectangle.

2. Roll dough to form even cylinder, stretching to 18-inch length.

3. Using bench scraper or chef's knife, cut cylinder into 16 pieces.

4. Using circular motion, gently form dough pieces into rounds.

5. Arrange rounds in pan, one in center, seven around edge.

Flavor-Packed Fresh Tomato Sauces

How do you make a sauce that does justice to the robust flavor of seasonal tomatoes?

≥ BY MATTHEW CARD ≤

The dog days of summer produce the only fresh tomatoes of the year fit for pairing with pasta. Packed with bracing acidity and sweet fruitiness, they taste the way tomatoes should yet rarely do. Seizing the opportunity, I splurged on several crates of these rare specimens and set out to create a few quick pasta sauces that would capitalize on their full, robust flavor.

Previously, the test kitchen has found that one of the best ways to prepare tomatoes for pasta sauces is to skin, seed, and chop them into small pieces before simmering them in a skillet with garlic and olive oil. With the skillet's ample cooking surface, it's only a matter of minutes before the excess moisture evaporates and the tomatoes gently slump into a hearty sauce. Any type of tomato tastes fine cooked this way: Ripeness, not variety, is key.

I quickly discovered that meek ingredients weren't going to cut it here; they simply dulled the liveliness of the tomatoes. So I cast the usual parsley and ricotta aside in favor of potent herbs and spices, cured meats, and assertive cheeses. Piney rosemary, smoky bacon, pungent feta, spicy pepperoncini, and similar ingredients pointed up the fresh qualities of these gutsy tomatoes yet gamely shared the spotlight. A cautious touch, however, was crucial; a spoonful too much threw the sauce out of whack, obscuring the tomato flavor. As with most things in life, balance really paid off.

FRESH TOMATO SAUCE WITH ROSEMARY AND BACON
MAKES ENOUGH TO SAUCE I POUND OF PASTA

Pancetta can be substituted for the bacon. Any short tubular pasta is well suited to this sauce. If your tomatoes are tart, you may need to add up to ½ teaspoon sugar.

- 6 ounces bacon (6 slices), cut crosswise into ½-inch strips
- 2 tablespoons extra-virgin olive oil
- 2 medium garlic cloves, minced or pressed through garlic press (about 2 teaspoons)
- ½ teaspoon minced fresh rosemary
- ½–¾ teaspoon hot red pepper flakes
- 3 pounds ripe round tomatoes, cored, peeled, seeded, and cut into ½-inch pieces (about 3¾ cups)
- 1 tablespoon chopped fresh parsley leaves
- ¼ teaspoon table salt
- ⅛ teaspoon ground black pepper
  Granulated sugar
- 2 ounces Parmesan cheese, shaved thin with vegetable peeler (about ¾ cup)

1. Cook bacon in 10-inch skillet over medium heat, stirring occasionally, until crisp, 8 to 10 minutes. Using slotted spoon, transfer bacon to paper-towel-lined plate. Pour off bacon fat from pan and discard.

2. Return skillet to medium-high heat. Add oil, swirl to coat pan, and add garlic, rosemary, and pepper flakes. Cook, stirring constantly, until garlic is fragrant but not browned, about 30 seconds. Stir in tomatoes and cook until tomato pieces lose their shape to form chunky sauce, about 10 minutes. Stir in parsley, salt, pepper, and sugar to taste. Toss sauce with pasta and serve, sprinkling Parmesan and reserved bacon over individual bowls.

FRESH TOMATO SAUCE WITH SALAMI, PEPPERONCINI, AND MOZZARELLA
MAKES ENOUGH TO SAUCE I POUND OF PASTA

Use spicy (not mild) pepperoncini to balance the richness of the sauce. Farfalle pasta is a good choice for this sauce. If your tomatoes are tart, you may need to add up to ½ teaspoon sugar.

- 3 tablespoons extra-virgin olive oil
- 2 medium garlic cloves, minced or pressed through garlic press (about 2 teaspoons)
- 3 pounds ripe round tomatoes, cored, peeled, seeded, and cut into ½-inch pieces (about 3¾ cups)
- 4 ounces salami, cut into ⅛-inch-thick slices, slices cut into half-moons, and half-moons cut into ¼-inch-wide strips
- 1 tablespoon chopped fresh oregano leaves
- ⅓ cup thinly sliced pepperoncini, drained and rinsed
- ¼ teaspoon table salt
- ⅛ teaspoon ground black pepper
  Granulated sugar
- 12 ounces fresh mozzarella, cut into ½-inch pieces and blotted dry

1. Heat 2 tablespoons oil and garlic in 10-inch skillet over medium heat until garlic is fragrant but not browned, 1 to 2 minutes. Stir in tomatoes; increase heat to medium-high and cook until tomato pieces lose their shape to form chunky sauce, about 10 minutes, stirring in salami after 8 minutes to heat through.

2. Stir in oregano, pepperoncini, salt, pepper, and sugar to taste. Toss sauce, mozzarella, and remaining tablespoon oil with pasta and serve.

FRESH TOMATO SAUCE WITH FENNEL AND ORANGE
MAKES ENOUGH TO SAUCE I POUND OF PASTA

Any short tubular or curly pasta works well with this sauce. If your tomatoes are tart, you may need to add up to ½ teaspoon sugar.

- 4 tablespoons extra-virgin olive oil
- 1 medium fennel bulb, trimmed of stalks, halved, cored, and cut into ¼-inch dice (about 1½ cups)
- 2 medium garlic cloves, minced or pressed through garlic press (about 2 teaspoons)
- ½ teaspoon fennel seed, lightly crushed
  Pinch saffron, crushed (optional)
- ⅛ teaspoon hot red pepper flakes
- 2 strips orange peel (each 3 by 1 inch) plus 3 tablespoons juice from 1 orange
- 3 pounds ripe round tomatoes, cored, peeled, seeded, and cut into ½-inch pieces (about 3¾ cups)
- 3 tablespoons chopped fresh basil leaves
- ¼ teaspoon table salt
- ⅛ teaspoon ground black pepper
  Granulated sugar

1. Heat 2 tablespoons oil in 10-inch skillet over medium-high heat until shimmering. Add fennel and cook, stirring occasionally, until softened and browned around edges, 4 to 6 minutes. Add garlic, fennel seed, saffron (if using), pepper flakes, and orange peel; cook, stirring constantly, until fragrant, about 30 seconds. Stir in tomatoes and cook until tomato pieces lose their shape to form chunky sauce, about 10 minutes

2. Remove and discard orange peel. Stir in orange juice, basil, salt, pepper, and sugar to taste. Toss sauce and remaining 2 tablespoons oil with pasta and serve.

Go to www.cooksillustrated.com
- Key in code 9063 for our recipe for **Fresh Tomato Sauce with Roasted Peppers, Toasted Garlic, and Paprika.**
- Key in code 9064 for our recipe for **Fresh Tomato Sauce with Mint, Feta, and Spinach.**
- Recipes available until March 1, 2007.

Better Roast Chicken and Vegetables

Roasting a few vegetables along with the chicken makes for an easy side dish, right? Greasy side dish is more like it. We set out to fine-tune this flawed Sunday-night classic.

> BY SARAH WILSON <

For roasted vegetables that are dripping with chicken flavor—not chicken grease—make sure the serving platter is the first place the chicken and vegetables meet.

Like communism or sunless tanning, roasting chicken and vegetables together is far more appealing in theory than in practice. It's a tempting proposition: With a chicken perched on a roasting rack dripping flavorful juices into the expanse below, it seems a shame not to toss in a few vegetables to soak up all that yummy, chickeny goodness. A bonus side dish, no fuss or forethought required.

Unfortunately, when it comes to chicken and vegetables, killing two birds with one stone usually means victimizing the veggies. They may be chock-full of chicken flavor, but they're also awash in greasy schmaltz and overcooked to a mushy consistency. Clearly, this classic Sunday-dinner combo required more than spur-of-the-moment improvisation. My goal was to come up with a recipe that gave each component the attention it deserved—not just the chicken. I wanted juicy meat, crispy-thin skin, and vegetables infused with chicken flavor, not just chicken fat.

Chicken Account

Even though the vegetables were no doubt the true victims here, the chicken had a few grievances of its own. Most *Cook's* roast chicken recipes call for a 3½-pound bird. That's fine for two or three people (or four on a diet), but I wanted enough chicken to feed a hungry family. So I opted for the big birds in my supermarket's poultry case—specifically, the "oven stuffer roasters." Weighing in at 6 to 8 pounds, these chickens would easily serve six.

Now that I was in big-bird territory, however, I had a new set of problems. First, while I'd planned to follow the test kitchen's usual chicken-roasting procedure—brining (to season the meat and keep it moist) and flipping (so the dark meat and white meat cook evenly)—I would have to adjust the times for this larger bird. Second, because mass-produced chickens generally taste bland, the test kitchen tends to splurge on chickens from boutique poultry purveyors (such as Empire or Bell & Evans), which offer superior flavor in exchange for slightly steeper prices. Unfortunately, these "boutique birds" mostly come in petite sizes; the big chickens in my supermarket are almost exclusively of the bland, mass-produced variety.

I tackled brining first. The test kitchen's standard formula for brining poultry is 1 cup of table salt and 1 cup of sugar in a gallon of water. With a 3½-pound chicken, it takes an hour for the brine to penetrate the meat fully. With an 18-pound turkey, it takes about six hours. I figured the brining time for my 6- to 8-pound roaster would fall somewhere in between. Sure enough, a few tests told me that the magic number was just under four hours. While that kind of wait may be OK for a once-a-year holiday feast, it seemed like overkill for a typical Sunday-night supper. Trying out various amounts of salt and sugar, I found that upping the concentration to 1½ cups of each (per gallon of water) gave me a fully seasoned chicken in just two hours.

Next, I tried adapting the "small bird" roasting method for this large chicken: basically, wing up for 20 minutes, the other wing up for 20 minutes, then breast up until done (about 20 minutes more). An additional 10 minutes or so for each step yielded evenly cooked white and dark meat. I experimented with various combinations of oven temperatures (starting out high, decreasing partway with cooking, and so on) but found that the best method was also the easiest: 400 degrees from start to finish.

This chicken had juicy, seasoned meat and crisp, well-rendered skin, but the bland flavor still left something to be desired. (Salt only enhances flavors if there are, in fact, any flavors to enhance.) First, I tried stuffing the cavity with aromatics—onions and fresh herbs—but nobody could taste a difference. Lemon and garlic were better but still too subtle. Taking a cue from a previous *Cook's* recipe, I tried adding a few garlic cloves and bay leaves to my brine. This really got tasters' attention. Gradually increasing the amounts of each, I found that spiking the brine with two full

Boosting a Bland Bird's Flavor

Mass-produced chickens are notoriously bland, and their more flavorful "boutique" counterparts aren't widely available in larger sizes. We solved the problem by adding two full heads of garlic and six bay leaves to the brine, along with the usual salt and sugar.

heads of crushed garlic and six bay leaves gave the chicken great flavor once cooked.

Surprisingly, the only thing my colleagues noticed was a huge improvement in chicken flavor, not garlicky meat perfumed by bay leaf. In fact, not one taster guessed my secret ingredient. What was going on? It turns out that the enzyme (called allinase) responsible for garlic's characteristic bite is deactivated in the presence of very high concentrations of salt. With its "garlicky" traits masked, the garlic in the brine contributed only its mellow, savory qualities to the chicken—in this case, just what the doctor ordered.

Grease Monkeying

Turning my attention to the vegetables, I stuck with the usual suspects—carrots, onions, parsnips, and potatoes. I knew from experience that roasting the cut-up vegetables right along with the chicken was problematic. The sheer volume of greasy juices overwhelmed them, if overcooking didn't kill them off first. Clearly, the vegetables needed less roasting time than the chicken, and I had to get rid of some of the grease. I tried pouring off all the juices from the roasting pan when the chicken was mostly done, adding the vegetables to a virtually fat-free pan. While this was a big improvement, the chicken continued to render fat as it finished cooking, making the vegetables too greasy still.

At this point, I was beginning to wonder whether grease-free, chicken-infused veggies were but a pipe dream. After all, the test kitchen had already figured out the secret to great caramelized vegetables—tossing them with some oil and salt and roasting them in a pan. In a separate pan, that is. Maybe the secret to great roast chicken and vegetables was to keep the chicken and vegetables as far away from each other as possible.

That's when I made my first real breakthrough. If I roasted the vegetables separately, I figured I could control precisely how much fat mingled with them. My idea was to use the test kitchen's existing recipe for roasted root vegetables, replacing the oil with an equal amount of chicken fat. Even better, if I timed things so the vegetables roasted during the chicken's half-hour rest (a step that helps redistribute juices throughout the meat), I could serve them piping-hot along with the chicken.

Taking a chicken's temperature can be tricky, no matter how good your thermometer. For the most precise readings, follow the procedures below. Also, it's important to test both breasts and both thighs in multiple spots.

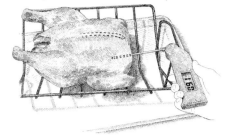

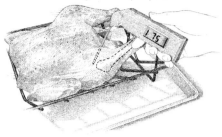

WHITE MEAT
Insert the thermometer into the thickest part of the breast from the neck end, keeping it parallel to the breastbone. The white meat is done when the temperature reaches 160 degrees.

DARK MEAT
Insert the thermometer at an angle into the thickest part of the thigh—located between the drumstick and breast—taking care not to hit bone. The dark meat is done when the temperature reaches 175 degrees.

With new hope, I plopped yet another chicken into the roasting pan, my cut-up vegetables at the ready. As soon as the chicken was finished cooking, I moved it to a cutting board to rest and tossed the vegetables with 3 tablespoons of chicken fat salvaged from the pan, transferring them to a baking sheet and into the oven. Thirty minutes later, disappointment loomed: The vegetables were greasy and poorly browned. Even worse, they barely tasted like chicken at all.

The browning problem I solved easily, by cranking up the heat from 400 degrees to 500 degrees. But the greasiness lingered, as did the puzzling lack of chicken flavor. Dejected, I was packing it in for the day when I noticed the dark, sticky *fond* (browned bits) encrusted on the bottom of the roasting pan. It was at that moment that I realized the error of my ways. Of course! It wasn't the chicken fat that contained all the flavor but the fond—the building block of flavor for every pan sauce I had ever made.

Flavor Saver

To take advantage of the fond, I first needed to preserve it—after an hour and a half of cooking, what had accumulated in the pan was either too hardened to use or just plain burned. Water added to the pan at the beginning evaporated too quickly. But by adding 1 cup of water at the one-hour mark (when the chicken is flipped breast side up), I was able to save the fond that

was already developing and ensure that the rest of the drippings would continue to enrich the liquid. When I substituted a cup of store-bought chicken broth for the water, the drippings ended up even richer.

Once the chicken was fully cooked (and safely removed from the pan), I poured the pan contents into a fat separator. I tossed the fat with the vegetables, but how was I going to introduce the defatted drippings—the sole agent of chicken flavor—to the vegetables? When added too early, the liquid hindered browning, giving me ultra-chickeny but utterly soggy vegetables. Experimenting with times and amounts, I got the best results when adding ½ cup of the defatted drippings to the vegetables after 25 minutes, then cranking up the oven to the broil setting for 10 minutes to get the veggies good and glazed, stirring them once partway through. As for the grease factor, I found that discarding the chicken fat completely in favor of plain vegetable oil made for less sodden vegetables and a cleaner taste.

A flawed improvisation no longer, this carefully composed version of roast chicken and vegetables had been transformed into a sophisticated meal fit for company (not just my forgiving family). Who would have thought that the secret to ultra-chickeny chicken and vegetables was to make sure the chicken and vegetables never met at all—at least not until they hit the plate?

RECIPE SHORTHAND: **Which Comes First, the Chicken or the Vegetables?**

1. Roast chicken, wing side up, for 30 minutes. **2.** Roast chicken, other wing side up, for 30 minutes. **3.** Flip chicken breast side up, pour broth into pan, and roast for 40 minutes. **4.** Transfer chicken to cutting board to rest, and pour drippings into fat separator. **5.** Reheat roasting pan while oven heats up to 500 degrees. **6.** Toss vegetables with oil, add to heated roasting pan, and roast for 25 minutes. **7.** Turn oven setting to broil and pour defatted drippings into pan, tossing with vegetables. Broil for 10 minutes.

ROAST CHICKEN WITH ROOT VEGETABLES
SERVES 4 TO 6

The times given in the recipe are designed to work with a 6- to 8-pound chicken. It's possible to roast a slightly smaller bird (around 5 pounds) by reducing the roasting time in step 4 to about 25 minutes, but if all you can find are 3- to 4-pound chickens, see the following recipe for Two Roast Chickens with Root Vegetables. Begin carving the chicken as soon as the vegetables are placed underneath the broiler. If using medium potatoes (2 to 3 inches in diameter), cut in half. If using large potatoes (3 to 4 inches in diameter), cut into quarters. We prefer a large, traditional (not nonstick) roasting pan for this recipe; if using a nonstick roasting pan, refrain from turning up the oven to broil when cooking the vegetables and stir them every 5 to 7 minutes to ensure they don't become too dark. If your broiler does not accommodate a roasting pan, continue to cook the vegetables at 500 degrees until done. You can substitute the following seasonal vegetables for any of those in the recipe: beets, celery root, fennel, rutabagas, and turnips; peel these vegetables (except for the fennel) and cut them into 2- to 3-inch pieces.

Chicken and Brine
- 1½ cups table salt
- 1½ cups sugar
- 2 medium heads garlic, outer papery skins removed, cloves separated, unpeeled, and crushed
- 6 bay leaves, crumbled
- 1 whole chicken (6 to 8 pounds), giblets removed and discarded
  Ground black pepper
- 1 cup low-sodium chicken broth, or more as needed

Vegetables
- 1 pound small (1½- to 2-inch diameter) red potatoes, scrubbed and unpeeled
- 1 pound medium carrots, peeled, cut into 2- to 3-inch pieces, tapered ends left whole, large upper portions halved lengthwise
- ½ pound parsnips, peeled, cut into 2- to 3-inch pieces, tapered ends left whole, large upper portions halved lengthwise
- ½ pound small (2- to 3-inch diameter) yellow onions, peeled, root end left intact, and quartered
- 3 tablespoons vegetable oil
- ½ teaspoon table salt
- ⅛ teaspoon ground black pepper

1. **FOR THE CHICKEN AND BRINE:** Dissolve salt and sugar in 1 gallon cold water in large container. Stir in garlic and bay; immerse chicken and refrigerate until fully seasoned, about 2 hours.

2. Adjust oven rack to middle position and heat oven to 400 degrees. Set V-rack in large flameproof roasting pan and lightly spray with nonstick cooking spray. Remove chicken from brine and thoroughly pat dry with paper towels.

3. Season chicken on all sides with pepper; set wing side up on prepared V-rack and roast for 30 minutes. Remove roasting pan from oven and, using 2 wads of paper towels, rotate chicken so other wing side faces up; continue to roast for 30 minutes.

4. Remove roasting pan from oven and, using 2 large wads paper towels, rotate chicken breast side up. Add 1 cup broth and continue to roast until chicken is golden brown and instant-read thermometer registers 160 degrees inserted in thickest part of breast and 175 degrees in thickest part of thigh, about 40 minutes. (If necessary, add more broth to maintain thin layer of broth on bottom of roasting pan.) Transfer chicken to cutting board and let rest, uncovered, while roasting vegetables; remove V-rack from roasting pan.

5. **FOR THE VEGETABLES:** While chicken is resting, adjust oven rack to middle position and increase oven temperature to 500 degrees. Using wooden spoon, scrape browned bits in roasting pan and pour liquid into fat separator. Return now-empty roasting pan to oven and heat until oven reaches 500 degrees, about 5 minutes. Toss vegetables with oil, salt, and pepper.

6. Scatter vegetables in single layer in roasting pan, arranging potatoes and onions cut side down. Roast, without stirring, for 25 minutes.

7. While vegetables are roasting, pour off ½ cup liquid from fat separator; discard remaining liquid and fat. Remove roasting pan from oven and heat broiler. Drizzle liquid over vegetables and broil, 5 minutes. Stir vegetables, coating well with reducing liquid, and continue to broil until tender and deep golden brown, about 5 minutes. Transfer vegetables to serving platter.

8. While vegetables are broiling, carve chicken. Transfer to platter with vegetables and serve.

TWO ROAST CHICKENS WITH ROOT VEGETABLES

If you can't find a large chicken at the market, it's possible to roast two 3- to 4-pound chickens using a similar method.

Follow recipe for Roast Chicken with Root Vegetables, substituting two 3- to 4-pound chickens for 6- to 8-pound chicken and reducing brining time to 1 hour. In step 3, reduce wing-side-up roasting time to 20 minutes per side. Continue to roast chickens as directed, reducing breast-side-up roasting time to 30 to 40 minutes.

TESTING EQUIPMENT: Roasting Racks

A roasting rack is as unglamorous as it is essential. It raises poultry and roasts out of the drippings, while giving the oven's heat easy access to the whole surface—a good start toward a well-rendered exterior. In a 1997 testing, we liked the V-shaped Norpro Nonstick Roasting Rack ($9.75). It holds roasts snugly in place, and we prefer its fixed shape, since adjustable racks have a nasty habit of adjusting when you least expect it. Recently, more V-racks have appeared on the market. Are any preferable to the model we've been using in the test kitchen?

Right away, we noted that not all V-racks are actually V-shaped. The slight bend on the Progressive V Shape Non-Stick Roasting Rack ($3.49) barely qualifies as a "V" and leaves no room for roasting vegetables underneath. The innovative Cuisipro Roast and Serve ($28.95) is shaped like a trough with a hinge at the center. Remove the dowel from the hinge and the rack comes apart, dropping the roast onto a platter or cutting board. While it worked fine, this rack was another that didn't elevate the roast enough, and its size (15 inches by 11½ inches) makes it a tight squeeze in all but the largest pan.

In addition to shape, handles were a decisive factor. Tall, vertical handles make removing the rack easy, even with bulky oven mitts. Horizontal handles, or no handles at all, make removal nearly impossible. In our tests, we also noticed that handle position matters. When located on the short sides of a rectangular rack they can get in the way of the roasting pan's handles. We prefer handles positioned on the long side of the rack.

The All-Clad Non-Stick Roasting Rack ($24.95) is our top choice. It's large enough to hold two small chickens and has the features we like. With its handles on the short side, the Norpro is a distant runner-up. If you're in the market for a new roasting pan, you should consider our favorite roaster, the Calphalon Contemporary Stainless All Season Pan ($99), which includes a rack that's just as good as the All-Clad model.

–Garth Clingingsmith

NEW FAVORITE
The sturdy All-Clad rack has good handles in a convenient location.

OLD FAVORITE
The Norpro rack would be better with handles on the long sides.

ALL WRONG
Shallow shape and no handles render the Progressive rack useless.

ALL IN ONE
Our favorite roasting pan, from Calphalon, includes a great rack.

Improving Sautéed Pork Tenderloin

Boneless, lean, and tender, pork tenderloin offers plenty of hope for the time-pressed weeknight cook. If only it offered plenty of flavor.

⇒ BY DAVID PAZMIÑO ⇐

With no bones, minimal fat, and wide availability, pork tenderloin has plenty going for it. When cooked properly, it has a tenderness rivaling that of beef tenderloin, the deluxe roast that gives us filet mignon. On the downside, this ultra-lean cut has an ultra-mild flavor that needs a major boost. Long marinades and hybrid searing/roasting techniques (the latter providing flavorful browning) help remedy such deficiencies, but they also take the home cook a long way from the realm of the no-fuss meal.

I wanted a recipe for a fast weeknight dinner, so I was left with only a small arsenal of tools at my disposal to enhance flavor and ensure juiciness. Skillets and quick pan sauces were in; brining, marinating, and heating a grill or oven were out.

Getting the Pork into Shape

The first problem was the tenderloin's oblong, tapered shape. Vacuum-sealed individually or in sets of two, the loins looked like neatly packed, identically sized sausages. Once unpacked, however, it became clear that they varied greatly in length (from 9 inches to 14 inches) and shape. And when packed in pairs, the two loins were almost guaranteed to be substantially different in weight, making it tricky to portion them out into equal servings. Tucking the tail end under the thicker section, then tying it into an evenly shaped roast, fixed that problem. But cooking the tenderloin whole (either pan-roasting or sautéing) took too much time—more than 30 minutes.

Slicing the tenderloin into thin medallions made for uniform thickness, but some pieces were nearly 3 inches wide while others were barely an inch. Attempts to cheat nature with creative bias slicing proved unreliable and tedious. What about cutting the smaller parts thicker and pounding them to equal width? More consistent, yes, but—thanks to the expanded surface area—they required sautéing in several batches.

Taking a cue from the more famous filet mignon, our "pork mignons" are thick-cut to keep them juicy and moist.

Overcooking was an even bigger problem with these sliced medallions. I wanted to get as much browning on the exterior as possible to provide textural contrast with the tender interior and to improve flavor. But with such thin slices, I had only two choices: overcooked medallions with a pronounced, flavorful sear or wan, gray disks. Neither was an acceptable compromise.

To get adequate browning without overcooking the interior, I next tried increasing the thickness of the medallions by increments—first half an inch, then ¾ inch, 1 inch, and so on—until they began to resemble miniature versions of beef tenderloin filets. At 2 inches thick, my "pork mignons" were developing a dark brown sear before the interiors had cooked through. At 1½ inches, the interior was cooked through but still juicy and the top and bottom surfaces were beautifully browned. These rounds also offered the advantage of fitting into a 12-inch skillet in one batch. Treating pork tenderloin like beef tenderloin was really doing the trick! Several tasters objected to leaving the sides unbrowned, so I made a point to stand the medallions on their sides (using tongs) during the searing process.

Cutting the pork into 1½-inch pieces left odd bits from both ends of the tenderloin, and even the slices from the central section were problematic, making for oblong pieces that would flop over and "flatten" awkwardly during cooking rather than maintaining their tidy cylindrical shape. To limit the number of odd pieces, I scored the section near the tail, creating a small flap of meat that folded underneath the larger half to yield the right-sized medallion (see the illustrations on page 15). To prevent the pork from flopping over, I took another cue from beef tenderloin and tied the meat with twine, which gave it much better structure. (Blanched bacon, wrapped around the thick medallions and fastened with toothpicks, was another effective method that also gave the dish a smoky flavor.)

Finishing Touches

At this point, my pork tenderloin medallions were juicy and nicely browned—and they could all be cooked in just one batch. But I wanted to boost the flavor even more. Unwilling to revisit the notion of a marinade, I decided to take advantage of the deep *fond* (the browned bits) left in the skillet by coming up with a few easy pan sauces to make while the medallions were given a five-minute rest, which allowed the juices to redistribute evenly.

Following the test kitchen's usual method for pan sauces, I cooked aromatics in the hot skillet until fragrant, deglazed the skillet with broth, then reduced the broth along with other flavorful ingredients. Given how mild pork tenderloin can be, I gravitated toward bold flavors. Raiding the pantry for staple items, I balanced the sweetness of maple syrup with balsamic vinegar and spicy whole grain mustard. For a more exotic—but still easy—spin on this sweet and sour theme, I

Good Pork, Bad Pork

While developing our recipe for pork tenderloin medallions, we struggled to achieve a deeply seared exterior without overcooking the interior. Our solution? Cut thicker medallions, which can spend more time in the pan.

GOOD
Great browning, moist interior.

BAD
Good browning, dry interior.

combined orange juice, hoisin sauce, ginger, and sesame oil, sprinkling chopped scallions over the medallions at the end for color and contrast (see Cook's Extra, page 14, for the recipe). Both of these sauces were ready in minutes.

My final sauce—a more complex mix of diced apples, apple cider, apple brandy, cinnamon, shallots, and thyme—wasn't thickening as much as I wanted during the pork's five-minute resting period. The solution was to cook most of the ingredients in a saucepan beforehand, then pour the reduced liquid into the skillet to finish.

THICK-CUT PORK TENDERLOIN MEDALLIONS
SERVES 4 TO 6

Serve with a pan sauce (recipes follow). We prefer natural to enhanced pork (pork that has been injected with a salt solution to increase moistness and flavor), though both will work in this recipe. Begin checking the doneness of smaller medallions 1 or 2 minutes early; they may need to be taken out of the pan a little sooner.

> 2   pork tenderloins (1 to 1¼ pounds each), trimmed of fat and silver skin, cut crosswise into 1½-inch pieces, and tied (see photo below); thinner end pieces removed and tied together according to illustrations above
> Kosher salt and ground black pepper
> 2   tablespoons vegetable oil

Season pork with salt and pepper. Heat oil in 12-inch skillet over medium-high heat until shimmering. Add pork cut side down and cook, without moving pieces, until well browned, 3 to 5 minutes. Turn pork and brown on second side, 3 to 5 minutes more. Reduce heat to medium. Using tongs, stand each piece on its side and cook, turning pieces as necessary, until sides are well browned and internal temperature registers 145 to 150 degrees on instant-read thermometer, 8 to 12 minutes. Transfer pork to platter and tent lightly with foil; let rest while making pan sauce (recipes follow), then serve.

MAPLE-MUSTARD SAUCE
MAKES ENOUGH TO SAUCE 2 PORK TENDERLOINS

> 2   teaspoons vegetable oil
> 1   medium onion, halved and sliced thin (about 1 cup)
> 1   cup low-sodium chicken broth
> ⅓   cup maple syrup
> 3   tablespoons balsamic vinegar
> 3   tablespoons whole grain mustard
> Table salt and ground black pepper

Pour off any fat from skillet in which pork was cooked. Add oil and heat skillet over medium heat until shimmering. Add onion and cook,

TECHNIQUE | TURNING THE END PIECE INTO A MEDALLION

After cutting the tenderloins into symmetrical 1½-inch medallions, you will inevitably have a few irregularly shaped pieces left over. The tapered end pieces can be scored, folded, and tied into medallions (as shown here). Tie any remaining smaller pieces together into a medallion shape, making sure top and bottom surfaces are flat.

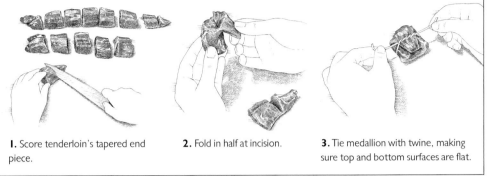

1. Score tenderloin's tapered end piece.

2. Fold in half at incision.

3. Tie medallion with twine, making sure top and bottom surfaces are flat.

stirring occasionally, until softened and beginning to brown, 3 to 4 minutes. Increase heat to medium-high and add broth; bring to simmer, scraping bottom of skillet with wooden spoon to loosen any browned bits. Simmer until liquid is reduced to ⅓ cup, 3 to 4 minutes. Add syrup, vinegar, mustard, and any juices from resting meat and cook until thickened and reduced to 1 cup, 3 to 4 minutes longer. Adjust seasonings with salt and pepper, pour sauce over pork, and serve.

APPLE CIDER SAUCE
MAKES ENOUGH TO SAUCE 2 PORK TENDERLOINS

Complete step 1 of this recipe either before or during the cooking of the pork, then finish the sauce while the pork rests.

> 1½   cups apple cider
> 1   cup low-sodium chicken broth
> 2   teaspoons cider vinegar
> 1   cinnamon stick
> 4   tablespoons unsalted butter, cut into 4 pieces
> 2   large shallots, minced (about ½ cup)
> 1   tart apple, such as Granny Smith, cored, peeled, and diced small
> ¼   cup Calvados or apple-flavored brandy
> 1   teaspoon minced fresh thyme leaves
> Table salt and ground black pepper

1. Combine cider, broth, vinegar, and cinnamon stick in medium saucepan; simmer over medium-high heat until liquid is reduced to 1 cup, 10 to 12 minutes. Remove cinnamon stick and discard. Set sauce aside until pork is cooked.

2. Pour off any fat from skillet in which pork was cooked. Add 1 tablespoon butter and heat over medium heat until melted and foaming subsides. Add shallots and apple and cook, stirring occasionally, until softened and beginning to brown, 1 to 2 minutes. Remove

skillet from heat and add Calvados. Return skillet to heat and cook about 1 minute, scraping bottom with wooden spoon to loosen browned bits. Add reduced cider mixture, any juices from resting meat, and thyme; increase heat to medium-high and simmer until thickened and reduced to 1¼ cups, 3 to 4 minutes. Off heat, whisk in remaining 3 tablespoons butter, and adjust seasonings with salt and pepper. Pour sauce over pork and serve immediately.

BACON-WRAPPED PORK TENDERLOIN MEDALLIONS

Place 12 to 14 slices bacon (1 slice for each pork medallion), slightly overlapping, in microwave-safe pie plate and cover with plastic wrap. Cook in microwave on high power until slices shrink and release about ½ cup fat but are neither browned nor crisp, 1 to 3 minutes. Transfer bacon to paper towels until cool, 2 to 3 minutes. Wrap each piece of pork with 1 slice bacon and secure with 2 toothpicks where ends of bacon strip overlap, inserting toothpicks on angle and gently pushing them through to other side (see photo, below). Season pork with pepper (do not salt) and proceed with step 2 of recipe for Thick-Cut Pork Tenderloin Medallions (time for searing sides may be slightly longer).

Two Tricks for Tidier Medallions

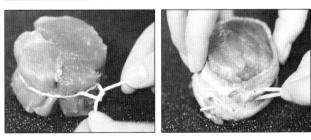

BUTCHER'S TWINE   **BACON 'TWINE'**

Thick medallions allow for more browning, but they can flop over in the pan. To prevent this, tie each piece with twine or a strip of parcooked bacon secured with two toothpicks.

Knowing When Food Is Done

Few kitchen mishaps are more frustrating than improper cooking. Here's how to cook food right every time.

THREE METHODS FOR DETERMINING DONENESS

Five Senses: Seasoned cooks rely on taste, touch, sight, smell, and even sound to know when foods are done. Novice cooks often forget that these five tools are always available.

Time: Many cooks get themselves in trouble by slavishly following times in recipes. All times are estimates, and actual times will vary with different ovens, stovetops, and grills. The exact size and initial temperature of ingredients will also dramatically affect their cooking time. In the test kitchen, we use timers to remind us to check foods early. If a recipe reads, "Bake for 60 minutes," set your timer for 45 or 50 minutes.

Temperature: In the test kitchen, we rely on digital instant-read thermometers. Dial-face thermometers are slow to register and can't read high temperatures associated with candy making or frying (most models cut off around 220 degrees). In addition, the sensor on dial-face thermometers is located at least 1 inch up from the tip, so these thermometers won't work in shallow liquids or thin cuts of meat. On digital thermometers, the sensor is located at the tip.

INSTANT-READ THERMOMETER
What to Buy: Our test kitchen winner is fast (it registers temperatures from −58 to 572 degrees in seconds), accurate, and perfectly proportioned (the folding probe is capable of reaching the very center of the largest roast). A recent test of nine inexpensive models found several reasonably priced thermometers with the features we like, although all were slower than our test kitchen winner.

★ TEST KITCHEN WINNER ★
THERMOWORKS Super-Fast Thermapen, $85

BEST BUY
CDN ProAccurate DTQ450, $17.95

KNOWING WHEN FISH, MEAT, AND POULTRY ARE DONE

This chart presents ideal serving temperatures. Since the temperature of meat will continue to rise as its rests, it should be taken off the heat just before it reaches the desired temperature. (This phenomenon doesn't occur with poultry and fish.) These temperatures (in degrees Fahrenheit) reflect our opinions regarding optimal flavor and juiciness. The U.S. Department of Agriculture recommends cooking beef, lamb, veal steaks and roasts, and fish to 145 degrees, pork and all ground meat to 160 degrees, and poultry to 180 degrees to eliminate potential food-borne pathogens.

	RARE	MEDIUM-RARE	MEDIUM	WELL-DONE
Fish	110	120	140	*
Red Meat (beef, lamb, veal)	125	130	140	160**
Pork	*	*	145	160**
Poultry (white meat)	*	*	*	160 to 165
Poultry (dark meat)	*	*	*	175

* Not recommended

** Recommended only for ground meat dishes, such as meat loaf.

JUDGING THE DONENESS OF FISH
You can use an instant-read thermometer to check doneness in thick fillets, but in most cases you have to resort to a more primitive test—nicking the fish with a paring knife and then peeking into the interior to judge color and flakiness. White fish (everything from cod to snapper) should be cooked to medium (that is, the flesh should be opaque but still moist and just beginning to flake). Salmon and scallops are best cooked to medium-rare (the center should still be translucent), while tuna is best cooked rare (only the outer layer is opaque while the rest of the fish is translucent).

TAKING THE TEMPERATURE OF A STEAK OR CHOP
Use tongs to hold the steak or chop aloft and insert the thermometer through the side of the meat. This method also works with burgers, boneless chicken breasts, and other chicken parts.

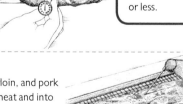

TAKING THE TEMPERATURE OF A ROAST
For many roasts (including beef tenderloin, pork tenderloin, and pork loin), it's possible to slide the probe right through the meat and into the pan, which will give you a false reading. To make sure that the probe stays in the meat, insert the thermometer at an angle. Push the probe deep into the roast and then slowly draw it out, looking for the lowest temperature to find the center of the meat.

TAKING THE TEMPERATURE OF A CHICKEN OR TURKEY
You need to check the thickest part of the thigh as well as the thickest part of the breast (see the illustrations on page 12). If roasting a stuffed bird, insert the thermometer directly into center of the cavity as well to make sure the stuffing has reached a safe temperature of 165 degrees.

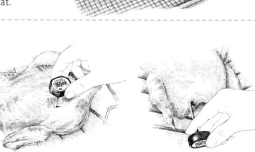

CARRYOVER EFFECT
When it comes to red meat and pork, judging doneness, even with a thermometer, involves some guesswork. That's because sometimes you aren't judging whether the food is ready to eat but whether it will be ready to eat once it has cooled or rested. For instance, to allow for juices to distribute themselves evenly, steaks, chops, and roasts should rest five to 20 minutes. (A steak needs less time than a big roast.) As meat rests, its temperature will climb. The thicker the cut, the more the temperature will rise. Also, food coming out of a very hot oven will have more residual heat than food coming out of a cooler oven. A thick roast cooked in a hot oven might experience a 10- or 15-degree temperature increase as it rests; the temperature of a thin steak may rise by 5 degrees or less.

KNOWING WHEN BAKED GOODS ARE DONE

CAKES, MUFFINS, AND QUICK BREADS

There are two ways to judge doneness in cakes, muffins, and quick breads.

1. Fully baked items should feel springy and resilient when the center is gently pressed. If your finger leaves an impression—or the center jiggles—the item is not done.

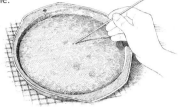

2. A skewer or toothpick should emerge fairly clean, with perhaps just a few crumbs attached. If you see moist batter, the item needs to bake longer.

COOKIES

We think most cookies are best when they are chewy. This means taking them out of the oven when they are slightly underdone—in fact, the cookies are often so soft they will droop over the end of a spatula (as shown below). Bake cookies on parchment and cool on baking sheet for a few minutes; after they have set up slightly, slide the parchment onto a cooling rack. If the cookies have crevices, the crevices should appear moist. When baking smooth cookies, look at the edges, which should be lightly browned; the center should be set but not fully dry.

BROWNIES

Overbaked brownies are dry and chalky and the chocolate flavor is diminished. Use the skewer test to determine doneness, but look for moist, sticky crumbs.

PUDDINGS AND CUSTARDS

Egg-based puddings and custards can curdle if cooked beyond 185 degrees. We take crème anglaise off the heat when the mixture registers 175 to 180, but when making the base for ice cream we push the temperature to 180 to 185 for maximum thickness. Baked custards, such as flan and crème brûlée, should jiggle (but not slosh) when gently shaken. This will occur between 170 and 175 degrees.

YEAST BREADS

Lean breads, such as country white and baguettes, are done when the internal temperatures measures 210 degrees. Richer loaves made with eggs and butter, such as brioche and challah, are done when the internal temperature measures 190 degrees. Breads with a modest amount of fat, such as American sandwich bread and rye bread, fall in between; they are done at 195 to 200 degrees.

For free-form loaves, tip the loaf up (with your hand shielded by an oven mitt or potholder) and insert the probe through the bottom crust into the center.

For bread baked in a loaf pan, insert the thermometer from the side, just above the pan edge, and direct it at a downward angle into the center of the loaf.

PIES AND PASTRIES

For pies and pastries, it's all about color. A well-browned crust is more flavorful than a blond one, and it won't be doughy in the middle. We bake all pies in glass pie plates so we can examine the bottom of the crust to determine doneness. When working with puff pastry or other flaky doughs, lift up the bottom of individual pieces and look for even browning.

CHEESECAKE

A cheesecake is done when the center just barely jiggles. Since this can be difficult to judge, try this tip.

Cheesecake is ready to come out of oven when the internal temperature reaches 150 degrees. (At higher temperatures, the texture will suffer.) If possible, insert the thermometer into the side of the cheesecake where it rises above the pan (otherwise, insert it into the center of the cake).

KNOWING WHEN OTHER FOODS ARE DONE

The following items offer some challenges in the kitchen. Here's how to know when they are done.

BEANS

For creamy, intact beans, turn off the heat before the beans are fully cooked. Cover the pot and let residual heat continue to soften the interior without any agitation from boiling water, which can rupture delicate skins.

EGGS

Most egg dishes provide visual cues when done, but not hard-cooked eggs. To keep that greenish ring from forming around the yolk, bring large eggs to a boil in a pot of water, turn off the heat, cover, and let them sit for exactly 10 minutes before transferring them to a bowl of ice water to stop the cooking process.

NUTS

Forget about trying to judge color when toasting nuts. When nuts are fragrant, they are done.

PASTA

Properly cooked pasta will have a slight bite (that is, it will be al dente). If in doubt, cut a piece in half. If you see a white core, the pasta needs more time. Many recipes suggest simmering the drained pasta in the sauce to help marry the two; if you plan on doing this (a good idea for many cream and broth-based sauces), undercook the pasta slightly.

POTATOES

Potatoes and other root vegetables are generally done when a skewer slides through them and meets little resistance. With peeled potatoes, the pieces should just break apart when pierced with a skewer or paring knife. When boiling whole potatoes, try lifting them out of the water with a paring knife; if the potato clings to the knife (even for an instant), it's not done yet.

RICE

It's not hard to make rice tender; fluffy rice is another matter. Rather than continuing to cook the rice and risk scorched or blown-out grains, place a folded kitchen towel between the pot and the lid and then set the covered pot aside for 10 minutes. Residual heat will continue to steam the rice while the towel absorbs excess moisture.

TIPS FOR USING A THERMOMETER

- Regularly check accuracy by leaving the probe in a bucket of ice water for a minute or two. If the temperature doesn't register 32 degrees Fahrenheit, use the calibration button (available on the brands recommended on page 16) to reset the thermometer.

- Slide the probe deep into the center of foods, making sure that the tip does not exit the food.

- Avoid bones, cavities (say, in a turkey), and pan surfaces, all of which will throw off the reading.

- Take more than one reading, especially in large roasts and turkeys.

Really Good Mushroom Lasagna

Exotic mushrooms and homemade pasta practically guarantee great mushroom lasagna—if you've got money to spend. But what if you have to rely on supermarket staples?

≥ BY SANDRA WU ≤

A great mushroom lasagna is much more than just another vegetarian lasagna—it might be the one entree a meat eater will consider ordering even when steak is on the menu. My research uncovered two distinct styles for this recipe. While American-style mushroom lasagnas are often loaded with red sauce and mozzarella, authentic Italian versions opt for Parmesan and creamy béchamel sauce (basically, milk thickened with butter and flour)—and no tomatoes.

After making several American-style recipes, I quickly dismissed them. The mushrooms were lost in the sea of tomato sauce and mozzarella. The Italian recipes put the emphasis on the mushrooms, but I had two problems with them. First, many called for esoteric and/or expensive wild mushrooms. (Fresh porcini rarely make it to my market, and I'm not about to put $39-per-pound mushrooms in a lasagna, anyway!) Second, these authentic recipes required lots of time. Every one I tried called for homemade pasta. Who wants to spend two hours mixing, rolling, boiling, shocking, and drying the dough for several dozen sheets of pasta, especially when another hour is needed to make the sauce? I was determined to make Italian-style mushroom lasagna approachable—and that meant widely available mushrooms and no-boil noodles.

Serious Mushroom Flavor

I decided to deconstruct the mushroom layer first. Wild mushrooms from my local gourmet market were great (see Cook's Extra, at right, for this recipe), but, I racked up a $48 mushroom bill—for one lasagna. The cheapest option in the supermarket, humble white button mushrooms, simply didn't have the heft or flavor to do the job. Widely available cremini mushrooms offered fuller mushroom flavor but still paled in comparison with the wild mushrooms. The supermarket produce aisle left me one option: portobellos. An unlikely choice, but it made sense, as portobellos have substantial flavor and texture. Sautéing the portobellos took forever and didn't do them justice. Roasting them in the oven kept them to one batch and better concentrated their flavors.

Packed with hearty portobellos, earthy porcini, and tangy fontina, this lasagna raises supermarket ingredients to flavorful heights.

Neither Too Rich nor Too Thin

I next tried to fix the dry, pasty noodles—the result when I simply substituted the no-boil noodles directly for homemade. Soaking the pasta in hot water for five minutes helped start the rehydration process, but the noodles were still sucking all the moisture out of my béchamel. Adding more milk to the béchamel solved the moisture problem, but tasters complained that the dairy flavor was overwhelming and called this effort "lasagna Alfredo." I hit upon a solution when I supplemented the milk with chicken broth to make a very loose béchamel sauce.

The sauce now had the right consistency, but the lasagna still needed more mushroom flavor. I was roasting 2 pounds of portobellos and couldn't really fit any more in a pan. What if I pumped up the flavor of the béchamel itself? Dried porcini were an obvious place to start; a packet costs just a few dollars and can add a lot of flavor. It seemed silly to throw out the hot water I was using to rehydrate the dried porcini, so I replaced the chicken broth in my béchamel sauce with this filtered liquid.

I was getting close, but my greedy tasters wanted a more intense mushroom experience. I borrowed an idea from classic French cooking, adding duxelles to my sauce. *Duxelles* is a fancy term for a simple idea. You chop button mushrooms finely and sauté them until the mushrooms form a concentrated paste. A quick addition of garlic and vermouth and this fragrant mixture was ready to merge with the sauce. I stirred the duxelles into my béchamel, and tasters were finally satisfied. To make things easier, I built my béchamel—now a mushroom béchamel—right on top of the duxelles, so I had just one pan to clean.

Balancing It Out

To balance the earthiness of the mushrooms, the dish needed additional sweet, sharp, salty, and bright elements. Sautéed red onions added just the right sweetness. As for the cheese, the traditional choice of Parmesan contributed a nice sharp, salty flavor, but it lacked the creamy, melting quality tasters clamored for. I tried combining Parmesan with a few varieties of semifirm cheese. Mozzarella and provolone provided creamy texture but not enough flavor. Italian fontina added a complementary buttery nuttiness that tasters liked, and it also melted beautifully, helping the layers adhere in a cohesive mass. Nutmeg, basil, and parsley rounded out the sauce.

As I waited for my baked lasagna to set up for slicing, I couldn't help but think that another sprinkling of fresh herbs couldn't hurt. A gremolata-like topping of minced parsley, basil, lemon zest, and garlic, added to the lasagna while it rested, contributed another layer of complexity and freshness. My mushroom lasagna might start out with humble supermarket ingredients, but there's nothing humble about the big, bold flavors it ends up with.

Go to www.cooksillustrated.com
- Key in code 9066 for our recipe for **Wild Mushroom Lasagna**.
- Key in code 9067 for our recipe for **Mushroom Lasagna with Pancetta and Sage**.
- Key in code 9068 for our recipe for **Mushroom Lasagna with Goat Cheese, Broccoli Rabe, and Sun-Dried Tomatoes**.
- Recipes available until March 1, 2007.

Supercharged Mushroom Lasagna from Supermarket Staples

Creating the ultimate mushroom lasagna isn't hard when you can find lots of exotic mushrooms—and have plenty of cash. With the right treatment, however, supermarket ingredients really do the trick. Roasting portobello mushrooms drives off excess liquid and concentrates their flavor. Fortifying the sauce with sautéed button mushrooms and chopped dried porcini (plus the liquid used to rehydrate them) makes for a triple hit of mushroom flavor. Opting for buttery fontina cheese and Parmesan puts the emphasis on flavor, as does a last-minute sprinkle of raw garlic, herbs, and lemon zest.

ROAST MUSHROOMS

FORTIFY SAUCE

UPGRADE CHEESE

ADD BRIGHTNESS

MUSHROOM LASAGNA
SERVES 10 TO 12

If Italian fontina is unavailable, use whole milk mozzarella rather than a rubbery Danish, Swedish, or American fontina. Whole milk is best in the sauce, but skim or low-fat milk also work.

- 1/2 ounce dried porcini mushrooms, rinsed well
- 1 cup water
- 2 pounds (about 10 medium) portobello mushroom caps, cleaned and cut into 2 by 1/4-inch slices
- 4 tablespoons olive oil
  Table salt and ground black pepper
- 2 large red onions, chopped medium (about 4 cups)
- 8 ounces button mushrooms, cleaned, stems trimmed, and broken into rough pieces
- 4 medium garlic cloves, minced or pressed through garlic press (about 1 tablespoon plus 1 teaspoon)
- 1/2 cup dry vermouth
- 3 tablespoons unsalted butter, plus additional for greasing pan
- 3 tablespoons unbleached all-purpose flour
- 3 1/2 cups milk (see note above)
- 1/4 teaspoon ground nutmeg
- 1/4 cup minced fresh parsley leaves
- 1/4 cup plus 2 tablespoons minced fresh basil leaves
- 8 ounces Italian fontina cheese, rind removed and shredded (about 2 1/4 cups)
- 1 1/2 ounces grated Parmesan cheese (about 3/4 cup)
- 12 no-boil lasagna noodles
- 1/2 teaspoon grated zest from 1 lemon

1. Cover porcini with water in microwave-safe bowl; cover with plastic wrap, cut several steam vents in plastic with paring knife, and microwave on high power for 30 seconds. Let stand until mushrooms soften, about 5 minutes. Lift mushrooms from liquid with fork and roughly chop (you should have about 3 tablespoons). Strain liquid through fine-mesh strainer lined with paper towel into medium bowl. Set mushrooms and liquid aside.

2. Adjust oven rack to middle position and heat oven to 425 degrees. Spread portobellos in even layer on rimmed baking sheet and drizzle with 2 tablespoons oil, tossing to coat mushrooms evenly; sprinkle with 1/2 teaspoon salt and 1/2 teaspoon pepper and toss again. Roast mushrooms until shriveled and all liquid has evaporated, about 30 minutes, stirring halfway through cooking time. Set aside to cool. (Do not turn off oven.)

3. While portobellos roast, heat 1 tablespoon oil in 12-inch nonstick skillet over medium-high heat until shimmering. Add onions, 1/4 teaspoon salt, and 1/4 teaspoon pepper and cook, stirring occasionally, until onions are browned around edges, about 10 minutes. Transfer onions to large bowl and set aside.

4. Meanwhile, process button mushrooms in food processor until uniformly coarsely chopped, about six 1-second pulses, stopping to scrape bowl as needed. Heat remaining tablespoon oil in now-empty skillet over medium-high heat until shimmering. Add chopped button mushrooms and cook, stirring occasionally, until browned and moisture has evaporated, 6 to 8 minutes.

5. Reduce heat to medium and stir in porcini mushrooms, 1 tablespoon garlic, 1 teaspoon salt, and 1 teaspoon pepper. Cook, stirring frequently, until garlic is fragrant, about 1 minute. Add vermouth and cook, stirring occasionally, until liquid has evaporated, 2 to 3 minutes.

6. Add butter and cook until melted. Add flour and cook, stirring constantly, about 1 minute. Add milk, scraping pan bottom to loosen browned bits. Add reserved porcini liquid and nutmeg. Increase heat to medium-high and bring mixture to boil. Reduce heat to medium-low and simmer until sauce reaches consistency of heavy cream, 10 to 15 minutes. Remove from heat and stir in 2 tablespoons parsley and 1/4 cup basil.

7. Combine fontina and Parmesan in medium bowl. Toss cooled portobello mushrooms with onions in large bowl. Place noodles in 13 by 9-inch ovensafe baking dish and cover with hot tap water; let soak 5 minutes, stirring occasionally to prevent sticking. Remove noodles from water and place in single layer on kitchen towel. Wipe baking dish dry and coat with butter.

8. Using rubber spatula, evenly distribute 1 cup mushroom sauce in bottom of baking dish; position 3 noodles on top of sauce. Spread 3/4 cup sauce evenly over noodles followed by 2 cups mushroom-onion mixture and 3/4 cup cheese. Repeat layering of noodles, sauce, mushroom-onion mixture, and cheese two more times. Place 3 remaining noodles on top of last layer of cheese. Spread remaining sauce over noodles and sprinkle with remaining cheese. Lightly spray large sheet of foil with nonstick cooking spray and cover lasagna. Bake until bubbling, about 20 minutes.

9. While lasagna is baking, combine remaining 2 tablespoons parsley, 2 tablespoons basil, and 1 teaspoon garlic with zest in small bowl. Increase oven temperature to 500 degrees, remove foil from lasagna, and continue to bake until cheese on top becomes spotty brown, 6 to 8 minutes. Remove lasagna from oven and immediately sprinkle evenly with herb mixture. Cool 15 minutes, then cut into pieces and serve.

TESTING EQUIPMENT:
Lasagna Pans

When making lasagna, we reach for an ordinary 13 by 9 by 2-inch Pyrex baking dish. But do specialized lasagna pans offer any advantages? The first thing we noticed about the five pans we tested was their size: They're big. The Mario Batali Extra Deep Lasagna Pan ($79.95) weighed in at 11 pounds—when empty—and holds 1 1/2 batches of our Mushroom Lasagna. Second, a pan holding several pounds of pasta, sauce, and cheese needs handles, which the Chicago Metallic Professional ($23.50) and Kaiser La Forme ($40) lacked. These two pans also featured dark nonstick surfaces that scorched the lasagna even at a lower oven temperature. In the end, we liked just one pan. The Metro 3 Piece Lasagna Pan Set ($19.99, includes spatula and roasting rack) is light colored, double handled, and big (14 1/4 by 10 1/2 by 4 inches) but not awkward. But since we don't mind the 2-inch depth of our trusty Pyrex Bakeware ($9.79) it remains the test kitchen standard.

–Garth Clingingsmith

BIGGER, NOT BETTER
This Metro pan is the best option for super sized lasagna recipes.

VERSATILE AND CHEAP
An inexpensive Pyrex baking dish is fine for regular lasagna recipes, including ours.

Chicken and Rice, Latino Style

Could we turn this all-day one-dish dinner into a fast but flavorful weeknight meal?

⋺ BY DAVID PAZMIÑO ⋹

The bold-flavored cousin of American-style chicken and rice, *arroz con pollo* (literally, "rice with chicken") is Latino comfort food at its most basic. Having grown up with arroz con pollo on the dinner table two or three times a month, I've had plenty of great versions: moist, tender chicken nestled in rice rich with peppers, onions, herbs, and deep chicken flavor—a satisfying one-dish meal.

Like most staples, however, arroz con pollo runs the gamut from the incredible to the merely edible, depending on how much time and effort you're willing to spend. The traditional method is to stew marinated chicken slowly with aromatic herbs and vegetables, creating a rich broth in which the rice is cooked once the chicken is fall-off-the-bone tender—terrific, yes, but also time-consuming. Quick versions speed things up by cooking the rice and chicken (often boneless) separately, then combining them just before serving. The trade-off is rice that's devoid of chicken flavor. My goal was to split the difference: to streamline the more time-consuming, traditional recipes for arroz con pollo without sacrificing great taste.

Chicken Coup

If I wanted chicken-infused rice, it was clear the chicken and the rice would have to spend some time together. But how long was long enough?

A few of the "quick" recipes I found called for simmering the chicken and rice together, chopping the chicken into small pieces that would be done in sync with the rice—in about half an hour. Was this my streamlined solution? The timing was right, but the results were not. The white meat and dark meat cooked unevenly, the skin was flabby, and, after 30 minutes, flavor infusion was minimal. Worse, the hacked-up chicken, replete with jagged bones, was wholly unappealing.

Regrouping, I decided to start with a traditional recipe and adjust things from there. I began by sautéing a mixture of chopped onions and green peppers (called a *sofrito*, the Latin American answer to the French *mirepoix* of carrots, onions, and celery). Once the vegetables softened, I added the chicken and a few cups

Quick versions of arroz con pollo usually sacrifice flavor for speed. Our version offers bold Latino flavors and takes about an hour.

of water, turned the burner to low, and let the chicken poach for an hour. Removing the chicken, I added the rice to the pot, and, 30 minutes later, the rice had absorbed every drop of the rich broth the chicken had left behind. I added the chicken back to rewarm for 10 minutes, then lifted the lid. Now this was chicken-infused rice!

Unfortunately, it was also a two-hour project—and I hadn't even factored in the traditional marinade yet. What's more, while the dark meat was moist and tender, the leaner white meat was in bad shape. In a vivid flashback to my childhood, I recalled fighting with my cousins at the dinner table over the thighs and the drumsticks. (The dry, stringy white meat had to be drenched in the wet beans served on the side.) Opting for all thighs meant uniform cooking times, shopping convenience (one big "value" pack), and the best chance for peace at the dinner table.

A new problem emerged: Thighs are laden with fat, and this made the dish greasy. Removing the skin helped, but the meat near the surface dried out and the flavor suffered. The answer was to trim away any visible pockets of waxy yellow fat and most of the skin, leaving just enough to protect the meat. I also replaced most of the

water I was adding with an equal amount of store-bought chicken broth, which made up for lost chicken flavor. After stewing for almost an hour, the skin was pretty flabby, so I removed it while the rice finished cooking. To make the chicken even more appealing, I took the additional step of removing the meat from the bones.

Rice and Spice

The two traditional rice choices for arroz con pollo are long grain and medium grain. While both were fine, tasters preferred the creamier texture of medium-grain rice. (See page 31 for the results of our tasting.) But medium-grain rice was not without its problems. The grains had a tendency to split and release too much starch, making the overall texture of the dish pasty. Giving the rice a stir partway through cooking helped keep any one layer from overcooking, as did removing the pot from the direct heat of the stovetop to the diffuse heat of the oven.

Traditionally, arroz con pollo has an orange hue that comes from infusing oil with *achiote*, a tropical seed also used for coloring cheddar cheese. Achiote is hard to find, so I experimented with substitutions. Turmeric and saffron looked right but tasted wrong—too much like curry or paella. (Achiote has no distinct flavor.) The solution was adding 8 ounces of canned tomato sauce along with the broth.

A common method for infusing this dish with Latino flavors is to marinate the chicken for a few hours or even overnight. A nice idea, but I couldn't spare the time. Instead, I tried a quick, 15-minute marinade with garlic, oregano, and white vinegar. The results were a step in the right direction. Tossing the chicken with olive oil, vinegar, and cilantro after pulling it off the bone—a postcooking "marinade"—gave it the additional boost it

SHOPPING: **The Rice Is Right**

For arroz con pollo, we prefer the sticky-yet-firm consistency of medium-grain rice. Although there are widely available brands that hail from many places, we found that Hispanic brands of rice had the best texture for this dish.

PHOTOGRAPHY: CARL TREMBLAY

needed. Capers, red pepper flakes, pimentos, and briny olives rounded out the flavors.

All of my efforts at streamlining this dish had brought the cooking time down to 90 minutes—an hour to stew the chicken and half an hour to cook the rice—a far cry from the half-day affair I'd faced at the start. But was this the best I could do? To shave off still more time, I tried adding the rice to the pot when the chicken still had half an hour to go. The chicken was fine, but the rice near the chicken pieces cooked unevenly. The solution to this problem was easy: Instead of giving the rice only one stir during cooking, I gave it a second stir to redistribute the ingredients. Now both the rice and the chicken were perfectly cooked in just over an hour. I finally had a rich, flavorful dish that tasted authentic, and I didn't have to wait for the weekend to enjoy it.

Maximum Flavor in Minimum Time

Many recipes for arroz con pollo call for hours of marinating, followed by hours of cooking. Here's how we shaved time without sacrificing taste.

MARINATE
Briefly marinating the chicken in garlic, vinegar, and herbs gave us a quick infusion of Latino flavors.

ENRICH
Stewing the chicken in store-bought chicken broth instead of water upped the chicken flavor.

DOUBLE UP
Adding the rice to the pot when the chicken was partially cooked saved us another half an hour.

MARINATE AGAIN
Tossing the chicken with a second marinade (after cooking) gave it the flavor boost it needed.

LATINO-STYLE CHICKEN AND RICE (ARROZ CON POLLO)
SERVES 4 TO 6

To keep the dish from becoming greasy, it is important to remove excess fat from the chicken thighs and trim the skin. To use long-grain rice instead of medium-grain, increase the water to ¾ cup in step 2.

- 6 medium garlic cloves, minced or pressed through garlic press (about 2 tablespoons)
  Table salt
- ½ teaspoon dried oregano
- 1 tablespoon plus 2 teaspoons distilled white vinegar
  Ground black pepper
- 8 bone-in, skin-on chicken thighs (3½ to 4 pounds), trimmed of excess skin and fat
- 2 tablespoons olive oil
- 1 medium onion, chopped fine (about 1 cup)
- 1 small green pepper, stemmed, seeded, and chopped fine (about ¾ cup)
- ¼ teaspoon hot red pepper flakes
- ¼ cup minced fresh cilantro leaves
- 1 (8-ounce) can tomato sauce
- 1¾ cups low-sodium chicken broth
- ¼ cup water
- 3 cups medium-grain rice
- ½ cup green manzanilla olives, pitted and halved
- 1 tablespoon capers
- ½ cup jarred pimentos, cut into 2 by ¼-inch strips
  Lemon wedges, for serving

1. Adjust oven rack to middle position and heat oven to 350 degrees. Place garlic and 1 teaspoon salt in large bowl; using rubber spatula, mix to make smooth paste. Add oregano, 1 tablespoon vinegar, and ½ teaspoon black pepper to garlic-salt mixture; stir to combine. Place chicken in bowl with marinade. Coat chicken pieces evenly with marinade; set aside for 15 minutes.

2. Heat 1 tablespoon oil in Dutch oven over medium heat until shimmering. Add onion, green pepper, and pepper flakes; cook, stirring occasionally, until vegetables begin to soften, 4 to 8 minutes. Add 2 tablespoons cilantro; stir to combine. Push vegetables to sides of pot and increase heat to medium-high. Add chicken to clearing in center of pot, skin side down, in even layer. Cook, without moving chicken, until outer layer of meat becomes opaque, 2 to 4 minutes. (If chicken begins to brown, reduce heat to medium.) Using tongs, flip chicken and cook on second side until opaque, 2 to 4 minutes more. Add tomato sauce, broth, and water; stir to combine. Bring to simmer; cover, reduce heat to medium-low, and simmer for 20 minutes.

3. Add rice, olives, capers, and ¾ teaspoon salt; stir well. Bring to simmer, cover, and place pot in oven. After 10 minutes, remove pot from oven and stir chicken and rice once from bottom up. Return pot to oven. After another 10 minutes, stir once more, adding ¼ cup water if rice appears dry and bottom of pot is beginning to burn. Cover and return pot to oven; cook until rice has absorbed all liquid and is tender but still holds its shape and temperature of chicken registers 175 degrees on instant-read thermometer, about 10 minutes longer.

4. Using tongs, remove chicken from pot; replace lid and set pot aside. Remove and discard chicken skin; using 2 spoons, pull meat off bones into large chunks. Using fingers, remove remaining fat or dark veins from chicken pieces. Place chicken in large bowl and toss with remaining tablespoon olive oil, remaining 2 teaspoons vinegar, remaining 2 tablespoons cilantro, and pimentos; season with salt and pepper to taste. Place chicken on top of rice, cover, and let stand until warmed through, about 5 minutes. Serve, passing lemon wedges separately.

LATINO-STYLE CHICKEN AND RICE WITH BACON AND ROASTED RED PEPPERS

1. Follow recipe for Latino-Style Chicken and Rice through step 1, substituting 2 teaspoons sweet paprika for oregano and sherry vinegar for white vinegar.

2. Fry 4 strips bacon, cut into ½-inch pieces, in Dutch oven over medium heat until crisp, 6 to 8 minutes. Using slotted spoon, transfer bacon to paper-towel-lined plate; pour off all but 1 tablespoon bacon fat. Continue with step 2, substituting 1 small red pepper, finely chopped, and 1 medium carrot, finely chopped, for green pepper and sautéing vegetables in bacon fat.

3. Continue with recipe, substituting ¼ cup minced fresh parsley leaves for cilantro, omitting olives and capers, and substituting ½ cup roasted red peppers, cut into 2 by ¼-inch strips, for pimentos. Garnish chicken and rice with reserved bacon before serving.

TECHNIQUE | TAKING THE MEAT OFF THE BONE

Removing the meat from the bones isn't hard when there's plenty of time for it to cool, but we wanted it fast. To spare our fingertips, we tried using a fork, but it tended to shred the meat rather than pull it apart intact. Our solution? Two spoons, which were much more gentle—and just as effective.

Rethinking Crêpes Suzette

Old-school French restaurants have mastered the fiery theatrics of this tableside treat for two. Could we adapt this classic for the home cook—and a tableful of hungry guests?

≥ BY REBECCA HAYS ≤

Not long ago, in an old-style French restaurant in New York City, I chose crêpes suzette for dessert. The theatrics began as soon as I placed my order, with the maitre d' wheeling up a tableside cart and setting about the business of rubbing sugar cubes on whole oranges. The scented sugar was melted in a large, shallow, copper suzette pan, and then several pats of butter and the juice of the oranges were added. The mixture bubbled into a luscious sauce in which crêpes were bathed and folded into quarters. Finally, the big finish: Splashes of Grand Marnier and cognac were set aflame, lighting up the dim surroundings.

The experience made me wonder why this classic dessert has fallen out of favor. What's not to like about the sophisticated combination of crêpes, oranges, liquor, and a showy flambé? And so I was inspired to bring crêpes suzette back to life for my next dinner party. I would develop a recipe to serve six since tableside preparations for only one or two diners are impractical for the home cook.

We sidestep sogginess by broiling our sugar-sprinkled crêpes, then spooning on the tangy orange sauce just before serving.

The French Connection

My first stop was the library, where I instinctively pulled a French cookbook by Julia Child from the shelves. (This dish is usually credited to the world's most famous French chef, Escoffier, though some suggest that a young chef accidently flambéed a skillet full of pancakes and named the dish after Suzette, mistress to the Prince of Wales.) I copied her recipe along with five others and started comparing ingredient lists. Crêpes consist mainly of flour, milk, and egg; the accompanying orange sauce of butter, sugar, orange juice, cognac, and orange liqueur. (I ignored specifications for suzette pans and used a skillet; I wasn't about to spend $200 on a single-purpose piece of cookware. See page 32 for our testing of electric crêpe makers.) After a morning of flipping crêpes and making sauces, I rounded up a few colleagues to witness the flambé step, which, as Julia warned, requires practice.

Tasters critiqued the sauces, calling them butter-heavy and overcooked, with a few tasting strongly of alcohol courtesy of an inferior flambé. Working with the test kitchen's favorite crêpe recipe, I scaled back the butter in a basic sauce and continued experimenting. When frozen orange juice concentrate, lemon juice, orange marmalade, and even grenadine syrup failed to improve things, I returned to square one. Adding uncooked orange juice and zest to the usual reduction of butter, sugar, and orange juice was the answer, yielding lively, multilayered flavors.

Faulty Ignition

Flambé science is simple enough. When alcohol is ignited, it reaches a temperature of about 500 degrees. This high heat causes a reaction in the sugars in the liquor, producing complex flavors that can't be achieved at the lower heat (180 degrees) of simmering. After a few shaky attempts at igniting my simmering dessert, I reached two important conclusions. First, the more crêpes in the pan, the more likely the alcohol will be quickly absorbed and then impossible to ignite. Second, the intensity of the flames is directly related to the heat in the pan.

Because I was preparing six servings and therefore had a very full skillet, I figured I'd have more success if I lit the sauce first and added the crêpes second. Yet even with this approach, the results were spotty at best. Minor variations in temperature had a dramatic effect on the results, which ranged from mere flickers (low heat) to a full-out blaze (high heat). Then it hit me: What if I simply removed the extraneous variables and started by flambéing the alcohol alone in the skillet? Voilà! This reversal (flambé first, build the sauce second) delivered great flavor, along with predictable flames.

As for the alcohol, cognac was a given. Grand Marnier is usually called for, but it's not the only orange liqueur, so I tried other options. Surprisingly, inexpensive and less alcoholic triple sec stole the show (see the tasting on page 23).

Preventing Sogginess

Although I had made good progress, I was having problems with crêpes that were bloated and soggy, having spent too much time swimming in sauce. This isn't much of a problem when the dessert is made rapidly for two people, but when six servings (12 crêpes) are called for, there is too much absorption time. The solution came from another well-known French chef, Jacques Pépin, who sprinkles unsauced crepes with sugar and then broils them. I followed his lead, first transferring the sauce in the skillet to a serving bowl, then arranging folded, sugared crêpes in the skillet. When they emerged from the oven, I drizzled on a bit of sauce and passed the remainder at the table. Though untraditional, this brûlée technique was a real hit, forming a crunchy, sugary barrier that provided textural contrast and partially protected the crêpes from the sauce.

I reviewed my recipe. Like most, it aimed for ultra-tender crêpes and so called for resting the batter to relax the gluten, a protein that can make batters and doughs tough. Would skipping this step prove beneficial, yielding sturdier crêpes more capable of standing up to the sauce (not to mention saving two hours of prep time)? I put together one last test, and, sure enough, tasters preferred the unrested crêpes, finding that once sauced they retained a more substantial texture than the rested batch.

CRÊPES SUZETTE
SERVES 6

It takes a few crêpes to get the heat of the pan right; your first two or three will almost inevitably be unusable. (To allow for practice, the recipe yields about 16 crepes; only 12 are needed for the dish.) A dry measuring cup with a ¼-cup capacity is useful for portioning the batter. Tasters had a slight preference for crêpes made with whole milk, but low-fat or skim milk can also be used. For tips on how to flambé, see page 30.

Crêpes
- 3 large eggs
- 1½ cups whole milk (see note above)
- ½ cup water
- 1½ cups (7½ ounces) unbleached all-purpose flour
- 2 tablespoons cognac
- 3 tablespoons sugar
- ½ teaspoon table salt
- 5 tablespoons unsalted butter, melted, plus extra for brushing pan

Orange Sauce
- 4 tablespoons cognac
- 6 tablespoons unsalted butter, cut into 6 pieces
- 4 tablespoons sugar
- 1¼ cups juice plus 1 tablespoon finely grated zest from 3 to 4 large oranges
- 2 tablespoons orange-flavored liqueur, preferably triple sec

1. **FOR THE CRÊPES:** Combine eggs, milk, water, flour, cognac, sugar, salt, and melted butter in blender until smooth batter forms, about 10 seconds. Transfer batter to medium bowl.

2. Using pastry brush, brush bottom and sides of 10-inch nonstick skillet very lightly with melted butter; heat skillet over medium heat. When butter stops sizzling, tilt pan slightly to right and begin pouring in scant ¼ cup batter. Continue to pour batter in slow, steady stream, rotating wrist and twirling pan slowly counterclockwise until pan bottom is covered with even layer of batter.

Cook until crêpe starts to lose opaqueness and turns spotty light golden brown on bottom, loosening crêpe from side of pan with rubber spatula, 30 seconds to 1 minute. To flip crêpe, loosen edge with rubber spatula and, with fingertips on top side, slide spatula under crêpe and flip. Cook until dry on second side, about 20 seconds.

3. Place cooked crêpe on plate and repeat cooking process with remaining batter, brushing pan very lightly with butter before making each crêpe. As they are done, stack crêpes on plate (you will need 12 crêpes). (Crêpes can be double-wrapped in plastic and refrigerated up to 3 days. If crêpes have been refrigerated, bring them to room temperature before making sauce.)

4. **FOR THE ORANGE SAUCE:** Adjust oven rack to lower-middle position and heat broiler. Add 3 tablespoons cognac to broilersafe 12-inch skillet; set over medium heat just until vapors begin to rise from cognac, about 5 seconds. Remove pan from heat and wave lit chimney match over cognac until it ignites; shake pan until flames subside. (Cognac should burn for about 15 seconds; re-ignite if flame dies too soon.)

5. Add butter, 3 tablespoons sugar, and 1 cup orange juice to cognac; simmer briskly over high heat, whisking occasionally, until many large bubbles appear and mixture reduces to thick syrup, 6 to 8 minutes. (You should have just over ½ cup sauce.) Transfer sauce to small bowl; do not wash skillet. Stir remaining ¼ cup orange juice, zest, liqueur, and remaining tablespoon cognac into sauce. Cover to keep warm.

6. **TO ASSEMBLE:** Fold each crêpe in half, then in half again to form wedge shape. Arrange 9 folded crêpes around edge of now-empty skillet, with rounded edges facing inward, overlapping as necessary to fit. Arrange remaining 3 crêpes in center of pan. Sprinkle crêpes evenly with remaining tablespoon sugar. Place skillet in oven and broil until sugar caramelizes and crêpes turn spotty brown, about 5 minutes. (Watch crêpes constantly to prevent scorching; turn pan as necessary.) Remove pan from oven and pour half of sauce over crêpes, leaving some areas unsauced. Transfer crêpes to individual serving dishes and serve immediately, passing extra sauce separately.

STEP-BY-STEP | MAKING CRÊPES

For the tenderest crêpes, most recipes call for resting the batter for two full hours to let the gluten relax. Given that our crêpes get crisped under a broiler and are then drenched in a sticky sauce, we wanted just the opposite. No need to rest the batter for our sturdier crêpes: Just mix and go.

1. Tilt buttered and heated nonstick skillet slightly to right and begin pouring in scant ¼ cup batter.

2. Continue tilting pan slowly, in counterclockwise motion, until a thin even crêpe is formed.

3. Loosen edge with heatproof rubber spatula and, with fingertips on top side, grab edge and flip.

Flambéed Cognac for a Crowd

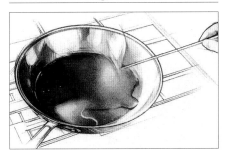

With just a few crêpes in the pan, it's not hard to ignite the cognac. With 12 crêpes, the alcohol gets absorbed too quickly—yielding a dozen boozy sponges. Our solution was to flambé the cognac separately, then build the sauce in the skillet, spooning it over the crêpes just before serving.

ILLUSTRATION: RANDY GLASS

Putting the Apple into Applesauce Cake

Applesauce cakes run the gamut from dense, chunky fruitcakes to gummy 'health' cakes that don't taste like much. How about an applesauce cake that tastes like apples?

> BY ERIKA BRUCE <

With all of its incarnations over the years, it is no surprise that applesauce cake suffers from an identity crisis. While its origins hark back to the chunky medieval fruitcake, in the years after World War I applesauce cake became a popular way to cut back on such hard-to-get ingredients as eggs, butter, and sugar without giving up dessert. In the health-crazed '60s, applesauce cake reemerged as a low-fat (applesauce mimics fat in some baked goods) and often flavorless option. More recently it's been offered up as a moist, rich, spice-laden cake. It's this last version that speaks of comfort to me: a simple cake to enjoy alongside a cup of afternoon tea.

But a quick survey of recipes representing this rich and tender style revealed that the applesauce cake still hasn't quite come into its own. Some recipes packed in dried fruit and nuts (a holdover from the fruitcake days?); others overdosed on the dried spices—a ploy to distract from a gummy or wet texture, perhaps. For me, applesauce cake conjures up more than an expectation of moist and tender spice cake: I wanted something that actually tasted like apples.

Easy Is as Easy Does
But before I could inject this cake with a dose of apple flavor, I needed to get the structure right. I started with a simple recipe (omitting any distracting nuts, raisins, or spices) of 1 cup applesauce, 1½ cups flour, 1 teaspoon baking soda, 1 cup sugar, 2 eggs, and 8 tablespoons butter. The most common mixing method for these butter-rich cakes was the creaming method, in which the butter and sugar are whipped together until light and fluffy, the eggs are added, and the dry ingredients alternated with the applesauce. The result was an elegant cake with a refined crumb. Tasters liked it, but it seemed like an awful lot of fuss for such a simple cake.

Could I just melt the butter, dump everything into a bowl, and stir it all by hand? Not unless I wanted a dense, heavy cake, apparently. The next

Go to www.cooksillustrated.com
- Key in code 90610 for the complete results of our **Applesauce Tasting**.
- Tasting results available until March 1, 2007.

Simple doesn't have to mean boring. Our Applesauce Snack Cake gets its pronounced apple flavor from three different sources.

simplest method I tried was the one often used for quick breads and muffins, in which a few extra minutes are spent mixing the wet ingredients separately, before gently adding the dry ingredients—but still by hand. When this cake emerged from the oven, it was clear that this method was a winner. A far cry from the refined crumb produced by creaming in a standing mixer, this cake's texture had a looser, more casual crumb that was better suited to a rustic snack cake.

Despite better structure, the texture remained somewhat gummy. I tried substituting vegetable oil (a common quick bread ingredient) for melted butter, but my efforts were for naught: While oil did keep the gumminess under control, tasters were not about to sacrifice buttery flavor for a slightly better texture. I fussed with the type and amount of leavener, adding some baking powder in hopes of quelling the gumminess with a more powerful rise, but the metallic aftertaste wasn't worth the modest improvement. In the end, the solution

was about as simple as it gets: reducing the eggs by one.

Upping the Apples
Since apple flavor was the main goal, my first step seemed the most obvious: Increase the applesauce. But as little as an extra half-cup reintroduced the gumminess. To combat the moisture, I tried both draining the applesauce and cooking off the moisture in a pan (each method alleviated a half-cup of liquid), but to no avail. The flavor of the applesauce was simply less noticeable and bright than before. Apparently, the flavor of applesauce (already cooked once) is a subtle thing—too subtle. While the applesauce was doing a fine job of providing the cake with moisture and tenderness, I would have to eke out more apple flavor from another source.

Fresh apples, whether shredded or diced, added a nice tart apple flavor, but they also added too much moisture. Apple butter, made from cooking apples down to a smooth, satiny paste, contributed a deep brown color yet disappointingly little flavor. Apple cider was my next bet, but I was wary of adding pure liquid to a recipe prone to being too moist. Reducing it to a syrup as a precautionary measure turned out to be key: The syrup contributed a pleasing sweetness and a slight tang without excess moisture. To compensate for the sweetness the cider added, I adjusted the sugar from 1 cup to just ⅔ cup.

A fellow test cook suggested adding dried apples to accent the apple flavor even further, but I was reminded of the unpleasantly chunky applesauce cakes from my initial tests. I tried

Past Lives of Applesauce Cake

Applesauce cakes have something of a fractured history, from the World War I–era fruitcake (left) to the '60s-style "health" cake (right) to the moist, buttery snack cake we prefer today.

CHUNKY AND DENSE   **LOW FAT AND BLAND**

PHOTOGRAPHY: CARL TREMBLAY

grinding them up into tiny pieces and adding them along with the applesauce. The apple flavor was significantly improved, but the bits of dried apple floated to the surface of the cake during baking, creating an odd top layer. Noticing my pan of cider simmering away, I tossed in the dried apples; not only did they absorb the cider, but they became plump and soft. A quick run through the food processor further unified the dried apples, cider, and applesauce. This triple-apple applesauce cake finally had the bright, recognizable taste of apple that I was after—without any compromise in texture.

And Everything Nice

While spices can easily become too much of a good thing, their use in moderation was welcome (the nuts and raisins were still out). Some applesauce cakes come adorned with a syrupy glaze or a creamy frosting, but I didn't want this cake

to be too sweet or rich. To achieve at least a modicum of textural contrast, I tried topping the cake first with a simple streusel and then with an even simpler topping of granulated sugar. Although I liked the simple, crunchy sugar best, a few tasters preferred the streusel version, so I kept that recipe as a variation.

After peeling away the many guises of applesauce cake, I had hit on an original that was simple in design yet bursting with honest apple flavor and warm spices. Identity crisis—at long last—averted.

APPLESAUCE SNACK CAKE
MAKES ONE 8-INCH SQUARE CAKE

This recipe can be easily doubled and baked in a 13 by 9-inch baking dish. If doubling the recipe, give the cider and dried apple mixture about 20 minutes to reduce and bake the cake for about 45 minutes. The cake is very moist, so it is best to err on the side of overdone when testing its doneness. The test kitchen prefers the rich flavor of cider, but apple juice can be substituted. Cooled leftovers can be wrapped in plastic wrap and stored at room temperature for up to 2 days.

- ¾ cup (2 ounces) dried apples, cut into ½-inch pieces
- 1 cup apple cider
- 1½ cups (7½ ounces) unbleached all-purpose flour
- 1 teaspoon baking soda
- ⅔ cup (4¾ ounces) sugar
- ½ teaspoon ground cinnamon
- ¼ teaspoon ground nutmeg
- ⅛ teaspoon ground cloves
- 1 cup unsweetened applesauce, room temperature
- 1 large egg, room temperature, lightly beaten
- ½ teaspoon table salt
- 8 tablespoons (1 stick) unsalted butter, melted and cooled slightly
- 1 teaspoon vanilla extract

1. Adjust oven rack to middle position; heat oven to 325 degrees. Cut 16-inch length parchment paper or aluminum foil and fold lengthwise to 7-inch width. Spray 8-inch square baking dish with nonstick cooking spray and fit parchment into dish, pushing it into corners and up sides; allow excess to overhang edges of dish.

2. Bring dried apples and cider to simmer in small saucepan over medium heat; cook until liquid evaporates and mixture appears dry, about 15 minutes. Cool to room temperature.

3. Whisk flour and baking soda in medium bowl to combine; set aside. In second medium

Apple Flavor 1-2-3

SAUCE
While applesauce added moisture, its flavor was too faint once baked.

CIDER
Reduced in a saucepan, cider added an apple kick without extra wetness.

DRIED
Dried apples infused the cake with flavor without gumming it up.

bowl, whisk sugar, cinnamon, nutmeg, and cloves. Measure 2 tablespoons sugar-spice mixture into small bowl and set aside for topping.

4. In food processor, process cooled dried-apple mixture and applesauce until smooth, 20 to 30 seconds, scraping sides of bowl as needed; set aside. Whisk egg and salt in large bowl to combine. Add sugar-spice mixture and whisk continuously until well combined and light colored, about 20 seconds. Add butter in three additions, whisking after each. Add applesauce mixture and vanilla and whisk to combine. Add flour mixture to wet ingredients; using rubber spatula, fold gently until just combined and evenly moistened.

5. Turn batter into prepared pan, smoothing top with rubber spatula. Sprinkle reserved 2 tablespoons sugar-spice mixture evenly over batter. Bake until wooden skewer inserted in center of cake comes out clean, 35 to 40 minutes. Cool on wire rack to room temperature, about 2 hours. Run knife along cake edges without parchment to release. Remove cake from pan by lifting parchment overhang and transfer to cutting board. Cut cake and serve.

GINGER-CARDAMOM APPLESAUCE SNACK CAKE

Follow recipe for Applesauce Snack Cake, omitting cinnamon, nutmeg, and cloves. Whisk ½ teaspoon ground ginger and ¼ teaspoon ground cardamom into sugar in step 3. Measure 2 tablespoons sugar-spice mixture into small bowl, add 1 tablespoon finely chopped crystallized ginger, and set aside for topping.

APPLESAUCE SNACK CAKE WITH OAT-NUT STREUSEL

Follow recipe for Applesauce Snack Cake through step 2. In step 3, measure 2 tablespoons sugar-spice mixture into medium bowl. Add 2 tablespoons brown sugar, ⅓ cup chopped pecans or walnuts, and ⅓ cup old-fashioned or quick oats. Work in 2 tablespoons softened unsalted butter by rubbing mixture between fingers until fully incorporated. Pinch mixture into hazelnut-sized clumps and sprinkle evenly over batter before baking.

The Cider Vinegar Rules

You can spend six cents an ounce for a jug of generic apple cider vinegar—or 20 times more for the fancy stuff. Does it matter? We tasted 10 brands to find out.

⋝ BY LISA McMANUS ⋜

Like the late comedian Rodney Dangerfield, apple cider vinegar gets no respect. While its glamorous cousins, balsamic and wine vinegar, commandeer premium supermarket shelf space—with bottle after exquisite-looking bottle—cider vinegar is often relegated to the bottom shelf alongside the inexpensive jugs of generic distilled white vinegar.

Such humble posturing reflects apple cider vinegar's equally humble beginnings. Apples were once the most commonly cultivated fruit in this country, and, until the early 20th century, cider vinegar was a natural byproduct of America's favorite beverage: hard (alcoholic) cider. From Colonial times until refrigeration came along, most American homes kept a barrel of apple cider vinegar for preserving foods.

Even though cider vinegar is now used more for brightening sauces and salad dressings than staving off spoilage, most cooks (including us) still opt for the most generic brand possible. As supermarkets have begun to offer a more varied selection—some in the vinegar aisle, some in the "natural foods" section—we wondered if it was time to change our tune. How much does cider vinegar brand matter? To find out, we purchased 10 brands available in supermarkets or by mail—six produced domestically, three from France, and one from Canada. We tasted them four ways: plain, in a Carolina-style barbecue sauce, in a pan sauce, and on romaine lettuce in a simple vinaigrette.

Fruitless Search

Right off the bat, it was plain that these were not identical products. Some vinegars were pale yellow, others deep gold, a few caramel colored. They also ranged from very cloudy to sparkling clear; one contained distinct reddish particles. Their tastes were varied, too, from slightly sweet and mellow to harsh and not sweet at all. The aroma and taste of apple were forthright in some, oddly missing in others.

Any hopes of a clear-cut victory along national lines were dashed as soon as the results were tallied. Of the two favorites, one was French (Maille), the other American (Spectrum Naturals Unfiltered). Could cloudiness or clarity be the winning factor? Cloudiness is a sign of unfiltered, unpasteurized vinegar, which still contains the "mother of vinegar," a gelatinous substance consisting of cellulose (plant fibers) and acetic bacteria (which ultimately produce vinegar). Clear vinegars are filtered. Again, tasters were split: One winner was clear, the other cloudy. Color? Wrong again: One was deep caramel, the other pale yellow.

Investigations into the manufacturing process proved similarly fruitless. Nine of the 10 vinegars are mass-produced in an acetator, a machine that can create 100 gallons of vinegar an hour. Only the Quebec vinegar (Verger Pierre Gingras) was made in the traditional way, with cider left in wooden barrels for at least a year to ferment first into alcohol, then into vinegar. While a small but vocal minority of tasters sang the praises of the distinctive complexity lent by barrel fermentation, most were put off by this artisanal vinegar's astringent, "musty" qualities. It finished toward the bottom of the pack along with two French vinegars that had similar flavor profiles. (Of course, this may say more about the American palate than the vinegars; in France, a refined "mustiness" isn't a flaw—it's a sought-after characteristic.)

A Spoonful of Sugar

My first important clue came not from the labels but from tasters' comments about what they liked about our winners. Praise abounded for the "sweet honey and caramel" notes of first-place Maille and the "appley sweetness" of second-place Spectrum Naturals Unfiltered. From the top brand to the bottom, sweetness—or lack thereof—was clearly an overriding concern for tasters. On a hunch, I sent all 10 vinegars to a laboratory to be analyzed for sugar content.

Two weeks later, the lab reports arrived, and the results cleared things up considerably. High sugar content correlated directly with taster preference. Maille and Spectrum Naturals Unfiltered—our two winning vinegars—were the sweetest of the group, with 1.31 and 1.56 grams of sugar (per 100-milliliter sample), respectively. The next three vinegars, in descending chart order, were White House (1.13 grams), Eden (0.75 grams), and Bragg (0.69 grams). The last-place Delouis (0.53 grams) had the lowest sugar level of the entire group—about one-third the amount of the winners.

Are some vinegar makers adding sugar to the mix to satisfy the American sweet tooth? Not quite. According to Karen Fahden of Sonoma Vinegar Works, a vinegar maker in Calistoga, Calif., vinegars like Spectrum Naturals come by their sugar naturally. The conversion of apple cider to vinegar is simply stopped before all the natural sugars are fermented. For instance, a vinegar maker catering to the French palate—which favors a drier, more tannic (and musty) profile—might let the fermentation continue undisturbed until almost all of the sugars have been converted. The results from our tasting indicate that a manufacturer catering to the American palate would be wise to leave some of the sugars intact. (The rise in popularity of balsamic vinegar during the past two decades is no doubt linked to its sweeter profile relative to that of wine vinegars.)

The one exception to the "sweeter is better" rule was the sixth-place Spectrum Naturals Filtered, sibling to our runner-up, which had plenty of sugar but did not fare so well. A call to an industry insider, Roger Fairchild, proprietor of Golden Valley Vinegars of Fruitland, Idaho, revealed one trick of the trade. "Vinegar making is as much an art as a science," Fairchild said. "Some days you make great vinegar, some days good vinegar, and other days it's not good at all." While he throws away the rare batch of poor vinegar that doesn't make the grade, he says other vinegar makers often filter mediocre vinegar to make it taste better. Filtering also makes the vinegar more appealing to consumers who associate a clear product with a pure one. But filtering, which removes apple solids and the mother of vinegar, also strips out much of the apple flavor. No wonder, then, that tasters consistently decried the "absence of apple flavor" in the Spectrum Naturals Filtered sample while praising Spectrum Naturals Unfiltered for its prominent fruitiness.

So sweetness counts when it comes to apple cider vinegar, but even generous sugar levels can't make up for a lack of apple flavor, a byproduct of filtering. For vinegars that performed well in every test, the tasting results point to the rich, smooth Maille and the sweet and tangy Spectrum Naturals Unfiltered. For those intrigued by the complexity of a French-style cider vinegar, the Verger Pierre Gingras (from Quebec) had several enthusiastic fans. But bear in mind that the majority of tasters found this vinegar unpleasantly "medicinal" (landing it in an unremarkable ninth place) and that its $19 price tag makes it a fairly high-priced gamble.

TASTING APPLE CIDER VINEGARS

Ten nationally available apple cider vinegars were sampled by 24 members of the *Cook's Illustrated* staff. The vinegars were tasted four ways: plain; in a Carolina-style vinegar-based barbecue sauce; in a pan sauce made with butter, cream, and shallots; and in a vinaigrette made with olive oil, salt, and pepper and served on romaine lettuce. Tasters judged the vinegars on their fruity, appley flavor, their balance of sweetness to tartness, and their complexity. Scores for the four tastings were combined to obtain overall rankings. Our tasters' preferences tended to track with the vinegars' sugar levels, reported here in grams per 100 milliliters. Most of the vinegars are available in supermarkets and natural foods stores. Mail-order sources for the winners are listed on page 32.

RECOMMENDED

MAILLE Apple Cider Vinegar
- $4.00 for 16.9 ounces (about 24 cents per ounce)
- Acidity: 5%
- Grams sugar per 100 ml: 1.31

Tasters raved about this French vinegar's "deep, warm" flavor profile and complex notes of honey, caramel, and sweet, "definite apple" taste. In the cream sauce, tasters liked this vinegar's "mellow, smooth cider flavor," which boasted a "good balance of richness and tang."

SPECTRUM NATURALS Organic Apple Cider Vinegar, Unfiltered
- $2.89 for 16 ounces (18 cents per ounce)
- Acidity: 5%
- Grams sugar per 100 ml: 1.56

Tasters liked the California-made Spectrum's sweetness, and indeed this vinegar had the highest sugar content of the group. But sweetness wasn't its only selling point. A "distinct apple flavor," a "floral" aroma, and "assertive, tangy" qualities also gave it an edge. Cooked in the cream sauce, Spectrum's strong apple taste came through with a "nice balance of tart and sweet."

RECOMMENDED WITH RESERVATIONS

WHITE HOUSE Apple Cider Vinegar
- $1.99 for 32 ounces (6 cents per ounce)
- Acidity: 5%
- Grams sugar per 100 ml: 1.13

American-made White House performed in the middle of the pack until the vinaigrette tasting, where it suddenly took top honors with a "good balance of acidity." But it was also downgraded for having "not much apple" flavor. Some found the acidity too much—"an aftertaste that burns."

EDEN Organic Apple Cider Vinegar
- $2.06 for 16 ounces (13 cents per ounce)
- Acidity: 5%
- Grams sugar per 100 ml: 0.75

While some tasters liked Eden's "pronounced apple cider profile" and light, mild, "pleasantly fruity flavor," most deemed it "mundane," "flat," "a little too subtle," and "almost unidentifiable" in the pan sauce and vinaigrette.

BRAGG Organic Apple Cider Vinegar
- $2.59 for 16 ounces (16 cents per ounce)
- Acidity: 5%
- Grams sugar per 100 ml: 0.69

A few tasters responded to this California vinegar's "good apple flavor" and "cidery" qualities, enjoying its "bright and vibrant" effect on the pan sauce. But uncooked, those strong notes came across as "harsh, medicinal," sour, bitter, and "unappealing."

RECOMMENDED WITH RESERVATIONS *(CONT.)*

SPECTRUM NATURALS Organic Apple Cider Vinegar, Filtered
- $3.09 for 16 ounces (19 cents per ounce)
- Acidity: 5%
- Grams sugar per 100 ml: 1.41

In each of the four tastings, the filtered Spectrum fared distinctly worse than its unfiltered sibling, with tasters complaining, "Where's the apple?" Others called it one-dimensional—"plain Jane."

VILUX Apple Cider Vinegar
- $4.50 for 25.4 ounces (18 cents per ounce)
- Acidity: 5%
- Grams sugar per 100 ml: 0.98

"Ick," wrote one succinct panelist. This French vinegar really riled up tasters, eliciting comments about its "Chloraseptic throat spray" qualities and "sour, moldy," "stale, musty," off-notes. In the pan sauce, it was "very bland."

HEINZ Apple Cider Vinegar
- $2.19 for 32 ounces (7 cents per ounce)
- Acidity: 5%
- Grams sugar per 100 ml: 0.60

The best panelists could muster for this ubiquitous American vinegar was to call it simple and mild: "No harm, no foul." Several decried it as "very acidic without much apple" flavor and complained about its "harsh, astringent" and "bitter aftertaste," which wound up with a "shocking finish."

VERGER PIERRE GINGRAS Apple Cider Vinegar
- $19.00 for 16 ounces ($1.19 per ounce)
- Acidity: 4.5%
- Grams sugar per 100 ml: 0.68

This wood-aged artisanal vinegar from Quebec was really a matter of taste. A few raved that it was "the best one yet; flavor is full, tasty!" But most complained that it smelled "awful," was "stinky," and imparted "burnt, ashy flavors" to the pan sauce. In the vinaigrette, it came across as "strange" and "medicinal."

DELOUIS Organic Apple Cider Vinegar
- $3.15 for 16.9 ounces (19 cents per ounce)
- Acidity: 5%
- Grams sugar per 100 ml: 0.53

Rated as "odd and clinical tasting" and "quite strong, maybe too much," this French vinegar had an "off, sour flavor" that was described as "gross" and "musty." It fared little better in the pan sauce, where it still had that slightly off flavor. In the vinaigrette and barbecue sauce, it was described as "unpleasant."

Should You Buy a Bargain Sauté Pan?

Paying top dollar for a saucepan or skillet isn't hard to justify. But how much should you spend on the infrequently used sauté pan?

≥ BY TODD DATZ ≤

Back in 2001, All-Clad was the winner of our testing of sauté pans, but now our top choice costs more than $180. While a sauté pan—basically, a lidded skillet with straight rather than flared sides—is essential when you pan-fry cutlets and braise chicken parts or vegetables, it seems like an awful lot of money for a pan that might see action just once or twice a week, even in a busy home kitchen. Given the dizzying number of choices in the cookware aisle these days, we wondered if we could get similar performance for less money.

To find out, we assembled a lineup of eight "bargain" brands to compete against the All-Clad: Cuisinart ($54.95), Emerilware ($69.95), Farberware ($69.99), Gourmet Standard ($73.36), Henckels ($79.95), Oneida ($29.99), Scanpan ($99.99), and Sitram ($49.99). Every pan had a capacity of 3 to 3½ quarts (fine for most tasks) and a traditional (rather than nonstick) cooking surface, the better choice for developing the sticky browned bits—*fond*—that give pan sauces and braises deep flavor.

Disparate but Equal

For our first test, we prepared white rice. An hour later, we had nine batches, each one just as fluffy as the next. When we sautéed chopped onions over medium heat, a few pans browned them very quickly, while others left them pale, but slightly adjusting the temperature easily corrected both tendencies. Evenly pan-fried chicken cutlets? Check. Nice pan sauce from the drippings? Check. As every pan passed every test without incident, we wondered how much we'd

Through Thick and Thin

As a group, the disk-bottomed pans in our lineup were more than twice as thick on the bottom as the clad-style pans. We found that the thicker the pan's bottom, the better it maintained a constant temperature—but it took a long time to get there. The thinner the bottom, the more quickly the pan responded to temperature changes, which can be a good or bad thing. To illustrate the difference, we had our local hardware store slice through the middle of our thinnest (left) and thickest (right) sauté pans.

THIN BOTTOM:
SUPERIOR RESPONSIVENESS

THICK BOTTOM:
SUPERIOR HEAT RETENTION

overspent on cookware over the years—until we had our first casualty.

During the crêpe-making session—an unconventional test for finding hot or cool spots on a pan's cooking surface—every pan produced perfect crêpes except one: The Sitram's crêpes turned dark brown around the edges. The problem was obvious. The thick aluminum disk stamped to the pan's bottom did not quite extend to its outer edge, leaving an unprotected ¾-inch ring.

If dark-edged crêpes were the Sitram's only problem, all would be forgiven. (Who but a *Cook's* equipment tester makes crêpes in a straight-sided pan?) But in a subsequent test—browning chicken thighs—that unprotected ring wreaked havoc again, burning the fond.

Fond, Farewell

Clearly, an expensive sauté pan isn't crucial for basic tasks. But what if we pushed these pans to their limits? After combing through the *Cook's* recipe archive, we had just the challenge: pan-seared steaks, cooked five minutes per side over very high heat (450 to 500 degrees). To see how well pans negotiated the fiery heat below versus the cold steaks above, we fastened a temperature probe to the cooking surface.

Our test taught us several lessons, the first of which revealed itself before the steaks even hit the pan. With the probes in place, we let the pans preheat until the surface reached 500 degrees. The variation in preheating times was shocking. From fastest to slowest: Scanpan (2:55), Gourmet Standard (3:07), All-Clad (3:11), Henckels (4:22), Cuisinart (4:45), Oneida (4:50), Sitram (5:00), Farberware (5:01). Emerilware? A whopping 7:36. No wonder the Emerilware had been on the slow side in some of the other tasks—it was probably still preheating!

The four fastest pans (Scanpan through Henckels) had one thing in common: clad-style construction, meaning that the entire pan is made of layers of stainless steel sandwiched around an aluminum core. The slowest five (Cuisinart through Emerilware) all had thick aluminum-core disks attached to the

bottom. Because the clad pans were much thinner on the bottom than the disk pans, they heated up more efficiently: At 0.05 inches thick, the Scanpan was the responsiveness champ, while the 0.30-inch-thick Emerilware—six times thicker—was the least responsive of all.

Of course, responsiveness is only part of the equation. A pan also needs to retain heat well. When the cold steaks hit the pan, the tables turned: The heat-retention champs were the Emerilware and the Farberware, two thick, disk-bottomed pans that kept the cooking surface between 450 degrees and 500 degrees for almost the full 10 minutes. The clad pans were much more volatile—dropping precipitously, then recovering, only to drop off again when we flipped the steaks. Despite the drama, the clad pans produced fine steaks, with the exception of the hyper-responsive Scanpan, which heated up to such extremes that it scorched the steaks and ruined the fond.

The steak test convinced us that the ideal sauté pan would balance responsiveness and heat retention—too much of one or the other meant either having to wait forever to get the pan hot enough or having to be super-vigilant in monitoring the temperature roller coaster. The clad-style All-Clad, Gourmet Standard, and Henckels and the disk-bottomed Oneida struck that balance well.

Design Matters

Although performance was our key concern, design details figured in as well. First, the size of the cooking surface matters. The pans tested ranged in cooking-surface diameter from 8½ to 10 inches, and that extra inch and a half is not insignificant: We easily fit a cut-up 3½-pound chicken in the larger pans, but the smaller models were too cramped to ensure proper browning.

Most pans had long metal handles that stayed cool, but the stubby Henckels handle heated up uncomfortably. Only one pan (Oneida) had a plastic handle, which stayed cool on the stovetop but precluded use in an oven hotter than 375 degrees. Five pans came with a "helper" handle, a small, loop-shaped second handle that made it easier to keep the pan level during transport. A dealbreaker? No. The occasional tiebreaker? Yes.

In the end, it turns out you can get a great sauté pan for less than $100. The modestly priced Gourmet Standard ($74) matched the performance of the All-Clad ($184) task for task.

We tested and evaluated eight "bargain" ($100 or less) sauté pans alongside our long-time (and expensive) favorite from All-Clad. We selected pans with a 3-quart capacity (or as close to it as we could find in each manufacturer's line) that were available in open stock according to the criteria below. All stovetop cooking tests were performed over 15,000-BTU gas burners on a Thermador range in our test kitchen. The pans are listed in order of preference.

WEIGHT: Without the lid.

DIAMETER OF COOKING SURFACE: Distance from interior wall to interior wall, as measured in the test kitchen.

THICKNESS: Of the pan bottoms, as measured in the test kitchen.

TIME TO HEAT: Time elapsed before the cooking surface reached 500 degrees when placed, empty, on a gas burner set to medium-high.

SAUTÉ SPEED: Average, fast, or slow, based on testers' observations of pan speed sautéing onions, searing chicken cutlets, browning chicken thighs, and searing steaks. A fast pan will require more attention from the cook than an average pan. If using a slow pan, you may need to increase the heat level.

PERFORMANCE: We sautéed chopped onions, cooked crêpes (to look for hot or cool spots), seared chicken cutlets, cooked white rice, and browned chicken thighs in two batches, making a pan sauce with the drippings. We measured heat responsiveness and heat retention by pan-searing two strip steaks and recording the temperature every 30 seconds. Scores of good, fair, or poor were assigned for each test, and the composite of these scores constitutes the overall performance rating for each pan.

DESIGN: Factors evaluated included whether the pan's weight and handle shape contribute to a feeling of maneuverability, the capacity to accommodate eight pieces of chicken without overlap, the handles' resistance to heat, and the shape and seal of the lid.

RECOMMENDED

All-Clad Stainless 3 Quart
PRICE: $183.95
MATERIALS: Stainless steel exterior and interior with complete aluminum core; stainless steel handle and lid

PERFORMANCE	
WEIGHT:	3 lb. 2 oz.
DIAMETER:	10"
THICKNESS:	0.08"
TIME TO HEAT:	3:11
SAUTÉ SPEED:	Average
PERFORMANCE:	★★★
DESIGN:	★★★

TESTERS' COMMENTS: Narrowly eked out another win thanks to as tiny a detail as its helper handle, a feature many staffers deemed crucial. Not to diminish its first-class performance: gorgeous sautéed onions, nicely browned steaks and cutlets, and impressive responsiveness. The most spacious cooking surface.

BEST BUY
Gourmet Standard Tri-Ply 10-Inch
PRICE: $73.36
MATERIALS: Stainless steel exterior and interior with complete aluminum core; stainless steel handle and lid

WEIGHT:	3 lb.
DIAMETER:	9½"
THICKNESS:	0.11"
TIME TO HEAT:	3:07
SAUTÉ SPEED:	Average
PERFORMANCE:	★★★
DESIGN:	★★★

If it weren't for the absence of a helper handle, the near-tie for first place might have broken in this modestly priced pan's favor. Aced every test thrown its way, and a thicker gauge helped it maintain composure in the steak test just a hair better than our winner.

RECOMMENDED WITH RESERVATIONS

Oneida Stainless Steel Cook & Pour 10-Inch Deep
PRICE: $29.99
MATERIALS: Stainless steel exterior and interior with aluminum disk base; Bakelite handle; glass lid

WEIGHT:	2 lb. 9 oz.
DIAMETER:	9½"
THICKNESS:	0.27"
TIME TO HEAT:	4:50
SAUTÉ SPEED:	Average
PERFORMANCE:	★★★
DESIGN:	★★

The cheapest pan surprised us by stumbling on nary a task, and testers appreciated the deep sides. Thanks to a plastic handle, it's ovensafe to only 375 degrees, and the construction had "a chintzy feel." But, hey—it's 30 bucks. No helper handle.

Cuisinart Chef's Classic Stainless 3½ Quart
PRICE: $54.95
MATERIALS: Stainless steel exterior and interior with aluminum disk base; stainless steel lid and handle

WEIGHT:	3 lb. 2 oz.
DIAMETER:	9"
THICKNESS:	0.21"
TIME TO HEAT:	4:45
SAUTÉ SPEED:	Fast
PERFORMANCE:	★★
DESIGN:	★★★

Aced the steak test, where it maintained a steady temperature better than most, and the crêpe cooked evenly. But keep an eye on the heat during delicate tasks: Once the thick base heated up, the sauté pace raced, yielding patches of overbrowned onions.

Henckels International Classic Clad 3 Quart
PRICE: $79.95
MATERIALS: Stainless steel exterior and interior with complete aluminum core; stainless steel handle and lid

WEIGHT:	2 lb. 9 oz.
DIAMETER:	8½"
THICKNESS:	0.13"
TIME TO HEAT:	4:22
SAUTÉ SPEED:	Slow
PERFORMANCE:	★★
DESIGN:	★★

Onions cooked evenly, and chicken cutlets browned well. But eight chicken pieces proved a tight fit, and the handle heated up quickly. The narrow surface also affected the pan's ability to maintain a consistent temperature during our steak test. No helper handle.

Emerilware Stainless Steel 3 Quart
PRICE: $69.95
MATERIALS: Stainless steel exterior and interior with triple-thick disk base of stainless steel, aluminum, and copper center; stainless steel handle; glass lid

WEIGHT:	4 lb. 8 oz.
DIAMETER:	9¼"
THICKNESS:	0.30"
TIME TO HEAT:	7:36
SAUTÉ SPEED:	Slow
PERFORMANCE:	★★
DESIGN:	★★

Slow and steady was this pan's motto, but it's not for the weak of arm—that composure comes from heaviness, more than a pound heavier than the next lightest pan. But the real deal breaker was the time it took to preheat: "Who wants to wait seven minutes every time you sear steaks?"

Scanpan 10¼-Inch Fusion 5
PRICE: $99.99
MATERIALS: Stainless steel exterior and interior with complete aluminum core; stainless steel handle and lid

WEIGHT:	3 lb. 2 oz.
DIAMETER:	9¾"
THICKNESS:	0.05"
TIME TO HEAT:	2:55
SAUTÉ SPEED:	Fast
PERFORMANCE:	★★
DESIGN:	★★

A veritable roller coaster, this pan plummeted in temperature when cold steaks were added, then heated up enough to burn the fond, yielding a bitter-tasting sauce. The thinnest pan bottom.

Farberware Advantage Stainless Steel 10 Inch
PRICE: $69.99
MATERIALS: Stainless steel interior and exterior with aluminum disk base; stainless steel handle and lid

WEIGHT:	3 lb. 7 oz.
DIAMETER:	8¾"
THICKNESS:	0.23"
TIME TO HEAT:	5:01
SAUTÉ SPEED:	Fast
PERFORMANCE:	★★
DESIGN:	★★

Browned the chicken cutlets with gusto, but overbrowned a good portion of the sautéed onions. Snug fit for the chicken. As with the Henckels and the Sitram, we would leave out a drumstick to ensure proper browning.

NOT RECOMMENDED

Sitram Profiserie 3.3-Quart Commercial Stainless Steel
PRICE: $49.99 (without lid); $14.99 for lid
MATERIALS: Stainless steel exterior and interior, aluminum disk base; stainless steel lid (sold separately)

WEIGHT:	2 lb. 8 oz.
DIAMETER:	8½"
THICKNESS:	0.30"
TIME TO HEAT:	5:00
SAUTÉ SPEED:	Slow
PERFORMANCE:	★★
DESIGN:	★

This pan's stamped disk bottom isn't flush with its sides, leaving an unprotected gap between the disk and the outer edge of the pan. The result? A dark brown outside ring on our crêpes and burnt chicken fond. No helper handle, a cramped cooking surface, and slow to preheat.

Fearless Flambé

Flambéing is more than just table-side theatrics: As dramatic as it looks, igniting alcohol actually helps develop a deeper, more complex flavor in sauces, thanks to flavor-boosting chemical reactions that occur only at the high temperatures reached in flambéing. But accomplishing this feat at home can be daunting. Here are some tips for successful—and safe—flambéing at home.

Be prepared: Turn off the exhaust fan, tie back long hair, and have a lid ready to smother dangerous flare-ups.

Use the proper equipment: A pan with flared sides (such as a skillet) rather than straight sides will allow more oxygen to mingle with the alcohol vapors, increasing the chance that you'll spark the desired flame. If possible, use long, wooden chimney matches, and light the alcohol with your arm extended to full length.

Ignite warm alcohol: If the alcohol becomes too hot, the vapors can rise to dangerous heights, causing large flare-ups once lit. Inversely, if the alcohol is too cold, there won't be enough vapors to light at all. We found that heating alcohol to 100 degrees Fahrenheit (best achieved by adding alcohol to a pan off heat, then letting it heat for five to 10 seconds) produced the most moderate, yet long-burning flames.

Light the alcohol off the heat: If using a gas burner, be sure to turn off the flame to eliminate accidental ignitions near the side of the pan. Removing the pan from the heat also gives you more control over the alcohol's temperature.

If a dangerous flare-up should occur: Simply slide the lid over the top of the skillet (coming in from the side of, rather than over, the flames) to put out the fire quickly. Let the alcohol cool down and start again.

If the alcohol won't light: If the pan is full of other ingredients, the potency of the alcohol can be diminished as it becomes incorporated. For a more foolproof flame, ignite the alcohol in a separate small skillet or saucepan; once the flame has burned off, add the reduced alcohol to the remaining ingredients.

Nature of the Yeast

Active dry yeast and rapid rise (instant) yeast may be similar in

SLEEPER CELLS
When substituting active dry yeast (above) for rapid rise (below), it's important to compensate for the "dead weight" of the inactive yeast cells.

appearance and origins (both are dried forms of live yeast), but substituting one for the other will yield vastly different results. When we baked our American Sandwich Loaf (May/June 1996), Multigrain Bread (March/April 2006), and Best American Dinner Rolls (see page 9) using equal amounts of each, the active dry batches consistently took longer to rise after mixing and after shaping—by almost 50 percent—and baked up denser than the rapid rise batches. Why? These two forms of yeast have different degrees of potency owing to differences in processing: Active dry yeast is dried at higher temperatures, which kills more of the exterior yeast cells (this yeast requires an initial activation in warm water), whereas rapid rise yeast is dried at more gentle temperatures (so it can be added directly to the dry ingredients).

What do you do if you have active dry in the cupboard and a recipe calls for rapid rise? Luckily, there's an easy fix: To compensate for the greater quantity of inactive yeast cells in the active dry yeast, simply use 25 percent more of it (for example, if the recipe calls for 1 teaspoon of instant yeast, use 1¼ teaspoons of active dry). The inverse holds true as well—use about 25 percent less rapid rise yeast in a recipe that calls for active dry. Also, don't forget to dissolve active dry yeast in a portion of the water from the recipe, heated to 105 degrees. Then let it stand for five minutes before adding it to the remaining wet ingredients. Skip this step if using instant yeast in recipes that call for active dry.

Substituting Canned Tomatoes for Fresh

Nothing tastes better than juicy, fresh tomatoes—on the rare occa-

---

'This Isn't the Prime Rib I Asked For': Two Solutions

While we found it most convenient simply to ask our butcher to separate the meat from the bones for our Grill-Roasted Prime Rib (see page 7), every so often we were faced with doing the task ourselves. And, on a few occasions, we could find only boneless prime rib, leaving us with an overbrowned roast, thanks to the lack of protective bone. Should either of these scenarios ever present itself, here are the test kitchen's solutions.

PROBLEM: The butcher fails to cut the meat off the bone.
SOLUTION: Do it yourself.

PROBLEM: The prime rib comes with no bone.
SOLUTION: Fashion a makeshift "foil bone."

I. Holding a meaty lobe in one hand and a sharp boning or chef's knife in the other, run the knife down the length of the first bone, following the contours as closely as possible, to separate it from the meat.

2. Flip the roast (so the uncut portion faces you). Holding the bones back with one hand, cut the meat from the remaining ribs. Once the meat is removed, proceed with seasoning and tying as directed in step I of the recipe.

I. Fold a 12- to 14-foot sheet of aluminum foil in half lengthwise and then in half lengthwise again; gently roll and scrunch it into a narrow tube. Coil the foil tube into a tight disk about 6 inches across. Flatten to form a rectangle.

2. Tie the foil "bone" to the roast (where the real bones were removed) and proceed with the recipe.

If you're making white rice as a side dish, any variety will do. But when a recipe calls specifically for long-grain (four to five times longer than wide), medium-grain (two to three times longer than wide), or short-grain rice (almost round), it's wise to use the right one—not only so the recipe's cooking time will work but also because each variety contributes a distinct texture to the dish. The test kitchen prefers medium-grain rice for saucy rice dishes such as jambalaya, gumbo, and arroz con pollo (see page 21): The exterior starches (of medium-grain rice) help thicken the sauce, yet the grains are firm and distinct enough to keep them from turning to mush.

The problem with medium-grain rice, we found, is unreliable labeling. When we purchased several brands of medium-grain rice for a taste test, we were surprised by the imprecision. (For instance, one brand labeled "medium grain" was really a sushi rice that matched our definition of short-grain rice in size and consistency.) All in all, we had the most consistent results with the Latin American brands in our lineup (rather than the Italian or Japanese), all of which had the starchy yet firm consistency we wanted. Our two favorite brands were Mi Casa and the widely available Goya.

---

sion that they're in season, that is. The pale, mealy options available during the rest of the year would ruin dishes like our fresh tomato sauces (see page 10). In fact, the test kitchen found that canned tomatoes make a better stand-in than those flavorless, off-season fresh options. For every pound of fresh tomatoes needed, simply substitute one 14.5-ounce can of drained diced tomatoes, plus 1 tablespoon of the drained liquid. And since canned diced tomatoes are firmer than fresh tomatoes, they should be pressed against the side of the pan with a wooden spoon to help them break down more naturally as they cook.

Mushy Mushrooms?

Conventional wisdom holds that you should never, ever wash mushrooms under running water. Their spongy nature allows them to soak up water, which makes them soft and slimy in the final dish. But the painstaking task of gingerly wiping every one of the mushrooms called for in our Mushroom Lasagna (see page 19) with a damp cloth—the method recommended by most experts—had us reconsidering just how crucial this maxim really is.

After testing both methods (a damp cloth versus a quick rinse in a colander under running water), we found that the rinsed mushrooms turned out just as good as the wiped ones in the lasagna, which made sense, given that they were cooked in a wet sauce. Our rule of thumb? Wash mushrooms right before cooking; if you let rinsed mushrooms sit around for longer than 10 or 15 minutes, the texture will begin to suffer.

Better Chicken Flipping

To flip a chicken or turkey during roasting (the test kitchen's preferred technique for ensuring even browning), we've always recommended grasping both ends with a generous handful of wadded-up paper towels. It's an effective method, but one that can be awkward and that can, on occasion, cause the skin to tear.

During testing for our Roast Chicken with Root Vegetables (see page 13), we came up with a hybrid technique that was even more reliable. Simply insert a sturdy metal or wooden spoon with a long handle and large head into the cavity of the bird. While guiding the other end of the chicken using paper towels, lift the spoon, flip the bird, then gently deposit it back onto the roasting rack. Just don't forget to remove the spoon before putting the bird back into the oven.

AS THE BIRD TURNS
A spoon is an unlikely—but highly effective—tool for flipping hot poultry during roasting.

Shrimp Potstickers

We weren't surprised when readers asked how they could modify our recipe for pork-filled **Potstickers** (March/April 2006) using shrimp instead. After all, shrimp is one of the most popular potsticker fillings in Chinese restaurants. We wondered if a straight substitution might work, but the filling was a disaster, oozing so much excess liquid that we couldn't seal the wrappers. Omitting one of the two egg whites improved the texture, but tasters complained that the filling was bland. We solved the flavor problem in two ways. First, we pulsed the shrimp in the food processor until almost pureed, a better consistency for absorbing the flavors of the garlic and ginger. Adding the fatty yolk along with the remaining egg white—to compensate for the leanness of shrimp compared with ground pork—gave these potstickers the flavor boost they needed.

Individual Blueberry Buckles

Several readers wondered if our recipe for **Blueberry Buckle** (July/August 2005) could be made into individual portions using a muffin pan. Turns out the easy answer is yes—until you try to turn them out. With so many blueberries, sticking is inevitable. We solved that problem in our original recipe with a quadruple-prepared pan (nonstick spray, parchment paper, more nonstick spray, and flour). That solution may be fine for a single cake pan, but it was a nonstarter when it came to 12 individual muffin cups. We had better luck with paper muffin liners, which kept the buckles from sticking. We also found it necessary to press the batter firmly to keep air pockets from forming.

BLUEBERRY MESS

PERFECT BUCKLE

An abundance of blueberries made sticking inevitable (top), but paper liners made perfect buckles for one (bottom).

Tea-Smoked Duck

In our recipe for **Oven-Smoked Barbecued Ribs** (January/February 2006), we found a great way to get the smoke flavor of the grill using a hot oven, a pizza stone, and ultra-smoky Lapsang Souchong tea. A few fans of the ribs asked whether the same method could be applied to other meats commonly cooked in a smoker, including duck. First, we had to account for the thick layer of fat underneath a duck's skin. Taking a cue from our **Crisp Roast Duck** recipe (November/December 1998), we started by steaming the duck in a covered roasting pan on top of the stove for 30 minutes, a technique we use to render the fat. (A full 1/2 cup of fat melted away!) From there, we figured we could substitute the steamed duck for the ribs. The dark meat was tender, but the delicate breast meat turned bone-dry. The solution was simple: After steaming, we separated the dark meat from the white. Once the tea smoke died out, we removed the breasts and roasted the legs 45 minutes longer. Finally, the breasts went under the broiler (along with the now-tender legs) to crisp the skin. The result was spicy, crispy skin and smoky, perfectly cooked meat, both white and dark.

–Compiled by Sarah Wilson

IF YOU HAVE A QUESTION about a recently published recipe, let us know. Send your inquiry, name, address, and daytime telephone number to Recipe Update, Cook's Illustrated, P.O. Box 470589, Brookline, MA 02447, or write to recipeupdate@bcpress.com.

COOK'S extra

Go to www.cooksillustrated.com
• Key in code 90611 for **Individual Blueberry Buckles**.
• Key in code 90612 for **Shrimp Potstickers**.
• Key in code 90613 for **Tea-Smoked Duck**.
• Recipes available until March 1, 2007.

⇒ BY GARTH CLINGINGSMITH ⇐

PRODUCT UPDATE Zyliss Garlic Press

Last year our favorite garlic press, the Zyliss Susi Deluxe, went out of production; its replacements are the Zyliss Jumbo ($16.95) and the Susi 2 ($13.49). Both have larger hoppers, with room for multiple cloves. The Susi 2 loses the original's blue plunger, used for cleaning—key for pressing unpeeled cloves. We pressed a full head of peeled garlic through the Susi 2 with ease, but a single unpeeled clove clogged it. Both models represent improvements, but the plunger makes the Jumbo our winner.

MEET THE PRESS
The Jumbo handles even super-sized garlic cloves.

EQUIPMENT UPDATE Silicone Pastry Brushes

When silicone pastry brushes first emerged, heat resistance (up to 600 degrees) and durability (bristles that don't break off) were their sole selling points. Their performance was poor. More egg wash and melted butter dropped onto the counter than got swabbed onto the food, thanks to thick, sparsely distributed bristles. But recently overhauled designs had us basting chickens, stirring hot sugar syrup, and brushing dough with butter and egg wash to see if the new models could match our favorite natural boar's-hair brush, made by Oxo ($5.99).

The Henckels ($11.95), Le Creuset ($9.95), and MIU France ($7.99) brushes were as chunky-bristled and nonabsorbent as ever. The other models faced the absorbency problem head on. Suction components (resembling bulb basters) provided impressive absorption but poor delivery: Baster-style brushes by Orka ($9.95) and Cuisipro ($10.95) spewed rather than gently swabbed. Decreasing bristle diameter was more effective. The Oxo Good Grips ($6.99), iSi Basics ($7.99), Progressive International ($11.99 for a set), and Williams-Sonoma ($16) models sported sleek 1-millimeter-thick bristles—the losers' bristles were twice as thick—giving them superior

LOST BY A HAIR
Oxo's natural boar's-hair model is a fine pastry brush—except when it sheds.

OUR NEW WINNER
The perforated flaps of Oxo's silicone brush trap liquid nicely and clean up easily.

absorption. Only the new Oxo rivaled our natural-bristled winner (its sibling), thanks to an ingenious innovation: a row of perforated flaps hidden among the bristles. The flaps trap liquid until the brush hits the food, working in much the same way as the plastic wand included in a child's bubble-blowing kit. Oxo's natural-bristle brush has the slightest edge in absorbency, but superior heat resistance, easier cleaning, and the promise of never again plucking stray boar's hairs out of pastry dough break the tie in the silicone's favor.

PRODUCT UPDATE Thermapen

Last year, we tested the new version of our favorite instant-read thermometer, the Standard Penetration Thermapen ($79), which promised faster readings—and, thus, less time hovering over a hot oven or grill. The thin, two-piece tip of the Super-Fast Thermapen ($85) was faster all right (five seconds versus 10), but also less durable. During testing we bent, then broke, the tip. As soon as we dismissed the new model, a *more* improved Super-Fast Thermapen (still $85) came out. This time, we had a winner: Its one-piece tip could still read in seconds, and it came out of testing in one piece.

EQUIPMENT TESTING Grill Grates

Our favorite gas grill, the Weber Genesis Silver A ($350), can now be equipped with various grates: stainless steel (the original), enameled steel, and enameled cast iron. Does grate style matter? Yes—as a steak-searing test (three minutes per side on a 500-degree grill) quickly proved. The difference came down to heat retention. When cool food hits the grill, the grate's temperature starts to drop; the key is how long it stays above 300 degrees (the minimum temperature for browning). The stainless and enameled stainless grates (each about 2 pounds) stayed above 300 degrees for just two minutes, which gave us great marks on one side of the steak but faint ones on the other. The heavy cast-iron grate (7½ pounds) stayed above 300 degrees for five minutes, long enough for great marks on both sides. The cast iron took 21 minutes to hit 500 degrees (the stainless grates took 15), but we'd rather wait a few minutes than lose out on the flavorful char. If you're in the market for a grill, purchase our favorite with the cast-iron-grate option (no extra cost). If you already have a Weber—and a spare $55—it's an upgrade we recommend.

DO YOU REALLY NEED THIS? Crêpe Makers

Most home cooks don't have a well-seasoned steel crêpe pan lying around, so cookware makers have come to the rescue with a bevy of home-crêperie solutions. Pans with convex cooking surfaces—like the NordicWare French Crepe Pan ($34.99), VillaWare's Crepe Maker ($39.99), and Maxim's Electric Crepe Maker ($34.99)—are heated (on the stove or electrically), then dipped into batter to yield thin, often misshapen crêpes. A higher-tech option, the Tibos Electric Crepe Maker, was expensive ($139.99) and difficult to use, thanks to an awkward batter "spreader device." We prefer a small (8- or 10-inch) nonstick skillet: It works like a seasoned classic, and you probably already own one.

Sources

The following are mail-order sources for items recommended in this issue. Prices were current at press time and do not include shipping and handling. Contact companies to confirm information or visit www.cooksillustrated.com for updates.

Page 3: ESCARGOT PLATE
- Stainless Escargot Plate: $6.99, item #6807, **Fante's Kitchen Wares Shop** (800-443-2683, www.fantes.com).

Page 13: ROASTING RACKS
- All-Clad Non-Stick Roasting Rack: $24.95, item #185681, and Calphalon Contemporary Stainless All Season Pan with Rack ($99.00), item #403913, **Cooking.com** (800-663-8810, www.cooking.com).

Page 27: APPLE CIDER VINEGAR
- Maille Apple Cider Vinegar: $4.00 for 16.9 ounces, item #B000E46MA4, **Amazon.com** (www.amazon.com).
- Spectrum Naturals Organic Apple Cider Vinegar, unfiltered: $13.04 for 1 gallon, item #B0000DJFBD, **Amazon.com**.

Page 29: SAUTÉ PANS
- All-Clad 3-Quart Sauté Pan with Loop Handle: $183.95, item #100183, **Cooking.com**.
- Gourmet Standard Professional 10" Sauté Pan with Lid: $73.36, item #AS11114, **The Knife Merchant** (800-714-8226, www.knifemerchant.com).

Page 32: GARLIC PRESS
- Zyliss Jumbo Garlic Press: $16.95, item #203174, **Cooking.com**.

Page 32: PASTRY BRUSH
- Oxo Silicone Pastry Brush: $6.99, item #1071062, **Oxo.com** (800-545-4411, www.oxo.com).

Page 32: GRILL GRATE
- Porcelain Enamel Cast Iron Gas Grill Grate: $55.00, item #9887, for Weber Genesis Silver A, **Weber** (800-446-1071, www.weber.com).

Page 32: THERMAPEN
- Super-Fast Thermapen: $85.00, item #211-076, **Thermo-Works** (800-393-6434, www.thermoworks.com).

RECIPES
September & October 2006

New Recipes Available on the Web

Recipes available until March 1, 2007. Go to www.cooksillustrated .com and enter the code listed after the recipe title.

www.cooksillustrated.com
Start your 14-day FREE TRIAL MEMBERSHIP
Go to CooksIllustrated.com/SubTrial Today!

Your free trial membership to CooksIllustrated.com includes all these benefits and much more:

- Access to all 14 years of *Cook's Illustrated* recipes.
- Up-to-date equipment ratings and supermarket ingredient taste tests.
- NEW! GOOGLE-powered search engine that helps you find it fast!
- Options to SAVE your "favorites," CREATE menus, and PRINT shopping lists.
- NEW! Menus for all occasions. Available only to Web site members.

Join our 110,000 members and enhance your subscription to *Cook's Illustrated* magazine with a Web site membership.

Go to CooksIllustrated.com/SubTrial to begin your no-risk 14-day FREE TRIAL.

AMERICA'S TEST KITCHEN
Public television's most popular cooking show

Join the millions of home cooks who watch our show, *America's Test Kitchen*, on public television every week. For more information, including recipes and program times, visit www.americastestkitchen.com.

Roast Chicken with Root Vegetables, 13

Mushroom Lasagna, 19

Arroz con Pollo, 21

Crêpes Suzette, 23

Best American Dinner Rolls, 9

Pork Tenderloin Medallions, 15

Grill-Roasted Prime Rib, 7

Tomato Sauce with Rosemary and Bacon, 10

Applesauce Snack Cake, 25

PHOTOGRAPHY: CARL TREMBLAY, STYLING: MARIE PIRAINO

Red Winesap

Northern Spy

Tolman Sweet

Stayman Winesap

Baldwin

McIntosh

Rhode Island Greening

Ben Davis

NEW ENGLAND HEIRLOOM APPLES

Cleaning Blender Jars

What's the best way to clean a blender jar? Can it go through the dishwasher?

KRISTI HAMADA
SOMERVILLE, MASS.

➤ Even blenders that are deemed dishwasher-safe may not be immune to shrinking or warping after enough trips through the dishwasher; especially vulnerable are rubber gaskets, which when damaged can cause leaking. To extend the life of your blender, we recommend hand-washing whenever possible. To make the job easier, especially when cleaning sticky or pasty ingredients such as peanut butter and hummus, we recommend an initial 20-second whir with hot tap water (enough to fill the bottom third of the jar) and a drop or two of dishwashing liquid to loosen any material trapped underneath the blades, then repeating once or twice with hot water only. To finish the job, unscrew the bottom of the jar and hand-wash each piece using a soapy sponge. For one-piece jar models, use a long, plastic-handled wand-style sponge to reach food stuck on the bottom or sides.

Panko Decoded

Many of your recipes call for panko. Is there a brand you prefer?

DANIEL SIEGEL
ROCHESTER, N.Y.

➤ To see if there really is a difference between the brands of this light, Japanese-style bread-crumb coating, we picked up four samples—Wel-Pac, Dynasty, Kikkoman, and Ian's—at Boston-area supermarkets and tested them in two recipes: baked chicken Parmesan and pan-fried breaded pork cutlets. Each brand worked fine in both baked and fried applications, but with slightly different textural qualities. While the Wel-Pac, Dynasty, and Kikkoman brands possessed a delicate crispness, the oil-free Ian's (purchased from a large natural foods supermarket) provided a much more substantial crunch. In the end, if a super-crunchy—rather than delicate and crisp—texture is what you're aiming for, choose Ian's. Otherwise, brand doesn't really matter.

Our tasters discovered that one brand of panko is crunchier than the rest.

Cooking with Nonalcoholic Beer

My favorite chili recipe calls for a bottle of beer. Can I use nonalcoholic beer?

WENDY BONNER
ALEXANDRIA, VA.

➤ Here in the test kitchen, we've tried using nonalcoholic beer in two of our recipes (carbonnade and beer-braised short ribs) and have had great success. Because both of these dishes are simmered over a long period of time, much of the alcohol in the beer is cooked off anyway. In the end, what's left is the beer's hoppy, malty flavor profile and little, if any, raw alcohol flavor. Therefore, swapping in a non-alcoholic beer makes sense. We like O'Doul's Amber Nonalcoholic Beer, which has a fruity sweetness that brings out the rich beefiness of these dishes. Because it is neither harsh nor overly sweet, it would probably be a great choice for your chili as well.

Can you really cook with nonalcoholic beer?

Parmesan versus Pecorino

What's the difference between Parmesan and Pecorino Romano cheeses? Some recipes call for either, and we're never sure which one to buy.

JOHN AND BARBARA KATORI
CHARLTON, MASS.

➤ Made from cow's milk, Parmesan is a hard, dry, aged cheese with a sharp, nutty flavor and a granular texture that lends itself to grating. Pecorino Romano, on the other hand, is an aged sheep's-milk cheese with a firm-to-hard, slightly grainy, oily texture and a salty, piquant flavor that borders on lemony. Pecorino Romano originated in the countryside just outside Rome. Other types of pecorino named for other regions of Italy can be found at specialty cheese shops or well-stocked supermarkets. Pecorino Sardo (from Sardinia) is soft and crumbly when freshly made but very similar to Pecorino Romano once ripened. Pecorino Toscano (from Tuscany) is creamy in texture when freshly made and becomes drier and chalkier as it ages.

Because Parmesan and Pecorino Romano cheeses have similar textures and flavors, they can generally be used interchangeably, especially when the amount called for is moderate. In larger quantities, however, Pecorino Romano can be fairly pungent (as we found to be the case in our recipe for spaghetti alla carbonara, which uses a full cup of cheese) and may require a small amount of Parmesan swapped in to balance its bold flavor. If you must choose between one cheese and the other, Parmesan is the more flexible choice for the broadest range of recipes.

Best Storage for Maple Syrup and Honey

This morning, we were looking at our container of maple syrup and noticed instructions to refrigerate after opening. Why does maple syrup need to be refrigerated but honey does not?

VISHAL THANIK
NEW YORK, N.Y.

➤ We've occasionally left maple syrup out on the countertop, only to find it spotted with mold a few weeks later, while a jar of honey sitting right next to it remained perfectly fine. Because of its high moisture level and lack of preservatives, maple syrup is a perishable food product that is susceptible to the growth of yeasts, molds, and bacteria. Refrigeration not only helps maple syrup retain its flavor but prevents microorganisms from growing as well. Unopened, maple syrup will last several years stored in a cool, dark place. Once opened, it will keep six months to a year in the refrigerator.

Honey, unlike maple syrup, is highly resistant to microbial growth because of its naturally low moisture content and slightly acidic nature. According to Harold McGee in his book *On Food and Cooking* (2004), when bees turn nectar into honey, an enzyme in the bees' saliva oxidizes some of the glucose (a simple sugar) to form gluconic acid (which increases the honey's acidity, making it less hospitable to microbes) and peroxides (which act as an antiseptic).

If kept tightly capped in a moisture-tight container, processed (that is, pasteurized) honey can be safely kept at room temperature (the National Honey Board recommends a range of 64 to 75 degrees Fahrenheit) for about two years. In the test kitchen's experience, however, it can be stored for even longer without flavor degradation. Refrigeration can cause processed honey

A VERMONT CHRISTMAS CAROL

As a young child, Martha was the pride and joy of the Skidmore family. She wanted for nothing—having acquired a mail-order dollhouse, pretty Sunday dresses, and a painted pony of even disposition—and as a young woman, she was indisputably the town beauty. Her picnic lunch was always the first one bid upon at the box socials, as the young man was buying not just her fried chicken and biscuits but the pleasure of her company as well. Both were said to be a bargain at $2.50. But chance did not always favor Martha Skidmore. She waited on a proposal of marriage from the young and handsome Phineas Lomberg until it was too late. Phineas finally settled down with a plainer, steadier woman, someone who would make the type of home that neighbors liked to visit for a molasses cookie or a bit of friendly gossip.

Phineas was the village carpenter. He was a tall, thin man who was loosely joined, his arms and legs having only a casual connection to his torso, as if his appendages might take off on their own were they offered half a chance. He lived on the back road next to the Woodcock place, and people had long ago stopped wondering when he was going to finish his own house, the one where his two sons, Eben and Hiram, had grown up long ago and where his wife, Rose, had taken to bed one day and never recovered. She was buried up in the cemetery above the Methodist Church, and on a clear day she still had a good view down the valley, past the ruins of the dance hall and Heard's store. His sons left to pursue their fortunes farther west, where the topsoil is deeper, the rocks are smaller, and, so they say, one needs just a bit less character to make a living.

As the years passed, Martha grew taller and more angular and her eyes narrowed from bearing witness to the ever-present manifestations of sin. The playthings of a happy childhood had long ago been forgotten, and she was now the loudest voice in the small church choir, despite John Wesley's instructions (printed in the front of the hymnal) regarding the importance of not raising one's voice above others. For Martha, everything was judged according to the book, a set of rules from which there was to be no deviation, and judge she did. The miller was guilty of coarse language. The blacksmith was gimlet-eyed for the red-headed teacher from Pawlet. Even the minister did not escape comment, as he was apt to find a deep pocket for an extra doughnut or two to enjoy on his long ride home from coffee hour. And she reserved her harshest criticism for Phineas, a man she reviled as besotted with forgetfulness and lack of respect for the Lord's good works.

The years passed slowly but Phineas's house grew no more finished. The pile of lumber in the yard was finally carpeted with weeds, the front door hung at an odd angle like a broken leg, and the side facing the road remained finished in tarpaper, not clapboard. But as a hired carpenter, Phineas acquired a keen eye for detail, fitting windows and doors until they opened and closed as if greased with butter, fashioning the joints in moldings so fine that they could not be seen with the naked eye. Yes, he might decide to put a window where a door was supposed to go, but one was well advised to simply enjoy the view, for his workmanship was a thing to be remarked upon. And it was said that Phineas had a keen eye for human affairs as well, using his carpenter's eye to sense when the foundation of a marriage needed a bit of stonework or when two people ought to be joined together like two beams of a bridge, one made of hardwood and the other soft, so they would grow strong together over time.

One year, the season of Advent came upon the small village and the minister's wife started rehearsals for the Christmas Eve service and hymn sing. As usual, Martha was in full voice, as if she were trying to single-handedly reach up to heaven to expose the sinners in the congregation. She

Christopher Kimball

never smiled, the corners of her mouth having turned earthward and her teeth seemingly sharper, adding bite to her righteous commentary. It was also noticed that Phineas was spending most of his time holed up in his workshop in the barn, working late into the night with no time given to the holiday festivities.

Christmas Eve arrived and the candlelight service was well-attended. The fresh cider had been pressed by the Skidmore boys, the coffeecakes were provided by the town baker, Marie, and there were tins overflowing with saucer-sized sugar cookies. Martha walked home alone as usual, past town hall, the town garage, and the forest-fire warden's house to her small, neat saltbox, set on a bank just above the Green River. It was a cold, crisp night with the sharp crunch of snow underfoot, and as Martha came up to her front porch she could just make out the shape of something unfamiliar.

Upon closer inspection she recognized a freshly painted dollhouse—a good likeness of her own home, but with a window where the front door ought to be. At first she was startled, as if she had glanced in a mirror only to see an unfamiliar face. But then the dollhouse warmed other memories, not just the ribbons and buttons of a happy childhood, but the pleasure of unexpected company, the taste of her mother's baking-powder biscuits, and the happy cadence of life in a small mountain town.

Martha smiled and then looked up past the rooftops and church spire and noticed a lone star in the east. In a small Vermont town, a carpenter had been at work, just like one so many years ago.

Walter Hard, who wrote about our part of Vermont in the 1930s, inspired this editorial. Two stories of particular interest are "The Carpenter" and "Sabbath Keeping."

FOR INQUIRIES, ORDERS, OR MORE INFORMATION:

www.cooksillustrated.com

At www.cooksillustrated.com, you can order books and subscriptions, sign up for our free e-newsletter, or renew your magazine subscription. Join the Web site and you'll have access to 14 years of *Cook's* recipes, cookware tests, ingredient tastings, and more.

COOKBOOKS

We sell more than 40 cookbooks by the editors of *Cook's Illustrated*. To order, visit our bookstore at www.cooksillustrated.com or call 800-611-0759 (or 515-246-6911 from outside the U.S.).

COOK'S ILLUSTRATED Magazine

Cook's Illustrated magazine (ISSN 1068-2821), number 83, is published bimonthly by Boston Common Press Limited Partnership, 17 Station St., Brookline, MA 02445. Copyright 2006 Boston Common Press Limited Partnership. Periodicals postage paid at Boston, Mass., and additional mailing offices, USPS #012487. POSTMASTER: Send address changes to Cook's Illustrated, P.O. Box 7446, Red Oak, IA 51591-0446. For subscription and gift subscription orders, subscription inquiries, or change-of-address notices, call 800-526-8442 in the U.S. or 515-247-7571 from outside the U.S., or write us at Cook's Illustrated, P.O. Box 7446, Red Oak, IA 51591-0446.

CONTENTS
November & December 2006

2nd PRINTING IN CHINA

www.cooksillustrated.com
HOME OF AMERICA'S TEST KITCHEN

Founder and Editor	Christopher Kimball
Editorial Director	Jack Bishop
Test Kitchen Director	Erin McMurrer
Managing Editor	Rebecca Hays
Senior Editors	Keith Dresser
	Lisa McManus
Associate Editors	Erika Bruce
	Charles Kelsey
	Sandra Wu
Copy Chief	India Koopman
Test Cooks	Garth Clingingsmith
	David Pazmiño
Market Research Manager	Melissa Baldino
Assistant Test Kitchen Director	Matthew Herron
Assistant Editor	Elizabeth Bomze
Editorial Assistant	Meredith Smith
Kitchen Assistants	Maria Elena Delgado
	Nadia Domeq
	Ena Gudiel
Editorial Intern	Lois Weinblatt
Contributing Editors	Matthew Card
	Dawn Yanagihara
Consulting Editors	Shirley Corriher
	Guy Crosby
	John Dewar
	Jasper White
	Robert L. Wolke
Proofreader	Jean Rogers
Web Managing Editor	Katherine Bell
Web Editor	Lindsay McSweeney
Editorial Manager, Books	Elizabeth Carduff
Senior Editors, Books	Julia Collin Davison
	Lori Galvin
Associate Editors, Books	Rachel Toomey
	Sarah Wilson
Test Cook, Books	Megan Wycoff
Assistant Editor, Books	Elizabeth Wray Emery
Design Director	Amy Klee
Art Director, Books	Carolynn DeCillo
Senior Designer, Web/Magazines	Julie Bozzo
Designers	Jay Layman
	Christine Vo
	Matthew Warnick
Staff Photographer	Daniel J. van Ackere
Vice President Marketing	David Mack
Circulation Director	Bill Tine
Fulfillment Manager	Carrie Horan
Circulation Assistant	Elizabeth Dayton
Direct Mail Director	Adam Perry
Product Operations Director	Steven Browall
E-Commerce Marketing Manager	Hugh Buchan
Marketing Copywriter	David Goldberg
Junior Developer	Doug Sisko
Customer Service Manager	Jacqueline Valerio
Customer Service Representatives	Julie Gardner
	Jillian Nannicelli
Vice President Sales	Demee Gambulos
Retail Sales Director	Jason Geller
Corporate Marketing Manager	Emily Logan
Partnership Account Manager	Allie Brawley
Marketing Assistant	Connie Forbes
Production Director	Guy Rochford
Senior Production Manager	Jessica L. Quirk
Project Manager	Anne Francis
Production Assistant	Lauren Pettapiece
Imaging & Color Specialist	Andrew Mannone
Technology & Operations Director	Aaron Shuman
Systems Administrator	S. Paddi McHugh
Chief Financial Officer	Sharyn Chabot
Human Resources Manager	Adele Shapiro
Controller	Mandy Shito
Office Manager	Saudiyah Abdul-Rahim
Receptionist	Henrietta Murray
Publicity	Deborah Broide

OYSTERS

OYSTERS Atlantic (or Eastern) oysters grow in waters along the East and Gulf coasts and tend to be large, crisp, and briny. Many are named for the bays, inlets, and ponds where they are found. Katama Bay and Marionpoint oysters hail from areas around Cape Cod, and Moonstone oysters are named for a beach in southern Rhode Island. Today, most varieties are farmed, but Wellfleet oysters, also from Cape Cod, are still harvested wild. Blue Points originally came only from Long Island, but the term is now used for oysters grown anywhere from Nova Scotia to the Gulf of Mexico. The warm waters of the Gulf can yield large, slightly rubbery, muddy-tasting oysters, such as the Louisiana, that are more suitable for cooking. The icy waters of the Pacific produce smaller oysters, with a vegetal or fruity flavor, such as the Fanny Bay and Stellar Bay, both from British Columbia. Originally from Japan but now farmed in the Pacific Northwest, Kumamoto oysters are very small, with a delicate, sweet flavor. Olympic Miyagi and Gold Creek oysters, from Puget Sound, are both meaty and clean tasting.

COVER (*Acorn Squash*): Elizabeth Brandon, BACK COVER (*Oysters*): John Burgoyne

For list rental information, contact: Specialists Marketing Services, Inc., 1200 Harbor Blvd., 9th Floor, Weehawken, NJ 07087; 201-865-5800.
Editorial Office: 17 Station St., Brookline, MA 02445; 617-232-1000; fax 617-232-1572. Subscription inquiries, call 800-526-8442.
Postmaster: Send all new orders, subscription inquiries, and change-of-address notices to Cook's Illustrated, P.O. Box 7446, Red Oak, IA 51591-0446.

NUMBER EIGHTY-THREE

NOVEMBER & DECEMBER 2006

COOK'S
ILLUSTRATED

Salt-Roasted Turkey

Olive Oil Olympics
Spain Crushes Italy

Do Manual Knife
Sharpeners Work?

Hearty Chicken Stew
Bacon, Red Wine, Deep Flavor

Ultimate
Beef Tenderloin

No-Bake
Pumpkin Pie
Easy, Light, and Fresh Tasting

Penne alla Vodka
Tomatoes, Cream, and Vodka

Arugula Salads
Best Green Bean Casserole
Chocolate Pots de Crème
Spices and Seasonings 101
Multigrain Pancakes

www.cooksillustrated.com

$5.95 U.S./$6.95 CANADA

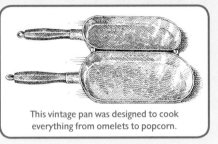

I purchased this odd hinged double pan at a local thrift store. When I asked what it was, I got responses ranging from a pan used to make cornpone to a primitive version of the pancake flipper pans sold on TV. Can you help me figure out what it is?

JON ORAVEC, PENDLETON, ORE.

➤ Your thrift-store find is neither a cornpone pan nor a pancake flipper. This hinged, wooden-handled, heavy-duty aluminum gadget is a vintage Double Fry Pan or Omelette Pan made by Super Maid Cook-Ware, a brand imported from Switzerland in the 1920s and '30s. In an old promotional booklet produced by the company, Super Maid touted its cookware line for its "extra thick sides and bottom[s]," which promoted "economical cooking" by conducting heat more efficiently. Food could thus cook "slowly and evenly, with very little gas."

Each side of the Double Fry Pan measures 10½ inches long, 5 inches wide, and 1½ inches deep. According to manufacturer instructions, the pan should be allowed to get very hot before the heat is reduced to fry food (with pan left open) or bake food (with pan closed shut) without sticking or scorching. Among the items recommended for cooking in the pan were omelets, cakes, biscuits, fish, and popcorn.

This vintage pan was designed to cook everything from omelets to popcorn.

to crystallize, or become cloudy, a phenomenon that can be reversed by heating the portion to be used in a water bath in a saucepan on top of the stove.

Sizing Up Pan Liners

I'm thinking about purchasing several Silpats for baking, but I'm pretty sure they won't fit into a few odd-sized pans I own. Can I cut them down to size?

ANNA LAW
CHICAGO, ILL.

➤ We've found that heavy-duty baking mats such as the Silpat nonstick pan liner work great if your baking sheet is exactly the right size for the mat. If the liner is too large and cannot lie flat in the pan, however, the edges may bow upward and leave an area of the liner without direct pan contact, thereby affecting browning (and occasionally breaking cookies). Unfortunately, because these heavy-duty liners are made of woven fiberglass strands (coated with silicone), they cannot be cut to fit. There's a danger that the sharp, exposed bristles will break off and become accidentally embedded in baked goods.

Two brands of lightweight reusable baking-pan liners that can be trimmed to size are KatchAll's Cook-Eze and Chef's Planet Bake Liner. After testing these liners, we found that although they were convenient, they were also less durable than their heavy-duty counterparts, creasing after just a few washes. While this may not be an issue for sturdy items like thick and chewy cookies, it can make or break thinner, more delicate items that need a smooth, even surface. If you're set on buy-ing a baking mat (great for delicate, sticky items like tuiles or lace cookies), make sure at least one of your baking sheets is an exact fit. For the rest of your pans, sticking to parchment paper is your best bet.

Better Day–Old Bread?

What is the best way to store an unfinished loaf of French bread?

MICHAEL SHERWOOD
WOOLWICH, MAINE

➤ Unless you store it correctly, there's often no good way to salvage a half-finished loaf of day-old French bread; your best bet is to use the stale pieces for bread crumbs, strata, or French toast. We tried several methods of keeping our leftover French bread fresh, both at room temperature and in the refrigerator: in its original paper bag, folded shut; wrapped tightly in aluminum foil; wrapped tightly in plastic wrap; and inside a large zipper-lock bag with the air pressed out.

Two days later, the room-temperature bread stored in the paper bag was hard, stale, and inedible. The foil-wrapped bread, on the other hand, was the best of the bunch. While it wasn't quite up to the standards of a fresh loaf (the crust had softened considerably and the interior crumb had gotten slightly chewier), it wasn't half bad, especially when crisped and "refreshed" for a few minutes in the toaster oven (or for five to seven minutes in a 375-degree oven). The bread stored in the zipper-lock bag was comparable, while the sample wrapped in plastic wrap—not quite as airtight as foil—was slightly staler. The refrigerated loaves didn't fare as well: They were drier, tougher versions of those left at room temperature.

So the next time you have a bit of baguette left over, store it at room temperature, tightly wrapped in foil or in a zipper-lock bag, and don't wait longer than a couple of days to eat it.

Rebaking Underbaked Cookies

I sometimes have difficulty determining whether a cookie is done baking or not. What happens if you take them out of the oven too early? Can you rebake them after they've cooled?

SHIRLEY MILLER
TAMPA, FLA.

➤ We purposely underbaked a few batches of chocolate chip cookies and sugar cookies by several minutes (to the point where they looked just done but really weren't), cooled them on a rack, and tried a few different methods to finish baking them.

First, we tried rebaking the cookies for about half the original baking time. Neither the sugar nor the chocolate chip cookies continued to spread on the baking sheet, and both remained raw in the centers. Next, we lowered the oven temperature by 50 degrees and rebaked them for the entire length of time called for in the recipe. This time, the sugar cookies were less "doughy" in the middle and the chocolate chip cookies were cooked through without being burned. The drawbacks? While no longer raw tasting, the cookies were noticeably tougher on the edges because of their extended stay in the oven. Last, we tried microwaving, a method known for cooking foods from the inside out. Unfortunately, at best the microwaved cookies were dense and dry in the center; at worst they were burned and brittle.

So if you accidentally underbake your cookies, your best bet at salvaging them is to bake them for a longer period of time at a slightly lower temperature.

FIRST BAKE: UNDERBAKED

SECOND BAKE: BAKED THROUGH

Putting an underbaked cookie (top) back in a lower-heat oven will allow it to puff to almost-normal size (below).

SEND US YOUR QUESTIONS We will provide a complimentary one-year subscription for each letter we print. Send your inquiry, name, address, and daytime telephone number to Notes from Readers, Cook's Illustrated, P.O. Box 470589, Brookline, MA 02447, or to notesfromreaders@bcpress.com.

Quick Tips

≥ COMPILED BY DAVID PAZMIÑO ≤

Quicker Pepper-Grinder Loading

Filling a pepper grinder usually means cleaning up wayward pepper-corns from the countertop or floor. Linda Leong of San Jose, Calif., keeps the peppercorns where they belong by fashioning a "funnel" from a plastic storage bag.

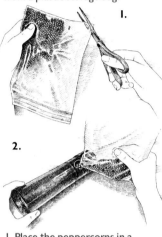

1. Place the peppercorns in a zipper-lock bag and snip off one corner with scissors.
2. With the snipped corner posi-tioned inside the grinder, fill to capacity.

No More Sticky Residue

Using a knife to cut dried fruit can leave a sticky residue on the blade, making it hard to cut the fruit evenly. Marian Ison of San Antonio, Texas, has better luck with kitchen shears dipped in hot water, shaking off any excess water before cutting the fruit.

Spreading Stiff Frosting

Trying to ice a cake with stiff frosting can yield unappealing flecks of torn-off cake. To keep things spreadable, Sarah Marren of Chicago, Ill., heats up a spatula or spoon in hot water before slathering on the frosting.

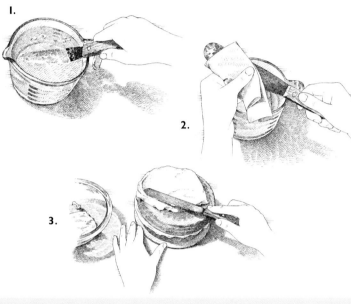

1. Dip the metal spatula (or spoon) into hot water for 5 seconds.
2. Remove and dry completely.
3. Spread the frosting on the cake, repeating the process as necessary.

Making the Grade(s)

To avoid having to drag out a ruler every time he wants a precise cut, Chris Dankulich of Boston, Mass., used a permanent marker to make gradations right on his cutting board.

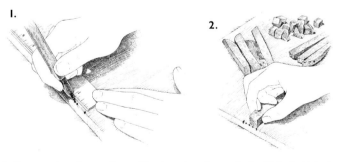

1. On one edge of a wooden cutting board, make marks for ¼ inch, ½ inch, ¾ inch, and 1 inch.
2. Place an item against the guide to check your knife work.

A New Way to Skin Hazelnuts

The most common way to remove the skins from toasted hazelnuts is to rub them off with a dish towel. After a marathon of baking holiday desserts, Susan Coppa of Concord, Calif., came up with a better method. She places the nuts on a wire rack set in a rimmed baking sheet, then lightly toasts them in a 350-degree oven for 10 to 15 min-utes. Once the hazelnuts are cool enough to touch, she rubs them against the rack, letting the skins fall onto the pan below.

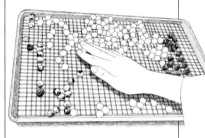

A Fresher Disposal

Tired of offending smells coming from the garbage disposal, Janet Vogenthaler of Denver, Colo., found a remedy in frozen vinegar.

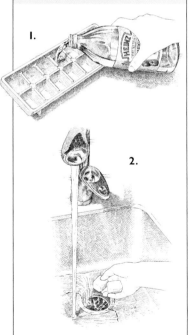

1. Fill an ice cube tray with distilled white vinegar and freeze until solid.
2. Toss a few cubes into an empty garbage disposal. With cold water run-ning, run the disposal until the cubes are ground up.

Send Us Your Tip We will provide a complimentary one-year subscription for each tip we print. Send your tip, name, address, and daytime telephone number to Quick Tips, Cook's Illustrated, P.O. Box 470589, Brookline, MA 02447, or to quicktips@bcpress.com.

ILLUSTRATION: JOHN BURGOYNE

Softening Cream Cheese with Ease

When she needs room-temperature cream cheese to make frosting and doesn't have time to wait, Tiffany Stephens of Longview, Wash., speeds things up by submerging the foil-wrapped package in a bowl of warm water for about 10 minutes, or until softened.

Safer Microwaving

Using plastic wrap to cover a plate of food for the microwave may be easy, but it also traps plenty of scalding steam that can rush out upon opening. Sarah Hilderbrand of Swampscott, Mass., forgoes the wrap in favor of inverted bowls (of various sizes), which she stores above her microwave.

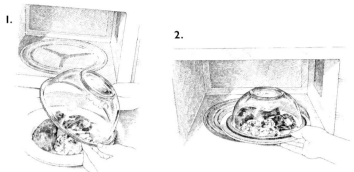

1. Place the food on a microwave-safe plate.
2. Position an inverted microwave-safe bowl over the food, transfer the plate to the microwave, and heat as desired.

Making Sugar Stick

Randi Crovets of Flushing, N.Y., came up with the following trick for keeping the colored sugar from falling off her holiday cookies.

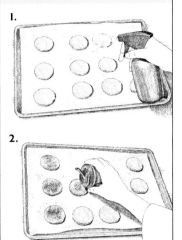

1. Using a spray bottle (a plant mister works well), spritz the cookies with a light coating of water.
2. Sprinkle on the colored sugar.

Sticking It to Stuck-On Food

Ruth Maples of Edina, Minn., has an effective solution for removing burnt-on food from her pots and pans.

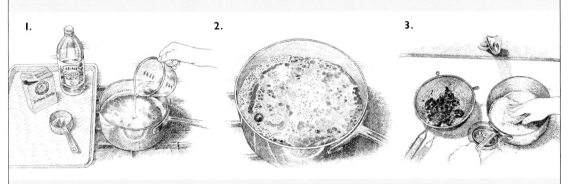

1. Fill the pan 2 inches high with water. Add ¼ cup baking soda and ¼ cup distilled white vinegar.
2. Bring to a boil and cook for 15 minutes. Turn off heat and let sit until cooled.
3. Drain the water and clean the pot as usual. If any burnt patches remain, repeat.

Foolproof Cookie Ornaments

The usual drill for turning cut-out cookies into ornaments for the Christmas tree is to poke a hole (for stringing) with a toothpick or skewer just before baking. But sometimes the hole closes up as the cookies expand. Elizabeth Chell of Hamilton Township, N.J., has better luck using a drinking straw, which removes enough of the dough to allow for expansion without completely closing the hole.

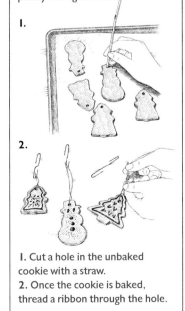

1. Cut a hole in the unbaked cookie with a straw.
2. Once the cookie is baked, thread a ribbon through the hole.

Removing Pesky Sausage Casing

Michael Cavaniola of Sag Harbor, N.Y., offers a simple tip for removing hard-to-peel casings from salami or soppressata.

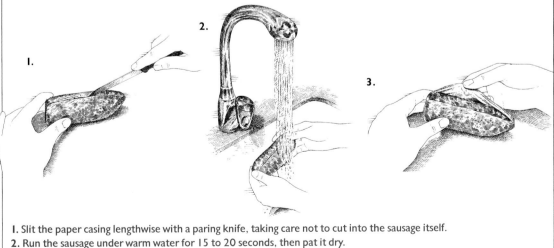

1. Slit the paper casing lengthwise with a paring knife, taking care not to cut into the sausage itself.
2. Run the sausage under warm water for 15 to 20 seconds, then pat it dry.
3. Pull the casing off in one piece.

Ultimate Beef Tenderloin

Beef tenderloin is perfect holiday fare. Add a rich stuffing and you've got the ultimate main course—at least in theory.

≽ BY SANDRA WU ≼

When I first got the assignment to work on a recipe for stuffed beef tenderloin, I figured I had it made. As I combed through a stack of recipes, I had visions of daily sessions spent carving into deeply charred crusts and tender, rosy-pink interiors to reveal generous caches of luxurious fillings—buttered lobster chunks, cognac-soaked chanterelles, truffled bread crumbs, and the like.

Once I stopped daydreaming and prepared these recipes, however, reality reared its ugly head. Much of the problem lay in the tenderloin's thin, tapered shape. By the time the thicker end reached medium-rare (about 30 minutes), the skinny end was overcooked. And forget about a nice crust—the exterior had hardly begun to brown at this point. The stuffing situation was even worse. The aforementioned "deluxe" fillings were either so chunky they fell out unceremoniously onto the platter upon carving or so absorbent they turned an unappealing blood-red (literally). Clearly, I had my work cut out for me if I wanted to make a stuffed beef tenderloin worthy of its reputation.

Fit to Be Tied

My first decision involved the cut of meat. I could go with the whole tenderloin or the center-cut roast, also known as the Châteaubriand, a fancy name to match the fancy price tag (about $17 a pound). At $13 a pound, the whole tenderloin definitely had the price advantage, but was it worth the headaches?

I knew from past experience that to get a sufficient crust, the tenderloin would have to spend some time in a hot skillet. Although the test kitchen (in previous recipes) has fit a whole tenderloin in a 12-inch skillet by coiling it tightly, that trick doesn't work so well when the tenderloin is bursting at the seams with stuffing. What's more, the tapered end of the tenderloin (called the tail) is too narrow to hold more than a few

COOK'S extra

Go to www.cooksillustrated.com
- Key in code 11061 for **Roast Beef Tenderloin with Dried Fruit and Nut Stuffing.**
- Recipe available until May 1, 2007.

A swirl of mushrooms, caramelized onion, and Madeira makes pricey tenderloin worth every penny.

teaspoons of stuffing. By contrast, I found that the almost perfectly cylindrical Châteaubriand fits comfortably in a 12-inch skillet, roasts at an even rate, and accommodates just as much stuffing in one end as the other. In this case, I decided, the higher per-pound price was worth it.

Starting with a basic sautéed-mushroom stuffing (a simplified version of the least disappointing filling from my initial tests—but more on that later), I tried a basic butterflying procedure, making one cut down the length of the Châteaubriand, opening it up like a book, spreading the filling on the meat, then tying the flaps back together with twine. This method wasn't bad, but the amount of stuffing it could manage was pretty skimpy. One colleague suggested I try "double-butterflying" the roast, making two cuts so that it opened up into three parts (like a business letter) rather than two parts (like a book). Sure enough, this modified butterflying technique (see illustrations on page 7) accommodated 50 percent more filling.

Searing the stuffed tenderloin in a skillet over medium-high heat for 10 minutes did a decent job of developing a crust, but my tasters wanted

more of a contrast between exterior and interior. Given the 15 or 20 additional minutes this long, narrow roast needed to cook up to temperature, the oven wasn't going to help much. Borrowing a trick the test kitchen has used for other beef roasts, I coated the exterior with kosher salt for a full hour before searing. Not only does the texture of the salt itself contribute to the crust, but an hour is enough time for the salt to begin breaking down the protein fibers of the outermost layer of meat, desiccating it to the point that it browns quickly.

Once seared, the tenderloin went into the oven on top of a rack-lined baking sheet (the elevation encourages uniform cooking). I found that a fairly hot oven (450 degrees) produced both a beautiful reddish-pink interior and the deepest, darkest crust in just 20 minutes.

Flavor, Flavor Everywhere

My initial round of tests had taught me a few things about how not to stuff a tenderloin. Lesson one: Don't stuff a beef roast with bread cubes; they turn into absorbent little sponges saturated with blood-red juices. Lesson two: Avoid bulky ingredients (such as buttered lobster chunks), which fall out of the roast in a heap as soon as you start carving.

Despite the advances I'd made, the roast could accommodate only about a cup of filling. To get the most mileage from this relatively small amount, it was clear that I needed the most concentrated flavors possible. The mushroom stuffing I'd been using thus far needed some work.

Replacing the button mushrooms with earthy cremini deepened the flavor, while pulsing the mushrooms in the food processor reduced their bulk. Caramelized onions contributed sweetness and bound the mushrooms into a thick, slightly sticky jam that was easy to spread across the surface of the butterflied beef—and helped it stay put upon carving. Minced garlic and a splash of Madeira rounded out the flavors. To give the stuffing an aesthetic boost, I added a layer of baby spinach before rolling and tying the roast.

I wondered if I could pack in a little more flavor. As a finishing touch, I added a rich, herb-studded compound butter, a traditional accompaniment for lean beef tenderloin.

PHOTOGRAPHY: CARL TREMBLAY

1. Insert chef's knife about 1 inch from bottom of roast and cut horizontally, stopping just before edge. Open meat like a book.

2. Make another cut diagonally into thicker portion of roast. Open up this flap, smoothing out butterflied rectangle of meat.

3. Spread filling evenly over entire surface, leaving ½-inch border on all sides. Press spinach leaves evenly on top of filling.

4. Using both hands, gently but firmly roll up stuffed tenderloin, making it as compact as possible without squeezing out filling.

5. Evenly space 8 pieces kitchen twine (each about 14 inches) beneath roast. Tie each strand tightly around roast, starting with ends.

With a swirl of intensely flavored stuffing in each bite and a potent butter permeating the deeply charred crust, this royal entree was finally worth its royal price.

ROAST BEEF TENDERLOIN WITH CARAMELIZED ONION AND MUSHROOM STUFFING
SERVES 4 TO 6

The roast can be stuffed, rolled, and tied a day ahead, but don't season the exterior until you are ready to cook it. This recipe can be doubled to make two roasts. Sear the roasts one after the other, cleaning the pan and adding new oil after searing the first roast. Both pieces of meat can be roasted on the same rack.

Stuffing
- 8 ounces cremini mushrooms, cleaned, stems trimmed and broken into rough pieces
- ½ tablespoon unsalted butter
- 1½ teaspoons olive oil
- 1 medium onion, halved and sliced ¼ inch thick
- ¼ teaspoon table salt
- ⅛ teaspoon ground black pepper
- 1 medium garlic clove, minced or pressed through garlic press (about 1 teaspoon)
- ½ cup Madeira or sweet Marsala wine

Beef Roast
- 1 beef tenderloin center-cut Châteaubriand (2 to 3 pounds), trimmed of fat and silver skin Kosher salt and ground black pepper
- ½ cup lightly packed baby spinach
- 3 tablespoons olive oil

Herb Butter
- 4 tablespoons unsalted butter, softened
- 1 tablespoon chopped fresh parsley leaves
- ¾ teaspoon chopped fresh thyme leaves
- 1 medium garlic clove, minced or pressed through garlic press (about 1 teaspoon)
- 1 tablespoon whole grain mustard
- ⅛ teaspoon table salt
- ⅛ teaspoon ground black pepper

1. **FOR THE STUFFING:** Process mushrooms in food processor until coarsely chopped, about six 1-second pulses. Heat butter and oil in 12-inch nonstick skillet over medium-high heat until foaming subsides. Add onion, table salt, and pepper; cook, stirring occasionally, until onion begins to soften, about 5 minutes. Add mushrooms and cook, stirring occasionally, until all moisture has evaporated, 5 to 7 minutes. Reduce heat to medium and continue to cook, stirring frequently, until vegetables are deeply browned and sticky, about 10 minutes. Stir in garlic and cook until fragrant, 30 seconds. Slowly stir in Madeira and cook, scraping bottom of skillet to loosen any browned bits, until liquid has evaporated, 2 to 3 minutes. Transfer onion-mushroom mixture to plate and cool to room temperature.

2. **FOR THE ROAST:** Following illustrations 1 and 2 above, butterfly roast. Season cut side of roast liberally with kosher salt and pepper. Following illustration 3, spread cooled stuffing mixture over interior of roast, leaving ½-inch border on all sides; lay spinach on top of stuffing. Following illustrations 4 and 5, roll roast lengthwise and tie.

3. In small bowl, stir together 1 tablespoon olive oil, 1½ teaspoons kosher salt, and 1½ teaspoons pepper. Rub roast with oil mixture and let stand at room temperature for 1 hour.

4. Adjust oven rack to middle position and heat oven to 450 degrees. Heat remaining 2 tablespoons olive oil in 12-inch skillet over medium-high heat until smoking. Add beef to pan and cook until well browned on all sides, 8 to 10 minutes total. Transfer beef to wire rack set in rimmed baking sheet and place in oven. Roast until instant-read thermometer inserted into thickest part of roast registers 120 degrees for rare, 16 to 18 minutes, or 125 degrees for medium-rare, 20 to 22 minutes.

5. **FOR THE BUTTER:** While meat roasts, combine butter ingredients in small bowl. Transfer tenderloin to cutting board; spread half of butter evenly over top of roast. Loosely tent roast with foil; let rest for 15 minutes. Cut roast between pieces of twine into thick slices. Remove twine and serve with remaining butter passed separately.

Upgrading Green Bean Casserole

The classic combo of frozen beans, condensed soup, and canned onions isn't bad. But for a holiday centered on homemade food, shouldn't every dish be great?

⇒ BY SARAH WILSON ⇐

Green bean casserole was originally created in the kitchens of the Campbell Soup Company in 1955, solely to feature one of its star products, condensed cream of mushroom soup. In fact, it's estimated that as many as 20 million portions of green bean casserole are served every year—a dozen of which are consumed by test kitchen staffers on Thanksgiving.

Fond memories of this dish notwithstanding, I was disappointed when I prepared the original recipe. Although not without merit—the concept of tender green beans, creamy "sauce," and a crisp, salty topping is a winning one—there's a bland and stodgy quality that comes from using nothing but processed convenience products: frozen green beans, canned condensed soup, and canned fried onions. Surely, with a little tinkering, I could come up with a casserole I would be proud to offer alongside the other homemade dishes at my holiday dinner table.

This classic dish gets a partial makeover with fresh beans and a homemade mushroom sauce.

The Beans

The original "green bean bake," as this casserole is sometimes called, uses frozen or canned beans. While both are easy to use, I felt certain that fresh green beans would make this casserole better without adding too much work. Just to be sure that people could tell the difference, the test kitchen held a formal tasting of fresh, frozen, and canned green beans, both plain and cooked in the casserole. Suffice it to say that the fresh beans won out. (For the full results of the tasting, see page 9.)

Armed with bushels of green beans, I first tried

adding raw beans to the almost-finished sauce so both could finish cooking simultaneously. Unfortunately, this method turned the beans a dull army green, and it was hard to avoid overcooking them. Next I tried steaming the beans, thinking they'd cook evenly in a lidded pot, but the results were just as problematic, with the added disadvantage that they were completely unseasoned.

Finally, I tried blanching—dropping the raw beans into boiling, salted water and cooking them until tender (about six minutes), then

"shocking" them (to stop the cooking) in an ice-water bath. Foolproof and straightforward, this method worked; the beans were perfectly cooked, consistent in texture, and colored a beautiful bright green. They were also nicely seasoned.

The Sauce

The product that inspired this recipe may be called a soup, but it is so thick (condensed) that it might as well be called a sauce. And while it may be concentrated in terms of consistency, in terms of mushroom flavor it's anything but. My upgraded version, I decided, should have a distinct mushroom flavor in addition to that rich, velvety consistency.

To begin, I sautéed a pound of sliced mushrooms in 2 tablespoons of butter, added an equal amount of flour (making a roux, a French technique for thickening sauces), then poured in 2½ cups of chicken broth. (Basically, I was making a mushroom variation on the classic French velouté sauce.) To finish the sauce, I added a half-cup of heavy cream. The flavor was great, but the texture was too loose for this casserole. Increasing the roux by half (3 tablespoons butter plus 3 tablespoons flour) was an improvement, but adjusting the proportions of chicken broth and heavy cream to 1½ cups each is what really did the trick, giving this sauce the right balance of savory and creamy.

Would fancier mushrooms make this casserole even more deluxe? Well, exotic wild mushrooms did make it a lot more expensive, but they contributed little extra flavor (thanks largely to the generous amount of cream). Likewise, dried porcini were not worth the minimal flavor difference, while portobellos made the sauce unappealingly dark. The one change I made to the mushrooms had nothing to do with flavor: Tasters preferred

RECIPE TESTING: Onion Toppings

We tested 20 different toppings for our green bean casserole. Here are some of the highlights.

TOO SLOW
Onions that were floured, then pan-fried, tasted great but took three batches and 45 minutes to make.

TOO LEATHERY
Shallots tossed with flour and baked were tough and chewy.

TOO EGGY
Shallots coated with flour and eggs and pan-fried were like an eggy onion pancake.

TOO GRITTY
Breaded-then-baked onions were gritty and grainy.

JUST RIGHT
A combination of canned fried onions and bread crumbs was easy and tasty.

PHOTOGRAPHY: CARL TREMBLAY

the rustic texture of unevenly broken mushroom pieces to the more elegant slices I'd been using, making for a quicker prep time (see "Breaking Mushrooms," page 30).

The Topping

Emboldened by the ease with which I'd upgraded this casserole on the bean and sauce fronts, I approached the fried-onion topping with optimism. Invented decades ago as a convenience product for topping casseroles, salads, and other dishes, Durkee's canned fried onions (now made by French's) are just what they sound like: thinly cut onions, dredged in flour, deep-fried in oil, salted generously, and air-dried for hours. Many tasters waxed nostalgic over their tender, airy crunch, but others derided their "commercial flavor." I figured a topping made from scratch would represent a marked improvement.

Following the French's model, I duly sliced up a few pounds of onions, dredged them in flour, and deep-fried them. I loved the flavor but not the time, mess, and half-gallon of oil I went through to get it. This is a side dish, after all, and I wanted to keep the preparation in concert with the rest of the meal. Next I tried shallow-frying the onions in a fraction of the oil, but the sliced onions shrank down to a quarter of their original mass—not nearly enough to top the casserole. And given that one batch took about 15 minutes to crisp properly, multiple batches were a nonstarter.

What about moving the proceedings to the oven? I tried baking the sliced, floured onions on a well-oiled rimmed baking sheet. This treatment gave the onions a crisp exterior, but the 40 minutes of oven time required also caused them to become dehydrated and chewy.

This topping upgrade was turning out to be a lot more difficult than I'd anticipated. Switching gears, I devised a test to see just how crucial the onions were to this casserole. I pulsed a few slices of bread in the food processor, tossed the crumbs with softened butter, and baked them right on top of my casserole. When the bubbling casserole emerged from the oven, I waited with bated breath. The outcome? Mixed. Tasters loved the buttery crunch of the homemade bread crumbs but missed the onion flavor.

Fine, then. I knew just the way to get some onion flavor into this casserole topping both quickly and ultra-conveniently. Keeping the bread-crumb topping mostly intact, I secretly added a few cups of those darned canned onions I'd failed to replicate (in a reasonable amount of time, that is). When this casserole came out of the oven, tasters completely overlooked the canned fried onions tucked among the homemade bread crumbs. What they did notice was the topping's great taste and texture. This was the green bean casserole they'd been hoping for!

It almost broke my heart to divulge the secret. But even the canned-food naysayers had to admit

that the freshly made buttered bread crumbs masked the "commercial" flavor they'd complained about earlier. My green bean casserole makeover was finally complete.

GREEN BEAN CASSEROLE

SERVES 10 TO 12

The components of the casserole can be prepared ahead of time. Store the bread-crumb topping in an airtight container in the refrigerator and combine with the onions just before cooking. Combine the beans and cooled sauce in a baking dish, cover with plastic wrap, and refrigerate for up to 24 hours. To serve, remove the plastic wrap and heat the casserole in a 425-degree oven for 10 minutes, then add the topping and bake as directed. This recipe can be halved and baked in a 2-quart (or 8-inch-square) baking dish. If making a half batch, reduce the cooking time of the sauce in step 3 to about 6 minutes (1¾ cups) and the baking time in step 4 to 10 minutes.

Topping

- 4 slices white sandwich bread, each slice torn into quarters
- 2 tablespoons unsalted butter, softened
- ¼ teaspoon table salt
- ⅛ teaspoon ground black pepper
- 3 cups canned fried onions (about 6 ounces)

Beans and Sauce

- Table salt
- 2 pounds green beans, ends trimmed, and halved
- 3 tablespoons unsalted butter
- 1 pound white button mushrooms, stems trimmed, wiped clean, and broken into ½-inch pieces (see illustrations on page 30)
- 3 medium garlic cloves, minced or pressed through garlic press (about 1 tablespoon)
- Ground black pepper
- 3 tablespoons all-purpose flour
- 1½ cups low-sodium chicken broth
- 1½ cups heavy cream

1. **FOR THE TOPPING:** Pulse bread, butter, salt, and pepper in food processor until mixture resembles coarse crumbs, about ten 1-second pulses. Transfer to large bowl and toss with onions; set aside.

2. **FOR THE BEANS AND SAUCE:** Adjust oven rack to middle position and heat oven to 425 degrees. Fill large bowl with ice water. Bring 4 quarts water to boil in large Dutch oven. Add 2 tablespoons salt and beans. Cook beans until bright green and crisp-tender, about 6 minutes. Drain beans in colander and plunge immediately into ice water to stop cooking. Spread beans on paper-towel-lined baking sheet to drain.

3. Add butter to now-empty Dutch oven and melt over medium-high heat until foaming subsides. Add mushrooms, garlic, ¾ teaspoon salt, and ⅛ teaspoon pepper; cook until mushrooms release moisture and liquid evaporates, about 6 minutes. Add flour and cook for 1 minute, stirring constantly. Stir in broth and bring to simmer, stirring constantly. Add cream, reduce heat to medium, and simmer until sauce is thickened and reduced to 3½ cups, about 12 minutes. Season with salt and pepper to taste.

4. Add green beans to sauce and stir until evenly coated. Arrange in even layer in 3-quart (or 13 by 9-inch) baking dish. Sprinkle with topping and bake until top is golden brown and sauce is bubbling around edges, about 15 minutes. Serve immediately.

Perfecting Penne alla Vodka

Splashes of vodka and cream can turn run-of-the-mill tomato sauce into luxurious restaurant fare—or a heavy, boozy mistake. We set out to fine-tune this modern classic.

⇒ BY REBECCA HAYS ⇐

Asked to develop a recipe for penne alla vodka, I phoned my Italian friends. Perhaps their grandmothers might share old family secrets? No such luck. Further research revealed that this unusual recipe for tomato sauce finished with vodka and cream isn't steeped in Italian tradition at all; rather, it's a mostly American creation, the winner of a 1970s recipe contest promoting vodka. An instant classic, penne alla vodka became a featured item on the menus of trendy restaurants, thanks to its simple yet well-thought-out blend of power ingredients. Cream provides luxurious richness. Red pepper flakes ratchet up the heat. Splashes of vodka heighten the flavor of the tomatoes without adding competing flavors.

As with most dishes that look simple on paper, this one finds success in its proportions and timing, as proved by a survey of recipes with identical ingredient lists. Some were absurdly rich, containing more cream than tomatoes; others added too much vodka too late, yielding soupy, boozy sauces. My goal was to fine-tune this modern classic to strike the right balance of sweet, tangy, spicy, and creamy.

Most recipes for penne alla vodka begin with a basic tomato sauce (canned tomatoes, garlic, and red pepper flakes sautéed in olive oil), but the textures run the gamut from thick-and-chunky to ultra-smooth. Tasters preferred a middle road, so I pureed half the tomatoes (which helped the sauce to cling nicely to the pasta) and cut the rest into chunks. With just 10 minutes of simmering, the sauce had a perfect consistency, but I noticed two recurring problems.

First, the mix of potent ingredients was overwhelming the flavor of the tomatoes, especially their sweetness, a crucial component of the balanced flavor profile I sought. Sautéed minced onion added the right touch of sweetness, and a tablespoon of tomato paste remedied the missing depth of the flavor.

Second, the vodka was out of whack. Besides cutting through the richness, vodka contributes another nuance to the sauce—what tasters identified as "zinginess." As silly as it sounds, the science backs it up. Raw alcohol is an irritant, creating a stinging sensation on the tongue and in the throat. When cooked, alcohol doesn't entirely evaporate, and a mild burning sensation (aka zinginess) is left behind. Many recipes add the vodka along with the heavy cream near the end, but no matter how much restraint I mustered, the sauce tasted boozy. Trial and error taught me to add a liberal amount of vodka along with the tomatoes so that the alcohol mostly—but not completely—cooked off.

To finish the sauce, I swirled in ½ cup of heavy cream for a luxurious but not over-the-top consistency. Letting the penne finish cooking in the sauce (a standard Italian method) encouraged cohesiveness. I garnished the pasta with chopped basil and grated Parmesan. Finally, I had a quick and delicious version of penne alla vodka that struck the flavor balance I'd been looking for. Give it a shot.

PENNE ALLA VODKA
SERVES 4

So that the sauce and pasta finish cooking at the same time, drop the pasta into boiling water just after adding the vodka to the sauce. If possible, use premium vodka; inexpensive brands will taste harsh in this sauce. Pepper vodka imparts a pleasant flavor and can be substituted for plain.

- 1 (28-ounce) can whole tomatoes, drained, liquid reserved
- 2 tablespoons olive oil
- ½ small onion, minced (about ¼ cup)
- 1 tablespoon tomato paste
- 2 medium garlic cloves, minced or pressed through garlic press (about 2 teaspoons)
- ¼–½ teaspoon hot red pepper flakes
  - Table salt
- ⅓ cup vodka
- ½ cup heavy cream
- 1 pound penne pasta
- 2 tablespoons finely chopped fresh basil leaves
  - Freshly grated Parmesan cheese, for serving

1. Puree half of tomatoes in food processor until smooth. Dice remaining tomatoes into ½-inch pieces, discarding cores. Combine pureed and diced tomatoes in liquid measuring cup (you should have about 1⅔ cups). Add reserved liquid to equal 2 cups.

2. Heat oil in large saucepan over medium heat until shimmering. Add onion and tomato paste and cook, stirring occasionally, until onions are light golden around edges, about 3 minutes.

Add garlic and pepper flakes; cook, stirring constantly, until fragrant, about 30 seconds.

3. Stir in tomatoes and ½ teaspoon salt. Remove pan from heat and add vodka. Return pan to medium-high heat and simmer briskly until alcohol flavor is cooked off, 8 to 10 minutes; stir frequently and lower heat to medium if simmering becomes too vigorous. Stir in cream and cook until hot, about 1 minute.

4. Meanwhile, bring 4 quarts water to boil in large Dutch oven over high heat. Add 1 tablespoon salt and pasta. Cook until just shy of al dente, then drain pasta, reserving ¼ cup cooking water, and transfer pasta back to Dutch oven. Add sauce to pasta and toss over medium heat until pasta absorbs some of sauce, 1 to 2 minutes, adding reserved cooking water if sauce is too thick. Stir in basil and adjust seasoning with salt. Divide among pasta bowls and serve immediately, passing Parmesan separately.

PENNE ALLA VODKA WITH PANCETTA

Heat 1 tablespoon olive oil in large saucepan over medium-high heat, add 3 ounces thinly sliced pancetta, cut into ½-inch pieces (about ½ cup), and cook until crisp, 6 to 8 minutes. Using slotted spoon, transfer pancetta to small bowl and set aside. Pour off all but 2 tablespoons fat from pan and continue with recipe for Penne alla Vodka, using fat in pan instead of oil in step 2, reducing salt to pinch in step 3, and adding reserved pancetta to sauce along with basil in step 4.

Penne from Heaven

Does vodka quality matter in our penne recipe? To find out, we conducted a taste test of sauces made with six brands of vodka, ranging in price from $6.99 to $34 per bottle. To our surprise, nine out of 10 tasters favored the sauce made with the most expensive vodka, noting a "fresher," "cleaner" flavor. It turns out that cheap vodkas are distilled only once to remove harsh tastes, while "premium" and "super-premium" brands are filtered three or more times—and you can taste the difference, even in a tomato sauce. You don't necessarily need to cook with Grey Goose (winner of this taste test), but don't ruin your sauce with rot-gut vodka you'd never drink on its own.

FOR MORE THAN JUST MARTINIS?

Rethinking Roast Turkey

We have brined thousands of turkeys over the years. But with limited room
in the refrigerator, was it time to develop a space-saving alternative?

≥ BY DAVID PAZMIÑO ≤

We've been advocating brining in the pages of this magazine for 13 years. During that time, what was once an obscure technique has become mainstream. Pick up almost any recent cookbook and you can read about the virtues of brining, which will keep turkey (as well as chicken and pork) tender and juicy by pumping it up with water and salt. So why do anything different?

Readers have sent us hundreds of letters over the years asking for brining alternatives. Let's face it, refrigerating a big turkey in a bigger bucket filled with cold water and salt isn't always practical, especially around the holidays, when most refrigerators are packed. A large beer cooler filled with ice packs is one way to get around the space issue, but many readers can't lift a cooler loaded down with gallons of water and a big turkey—and disinfecting the cooler afterward is no easy matter. We were stuck. Brining is the best way to guarantee a moist turkey, but it isn't always the most practical way.

We seriously began to rethink our brine-at-all-costs philosophy while developing our recipe for Spice-Rubbed Picnic Chicken (July/August 2006). We found that salting, a kind of "dry-brining" in which we rubbed the chicken with salt and let it rest in the refrigerator for several hours, not only seasoned the meat but also helped keep it moist. How does salting do its work? Initially, the salt draws out moisture from the meat, and this moisture mixes with the salt to form a shallow brine. Over time, the salt migrates from the shallow brine into the meat, just as it does in our usual brining technique. Once inside the meat, the salt changes the structure of the muscle fibers so that the meat is able to hold on to more water—even in a hot oven. But we had taken our first stab at salting with pieces of cut-up chicken. Would it work with a whole turkey? If it did, would the salted turkey taste as good as a brined one?

The Rubdown

Heading into the test kitchen, I already knew a few things about salting poultry: It is more effective when the salt is applied directly to the

A new salting technique yields moist, juicy meat and eliminates the need for a messy brining bucket.

meat, not the skin, and, just as in brining, the amount of time the bird is exposed to the salt is important. Getting the salt under the skin was easy. After using a chopstick or the handle of a wooden spoon to separate the skin from the meat (this worked better than my fingers, which tended to tear the skin), I had ample room to give the turkey a proper salt rubdown. Starting with ¼ cup, I proceeded to rub table salt on the meat under the skin and in the cavity, then wrapped the bird up, and refrigerated it for 12 hours. Using our much-tested single-flip roasting technique, I cooked the turkey at 425 degrees with the breast down for 45 minutes, then flipped the breast up, lowered the temperature to 325 degrees, and continued roasting until the meat was done. The results? The outer layers of meat were well seasoned, but there was little salt flavor much beyond that. As one taster said, "Salty on the outside but bland everywhere else."

Switching to larger-grained kosher salt (which is easier to rub over the meat without leaving salty pockets), I began to increase the amount of salt, but I quickly found that more salt just made the problem worse. Regrouping, I scaled back the kosher salt to ⅓ cup and tried gradually increasing the salting time instead. Because 12 hours had yielded ho-hum results, I tried leaving the salt on for 24, 48, 72, and 96 hours. Whereas the birds that were salted for only 12 hours had a salty crust with a moderately moist and slightly flavored interior, the turkeys salted for 72 and 96 hours were overly salty, with

---

SCIENCE: Journey to the Center of the Bird

Weighing salted and unsalted birds both before and after roasting convinced me that salting could indeed help turkey retain moisture and produce a juicier bird. But a few naysayers wanted visual proof that the salt was worth the effort.

My first thought was to mix either food coloring or turmeric with the salt, but the color compounds in both were too large to pass through muscle cells in the meat. Next I attached an electric meter to the turkey and ran electricity through the breast to determine where the salt had penetrated, but the tests produced inconsistent results. I needed a compound that once dissolved would travel the same path as the salt to the center of the meat. The two likely candidates were tincture of iodine and copper sulfate, both vibrantly colored inorganic salts. The test with rust-colored iodine did not work, but the turkey coated with the blue copper sulfate lit up like a roadmap of salt penetration: The meat was dyed blue from the skin to the bone. Don't try this at home—copper sulfate is poisonous—but I finally convinced even the most stubborn kitchen skeptics that salting works. –D.P.

WEIRD SCIENCE
We rubbed a turkey with salt dyed blue, waited 24 hours, then removed pieces to track salt penetration.

Icing It Down

Cooling the breast down with ice ensures that it will cook more slowly than the legs and thighs, preventing the meat from drying out. Place bags of ice underneath the breast and inside both the large cavity and the neck area.

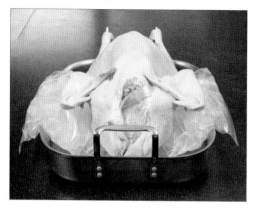

a jerky-like appearance. The turkeys salted for 24 and 48 hours were the perfect compromise: Most of the meat was nicely seasoned, and it was pretty moist.

There were, however, some salty pockets, especially in the deep valleys between the thighs and breast. Rinsing away excess salt before roasting solved this problem but left the skin flabby and soft. Blotting up the excess moisture ensured that the roasted bird would emerge from the oven crisp and brown.

Now for the moment of truth: comparing the salted bird with one that had been brined. First the bad news. Tasters found the brined turkey to be moister, and the numbers confirmed their impression. While a brined bird shed 19 percent of its initial weight in the oven, a salted bird shed 22 percent of its out-of-the-package weight. (A bird that is neither brined nor salted will shed 28 percent of its initial weight in the oven.)

Although salting couldn't quite compete with brining as a way to pump moisture into a turkey, it more than held its own in terms of flavor. In fact, most tasters chose the salted turkey over the brined for its "fuller turkey flavor." It "actually tastes like turkey," said one. Several tasters also preferred the more "natural" texture of the salted bird, even if the meat was a bit dry. If only I could find a way to make a salted bird retain a bit more moisture without pumping it up with water or slathering on extra gravy, I knew I would have a winning formula.

The Cool-down

I had one more trick up my sleeve. The dryness problem in the salted turkey was confined to the breast meat. (The fat in dark thigh and leg meat makes dryness a minimal concern.) Ideally, the breast should be cooked to 160 degrees and the thigh to 175 degrees, but these two temperatures are hard to achieve simultaneously, even when the bird is roasted breast side down (which gives

it some protection from the direct heat of the oven). Some time ago, I heard a radio interview with food scientist Harold McGee, who said he dealt with the temperature differential between breast and thigh by chilling the breast on ice. He explained that if the temperature of the breast was lower than the temperature of the thigh before the turkey went into the oven, that differential would be easier to maintain as the turkey roasted. McGee's idea sounded great, but how would I ice just the breast?

I tried to attach ice packs to the breast with masking tape, but they slid down onto the legs and thighs, parts of the bird that I did not want to cool down. Attaching the ice bags with duct tape and an athletic bandage (what was I thinking?) was more effective, but my colleagues joked that it looked like I was holding the bird hostage. Snickers aside, one thing was sure: Icing the breast was having an effect. The breast meat on this bandaged bird cooked up moist and juicy. If only I could ice the bird with less fuss.

One day, after filling several gallon-sized zipper-lock bags with ice, two bags were left in the bottom of a bowl. I had to wonder why

I had spent so much time trying to attach ice packs to the breast when—as I now realized—I simply could have placed the turkey, breast side down, on top of two ice bags. No wrapping, no fuss. After the first try, I knew this method was a keeper. It also allowed the thighs and legs to warm up faster, since they were now facing up. Wanting to chill the breast more thoroughly, I stuffed one small bag of ice in the cavity and placed another against the breast under the skin of the neck. The effect of all this icing was pretty dramatic. While the breast and leg were the same temperature (41 degrees) when the turkey first came out of the refrigerator, the breast, after an hour on ice, dropped to 36 degrees, while the un-iced leg had risen to 43 degrees. That 7-degree head start for the leg meant the turkey could stay in the oven long enough to fully cook the dark meat without drying out the white meat.

But had I convinced the test kitchen that salting could rival brining? When tasted head-to-head one last time, both turkeys were well liked. Tasters who wanted more moisture still favored the brined bird (which was still ever so slightly juicier), while those wanting a more natural turkey texture and flavor

---

STEP-BY-STEP | HOW TO SALT A TURKEY

Rubbing the meat with salt 24 to 48 hours prior to cooking flavors the turkey and breaks down some of the proteins, allowing them to retain more moisture. It's imperative that you massage the salt evenly inside the cavity and directly onto the meat.

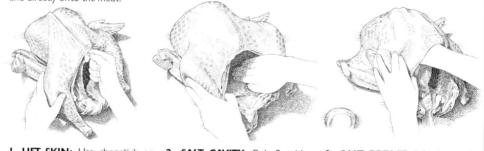

1. LIFT SKIN: Use chopstick or thin wooden spoon handle to separate skin from meat over breast, legs, thighs, and back.

2. SALT CAVITY: Rub 2 tablespoons kosher salt inside main cavity.

3. SALT BREAST: Lift skin and apply 1 tablespoon kosher salt over each breast half, placing half of salt on each end of each breast, then massaging salt evenly over meat.

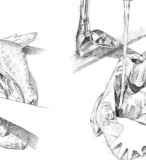  

4. SALT EACH LEG: Apply 1½ teaspoons kosher salt to each leg, adding half of salt while bird is breast up, flipping bird, and then applying remaining salt to underside of thigh.

5. RINSE: After 24 to 48 hours, rinse bird well to remove excess salt trapped under skin.

6. DRY: Use paper towels to blot excess moisture from skin so it can crisp and brown in oven.

picked the salted and iced version. One thing, however, was perfectly clear: Brining now had a strong contender, which also happened to take up much less space in the refrigerator.

ROAST SALTED TURKEY
SERVES 10 TO 12

This recipe was developed and tested using Diamond Crystal Kosher Salt. If you have Morton's Kosher Salt, which is denser than Diamond Crystal, use only 4½ teaspoons of salt in the cavity, 2¼ teaspoons of salt per each half of the breast, and 1 teaspoon of salt per leg. Table salt is too fine and not recommended for this recipe. If you are roasting a kosher or self-basting turkey (such as a frozen Butterball), do not salt it; it already contains a good amount of sodium.

- 1 turkey (12 to 14 pounds), giblets and neck reserved for gravy, if making
- 5 tablespoons kosher salt (see note above)
- 1 (5-pound) bag ice cubes
- 4 tablespoons unsalted butter, melted

1. Following illustration 1 on page 12, carefully separate turkey skin from meat on breast, legs, thighs, and back; avoid breaking skin. Following illustrations 2 through 4, rub 2 tablespoons salt evenly inside cavity of turkey, 1 tablespoon salt under skin of each breast half, and 1½ teaspoons salt under skin of each leg. Wrap turkey tightly with plastic wrap; refrigerate 24 to 48 hours.

2. Remove turkey from refrigerator. Following illustrations 5 and 6, rinse off excess salt between meat and skin and in cavity, then pat dry inside and out with paper towels. Add ice to two 1-gallon zipper-lock bags until each is half full. Place bags in large roasting pan and lay turkey breast side down on top of ice. Add ice to two 1-quart zipper-lock bags until each is one-third full; place one bag ice in cavity of turkey and other bag in neck cavity. (Make sure that ice touches breast only, not thighs or legs; see photo on page 12.) Keep turkey on ice for 1 hour (roasting pan should remain on counter).

3. Meanwhile, adjust oven rack to lowest position and heat oven to 425 degrees. Line large V-rack with heavy-duty foil and use paring knife or skewer to poke 20 to 30 holes in foil.

4. Remove turkey from ice and pat dry with paper towels (discard ice). Tuck tips of drumsticks into skin at tail to secure and tuck wingtips behind back. Brush turkey breast with 2 tablespoons butter. Set prepared V-rack in roasting pan; set turkey breast side down on V-rack; brush back and legs with remaining 2 tablespoons butter. Roast for 45 minutes.

5. Remove roasting pan with turkey from oven (close oven door to retain oven heat); reduce oven temperature to 325 degrees. Using clean potholders or kitchen towels, rotate turkey breast side up; continue to roast until thickest part of breast registers 160 degrees and thickest part of thigh registers 170 to 175 degrees on instant-read thermometer, 1 to 1½ hours longer. Transfer turkey to carving board; let rest 30 minutes. Carve and serve.

ROAST SALTED TURKEY FOR A CROWD
SERVES 14 TO 16

To roast 15- to 18-pound turkey, follow recipe for Roast Salted Turkey, increasing salt rubbed into cavity to 3 tablespoons (6¾ teaspoons if using Morton's salt) and into each breast half to 1½ tablespoons (3¾ teaspoons if using Morton's). Increase roasting time in step 4 to 1 hour; reduce oven temperature to 325 degrees, flip turkey, and continue roasting until it reaches proper internal temperature, 1½ to 2 hours longer.

EQUIPMENT TESTING: **Carving Boards**

As the centerpiece of the traditional Thanksgiving meal, the turkey—and the bearing of the turkey to the table—inspires in many minds the tableau Norman Rockwell painted in *Freedom from Want.* What his painting neglects to show, however, is the head of the table struggling to slice that huge bird on its coaster-like china platter. Seasoned cooks know that turkey carving is best done in the kitchen—and requires a sturdy board. We tested eight carving boards to determine which should be entrusted with the holiday bird.

A modest 15-pound turkey measures roughly 16 inches long, a fact that put two 18-inch boards out of the running. After half an hour's rest, our birds shed roughly half a cup of liquid, which flooded the shallow channels on two other boards.

The deeper, wider trenches on the Williams-Sonoma Medium Reversible Carving Board ($58) and the Ironwood Memphis Cutting Board ($79.95) were far more effective at trapping juices. What's more, both boards featured meat-anchoring mechanisms that kept the main course from sliding around en route from countertop to tabletop. The Williams-Sonoma featured a deep, oval-shaped central well where the turkey rested snugly, while the Ironwood Memphis had convex rows of pyramid points that gently gripped the turkey. Where the Williams-Sonoma board bested its rival, however, was in its versatility. The Ironwood Memphis, even with its generous surface area (22 by 15 inches) and sturdy, padded feet, was no match for the Williams-Sonoma, which with one flip could be used to accommodate a flank steak or tenderloin roast. And our winning board is elegant enough even for Rockwell's table. –Elizabeth Bomze

OUR FAVORITE
Williams-Sonoma Medium
Reversible Carving Board, $58
An oval well holds the turkey snugly, with ample room for carving.

FOR TURKEY ONLY
Ironwood Memphis Cutting Board, $79.95
Rows of pyramid points grip the turkey but render the board useless for anything but poultry carving.

PRONE TO FLOODING
Oxo's Carving and Cutting Board, $19.99
Turkey juices overwhelmed the shallow channels on this polypropylene board.

TOO SHORT
Catskill Craftsmen Carving Board with Feet and Groove, $20.33
This 18-inch board is barely longer than a small turkey.

Not All Kosher Salt Is the Same

Unlike table salt, kosher salt is fairly easy to spread and won't clump, so it is a must in our turkey recipe. But the two leading brands of kosher salt are not the same. Because of its more open crystal structure, a teaspoon of Diamond Crystal actually contains less salt than a teaspoon of Morton's Kosher. Use this reference guide to convert measurements.

1 tablespoon = 2¼ teaspoons
Diamond Crystal   Morton's

Multigrain Pancakes Worth Eating

Bland, dense, and gummy, most multigrain pancakes are more about appeasing your diet than pleasing your palate. We wanted flavorful, fluffy, and healthful flapjacks.

≥ BY MATTHEW CARD ≤

While I have always liked the wholesome flavor and hearty texture of multigrain breads, cereals, and baked goods, I've never quite cottoned to multigrain pancakes. Every version I ever tasted was bland and gummy, dense and chewy, or just unpalatably wholesome. First thing in the morning, I want breakfast, not penance.

That being said, I want to love them. I really do. Theoretically, nothing sounds better to me than a tall stack of complexly flavored, light, and fluffy multigrain pancakes—a breakfast I could enjoy eating and feel good about eating, too. In reality, of course, that's a pretty tall order. Leaden whole wheat, oats, barley, buckwheat, and the like don't lighten up so easily. Ever the test cook, I wondered what sort of kitchen alchemy could make a light, full-flavored pancake viable.

Flour Arrangement

There are a lot of multigrain pancake recipes out there, each one producing a batch of pancakes heavier than the last. A couple of the recipes I tried made for good flavor, but the pancakes' dense texture seemed beyond redemption. I did manage to dig up one or two recipes that were light. Their secret? Skimp on the grains. An easy, unsatisfactory solution: Multigrain pancakes should contain a multitude of whole grains, not a token spoonful. So where was I to start? Square

What's the secret to tall, fluffy pancakes packed with rich multigrain flavor?

one, with my favorite buttermilk pancake recipe. Perhaps I could adapt it to suit my needs.

After a good deal of trial and error, I felt like I was getting someplace. A mix of whole wheat flour and all-purpose flour punctuated with a variety of grains—oats, rye flakes, wheat germ, and more—tasted pretty good and wasn't horribly dense. And the mixing method couldn't have been easier: Blend the wet and dry ingredients independently, then whisk the two together just before cooking.

Sounds good, but the ingredient list was far too long, and the more flours and grains I added (in miniscule amounts), the better the pancakes tasted. A loaf of bread, maybe, was worth such an investment of time and effort, but pancakes? It felt like I was turning pancakes into a complicated affair when they should be a quick, mindless project, the sort of thing you can whip up while simultaneously brewing coffee, skimming the paper, and entertaining a demanding toddler.

Cereal Saves the Day

There had to be an easier way. I found several different grain mixes at the store that looked promising. While they were designed for hot cereal, I wondered if I could substitute a portion for the grains I had been adding to the pancakes. (A similar strategy had worked well with our Multigrain Bread recipe; see March/April 2006.) No such luck. Even after a long soak in the pancake's liquid components, the hard grains—coarse cornmeal and chewy barley—didn't sufficiently hydrate, and the pancakes were unpleasantly gritty, as if somebody had thrown a handful of sand into the batter while I wasn't looking. Prolonged cooking seemed to be the only way to soften the grains, but making a mush with the cereal before adding it to the pancake batter—a method that works well with cornbread—yielded very gummy, dense pancakes.

Hot cereal may not have worked, but what about cold cereal? The shelves of any supermarket are lined with dozens of different multigrain cereals, some certainly more "wholesome" than others. I read labels and bought a few that were highest in grain content and lowest in sugar.

Flake-style cereals, like Wheaties, almost dissolved into the batter and gave the pancakes an appealing chewiness. Hard, crunchy cereals, like Grape-Nuts and granola, made pancakes that were far too textured for my taste. While promising, none of the cereals I tried offered the depth of flavor (or variety of grains) I'd hoped for.

Then I found muesli. Made from raw whole oats, wheat germ, rye flakes, barley, toasted nuts, and dried fruit, it had everything I wanted in one convenient package. And that convenience translated to great flavor—far superior to anything I'd achieved in previous tests. The dried fruit and toasted nuts—usually almonds and/or hazelnuts—provided a huge flavor boost.

Flavor was one thing, but texture was something different altogether. The pancakes prepared with whole muesli were too chewy and had a gummy texture more befitting a bowl of oatmeal

Multigrain Makeover

Some multigrain pancake recipes load up on unprocessed grains—great for flavor but bad for texture. To avoid gummy, chewy pancakes, we made our own multigrain "flour" by processing store-bought muesli cereal in a food processor. To give our pancakes a subtle hint of that hearty whole grain texture, we added a few tablespoons of unprocessed muesli to the batter.

TOO TOOTHSOME
Pancakes made with unprocessed muesli had great flavor but too much chew.

PERFECT COMBO
Processing some muesli into "flour" and leaving some whole gave us great texture.

Let That Batter Rest

To get light, fluffy pancakes, it's important to let the batter rest while the pan heats (a full five minutes). The flour needs this time to absorb all the liquid, thus ensuring that the batter sets up properly. Skip this step and the pancakes will run together in the pan (left) and cook up flat, not to mention misshapen. Properly rested batter will maintain its shape when poured into the pan and will produce tall and fluffy pancakes (right).

UNRESTED   RESTED

than a stack of pancakes. Soaking the muesli in the liquid components of the batter to soften it remedied the chewiness but did little for the gumminess.

If whole muesli wasn't going to deliver a fluffy texture, what about grinding it fine into a homemade "flour"? I tossed a couple of cups into the food processor and let the muesli whirl until the cereal was reduced to a coarse meal. I replaced roughly half of the all-purpose and whole wheat flour in my working recipe with the ground muesli, and the resulting pancakes were almost as light as I wanted them. Proper leavening, perhaps, could make them perfect.

Lighten Up

Pancakes can be leavened naturally with whipped egg whites or chemically with baking powder and/or soda. I wasn't thrilled by the prospect of separating and whipping egg whites, but I was determined to test this method. To my relief, egg whites didn't seem up to the task. This dense batter needed the power of chemical leavening.

Many chemically leavened pancake recipes include both baking powder and soda, especially when they're bulked up with heavy grains. It may seem redundant, but the combination makes for fail-safe leavening and thorough browning. (In addition to acting as a leavener, baking soda is a browning agent—a fact that a quick test reconfirmed.) I experimented with varying volumes of both powder and soda and concluded that a substantial 2¼ teaspoons powder and ½ teaspoon soda yielded the fluffiest pancakes.

The texture was now spot-on and the flavor more than decent, but I couldn't help but think I could improve it with some tweaking. A little butter rounded out the grains' rough edges, and a splash of vanilla added depth. Most pancake recipes go light on the sweetener (that's what the syrup's for, after all), but I found that a couple

tablespoons of brown sugar went far in emphasizing the earthiness of the grains.

I thought I was done, but a few of my tasters thought that the buttermilk was a bit too sour, impinging on the flavor of the grains. If I did away with it entirely, I would have to rethink the leavening—no thanks. But what if I simply used a less acidic-tasting blend of milk and lemon juice? That was the answer. The milk and lemon juice mixture made for a surprisingly cleaner, richer tasting pancake with—as an unexpected bonus—an even lighter texture.

Perfect multigrain pancakes? Perhaps too perfect. Some test cooks thought they were going down too easy and favored the addition of a little whole muesli to the batter for a bit more chew. A teasing reminder, perhaps, of how far these pancakes had come from their dense beginnings.

MULTIGRAIN PANCAKES
MAKES ABOUT SIXTEEN 4-INCH PANCAKES,
SERVING 4 TO 6

Familia-brand no-sugar-added muesli is the best choice for this recipe. If you can't find Familia, look for Alpen or any no-sugar-added muesli. (If you can't find muesli without sugar, muesli with sugar added will work; reduce the brown sugar in the recipe to 1 tablespoon.) Mix the batter first and then heat the pan. Letting the batter sit while the pan heats will give the dry ingredients time to absorb the wet ingredients, otherwise the batter will be runny. Unless you have a pastry brush with heatproof bristles, a paper towel is the best means of coating the pan surface with oil. Pancakes will hold for 20 minutes when placed on a greased rack set on a baking sheet in a 200-degree oven. Serve with maple syrup or Apple, Cranberry, and Pecan Topping (recipe follows).

4	teaspoons juice from 1 lemon
2	cups whole milk
1¼	cups (6 ounces) plus 3 tablespoons no-sugar-added muesli (see note above)
¾	cup (3¾ ounces) unbleached all-purpose flour
½	cup (2¾ ounces) whole wheat flour
2	tablespoons light or dark brown sugar
2¼	teaspoons baking powder
½	teaspoon baking soda
½	teaspoon table salt
2	large eggs
3	tablespoons unsalted butter, melted and cooled
¾	teaspoon vanilla extract
	Vegetable oil

1. Whisk lemon juice and milk together in medium bowl or 4-cup measuring cup; set aside to thicken while preparing other ingredients.

2. Process 1¼ cups muesli in food processor until finely ground, 2 to 2½ minutes; transfer to large bowl. Add remaining 3 tablespoons

unground muesli, flours, brown sugar, baking powder, baking soda, and salt; whisk to combine.

3. Whisk eggs, melted butter, and vanilla into milk until combined. Make well in center of dry ingredients in bowl; pour in milk mixture and whisk very gently until just combined (few streaks of flour and lumps should remain). Do not overmix. Allow batter to sit while pan heats.

4. Heat 12-inch nonstick skillet over medium-low heat for 5 minutes. Add 1 teaspoon oil and brush to coat skillet bottom evenly. Following instructions below, add 1 tablespoon batter to gauge temperature of pan. Pour ¼ cup batter onto 3 spots in skillet, using bottom of ladle to spread batter smooth if necessary. Cook pancakes until small bubbles begin to appear evenly over surface, 2 to 3 minutes. Using thin, wide spatula, flip pancakes and cook until golden brown on second side, 1½ to 2 minutes longer. Serve immediately. Repeat with remaining batter, brushing surface of pan lightly with oil between batches and adjusting heat if necessary.

APPLE, CRANBERRY, AND PECAN TOPPING
SERVES 4 TO 6

The test kitchen prefers semifirm apples such as Fuji, Gala, or Braeburn for this topping. Avoid very tart types like Granny Smith and soft varieties like McIntosh.

3½	tablespoons cold unsalted butter
3	medium apples, peeled, cored, and cut into ½-inch pieces (about 4 cups) (see note above)
	Pinch table salt
1	cup apple cider
½	cup dried cranberries
½	cup maple syrup
½	teaspoon vanilla extract
1	teaspoon juice from 1 lemon
¾	cup pecans, toasted and chopped coarse

Melt 1½ tablespoons butter in large skillet over medium-high heat. Add apples and salt; cook, stirring occasionally, until softened and browned, 7 to 9 minutes. Stir in cider and cranberries; cook until liquid has almost evaporated, 6 to 8 minutes. Stir in maple syrup and cook until thickened, 4 to 5 minutes. Add vanilla, lemon juice, and remaining butter; whisk until sauce is smooth. Serve with toasted nuts.

Pancakes 101: Is the Pan Ready?

The best way to determine when the skillet is ready is to make a test pancake the size of a half-dollar (use 1 tablespoon of batter). If after one minute the pancake is golden brown, the pan is ready. If the bottom of the pancake remains blond—or is close to burning—adjust the heat accordingly.

Spices 101

Throwing away that antique jar of ground pepper is only the first step. Here's our guide to getting the most flavor from your spice rack. BY KEITH DRESSER

SPICE RUBS

Sprinkle spice rubs over food and then gently massage in the seasonings to make sure they adhere. As a general rule, use about 1 tablespoon of rub per portion of meat or poultry and 1 teaspoon of rub per portion of fish. Although rubs can be applied right before cooking, we've discovered that the flavor of the spices penetrates deeper into the food if given time. Refrigerate rubbed meat for at least an hour to maximize the return (large cuts of meat can sit overnight for a spicier, more intense flavor). See Cook's Extra on page 17 for some of our favorite spice rubs.

ESSENTIAL SPICES

In the test kitchen we stock more than 50 different spices, but we seem to reach for the same dozen bottles over and over again. Here's what you need to know about these essential spices. (Pepper is so important that it merits a separate discussion; see page 17.)

Cardamom

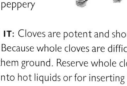

WHAT YOU NEED TO KNOW: Whole cardamom consists of a green seed pod that holds about 20 small black seeds. While cardamom is available ground, the whole pods have a superior flavor and aroma.

HOW TO USE IT: Since the flavor resides in the small seeds, it is necessary to crush the whole pods before using them.

Cayenne Pepper

WHAT YOU NEED TO KNOW: Originally made from cayenne peppers, this spice is now made from a variety of ground dried chiles. Cayenne pepper is rich with volatile oils, making it susceptible to flavor loss within a few months.

HOW TO USE IT: Intensity varies from brand to brand, so add a small amount, taste, and adjust seasoning.

Chili Powder

WHAT YOU NEED TO KNOW: Most brands are a blend of 80 percent ground dried chiles with garlic powder, oregano, and cumin. Chili powders made solely from chiles can be found in ethnic markets and are usually labeled by type of chile (such as ancho chile powder or chipotle chile powder).

HOW TO USE IT: Because chili powder is a blend of spices, it should be "bloomed" in hot oil to bring out its complex flavors.

★TEST KITCHEN WINNER★ Spice Islands Chili Powder

Cinnamon

WHAT YOU NEED TO KNOW: True cinnamon, or Ceylon cinnamon, is made from the dried bark of a tropical evergreen tree and can be difficult to find in American markets. What most cooks think of as cinnamon is actually cassia, made from the bark of a similar evergreen. Cassia has a darker color and a more pungent flavor than true cinnamon, which we find too mild and not worth seeking out.

HOW TO USE IT: Cinnamon is one of the few spices that we prefer to buy ground. Save whole cinnamon sticks for infusing flavor into hot liquids.

★TEST KITCHEN WINNER★ Penzeys China Cassia Cinnamon

Cloves

WHAT YOU NEED TO KNOW: Cloves are the dried unopened flower buds of a species of evergreen tree and boast a sweet, peppery flavor.

HOW TO USE IT: Cloves are potent and should be used sparingly. Because whole cloves are difficult to grind, we buy them ground. Reserve whole cloves for infusing flavor into hot liquids or for inserting into ham.

Coriander

WHAT YOU NEED TO KNOW: Coriander is the seed of the plant that produces the herb cilantro. Coriander is sold whole and ground, but whole seeds provide a more vibrant, complex flavor.

HOW TO USE IT: Toasting whole coriander helps to release its flavor and aroma.

Cumin

WHAT YOU NEED TO KNOW: Cumin is a highly aromatic spice that comes from a plant in the parsley family.

HOW TO USE IT: If time allows, we like to toast and grind whole cumin seeds; this gives the spice a more complex peppery flavor than when purchased ground.

★TEST KITCHEN WINNER★ McCormick Gourmet Collection Ground Cumin

Curry Powder

WHAT YOU NEED TO KNOW: Curry powder is a blend of spices. Because there is no standard formula, flavors vary from brand to brand. Most formulas include cardamom, chiles, cumin, fennel, fenugreek, nutmeg, and turmeric, which gives curry its characteristically yellow color.

HOW TO USE IT: For general cooking, we prefer a mild curry powder; hot curry powder, which contains more chiles, can be overpowering. Curry powder should be sautéed in hot oil to "bloom" its flavor.

★TEST KITCHEN WINNER★ Tone's Curry Powder

Nutmeg

WHAT YOU NEED TO KNOW: Nutmeg is the dried seed-like kernel of an evergreen tree. Its warm, spicy flavor accentuates sweetness in recipes. The lacy membrane that covers nutmeg, when dried and ground, becomes the spice mace.

HOW TO USE IT: Nutmeg loses its aroma when ground, so it's best to buy whole nutmeg and grate it when needed. Just keep in mind that a little goes a long way.

Paprika

WHAT YOU NEED TO KNOW: Paprika is a fine powder made by grinding dried red peppers. Its flavor and pungency can range from mild to hot, depending on what type of pepper is used and how much of the placenta (the white veins) is ground with the pepper.

HOW TO USE IT: We prefer the complexity of sweet paprika, especially brands from Hungary and Spain, which have a slightly fuller flavor than domestic varieties.

★TEST KITCHEN WINNER★ Penzeys Hungary Sweet Paprika

Saffron

WHAT YOU NEED TO KNOW: Saffron, the world's most expensive spice, is the hand-harvested stigma of a variety of crocus. Buy red saffron threads that are devoid of yellow and orange. Saffron can also be purchased powdered, but because ground saffron is often mixed with other ingredients, it should be bought from a reputable source. While Spanish saffron is often considered superior, we prefer the flavor of domestic saffron produced in Pennsylvania.

HOW TO USE IT: To release flavor, crush saffron threads with your fingers before adding them to a dish. Use sparingly; too much will impart a metallic taste.

ILLUSTRATION: JOHN BURGOYNE

ALL ABOUT PEPPER

Black pepper is the most important spice in your pantry. This berry grows in a spike-like cluster on a climbing vine that is indigenous to the tropics. The berries are picked when green and then sun-dried until they become the dry, hard, blackish kernels we know as peppercorns.

What to Buy

What's the best brand of ground black pepper? There isn't one: As soon as peppercorns are cracked, they begin losing the volatile compounds that give them bold aroma and subtle flavor; soon enough, all that's left is a nonvolatile compound called piperine, which gives the sensation of "hotness" but little else. For that reason, we consider whole peppercorns—ground to order in a pepper mill—the only viable option. While gourmet stores carry black peppercorns with exotic names (Malabar, Sarawak, and the like) and origins, we've found the differences to be almost imperceptible.

★TEST KITCHEN WINNER★ McCormick/Schilling Whole Black Pepper

WHITE PEPPER

The berries used to make white pepper are the same as those used to make black pepper, but they are harvested at a riper stage. The hulls are then removed and with them goes some of the heat characteristic of black pepper. White peppercorns are often used when the appearance of a dish would be marred by flecks of black. Many Asian recipes rely on the fragrant, citrusy flavor of white pepper. We use white pepper so infrequently that we can't justify purchasing a pepper mill for the sole purpose of grinding it, nor can we be bothered emptying and then refilling the black-pepper mill. Instead, we buy ground white pepper and replenish our stock when the pepper loses its fragrance.

Pepper Mills

We've used our share of wrist-wrenching pepper mills in an attempt to render whole peppercorns to ground pepper. Our favorite pepper mill has a huge capacity, is easily adjustable, and works with astonishing speed.

★TEST KITCHEN WINNER★
Unicorn Magnum Plus Peppermill, $45

Crushing Peppercorns

Many recipes call for coarsely crushed peppercorns, something that most pepper mills can't produce. Here are two ways of achieving uniformly crushed peppercorns.

Skillet: Spread the peppercorns on a cutting board and, using a rocking motion, crush them with the back of a clean, heavy pan.

Rolling Pin: Spread the peppercorns in an even layer in a zipper-lock bag, then whack them with a rolling pin or meat pounder.

BUYING AND STORING SPICES

In most cases, purchasing whole spices and grinding them is preferable to buying ground spices. Whole spices have a longer shelf life (about twice that of ground spices), and most fresh-ground spices also have superior aroma and flavor. Whether whole or ground, spices should be bought in the smallest quantities available. It also pays to check the expiration date.

When storing spices, the biggest mistake cooks make is keeping them close to the stove. Heat and moisture quickly shorten the shelf life of spices, leaving them dull; keep spices in a cool, dark, dry place in a well-sealed container.

Using stick-on dots, write the name and purchase date on top of the spice jar. This will tell you how long you've had the spice and will make it easier to find the spice you want when they are stored in a drawer.

PUMPING UP THE FLAVOR

We often toast or bloom spices to release their volatile oils and fullest flavor.

Toasting

The process of dry-toasting spices is normally reserved for whole spices that are then ground into a fine powder. To toast spices, put them in a small skillet without any oil and set the skillet over medium heat. Shake the skillet occasionally to prevent scorching and toast until they are fragrant, 1 to 3 minutes. Cool slightly before grinding.

Blooming

To intensify the flavor of commercially ground spices, cook them for a minute or two in a little butter or oil—before any liquid is added to the recipe. (If the recipe calls for sautéing onions or other aromatics, add the spices to the skillet when the vegetables are nearly cooked.) This step is particularly important with spice mixtures, such as chili powder and curry powder, where it's crucial to develop their complex flavors. (Whole spices can also be bloomed in oil or butter. This is a common technique used at the start of many Indian recipes. The spices should be discarded before the dish is served.)

SPICE GRINDERS

To reap the benefits of whole spices, you need a device that transforms them into a fine, even powder. While there are many gadgets available for such a task, we've determined that the best tool for the job is a coffee grinder. An inexpensive blade grinder produces consistently good results with little effort. If possible, keep one grinder for coffee, another for spices.

★TEST KITCHEN WINNER★
Krups Fast-Touch Coffee Mill, Model 203, $17.95

COOK'S extra

Go to www.cooksillustrated.com
- Key in code 11062 for **Favorite Spice Rubs** for chicken, pork, beef, lamb, and fish.
- Key in code 11063 for **Dry Rub for Barbecue**.
- Recipes available until May 1, 2007.

How to Clean a Spice Grinder

A quick wipe with a brush or cloth is usually sufficient to clean the test kitchen's grinder. Sometimes, however, spice residues remain even after wiping. Because most grinders can't be immersed in water, we developed a technique for "dry cleaning" that sufficiently removes all traces of residue.

Add several tablespoons of raw white rice to the grinder and pulverize to a fine powder. The rice powder will absorb residual spice particles and oils. Discard the rice powder; your grinder will be clean.

Simplifying Coq au Vin

White-tablecloth restaurants have hijacked this simple chicken and wine stew, making it a fussy, time-consuming affair. Could we return this dish to its humble roots?

≥ BY SANDRA WU ≤

Originally made with roosters no longer suitable for breeding, coq au vin (chicken stewed in red wine) began life as provincial peasant fare. Simmered for hours, the tough, old fowl soaked up the wine's rich flavor as the acidic liquid gently broke down the sinewy fibers. Local mushrooms, herbs, and onions—perhaps a little bit of pork fat—rounded out this simple stew.

Once well-heeled bistro patrons replaced peasants as the primary consumers of this dish, the recipes started to get fancy. Very fancy. Combing through classic French cookbooks, I found one ambitious recipe that called for reducing veal stock with wine and vegetables, sautéing lardons (diced bacon), browning chicken pieces in the rendered fat, deglazing the pan, straining out the solids, thickening the sauce with pureed chicken livers and beurre manié (butter-flour paste), adding in new vegetables, then flambéing the whole thing with cognac. Rich and complex, yes, but way beyond the pale for home cooking.

Some modern versions (including our own recipe from 1999) get the process down to a few hours. Yet even these "streamlined" recipes seem to be caught in the trappings of haute cuisine. After all, coq au vin is just chicken stew, right? I wanted to return this dish to its roots, simplifying the recipe to the point where I wouldn't have to wait for a formal dinner party to serve it.

Poultry Matter

Ignoring the oddball all-day extravaganzas, I carefully studied the typical 2½-hour coq au vin recipes, and kept my eyes peeled for places to pare down. The basic process was to cook bacon in a Dutch oven, sauté a cut-up chicken with mirepoix vegetables (carrots, celery, onions) in the rendered fat, then simmer the parts in red wine, herbs, and chicken stock, adding pearl onions and mushrooms as a garnish.

A Rooster in Every Pot

Old-fashioned coq au vin wasn't fancy. It took hours to cook, but only so the tough, past-its-prime rooster originally used in this dish (coq is French for "rooster") would eventually become tender. Even though "modern" coq au vin recipes opt for faster-cooking chickens, most tend to take just as long, using the drawn-out time frame to fancy up this rustic stew.

Red wine, mushrooms, and bacon transform chicken thighs into a rich, hearty stew. Serve with mashed potatoes to soak up every drop of the sauce.

I homed in on the chicken. Opting for precut chicken parts rather than cutting up a whole chicken myself was a start, but saving 10 minutes wasn't exactly the major overhaul I was going for. Some recipes call for breasts and whole legs, the latter needing about an hour to turn adequately tender. Swapping out legs for thighs—which cook in just 40 minutes—proved a better option. (The breast pieces needed only 25 minutes.)

Two hours represented a modest improvement over the original 2½, but I thought I could do better. I decided to try using boneless, skinless breasts and thighs. Sautéing them quickly in bacon fat, then adding red wine, I found that just 25 minutes produced thighs that were fall-apart tender and packed with wine flavor. The breasts, on the other hand, were a parched disaster. Adding the breasts for only the last 10 minutes of

cooking kept them reasonably moist, but with so little time to absorb the wine's flavor, they came out tasting like plain poached chicken. My decision was made: boneless thighs yes, breast meat no.

Getting Saucy

Unfortunately, opting for no bones and no skin had robbed the stew of some of its complexity and flavor. In addition, after just 25 minutes of simmering, the full bottle of red wine I was using still tasted boozy and astringent.

To get fuller, rounder, less astringent flavor quickly, I tried reducing the wine, bulked up with some chicken broth (to compensate for the diminished chicken flavor), in a separate saucepan before adding it to the stew. This trick worked beautifully. While the liquid reduced, I could cook the bacon, render its fat, and brown the chicken and vegetables, saving precious minutes. What's more, by the time I added the reduced wine-broth mixture to the stew, its flavors had concentrated and the boozy taste had cooked off considerably.

Some recipes call for sautéing carrots and onions for flavor, straining them out once they turn to mush, then folding in a separately browned batch of blanched pearl onions and button mushrooms. Because of my much shorter simmering time, I found that the onions and mushrooms could remain in the pot from beginning to end (making that initial batch of vegetables unnecessary). As for the type of onions and mushrooms, cremini mushrooms were favored over buttons for their earthier flavor, and tasters thought frozen pearl onions were nearly as good as fresh; the quicker prep time for the frozen variety gave them the winning edge—and made my recipe 15 minutes shorter. Minced garlic and tomato paste provided additional depth. Finally, I found that adding the crisped bacon to the braising liquid (rather than saving it to garnish the finished dish) helped extract its meaty, savory flavor, allowing it to permeate the entire stew.

To thicken the sauce, some older recipes call for whisking in chicken's blood or a beurre manié. I wasn't too keen on adding blood—or looking for a place that sells it—and a beurre manié seemed fussy. Instead, I opted for the just as authentic (but simpler) roux method, adding flour with the vegetables while they browned in butter. After reducing the sauce for a few minutes, I finally had the thick, glossy texture I was after.

As a final test, I pitted my streamlined coq au vin—now pared down to a truly manageable 90 minutes—against the 2½-hour project I had started with. Most tasters marveled at how close I'd come to matching the flavor of the original in 40 percent less time, but my pickier colleagues found this quicker version too lean and somewhat lacking in deep wine flavor. The solution was simple enough. I reserved 1 tablespoon of uncooked wine to stir in at the end and finished the sauce with 2 tablespoons of cold butter.

Rich, bacony, and brimming with red wine flavor, this simplified coq au vin had finally escaped its haute-cuisine trappings to move closer—at least in spirit—to its original, humble roots. No past-its-prime rooster required.

MODERN COQ AU VIN
(CHICKEN IN RED WINE SAUCE)
SERVES 4 TO 6

A medium-bodied, fruity red wine such as Pinot Noir or Rhône Valley Grenache is best for this recipe. Avoid bold, heavily oaked red wine varietals like Cabernet and light-bodied wines like Beaujolais. To use fresh pearl onions, trim the root and stem end of each onion and discard. Boil for 1 minute, shock in ice water, then peel a thin strip from root to stem. Remove any remaining outer skin (it's like peeling off a jacket). If neither frozen nor fresh pearl onions are available, substitute one large onion cut into ½-inch pieces. (Do not use jarred pearl onions, which will turn mushy and disintegrate into the sauce.) Serve the stew with egg noodles or mashed potatoes.

1	bottle medium-bodied red wine (see note above)
2	cups low-sodium chicken broth
10	sprigs fresh parsley plus 2 tablespoons minced fresh parsley leaves
2	sprigs fresh thyme
1	bay leaf
4	ounces bacon, preferably thick-cut, cut crosswise into ¼-inch pieces
2½	pounds boneless skinless chicken thighs, trimmed of excess fat and cut in half crosswise Table salt and ground black pepper
5	tablespoons unsalted butter
24	frozen pearl onions, thawed, drained, and patted dry (about 1 cup) (see note above)
8	ounces cremini mushrooms, wiped clean, stems trimmed, halved if small and quartered if large
2	medium garlic cloves, minced or pressed through garlic press (about 2 teaspoons)
1	tablespoon tomato paste
2	tablespoons all-purpose flour

How We Did It: Coq au Vin in 90 Minutes

Butchering, chopping, browning, straining, simmering, thickening . . . most coq au vin recipes require almost three hours from start to finish. We came up with some shortcuts to keep this simple stew under control.

NO BONES
Opting for boneless thighs rather than bone-in legs shaved more than 30 minutes from the cooking time.

TWO POTS
We reduced the wine, stock, and herbs in a separate saucepan while browning the meat and vegetables.

1. Bring all but 1 tablespoon wine (reserve for later use), broth, parsley sprigs, thyme, and bay to simmer in large saucepan over medium-high heat. Cook until reduced to 3 cups, about 25 minutes. Discard herbs.

2. Meanwhile, cook bacon in large Dutch oven over medium heat until browned, 7 to 8 minutes. Using slotted spoon, transfer bacon to paper-towel-lined plate. Reserve 2 tablespoons fat in small bowl; discard remaining fat.

3. Lightly season chicken with salt and pepper. Heat 1 tablespoon reserved bacon fat in Dutch oven over medium-high heat until just smoking. Add half of chicken in single layer and cook until lightly browned, about 2 minutes per side. Transfer to plate and repeat with remaining chicken and 1 tablespoon bacon fat.

4. Melt 3 tablespoons butter in now-empty Dutch oven over medium-high heat. When foaming subsides, add pearl onions and mushrooms; cook, stirring occasionally, until lightly browned, 5 to 8 minutes. Reduce heat to medium, add garlic, and cook until fragrant, about 30 seconds. Add tomato paste and flour; cook, stirring frequently, until well combined, about 1 minute.

5. Add reduced wine mixture, scraping bottom of pot with wooden spoon to loosen browned bits; add ¼ teaspoon pepper. Return chicken, any accumulated juices, and reserved bacon to pot; increase heat to high and bring to boil. Reduce heat to medium-low, cover pot, and simmer until chicken is tender, about 25 minutes, stirring halfway through cooking time.

6. Using slotted spoon, transfer chicken to large bowl; tent with foil to keep warm. Increase heat to medium-high and simmer sauce until thick and glossy and measures 3¼ cups, about 5 minutes. Off heat, stir in remaining 2 tablespoons butter and reserved 1 tablespoon wine. Season to taste with salt. Return chicken to pot and top with minced parsley. Serve immediately.

EQUIPMENT TESTING: **Wine Openers**

In our 1997 testing of corkscrews, the test kitchen came down solidly on the lever-style design (eventually popularized by Metrokane's "Rabbit" corkscrew) as the ultimate tool for removing the cork from a wine bottle. At $150, our winning Le Creuset Screwpull Lever LX was also very expensive. Since that time, other lever-style options have flooded the market—some at much more attractive price points. We gathered 13 contenders (ranging in price from $12.95 to $134.95) to see just how low you can go and still get great performance.

At a glance, 12 of the 13 models were virtually identical and all pulled out corks competently. What separated the good from the great, however, was lever length. The increased leverage (we like 6½ inches or longer) means you need less brute strength to open the bottle; still, even the corkscrew with the shortest lever (the curvy 5½ inches on the Bonjour Chateau Royale, $69.99) was workable. The longest lever (7¼ inches) was on the cheapest model, the Zoom Corkscrew from the Wine Enthusiast ($12.95).

The one innovative wine opener, the Screwpull Trigger ($79.95) has an ingenious slip-over sleeve design, which helps center the screw over the bottle opening—you squeeze the "trigger" to secure the bottle. This new feature streamlines an already speedy process, making this model our new "ultimate" choice. That said, the $12.95 Zoom Corkscrew will keep the wine flowing. –Garth Clingingsmith

ULTIMATE OPENER
The **Screwpull Trigger** ($79.95) has a few innovative touches that justify its price.

BEST BUY
The **Wine Enthusiast Zoom Corkscrew** ($12.95) rivals the expensive models—for the frugal gadget hound.

TOO SHORT
The stumpy handle on the **Bonjour Chateau Royale** ($69.99) provided less-than-ideal leverage.

No-Bake Pumpkin Pie

A no-bake pumpkin pie sounds appealing, but not if the filling is starchy or dense.
Could we reformulate this recipe and make it worthy of the holiday table?

≥ BY ERIKA BRUCE ≤

With its spiced custard filling and buttery pastry crust, a baked pumpkin pie is utterly traditional. But it's not the only kind of pumpkin pie you can put on the holiday table. Although unheralded, the no-bake pumpkin pie has a couple of benefits not offered by its traditional counterpart, one being a much easier, press-in crumb crust that requires just 15 minutes of oven time, another being a creamier filling with a fresher, brighter pumpkin flavor. No need to roll out pie dough or tie up your oven? Sounds like the perfect recipe for a busy holiday.

But every good recipe has bad versions. For no-bake pumpkin pies this translates to crumbly crusts and poorly textured fillings. Some fillings are thickened with so much gelatin that they become rubbery. Others use cream cheese as the binding agent and end up dense and chalky. I wanted creaminess, but I also wanted lightness. While chiffon-style pies are certainly light, the addition of whipped egg whites makes them fluffy, even spongy—not what I wanted. Despite these obstacles, the promise of producing a creamy pumpkin pie without the hassle of making pie pastry was appealing. Surely I could resolve these texture issues.

A crumb crust and no-bake filling yield an easy pie that's lighter and fresher than the classic version.

Texture Treatment
Lucky for me, I already had a strong foundation—a simple and sturdy *Cook's* recipe for graham cracker crust (Summer Berry Pie, July/August, 2003). To this I added a barebones filling of 1 can pumpkin, ⅔ cup sugar, and ½ cup each of milk and heavy cream (the same ratio used in our baked pumpkin pie). I also needed the right thickener. Of all the thickeners used in no-bake pies, the most common are gelatin (which is melted) and cornstarch (cooked on the stovetop). Although I widened the playing field to test tapioca, arrowroot, and even potato

starch, gelatin ended up as the victor. And I learned that gelatin should be used modestly. Whereas most recipes called for more than a tablespoon (resulting in pies with a tough, rubbery texture), I found that just 2 teaspoons produced a pie that could be neatly sliced without being excessively stiff.

Now that my pie filling was holding together, my tasters shifted their complaints to the fibrous texture of the pumpkin. Despite being labeled "pureed," canned pumpkin is not truly smooth. A quick whirl in the food processor yielded a silky mixture worthy of the label.

Although the consistency of my pie was better, it needed more richness. Switching from a blend of milk and heavy cream to all heavy cream was an improvement. Next I tried whipping the cream and folding it into the filling. Although the texture was lighter and fluffier, the pumpkin and the cream never really melded but instead settled into an unattractive mottled appearance. Pureeing some of the cream with the pumpkin lightened the filling just a bit and helped to unify the ingredients.

My filling was getting pretty good, but my tasters clamored for a richer and more velvety texture—like that of a baked pumpkin pie. Comparing the ingredient lists of my no-bake recipe and the test kitchen's favorite baked pumpkin pie, I saw one major difference: My no-bake recipe didn't contain eggs. I had rejected chiffon-style pies because the whipped whites made them too mousse-like and insubstantial. But what if I kept the yolks and cooked them with the sugar and cream to form a simple custard? I had to heat the cream anyway to dissolve the sugar. After a few tests I found that three yolks gave my pie filling the luxurious texture my tasters and I sought.

Flavor Fix
Rich, creamy, and smooth, this pie filling now needed a refined flavor to match its texture. To add some complexity, I included some spices. A mix of ground cinnamon, ginger, nutmeg, and cloves tasted best, but because they weren't cooked their raw flavors quickly became hot and harsh. I decreased the amount, but the harshness persisted. Next I tried heating them in the cream; this softened their hard edge while drawing out

Two Problem Pies
We wanted a rich and creamy filling. Many of the recipes we tested fell short of this goal, like these two flawed examples.

TOO PASTY   TOO SPONGY

Cornstarch makes the filling pasty and gritty (left), while whipped egg whites produce a spongy filling (right).

Pumpkin Pie, Reimagined

What makes our no-bake filling rich and creamy? Here are two key steps.

MAKE A CUSTARD
A quick custard with egg yolks adds velvety richness but little work.

PUREE THE PUMPKIN
Whipping the pumpkin with cream creates a lighter, smoother filling.

more of their heady, fragrant qualities.

To offset the spices, I tried adding some high flavor notes. Lemon juice was too sour and bourbon too boozy, but orange juice was both bright and delicate enough to be added uncooked to the mix. Combined with a touch of vanilla extract, it added a sweet, perfumed punch (and served double duty to soften the gelatin before it was melted into the custard). Last, I switched from granulated to brown sugar, sure that it would add a welcome hint of molasses. In fact, tasters thought it muddied the pie, preferring the former for its clean flavor.

With these last adjustments, my no-bake pie was finally good enough to take its place on the holiday dessert table. Yes, you need to cook the

---

TECHNIQUE

PERFECT CRUMB CRUST

Crumb crusts come together in just seconds, but they can sometimes fall apart. Here's how to make a neat and sturdy crust.

Using a flat-bottomed measuring cup, gently press down on the crumbs in the center of the pie plate and then work toward the sides. Tilting the measuring cup, press the sides while squaring off the top edge with your thumb.

---

filling on the stovetop, but the pie requires just 15 minutes of baking, leaving the oven free for roast turkey and all those holiday side dishes.

NO-BAKE PUMPKIN PIE
SERVES 8

The crust can be baked, cooled, wrapped tightly in plastic wrap, and stored at room temperature for one day. Serve with lightly sweetened whipped cream.

Graham Cracker Crust

- 5 ounces graham crackers (9 whole crackers), broken into large pieces
- 2 tablespoons sugar
- 5 tablespoons unsalted butter, melted and warm

Pumpkin Filling

- 3 tablespoons cold orange juice
- 2 teaspoons vanilla extract
- 2 teaspoons gelatin (from 1 package)
- 1 cup cold heavy cream
- 2/3 cup (4¾ ounces) sugar
- ¾ teaspoon table salt
- 1 teaspoon ground cinnamon
- ½ teaspoon ground ginger
- ¼ teaspoon ground nutmeg
- ⅛ teaspoon ground cloves
- 3 large egg yolks
- 1 (15-ounce) can plain pumpkin puree (1¾ cups)

1. **FOR THE CRUST:** Adjust oven rack to lower-middle position and heat oven to 325 degrees.

2. Pulse crackers and sugar in food processor until evenly and finely ground, about fifteen 2-second pulses (you should have 1 cup crumbs). Add warm butter in steady stream through feed tube while pulsing until crumbs are evenly moistened and resemble damp sand. Transfer crumbs to 9-inch pie plate and spread evenly over bottom and sides; wipe out food processor bowl and reserve. Using flat-bottomed ramekin or dry measuring cup, press and smooth crumbs into pie plate (see illustration, at left). Bake until fragrant and browned around edges, 15 to 18 minutes. Cool completely on wire rack.

3. **FOR THE FILLING:** Stir orange juice and vanilla together in medium bowl. Sprinkle gelatin over orange juice mixture and set aside to thicken, about 5 minutes.

4. Combine ½ cup heavy cream, ⅓ cup sugar, salt, and spices in small saucepan. Cook over medium-low heat until bubbles form at edges; remove from heat. Whisk remaining ⅓ cup sugar and yolks together in medium bowl until pale and slightly thickened. Slowly pour hot cream into yolk mixture, whisking constantly. Return mixture to pan and cook over medium-low heat, stirring constantly and scraping bottom of pot with heatproof spatula, until custard is thickened and registers 175 to 180 degrees on instant-read

---

---

thermometer, about 2 minutes. (When properly cooked, custard should form slight ridge on tip of spatula when bottom of pan is scraped and spatula is lifted.) Immediately pour custard over gelatin mixture and stir until smooth and gelatin has completely dissolved.

5. Puree pumpkin in food processor until smooth, 10 to 15 seconds. With machine running, add remaining ½ cup heavy cream through feed tube in steady stream. Scrape sides of bowl and process for additional 10 to 15 seconds. Add pumpkin mixture to custard mixture and stir until completely smooth. Transfer filling to cooled crust. Chill pie, uncovered, until filling is just set, about 3 hours. Cover pie with plastic wrap and continue to chill until fully set, at least 6 and up to 24 hours. Cut pie into wedges and serve.

Easy Chocolate Pots de Crème

Forget the water bath and slow baking. We found a way to make this classic French chocolate custard faster, simpler, and better.

⇒ BY DAWN YANAGIHARA ⇐

Chocolate pot de crème and I have a history. In culinary school, I became smitten with it. Some years later, during a stint as a pastry chef in a Minneapolis bistro, I put this French take on chocolate pudding on the dessert menu, and it was a smash hit. So what is chocolate pot de crème, you ask? Think crème brûlée, without the caramelized-sugar crust but enriched with dark chocolate. This decadent dessert boasts a satiny texture and intense chocolate flavor. Classically, pots de crème are made in petite lidded pots, but individual ramekins are the contemporary vessels. These rich chocolaty custards are served in small portions because more would be too much.

Because this dessert was such a hit among customers as well as the restaurant's owner, I made batches upon batches. Unfortunately, the recipe I was using was so finicky and laborious that I quickly grew tired of making it. And so when I left that job, I also left chocolate pot de crème.

A decade elapsed, during which I hadn't given much thought to pot de crème. But one winter day, as I was trying to design a nice holiday menu, I remembered pot de crème and realized that it makes the perfect holiday dessert: It can be made in advance, and it meets the richness and elegance required of holiday desserts.

I decided that I wanted to reconnect with chocolate pot de crème, but on different terms. The recipe from my restaurant days required a large roasting pan that accommodated all the ramekins and a hot water bath that threatened to splash the custards every time the pan was moved. In addition, the individual custards didn't always cook at the same rate, which meant going in and out of the oven multiple times to gauge doneness and plucking hot ramekins from the water bath only to have them drip onto their neighbors.

I wanted a simpler recipe that would be as user-friendly as possible. I started by scouring cookbooks and online sources. Not surprisingly, the ingredients were more or less the same across the board: chocolate, eggs, sugar, and cream (or other such dairy). The bigger difference lay in the ratio of ingredients and the way the custard was cooked. Most of the recipes employed the usual

Finish these rich custards with a dollop of whipped cream and a sprinkling of shaved bittersweet chocolate.

treatment for baked custard: a hot water bath and a moderately low oven. But two out of the 20 or so recipes I found employed an unconventional method in which the custard is cooked on the stovetop in a saucepan, then poured into ramekins. Very interesting.

The Dark Side

Using the standard baked custard method for the time being, I went to work on ingredients, which I needed to scale down from my restaurant recipe. I started with the dairy. To serve eight, a chocolate pot de crème recipe requires about 2 cups of milk, half-and-half, or heavy cream. The richest of recipes use heavy cream exclusively, but most call for a combination of cream and milk. I tested it all, in different ratios, and decided that 1½ cups of cream and ¾ cup of half-and-half had just the right amount of richness and body.

Next, eggs, which enrich and help thicken the custard. Yolks are the norm. I experimented with as many as eight and as few as four. Five was the right number to make a luxurious custard. This is fewer than what many recipes call for,

but I wanted to use a lot of chocolate, and I knew that would also help the custard to set up.

Intensity of flavor was key, so I passed over milk chocolate and semisweet chocolate because I knew they'd be too mild. Cocoa powder and unsweetened chocolate were too gritty, so I focused my testing on bittersweet chocolate. With only 4 ounces of bittersweet chocolate, the pot de crème was too milky; with a whole pound, it was unpalatably rich. My taste tended toward a recipe made with 12 ounces—it was incredibly thick and chocolaty—but since most tasters couldn't abide the heavy texture, I went with

SCIENCE: **Skip the Scalding**

Crème anglaise is a classic French preparation for a pourable custard that's used as a dessert sauce or as a base for ice creams and Bavarians. It's also the base for our chocolate pots de crème. The procedure for making crème anglaise that's taught in cooking schools everywhere goes like this: The cream (or half-and-half or milk) is *scalded* (that is, brought to a boil); the yolks and sugar are *ribboned* (that is, whisked together until light in color and the sugar dissolves); the yolk/sugar mixture is *tempered* (that is, some of the hot scalded cream is slowly whisked in to prevent the yolks from scrambling); the tempered mixture is returned to the saucepan; and the custard is cooked gently with constant stirring.

A fan of shortcuts, I tried making the crème anglaise base for my chocolate pots de crème without scalding the cream and tempering the eggs. Basically, I took cold or room-temperature ingredients, whisked them together, then cooked the mixture as usual. The result? A perfectly good crème anglaise. Why would this lazy-man's method work just as well as a classic and more complicated method?

It turns out the scald-and-temper method is scientifically out of date. This technique was developed to ensure smooth, uncurdled crème anglaise at a time when the quality of cream and milk was inconsistent. The unpasteurized and unhomogenized dairy products of yesteryear were more susceptible to curdling when they met heat. Today, dairy simply does not need to be scalded to check quality, and, consequently, there's no need to temper the egg yolks since they can be combined with the cold cream. –D.Y.

10 ounces. With only one exception, this was at least 50 percent more chocolate than in any other recipe that I encountered.

Causing a Stir

It was now time to settle the matter of cooking method. Using the same ingredients, I made two versions of pots de crème. I baked one in a moderately low oven in a water bath, covered with foil to prevent the surface of the custards from drying out; the other I made on the stovetop in the style of a stirred custard, or crème anglaise in the culinary vernacular.

It was unequivocal. The crème anglaise method was immensely easier than the traditional (and cumbersome) baking method—and the results were close to identical. (The baked custards were ever so slightly firmer and more set than the stirred ones, but tasters weren't the least bit concerned.) What wasn't identical was the hassle factor: The crème anglaise method was easy and reliable. The eggs, sugar, and dairy are cooked on the stovetop, the resulting custard is poured over the chocolate, then the mixture is gently whisked until combined. The only equipment required is a saucepan and a heatproof spatula, no roasting pan and no water bath. To boot, when cooked on the stovetop the pots de crème were made in a fraction of the time they took to bake.

It took 10 years, but I once again embrace chocolate pots de crème, especially this simplified recipe. This elegant dessert has finally reclaimed its place in my culinary repertoire and will probably show up at holiday dinners from now on.

CHOCOLATE POTS DE CRÈME
SERVES 8

We prefer pots de crème made with 60 percent cocoa bittersweet chocolate (our favorite brands are Ghirardelli, Callebaut, Valrhona, and El Rey), but 70 percent bittersweet chocolate can also be used. If using a 70 percent bittersweet chocolate (we like Lindt, El Rey, and Valrhona), reduce the amount of chocolate to 8 ounces. A tablespoon of strong brewed coffee may be substituted for the instant espresso and water. Covered tightly with plastic wrap, the pots de crème will keep for up to 3 days in the refrigerator, but the whipped cream must be made just before serving.

Pots de Crème
- 10 ounces bittersweet chocolate (see note above), chopped fine
- 5 large egg yolks
- 5 tablespoons sugar
- ¼ teaspoon table salt
- 1½ cups heavy cream
- ¾ cup half-and-half
- 1 tablespoon vanilla extract
- ½ teaspoon instant espresso mixed with 1 tablespoon water

ILLUSTRATION: RANDY GLASS

An instant-read thermometer is the most reliable way to judge when crème anglaise has reached the proper temperature of 175 to 180 degrees. But you can also judge the progress of a custard sauce by its thickness. Dip a wooden spoon into the custard and run your finger across the back. (Yes, this old-fashioned method really does work.)

NOT YET
When its temperature is between 165 and 170 degrees, the custard will still be thin, and a line drawn on the back of the spoon will not hold.

READY
When its temperature is between 175 and 180 degrees, the custard will coat the spoon, and the line will maintain neat edges.

TOO FAR
When its temperature goes above 180 degrees, small chunks will become visible in the curdled custard.

Whipped Cream
- ½ cup cold heavy cream
- 2 teaspoons sugar
- ½ teaspoon vanilla extract

Garnish (optional)
- Cocoa for dusting
- Chocolate shavings for sprinkling

1. **FOR THE POTS DE CRÈME:** Place chocolate in medium heatproof bowl; set fine-mesh strainer over bowl and set aside.

2. Whisk yolks, sugar, and salt in medium bowl until combined; whisk in heavy cream and half-and-half. Transfer mixture to medium saucepan. Cook mixture over medium-low heat, stirring constantly and scraping bottom of pot with wooden spoon, until thickened and silky and custard registers 175 to 180 degrees on instant-read thermometer, 8 to 12 minutes (see photos, above). Do not let custard overcook or simmer.

3. Immediately pour custard through strainer over chocolate. Let mixture stand to melt chocolate, about 5 minutes. Whisk gently until smooth, then whisk in vanilla and espresso. Divide mixture evenly among eight 5-ounce ramekins. Gently tap ramekins against counter to remove air bubbles.

4. Cool pots de crème to room temperature, then cover with plastic wrap and refrigerate until chilled, at least 4 hours or up to 72 hours. Before serving, let pots de crème stand at room temperature 20 to 30 minutes.

5. **FOR THE WHIPPED CREAM:** Using hand mixer or standing mixer fitted with whisk attachment, beat cream, sugar, and vanilla on low speed until bubbles form, about 30 seconds. Increase speed to medium; continue beating until beaters leave trail, about 30 seconds longer. Increase speed to high; continue beating until nearly doubled in volume and whipped cream forms soft peaks, 30 to 45 seconds longer.

6. Dollop each pot de crème with about 2 tablespoons whipped cream; garnish with cocoa or chocolate shavings, if using. Serve.

STEP-BY-STEP | FOOLPROOF POTS DE CRÈME

For our recipe, all the action takes place on the stovetop and counter so you can see what's happening. In contrast, traditional recipes call for baking the custards in a messy water bath (to prevent overcooking) and rely on tricky visual clues rather than a thermometer to determine doneness.

1. MAKE ANGLAISE
Heat egg yolks, sugar, salt, cream, and half-and-half to 175 to 180 degrees.

2. MELT CHOCOLATE
Pour warm anglaise through strainer and into bowl with chocolate.

3. WHISK TO COMBINE
After 5 minutes, whisk gently to combine anglaise and chocolate.

4. POUR AND CHILL
Divide chocolate custard among ramekins and refrigerate until set.

Better Arugula Salads

A surprise ingredient guarantees salads that are lively but not harsh.

⇒ BY REBECCA HAYS ⇐

Unlike everyday (read: bland) iceberg, romaine, or butter lettuce, spicy arugula is more than just a leafy backdrop for salad garnishes. Yet that complex, peppery flavor also makes arugula something of a challenge to pair with other ingredients. To figure out the best way to temper this assertive green, I headed to the test kitchen with a stack of representative recipes.

Combinations with harsh, one-dimensional flavor profiles (arugula, radishes, and lemon-buttermilk dressing, for example) were left mostly uneaten. Salads containing fruit and cheese, however, were devoured, the sweet and salty notes offering nice counterpoints to the sharp, peppery arugula. Tasters also liked salads with crunchy elements.

I started at square one: the vinaigrette. Many recipes rely on ingredients like mustard to help the emulsion along. Mustard was clearly wrong—too spicy to partner with peppery arugula—but what if I chose an emulsifier that contributed sweetness? I added a drizzle of honey to a basic vinaigrette, and this worked well. But my wheels kept turning. How about adding a spoonful of jam instead of honey? This idea hit the mark: The jam added fruity sweetness, pulling the flavors of the salad right in line.

To echo the flavor of the fruity vinaigrettes, I next experimented with adding winter fruits to the salad. After some trial and error, I settled on dried figs plumped with balsamic vinegar for one salad, fresh red grapes for another, and juicy orange sections for a third.

Now that I had the sweet and spicy/peppery bases adequately covered, choosing the salty and crunchy components was a snap. Cured meat and crumbled cheese offered stark but appealing salty contrast. Finally, slivers of raw fennel along with toasted nuts delivered just the right amount of crunch.

ARUGULA SALAD WITH FIGS, PROSCIUTTO, WALNUTS, AND PARMESAN
SERVES 6

Although frying the prosciutto adds crisp texture to the salad, if you prefer, you can simply cut it into ribbons and use it as a garnish. Honey can be substituted for the jam in any of these salad recipes.

- 4   tablespoons extra-virgin olive oil
- 2   ounces thinly sliced prosciutto, cut into ¼-inch-wide ribbons
- 1   tablespoon raspberry jam
- 3   tablespoons balsamic vinegar
- ½   cup dried figs, stems removed, fruit chopped into ¼-inch pieces
- 1   small shallot, minced very fine (1 tablespoon)
       Table salt and ground black pepper
- 5   ounces lightly packed baby arugula (8 cups)
- ½   cup chopped walnuts, toasted
- 2   ounces Parmesan cheese, shaved into thin strips with vegetable peeler

1. Heat 1 tablespoon oil in 10-inch nonstick skillet over medium heat; add prosciutto and fry until crisp, stirring frequently, about 7 minutes. Using slotted spoon, transfer to paper-towel-lined plate and set aside to cool.

2. Whisk jam and vinegar in medium microwave-safe bowl; stir in figs. Cover with plastic wrap, cut several steam vents in plastic, and microwave on high until figs are plump, 30 seconds to 1 minute. Whisk in remaining 3 tablespoons oil, shallot, ¼ teaspoon salt, and ⅛ teaspoon pepper; toss to combine. Let cool to room temperature.

3. Toss arugula and vinaigrette in large bowl; adjust seasonings with salt and pepper. Divide salad among individual plates; top each with portion of prosciutto, walnuts, and Parmesan. Serve immediately.

ARUGULA SALAD WITH GRAPES, FENNEL, GORGONZOLA, AND PECANS
SERVES 6

- 4   teaspoons apricot jam
- 3   tablespoons white wine vinegar
- 3   tablespoons extra-virgin olive oil
- 1   small shallot, minced very fine (1 tablespoon)
       Table salt and ground black pepper
- ½   small fennel bulb, cored, trimmed of stalks, and sliced very thin (about 1 cup); fronds chopped coarse (about ¼ cup)
- 5   ounces lightly packed baby arugula (8 cups)
- 6   ounces red seedless grapes, halved lengthwise (about 1 cup)
- 3   ounces Gorgonzola cheese, crumbled (¾ cup)
- ½   cup chopped pecans, toasted

Whisk jam, vinegar, oil, shallot, ¼ teaspoon salt, and ¼ teaspoon pepper in large bowl. Toss fennel with vinaigrette; let stand 15 minutes. Add arugula, fennel fronds, and grapes; toss and adjust seasonings with salt and pepper. Divide salad among individual plates; top each with portion of Gorgonzola and pecans. Serve immediately.

ARUGULA SALAD WITH ORANGES, FETA, AND SUGARED PISTACHIOS
SERVES 6

The sugared pistachios can be made ahead and stored in an airtight container at room temperature. You can substitute an equal amount of roughly chopped toasted pistachios.

Sugared Pistachios
- ½   cup whole shelled pistachios
- 1   large egg white, lightly beaten
- ⅓   cup sugar

Salad
- 5   teaspoons orange marmalade
- 2   tablespoons plus 2 teaspoons juice from 1 lemon
- 3   tablespoons extra-virgin olive oil
- 1   small shallot, minced very fine (1 tablespoon)
- 1   tablespoon minced fresh mint leaves
       Table salt and ground black pepper
- 5   ounces lightly packed baby arugula (8 cups)
- 2   large oranges, peeled, cut into segments, segments halved and drained to remove excess juice
- 3   ounces feta, crumbled (¾ cup)

1. FOR THE SUGARED PISTACHIOS: Adjust oven rack to middle position and heat oven to 325 degrees. Toss pistachios with egg white in small bowl. Using slotted spoon, transfer nuts to 8-inch-square baking pan lined with parchment paper; discard excess egg white. Add sugar and stir until nuts are completely coated. Bake, stirring mixture every 5 to 10 minutes, until coating turns nutty brown, 25 to 30 minutes. Transfer nuts to plate in single layer to cool.

2. FOR THE SALAD: Whisk marmalade, lemon juice, oil, shallot, mint, ¼ teaspoon salt, and ⅛ teaspoon pepper in large bowl. Add arugula and oranges; toss and adjust seasonings with salt and pepper. Divide salad among individual plates; top each with portion of feta and sugared pistachios. Serve immediately.

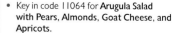

COOK'S extra

Go to www.cooksillustrated.com
- Key in code 11064 for **Arugula Salad with Pears, Almonds, Goat Cheese, and Apricots.**
- Recipe available until May 1, 2007.

The Best Way to Sharpen Your Knives

When your kitchen knives go dull, is there a quick, cheap, and easy way to restore their cutting edge and get back to cooking?

≥ BY LISA McMANUS ≤

The first time you pick up a truly sharp knife and slice through food, it's a revelation. If you are like many home cooks who have been soldiering on with a drawer full of dull knives, you suddenly realize that cooking just got a lot easier. But even the most expensive, well-made knives lose their sharpness quickly when used regularly. And it doesn't take months, or even weeks: A knife can go dull in just a few minutes, especially if you're cutting through tough materials, such as bone.

What's the best way to maintain that snappy edge that makes light work of chopping and slicing? First, it's important to note that there's a difference between tuning up a relatively sharp knife and sharpening a dull knife (see illustrations at right). A so-called sharpening steel, the metal rod sold with most knife sets, doesn't sharpen at all: It's a tune-up device. As you cut with a sharp knife, the thin cutting edge of the blade can actually turn to the side, making your blade seem duller than it is. Running the knife blade over the steel, as most professional chefs do each time they're about to use a knife, simply realigns that edge and makes it straight again. It can't reshape a truly dull blade that's rounded and worn down. That's when you need a sharpener that can cut away metal and restore the standard 20-degree angle of each side of the edge.

To reshape the edge of a dull knife, you have a few choices, depending on the amount of effort, skill, and money you want to invest. You can send it out (inconvenient, even if you can find someone to do it). You can use a whetstone (very difficult for anyone but a professional). But the best option for most home cooks is to buy a tool (either electric or manual) that does most of the work for you.

Based on previous kitchen tests (March/April 1997), we've said that electric knife sharpeners are the most reliable choice for home cooks. In 1997, we recommended the Chef'sChoice Model 110 for its easy, reliable sharpening of even the dullest knives. But since that time, new electric sharpeners have come on the market, both from EdgeCraft, maker of Chef'sChoice, and other companies. Are any better than the trusty machine we've used in the test kitchen for nearly a decade? Given that most electric sharpeners cost around $100, we thought it was also time to revisit manual sharpeners, many of which

are available for a fraction of the cost. Is there an inexpensive gem out there?

Designing the Tests

Most sharpeners, both electric and manual, start their work with a coarse material and progress through stages of finer material to polish the edge. In general, the hardest material is diamond, followed by tungsten carbide, followed by high-alumina ceramic, followed by steel. Hardness isn't everything, though; the material is only as good as the angle of the knife being swiped against it, so the design of the sharpener is important. Some models guarantee that even an inexperienced user will get the right angle; other models make this more a matter of chance.

To level the playing field for our testing, we wanted to start with knives of equal dullness. Looking to simulate the condition of knives that have been used for about a year without sharpening, we turned for advice to Stoddard's, a cutlery shop in Boston. Although the company has been in the business of sharpening knives since the early 1800s, owner David Marks good-naturedly agreed to "dull" dozens of new knives over the course of our testing. On a 220-grit whetstone, he used a heel-to-tip rocking motion that mimics a chef's slicing, repeating this motion 45 times for each knife. Marks also used a diamond slipstone to cut 1/16-inch notches in each blade near the heel and near the tip, where he said he often sees nicks appearing in chef's knives that have been roughly used—the kind of damage that might occur if you use your knife to hack through chicken bones or frozen foods.

Back in the test kitchen, we confirmed the knives' dullness by attempting to slice through a sheet of paper—without success. Following the manufacturers' instructions, we sharpened one knife on each sharpener and tried again to slice paper—with decidedly better results. We used the sharp knives to cut paper-thin slices of ripe tomato and chiffonade fresh basil leaves. In the final test, we measured how long it took to regrind the blades and smooth out those notches—a measure

The Life Cycle of a Knife

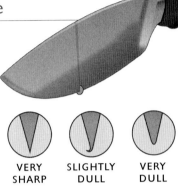

A sharp edge (left) will make quick work of slicing and chopping. However, even a few minutes of cutting can make the edge roll over (center), making the blade feel slightly dull. A quick steeling or sharpening will remove the folded edge and return the knife to its original sharpness. After significant use, the sharp angles on the edge will become rounded and very dull (right). At this point, it will take much more effort to use the knife and the edge will bruise food as it cuts. The knife needs an entirely new edge and will require significant work to become sharp again.

VERY SHARP   **SLIGHTLY DULL**   **VERY DULL**

of how well the sharpeners could repair severe damage.

Electric Performance

As in our earlier tests, most of the electric sharpeners were up to the job (see chart on page 26). Only one, the Kershaw Electric Knife Sharpener ($59.95), failed to restore a good cutting edge. The Waring PRO KS80 ($99.95) aced the paper, tomato, and basil tests, but it also cut a quarter-inch scoop, or swale, out of the heel because the knife dropped down onto the grinding wheel each time it was inserted. The heel of the blade thus no longer made contact with the cutting board, making it unusable. The Presto EverSharp 8800, the least expensive electric at $39.95, restored a sharp but "moderately rough" edge to the knife that one tester described as "chewed up." Its loud motor stalled frequently and alarmingly, halfway up the blade, whenever we failed to keep a very light touch on the knife.

As for Chef'sChoice, our old model 110 ($79.95) performed well, but improvements on its newer siblings made them quicker and easier to use. In addition to taking less time and trouble to reach a fine edge, the new models feature spring-loaded blade guides that allow no ambiguous wiggle room as they hold the blade against the sharpening wheels at the proper angle, replacing the trickier magnetic guides on the 110. The sharpening wheels on newer models also reach closer to the edge of the machine, ensuring that the sharpening extends all the way to the end of a knife.

Overall, we preferred the sharper, finer, more polished edge we got with the Chef'sChoice 130 ($139), the quietest and smoothest of the six electric sharpeners we tested. It sharpened dulled knives quickly. We also liked its nonmotorized slot, which operates like a sharpening steel. Because many people have a hard time mastering the motion needed to use a traditional steel, this is an easy way to get the benefit of steeling. To keep your knives in prime condition, you would keep this sharpener on the counter and use the built-in steel just as professional chefs do, right before—and every time—you use your knives. If money is no object, the Chef'sChoice Model 130 is our new electric sharpener of choice. If your budget is more modest, the 110 is still worth buying and will keep your knives in top condition.

Going Manual

Manual sharpeners share some similarities: In size, most are a little bigger than a desktop stapler, and the sharpening material used may be diamond, steel, ceramic, tungsten carbide, or a combination of these. In most manual sharpeners, the sharpening material is enclosed in a plastic or metal body, with one, two, or three angled openings for the knife to be drawn through. In a few models, the sharpener consists of a base that holds the exposed honing material, such as ceramic sticks, in a V-shape that the knife is drawn against.

Could manual sharpeners hold a candle to the electric models we tested? In a word, yes. A few made admirably quick and thorough work of basic sharpening tasks and did so for a fraction of the price of an electric sharpener.

Coming out on top in our testing was the AccuSharp Knife and Tool Sharpener ($11.71), a simple plastic, hand-held device with a single tungsten carbide V-shaped blade. The AccuSharp produces metal shavings as you draw it over the knife, which you hold against the countertop with the cutting edge up. Once testers got over the strangeness of "straddling" the blade with the sharpener, they found themselves "surprised at how quickly this works," noting that it was "really easy to use . . . I'm impressed."

The second-place model, Anolon's Universal Sharpener ($29.95), has three sets of ceramic stones, from coarse to fine, in a plastic housing that you fill with water to keep the stones from clogging with metal filings, a common problem with ceramic. Testers remarked that it was "very easy, no pressure required," to make the knife cut through paper ("like butter") and that it was "no effort" to slice through tomatoes.

Another single-slot device, the Chantry Knife Sharpener ($39.95), took third place. Inside a sturdy metal casing, two spring-loaded steel rods

---

RATINGS	
GOOD:	★★★
FAIR:	★★
POOR:	★

RATING ELECTRIC KNIFE SHARPENERS

HIGHLY RECOMMENDED	TEST CRITERIA		TESTERS' COMMENTS
Chef'sChoice Model 130 PRICE: $139 SHARPENING MATERIAL: Diamond, with three slots, coarse, fine, and non-motorized butcher steel	STROKES TO SHARPEN: PERFORMANCE: NOTCH REMOVAL: EASE OF USE:	6 ★★★ 21 strokes ★★★	This quiet model is the Rolls-Royce of sharpeners. Spring-loaded blade guides make sharpening foolproof. One slot works like a sharpening steel but removes all guesswork from the usual steeling motion.
RECOMMENDED			
Chef'sChoice Model 120 PRICE: $129.95 SHARPENING MATERIAL: Diamond, with three slots, coarse, medium, and fine	STROKES TO SHARPEN: PERFORMANCE: NOTCH REMOVAL: EASE OF USE:	15 ★★★ 28 strokes ★★★	Very easy to operate; spring-loaded blade guides make sharpening fool-proof. Knife seems to "fall" somewhat jarringly into first slot.
RECOMMENDED WITH RESERVATIONS			
Chef'sChoice Model 110 PRICE: $79.95 SHARPENING MATERIAL: Diamond, with three slots, coarse for pre-sharpening, medium, and fine	STROKES TO SHARPEN: PERFORMANCE: NOTCH REMOVAL: EASE OF USE:	34 ★★★ 19 strokes ★★	Does the job at a reasonable price, although somewhat noisily. Instructions are a bit confusing and magnetic guides could control blade angle more easily. Grinding elements are set in from edge of machine and miss the heel on knives.
Presto EverSharp 8800 PRICE: $39.95 SHARPENING MATERIAL: "Sapphirite" (aluminum oxide, a ceramic), with two slots, coarse and fine	STROKES TO SHARPEN: PERFORMANCE: NOTCH REMOVAL: EASE OF USE:	6 ★★ 22 strokes ★	Very loud, and stalled when testers applied any pressure. Appeared to scuff blades.
NOT RECOMMENDED			
Waring PRO KS80 PRICE: $99.95 SHARPENING MATERIAL: Alumina (a ceramic), with three slots of coarse, fine, and strop/polish	STROKES TO SHARPEN: PERFORMANCE: NOTCH REMOVAL: EASE OF USE:	9 ★★ 137 strokes ★★	Grinding wheels on this large, quiet machine are set in too far from end of slot, so user can't hone entire blade edge. Knife dropped onto wheel, causing "scoop" to develop near heel end.
Kershaw Electric Knife Sharpener PRICE: $59.95 SHARPENING MATERIAL: Ceramic, single slot with sharpening cartridge containing coarse and fine stones	STROKES TO SHARPEN: PERFORMANCE: NOTCH REMOVAL: EASE OF USE:	7 ★ 143 strokes ★	Loud, "nerve-wracking" metallic noise. Grinding action sharpened at tip and heel of knife but not in middle, eventually ruining our knife. Crucial operation instructions found only on DVD. Can only operate two minutes at a time.

How We Rated the Sharpeners

We tested 12 manual knife sharpeners (right) and six electric knife sharpeners (left) and evaluated them according to the criteria below. In each chart, the knives are listed in order of preference.

PRICE: Purchase price online or at Boston-area retail outlets.

SHARPENING MATERIAL: The material(s) in the sharpener that hones the knife edge.

STROKES TO SHARPEN: We used new 8-inch Victorinox Forschner Fibrox chef's knives (test kitchen favorites) dulled to a uniform level on a 220-grit whetstone. We sharpened the dulled knives according to manufacturer instructions, counting the number of strokes. (Note: The numbers are an average based on results from multiple testers and may vary based on the skill level of the individual operator.)

PERFORMANCE: We tested the dulled and sharpened knives by cutting a sheet of paper, cutting thin slices of tomato, and cutting fresh basil into a chiffonade (fine strips). Scores of good, fair, or poor were assigned for each test.

NOTCH REMOVAL: To see if the sharpeners could rescue damaged knives, we used a diamond slipstone to cut two 1/16-inch notches (one near the heel, the other near the tip) in each blade and then attempted to remove the notches with the sharpeners. None of the manual sharpeners passed this test; for electric models we've noted the number of strokes needed to remove both notches.

EASE OF USE: Factors include whether operating the device was easy and comfortable, instructions were clear, and overall time and steps necessary to sharpen were reasonable.

are crossed at a 40-degree angle; the knife is pressed down as you saw it back and forth, as if cutting a loaf of bread. Its simplicity and sharp edge appealed to testers.

Clearly the sharpening material was not what set these sharpeners ahead of the others. In each case they won over testers with a combination of good results and ease of use—not always a given with a manual sharpener. Some of the low-rated models were nearly as expensive as an electric but took a lot more work and time to do the job. Other low-rated models were squeaky, jerky, awkward, or even useless.

No Smooth Operators

Now for the bad news: While some of the manual sharpeners could restore a respectable edge to the knives, not one removed the notches. In the attempt, we put the knives through each device 300 times, with no visible effect. What does this mean? Manual sharpeners take off a good deal less metal than electric sharpeners and simply cannot remove enough, in a reasonable amount of time, to restore a nicked or damaged knife. For these knives (and undoubtedly you have several), an electric sharpener is the only choice.

Should you bother buying a manual knife sharpener? The better options will help you maintain new knives and are fine with moderately dull blades. At $11.71, the appeal of the easy-to-operate AccuSharp is clear. But be prepared to pay a professional to handle your more challenging sharpening needs. In the long run, an electric sharpener is a good investment, if you can make the initial cash outlay. If not, pick up a cheap manual sharpener. The best ones are far superior to steeling rods and will keep many of your knives in decent shape.

TECHNIQUE | ARE YOUR KNIVES DULL?

Here's a quick way to find out if your knives need to be sharpened. Hold a sheet of plain paper and slice into the top with your knife. Does the knife glide through the paper? If you need to saw at the edge, or if the paper rips, your knife needs sharpening.

RATING MANUAL KNIFE SHARPENERS

RECOMMENDED

	TEST CRITERIA		TESTERS' COMMENTS
AccuSharp Knife and Tool Sharpener PRICE: $11.71 SHARPENING MATERIAL: Tungsten carbide V-shaped single blade	STROKES TO SHARPEN: PERFORMANCE: NOTCH REMOVAL: EASE OF USE:	20 ★★★ ★ ★★★	Establishes a sharp edge quickly and easily. This compact sharpener must be drawn over the exposed knife blade, which gave users some pause, at least initially.
Anolon Universal Knife Sharpener 3-Stage Wet Stone PRICE: $29.95 SHARPENING MATERIAL: Three slots with ceramic stones, coarse to fine; uses water	STROKES TO SHARPEN: PERFORMANCE: NOTCH REMOVAL: EASE OF USE:	42 ★★★ ★ ★★★	Smooth, easy motion yields very sharp, polished blade. Handle is especially comfortable. Must fill with water before each use.
Chantry Knife Sharpener PRICE: $39.95 SHARPENING MATERIAL: Steel, crossed and spring-loaded	STROKES TO SHARPEN: PERFORMANCE: NOTCH REMOVAL: EASE OF USE:	20 ★★★ ★ ★★★	Heavy metal casing on this fast, simple sharpener is durable and stays put. Instructions are vague.

RECOMMENDED WITH RESERVATIONS

	TEST CRITERIA		TESTERS' COMMENTS
Chef'sChoice 460 Multi-Edge Diamond Hone Sharpener PRICE: $29.95 SHARPENING MATERIAL: Industrial diamond in two slots, coarse and fine	STROKES TO SHARPEN: PERFORMANCE: NOTCH REMOVAL: EASE OF USE:	60 ★★★ ★ ★★	This lightweight model must be held down, but it did yield a sharp edge. Wheels indicating correct blade angle never turned as described, and knives didn't move smoothly.
Spyderco Tri-Angle Sharpmaker PRICE: $47.20 SHARPENING MATERIAL: Four triangular ceramic rods, two medium and two fine	STROKES TO SHARPEN: PERFORMANCE: NOTCH REMOVAL: EASE OF USE:	160 ★★★ ★ ★	Although overly complex (the instruction booklet has 28 pages!), slow to operate, and difficult to control, this model did produce a sharp edge—eventually.
Wüsthof Knife-Life 3-Stage Knife and Scissor Sharpener PRICE: $19.95 SHARPENING MATERIAL: Two slots, tungsten carbide and ceramic	STROKES TO SHARPEN: PERFORMANCE: NOTCH REMOVAL: EASE OF USE:	30 ★★★ ★ ★	Quick to operate, but performance is a notch below the better options. Knives sharpened with this tool tore, rather than sliced, tomatoes.

NOT RECOMMENDED

	TEST CRITERIA		TESTERS' COMMENTS
Füri Tech Edge Professional Sharpening System PRICE: $89.95 SHARPENING MATERIAL: Three interchangeable sharpening tools, one tungsten carbide and two diamond, medium and fine	STROKES TO SHARPEN: PERFORMANCE: NOTCH REMOVAL: EASE OF USE:	110 ★★★ ★ ★	Although this model put a fairly sharp edge on knives, the jumpy, jerky motion of the tungsten tool damaged the blade edge. The gripper in the handle broke in several test samples.
Global MinoSharp Plus Knife Sharpener, Model 440 PRICE: $48.95 SHARPENING MATERIAL: Two slots with ceramic stones, coarse and fine; uses water	STROKES TO SHARPEN: PERFORMANCE: NOTCH REMOVAL: EASE OF USE:	44 ★★ ★ ★★	Uncomplicated, but sharpening motion is jerky and produces blade that's not sharp enough. Must fill with water before each use.
Henckels TwinSharp Select Knife Sharpener PRICE: $39.95 SHARPENING MATERIAL: Two slots, coarse steel and fine ceramic	STROKES TO SHARPEN: PERFORMANCE: NOTCH REMOVAL: EASE OF USE:	30 ★★ ★ ★★	Knife squeaks unpleasantly as it goes through steel slot. Easy to use, but results are so-so.
Meyerco Sharpen-It PRICE: $29.99 SHARPENING MATERIAL: Two slots, tungsten carbide and ceramic	STROKES TO SHARPEN: PERFORMANCE: NOTCH REMOVAL: EASE OF USE:	90 ★★ ★ ★	This pocket-size sharpener was hard to manipulate, and instructions were poorly written. Blade drags in tungsten slot.
Lansky Crock Stick Two-Stage Professional Knife Sharpener PRICE: $39.99 SHARPENING MATERIAL: Ceramic rods, coarse and fine	STROKES TO SHARPEN: PERFORMANCE: NOTCH REMOVAL: EASE OF USE:	110 ★★ ★ ★	Complicated hand motion feels unnatural. Sharpening rods quickly became smooth, and cleaning as instructed didn't restore abrasive feel.
Chicago Cutlery MagnaSharp Mouse Knife Sharpener PRICE: $7.99 SHARPENING MATERIAL: Ceramic rods, single slot	STROKES TO SHARPEN: PERFORMANCE: NOTCH REMOVAL: EASE OF USE:	50 ★ ★ ★	Compact unit emits terrible squeaking noise. Felt like knife was being dragged over plastic housing, not sharpening tool. One sample didn't work; others were not much better.

Are Italian Olive Oils Really That Good?

When it's time to pay big bucks for an extra-virgin olive oil, many cooks automatically reach for boutique Tuscan oils. Should they?

⋺ BY LISA McMANUS ⋹

To fully appreciate the complex flavor of extra-virgin olive oil, you want to taste it straight from the bottle, or, at most, just barely warmed. In the test kitchen, we drizzle it over fish, vegetables, soups, pasta dishes, salads, and more. In 2001, we tasted inexpensive supermarket oils and proclaimed DaVinci ($12.99 per liter) our favorite. In subsequent tastings, DaVinci has continued its dominance over other mass-market brands.

But what if price isn't your first consideration? Does more money buy better olive oil? If so, how do you choose among the hundreds of boutique oils sold in fancy bottles at even fancier prices?

When Americans want extra-virgin olive oil, we generally buy Italian. Seven of the top 10 olive oils sold in the United States are Italian. But a growing number of extra-virgin olive oils from other countries now fill store shelves, including more offerings from Spain, the top olive-growing nation, and Greece. There are even oils from California. Gathering a lineup of 10 best-selling boutique extra-virgin olive oils from a variety of countries, priced at $20 to $56 per liter, we stripped them of their stylish labels and put them through the rigors of a blind tasting, sampling them plain, with French bread, and drizzled over fresh mozzarella.

High Standards

Sipped straight up from little cups, the extra-virgin olive oils in our lineup offered a pleasingly wide range of flavors, from fruity and "olive-y" to mild, buttery, and mellow to powerfully green, grassy, and pungent. Why does olive oil have such a wide-ranging flavor profile?

Experts agree that the type of olive, the time

of harvest (earlier means greener, more bitter, and pungent; later, more mild and buttery), and processing are the biggest factors. As one expert pointed out, olive oil is really just olive juice, and the quickest, gentlest extraction yields the truest flavors. The best-quality oil comes from olives picked at their peak—deciding exactly when to pick is the chief art of olive oil makers—and processed as quickly as possible without heat (which can coax more oil from the olives but at the expense of flavor).

Bottle labels often tout an oil's "low acidity." All extra-virgin oils must have less than 0.8 percent free oleic acid by agreement of the International Olive Oil Council (IOOC). We sent the oils in our tasting to an independent lab and found that they all met this standard. We also had the lab analyze the oils for peroxide levels—the industry test for oxidation caused by improper handling and/or storage—and, again, all were well within the IOOC standard.

Balancing Act

If all of the extra-virgin oils we tasted were technically fine—at least according to lab tests—why had tasters found such a variety of flavors? And why did tasters' scores reveal some clear winners—and some clear losers?

The big loser in our tasting was DaVinci, our favorite inexpensive oil, which finished dead last. Although disappointed, we weren't really surprised. This oil may be better than the other cheap options, but it couldn't compete with high-end products. Olive oil has been produced for centuries, and it makes sense that companies that take the time to make oil in small batches have figured out some secrets to distinguish their oils from mass-market products. At least when it comes to olive oil, high prices buy more than just pretty bottles.

We were surprised, however, that tasters were not impressed with the high-end Italian oils, which finished in fifth through eighth place. Our two top finishers came from Spain, the third from Greece. We needed to explain these unexpected findings.

As we tallied our tasting results, we realized that our two favorite oils—both praised by tasters for their fairly assertive yet well-balanced flavor—were made with a blend of olives. The Columela and Núñez de Prado oils are a mix of intense Picual and mild Hojiblanca olives (the Núñez also adds delicate-flavored Picudo olives), creating a "fruity" olive oil with no elements that were perceived as too strong tasting—or too mild. By contrast, the other two Spanish oils we tasted, L'Estornell and Pons, were made with only the mild-mannered Arbequina olive, and they rated much less favorably.

Darrell Corti, owner of Corti Brothers store in Sacramento, Calif., and chairman of olive oil judging at the Los Angeles County Fair, the top domestic and international olive oil competition in the United States, told us that producers often blend extra-virgin oils from olives with distinct flavors to create the overall flavor profile they want. According to Corti, the best oil is often made from a blend of varietals; the blend may consist of several oils, each one made from a single varietal (known as monocultivar, or single-olive, oils), or from a "field blend," in which different types of olives are picked and then processed together to create a single oil.

Was blending the answer we sought? Maybe not. Ranking nearly as high as the top Spaniards was a Greek oil, Terra Medi, made only with Koroneiki olives. It's not a blend, yet its balanced character and fruity, rounded flavor, with no harsh notes, made it similar in profile to the two top oils. Additionally, while some of the so-so Italian oils were made from single varietals, others were blends. So blending alone doesn't guarantee great oil.

The choice of olives is one factor that makes a particular oil more or less appealing. However, with their characteristic green, intense olive flavor and peppery aftertaste, the Italian oils had a few vocal supporters, but the majority of tasters felt that the oils' harsh pungency overwhelmed the olive flavor. The worst offender in this regard was a California oil, McEvoy Ranch, made with a blend of six Tuscan olives in the style of the Italian oils. This highly assertive oil turned off the majority of our tasters.

Green Monsters

What makes the Italian and Italian-style extra-virgin olive oils so pungent and green? According to

What about Cheap Olive Oil?

Among leading supermarket olive oils, DaVinci ($12.99 per liter) has won several taste tests in recent years and is the test kitchen's favorite. Bottled in Italy but made from a virtual United Nations of oils, this mass-market brand was tasted alongside the expensive oils on page 29 and earned praise for its "bright," "fruity" flavor. In the end, however, it paled in comparison to the pricey competition and finished in last place. Tasters deemed it "pleasant" but "not complex." For recipes where olive oil is heated or must compete with strong flavors, we'll stick with DaVinci, but for drizzling over foods just before serving, the test kitchen is ready for an oil change.

LESS MONEY, LESS FLAVOR

Paul Vossen of the University of California Cooperative Extension in Sonoma, an IOOC-certified olive oil taster, Italian oils came by their signature flavor profile out of necessity—and producers then made it a virtue.

"Tuscany has frost problems, or potential frost problems, so their law requires that they harvest their olives early—by a certain date—and that means they have a green olive oil that is bitter and pungent," said Vossen. "So the Italians just convinced the world that that's how extra-virgin olive oil is supposed to taste. It's marketing. Once you realize that and put it in context, and take it with a grain of salt . . . yes, they make absolutely fabulous extra-virgin olive oils in Italy, but it's really just one style."

Darrell Corti agreed. "Americans have been told that they should like very bitter oils, but they don't really like them. The Tuscan oils are bitter."

In recognition of the variety of extra-virgin olive oil styles, this year the Los Angeles County Fair judging panel, of which Vossen is a member, adopted a new European standard, dividing the oils into three categories based on flavor intensity: light fruity intensity, medium fruity intensity, and intense fruitiness.

As the Italian style moves into a less dominant role, other styles of oil are moving in, most notably those from Spain. "For many years, Spain was the poorest part of Europe, especially in the south," said Vossen, "and they're coming out of that now. They used to be only concerned about bulk oil production, while the Italians (Spain's biggest customer) would buy their oil and blend and refine it and craft a good olive oil out of it." Spanish extra-virgin olive oils are coming into their own, he said. "They're making fabulous olive oils right now."

In the end, balance turned out to be the key factor that determined the winners of our tasting, and we found it in Spanish oils, not Italian oils. Our tasters preferred oils of medium fruity intensity. Italian oils generally fall into the intense category.

In the test kitchen, we'll keep our DaVinci on hand for everyday use, but we'll stock up on our preferred medium fruity Spanish oil, too. With the top-ranked Columela coming in at about half the price of second-place Núñez de Prado, the former is our new test kitchen favorite when we want an extra-virgin olive oil with high-end flavor but don't want to break the bank to pay for it.

TASTING EXTRA-VIRGIN OLIVE OILS

Twenty *Cook's Illustrated* staff members tasted 10 nationally available extra-virgin olive oils priced at more than $20 per liter, along with DaVinci, the test kitchen's favorite inexpensive supermarket extra-virgin oil. We tasted them plain, on French bread, and drizzled over fresh mozzarella. Tasters rated each sample for olive flavor, complexity, and overall appeal. Brands are listed below in order of preference. Most of the oils are available in supermarkets. Mail-order sources for the top three appear on page 32.

RECOMMENDED

COLUMELA EXTRA VIRGIN OLIVE OIL
➤ Country of Origin: **SPAIN**
➤ $22 for 25.4 ounces (about $29/liter)
A blend of intense Picual and mild Hojiblanca olives, this oil took top honors for its fruity flavor and excellent balance. One taster summed it up: "Bold olive flavor, slightly fruity, medium-to-heavy texture: This is what I think of when I think EVOO." Another taster simply wrote, "Fantastic."

NÚÑEZ DE PRADO ORGANIC EXTRA VIRGIN OLIVE OIL
➤ Country of Origin: **SPAIN**
➤ $27.99 for 16.9 ounces (about $56/liter)
"Nutty, fruity, good, with a lot of flavor" was the consensus on this "well-rounded" oil made with Picual, Hojiblanca, and Picudo olives. One taster noted that it "packs a lot of olive taste." Another raved, "Olives, grass, herbs, rich, not much bite: Perfect!"

TERRA MEDI EXTRA VIRGIN OLIVE OIL
➤ Country of Origin: **GREECE**
➤ $9.95 for 17 ounces (about $20/liter)
"Rich, olive-y, delicious," wrote one taster. "Complex, rich, without being bitter," said another. Like the other top oils, this one (made with fruity Koroneiki olives) was praised for having a "great balance of flavor" and a "slightly peppery," "buttery" taste.

RECOMMENDED WITH RESERVATIONS

L'ESTORNELL EXTRA VIRGIN OLIVE OIL
➤ Country of Origin: **SPAIN**
➤ $21.99 for 25.3 ounces (about $29/liter)
Made with mild, sweet Arbequina olives, this organic oil won tasters over with "lots of olive flavor," but it lost favor with a few for having "sour" and "slightly off" notes. Many agreed with tasters who found it "pretty mild" and even "bland."

OLIO VERDE OLIO EXTRA VERGINE DI OLIVA
➤ Country of Origin: **ITALY**
➤ $10.50 for 500 ml ($21/liter)
"A complex and spicy finish," said one taster who enjoyed this Sicilian oil pressed from the early-harvest Nocellara del Belice olive, which gives the oil its characteristic "super-grassy" flavor. While many loved its "earthy, pungent" flavor, others found its "slightly bitter" profile "too much."

RECOMMENDED WITH RESERVATIONS (cont.)

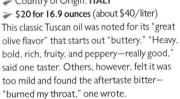

LUCINI PREMIUM SELECT EXTRA VIRGIN OLIVE OIL
➤ Country of Origin: **ITALY**
➤ $14.79 for 500 ml ($29.58/liter)
"Nutty" and "huge," with a "really good flavor: olive-y, buttery, fruity, and bold," said tasters, who liked this oil made from a blend of Frantoio, Pendolino, Moraiolo, and Leccino olives. Some found it to have a "really bitter aftertaste" that was "too acidic," while others liked its "lingering punch of pepper."

MONINI GRANFRUTTATO EXTRA VIRGIN OLIVE OIL
➤ Country of Origin: **ITALY**
➤ $11.49 for 500 ml ($22.98/liter)
Tasters generally liked this "peppery, bold," and "pungent" oil, which is made with a blend of olives, including Moraiolos that are picked when they are fully ripe. But some complained that it was "greasy," with "lingering bitterness," and "not too complex," even "slightly inelegant."

BADIA A COLTIBUONO EXTRA VIRGIN OLIVE OIL
➤ Country of Origin: **ITALY**
➤ $20 for 16.9 ounces (about $40/liter)
This classic Tuscan oil was noted for its "great olive flavor" that starts out "buttery." "Heavy, bold, rich, fruity, and peppery—really good," said one taster. Others, however, felt it was too mild and found the aftertaste bitter—"burned my throat," one wrote.

PONS EXTRA VIRGIN OLIVE OIL
➤ Country of Origin: **SPAIN**
➤ $21 for 500 ml ($42/liter)
Arbequina olives are used to create this oil, which tasters described as "rich, buttery, and full bodied," but also "mellow and not assertive." One taster commented, "Mild, but good. Subtle." Another panelist wrote, "EVOO-lite." Those who prefer oils with more robust flavor called it "bland."

McEVOY RANCH EXTRA VIRGIN OLIVE OIL
➤ Country of Origin: **UNITED STATES**
➤ $18.99 for 375 ml ($50.64/liter)
This organic oil from northern California is a blend of six Tuscan olives. Some tasters liked its "nutty" and "green" flavors, while others found its strong taste overpowering: "too pungent" and "no olive fruit, all chemical and bitter." Another wrote, "Packs some serious heat if you're into that sort of thing."

⇒ BY ERIKA BRUCE ⇐

How to Measure Greens

We often get questions about how to accurately measure greens for salads, which is why we always give both an ounce measure and a cup measure in recipes. But when we tried to convert our usual formula of 2 ounces (or 2 cups) of lightly packed greens per serving to our arugula salads (page 24), we ended up with more greens than we could eat. That's because our original calculation was based on head lettuce, which is actually heavier (because of its higher water content) than arugula. For lighter, fluffier baby greens, such as baby spinach, mesclun, and arugula, we found that less was more: One ounce of lightly packed baby greens will yield roughly 1½ cups, just enough for one serving.

PERFECTLY PACKED
Five ounces of lightly packed
baby greens yields about 8 cups.

But this begs another question: If you don't have a scale and are using the cup measurement, what exactly does "lightly" packed mean? The reason we don't just call for a more accurate measure of "tightly" packed greens, pressed firmly into the cup, as is done with brown sugar, is that this method would bruise delicate leafy greens. To lightly pack greens, simply drop them by the handful into a measuring cup and then gently pat down, using your fingertips rather than the palm of your hand.

Makeshift Carving Board

Good carving boards (see "Carving Boards" on page 13) come with a handy well in the center and a moat around the edges to capture juices from the meat that would otherwise drip onto the countertop and floor.

TECHNIQUE | QUICKER VEGETABLE PREP

While developing our recipe for Green Bean Casserole (page 9), we came up with the following methods for quickly preparing mushrooms and green beans.

BREAKING MUSHROOMS
I. Using your thumb, pop the caps off their stems.

2. Squeeze both the stem and the cap between your thumb and forefinger to break each into pieces.

TRIMMING GREEN BEANS
Line up about 8 beans in a row on a cutting board. Trim about ½ inch from each end, then cut the beans in half.

But when we had to carve a half-dozen turkeys at once for our Roast Salted Turkey (page 13), we ran out of proper boards. Our solution was to simply substitute a flat cutting board placed inside a rimmed baking sheet; the raised sides kept the juices from leaking out as we carved.

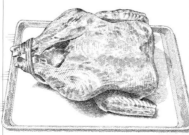

If you find yourself without a real carving board, set a regular flat cutting board inside a rimmed baking sheet.

Stay Hydrated

Most recipes that call for gelatin also ask the cook to hydrate it—that is, mix it with a small amount of cold water and let it sit before being dissolved in hot liquid. Why? It's known that adding powdered gelatin directly to hot liquid can cause the exterior of the gelatin granules to hydrate quickly and develop a coating that keeps the center of the granules from absorbing water. Direct immersion in hot liquid may

also cause the granules to clump, inhibiting full dissolution. As a result, the gelatin is thought to lose some of its ability to absorb water and thicken a liquid mixture.

We put this theory to the test by making plain gels using water and either hydrated or nonhydrated gelatin. The results? Both gels set up perfectly and had the same viscosity. So why hydrate?

It turns out that hydrating gelatin, like looking both ways before crossing the street, is merely a precautionary measure. If gelatin is

added to enough very hot (but not boiling) water and stirred vigorously, as it was in our test, then it will completely dissolve and swell to its full potential, even without being hydrated first. Problems may arise if the liquid-to-gelatin ratio is low, as it is in many recipes, including our No-Bake Pumpkin Pie (page 21), or if the gelatin is to be added to a cold mixture, such as whipped cream. In these instances, it is always best to hydrate each teaspoon of gelatin in at least 1 tablespoon of cool liquid before continuing with the recipe.

SHOPPING: **Canned Pumpkin**

Aside from its status as a Thanksgiving classic, pumpkin pie gets points for taking a plain canned good and dressing it up. To be sure we were opening the best canned pumpkin for our No-Bake Pumpkin Pie (page 21), we asked 10 tasters to sample pies made from three brands: One-Pie, Libby's, and Farmer's Market Organic.

Libby's and One-Pie ended up in a dead heat. While some tasters favored the "creamy" texture and "mild sweetness" of Libby's, others preferred the slightly "denser" texture and "sharper" pumpkin flavor of One-Pie. Farmer's Market was disqualified for its unpleasantly "vegetal" and "chalky" flavor.

LABEL LINGO
Read labels to make sure you're
buying plain pumpkin (left),
not pumpkin pie mix (right).

Whichever brand you choose, study the label carefully. Our supermarket stocks canned pumpkin from both Libby's and Farmer's Market that's already been spiced and sweetened. These products, marked as "pie mix" but looking very much like the cans of plain pumpkin, are a recipe for a soupy and overly sweet disaster.

—Elizabeth Bomze

TECHNIQUE | WHICH KNOT IS BEST?

With so many roasts to tie during recipe development for stuffed beef tenderloin (page 7), we decided to test the three tying methods featured in most culinary textbooks: the **surgeon's knot** (basically a looped double knot), the **butcher's knot** (a type of slipknot), and the **half-hitch knot** (made in a series along a continuous length of twine). While the latter made for the most attractive presentation of the cooked stuffed roast (the twine is looped around the roast several times and each loop is connected on both the top and the bottom, creating a very secure net), it took us multiple tries to get the hang of it, and it was tricky maneuvering a stuffed roast. The butcher's knot was also difficult to get right every time. Our favorite knot by far was also the most basic—the surgeon's knot. Single pieces of twine are wrapped around the roast at 1½-inch intervals and tied in an initial double loop, which holds the twine in place while a second knot is completed.

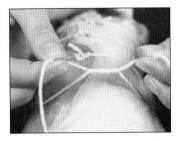 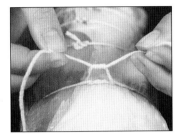

1. Begin by tying a knot as if tying a bow. Pull one end through the loop again.

2. Make a second knot on top of the first knot.

TASTING: The Ultimate Cooking Wine

Granted, a cardboard box may not look as classy as a slender green bottle, but we wondered if boxed wine could compete with bottled wine when used in cooking. First employed in Australia and Europe and now widely available in the United States, spigot-released boxed wine is both inexpensive and convenient, and it has a long shelf life, which makes it appealing to the cook who may need only the occasional cup.

To find out if boxed wine belongs in the kitchen, we tasted an array of boxed varietals ranging in price from $12.99 to $19.99 for three- or five-liter boxes, including Shiraz, Merlot, and Burgundy. As a control, we included a $10 bottle of the Côtes du Rhône we often use in the test kitchen for cooking. Sampled fresh out of the box, some of the wines did not impress, tasting sweet, simple, and sangria-like. But others were quite good, and tasters actually preferred them to the bottled wine. For the next test, we used each of the wines in our Modern Coq au Vin (page 19) and a red wine pan sauce. To our surprise, all of the sauces—even those made with the wines we didn't like straight from the box—were fine.

After the bottles and boxes had been open for two weeks, we tasted them in pan sauce again. As expected, the recorked bottle of Côtes du Rhône had skunked, depreciating to a flat, alcohol-flavored sourness, but the boxed wines were still going strong. Even at a full seven weeks, the unrefrigerated boxed wines were fine for cooking.

How do boxed wines stay fresh for so long? An airtight, bladder-like plastic sac collapses as wine is removed (the box is there only for stackability and portability), making the wine less susceptible to oxidation. Price is another plus: Those we tested cost the equivalent of $2 to $5 a bottle.

—Elizabeth Bomze

Do boxed wines stack up to bottled when used in cooking?

RECIPE UPDATE

Multigrain Dinner Rolls

Several readers asked to turn our **Multigrain Sandwich Bread** (March/April 2006) into dinner rolls. Simply cutting the proofed dough into smaller portions didn't work because the crust on this hearty dough overwhelmed the small amount of soft interior bread. We tried baking the rolls in larger pieces to cut down on the crust-to-interior ratio. But when proofed and baked, the dough looked more like small loaves than individual rolls.

We had more success when we divided the dough into 18 equal pieces, formed each one into a ball, and then spaced them evenly in two baking dishes. When proofed and then baked, the dough balls grew into one another to create a cluster of dinner rolls that easily pulled apart. Best of all, the crust formed on just the tops and bottoms of the rolls, so the ratio of crisp crust to soft interior was just right.

Bake rolls in a tightly packed dish to minimize the amount of crust on each roll.

Baked Orange-Flavored Chicken

Readers who found themselves intimidated by the thought of frying chicken for our **Orange-Flavored Chicken** recipe (May/June 2005) wondered if there was a "no-fry" method that would achieve the same tender meat and crispy coating as the original. To find out, we pulled out a baking sheet and cranked up the oven.

With a generous coating of egg white and cornstarch, we baked the bite-sized chicken pieces in a 500-degree oven—but the crust was barely forming when these small pieces of chicken were done. Leaving these boneless, skinless thighs whole proved cumbersome; by halving the thighs and preheating our baking sheet with the oil on it, we had good crust formation by the time the chicken finished cooking. Unfortunately, the crust was tough and brittle in places, mostly where the egg white and cornstarch had accumulated. Our solution was to drain the egg mixture off of the chicken pieces, then dredge them in a 50–50 mixture of flour and cornstarch, being sure to shake off any extra. The thin, even coating cooked up crispy, crunchy, and tender.

Pear Strudel

We weren't surprised when readers asked how they could modify our recipe for **Apple Strudel** (September/October 2003) to use pears instead. A quick test of the different varieties available in our supermarket demonstrated that Bosc pears hold their shape when ripe and are best suited for this strudel; Bartlett pears are acceptable, but they have a tendency to become soft when ripe, making them difficult to handle in this recipe. To balance the sweetness of the pears, we doubled the lemon juice to 2 teaspoons. We also substituted Poire William (a crystal-clear eau de vie made from pears) for the Calvados to keep the flavors in sync.

—Compiled by Sarah Wilson

IF YOU HAVE A QUESTION about a recently published recipe, let us know. Send your inquiry, name, address, and daytime telephone number to Recipe Update, Cook's Illustrated, P.O. Box 470589, Brookline, MA 02447, or to recipeupdate@bcpress.com.

Go to www.cooksillustrated.com
- Key in code 11065 for **Multigrain Dinner Rolls**.
- Key in code 11066 for **Baked Orange-Flavored Chicken**.
- Key in code 11067 for **Pear Strudel**.
- Recipes available until May 1, 2007.

EQUIPMENT CORNER

⇒ BY GARTH CLINGINGSMITH AND ELIZABETH BOMZE ⇐

EQUIPMENT TESTING: Nutcrackers

Classic V-shaped nutcrackers rely on hand strength and patience for precision cracking. In search of a better way, we sat down to 5 pounds of mixed nuts and six new nutcracker designs.

Testers had the best luck with a product called Reed's Rocket ($21.99). This nutcracker looks like it belongs in a garage—you push down on a handle to crush a nut between two pistons. The Rocket's long base and handle provide good leverage and control, and it is highly adjustable; it found no nut too tough to crack.

SMASHING SUCCESS
The Reed's Rocket is an unusual but highly effective nutcracker.

DO YOU REALLY NEED THIS?
Turkey Brining Bags

Brining a turkey is a great way to ensure a moist, fully seasoned bird, but where do you put a 5-gallon bucket when the refrigerator is already stuffed to the gills with holiday foods? A turkey brining bag seemed like a nice idea; it should be a lot easier to make room for a flexible container that isn't much bigger than the turkey. Unfortunately, the brining bags we tried were fraught with problems—slippery, floppy, and tough to fill with turkey and brine. Although designed for storing sweaters and pillows, Ziploc Big Bags XL ($5.79 for four) are foodsafe and, at 2 feet by 1.7 feet, they're the perfect size for turkey brining. In addition, the flat bottom keeps the bag steady during filling, and a handle provides a tighter grip on the slippery plastic.

EQUIPMENT UPDATE:
Candy/Deep-Fry Thermometers

For candy making and deep-frying, digital thermometers are best: quick to respond, precise, and easy to read. Still, we weren't quite satisfied even with our favorite of the models tested for the May/June 2006 issue, the Maverick's Redi-Chek Oil & Candy Thermometer ($34.95), which was tall and top-heavy. Testers wanted something more like our favorite thermometer for roasts, the Polder Digital Cooking Timer/

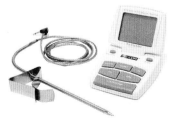

SWEET THERMOMETER
The clip makes this model our first choice for candy making.

Thermometer ($19.99), in which a long wire separates the "brains" from the business end. We'd use the Polder for candy or frying but couldn't find a way to secure the probe to the side of the pot. Then we found the CDN Digital Cooking Thermometer and Timer ($24.95). It's similar to the Polder but comes with a mounting clip that lets you attach the probe to your pan. An on/off switch would be nice (to save batteries over time), but it still gets our top recommendation for its clip-on ease.

DO YOU REALLY NEED THIS?
Hot/Cold Trivets

If you've ever been the last one in line at the buffet table, you know how disappointing it is to ladle out a bowlful of tepid stew. We purchased two thermal trays designed to remedy this problem. The Oggi Thermal HotCold Tray ($39.99) is a stainless steel platter with a gel core; the Icy-Cools Hot/Cold Trivet ($16.99) is a water-filled plastic quilt. Unfortunately, steaming-hot soup set on the Icy-Cools trivet actually lost heat faster than

COOL TRIVET
The Icy-Cools trivet keeps cold foods nicely chilled.

soup set atop a regular potholder (thanks to the microfiber sleeve that surrounds the heated trivet); the Oggi platter wasn't much better. Under bowls of yogurt and potato salad, however, the frosty Oggi platter did a good job and the Icy-Cools trivet was even more effective, actually lowering the temperatures of these foods. The latter is a worthwhile investment for summer barbecues and other events where you want to keep cold foods chilled. As for hot foods, we'll be hustling to the buffet table until a more functional product comes along.

EQUIPMENT UPDATE: Unicorn Minimill

The maker of the test kitchen's top-rated Unicorn Magnum Plus and Unicorn Magnum Pepper Mills has fashioned an elf-like mill fit for a slender pocket or purse. Filling the tablespoon-capacity Unicorn Minimill ($17.50) demands nimble fingers; twisting a coin in the head's built-in slot loosens the lid easily enough, but it takes a few practice rounds (and a few peppercorns lost to the floor) to master the tasks of steadying the shaft-like base with your forefinger while pouring in the peppercorns and then affixing the crown. Once assembled, however, the mill supplies enough perfectly ground pepper (coarse, medium, or fine) for many meals.

Sources

The following items are recommended in this issue. Prices were current at press time and do not include shipping. Contact companies to confirm prices and availability. Visit www.cooksillustrated.com for updates.

Page 7: KITCHEN SHEARS
- Messermeister Take-Apart Kitchen Shears: $23.99, item #5866, **Fante's Kitchen Wares Shop (800-443-2683, www.fantes.com).**
- Wüsthof Come-Apart Kitchen Shears: $19.95, item #5558, **Cutlery and More (www.cutleryandmore.com).**

Page 13: CARVING BOARD
- Williams-Sonoma Medium Reversible Carving Board: $58, item #36-635698, **Williams-Sonoma (877-812-6235, www.williams-sonoma.com).**

Page 19: WINE OPENERS
- Screwpull Trigger Wine Opener Set: $79.95, item #36-7078876, **Williams-Sonoma.**
- Zoom Corkscrew: $12.95, item #4182202, **The Wine Enthusiast (800-356-8466, www.wine enthusiast.com).**

Page 21: PIE SERVER
- Oxo Steel Pie Server: $7.95, item #145074, **Cooking.com (800-663-8810, www.cooking.com).**

Pages 26–27: KNIFE SHARPENERS
- Chef'sChoice Professional Sharpening Station Model 130: $139, item #CC130, **Cutlery and More.**
- AccuSharp Knife and Tool Sharpener: $11.71, item #61739, **Ace Hardware (866-290-5334, www.ace hardware.com).**
- Anolon Universal Knife Sharpener 3-Stage Wet Stone: $29.95, item #548540, **Cooking.com.**
- Chantry Knife Sharpener: $39.95, item #550B, **Cutlery and More.**

Page 29: EXTRA-VIRGIN OLIVE OILS
- Columela Extra Virgin Olive Oil: 25.4 oz. for $22, item #005100, **Salumeria Italiana (800-400-5916, www.salumeriaitaliana.com).**
- Núñez de Prado Organic Extra Virgin Olive Oil, 16.9 oz. for $27.99, **Colors of Spain (www.colorsofspain.com).**
- Terra Medi Extra Virgin Olive Oil, 17oz. for $9.95, item #203416, **Crate and Barrel (800-967-6696, www.crateandbarrelcom).**

Page 32: NUTCRACKER
- Reed's Rocket Nut Cracker: $21.99, item #6021, **Fante's.**

Page 32: TURKEY BRINING BAG
- Ziploc Big Bags XL: $5.79 for four, **Drugstore.com (800-378-4786, www.drugstore.com). Also at some supermarkets and Home Depot.**

Page 32: CANDY/DEEP-FRY THERMOMETER
- CDN Digital Cooking Thermometer and Timer: $24.95, model DTTC, **Kitchen Kaboodle (800-366-0161, www.kitchenkaboodle.com).**

Page 32: HOT/COLD TRIVET
- Icy-Cools FoodFresh Hot/Cold Trivet: $16.99, ASIN #B0009K6YA6, **Amazon.com.**

Page 32: PEPPER MILL
- Unicorn Minimill: $17.50, **Unicorn (800-634-8881, www.peppergun.com).**

RECIPES
November & December 2006

New Recipes Available on the Web

The following recipes are available free until May 1, 2007. Go to www.cooksillustrated.com and enter the code listed after the recipe title.

Multigrain Pancakes, 15

Roast Salted Turkey, 13

Stuffed Beef Tenderloin, 7

Penne alla Vodka, 10

Arugula Salad with Grapes, Fennel, Gorgonzola, and Pecans, 24

Green Bean Casserole, 9

Coq au Vin, 19

Chocolate Pots de Crème, 23

No-Bake Pumpkin Pie, 21

PHOTOGRAPHY: CARL TREMBLAY, STYLING: MARIE PIRAINO

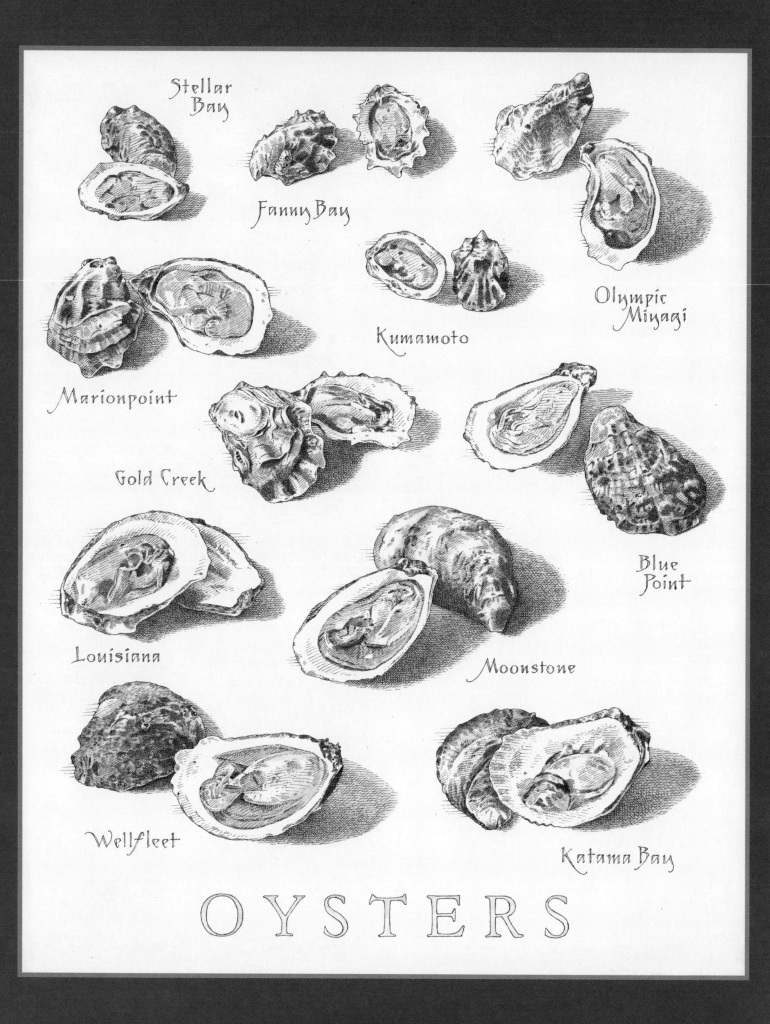

Stellar Bay

Fanny Bay

Kumamoto

Olympic Miyagi

Marionpoint

Gold Creek

Blue Point

Louisiana

Moonstone

Wellfleet

Katama Bay

OYSTERS